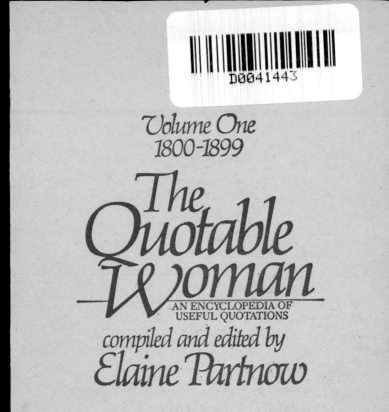

Volume One
1800-1899

The Quotable Woman

AN ENCYCLOPEDIA OF USEFUL QUOTATIONS

compiled and edited by
Elaine Partnow

PINNACLE BOOKS   LOS ANGELES

THE QUOTABLE WOMAN: VOLUME ONE

Copyright © 1977 by Elaine Partnow

A Pinnacle Books edition, published by special arrangement with Corwin Books.

First printing, October 1980

ISBN: 0-523-40859-5

Printed in the United States of America

PINNACLE BOOKS, INC.
2029 Century Park East
Los Angeles, California 90067

Liberated Ladies

"Thus far women have been mere echoes of men. . . . The free woman is as yet a dream of the future."—*Elizabeth Cady Stanton*

"Men are like the earth and we are the moon; we turn always one side to them and they think there is no other. . . ."—*Olive Schreiner*

"For an actress to be a success she must have the face of Venus, the brains of Minerva, the grace of Terpsichore, the memory of Macaulay, the figure of Juno, and the hide of a rhinoceros."
—*Ethel Barrymore*

". . . considering how dangerous everything is nothing is really frightening."—*Gertrude Stein*

"Too much of a good thing can be wonderful."
—*Mae West*

"Blessed is the man who, having nothing to say, abstains from giving wordy evidence of the fact."
—*George Eliot*

"Those men and women are fortunate who are born at a time when a great struggle for human freedom is in progress."—*Emmeline Pankhurst*

This book is dedicated
in memoriam
to my mother
Jeanette Bernstein Partnow
1912–1973
who gifted me with the joy of reading

Contents

Acknowledgments

The following have given their permission for inclusion of extracts from the works named; this permission is gratefully acknowledged.

Bantam Books, Inc. From *The Feminist Papers: From Adams to de Beauvoir*. Edited and with Introductory Essays by Alice S. Rossi. Copyright © 1973 by Alice S. Rossi. Published by Columbia University Press and Bantam Books, Inc. Reprinted by permission of Bantam Books, Inc.

Thomas Y. Crowell Company, Inc. Reprinted from *Poems From the Hebrew* by Robert Mezey. Copyright © 1973 by Robert Mezey. With permission of Thomas Y. Crowell Co., Inc.

Dodd, Mead & Company. From *India's Love Lyrics* by Laurence Hope. Copyright © 1922. Used by permission.

Farrar, Straus & Giroux, Inc. From *My Mother's House* by Colette, translated by Una Vicenzo Troubridge and Enid McLeod. Copyright © 1953 by Farrar, Straus and Young, Inc. Reprinted with the permission of Farrar, Straus & Giroux, Inc.

Harcourt Brace Jovanovich, Inc. From *A Room of One's Own* by Virginia Woolf. Copyright © 1929 by Harcourt Brace Jovanovich, Inc.; copyright © 1957 by Leonard Woolf. Reprinted by permission of the publisher.
Also: Drew, Elizabeth, *The Modern Novel* (1926). Fisher, Dorothy Canfield, *The Bent Twig* (1915); *Her Son's Wife* (1926); *The Deepening Stream* (1930); *Bonfire* (1933); *Seasoned Timber* (1939). Glasgow, Ellen, *In This Our Life* (1941). Meyer, Agnes E., *Journey Through Chaos* (1943). Porter, Katherine Anne, *Flowering Judas and Other Stories* (1930); *Old Mortality* (1936); *Noon Wine* (1937); *Pale Horse, Pale Rider* (1939). Roarke, Constance, *The Trumpets of Jubilee* (1927); *American Humor* (1931). Widdemer, Mar-

REFERENCE SOURCES

The author wishes to express her indebtedness to the following reference works, catalogs, and indices for the invaluable aid they provided in compiling this book.

The Academic Who's Who, 1973–1974
American Architects Directory, 1970
American Authors and Books
The American Heritage Dictionary, 1969, 1970
American Men and Women of Science: Behavioral and Social Sciences, 12th ed.
American Psychological Association Directory, 1974
Bartlett's Familiar Quotations (several editions)
The Biographical Encyclopedia and Who's Who of the American Theater, 1966
Biography Index, Vols. 1–9 and Sept. 1973–Aug. 1975
Books in Print (several editions)
Brown University Library Catalog of American Poetry and Plays
Chamber's Biographical Dictionary, 1969
The Columbia Encyclopedia, 3rd ed., 1963
Contemporary Authors, Vols. 1–56
Current Biography, 1940–1975
Cumulative Book Index (several editions)
Dictionary of American Biography, Vols. 1–10, 1933
Dictionary of American Scholars
Dictionary of Authors

Dictionary of National Biography, Vols. 1–22 and 1901–1960

Dictionary of North American Authors

Encyclopedia Britannica, 1953

Encyclopedia of American Biography, 1974

The Great Quotations, 1967

The Home Book of Quotations

Index to Literary Biographies, Vols. 1 & 2, 1975

Index to Women, 1970

International Directory of Psychologists, 1966

Leaders in Education

Los Angeles Public Library Catalog

National Cyclopedia of American Biography

National Faculty Directory, Vols. 1 & 2, 1975

National Union Catalog

New York Times Obituary Index

The Oxford Dictionary of Quotations, 2nd ed., 1955

The Penguin Book of Modern Quotations

Reader's Guide to Periodical Literature

Roget's International Thesaurus, 3rd ed., 1962

Southern California Answering Network

UCLA Card Catalog

USC Card Catalog

Webster's American Biographies, 1974

Webster's Biographical Dictionary, 1972

Webster's New Twentieth Century Dictionary, 2nd ed., unabridged, 1971

Webster's New World Thesaurus, 1974

Who Was Who in America, 1607–1973

Who's Who, 1897–1975

Who's Who in America, 38th ed.

Who's Who in American Education

Who's Who in American Politics, 4th ed.

Who's Who in American Women, 1974–1975

Who's Who in France, 12th ed.

Who's Who in Germany, 5th ed.

Who's Who in Government, 2nd ed.

Who's Who in the Theatre, 15th ed.

Who's Who in the World, 1974

World Book Encyclopedia, 1972

Writer's Dictionary

Introduction

What makes anyone quotable? To have been at some time in the public eye, to have had wit, a way with words, been able to make a cogent observation in few words, to have hit hard in wrath or fervor! The choice of such quotations is probably determined both by the prestige of the quoted person and by the intrinsic worth of the quotation itself.

The case of *The Quotable Woman* is something else. It bears witness to an exhaustive study of the thought of women in virtually every walk of life and in most of communicative society, selected and distilled; but the selection is not made on the basis of exterior criteria of relative values nor according to the preferences of the author of the book, Elaine Partnow. Her inclusiveness [in Volumes One and Two] takes us chronologically from Catharine Esther Beecher, born in 1800 to Denise M. Boudrot, 1952, and in diversity from Mme. Chiang Kai-Shek to Amelia Earhart, from Margaret Mead to Golda Meir, from Zsa Zsa Gabor to Simone de Beauvoir.

What Ms. Partnow has achieved over and above the standard guidelines of a *Bartlett's* kind of volume is to make the quotations representative of the *total* woman—at least that is the impression she conveys to me relative to the women I recognize and know in her list. I found only one important woman absent from her roster: Nathalie Sarraute, the French novelist who in her quiet way has revolutionized the modern novel, and who does not get involved in women's movements. No grandiose statements have come from her direction, yet in her book of critical writings, entitled *Era of Suspicion,* she has provided our time with a label that may become as memorable as W. H. Auden's "age of anxiety" which characterized an earlier period. [This infraction has been remedied in Volume Two.]

Ms. Partnow's international optic has included most

other women of note by giving the reader telling excerpts from their writings and communications; the space allotted to each and the length of the passage are determined, as far as I can judge, by the pertinence and strength of the remarks. There are perhaps too many movie stars—but that is the circle she is closest to, and if I do not find enough scholars and educators that is my own professional bias. All anthologies bear the imprint of the collector, and out of this one Ms. Partnow emerges with a great deal of good sense, a great deal of faith in women's wisdom, and approval of their positive thinking. Many of the current women's liberation leaders are represented but not to the exclusion of those of another age. We read with pleasure [in Volume One] Emma Goldman's comprehension of what real liberation is: "true emancipation begins neither at the polls nor in courts. It begins in woman's soul," in *Tragedy of Women's Emancipation*. We are encouraged by Helen Gahagan Douglas' conviction [in Volume Two]: "I know the force women can exert in directing the course of events." We wish *that* time would come sooner than it has!

The reader will realize, indeed, how many substantial women had distinguished careers as writers, artists, and publicists before the fanfare about the "new" woman. Hopefully, the availability of these volumes will encourage speechwriters to look for words of wisdom to quote from famous women as they do from men. As a matter of fact, one of the greatest disadvantages that women have suffered in gaining entry into the mainstream of public life, intellectually and socially, beyond the limits of quotas and tokenism, has been their inability to penetrate the consciousness and frame of reference of the central intelligence of society.

The Quotable Woman should henceforth find its place next to *Webster's Dictionary* on executive desks of thinkers, writers, movers, and shakers.

Beginning with a cursory reading, quickly you become absorbed, and as you read on and on, and follow the passage of the years, you realize that women's concerns follow closely those of men, that interests are not determined by sex but by the human condition. According to Ms. Partnow's meticulous analytical subject index, the most numerous of quotable reflections concern the self, life, love, marriage, children, death, war, and God. Ms. Partnow has allowed the poets among the women to speak in verse. She has wisely avoided aphorisms, and when she extracts from speeches and essays she deftly averts fragmentation; she succeeds in providing the reader with a clear-cut unity of thoughts. She also whets the appetite and is apt to send us to library shelves for further reading from the women quoted.

Let us hope that preachers, commencement speakers, and political speech writers, along with government agencies and groups searching for women executives, college presidents, etc., will have recourse to this valuable guide to the mind and heart of the modern woman, and that as a reference book it may turn into *the portable woman.*

—Anna Balakian

Anna Balakian is Professor of French and Comparative Literature at New York University, author of four books on surrealism and symbolism, and of over a hundred essays on modern literature, and is currently President of the American Comparative Literature Association.

Preface

There is some controversy over the very concept of anthology and abridgment. In her anthology *The Feminist Papers,* Alice Rossi says, "Abridgment of any published book or essay is an assault, a cutting or pruning by one mind of the work of another." A flip of the coin and we find Louise Imogen Guiney's opinion that "quotations . . . from the great old authors are an act of filial reverence," expressed in an article she wrote for *Scribner's.* Since the coin will probably land on its edge, perhaps one should go along with Elizabeth Janeway, who wrote in *The Writer's Book*: "As long as mixed grills and combination salads are popular, anthologies will undoubtedly continue in favor."

And so they have. One of the most popular forms of anthology has been books of quotations. In January of 1974 the idea for *The Quotable Woman* crystallized in my mind's eye—not as a feminist book, nor a book of feminists; not as a "woman's book," nor a book for women only—but a book of women, by women, for everyone.

For more than a hundred years now women have been "les frondeuses" for abolition, children's rights, unionism, and more. From their first embryonic struggles for suffrage to today's fight for the Equal Rights Amendment, woman's impact on society has been felt in all its spheres—the arts, politics, theater, literature; they've even altered the structure of the family. Yet, despite their impact, there has not been one single encyclopedic volume from which we could cull the contemplations, insights, and instructions of the daring women who have braved these good fights—at no uncertain risks, if not always of their lives, certainly of their reputations. Not one dusty offering have we from the patriarchal archives of our nation's libraries.

The staggering dearth of women in so many well-known books of quotations prompted me to compile the chart shown on the next page.

A few of the greats were there—Dickinson, Stein, Woolf—along with a few obscure poets who wrote of hearts and flowers, but that was it! Where were the great female revolutionaries, educators, and artists? The adventurers, the feminists, the Third World women? I was appalled—and determined to accomplish what I'd set out to do.

My ground rules for choosing the contributors were based on reputation, remarkability, quotability, and availability of their work. Also, the attempt was made to be as representative of as many professions and nations as possible, though writers and poets, American and English, do predominate.

BOOK	TOTAL CONTRIBUTORS	PERCENTAGE OF WOMEN	TOTAL QUOTES	PERCENTAGE OF WOMEN
Bartlett's Familiar Quotations	2,000	7½ %	117,000	½ %
The Oxford Book of Quotations	1,500	8½	40,000	1
The New Dictionary of Thoughts	1,800	10	20,000	2½
Home Book of Quotations*		10		5½
Contemporary Quotations*		16		
Best Quotations for All Occasions*		5		¾

I used many standard guides to create my bibliography—the *Encyclopedia Britannica*, reputable anthologies—and many off-beat guides as well: small presses, feminist bibliographies, *Rolling Stone*.† I estimate having made use of some 3,500 books and innumerable periodicals.

The quotations were chosen for various reasons—some for their lyricism, some for their uniqueness and piquancy, some because they were revelatory of the author's character, some because they were memorable and pertinent. Considered were infamous quotations, celebrated quota-

* Random samples.

† A list of all reference works used in my research can be found on pp. xi-xii.

tions, inventive quotations, and always, always usable quotations. A conscious effort was maintained to be as objective and eclectic as possible.

If usability was one of the criteria used in selecting the quotations, it was the only criterion used in compiling the Subject Index. Breaking from the tradition of indexing quotations by key words or phrases, I have attempted to synthesize the meaning of each quotation into one or more classifications.

If "Graceless, Pointless, Feckless and Aimless waited their turn to be milked" (from *Conference at Cold Comfort Farm* by Stella Gibbons) is indexed as "graceless" it gives little help to a reader who wants to illustrate a point. Indexing of this nature may amount to little more than a gargantuan vestigial organ. The same is true of the "by subject" method of indexing in which, for example, George Eliot's "An ass may bray a good while before he shakes the stars down" will be placed under the heading of "fool." Somewhat helpful, yes, but not nearly so much as indexing it under "braggart" and "egotist."

I like an index that is practical and usable, one that tells the reader what the quotation is *about*. Of course, there are shortcomings to this type of index. The reader searching for that favorite old quotation whose author is forgotten must try to duplicate my thinking processes to find "Graceless and Pointless . . ." classified under "cows" (of necessity) as well as under "passivity," the point of the phrase. One might object—no, no "idleness" is more to the point. I can only ask the reader to use her/his imagination and/or thesaurus, as I did. To have indexed all possible synonymous meanings as well as multiple meanings would have produced an elephantine index. Still, most quotations are classified under at least two different subjects, and some under three or four.

This Subject Index is not meant, however, to categorically pigeonhole the thoughts expressed in the quotations—simply to serve as a guide. There is a not so subtle philosophical difference in this approach which ironically makes the index both more arbitrary and more useful while implying—with some justification—that the key word/phrase method tends to serve the book, not the reader.

It seemed propitious to present the contributors chronologically, to project a sense of history and give the reader a perspective on where women in general have been and where they are going. It offers insight into changes in ideas, language (original spellings and idiosyncrasies of speech have been maintained), the use of newly gained freedoms—even in the popularity of first names. Thus, the chronological order is one more useful tool.

The frustration of tracking down biographical data on "lost" women was at times maddening. Scores of letters were sent to women in care of publishers, agents, and various organizations. Information was sought in the biographies of a contributor's husband, son, brother, or great-grandnephew. Years of birth were most elusive. Occasionally, when faced with a missing chink in the biographical or bibliographical armor, I included the woman or quotation anyway. Rather than lose fine contributors and good quotations to be true to form, I chose to be true to the women.

Through all this sleuthing I have come to feel that the public regards women in past and current history very much like fine character actors—we recognize them but do not know their names; we need them but do not pay them homage; we make demands on them but do not document their contributions. I hope that the quotations garnered here will counteract some of those lapses, that they will stimulate reading and study, that they will help retrieve "lost" women and help "found" women get some of their own back.

The most difficult part of an impossible task was, simply, to stop. This is—and probably always will be—an unfinished work. For every woman included, five, ten, twenty more could be added. Among those most frequently missing are non-English speaking women. The highly prolific Marie von Ebner-Eschenbach, for example, is sorely underrepresented because so few English translations of her works could be found. I even had difficulty finding translations of George Sand! But at least these women are represented—there were dozens more I wanted to include, but I could find nothing by them available in English. Helplessly, I was forced to eliminate one woman after another.

Many talented and deserving women whose works were collaborations with male partners also had to be ignored. And several distinguished scientists and mathematicians were left out because, though the women were/are memorable, I could find nothing "quotable"—at least nothing most of us could understand. And quotability is the principal measure for inclusion in *The Quotable Woman.*

As this is a book of learning and sharing, I'd like to take some space to thank the people who contributed to its making:

To the women who worked as my assistants and co-workers, who went beyond the tasks asked of them, working golden time for grey wages: Janine Watson, Paula Gray, Krista Michaels, Hazel Medina and, most especially, Georgia Griggs, my right—and left—hand;

To the one who saw me through it all, and held me up a good part of the time: Turner Browne, my friend, my husband;

To family, friends, and associates who supported me and advised me: Al and Sylvia Partnow, Judith and Herb Hyman, Susan Partnow, Barry Ganapol, Alejandro Grattan, Aniko Klein, Stanley Corwin, Marcy Posner, Beth Sue Rose, and all the staff at Corwin Books, Bob Garfield, Beverly Iser, Annett H. Welles, Gilda Cohen, Michele Kort, Robin Pearl, Ann and Burt Witkovsky, and Connell Cowan;

To the librarians and information service of the Los Angeles City Public Library's Main Branch, and to the Graduate Reserve Desk and general facilities of UCLA's Research Library;

To all of them—a hearty and keenly felt thanks.

But most of all I am indebted to the women who made this book possible—the contributors. Thank you, sisters.

Elaine Partnow
Los Angeles

How to Use This Book

The women quoted are presented in chronological order according to the year of their birth, beginning with the year 1800, and alphabetically within each year. Each has been given a contributor number; these numbers appear in the headings for each page in the Quotations section, and are used in the Biographical and Subject Indices rather than page numbers.

Firm birth and/or death dates are not known for every woman. When it was possible to make an accurate guess, a date followed by a question mark is given. If this was not possible, the women were given "flourished" decade dates (e.g., fl. 1850s), meaning that as near as can be figured they were most active in a certain decade. Such women are grouped together at the beginning of that decade's entries. If it is not known when a woman died but it is probable that she is no longer living, there is a question mark instead of a death date.

The quotations for each woman are presented chronologically according to the copyright date or publication date of the source. If the source was published after a woman's death, it is followed by a "p" (e.g., 1873p), indicating that it is posthumous. If only an approximate year of publication is known, the date is preceded by "c" for circa (e.g., c.1843). Parenthetical dates within a source indicate the time at which the quotation was originally spoken or written, whereas dates appearing in quotation marks indicate chapter or section titles in the sources.

In some cases no date could be found for a quotation (especially true for some poems and essays); these quotations follow the dated sources, separated from them by three asterisks across the column, and are listed alphabetically, by the first word of each new quotation.

When possible, the location of the quotation within the source is given—that is, the part, chapter, act, scene, etc.

If, however, a quote was derived from somewhere other than the source itself—for example, from a book review—and the precise location is not known, it precedes those quotations that are more specifically designated. Of course, many books have no chapter or part numbers or headings, and so locations cannot be specified for these.

Abbreviations used in source citations are: Vol.—volume; Pt.—part; Bk.—book; Ch.—chapter; St.—stanza; Sec.—section; No.—number; Sc.—scene; l.—line c.—circa; p.—posthumous; ed.—editor.

When a quotation was taken from a book, article, or any work by a writer other than our contributor, it is indicated by the words "quoted in" followed by the source and its author. In the instance of anthological works "quoted in" is not used, but editors are indicated.

Quote marks around a quotation indicate that it is from dialogue spoken by a character in a work of fiction. Except for exchanges of dialogue, original paragraphing is not indicated.

For information concerning the Biographical and Subject Indices, see notes preceding each index.

I would venture to guess that Anon,
who wrote so many poems without signing
them, was often a woman.
—*Virginia Woolf*

American women are not the only people
in the world who manage to lose track
of themselves, but we do seem to
mislay the past in a singularly
absent-minded fashion.
—*Elizabeth Janeway*

The signals of the century
Proclaim the things that are to be—
The rise of woman to her place,
The coming of a nobler race.
—*Angela Morgan*

The Quotations

1. Catharine Esther Beecher
(1800–1878)

1 Woman's great mission is to train immature, weak, and
ignorant creatures to obey the laws of God; the physical, the intellectual, the social, and the moral—first in
the family, then in the school, then in the neighborhood, then in the nation, then in the world. . . .
"An Address to the Christian Women of America," *Woman Suffrage and Women's Professions*
1871

2 To open avenues to political place and power for all
classes of women would cause [the] humble labors of
the family and school to be still more undervalued and
shunned. Ibid.

3 . . . as if *reasoning* were *any kind* of writing or talking
which tends to convince people that some doctrine or
measure is true and right. Ibid.

4 How many young hearts have revealed the fact that
what they had been trained to imagine the highest
earthly felicity was but the beginning of care, disappointment, and sorrow, and often led to the extremity
of mental and physical suffering.
Ibid., "Statistics of Female Health"

5 The delicate and infirm go for sympathy, not to the
well and buoyant, but to those who have suffered like
themselves. Ibid.

2. Julia Crawford
(1800–1885)

1 Kathleen Mavourneen! The grey dawn is breaking
The horn of the hunter is heard on the hill.
"Kathleen Mavourneen," St. 1   *1835*

2

2 Oh! Hast thou forgotten how soon we must sever?
     Oh! Hast thou forgotten this day we must part?
   It may be for years, and it may be forever;
     Then why art thou silent, thou voice of my heart?
                                  Ibid.

3. Frederika Bremer
(1801–1865)

1 Thou mayest own the world, with health
   And unslumbering powers;
   Industry alone is wealth,
   What we do is ours.

                        "Home"   *1885*

4. Jane Welsh Carlyle
(1801–1866)

1 He [Thomas Carlyle] has his talents, his vast and cultivated mind, his vivid imagination, his independence of
   soul and his high-souled principles of honour. But
   then—ah, these Buts! Saint Preux never kicked the fire-
   irons, nor made puddings in his tea cup.
           Letter to Friend (July, 1821), *Letters
                   and Memorials*   *1883p*

2 If they had said the sun and the moon was gone out of
   the heavens, it could not have struck me with the idea
   of a more awful and dreary blank in the creation than
   the words: Byron is dead.
           Ibid., Letter to Thomas Carlyle (1824)

3 . . . the only thing that makes one place more attractive to me than another is the quantity of *heart* I find
   in it. . . .
                   Ibid., Letter (1829)

4 Medical men all over the world having merely entered
   into a tacit agreement to call all sorts of maladies people are liable to, in cold weather, by one name; so that
   one sort of treatment may serve for all, and their practice thereby be greatly simplified.
          Ibid., Letter to John Welsh (March 4, 1837)

5 Some new neighbors, that came a month or two ago, brought with them an accumulation of all the things to be guarded against in a London neighborhood, viz., a pianofort, a lap-dog, and a parrot.

Ibid., Letter to Thomas Carlyle's Mother (May 6, 1839)

6 . . . I can see that the Lady has a genius for ruling, whilst I have a genius for *not being ruled*.

Ibid., Letter to Thomas Carlyle (1845)

7 It is sad and wrong to be so dependent for the life of my life on any human being as I am on you; that I cannot by any force of logic cure myself at this date, when it has become second nature. If I have to lead another life in any of the planets, I shall take precious good care not to hang myself round any man's neck, either as a locket or a millstone.

Ibid. (1850)

8 Never does one feel oneself so utterly helpless as in trying to speak comfort for great bereavement. I will not try it. Time is the only comforter for the loss of a mother.

Ibid. (December 27, 1853)

9 If peace and quietness be not in one's own power, one can always give oneself at least bodily fatigue—no such bad *succe daneum** after all.

Ibid., Journal Entry (October 23, 1855)

10 When one has been threatened with a great injustice, one accepts a smaller as a favour.

Ibid. (November 21, 1855)

11 All that senseless singing of *Te Deum* before the battle has begun!

Ibid., Letter

12 It's [society] like seasickness: one thinks at the time one will never risk it again, and then the impression wears off and one thinks perhaps one's constitution has changed and that this time it will be more bearable.

Ibid.

* * *

13 Of all God's creatures, Man alone is poor.

"To a Swallow Building Under Our Eaves"

* Substitution.

4

5. Lydia M. Child
(1802–1880)

1 In most nations the path of antiquity is shrouded in
darkness, rendered more visible by the wild, fantastic
light of fable; but with us, the vista of time is luminous
to its remotest point.

Hobomok, Ch. 1   *1824*

2 The old men gazed on them in their loveliness, and
turned away with that deep and painful sigh, which the
gladness of childhood, and the transient beauty of
youth, are so apt to awaken in the bosom of the aged.

Ibid., Ch. 8

3 "The fact is, passengers to heaven are in haste, and will
walk one way or the other. If a man doubts of his way,
Satan is always ready at hand to help him to a new set
of opinions at every stage. . . ."   Ibid., Ch. 13

4 England may as well dam up the waters from the Nile
with bulrushes as to fetter the step of Freedom, more
proud and firm in this youthful land. . . .

The Rebels, Ch. 4   *1825*

5 I sometimes think the gods have united human beings
by some mysterious principle, like the according notes
of music. Or is it as Plato has supposed, that souls originally one have been divided, and each seeks the half it
lost?

Philothea: A Romance, Ch. 1   *1836*

6 Every human being has, like Socrates, an attendant
spirit; and wise are they who obey its signals. If it does
not always tell us what to do, it always cautions us
what not to do.   Ibid., Ch. 6

7 No music is so pleasant to my ears as that word—
father. Zoroaster tells us that children are a bridge joining this earth to a heavenly paradise, filled with fresh
springs and blooming gardens. Blessed indeed is the
man who hears many gentle voices call him father!

Ibid., Ch. 19

8 Now twilight lets her curtain down
And pins it with a star.

Obituary for MacDonald Clark   *1842*

5

9 Whoso does not see that genuine life is a battle and a march has poorly read his origin and his destiny.

Letters from New York, Vol. I   1852

10 It is right noble to fight with wickedness and wrong; the mistake is in supposing that spiritual evil can be overcome by physical means.

Ibid.

11 Not in vain is Ireland pouring itself all over the earth. . . . The Irish, with their glowing hearts and reverent credulity, are needed in this cold age of intellect and skepticism.

Ibid., No. 33 (December 8, 1842)

12 None speaks of the bravery, the might, or the intellect of Jesus; but the devil is always imagined as being of acute intellect, political cunning, and the fiercest courage.

Ibid.

13 But now I have lost the power of looking merely on the surface. Everything seems to me to come from the Infinite, to be filled with the Infinite, to be tending toward the Infinite.

Ibid.

14 The more women become rational companions, partners in business and in thought, as well as in affection and amusement, the more highly will men appreciate *home*—that blessed work, which opens to the human heart the most perfect glimpse of Heaven, and helps to carry it thither, as on an angel's wings.

Ibid., No. 34 (January, 1843)

15 Spiritual bloom and elasticity are . . . injured by modes of life untrue to nature.

Ibid., Vol. II, No. 31 (December 31, 1844)

16 Use is the highest law of our being, and it cannot be disobeyed with impunity.

Ibid.

17 So he began to be very thoughtful about every action of his life; and if he felt uneasy about anything he was tempted to do, he said to himself, "This is the inward light, showing me that the thing is wrong. I will not do it." Pursuing this course, he became careful not to do

anything which did not bring peace to his soul; and as the soul can never be peaceful when it disobeys God, he was continually travelling toward Zion while he strove to follow this inward light in his soul; and the more humbly he tried to follow it, the clearer the light became.

"William Boen," *The Freedmen's Book*   1865

18 But men never violate the laws of God without suffering the consequences, sooner or later.

Ibid., "Toussaint L'Ouverture"

19 There are not many people who are conscientious about being kind in their relations with human beings; and therefore it is not surprising that still fewer should be considerate about humanity to animals. . . . The fact is, reasonable and kind treatment will generally produce a great and beneficial change in vicious animals as well as in vicious men.

Ibid., "Kindness to Animals"

20 Ah, my friend, that is the only true church organization, when heads and hearts unite in working for the welfare of the human race!

Letter to Theodore Weld   *1880*

* * *

21 Genius hath electric power
Which earth can never tame.

"Marius Amid the Ruins of Carthage"

22 Over the river and through the wood,
To grandfather's house we'll go.

"Thanksgiving Day," St. 1

6. Dorothea Dix
(1802–1887)

1 The present state of insane persons, confined within this commonwealth, in cages, closets, cellars, stalls, pens! Chained, naked, beaten with rods, and lashed into obedience.

Memorial to the Legislature of Massachusetts   1843

2 I think even lying on my bed I can still do something.

Attributed   *July 17, 1887*

7

3 In a world where there is so much to be done, I felt strongly impressed that there must be something for me to do.

Letters from New York, Vol. II (1852), Lydia Maria Child, ed.   *December 31, 1944p*

* * *

4 I have myself seen more than nine thousand idiots, epileptics and insane in the United States . . . bound with galling chains, bowed beneath fetters, lacerated with ropes, scourged with rods.

First Petition to Congress

7. Letitia Landon
(1802–1838)

* * *

1 As beautiful as woman's blush—
As evanescent too.

"Apple Blossoms"

2 Childhood, whose very happiness is love.

"Erinna"

3 Few, save the poor, feel for the poor.

"The Poor"

4 I loved him too as woman loves—
Reckless of sorrow, sin or scorn.   "The Indian Bride"

5 We might have been—These are but common words,
And yet they make the sum of life's bewailing.

"Three Extracts from the Diary of a Week"

6 Were it not better to forget
Than but remember and regret?   "Despondency"

8. Harriet Martineau
(1802–1876)

1 If a test of civilisation be sought, none can be so sure as the condition of that half of society over which the other half has power—from the exercises of the right of the strongest.

"Women," *Society in America,* Vol. III   *1837*

2 . . . there is no country in the world where there is so much boasting of the "chivalrous" treatment she enjoys. . . . In short, indulgence is given her as a substitute for justice.

Ibid.

3 There is a profusion of some things being taught which are supposed necessary because everybody learns them. . . . But what is given is, for the most part, passively received; and what is obtained is, chiefly, by means of the memory.

Ibid.

4 Religion is a temper, not a pursuit.

Ibid.

5 . . . the sum and substance of female education in America, as in England, is training women to consider marriage as the sole object in life, and to pretend that they do not think so.

Ibid.

6 . . . fidelity to conscience is inconsistent with retiring modesty. If it be so, let the modesty succumb. It can be only a false modesty which can be thus endangered.

Ibid.

7 Persecution for opinion, punishment for all manifestations of intellectual and moral strength, are still as common as women who have opinions and who manifest strength. . . .

Ibid.

8 If there is any country on earth where the course of true love may be expected to run smooth, it is America.

Ibid., "Marriage"

9 Marriage . . . is still the imperfect institution it must remain while women continue to be ill-educated, passive, and subservient. . . .

Ibid.

10 . . . the early marriages of silly children . . . where . . every woman is married before she well knows how serious a matter human life is.

Ibid.

11 In no country, I believe, are the marriage laws so iniquitous as in England, and the conjugal relation, in consequence, so impaired.

Ibid.

9

12 . . . nobody, I believe, defends the arrangement by which . . . divorce is obtainable only by the very rich. The barbarism of granting that as a privilege . . . !

Ibid.

13 Retribution is known to impend over violations of conjugal duty.

Ibid.

14 It is clear that the sole business which legislation has with marriage is with the arrangements of property; to guard the reciprocal rights of the children of the marriage and the community. There is no further pretence for the interference of the law, in any way.

Ibid.

15 I have no sympathy for those who, under any pressure of circumstances, sacrifice their heart's-love for legal prostitution.

Ibid.

16 Any one must see at a glance that if men and women marry those whom they do not love, they must love those whom they do not marry.

Ibid.

17 Laws and customs may be creative of vice; and should be therefore perpetually under process of observation and correction: but laws and customs cannot be creative of virtue: they may encourage and help to preserve it; but they cannot originate it.

Ibid.

18 For my own part, I had rather suffer any inconvenience from having to work occasionally in chambers and kitchen . . . than witness the subservience in which the menial class is held in Europe.

Ibid., "Occupation"

19 Readers are plentiful: thinkers are rare.

Ibid.

20 They are better educated by Providence than by men.

Ibid.

21 Their charity is overflowing, if it were but more enlightened. . . .

Ibid.

22 . . . but is it not the fact that religion emanates from the nature, from the moral state of the individual? Is it not therefore true that unless the nature be completely exercised, the moral state harmonised, the religion cannot be healthy?

Ibid.

23 During the present interval between the feudal age and the coming time, when life and its occupations will be freely thrown open to women as to men, the condition of the female working classes is such that if its sufferings were but made known, emotions of horror and shame would tremble through the whole of society.

Ibid.

24 What office is there which involves more responsibility, which requires more qualifications, and which ought, therefore, to be more honourable, than that of teaching?

Ibid.

25 The progression or emancipation of any class usually, if not always, takes place through the efforts of individuals of that class. . . .

Ibid.

26 . . . is it to be understood that the principles of the Declaration of Independence bear no relation to half of the human race?

Ibid.

27 . . . I declare that if we are to look for a hell upon earth, it is where polygamy exists: and that, as polygamy runs riot in Egypt, Egypt is the lowest depth of this hell.

"The Harem," *Eastern Life: Present and Past*   1848

28 Everywhere they [Egyptian women] pitied us European women heartily. . . . They think us strangely neglected in being left so free, and boast of their spy system and imprisonment as tokens of the value in which they are held.

Ibid.

29 I am sure that no traveler seeing things through author spectacles can see them as they are. . . .

Harriet Martineau's Autobiography, Vol. I   *1877p*

30 . . . in the history of human affections . . . the least satisfying is the fraternal. Brothers are to sisters what sisters can never be to brothers as objects of engrossing and devoted affection.

Ibid.

31 I am in truth very thankful for not having married at all.   Ibid.

11

32 The veneration in which I hold domestic life has always shown me that that life was not for those whose self respect had been early broken down, or had never grown.

Ibid.

33 The older I have grown, the more serious and irremediable have seemed to me the evils and disadvantages of married life as it exists among us at this time.

Ibid.

9. Marjory Fleming
(1803–1811)

1 but gently said Marjory
go into another room and
think what a great crime
you are committing
letting your temper
git the better of you
    Diary of Marjory Fleming, St. 1 (1811)   *1934p*

2 the most Devilish thing is 8 times 8
and 7 times 7 it is what nature itselfe
cant endure. . . .

Ibid.

3   love is a very
papithatick thing as well as
troubelsom and tiresome. . . .

Ibid.

4 To Day I pronounced a
word which should never
come out of a ladys lips it was
that I called John a Impu-
dent Bitch. . . .

Ibid., St. 3

5 Sentiment is what I am not acquainted with.

Ibid.

6 I confess that I have been
more like a little young
Devil then a creature. . . .

Ibid.

10. Marie Lovell
(1803–1877)

1 PARTHENIA. Clear be mine eyes, and thou, my soul, be steel!

Ingomar, the Barbarian, Act I   *1896p*

2 INGOMAR. Freedom is hunting, feeding, danger;
that, that is freedom—that it is which makes
the veins to swell, the breast to heave and glow.
Aye, that is freedom,—that is pleasure—life!

Ibid., Act II

3 INGOMAR. —This is slavery
that gives thee freedom, brings along with it
so rich a treasure of consoling joy, liberty shall be poor
and worthless by its side.

Ibid., Act V

11. Maria McIntosh
(1803–1878)

1 Beneficent Nature, how often does the heart of man, crushed beneath the weight of his sins or his sorrows, rise in reproach against thine unchanged serenity!

Two Lives, Ch. 1   *1846*

2 "Now, Jessie, there is some beauty and some goodness in every thing God has made, and he who has a pure conscience is like one looking into a clear stream; he sees it all; while him who has a bad conscience, all things look as you say they did in the muddy stream—black and ugly."

"Jessie Graham," *Aunt Kitty's Tales*   *1847*

3 ". . . there is selfishness in our hearts as long as we live; but while you watch over yourself, and pray earnestly to God against it, He will give you power always to act generously—to subdue your selfish feelings."

Ibid., "Florence Arnott"

4 To the inhabitants of the Southern States, not only the New Englander, but everyone who dwelt north of the Potomac was a Yankee—a name which was with him a

synonym of meanness, avarice and low cunning—while the native of the Northern States regarded his southern fellow-citizens as an indolent and prodigal race, in comparison with himself but half civilized, and far better acquainted with the sword and the pistol than with any more useful instrument.

The Lofty and the Lowly, Ch. 1   *1852*

5 Why is it that the young, ingenuous soul shrinks so from the disclosure of its first, earnest views of the relations in which it stands to God and man—to its Creator and its fellow-creatures?

Ibid., Ch. 16

6 ". . . it is only death which is hopeless. . . ."

Ibid., Ch. 19

12. Susanna Moodie
(1803–1885)

1 I had heard and read much of savages, and have since seen, during my long residence in the bush, somewhat of uncivilized life, but the Indian is one of Nature's gentlemen—he never says or does a rude or vulgar thing. The vicious, uneducated barbarians, who form the surplus of overpopulace European countries, are far behind the wild man in delicacy of feeling or natural courtesy.

Roughing It in the Bush, Ch. 1   *1852*

2 A nose, kind sir! Sure, Mother Nature,
With all her freaks, ne'er formed this feature.
If such were mine, I'd try and trade it,
And swear the gods had never made it.
Ibid., "Old Satan and Tom Wilson's Nose," Ch. 6

3 I have a great dislike to removing, which involves a necessary loss, and is apt to give to the emigrant roving and unsettled habits.

Ibid., Ch. 12

4 But hunger's good sauce.

Ibid.

5 "I have no wish for a second husband. I had enough of the first. I like to have my own way—to lie down mistress, and get up master."

Ibid.

14

6 The pure beauty of the Canadian water, the somber but august grandeur of the vast forest that hemmed us in on every side and shut us out from the rest of the world, soon cast a magic spell upon our spirits, and we began to feel charmed with the freedom and solitude around us.

Ibid., Ch. 13

7 When hands are tightly clasped, 'mid struggling sighs
And streaming tears, those whisper'd accents rise,
   Leaving to God the objects of our care
In that short, simple, comprehensive prayer—
ADIEU!

Ibid., Ch. 25

8 I have given you a faithful picture of a life in the backwoods of Canada. . . . To the poor, industrious working man it presents many advantages; to the poor gentleman, *none*! The former works hard, puts up with coarse, scanty fare, and submits, with a good grace, to hardships that would kill a domesticated animal at home. Thus he becomes independent. . . . The gentleman can neither work so hard, live so coarsely, nor endure so many privations as his poorer but more fortunate neighbor.

Ibid.

9 Ah, Hope! what would life be, stripped of thy encouraging smiles, that teach us to look behind the dark clouds of to-day, for the golden beams that are to gild the morrow.

Life in the Clearing, Ch. 1   *1853*

10 To wean a fellow-creature from the indulgence of a gross sensual propensity, as I said before, we must first convince the mind: the reform must commence there. Merely withdrawing the means of gratification, and treating a rational being like a child, will never achieve a great moral conquest.

Ibid., Ch. 2

11   This is my tale of woe; and if thou wilt
Be warn'd by me, this sparkling cup resign;
A serpent lurks within the ruby wine,
   Guileful and strong as him who erst betray'd
The world's first parents in their bowers of joy.

Ibid., "The Drunkard's Return"

12 The want of education and moral training is the only
    real barrier that exists between the different classes of
    men. Nature, reason, and Christianity recognize no
    other. Pride may say Nay; but Pride was always a liar,
    and a great hater of the truth.

    Ibid., Ch. 3

13 What a wonderful faculty is memory!—the most myste-
    rious and inexplicable in the great riddle of life; that
    plastic tablet on which the Almighty registers with
    unerring fidelity the records of being, making it the
    depository of all our words, thoughts, and deeds—this
    faithful witness against us for good or evil. . . .

    Ibid., Ch. 15

14 Large parties given to very young children, which are
    so common in this country [Canada], are very per-
    nicious in the way in which they generally operate upon
    youthful minds. They foster the passions of vanity and
    envy, and produce a love of dress and display which is
    very repulsive in the character of a child.

    Ibid., Ch. 19

15 The emigrant's hope of bettering his condition, and se-
    curing a sufficient competence to support his family, to
    free himself from the slighting remarks too often hurled
    at the poor gentleman by the practical people of the
    world, which is always galling to a proud man, but
    doubly so when he knows that the want of wealth con-
    stitutes the sole difference between him and the more
    favoured offspring of the same parent stock.

    "Canada: A Contrast"   *1871*

13. Sarah Power Whitman
(1803–1878)
* * *

1 And evening trails her robes of gold
   Through the dim halls of the night.   "Summer's Call"

2 Raven from the dim dominions
      On the Night's Plutonian shore,
   Oft I hear thy dusky pinions
      Wave and flutter round my door.   "The Raven"

3 Star of resplendent front! Thy glorious eye
   Shines on me still from out yon clouded sky.
   "Arcturus (To Edgar Allen Poe)"

14. Delphine de Girardin
(1804–1855)

1 Business is other people's money.
Marguerite, Vol. II   *1852*

15. George Sand
(1804–1876)

1 She is Choice at odds with Necessity; she is Love blindly butting its head against all the obstacles set in its path by civilization.

Indiana, Preface   *1832*

2 "I know that I am a slave, and you are my lord. The law of this country has made you my master. You can bind my body, tie my hands, govern my actions: you are the strongest, and society adds to your power; but with my will, sir, you can do nothing. God alone can restrain it and curb it. Seek then a law, a dungeon, an instrument of torture, by which you can hold it, it is as if you wished to grasp the air, and seize vacancy."

Ibid.

3 She did not love her husband, for the very reason that love had been imposed upon her as a duty, and that to resist all forms of moral constraint had become, with her, a second nature, a principle of behavior, a law of conscience. . . .

Ibid.

4 "How shall I free myself from this marble envelope which grips me round the knees, and holds me as totally imprisoned as a corpse by its tomb?"
Leila, Vol. I   *1833*

5 "Where love is absent there can be no woman."

Ibid.

6 I had forgotten how to be young, and Nature had forgotten to awaken me. My dreams had moved too much in the world of sublimity, and I could no longer descend to the grosser level of fleshly appetites. A complete divorce had come about, though I did not realize it, between body and spirit.   Ibid., Vol. II

17

7 What led to my loving him for so long . . . was a feverish irritation which took possession of my faculties as a result of never achieving personal satisfaction.

Ibid.

8 Desire, in my case, was an ardour of the spirit which paralysed the power of the senses even before they had been awakened, a savage ecstasy which took possession of my brain, and became exclusively concentrated there.

Ibid.

9 Having let my longings float away towards the land of dreams, I ended by following them in a fancy, seizing them on the wing and imperiously demanding of them, if not happiness at least the ephemeral emotion of a few days. . . .

Ibid.

10 As things are, they [women] are ill-used. They are forced to live a life of imbecility, and are blamed for doing so. If they are ignorant, they are despised, if learned, mocked. In love they are reduced to the status of courtesans. As wives they are treated more as servants than as companions. Men do not love them: they make use of them, they exploit them, and expect, in that way, to make them subject to the law of fidelity.
"La Fauvette du Docteur," *Almanach du Mois   November, 1844*

11 "And yet," plied [sic] my friend, "nature has not changed. The night is still unsullied, the stars still twinkle, and the wild thyme smells as sweetly now as it did then. . . . We may be afflicted and unhappy, but no one can take from us the sweet delight which is nature's gift to those who love her and her poetry."
La Petite Fadette, Preface   *1848*

12 Oh God! protect those who will the good, cast down those who intend evil. . . . Destroy the blind rule of the scribes and pharisees, and open a way for the traveller who seeks Thy holy places.
Souvenirs de 1848   1848

13 No one makes a revolution by himself; and there are some revolutions, especially in the arts, which humanity, accomplishes without quite knowing how, because it is everybody who takes them in hand.
The Haunted Pool, Preface   *1851*

14 Art is not a study of positive reality, it is the seeking for ideal truth. . . .

Ibid., Ch. 1

15 It is sad, no doubt, to exhaust one's strength and one's days in cleaving the bosom of this jealous earth, which compels us to wring from it the treasures of its fertility, when a bit of the blackest and coarsest bread is, at the end of the day's work, the sole recompense and the sole profit attaching to so arduous a toil.

Ibid., Ch. 2

16 He who draws noble delights from the sentiments of poetry is a true poet, though he has never written a line in all his life.

Ibid.

17 I see upon their [peasants'] noble brows the seal of the Lord, for they were born kings of the earth far more truly than those who possess it only from having bought it.

Ibid.

18 "One never knows how much a family may grow; and when a hive is too full, and it is necessary to form a new swarm, each one thinks of carrying away his own honey."

Ibid., Ch. 4

19 "Parents . . . sacrifice all the time of youth, which is the best, to forseeing what will happen to one at the age when one is no longer good for anything, and when it makes little difference whether one ends in one way or another."

Ibid., Ch. 13

20 "Thus far my daughter has understood very clearly that the best part of her life would be that which she spent in allowing herself to be courted, and she did not feel in haste to become the servant of one man, when she can command several. Therefore, so long as the game pleases her, she can amuse herself; but if you pleasure her better than the game, the game can cease."

Ibid.

21 For everything, alas! is disappearing. During even my own lifetime there has been more progress in the ideas and customs of my village than had been seen during centuries before the Revolution.   Ibid., Appendix

22 It is extraordinary how music sends one back into memories of the past—and it is the same with smells.
Story of My Life, Vol. I   *1856*

23 . . . since it always happens that one gives form and substance to the dangers upon which one broods to excess, the dread of the possibility became an accurate forecast of the future.

Ibid.

24 My heart once captured [by religion], I deliberately and, with a sort of frantic joy, showed reason the door. I accepted everything, I believed everything, without a struggle, without any consciousness of suffering, without regret, and without false shame. How could I blush for what I had learned to adore?

Ibid., Vol. III

25 Marriage is the ultimate goal of love. When love ceases, or is absent from the beginning, all that remains is sacrifice. . . . All very well for those who understand sacrifice . . . there is probably no middle way between the strength of the great-hearted, and that convenient negative attitude in which the poor-spirited find refuge—or, rather, there is a middle way, and its name is despair.

Ibid., Vol. IV

26 I regard as mortal sin not only the lying evidence of the senses in matters of love, but also the illusion which the senses seek to create where love is not whole or complete. One must love, say I, with all of one's self—or live a life of utter chastity.

Ibid.

27 The whole secret of the study of nature lies in learning how to use one's eyes. . . .
Nouvelles Lettres d'un Voyageur   *1869*

28 Classification is Ariadne's clue through the labyrinth of nature.

Ibid.

29 "I hated the pride of men of rank, and thought that I should be sufficiently avenged for their disdain if my genius raised me above them. Dreams and illusions all! My strength has not equalled my mad ambition. I have remained obscure; I have done worse—I have touched success, and allowed it to escape me. I thought myself

20

great, and I was cast down to the dust; I imagined that I was almost sublime, and I was condemned to be ridiculous. Fate took me—me and my audacious dreams—and crushed me as if I had been a reed. I am a most wretched man!"

"The Marquise" *1869*

30 The beauty that addresses itself to the eyes is only the spell of the moment; the eye of the body is not always that of the soul.

Handsome Lawrence, Ch. 1 *1872*

31 A man is not a wall, whose stones are crushed upon the road; or a pipe, whose fragments are thrown away at a street corner. The fragments of an intellect are always good.

Ibid., Ch. 2

32 Be prudent, and if you hear . . . some insult or some threat . . . have the appearance of not hearing it.

Ibid.

33 Consciousness lies in the consciousness we have of it, and by no means in the way the future keeps its promises.

Ibid., Ch. 3

34 Universal suffrage, that is to say the expression of the will of all, whether for good or ill, is a necessary safety-valve. Without it, you will get merely successive outbreaks of civil violence. This wonderful guarantee of security is there to our hands. It is the best social counterweight so far discovered.

Impressions et Souvenirs *1873*

35 There is only one happiness in life, to love and be loved. . . .

Letter to Lina Calamatta (March 31, 1862),
Correspondence, Vol. IV *1883p*

36 The constant winds of petty appetite dissipate the power of response.

Ibid., Letter to Flaubert
(November 30, 1866)

37 One is happy as a result of one's own efforts, once one knows the necessary ingredients of happiness—simple tastes, a certain degree of courage, self denial to a point, love of work, and, above all, a clear conscience. Happiness is no vague dream, of that I now feel certain.

Ibid., Vol. V

38 Faith is an excitement and an enthusiasm: it is a condition of intellectual magnificence to which we must cling as to a treasure, and not squander on our way through life in the small coin of empty words, or in exact and priggish argument. . . .

Ibid., Letter to Des Planches
(May 25, 1866)

39 One wastes so much time, one is so prodigal of life, at twenty! Our days of winter count for double. That is the compensation of the old.

Ibid., Letter to Joseph Dessauer
(July 5, 1868)

40 I have had my belly full of great men (forgive the expression). I quite like to read about them in the pages of Plutarch, where they don't outrage my humanity. Let us see them carved in marble or cast in bronze, and hear no more about them. In real life they are nasty creatures, persecuters, temperamental, despotic, bitter and suspicious.

Correspondence Vol. II   *1895p*

41 Liszt said to me today that God alone deserves to be loved. It may be true, but when one has loved a man it is very different to love God.

Intimate Journal (1834)   *1926p*

42 I realize that when one no longer loves, one no longer loves.

Ibid.

43 The capacity for passion is both cruel and divine. The sufferings of love should ennoble, not degrade. Pride is of some use here.   Ibid.

44 But if these people of the future are better than we are, they will, perhaps, look back at us with feelings of pity and tenderness for struggling souls who once divined a little of what the future would bring.

Ibid.

45 What sort of life do *you* lead, my fine men and women in the street? What has become of your eyes, your ears, your memories? You call me a cynic because I see and remember, and because I would blush to owe to blindness that sham kindliness which makes you at once fools and knaves. . . .

Ibid.

46 Can one ever really sum one's self up? Does one ever truly know oneself? Is one ever a *person*? I can no longer feel any certainty in these matters. I have the feeling now that one changes from day to day, and that after a few years have passed one has completely altered. Examine myself as I may, I can no longer find the slightest trace of the anxious, agitated individual of those years, so discontented with herself, so out of patience with others.

Ibid.

47 He is unaware that any man who is adored as a god is deceived, mocked and flattered.

Ibid. (June 13, 1837)

48 Immodest creature, you do not want a woman who will accept your faults, you want one who pretends that you are faultless—one who will caress the hand that strikes her and kiss the lips that lie to her.

Ibid.

49 Stupid men—you who believe in laws which punish murder by murder and who express vengeance in calumny and defamation!

Ibid.

50 In spite of occasional moods of disgust, in spite of periods of laziness and exhaustion which break in upon my work, in spite of the more than modest way in which I live, I know that I have found fulfillment. I have an object in life, a task, a—let me be frank and say a passion. The trade of authorship is a violent, and indestructible obsession.

Letter to Jules Boucoiran (March 4, 1831),
The Letters of George Sand   1930p

51 Search as I may for the remedies to sore injustice, endless misery, and the incurable passions which trouble the union of the sexes, I can see *no* remedy but the power of breaking and reforming the marriage bond.

Ibid., Letter to Abbé de Lamennais (c. 1836–1837)

52 Whether it be by the law, whether by generally recognised morality, whether by opinion or by prejudice the fact remains that woman having given herself to man is either enchained or considered a culprit.

Ibid., Letter to Mlle. Leroyer de Chantepie

53 For me Communism is the ideal which all progressive societies must set as their goal. It is a religion which will be a living reality centuries from now.

Quoted in *Women: A Journal of Liberation* Fall, 1970p

54 No religion can be built on force.

Ibid.

* * *

55 Education will in time be the same for men and women, but it will be in the female heart par excellence, as it always has been, that love and devotion, patience and pity, will find their true home. On woman falls the duty, in a world of brute passions, of preserving the virtues of charity and the Christian spirit. . . . when women cease to play that role, life will be the loser.

Impressions Littéraires

56 Men do not wish to be shown for what they are, nor to be made to laugh at the masks they have assumed. If you are no longer capable of love, then you must lie, or draw a veil so close about you that no eye can penetrate it. You must treat your heart as ageing libertines treat their bodies—hide it beneath the disguise of paint and subterfuge.

Sketches and Hints

57 She prided herself on being educated, erudite and eccentric. She had read a little of everything, even of politics and philosophy, and it was curious to hear her bringing out as her own, for the delectation of the ignorant, things that she had read that same morning in a book, or had heard the night before from the lips of some serious-minded man of her acquaintance.

"Horace"

58 The old woman I shall become will be quite different from the woman I am now. Another *I* is beginning, and so far I have not had to complain of her.

Isadora, Vol. II

16. Sarah Flower Adams
(1805–1848)

* * *

1 And joys and tears alike are sent
  To give the soul fit nourishment.
  As comes to me or cloud or sun,
  Father! thy will, not mine, be done.
                "He Sendeth Sun, He Sendeth Shower"

2 Once have a priest for enemy, goodbye
  To peace.
                    Vivia Perpetua, Act III, Sc. 2

3 Though like the wanderer,
    the sun gone down,
  Darkness be over me,
    my rest a stone;
  Yet in my dreams I'd be
  Nearer, my God, to Thee,
    Nearer to Thee.
              "Nearer, My God, to Thee," St. 2

17. Jeanne-Françoise Deroin
(1805–1894)

1 Because the revolutionary tempest, in overturning at
the same time the throne and the scaffold, in breaking
the chain of the black slave, forgot to break the chain
of the most oppressed of all—of Woman, the pariah of
humanity. . . .
      Letter from Prison of St. Lazare (Paris, June 15,
      1851), Written with Pauline Roland; Quoted in
      History of Woman Suffrage, Vol. I, by Elizabeth
      Cady Stanton, Susan B. Anthony, and Mathilda
      Gage   *1881*

2 We have, moreover, the profound conviction that only
by the power of association based on solidarity—by the
union of the working classes of both sexes to organize
labor—can be acquired, completely and pacifically, the
civil and political equality of women, and the social
right for all.   Ibid.

18. Angelina Grimké
(1805–1879)

1 I know you do not make the laws, but I also know that *you are the wives and mothers, the sisters and daughters of those who do.* . . .

> "Appeal to the Christian Women of
> the South," *The Anti-Slavery Examiner*
> *September, 1836*

2 I have not placed reading before praying because I regard it more important, but because, in order to pray aright, we must understand what we are praying for. . . .

> Ibid.

3 . . . when the books and papers of the Anti-Slavery Society were thrown out of the windows of their office, one individual laid hold of the Bible and was about tossing it out to the ground, when another reminded him that it was the Bible he had in his hand. *"O! 'tis all one,"* he replied, and out went the sacred volume, along with the rest. We thank him for the acknowledgment.

> Ibid.

4 It is through the tongue, the pen, and the press that truth is principally propagated.

> Ibid.

5 So precious a talent as intellect never was given to be wrapt in a napkin and buried in the earth.

> Ibid.

6 . . . we are commanded to love God with *all our minds,* as well as with all our hearts, and we commit a great sin if we *forbid or prevent* that cultivation of the mind in others which would enable them to perform this duty.

> Ibid.

7 What was the conduct of Shadrach, Meshach and Abednego? . . . Did these men *do right in disobeying the law* of their sovereign? Let their miraculous deliverance from the burning fiery furnace answer. . . .

> Ibid.

8 Duty is ours and events are God's.

Ibid.

9 If a law commands me to *sin I will break it*; if it calls me to *suffer*, I will let it take its course *unresistingly*. The doctrine of blind obedience and unqualified submission to any human power, whether civil or ecclesiastical, is the doctrine of despotism, and ought to have no place 'mong Republicans and Christians.

Ibid.

10 Slavery always has, and always will, produce insurrections wherever it exists, because it is a violation of the natural order of things, and no human power can much longer perpetuate it. . . .

Ibid.

11 . . . there is something in the heart of man which *will bend under moral suasion*. There is a swift witness for truth in his bosom, which *will respond to truth* when it is uttered with calmness and dignity.

Ibid.

12 Our fathers waged a bloody conflict with England, because *they* were taxed without being represented. . . . *They* were not willing to be governed by laws which *they* had no voice in making; but this is the way in which women are governed in this Republic.
Letter No. 11, *Letters to Catherine Beecher*,
Isaac Knapp, ed.   *1836*

13 I am not afraid to trust my sisters—not I.

Ibid.

14 Human beings have *rights*, because they are *moral* beings: the rights of *all* men grow out of their moral nature; and as all men have the same moral nature, they have essentially the same rights.
Ibid., Letter No. 12

15 When human beings are regarded as *moral* beings, *sex*, instead of being enthroned upon the summit, administrating upon rights and responsibilities, sinks into insignificance and nothingness. . . .

Ibid.

16 Hitherto, instead of being a help meet to man, in the highest, noblest sense of the term, as a companion, a co-worker, an equal; she has been a mere appendage of

his being, an instrument of his convenience and pleasure, the pretty toy with which he whiled away his leisure moments, or the pet animal whom he humored into playfulness and submission.

Ibid.

17 I recognize no rights but *human* rights—I know nothing of men's rights and women's rights; for in Christ Jesus there is neither male nor female. It is my solemn conviction that, until this principle of equality is recognized and embodied in practice, the church can do nothing effectual for the permanent reformation of the world.

Ibid.

18 Ought God to be *all in all* to us on *earth*? I thought so, and am frightened to find He is not, that is, I feel something else is necessary to my happiness. I laid awake thinking why it was that my heart longed and panted and reached after you as it does. Why my Savior and my God is not enough to *satisfy* me. Am I sinning, am I ungrateful, *am I an* IDOLATOR? I trust I am not, and yet—but I cannot tell how I feel. I am a mystery to myself.

> Letter to Theodore Dwight Weld (February, 1838), *Letters of Theodore Dwight Weld, Angelina Grimké Weld, and Sarah Grimké, 1822–1844*, Vol. II, Gilbert Hobbs Barnes and Dwight L. Dumond, eds. *1934p*

19 . . . thou art blind to the danger of marrying a woman who feels and acts out the principle of equal rights. . . .

Ibid.

19. Elizabeth Barrett Browning
(1806–1861)

1 Eve is a twofold mystery. . . .
> "The Poet's Vow," Pt. I, St. 1, *The Seraphim and Other Poems* *1883*

2   Is it thus,
Ambition, idol of the intellect?
Shall we drink aconite,* alone to use

* Poisonous plant.

Thy golden bowl? and sleep ourselves to death—
To dream thy visions about life?

Ibid., "The Student," 1. 56

3 O earth the thundercleft, windshaken, where
   The louder voice of "blood and blood" doth rise,
   Hast thou an altar for this sacrifice?

Ibid., "The Seraphim," Pt. I, 1. 288

4   But since he had
   The genius to be loved, why, let him have
   The justice to be honored in his grave.

"Crowned and Buried," St. 27,
Athenoeum   July 4, 1840

5 And lips say "God be pitiful,"
   Who ne'er said "God be praised."

"The Cry of the Human," St. 1,
Graham's American Magazine   1842

6 And I smiled to think God's greatness flowed around
     our incompleteness—
   Round our restlessness, His rest.

"Rhyme of the Duchess May," St. 11,
Poems of 1844   1844

7 Do ye hear the children weeping, O my brothers,
   Ere the sorrow comes with the years?

Ibid., "The Cry of the Children," St. 1

8 But the child's sob in the silence curses deeper
   Than the strong man in his wrath.

Ibid., St. 13

9 Experience, like a pale musician, holds
   A dulcimer of patience in his hand. . . .

Ibid., "Perplexed Music"

10 I tell you, hopeless grief is passionless. . . .

Ibid., "Grief"

11 Our Euripides, the human,
   With his droppings of warm tears,
   And his touches of things common
   Till they rose to touch the spheres!

Ibid., "Wine of Cyprus," St. 12

12 Poets ever fail in reading their own verses to their
   worth.

Ibid., "Lady Geraldine's Courtship," St. 42

13 Then we talked—oh, how we talked! her voice so cad-
     enced in the talking,
  Made another singing—of the soul! a music without
     bars. . . .   *Ibid.*, St. 45

14   behold me! I am worthy
  Of thy loving, for I love thee!
                              Ibid, St. 79

15 Therefore to this dog will I,
  Tenderly not scornfully,
    Render praise and favor. . . .
               Ibid., "To Flush, My Dog," St. 14

16 There Shakespeare, on whose forehead climb
  The crowns o' the world: O eyes sublime
  With tears and laughters for all time!
             Ibid., "A Vision of Poets," 1. 298

17 Life treads on life, and heart on heart;
  We press too close in church and mart
  To keep a dream or grave apart. . . .
             Ibid., Conclusion, 1. 820

18 "Knowledge by suffering entereth
  And Life is perfected by death."
                        Ibid., 1. 929

19 Thou large-brained woman and large-hearted man. . . .
           Ibid., "To George Sand, A Desire"

20 "Yes," I answered you last night;
  "No," this morning, sir, I say:
  Colors seen by candle-light
    Will not look the same by day.
            Ibid., "The Lady's 'Yes,' " St. 1

21 By thunders of white silence, overthrown. . . .
               "Hiram Powers' Greek Slave,"
                 Poems of 1850   *1850*

22 "Guess now who holds thee?"—"Death," I said. But
     there,
  The silver answer rang,—"Not Death, but Love."
        Sonnets from the Portuguese, I   *1850*

23 Go from me. Yet I feel that I shall stand
  Henceforward in thy shadow.
                        Ibid., VI

24   What I do
And what I dream includes thee, as the wine
Must taste of its own grapes.

Ibid.

25 If thou must love me, let it be for nought
Except for love's sake only.

Ibid., XIV

26 Say thou dost love me, love me, love me—toll
    The silver iterance!—only minding, Dear,
To love me also in silence, with thy soul.

Ibid., XXI

27 God only, who made us rich, can make us poor.

Ibid., XXIV

28 Because God's gifts put man's best dreams to shame.

Ibid., XXVI

29 How do I love thee? Let me count the ways.
I love thee to the depth and breadth and height
My soul can reach. . . .

Ibid., XLIII

30 I love thee with a love I seemed to lose
With my lost saints,—I love thee with the breath,
Smiles, tears, of all my life!—and, if God choose.
I shall but love thee better after death.

Ibid.

31   Women know
The way to rear up children (to be just),
They know a simple, merry, tender knack
Of tying sashes, fitting baby-shoes,
And stringing pretty words that make no sense. . . .

Aurora Leigh, Bk. I, 1. 47   *1857*

32   Life, struck sharp on death,
Makes awful lightning.

Ibid., 1. 210

33   the beautiful seems right
By force of Beauty, and the feeble wrong
Because of weakness.

Ibid., 1. 753

34 Whoever loves true life, will love true love.

Ibid., 1. 1066

35   Men do not think
Of sons and daughters, when they fall in love. . . .
                        Ibid., Bk II, 1. 608

36   If I married him,
I should not dare to call my soul my own
Which so he had bought and paid for. . . .
                              Ibid., 1. 785

37 God answers sharp and sudden some prayers,
And thrusts the thing we have prayed for in our face,
A gauntlet with a gift in 't.—Every wish
Is like a prayer, with God.   Ibid., 1. 952

38 How many desolate creatures on the earth
Have learnt the simple dues of fellowship
And social comfort, in a hospital. . . .
                    Ibid., Bk. III, 1. 1122

39   For poets (bear the word),
Half-poets even, are still whole democrats. . . .
                    Ibid., Bk. IV, 1. 413

40 A little sunburnt by the glare of life. . . .
                        Ibid., 1. 1140

41   Measure not the work
Until the day's out and the labor done. . . .
                    Ibid., Bk. V, 1. 76

42 Men get opinions as boys learn to spell,
By reiteration chiefly. . . .   Ibid., Bk. VI, 1. 6

43 Since when was genius found respectable?
                        Ibid., 1. 275

44   Earth's crammed with heaven,
And every common bush afire with God;
But only he who sees, takes off his shoes—
The rest sit round it and pluck blackberries. . . .
                    Ibid., Bk. VII, 1. 820

45 (Sweet cousin, walls must get the weather stain
Before they grow the ivy!)   Ibid., Bk. VIII, 1. 694

46   Genuine government
Is but the expression of a nation, good
Or less good—even as all society,
Howe'er unequal, monstrous, crazed and cursed,
Is but the expression of men's single lives,
The loud sum of the silent units.   Ibid., 1. 867

47 Alas, this Italy has too long swept
    Heroic ashes up for hour-glass sand. . . .
       Casa Guidi Windows, Pt. I, 1. 187   *1851*

48   If we tried
To sink the past beneath our feet, be sure
    The future would not stand.
                        Ibid., 1. 416

49   But "Live the People," who remained and must,
The unrenounced and unrenounceable.
    Long live the people! How they lived! and
      boiled
And bubbled in the cauldron of the street. . . .
                 Ibid., Pt. II, 1. 115

50   That tree of liberty, whose fruit is doubted,
Because the roots are not of nature's granting!
    A tree of good and evil: none, without it,
Grow gods; alas and, with it, men are wanting!

    O holy knowledge, holy liberty,
O holy rights of nations! If I speak
    These bitter things against the jugglery
Of days that in your names proved blind and
      weak,
    It is that tears are bitter.
                     Ibid., 1. 179

51   "What monster have we here?
A great Deed at this hour of day?
A great just Deed—and not for pay?
    Absurd,—or insincere."
              "A Tale of Villafrance," St. 4,
       Athenoeum   *September 24, 1859*

52 For civilization perfected
    Is fully developed Christianity.
              "Italy and the World," St. 11,
       Poems Before Congress   *1860*

53 The thinkers stood aside
    To let the nation act.
          Ibid., "Napoleon III in Italy," St. 3

54 And each man stands with his face in the light
    Of his own drawn sword,
Ready to do what a hero can.   Ibid., St. 8

55 The world goes whispering to its own,
   "This anguish pierces to the bone;"
   And tender friends go sighing round,
   "What love can ever cure this wound?"
   My days go on, my days go on.
           "De Profundis," St. 5, *Last Poems*   1862

56 Grief may be joy misunderstood;
   Only the Good discerns the good.
                      Ibid., St. 21

57   We walked too straight for fortune's end,
    We loved too true to keep a friend;
  At last we're tired, my heart and I.
          Ibid., "My Heart and I," St. 9

20. Maria Weston Chapman
(1806–1885)

1 As *wives* and *mothers*, as *sisters* and *daughters*, we are deeply responsible for the influence we have on the human race. We are bound to exert it; we are bound to urge man to cease to do evil, and learn to do well. We are bound to urge them to regain, defend and preserve inviolate the rights of all, especially those whom they have most deeply wronged.

                Address, Boston Female
           Anti-Slavery Society, *Liberator*
                 August 13, 1836

2 Let us rise in the moral power of womanhood; and give utterance to the voice of outraged mercy, and insulted justice, and eternal truth, and mighty love and holy freedom. . . .

                      Ibid.

3 Grudge no expense—yield to no opposition—forget fatigue—till, by the strength of prayer and sacrifice, the spirit of love shall have overcome sectional jealousy, political rivalry, prejudice against color, cowardly concession of principle, wicked compromise with sin, devotion to gain, and spiritual despotism. . . .

                      Ibid.

4 My disgust was unutterable . . . at the stupid schemes by which selfish men were then, as now, trying to make capital for themselves out of the sacred cause of human

rights. . . . Hear them clamorously and meanly taking advantage of ignorance, for the promotion of self-interest.

Address, "How Can I Help to
Abolish Slavery," New York   *1855*

5 In a republican land the power behind the throne is *the* power.

Ibid.

6 Don't drag the engine, like an ignoramus, but bring wood and water and flame, like an engineer.

Ibid.

7 Slavery can only be abolished by raising the character of the people who compose the nation; and *that* can be done only by showing them a higher one.

Ibid.

8 We may draw good out of evil; we must not do evil, that good may come.

Ibid.

21. Juliette Drouet
(1806–1883)

1 I love you [Victor Hugo] *because* I love you, because it would be impossible for me not to love you. I love you without question, without calculation, without reason good or bad, faithfully, with all my heart and soul, and every faculty.

Letters to Victor Hugo (1833)   *1915p*

2 It is wicked of me to torment you, yet I cannot help myself. My offence goes by the name of "jealousy."

Ibid. (1834)

3 If I were a clever woman, my gorgeous bird, I could describe to you how you unite in yourself the beauties of form, plumage, and song!

Ibid. (1835)

4 Love exalts as much as glory does.

Ibid. (January 21, 1838)

5 There are no wrinkles in the heart, and you will see my face only in the reflection of your attachment, eh, Victor, my beloved?   Ibid. (November 19, 1841)

35

6 In my opinion, infidelity does not consist in action only; I consider it already accomplished by the sole fact of desire.

Ibid. (April 4, 1847)

7 I come to fetch my heart where I left it, that is to say in yours.

Ibid. (December 14, 1881)

22. Mary Ann Dwight
(1806–1858)

1 Janus was invoked at the commencement of most actions; even in the worship of the other gods the voterie began by offering wine and incense to Janus. The first month in the year was named from him; and under the title of Matutinus he was regarded as the opener of the day.

"Janus," Grecian and Roman　　1849

23. Flora Hastings
(1806–1839)

* * *

1 Grieve not that I die young. Is it not well
To pass away ere life hath lost its brightness?

"Swan Song"

24. Nomura Motoni
(1806–1867)

1 The whistle of the samurai's arrow is changing today to the thunder of cannon.

Untitled Poem　　1855

2 This is a world that cages all warblers with a beautiful voice.

Untitled Poem　　1861

3 Many are the victims of the waves that rush in, then out of the beach.

Untitled Poem　　1861

4 The song of the warbler, joyful at his release, has drawn forth the cry of many other birds.

Untitled Poem　　1863

25. Julia Pardoe
(1806–1862)

1 Raising his truncheon above his head, he broke it in
the centre, and throwing the pieces among the crowd,
exclaimed in a loud voice, "Le roi est mort!" Then
seizing another staff, he flourished it in the air as he
shouted, "Vive le Roi!"

Life of Louis XIV, Vol. III   *1947*

* * *

2 The heart is a free and fetterless thing—
A wave of the ocean, a bird on the wing.

"The Captive Greek Girl"

26. Elizabeth Oakes Smith
(1806–1893)

* * *

1 Faith is the subtle chain
Which binds us to the infinite.

"Faith"

2 My friends, do we realize for what purpose we are con-
vened? Do we fully understand that we aim at nothing
less than an entire subversion of the present order of
society, a dissolution of the whole existing social com-
pact?   Speech

3 Yes, this is life, and everywhere we meet,
Not victor crowns, but wailings of defeat.

"The Unattained"

27. Lady Dufferin
(1807–1867)

1 The poor make no new friends.
"Lament of the Irish Emigrant"   *1894p*

2 They say there's bread and work for all,
And the sun shines always there:
But I'll not forget old Ireland,
Were it fifty times as fair.   Ibid.

28. Frances Dana Gage
(1808–1884)

* * *

1 The home we first knew on this beautiful earth,
The friends of our childhood, the place of our birth,
In the heart's inner chamber sung always will be,
As the shell ever sings of its home in the sea.

"Home"

29. Caroline Sheridan Nordon
(1808–1877)

1 God made all pleasures innocent.
The Lady of LaGrarye, Pt. I   *1862*

2 Until I truly loved, I was alone.

Ibid., Pt. II

3 They serve God well, who serve his creatures.
Ibid., Conclusion

* * *

4 A soldier of the legion lay dying in Algiers—
There was a lack of woman's nursing,
There was dearth of woman's tears.

"Bingen on the Rhine," St. 1

5 O Friend, I fear the lightest heart makes sometimes
heaviest mourning.

Ibid.

6   . . . (for ere the moon be risen
My body will be out of pain—my soul be out of
prison). . . .   Ibid.

7 I do not love thee!—no! I do not love thee!
And yet when thou art absent I am sad.

"I Do Not Love Thee"

8 Love not! Love not! Ye hapless sons of clay;
Hope's gayest wreaths are made of earthly flowers—
Things that are made to fade and fall away,
Ere they have blossomed for a few short years.

"Love Not"

9 My beautiful, my beautiful! That standest meekly by,
With thy proudly-arched and glossy neck, and dark
and fiery eye!
"The Arab's Farewell to His Steed"

10 The stranger hath thy bridle-rein, thy master hath his
gold;—
Fleet limbed and beautiful, farewell; thou'rt sold, my
steed, thou'rt sold.   Ibid.

30. Fanny Kemble
(1809–1893)

1 . . . children are made of eyes and ears, and nothing,
however minute, escapes their microscopic observation.
Journal of a Residence
on a Georgian Plantation in 1838–1839,
John Scott, ed.   *1961p*

2 Just in proportion as I have found the slaves on this
plantation intellectual and advanced beyond the general brutish level of the majority, I have observed this
pathetic expression of countenance in them, a mixture
of sadness and fear, the involuntary exhibition of the
two feelings, which I suppose must be the predominant
experience of their whole lives, regret and apprehension. . . .   Ibid.

3 For the last four years of my life that preceded my
marriage I literally coined money, and never until this
moment, I think, did I reflect on the great means of
good, to myself and others, that I so gladly agreed to
give up forever for a maintenance by the unpaid labor
of slaves—people toiling . . . unpaid.   Ibid.

4 This is no place for me, since I was not born among
slaves, and cannot bear to live among them.
Ibid.

* * *

5 A sacred burden is this life ye bear;
Look on it; lift it; bear it solemnly;
Fail not for sorrow; falter not for sin;
But onward, upward, till the goal ye win.
"Lines to the Young Gentlemen
Graduates at Lenox Academy,
Massachusetts"

6 Better trust all and be deceived,
    And weep that trust, and that deceiving,
Than doubt one heart that, if believed,
    Had blessed one's life with true believing.

"Faith"

7 Maids must be wives and mothers, to fulfill
The entire and holiest end of woman's being.

"Woman's Heart"

8 Nature lay frozen dead,—and still and slow,
A winding sheet fell o'er her body fair,
Flakey and soft, from his wide wings of snow.

"Winter"

9 What shall I do with all the days and hours
    That must be counted ere I see thy face?
How shall I charm the interval that lowers
    Between this time and that sweet time of grace?

"Absence"

31. Margaret Fuller
(1810–1850)

1 . . . not a few believe, and men themselves have expressed the opinion, that the time is come when Euridice is to call for an Orpheus, rather than Orpheus for Euridice; that the idea of man, however imperfectly brought out, has been far more so than that of woman, and that an improvement in the daughters will best aid the reformation of the sons of this age.

"The Great Lawsuit. Man Versus Men.
Woman Versus Women," The Dial
July, 1843

2 "You are not the head of your wife. God has given her a mind of her own."
    "I am the head and she is the heart."
    "God grant you play true to one another then."

Ibid.

3 And knowing that there exists, in the world of men, a tone of feeling towards women as towards slaves, such as is expressed in the common phrase, "Tell that to women and children." . . .

Ibid.

4 The female Greek, of our day, is as much in the street as the male, to cry, What news?

Ibid.

5 For human beings are not so constituted, that they can live without expansion; and if they do not get it one way, must another, or perish.

Ibid.

6 If the negro be a soul, if the woman be a soul, apparelled in flesh, to one master only are they accountable.

Ibid.

7 In every-day life the feelings of the many are stained with vanity. Each wishes to be lord in a little world, to be superior at least over one; and he does not feel strong enough to retain a lifelong ascendant over a strong nature. Only a Brutus would rejoice in a Portia. . . .

Ibid.

8 Two persons love in one another the future good which they aid one another to unfold.

Ibid.

9 Plants of great vigor will almost always struggle into blossom, despite impediments. But there should be encouragement, and a free genial atmosphere for those of more timid sort, fair play for each in its own kind.

Ibid.

10 The well-instructed moon flies not from her orbit to seize on the glories of her partner.

Ibid.

11 George Sand smokes, wears male attire, wishes to be addressed as Mon frère; perhaps, if she found those who were as brothers indeed, she would not care whether she were a brother or sister.

Ibid.

12 Harmony exists in difference no less than in likeness, if only the same key-note govern both parts.

Ibid.

13 It has been seen that as the loss of no bond ought to destroy a human being, so ought the missing of none to hinder him from growing.

Ibid.

14 The especial genius of women I believe to be electrical in movement, intuitive in function, spiritual in tendency.

Ibid.

15 Male and female represent the two sides of the great radical dualism. But, in fact, they are perpetually passing into one another. Fluid hardens to solid, solid rushes to fluid. There is no wholly masculine man, no purely feminine woman.

Ibid.

16 Nature provides exceptions to every rule.

Ibid.

17 Union is only possible to those who are units. To be fit for relations in time, souls, whether of man or woman, must be able to do without them in the spirit.

Ibid.

18 It is a vulgar error that love, *a* love, to woman is her whole existence; she is also born for Truth and Love in their universal energy. *Ibid.*

19 What I mean by the Muse is that unimpeded clearness of the intuitive powers, which a perfectly truthful adherence to every admonition of the higher instinct would bring to a finely organized human being.
Woman in the 19th Century   1845

20 It should be remarked that, as the principle of liberty is better understood, and more nobly interpreted, a broader protest is made in behalf of women. As men become aware that few [of them] have had a fair chance, they are inclined to say that no women have had a fair chance. *Ibid.*

21 What woman needs is not as a woman to act or rule, but as a nature to grow, as an intellect to discern, as a soul to live freely and unimpeded, to unfold such powers as were given her when we left our common home.

Ibid.

22 If any individual live too much in relations, so that he becomes a stranger to the resources of his own nature, he falls, after a while, into a distraction, or imbecility, from which he can only be cured by a time of isolation, which gives the renovating fountains time to rise up. With a society it is the same. *Ibid.*

23 It does not follow because many books are written by persons born in America that there exists an American literature. . . . Before such can exist, an original idea must animate this nation and fresh currents of life must call into life fresh thoughts along its shores.

Quoted in the *New York Tribune*   *1846*

24 Truth is the nursing mother of genius.

Ibid.

25 . . . the public must learn how to cherish the nobler and rarer plants, and to plant the aloe, able to wait a hundred years for its bloom, or its garden will contain, presently, nothing but potatoes and pot-herbs.

Ibid.

26 Essays, entitled critical, are epistles addressed to the public, through which the mind of the recluse relieves itself of its impressions.

"A Short Essay on Critics," *Art,*
Literature and the Drama   1858p

27 The critic is the historian who records the order of creation. In vain for the maker, who knows without learning it, but not in vain for the mind of his race.

Ibid.

28 POET. Yes, that is always the way. You understand me, who never have the arrogance to pretend that I understand myself.

Ibid., "A Dialogue"

29 It is not because the touch of genius has roused genius to production, but because the admiration of genius has made talent ambitious, that the harvest is still so abundant.

Ibid., "The Modern Drama"

30 'Tis, indeed, hard to believe that the drama, once invented, should cease to be a habitual and healthy expression of the mind. . . . But . . . no form of art will succeed with him to whom it is the object of deliberate choice. It must grow from his nature. . . .

Ibid.

31 . . . there are two modes of criticism. One which . . . crushes to earth without mercy all the humble buds of Phantasy, all the plants that, though green and fruitful, are also a prey to insects or have suffered by drouth. It

weeds well the garden, and cannot believe the weed in its native soil may be a pretty, graceful plant. There is another mode which enters into the natural history of every thing that breathes and lives, which believes no impulse to be entirely in vain, which scrutinizes circumstances, motive and object before it condemns, and believes there is a beauty in natural form, if its law and purpose be understood.   Ibid., "Poets of the People"

32 The lives of the musicians are imperfectly written for this obvious reason. The soul of the great musician can only be expressed in music. . . . We must read them in their works; this, true of artists in every department, is especially so of the high priestesses of sound.

Ibid., "Lives of the Great Composers"

33 We cannot have expression till there is something to be expressed.   Ibid., "American Literature"

34 This was one of the rye-bread days, all dull and damp without.

Diary Entry, *Life of Margaret Fuller-Ossoli,* Ch. 7, Thomas Wentworth Higginson, ed.   *1884p*

35 For precocity some great price is always demanded sooner or later in life.   Ibid., Ch. 18

36 Genius will live and thrive without training, but it does not the less reward the watering-pot and pruning-knife.

Ibid.

37 It is so true that a woman may be in love with a woman, and a man with a man. It is pleasant to be sure of it, because it is undoubtedly the same love that we shall feel when we are angels, when we ascend to the only fit place for the Mignons, where *sie fragen nicht nach Mann und Weib.*

Quoted in *Margaret Fuller, Whetstone of Genius* by Mason Wade   *1940p*

38 I myself am more divine than any I see.

Letter to Emerson (March 1, 1838), *The Feminist Papers,* Alice Rossi, ed.   *1973p*

39 . . . men are called on from a very early period to reproduce all that they learn. . . . But women learn without any attempt to reproduce. Their only reproduction is for purposes of display.

Ibid., Lecture, "Conversations" (1839)

40 Beware of over-great pleasure in being popular or even beloved.

Ibid., Letter to Her Brother, Arthur (December 20, 1840)

41 What a difference it makes to come home to a child!
Ibid., Letter to Friends (1849)

42 They [the Irish] are looked upon with contempt for their want of aptitude in learning new things; their ready and ingenious lying; their eye-service. These are the faults of an oppressed race, which must require the aid of better circumstances through two or three generations to eradicate. . . .

Ibid., Untitled Essay

43 Ye cannot believe it, men; but the only reason why women ever assume what is more appropriate to you is because you prevent them from finding out what is fit for themselves. Were they free . . . to develop the strength and beauty of women, they would never wish to be men.

Ibid.

32. Elizabeth Gaskell
(1810–1865)

1 A man . . . is *so* in the way in the house!
Cranford, Ch. 1   1853

2 Bombazine would have shown a deeper sense of her loss.

Ibid.

3 There, economy was always "elegant," and money-spending always "vulgar" and ostentatious—a sort of sour grapeism, which made us very peaceful and satisfied.
Ibid.

4 Correspondence, which bears much the same relation to personal intercourse that the books of dried plants I sometimes see ("Hortus Siccus," I think they call the thing) do to the living and fresh flowers in the lanes and meadows. . . .
Ibid., Ch. 3

5 One gives people in grief their own way.

Ibid., Ch. 6

6 A little credulity helps one on through life very smoothly.

Ibid., Ch. 11

7 I'll not listen to reason. . . . Reason always means what someone else has got to say.

Ibid., Ch. 14

8 What's the use of watching? A watched pot never boils.
Mary Barton, Ch. 31   *1932p*

33. Ernestine Rose
(1810–1892)

1 Oh, she [Frances Wright] had her reward!—that reward of which no enemies could deprive her, which no slanders could make less precious—the eternal reward of knowing that she had done her duty; the reward springing from the consciousness of right, of endeavoring to benefit unborn generations.

> Convention Speech, "Petitions Were Circulated" (1860), Quoted in *History of Woman Suffrage,* Vol. I, by Elizabeth Cady Stanton, Susan B. Anthony, and Mathilda Gage   *1881*

34. Fanny Fern
(1811–1872)

* * *

1 The way to a man's heart is through his stomach.
"Willis Parton"

35. Frances Sargent Osgood
(1811–1850)

* * *

1 Work—for some good, be it ever so slowly;
Cherish some flower, be it ever so lowly;
Labor!—all labor is noble and holy!
Let thy great deeds be thy prayer to thy god!
"Laborare Est Orare," St. 6

36. Harriet Beecher Stowe
(1811–1896)

1 "Well, I've got just as much conscience as any man in business can afford to keep—just a little, you know, to swear by as 't were. . . ."

Uncle Tom's Cabin, Ch. 1   1852

2 So long as the law considers all these human beings, with beating hearts and living affections, only as so many *things* belonging to the master—so long as the failure, or misfortune, or imprudence, or death of the kindest owner, may cause them any day to exchange a life of kind protection and indulgence for one of hopeless misery and toil—so long it is impossible to make anything beautiful or desirable in the best-regulated administration of slavery.

Ibid.

3 "I b'lieve in religion, and one of these days, when I've got matters tight and snug, I calculate to 'tend to my soul, and them are matters: and so what's the use of doin' any more wickedness than's re'lly necessary?—it don't seem to me it's 'tall prudent."

Ibid., Ch. 8

4 "Treat 'em like dogs, and you'll have dogs' works and dogs' actions. Treat 'em like men, and you'll have men's works."   Ibid., Ch. 11

5 If ever Africa shall show an elevated and cultivated race—and come it must, some time, her turn to figure in the great drama of human improvement—life will awake there with a gorgeousness and splendour of which our cold western tribes faintly have conceived.

Ibid., Ch. 16

6 "Who was your mother?"
   "Never had none!" said the child, with another grin.
   "Never had any mother? What do you mean? Where were you born?"
   "Never was born!" persisted Topsy. . . .
   "Do you know who made you?"
   "Nobody, as I knows on," said the child with a short laugh . . . "I 'spect I grow'd. Don't think nobody never made me."

Ibid., Ch. 20

47

7 "Cause I's wicked—I is. I's mighty wicked, any how. I can't help it."

Ibid.

8 Whipping and abuse are like laudanum: You háve to double the dose as the sensibilities decline.

Ibid.

9 For how imperiously, how coolly, in disregard of all one's feelings, does the hard, cold, uninteresting course of daily reality move on!

Ibid., Ch. 28

10 "Knows all that, Mas'r St. Clare; Mas'r's been too good: but, Mas'r, I'd rather have poor clothes, poor house, poor everything, and have 'em *mine*, than have the best, and have 'em any man's else! I had so, Mas'r; I think it's natur, Mas'r!"

Ibid.

11 Who can speak the blessedness of that first day of freedom? Is not the *sense* of liberty a higher and finer one than any of the five? To move, speak, and breathe, go out and come in, unwatched and free from danger! Who can speak the blessings of that rest which comes down on the free man's pillow, under laws which ensure to him the rights that God has given to man?

Ibid., Ch. 37

12 No one is so thoroughly superstitious as the godless man.

Ibid., Ch. 39

13 The longest day must have its close—the gloomiest night will wear on to a morning. An eternal, inexorable lapse of moments is ever hurrying the day of the evil to an eternal night, and the night of the just to an eternal day.

Ibid., Ch. 40

14 "They wanted us all to be like snow-flakes, and all that. And they were quite high, telling they wouldn't marry this, and they wouldn't marry that, till, at last, I made them a courtesy, and said, 'Gentlemen, we ladies are infinitely obliged to you, but *we* don't intend to marry people that read naughty books, either. Of course, you know, "snow-flakes don't like soot!"'"

Dred, Ch. 1   *1856*

15   "Ah, Miss Nina, we mustn't 'spect more of folks than dere is in them."

"Expect? I don't expect."

"Well, bless you, honey, bless you, honey, when you knows what folks *is*, don't let's worry. Ye can't fill a quart cup out of a thimble, honey, no way you can fix it. Dere's just where 'tis."   Ibid., Ch. 6

16   "They breed like rabbits! What God Almighty makes such people for, I don't know! I suppose He does. But there's these poor miserable trash have children like sixty; and there's folks living in splendid houses, dying for children, and can't have any. If they manage one or two, the scarlet-fever or whooping cough makes off with 'em. Lord bless me, things go on in a terrible mixed-up way in this world."

Ibid., Ch. 17

17   "Oh, I think," said Clayton, "the African race evidently are made to excel in that department which lies between the sensuousness and the intellectual—what we call the elegant arts. These require rich and abundant animal nature, such as they possess; and if ever they become highly civilised, they will excel in music, dancing and elocution."   Ibid., Ch. 29

18   He declared that the gold made in it [slavery] was distilled from human blood, from mother's tears, from the agonies and dying groans of gasping, suffocating men and women, and that it would sear and blister the soul of him that touched it; in short, he talked as whole-souled, impractical fellows are apt to talk about what respectable people sometimes do. Nobody had ever instructed him that a slave-ship, with a procession of expectant sharks in its wake, is a missionary institution, by which closely-packed heathen are brought over to enjoy the light of the Gospel.

The Minister's Wooing, Ch. 1   *1859*

19   So we go, so little knowing what we touch and what touches us as we talk! We drop out a common piece of news, "Mr. So-and-so is dead, Miss Such-a-one is married, such a ship has sailed," and lo, on our right hand or on our left, some heart has sunk under the news silently—gone down in the great ocean of Fate, without even a bubble rising to tell its drowning pang. And this—God help us!—is what we call living!

Ibid., Ch. 4

20 And ever and anon came on the still air the soft eternal pulsations of the distant sea—sound mournfulest, most mysterious, of all the harpings of Nature. It was the sea—the deep, eternal sea—the treacherous, soft, dreadful, inexplicable sea. . . .

Ibid., Ch. 5

21 There are some people who receive from Nature as a gift a sort of graceful facility of sympathy, by which they incline to take on, for the time being, the sentiments and opinions of those with whom they converse, as the chameleon was fabled to change its hue with every surrounding. Such are often supposed to be willfully acting a part, as exerting themselves to flatter and deceive, when in fact they are only framed so sensitive to the sphere of mental emanation which surrounds others that it would require an exertion not in some measure to harmonize with it. In approaching others in conversation, they are like a musician who joins a performer on an instrument—it is impossible for them to strike a discord; their very nature urges them to bring into play faculties according in vibration with those another is exerting.

Ibid., Ch. 16

22 All systems [of thought] that deal with the infinite are, besides, exposed to danger from small, unsuspected admixtures of human error, which become deadly when carried to such vast results. The smallest speck of earth's dust, in the focus of an infinite lens, appears magnified among the heavenly orbs as a frightful monster.

Ibid., Ch. 23

23 Slavery, it is true, was to some extent introduced into New England, but it never suited the genius of the people, never struck deep root, or spread so as to choke the good seed of self-helpfulness. . . . People, having once felt the thorough neatness and beauty of execution which came of free, educated, and thoughtful labor, could not tolerate the clumsiness of slavery.

"The Lady Who Does Her Own Work," *Atlantic Monthly* 1864

24 Everyone confesses in the abstract that exertion which brings out all the powers of body and mind is the best thing for us all; but practically most people do all they can to get rid of it, and as a general rule nobody does much more than circumstances drive them to do.

Ibid.

25 . . . these remarkable women of olden times are like the ancient painted glass—the art of making them is lost; my mother was less than her mother, and I am less than my mother.

Ibid.

26 They come here feeling that this is somehow a land of liberty, and with very dim and confused notions of what liberty is.

Ibid.

27 The great danger of all this, and of the evils that come from it, is that society by and by will turn as blindly against female intelligent culture as it now advocates it, and, having worked disproportionately one way, will work disproportionately in the opposite direction.

Ibid., "Servants"

28 . . . women are the real architects of society.

Ibid., "Dress, or Who Makes the Fashions"

29 One would like to be grand and heroic, if one could; but if not, why try at all? One wants to be *very* something, *very* great, *very* heroic; or if not that, then at least very stylish and very fashionable. It is this everlasting mediocrity that bores me.

Ibid.

30 Many a humble soul will be amazed to find that the seed it sowed in weakness, in the dust of daily life, has blossomed into immortal flowers under the eye of the Lord.

Ibid., "The Cathedral"

31 What makes saintliness in my view, as distinguished from ordinary goodness, is a certain quality of magnanimity and greatness of soul that brings life within the circle of the heroic.

Ibid.

32 . . . she never saw her hero, and so never married.

Ibid.

33 In a good old age, Death, the friend, came and opened the door of this mortal state, and a great soul, that had served a long apprenticeship to little things, went forth into the joy of its Lord; a life of self-sacrifice and self-abnegation passed into a life of endless rest.

Ibid.

34 The pain of the discipline is short, but the glory of the fruition is eternal.

Ibid.

35 "Take us the foxes, the little foxes, that spoil the vines: for our vines have tender grapes." . . . "Little Foxes," by which I mean those unsuspected, unwatched, insignificant *little* causes that nibble away domestic happiness, and make home less than so noble an institution should be. . . . The reason for this in general is that home is a place not only of strong affections, but of entire unreserve; it is life's undress rehearsal, its backroom, its dressing room, from which we go forth to more careful and guarded intercourse, leaving behind us much *debris* of cast-off and everyday clothing.

Little Foxes, Ch. 1   *1865*

36 Irritability is, more than most unlovely states, a sin of the flesh. . . . It is a state of nervous torture; and the attacks which the wretched victim makes on others are as much a result of disease as the snapping and biting of a patient convulsed with hydrophobia.

Ibid., Ch. 2

37 I am speaking now of the highest duty we owe our friends, the noblest, the most sacred—that of keeping their own nobleness, goodness, pure and incorrupt. . . . If we *let* our friend become cold and selfish and exacting without a remonstrance, we are no true lover, no true friend.

Ibid., Ch. 3

38 Wrath and bitterness speak themselves and go with their own force; love is shame-faced, looks shyly out of the window, lingers long at the doorlatch.

Ibid.

39 The bitterest tears shed over graves are for words left unsaid and deeds left undone.

Ibid.

40 . . . the obstinacy of cleverness and reason is nothing to the obstinacy of folly and inanity.

Ibid., Ch. 4

41 A little reflection will enable any person to detect in himself that *setness in trifles* which is the result of the unwatched instinct of self-will and to establish over himself a jealous guardianship.

Ibid.

42 Now, if the principle of toleration were once admitted into classical education—if it were admitted that the great object is to read and enjoy a language, and the stress of the teaching were placed on the few things absolutely essential to this result, if the tortoise were allowed time to creep, and the bird permitted to fly, and the fish to swim, towards the enchanted and divine sources of Helicon—all might in their own way arrive there, and rejoice in its flowers, its beauty, and its coolness.

Ibid., Ch. 5

43 Every human being has some handle by which he may be lifted, some groove in which he was meant to run; and the great work of life, as far as our relations with each other are concerned, is to lift each one by his own proper handle, and run each one in his own proper groove.

Ibid.

44 "For my part," said my wife, "I think one of the greatest destroyers of domestic peace is Discourtesy. People neglect, with their nearest friends, those refinements and civilities which they practice with strangers."

Ibid., Ch. 6

45 Yet there are persons who keep the requirements of life strained up always at concert pitch and are thus worn out, and made miserable all their days by the grating of a perpetual discord.

Ibid., Ch. 7

46 It lies around us like a cloud,
    A world we do not see;
Yet the sweet closing of an eye
    May bring us there to be.
                    "The Other World," St. 1   1867

47 One must be very much of a woman for whom a man can sacrifice the deepest purpose of his life without awaking to regret it.

Old Town Folks, Ch. 2   1869

48 The burning of rebellious thoughts in the little breast, of internal hatred and opposition, could not long go on without slight whiffs of external smoke, such as mark the course of subterranean fire.

Ibid., Ch. 11

49 These words dropped into my childish mind as if you should accidentally drop a ring into a deep well. I did not think of them much at the time, but there came a day in my life when the ring was fished up out of the well, good as new.

Ibid., Ch. 25

50 All men are lovers of sunshine and spring gales, but they are no one's in particular; and he who seeks to hold them to one heart finds his mistake.

Ibid., Ch. 36

51 All my life my desire to visit the beautiful places of this earth has been so intense, that I cannot but hope that after my death I shall be permitted to go and look at them.

"Household Papers and Stories,"
The Writings of Harriet Beecher Stowe,
Vol. III   *1896*

52 . . . talent, especially in a woman, creates a zest for variety that the deepest passion cannot entirely supply. A monotonous life, even in the bosom of content, dismays a mind so constituted.

Quoted in *The Trumpets of Jubilee*
by Constance Roarke   *1927p*

37. Sarah Boyle
(1812–1869)

* * *

1 Here I come creeping, creeping everywhere. . . .
"The Voice of Grass"

38. Sarah Ellis
(1812–1872)

1 To act the part of a true friend requires more conscientious feeling than to fill with credit and complacency any other station or capacity in social life.
Pictures of Private Life, Ch. 4   *1834*

39. Ann Preston
(1813–1872)

1 Wherever it is proper to introduce women as patients, there also it is in accordance with the instinct of truest womanhood for women to appear as physicians and students.
> Quoted in *The Liberated Woman's Appointment Calendar*, Lynn Sherr and Jurate Kazickas, eds. *1975p*

40. Ellen Wood
(1813–1887)

1 Years ago, by dint of looking things steady in the face, and by economizing, he might have retrieved his position; but he had done what most people do in such cases—put off the evil day *sine die*, and gone on increasing his enormous list of debts. The hour of exposure and ruin was now advancing fast.
> *East Lynne* (novel), Ch. 1   *1861*

2 Petty ills try the temper worse than great ones.
> Ibid., Ch. 16

3 When folks act childishly, they must be treated as children.
> Ibid., Ch. 37

4 Nothing but stabs; nothing but stabs! Was her punishment ever to end?
> Ibid., Ch. 40

5 LEVISON. But there are moments when our hearts' dearest feelings break through the conventionalities of life, and betray themselves in spite of our sober judgment.
> *East Lynne* (play), Act II, Sc. 1   *1862*

6 ARCHIBALD. A woman may almost as well love herself as suffer herself to love unsought.
> Ibid.

7 LEVISON. All strategems are fair in love and war.
> Ibid., Act III, Sc. 2

8 "Afflictions are of two kinds—as I class them. The one
we bring upon ourselves, through our own misconduct;
the other is laid upon us by God for our real advantage. Yes, my boys, we receive many blessings in disguise. Trouble of this sort will only serve to draw out
your manly energies, to make you engage vigorously in
the business of life, to strengthen your self-dependence
and your trust in God."

The Channings, Vol. I, Ch. 3   *1862*

9 Things often seem to go by the rule of contrary.

Ibid., Ch. 8

10 One thing is certain: that natures are not all formed to
feel in a like degree. While the shock of some great
trouble, whether anticipated or falling unexpectedly, as
the case may happen, is passed over lightly by one
man—hardly seen when it comes; to another it is as a
terrible agony, shattering the spirit for the time, leaving
its marks until death.

Our Children   1876

11 Life has become to the most of us one swift, headlong
race—a continuous fight in which there is so much to
do that the half of it has to be left undone. . . . It is
not so much what we have done amiss, as what we
have left undone, that will trouble us, looking back.

Ibid.

12 We are truly indefatigable in providing for the needs of
the body, but we starve the soul.

About Ourselves, Ch. 1   *1883*

41. Anne Botta
(1815–1891)

* * *

1 The honey-bee that wanders all day long . . .
Seeks not alone the rose's glowing breast,
The lily's dainty cup, the violet's lips,
But from all rank and noxious weed he sips
The single drop of sweetness closely pressed
Within the poison chalice.

"The Lesson of the Bee"

42. Julia Margaret Cameron
(1815–1879)

1 I longed to arrest all beauty that came before me, and
at length the longing has been satisfied.
Annals of My Glass House   1874

43. Eliza Farnham
(1815–1864)

1 The ultimate aim of the human mind, in all its efforts,
is to become acquainted with Truth.
Woman and Her Era, Pt. I, Ch. 1   *1864*

2 Our own theological Church, as we know, has scorned
and vilified the body till it has seemed almost a reproach and a shame to have one, yet at the same time
has credited it with power to drag the soul to perdition.
Ibid.

3 Again the human face is the organic seat of beauty.
. . . It is the register of value in development, a record
of Experience, whose legitimate office is to perfect the
life, a legible language to those who will study it, of the
majestic mistress, the soul. . . .

Ibid.

4 Each of the Arts whose office it is to refine, purify,
adorn, embellish and grace life is under the patronage
of a Muse, no god being found worthy to preside over
them.

Ibid., Pt. II, Ch. 1

44. Elizabeth Phelps
(1815–1852)

1 She found out there was no doctor for her like Dr.
"Have-To."
"What Sent One Husband to California,"
The Tell-Tale   *1853p*

2 "You gentlemen," said she, "have such odd ideas of
house-cleaning! You imagine you can do it up just as

57

you buy and sell—so much labor for so much money. Now, the fact is, the simple labor is the easiest part of it. It is the getting ready for labor—contriving, planning arranging—that is so wearisome."

Ibid., "The Old Leather Portfolio"

3 Put in *your* oar, and share the sweat of the brow with which you must both start up the stream. You will richly enjoy the rest, when you reach the harbor.

Ibid., "First Trials of a Young Physician"

45. Elizabeth Cady Stanton
(1815–1902)

1 . . . we still wonder at the stolid incapacity of all men to understand that woman feels the invidious distinctions of sex exactly as the black man does those of color, or the white man the more transient distinctions of wealth, family, position, place, and power; that she feels as keenly as man the injustice of disfranchisement.

History of Woman Suffrage,
Vol. I, with Susan B. Anthony
and Mathilda Gage   *1881*

2 . . . the impassable gulf that lies between riches and poverty.

Ibid.

3 It is impossible for one class to appreciate the wrongs of another.

Ibid.

4 And here is the secret of the infinite sadness of women of genius; . . . [she] must ever be surprised and aggravated with his assumptions of leadership and superiority, a superiority she never concedes, an authority she utterly repudiates.

Ibid.

5 In a republic where all are declared equal an ostracised class of half of the people, on the ground of a distinction founded in nature, is an anomalous position, as harassing to its victims as it is unjust, and as contradictory as it is unsafe to the fundamental principles of a free government.

Ibid.

6 But standing alone we learned our power; we repudiated man's counsels forevermore; and solemnly vowed that there should never be another season of silence until we had the same rights everywhere on this green earth, as man.

Ibid.

7 But when at last woman stands on an even platform with man, his acknowledged equal everywhere, with the same freedom to express herself in the religion and government of the country, then, and not until then, . . . will he be able to legislate as wisely and generously for her as for himself.

Ibid.

8 The prolonged slavery of women is the darkest page in human history.

Ibid.

9 But if a chivalrous desire to protect woman has always been the mainspring of man's dominion over her, it should have prompted him to place in her hands the same weapons of defense he has found to be most effective against wrong and oppression.

Ibid.

10 . . . woman's discontent increases in exact proportion to her development.

Ibid.

11 Like all disfranchised classes, they began by asking to have certain wrongs redressed, and not by asserting their own right to make laws for themselves.

Ibid.

12 It requires philosophy and heroism to rise above the opinion of the wise men of all nations and races. . . .

Ibid.

13 The creeds of all nations make obedience to man the corner-stone of her religious charter.

Ibid.

14 Though woman needs the protection of one man against his whole sex, in pioneer life, in threading her way through a lonely forest, on the highway, or in the streets of the metropolis on a dark night, she sometimes needs, too, the protection of all men against this one.

Ibid.

15 The ignorance and indifference of the majority of women, as to their status as citizens of a republic, is not remarkable, for history shows that the masses of all oppressed classes, in the most degraded conditions, have been stolid and apathetic until partial success had crowned the faith and enthusiasm of the few.

Ibid.

16 Sex pervades all nature, yet the male and female tree and vine and shrub rejoice in the same sunshine and shade. The earth and air are free to all the fruits and flowers, yet each absorbs what best ensures its growth.

Ibid.

17 Wherever the skilled hands and cultured brain of women have made the battle of life easier for man, he has readily pardoned her sound judgment and proper self-assertion.

Ibid.

18 Conceding to women wisdom and goodness, as they are not strictly masculine virtues, and substituting moral power for physical force, we have the necessary elements of government for most of life's emergencies.

Ibid.

19 The queens in history compare favorably with the kings.

Ibid.

20 . . . there is no force in the plea, that "if women vote they must fight." Moreover, war is not the normal state of the human family in its higher development, but merely a feature of barbarism lasting on through the transition of the race, from the savage to the scholar.

Ibid.

21 The virtue of patriotism is subordinate in most souls to individual and family aggrandizement.

Ibid.

22 A mind always in contact with children and servants, whose aspirations and ambitions rise no higher than the roof that shelters it, is necessarily dwarfed in its proportions.

Ibid.

23 Womanhood is the great fact in her life; wifehood and motherhood are but incidental relations. *Ibid.*

24 But the love of offspring . . . tender and beautiful as it is, can not as a sentiment rank with conjugal love.

Ibid.

25 Two pure souls fused into one by an impassioned love—friends, counselors—a mutual support and inspiration to each other amid life's struggles, must know the highest human happiness;—this is marriage; and this is the only corner-stone of an enduring home.

Ibid.

26 They who give the world a true philosophy, a grand poem, a beautiful painting or statue, or can tell the story of every wandering star . . . have lived to a holier purpose than they whose children are of the flesh alone, into whose minds they have breathed no clear perceptions of great principles, no moral aspiration, no spiritual life.

Ibid.

27 . . . the woman is uniformly sacrificed to the wife and mother.

Ibid.

28 The more complete the despotism, the more smoothly all things move on the surface.

Ibid.

29 As the most ignorant minds cling with the greatest tenacity to the dogmas and traditions of their faith, a reform that involves an attack on that stronghold can only be carried by the education of another generation. Hence the self-assertion, the antagonism, the rebellion of women, so much deplored in England and the United States, is the hope of our higher civilization.

Ibid.

30 Modern inventions have banished the spinning-wheel, and the same law of progress makes the woman of to-day a different woman from her grandmother.

Ibid.

31 *Declaration of Sentiments:* . . . We hold these truths to be self-evident: that all men and women are created equal. . . .   Ibid.

32 *Declaration of Sentiments:* Now, in view of this entire disfranchisement of half the people of this country, through social and religious degradation—in view of

the unjust laws above mentioned, and because women do feel themselves aggrieved, oppressed, and fraudulently deprived of their most sacred rights, we insist that they have immediate admission to all the rights and privileges which belong to them as citizens of the United States.

Ibid.

33 *Declaration of Sentiments: Resolved,* That such laws as conflict, in any way, with the true and substantial happiness of women, are contrary to the great precept of nature and of no validity, for this is "superior in obligation to any other."

Ibid.

34 *Declaration of Sentiments: Resolved,* That all laws which prevent women from occupying such a station in society as her conscience shall dictate, or which place her in a position inferior to that of man, are contrary to the great precept of nature, and therefore of no force or authority.

Ibid.

35 *Declaration of Sentiments: Resolved,* That the same amount of virtue, delicacy, and refinement of behavior that is required of woman in the social station, should also be required of man, and the same transgressions should be visited with equal severity on both man and woman.

Ibid.

36 *Declaration of Sentiments: Resolved, therefore,* That, being invested by the Creator with the same capabilities, and the same consciousness of responsibility for their exercises, it is demonstrably the right and duty of woman, equally with man, to promote every righteous cause by every righteous means . . . and this being a self-evident truth growing out of the divinely implanted principles of human nature, any custom or authority adverse to it, whether modern or wearing the hoary sanction of antiquity, is to be regarded as a self-evident falsehood, and at war with mankind.

Ibid.

37 She [Susan B. Anthony] supplied the facts and statistics, I the philosophy and rhetoric, and together we have made arguments that have stood unshaken by the storms of thirty long years. Ibid.

38 The tyrant, Custom, has been summoned before the bar of Common-Sense. His majesty no longer awes the multitude—his sceptre is broken—his crown is trampled in the dust—the sentence of death is pronounced upon him.

Ibid., Speech, New York State
Legislature (1854)

39 You who have read the history of nations, from Moses down to our last election, where have you ever seen one class looking after the interests of another?

Ibid. (1860)

40 Reformers can be as bigoted and sectarian and as ready to malign each other, as the Church in its darkest periods has been to persecute its dissenters.

Ibid., "The Kansas Campaign of 1867"

41 There never was a more hopeful interest concentrated in the legislation of any single State, than when Kansas submitted the two propositions to her people to take the words "white" and "male" from her Constitution.

Ibid.

42 . . . mothers of the race, the most important actors in the grand drama of human progress. . . .

Ibid.

43 Having gleefully chased butterflies in our young days on our way to school, we thought it might be as well to chase them in our old age on the way to heaven.

Ibid., "The Newport Convention"

44 The *ennui* and utter vacuity of a life of mere pleasure is fast urging fashionable women to something better. . . .

Ibid.

45 . . . they had souls large enough to feel the wrongs of others. . . . Ibid., "Seneca Falls Convention"

46 The Bible teaches that woman brought sin and death into the world, that she precipitated the fall of the race, that she was arraigned before the judgment seat of Heaven, tried, condemned and sentenced. Marriage for her was to be a condition of bondage, maternity a period of suffering and anguish, and in silence and subjection, she was to play the role of a dependent on man's bounty for all her material wants. . . .

The Woman's Bible, Pt. I   *1895*

47 If the Bible teaches the equality of women, why does the church refuse to ordain women to preach the gospel, to fill the offices of deacons and elders, and to administer the Sacraments . . . ?

Ibid.

48 Why is it more ridiculous to arraign ecclesiastics for their false teaching and acts of injustice to women, than members of Congress and the House of Commons?

Ibid.

49 Come, come, my conservative friend, wipe the dew off your spectacles, and see that the world is moving.

Ibid.

50 For so far-reaching and momentous a reform as her complete independence, an entire revolution in all existing institutions is inevitable.

Ibid.

51 Reformers who are always compromising, have not yet grasped the idea that truth is the only safe ground to stand upon.

Ibid.

52 So long as tens of thousands of Bibles are printed every year, and circulated over the whole habitable globe, and the masses in all English-speaking nations revere it as the word of God, it is vain to belittle its influence.

Ibid.

53 The Bible cannot be accepted or rejected as a whole, its teachings are varied and its lessons differ widely from each other.

Ibid.

54 The Bible and Church have been the greatest stumbling blocks in the way of woman's emancipation.

Quoted in *Free Thought Magazine*
September, 1896

55 The whole tone of Church teaching in regard to women is, to the last degree, contemptuous and degrading.

Ibid.   *November, 1896*

56 The memory of my own suffering has prevented me from ever shadowing one young soul with the superstitions of the Christian religion.

Eighty Years and More   *1898*

57 It is a proud moment in a woman's life to reign supreme within four walls, to be the one to whom all questions of domestic pleasure and economy are referred.

Ibid.

58 Though motherhood is the most important of all the professions—requiring more knowledge than any other department in human affairs—there was no attention given to preparation for this office.

Ibid., Rev. Ed.   *1902*

59 . . . I had . . . as little faith in the popular theories in regard to babies as on any other subject. I saw them, on all sides, ill half the time, pale and peevish, dying early, having no joy in life. . . . Everyone seemed to think these inflictions were a part of the eternal plan—that Providence had a kind of Pandora's box, from which he scattered these venerable diseases most liberally among those whom he especially loved.

Ibid.

60 The life and well-being of the race seemed to hang on the slender thread of such traditions as were handed down by ignorant mothers and nurses.

Ibid.

61 Besides the obstinacy of the nurse, I had the ignorance of the physicians to contend with.

Ibid.

62 They smiled at each other, and one said, "Well, after all, a mother's instinct is better than a man's reason." "Thank you, gentlemen, there was no instinct about it. I did some hard thinking. . . ."

Ibid.

63 So closely interwoven have been our lives, our purposes, and experiences that, separated, we have a feeling of incompleteness—united, such strength of self-assertion that no ordinary obstacles, differences, or dangers ever appear to us insurmountable.

Ibid.

64 I am at a boiling point! If I do not find some day the use of my tongue on this question I shall die of an intellectual repression, a woman's rights convulsion.

Elizabeth Cady Stanton, Vol. II,
Theodore Stanton and Harriot
Stanton Blatch, eds.   *1922p*

65 Dear me, how much cruel bondage of mind and suffering of body poor woman will escape when she takes the liberty of being her own physician of both body and soul!

Ibid.

66 I never felt more keenly the degradation of my sex. To think that all in me of which my father would have felt a proper pride had I been a man, is deeply mortifying to him because I am a woman.

Ibid.

67 I think if women would indulge more freely in vituperation, they would enjoy ten times the health they do. It seems to me they are suffering from repression.

Ibid.

68 . . . one of the best gifts of the gods came to me in the form of a good, faithful housekeeper.

Ibid.

69 Last evening we spoke of the propriety of women being called by the names which are used to designate their sex, and not by those assigned to males. . . . I have very serious objections, dear Rebecca, to being called Henry. There is a great deal in a name. . . . The custom of calling women Mrs. John This and Mrs. Tom That, and colored men Sambo and Zip Coon, is founded on the principle that white men are lords of all. I cannot acknowledge this principle as just; therefore, I cannot bear the name of another.

Ibid., Letter to Rebecca R. Eyster
(May 1, 1847)

70 Man in his lust has regulated long enough this whole question of sexual intercourse. Now let the mother of mankind, whose prerogative it is to set bounds to his indulgence, rouse up and give this whole matter a thorough, fearless examination.

Ibid., Letter to Susan B. Anthony (1853)

71 Women's degradation is in man's idea of his sexual rights.

Ibid. (1860)

72 I shall not grow conservative with age.

Ibid.

73 I have no sympathy with the old idea that children owe such immense gratitude to their parents that they can

never fulfill their obligations to them. I think the obligation is all on the other side. Parents can never do too much for their children to repay them for the injustice of having brought them into the world, unless they have insured them high moral and intellectual gifts, fine physical health, and enough money and education to render life something more than one ceaseless struggle for necessities.   Ibid., Diary Entry (1880)

74 I have come to the conclusion that the first great work to be accomplished for women is to revolutionize the dogma that sex is a crime, marriage a defilement and maternity a bane.   Ibid. (1881)

75 I have been into many of the ancient cathedrals—grand, wonderful, mysterious. But I always leave them with a feeling of indignation because of the generations of human beings who have struggled in poverty to build these altars to the unknown god.

Ibid. (1882)

76 I am weary seeing our laboring classes so wretchedly housed, fed, and clothed, while thousands of dollars are wasted every year over unsightly statues. If these great men must have outdoor memorials let them be in the form of handsome blocks of buildings for the poor.

Ibid. (1886)

77 Our trouble is not our womanhood, but the artificial trammels of custom under false conditions. We are, as a sex, infinitely superior to men, and if we were free and developed, healthy in body and mind, as we should be under natural conditions, our motherhood would be our glory. That function gives women such wisdom and power as no male ever can possess. When women can support themselves, have their entry to all the trades and professions, with a house of their own over their heads and a bank account, they will own their bodies and be dictators in the social realm.

Ibid. (1890)

78 I asked them why . . . one read in the synagogue service every week the "I thank thee, O lord, that I was not born a woman." ". . . It is not meant in an unfriendly spirit, and it is not intended to degrade or humiliate women." "But it does, nevertheless. Suppose the service read, 'I thank thee, O Lord, that I was not born a jackass.' Could that be twisted in any way into a compliment to the jackass?"   Ibid. (1895)

79 Men as a general rule have very little reverence for trees.   Ibid. (1900)

80 In a word, I am always busy, which is perhaps the chief reason why I am always well.

                 Ibid.

81 The growth of the mind should mean as much in citizenship as the growth of the body; perhaps even more.
                 Ibid. (1902)

82 I do not know whether the world is quite willing or ready to discuss the question of marriage. . . . I feel, as never before, that this whole question of women's rights turns on the pivot of the marriage relation, and, mark my word, sooner or later it will be the topic for discussion. I would not hurry it on, nor would I avoid it.

             Letter to Susan B. Anthony (1853),
        Feminism, Mariam Schneir, ed.   *1972p*

83 We who like the children of Israel have been wandering in the wilderness of prejudice and ridicule for forty years feel a peculiar tenderness for the young women on whose shoulders we are about to leave our burdens.
       Ibid., Speech, International Council
                     of Women (1888)

84 Thus far women have been the mere echoes of men. Our laws and constitutions, our creeds and codes, and the customs of social life are all of masculine origin. The true woman is as yet a dream of the future.

                 Ibid.

85 No matter how much women prefer to lean, to be protected and supported, nor how much men desire to have them do so, they must make the voyage of life alone, and for safety in an emergency, they must know something of the laws of navigation.
            Ibid., Speech, "Solitude of Self,"
       House Judiciary Committee (1892)

46. Harriet Tubman
(1815?–1913)

1 When I found I had crossed dat *line*, I looked at my hands to see if I was de same pusson. There was such a

glory ober ebery ting; de sun came like gold through the trees, and ober the fields, and I felt like I was in Heaben.

Quoted in *Scenes in the Life of Harriet Tubman* by Sarah H. Bradford   *1869*

2 I had crossed the line, I was *free*; but there was no one to welcome me to the land of freedom. I was a stranger in a strange land; and my home, after all, was down in Maryland; because my father, my mother, my brothers, and sisters, and friends were there. But I was free, and *they* should be free. I would make a home in the North and bring them there, God helping me.

Ibid.

3 Don't you think we colored people are entitled to some credit for that exploit, under the lead of the brave Colonel Montgomery? We weakened the rebels somewhat on the Combahee River, by taking and bringing away *seven hundred and fifty-six* head of their most valuable live stock, known up in your region as "contrabands," and this, too, without the loss of a single life on our part, though we had good reason to believe that a number of rebels bit the dust. Of these seven hundred and fifty-six contrabands, nearly or quite all the able-bodied men have joined the colored regiments here. . . .

Ibid., Article in the *Boston Commonwealth* (June 30, 1863)

4 I tink dar's many a slaveholder'll git to Heaven. Dey don't know no better. Dey acts up to de light dey hab. You take dat sweet little child—'pears more like an angel dan anyting else—take her down dere, let her nebber know nothing 'bout niggers but they was made to be whipped, an' she'll grow up to use the whip on 'em jus' like de rest. No, Missus, it's because dey don't know no better.

Ibid.

5 I had reasoned this out in my mind, there was two things I had a right to, liberty and death. If I could not have one, I would have the other, for no man should take me alive.

Quoted in "Lost Women: Harriet Tubman—The Moses of her People" by Marcy Galen. *Ms. August, 1973p*

47. Charlotte Brontë
(1816–1855)

1 Life, believe, is not a dream
 So dark as sages say;
Oft a little morning rain
 Foretells a pleasant day.

       "Life," St. 1 *1846*

2 The human heart has hidden treasures,
 In secret kept, in silence sealed;—
The thoughts, the hopes, the dreams, the pleasures,
 Whose charms were broken if revealed.

      "Evening Solace," St. 1 *1846*

3 Conventionality is not morality. Self-righteousness is not religion. To attack the first is not to assail the last. To pluck the mask from the face of the Pharisee is not to lift an impious hand to the Crown of Thorns.

      Jane Eyre, Preface *1847*

4 Vain favour! coming, like most other favours long deferred and often wished for, too late!

         Ibid., Ch. 3

5 Something of vengeance I had tasted for the first time; as aromatic wine it seemed, on swallowing, warm and racy: its after-flavour, metallic and corroding, gave me a sensation as if I had been poisoned.

         Ibid., Ch. 4

6 It is in vain to say human beings ought to be satisfied with tranquillity: they must have action; and they will make it if they cannot find it. Millions are condemned to a stiller doom than mine, and millions are in silent revolt against their lot. Nobody knows how many rebellions besides political rebellions ferment in the masses of life which people earth.

        Ibid., Ch. 12

7 My help had been needed and claimed; I had given it: I was pleased to have done something; trivial, transitory though the deed was, it was yet an active thing, and I was weary of an existence all passive.

           Ibid.

8 . . . if you are cast in a different mould to the majority, it is no merit of yours: Nature did it.

Ibid., Ch. 14

9 Little girl, a memory without blot or contamination must be an exquisite treasure—an inexhaustible source of pure refreshment: is it not?

Ibid.

10 "Dread remorse when you are tempted to err, Miss Eyre: remorse is the poison of life."

Ibid.

11 "I grant an ugly *woman* is a blot on the fair face of creation; but as to the *gentlemen*, let them be solicitous to possess only strength and valour: let their motto be:—Hunt, shoot, and fight: the rest is not worth a fillip."

Ibid., Ch. 17

12 "Reason sits firm and holds the reins, and she will not let the feelings burst away and hurry her to wild chasms. The passions may rage furiously, like true heathens, as they are; and the desires may imagine all sorts of vain things, but judgment shall still have the last word in every argument, and the casting vote in every decision."

Ibid., Ch. 19

13 ". . . as much good-will may be conveyed in one hearty word as in many."   Ibid., Ch. 21

14 "You had no right to be born; for you make no use of life. Instead of living for, in, and with yourself, as a reasonable being ought, you seek only to fasten your feebleness on some other person's strength. . . ."

Ibid.

15 Feeling without judgment is a washy draught indeed; but judgment untempered by feeling is too bitter and husky a morsel for human deglutition [sic].

Ibid.

16 "Laws and principles are not for the times when there is no temptation: they are for such moments as this, when body and soul rise in mutiny against their rigour; stringent are they; inviolate they shall be. If at my individual convenience I might break them, what would be their worth?"   Ibid., Ch. 28

17 The soul, fortunately, has an interpreter—often an unconscious, but still a truthful interpreter—in the eye.

Ibid.

18 "I hold that the more arid and unreclaimed the soil where the Christian labourer's task of tillage is appointed him—the scantier the meed his toil brings—the higher the honour."

Ibid., Ch. 30

19 One does not jump, and spring, and shout hurrah! at hearing one has got a fortune, one begins to consider responsibilities, and to ponder business. . . .

Ibid., Ch. 33

20 Reader, I married him.

Ibid., Ch. 38

21 Prejudices, it is well known, are most difficult to eradicate from the heart whose soil has never been loosened or fertilized by education; they grow there, firm as weeds among stones.

Ibid.

22 An abundant shower of curates has fallen upon the north of England.

Shirley, Ch. 1   *1849*

23 Give him rope enough and he will hang himself.

Ibid., Ch. 3

24 Look twice before you leap.

Ibid., Ch. 9

25 Like March, having come in like a lion, he purposed to go out like a lamb.

Ibid., Ch. 15

26 . . . nothing moved her [Emily Brontë] more than any insinuation that the faithfulness and clemency, the long-suffering and loving-kindness which are esteemed virtues in the daughters of Eve, become foibles in the sons of Adam. She held that mercy & forgiveness are the divinest attributes of the Great Being who made both man and woman, and that what clothes the Godhead in glory, can disgrace no form of feeble humanity.

Preface to *Wuthering Heights* by
Emily Brontë   *1850*

27 But this I know; the writer who possesses the creative
gift owns something of which he is not always master—
something that at times strangely wills and works for
itself. . . . If the result be attractive, the World will
praise you, who little deserve praise; if it be repulsive,
the same World will blame you, who almost as little
deserve blame.   Ibid.

28 Alfred and I intended to be married in this way almost
from the first; we never meant to be spliced in the
hum-drum way of other people.
                        Villette, Ch. 42   *1853*

48. Frances Brown
(1816–1864)

* * *

1 Oh! those blessed times of old! with their chivalry and
    state;
I love to read their chronicles, which such brave deeds
    relate. . . .
            "Oh! The Pleasant Days of Old," St. 7

49. Charlotte Saunders Cushman
(1816–1876)

1 To me it seems as if when God conceived the world,
that was Poetry; He formed it, and that was Sculpture;
He colored it, and that was Painting; He peopled it
with living beings, and that was the grand, divine, eternal Drama.
                        Quoted in *Charlotte Cushman*
                        by Emma Stebbins   *1879p*

2 Art is an absolute mistress; she will not be coquetted
with or slighted; she requires the most entire self-
devotion, and she repays with grand triumphs.
                                    Ibid., Ch. 10

* * *

3 There is a God! the sky his presence snares,
        His hand upheaves the billows in their mirth,
Destroys the mighty, yet the humble spares
        And with contentment crowns the thought of worth.
                                    "There Is a God"

73

50. Ellen Sturgis Hooper
(1816–1841)

* * *

1 I slept, and dreamed that life was Beauty;
  I woke, and found that life was Duty.
"Beauty and Duty"

2 The straightest path perhaps which may be sought,
  Lies through the great highway men call "I ought."
"The Straight Road"

51. Eliza "Mother" Stewart
(1816–1908)

1 No power on earth or above the bottomless pit has
such influence to terrorize and make cowards of men
as the liquor power. Satan could not have fallen on a
more potent instrument with which to thrall the world.
Alcohol is king!
Memories of the Crusade, Ch. 1   *1888*

2 But you must know the class of sweet women—who
are always so happy to declare "they have all the rights
they want"; "they are perfectly willing to let their husbands vote for them"—are and always have been numerous, though it is an occasion for thankfulness that
they are becoming less so.
Ibid., Ch. 7

52. Jane Montgomery Campbell
(1817–1879)

* * *

1 We plough the fields and scatter
  The good seed on the land,
  But it is fed and watered
  By God's Almighty hand.
"We Plough the Fields," *Garland of Songs*

2 He paints the wayside flower,
  He lights the evening star.
Ibid.

53. Mrs. Cecil Frances Alexander
(1818–1895)

* * *

1 Jesus calls us, o'er the tumult
  Of our life's wild, restless sea.   "Jesus Calls Us"

2 The rich man at his castle,
    The poor man at his gate,
  God made them, high or lowly,
    And ordered their estate.   "All Things Bright"

3 All things bright and beautiful,
  All creatures great and small,
  All things wise and wonderful,
  The Lord God made them all.   Ibid.

54. Amelia Jenks Bloomer
(1818–1894)

1 Another cannot make fit to eat without wine or
  brandy. A third must have brandy on her apple dumplings, and a fourth comes out boldly and says she likes
  to drink once in a while herself too well. What flimsy
  excuses these! brandy and apple dumplings forsooth!
  That lady must be a wretched cook indeed who cannot
  make apple dumplings, mince pie or cake palatable
  without the addition of poisonous substances.
                              Water Bucket   *1842*

2 Like the beautiful flower from which it derives its
  name, we shall strive to make *The Lily* [a newspaper]
  the emblem of "sweetness and purity"; and may heaven
  smile on our attempt to advocate the great cause of
  Temperance reform!
                      The Lily   *January 1, 1849*

3 Man represents us, legislates for us, and now holds
  himself accountable for us! How kind in him, and what
  a weight is lifted from us! We shall no longer be an-
  swerable to the laws of God or man, no longer be
  subject to punishment for breaking them, no longer be
  responsible for any of our doings.
                          Ibid.   *March, 1850*

4 Ah, how steadily do they who are guilty shrink from reproof!

Ibid.   April, 1853

5 The costume of women should be suited to her wants and necessities. It should conduce at once to her health, comfort, and usefulness; and, while it should not fail also to conduce to her personal adornment, it should make that end of secondary importance.

Letter to Charlotte A. Joy   June 3, 1857

55. Emily Brontë
(1818–1848)

1 Faithful, indeed, is the spirit that remembers
After such years of change and suffering!

"Remembrance"   1846

2 Once drinking deep of that divinest anguish,
How could I seek the empty world again?

Ibid.

3 I'll walk where my own nature would be leading—
It vexes me to choose another guide. . . .

"Often Rebuked"   1846

4 Love is like the wild rose-briar;
    Friendship like the holly-tree.
The holly is dark when the rose-briar blooms,
    But which will bloom most constantly?

"Love and Friendship"   1846

5 No coward soul is mine,
No trembler in the world's storm-troubled sphere:
I see Heaven's glories shine,
And faith shines equally, arming me from fear.

"Last Lines"   1846

6 Vain are the thousand creeds
That move men's hearts: unutterably vain. . . .

Ibid.

7 Though earth and man were gone,
And suns and universes ceased to be,
And Thou wert left alone,
Every existence would exist in Thee.

Ibid.

8 There is not room for Death.

Ibid.

9 Oh! dreadful is the check—intense the agony—
When the ear begins to hear, and the eye begins to see;
When the pulse begins to throb, the brain to think
again;
The soul to feel the flesh, and the flesh to feel the
chain.
"The Prisoner"   1846

10 Sleep not, dream not; this bright day
Will not, cannot, last for aye;
Bliss like thine is bought by years
Dark with torment and with tears.
"Sleep Not," St. 1   1846

11 "Wretched inmates!" I ejaculated, mentally, "you deserve perpetual isolation from your species for your
churlish inhospitality."
Wuthering Heights, Ch. 2   1847

12 "I am now quite cured of seeking pleasure in society,
be it country or town. A sensible man ought to find
sufficient company in himself."
Ibid., Ch. 3

13 "Proud people breed sad sorrows for themselves."
Ibid., Ch. 7

14 "A good heart will help you to a bonny face, my lad
. . . and a bad one will turn the bonniest into something worse than ugly."
Ibid.

15 "A person who has not done one half his day's work by
ten o'clock, runs a chance of leaving the other half undone."   Ibid.

16 "My love for Linton is like the foliage in the woods:
time will change it, I'm well aware, as winter changes
the trees. My love for Heathcliff resembles the eternal
rocks beneath: a source of little visible delight, but necessary. Nelly, I *am* Heathcliff!"   Ibid., Ch. 9

17 "The tyrant grinds down his slaves and they don't turn
against him; they crush those beneath them."
Ibid., Ch. 11

18 "Having levelled my palace, don't erect a hovel and
complacently admire your own charity in giving me
that for a home."   Ibid.

77

19 Any relic of the dead is precious, if they were valued living.

Ibid., Ch. 13

20 "And we'll see if one tree won't grow as crooked as another with the same wind to twist it!"

Ibid., Ch. 17

21 Good things lost amid a wilderness of weeds, to be sure, whose rankness far over-topped their neglected growth; yet, notwithstanding, evidence of a wealthy soil, that might yield luxuriant crops under other and favourable circumstances.

Ibid., Ch. 18

22 I lingered round them [tombstones], under that benign sky: watched the moths fluttering among the heath and harebells; listened to the soft wind breathing through the grass; and wondered how anyone could ever imagine unquiet slumbers for the sleepers in that quiet earth.

Ibid., Conclusion

56. Emily Collins
(1818?–1879?)

1 . . . from the earliest dawn of reason I pined for that freedom of thought and action that was then denied to all womankind. I revolted in spirit against the customs of society and the laws of the State that crushed my aspirations and debarred me from the pursuit of almost every object worthy of an intelligent, rational mind.

"Reminiscences of Emily Collins," Quoted in *History of Woman Suffrage*, Vol. I, by Elizabeth Cady Stanton, Susan B. Anthony, and Mathilda Gage

1881p

2 It is ever thus; where Theology enchains the soul, the Tyrant enslaves the body.

Ibid.

3 Every argument for the emancipation of the colored man was equally one for that of women; and I was surprised that all Abolitionists did not see the similarity in the condition of the two classes.

Ibid.

4 We breathe a freer, if not a purer, atmosphere here among the mountains than do the dwellers in cities,—have more indeed, are less subject to the despotism of fashion, and are less absorbed with dress and amusements.

> Ibid., Letter to Sarah C. Owen (October 23, 1848)

5 Moral Reform and Temperance Societies may be multiplied *ad infinitum*, but they have about the same effect upon the evils they seek to cure as clipping the top of a hedge would have toward extirpating it.

> Ibid.

6 People are more willing to be convinced by the calm perusal of an argument than in a personal discussion.

> Ibid.

7 From press, and pulpit, and platform, she was taught that "to be unknown was her highest praise," that "dependence was her best protection," and "her weakness her sweetest charm."

> Ibid.

57. Eliza Cook
(1818–1889)

* * *

1 Better build schoolrooms for "the boy,"
Than cells and gibbets for "the man."
> "A Song for the Ragged Schools," St. 12

2 Hunger is bitter, but the worst
Of human pangs, the most accursed
Of Want's fell scorpions, is thirst.

> "Melaia"

3 I love it—I love it, and who shall dare
To chide me for loving that old Arm-chair?
> "The Old Arm-Chair"

4 Let Reason become your employer,
And your body be ruled by your soul.
> "Where There's a Will There's a Way," St. 3

5 Oh! Much may be done by defying
The ghosts of Despair and Dismay;
And much may be gained by relying
On "Where there's a will there's a way." Ibid., St. 4

6 Oh! better, then, to die and give
   The grave its kindred dust,
Than live to see Time's bitter change
   In those we love and trust.

"Time's Changes"

7 Oh, how cruelly sweet are the echoes that start
When Memory plays an old tune on the heart!
"Old Dobbin," St. 16, *The Journal*, Vol. IV

8 On what strange stuff Ambition feeds!

"Thomas Hood"

9 Spring, Spring, beautiful Spring.

"Spring"

10 There's a star in the West* that shall never go down
   Till the Records of Valour decay,
We must worship its light though it is not our own,
   For liberty burst in its ray.

"There's a Star in the West"

11 Though language forms the preacher,
   'Tis "good works" make the man.

"Good Works"

12 'Tis a glorious charter, deny it who can,
That's birthed in the words, "I'm an Englishman."
"An Englishman"

13 'Tis well to give honour and glory to Age,
   With its lessons of wisdom and truth;
Yet who would not go back to the fanciful page,
   And the fairytale read but in youth?

"Stanzas"

14 Who would not rather trust and be deceived?
"Love On"

15 Whom do we dub as Gentleman? The
   Knave, the fool, the brute—
If they but own full tithe of gold, and
   Wear a courtly suit.

"Nature's Gentleman," St. 1

16 Why should we strive, with cynic frown,
To knock their fairy castles down?
"Oh! Dear to Memory"

* Referring to George Washington.

58. Mary A. E. Green
(1818?–1895)

1 Of all the royal daughters of England who, by the
weight of personal character, or the influence of advan-
tageous circumstances, had exercised a permanent
bearing on its destiny, few have occupied so prominent
a place as Elizabeth, queen of bohemia, the high-
minded but ill-fated daughter of James I.
Elizabeth, Queen of Bohemia, Ch. 1   *1855*

59. Mary Elizabeth Hewitt
(1818–?)

1 A sumptuous dwelling the rich man hath.
    And dainty is his repast;
But remember that luxury's prodigal hand
    Keeps the furnace of toil in blast.
      "A Plea for the Rich Man," *Poems*, St. 3   *1853*

2 Ah me! poor heart! that love like thine
    Should seek with dreams to be content!

With dreams—and what is life, alas
    But of the visions that we see?
Shadows of love, and hope, that pass
    To mock us, like my dream of thee.
      Ibid., "Leonora Thinking of Tasso," Sts. 4–5

3 And I shall hear thy song resound,
Till from his shackles man shall bound
    And shout exultant, "LIBERTY!"
      Ibid., "The Songs of Our Land," St. 12

4 Then hail! thou noble conqueror!
    That, when tyranny oppressed,
Hewed for our fathers from the wild
    A land wherein to rest.
      Ibid., "The Axe of the Settler," St. 5

60. Mary Todd Lincoln
(1818–1882)

1 The change from this gloomy earth, to be forever reunited to my idolized husband & my darling Willie, would be happiness indeed!

> Letter to Mrs. Slataper (September 29, 1868) *The Mary Lincoln Letters,* Justin G. Turner, ed. *1956p*

2 I am convinced, the longer I live, that life & its blessings are not so entirely unjustly distributed [as] when we are suffering greatly, we are inclined to suppose. My home for so many years was so rich in love and happiness; now I am so lonely and isolated—whilst others live on in a careless lukewarm state—not appearing to fill Longfellow's measure: "Into each life, some rain must fall."

> Ibid.

3 Beautiful, glorious Scotland, has spoilt me for every other country!

> Ibid. (August 21, 1869)

4 My feelings & hopes are all so sanguine that in this dull world of reality 'tis best to dispell our delusive daydreams as soon as possible.

> Letter to Mercy Levering (July 23, 1840), *Mary Todd Lincoln: Her Life and Letters,* Justin G. Turner, ed. *1972p*

5 My evil genius Procrastination has whispered me to tarry 'til a more convenient season. . . .

> Ibid. (June, 1841)

6 Clouds and darkness surround us, yet Heaven is just, & the day of triumph will *surely* come, when justice & truth will be vindicated. Our wrongs will be made right, & we will once more, taste the blessings of freedom, of which the degraded rebels, would deprive us.

> Ibid., Letter to James Gordon Bennett (October 25, 1861)

61. Maria Mitchell
(1818–1889)

1 Why can not a man act himself, be himself, and think
for himself? It seems to me that naturalness alone is
power; that a borrowed word is weaker than our own
weakness, however small we may be.

> Diary Entry (1867), *Maria Mitchell,*
> *Life, Letters, and Journals,* Phebe
> Mitchell Kendall, ed.   *1869p*

2 We travel to learn; and I have never been in any country where they did not do something better than we do
it, think some thoughts better than we think, catch
some inspiration from heights above our own.

> Ibid. (July, 1873)

3 This ignorance of the masses leads to a misconception
in two ways; the little that a scientist can do, they do
not understand—they suppose him to be god-like in his
capacity, and they do not see results; they overrate him
and they underrate him—they underrate his work.

> Ibid. (1874)

4 For women there are, undoubtedly, great difficulties in
the path, but so much the more to overcome. First, no
woman should say, "I am but a woman!" But a
woman! what more can you ask to be?

> Ibid., Address to Students (1874)

5 The whole system is demoralizing and foolish. Girls
study for prizes and not for learning, when "honors"
are at the end. The unscholarly motive is wearying. If
they studied for sound learning, the cheer which would
come with every day's gain would be health-preserving.

> Ibid. (March 13, 1882)

6 . . . to-day I am ready to say, "Give no scholarships
at all." I find a helping-hand lifts the girl as crutches
do; she learns to like the help which is not self-help. If
a girl has the public school, and wants enough to learn,
she will learn. It is hard, but she was born to hard-
ness—she cannot dodge it. Labor is her inheritance.

> Ibid. (February 10, 1887)

7 Health of body is not only an accompaniment of health
of mind, but is the cause; the converse may be true—

that health of mind causes health of body; but we all know that intellectual cheer and vivacity act upon the mind. If the gymnastic exercise helps the mind, the concert or the theatre improves the health of the body.

Ibid.

8 . . . I do think, as a general rule, that teachers talk too much! A book is a very good institution! To read a book, to think it over, and to write out notes is a useful exercise; a book which will not repay some hard thought is not worth publishing.   Ibid. (July, 1887)

9 Every formula which expresses a law of nature is a hymn of praise to God.

Inscription on Bust in the Hall of Fame   *1905p*

62. Elizabeth Prentiss
(1818–1878)

* * *

1   Sleep, baby, sleep!
Thy father's watching the sheep,
Thy mother's shaking the dreamland tree,
And down drops a little dream for thee.
        Sleep, baby, sleep.

"Cradle Song"

63. Lucy Stone
(1818–1893)

1 I know not what you believe of God, but I believe He gave yearnings and longings to be filled, and that He did not mean all our time should be devoted to feeding and clothing the body.

Speech, "Disappointment Is the Lot of Women" (October 17–18, 1855), Quoted in *History of Woman Suffrage*, Vol. I, by Elizabeth Cady Stanton, Susan B. Anthony, and Mathilda Gage

1881

2 In education, in marriage, in religion, in everything disappointment is the lot of women. It shall be the business of my life to deepen this disappointment in every woman's heart until she bows down to it no longer.

Ibid.

3 The widening of woman's sphere is to improve her lot. Let us do it, and if the world scoff, let it scoff—if it sneer, let it sneer. . . .   Ibid.

4 We want rights. The flour-merchant, the house-builder, and the postman charge us no less on account of our sex; but when we endeavor to earn money to pay all these, then, indeed, we find the difference.

Ibid.

5 I expect some new phases of life this summer, and shall try to get the honey from each moment.
                              Quoted in *Antoinette Brown*
                              Blackwell: Biographical Sketch by
                              Sarah Gilson   *1909p*

6 Because I know that I shall suffer, shall I, for this, like Lot's wife, turn back? No, mother, if in this hour of the world's need I should refuse to lend my aid, however small it may be, I should have no right to think myself a Christian, and I should forever despise Lucy Stone. If, while I hear the wild shriek of the slave mother robbed of her little ones, or the muffled groan of the daughter spoiled of her virtue, I do not open my mouth for the dumb, am I not guilty?
          Letter to Her Mother (c.1847), Quoted in *Morning Star*, Pt. II, Ch. 6, by Elinor Rice Hays
                                                    1961p

7 I was a woman before I was an abolitionist. I must speak for the women.   Ibid. (c. 1848)

8 The privations I have learned to endure, and the isolation, I scarcely regret; while the certainties that I am *living usefully* brings a deep and *abiding* happiness.
          Ibid., Letter to Henry Blackwell   (c. 1849)

9 "We, the people of the United States." Which "We, the people"? The women were not included.
          Ibid., Speech, *New York Tribune* (April, 1853)

10 My heart aches to love somebody that shall be all its own . . . [but] I shall not be married ever. I have not yet seen the person whom I have the slightest wish to marry, and if I had, it will take longer than my lifetime for the obstacles to be removed which are in the way of a married woman having any being of her own.
          Ibid., Ch. 9, Letter to Nette Brown (1853)

11 Our victory is sure to come, and I can endure anything but recreancy to principle.

> Ibid., Pt. III, Ch. 19

12 I think God rarely gives to one man, or one set of men, more than *one* great moral victory to win.

> Ibid. (c.1867)

64. George Eliot
(1819–1880)

1 Any coward can fight a battle when he's sure of winning; but give me the man who has pluck to fight when he's sure of losing. That's my way, sir; and there are many victories worse than a defeat.

> *Janet's Repentance,* Ch. 6   1857

2 Opposition may become sweet to a man, when he has christened it persecution.

> Ibid., Ch. 8

3 In every parting scene there is an image of death.

> "Amos Barton," *Scenes of Clerical Life*   1858

4 Animals are such agreeable friends—they ask no questions, they pass no criticisms.

> Ibid., "Mr. Gilfi's Love Story"

5 It's but little good you'll do a-watering the last year's crop.

> *Adam Bede,* Ch. 18   1859

6 It was a pity he couldna be hatched o'er again, an' hatched different.

> Ibid.

7 A patronizing disposition always has its meaner side.

> Ibid., Ch. 28

8 Our deeds determine us, as much as we determine our deeds.

> Ibid., Ch. 29

9 It's them as take advantage that get advantage i' this world.

> Ibid., Ch. 32

10 A maggot must be born i' the rotten cheese to like it.

> Ibid.

11 He was like a cock, who thought the sun had risen to hear him crow.

Ibid., Ch. 33

12 We hand folks over to God's mercy, and show none ourselves.

Ibid., Ch. 42

13 I'm not denyin' the women are foolish: God Almighty made 'em to match the men.

Ibid., Ch. 43

14 I'm not one o' those as can see the cat 'i the dairy an' wonder what she's come after.

Ibid., Ch. 52

15 Anger and jealousy can no more bear to lose sight of their objects than love.

The Mill on the Floss, Bk. I, Ch. 10   *1860*

16 The law's made to take care o' raskills.

Ibid., Bk. III, Ch. 4

17 I've never any pity for conceited people, because I think they carry their comfort about them.

Ibid., Bk. V, Ch. 4

18 In their death they were not divided.

Ibid.

19 The happiest women, like the happiest nations, have no history.

Ibid., Bk. VI, Ch. 3

20 I should like to know what is the proper function of women, if it is not to make reasons for husbands to stay at home, and still stronger reasons for bachelors to go out.

Ibid., Ch. 6

21 Jealousy is never satisfied with anything short of an omniscience that would detect the subtlest fault of the heart.

Ibid., Ch. 10

22 We are not apt to fear for the fearless, when we are companions in their danger.

Ibid., Bk. VII, Ch. 5

23 Nothing is so good as it seems beforehand.

Silas Marner, Ch. 18   *1861*

24 There is a mercy which is weakness, and even treason
against the common good.

Romola   *1863*

25 Marriage must be a relation either of sympathy or of
conquest.

Ibid., Ch. 48

26 An ass may bray a good while before he shakes the
stars down.

Ibid., Ch. 50

27 There are glances of hatred that stab, and raise no cry
of murder.

Felix Holt, the Radical, Introduction   *1866*

28 In all private quarrels the duller nature is triumphant
by reason of dullness.

Ibid., Ch. 9

29 The beginning of compunction is the beginning of a
new life.

Ibid., Ch. 13

30 In our springtime every day has its hidden growth in
the mind, as it has in the earth when the little folded
blades are getting ready to pierce the ground.

Ibid., Ch. 18

31 One way of getting an idea of our fellow-countrymen's
miseries is to go and look at their pleasures.

Ibid., Ch. 28

32 But is it what we love, or how we love,
That makes true good?

"The Spanish Gypsy," Bk. I   *1868*

33 'Tis what I love determines how I love.

Ibid.

34 Death is the king of this world: 'tis his park
Where he breeds life to feed him. Cries of pain
Are music for his banquet.   Ibid., Bk. II

35 Best friend, my well-spring in the wilderness!

Ibid., Bk. III

36 Kisses honeyed by oblivion. . . .   Ibid.

37   What if my words
Were meant for deeds?   Ibid.

38 Our words have wings, but fly not where we would.

Ibid.

39   Women know no perfect love:
Loving the strong, they can forsake the strong;
Man clings because the being whom he loves
Is weak and needs him.

Ibid.

40 Prophecy is the most gratuitous form of error.

Middlemarch, Ch. 10   *1871–1872*

41 If we had keen vision of all that is ordinary in human life, it would be like hearing the grass grow or the squirrel's heart beat, and we should die of that roar which is the other side of silence.

Ibid., Ch. 22

42 What loneliness is more lonely than distrust?

Ibid., Ch. 44

43 Our deeds still travel with us from afar,
And what we have been makes us what we are.

Ibid., Ch. 70

44 Truth has rough flavors if we bite it through.

Armgart, Sc. 2   *1871*

45 . . . a woman's heart must be of such a size and no larger, else it must be pressed small, like Chinese feet. . . .

Daniel Deronda   *1876*

46 Gossip is a sort of smoke that comes from the dirty tobacco-pipes of those who diffuse it; it proves nothing but the bad taste of the smoker.

Ibid.

47 The Jews are among the aristocracy of every land; if a literature is called rich in the possession of a few classic tragedies, what shall we say to a national tragedy lasting for fifteen hundred years, in which the poets and actors were also the heroes.

Ibid.

48 A difference of taste in jokes is a great strain on the affections.

Ibid., Bk. II, Ch. 15

49 Men's men: gentle or simple, they're much of a muchness.   Ibid., Bk. IV, Ch. 31

50 Friendships begin with liking or gratitude—roots that can be pulled up.

Ibid., Ch. 32

51 The reward of one duty is the power to fulfill another.

Ibid., Bk. VI, Ch. 46

52 Blessed is the man who, having nothing to say, abstains from giving wordy evidence of the fact.

The Impressions of Theophrastus Such, Ch. 4 *1879*

53 One may prefer fresh eggs, though laid by a fowl of the meanest understanding, but why fresh sermons?

Ibid., "Looking Backward"

54 Life is too precious to be spent in this weaving and unweaving of false impressions, and it is better to live quietly under some degree of misrepresentation than to attempt to remove it by the uncertain process of letter-writing.

Letter to Mrs. Peter Taylor (June 8, 1856), *George Eliot's Life as Related in Her Letters and Journals* *1900p*

55 Few women, I fear, have had such reason as I have to think the long sad years of youth were worth living for the sake of middle age.

Ibid. (December 31, 1857)

56 The years seem to rush by now, and I think of death as a fast approaching end of a journey—double and treble reason for loving as well as working while it is day.

Ibid., Letter to Miss Sara Hennell (November 22, 1861)

57 I have the conviction that excessive literary production is a social offence.

Ibid., Letter to Alexander Main (September 11, 1871)

58 I like not only to be loved, but also to be told that I am loved. I am not sure that you are of the same kind. But the realm of silence is large enough beyond the grave. This is the world of literature and speech, and I shall take leave to tell you that you are very dear.

Ibid., Letter to Mrs. Burne-Jones (May 11, 1875)

59 To fear the examination of any proposition appears to
me an intellectual and moral palsy that will ever hinder
the firm grasping of any substance whatever.
The George Eliot Letters   1954p

* * *

60 Oh may I join the choir invisible
Of those immortal dead who live again
In minds made better by their presence.
"Oh May I Join the Choir Invisible," *Poems*

61   May I reach
That purest heaven, be to other souls
The cup of strength in some great agony.

Ibid.

62   'Tis God gives skill,
But not without men's hands: He could not make
Antonio Stradivari's violins
Without Antonio.
Ibid., "Stradivarius," 1. 140

65. Julia Ward Howe
(1819–1910)

1 Mine eyes have seen the glory
Of the coming of the Lord
He is trampling out the vintage
Where the grapes of wrath are stored.
He hath loosed the fateful lightning
Of His terrible, swift sword;
His truth is marching on!
"Battle Hymn of the Republic"   *1862*

2 In the beauty of the lilies
Christ was born across the sea,
With a glory in His bosom
That transfigures you and me:
As He died to make men holy,
Let us die to make men free;
His truth is marching on!

Ibid.

* * *

3 O Land, the measure of our prayers,
Hope of the world in grief and wrong!
"Our Country"

4 'Twas red with the blood of freemen and white with the
    fear of the foe;
And the stars that fit in their courses 'gainst tyrants its
    symbols know.

"The Flag"

66. Harriet Sewall
(1819–1889)

* * *

1 Why thus longing, thus forever sighing
    For the far-off, unattain'd, and dim,
While the beautiful all round thee lying
    Offers up its low, perpetual hymn?

"Why Thus Longing?"

67. Queen Victoria
(1819–1901)

1 We are not interested in the possibilities of defeat.

Letter to A. J. Balfour   1899

2 We are not amused.

Notebooks of a Spinster Lady   1900

3 I sat between the King and Queen. We left supper soon.
My health was drunk. I then danced one more quad-
rille with Lord Paget. . . . I was *very* much amused.

Journal Entry (June 16, 1833), The Girlhood of
Queen Victoria, Vol. I, Viscount Esher, ed.

1912p

4 . . . I *too well* know its truth, from experience, that
whenever any poor Gipsies are encamped anywhere
and crimes and robberies &c. occur, it is invariably laid
to their account, which is shocking; and if they are always looked upon as vagabonds, how *can* they become
good people?

Ibid. (December 29, 1836)

5 *Russia* having *failed*, she *must see* that she *cannot*
again *attempt* a similar *coup d'état*. One of the first
conditions should therefore be to bring about a reconciliation. . . . Russia has gravely compromised her-

self. . . . She will therefore be more easily worked upon, for she cannot avow such monstrous conduct.

> Letter to Marquis of Salisbury (August 25, 1886), *The Letters of Queen Victoria,* Vol. I, George Earle Buckle, ed.
>
> *1930p*

6 The Queen is most anxious to see the Government strengthened and supported, and she *does* think that want of firmness in the leader of the House of Commons is most detrimental to it.

> Ibid. (June 27, 1890)

7 . . . now let me entreat you seriously not to do this, not to let your feelings (very natural and usual ones) of momentary irritation and discomfort be seen by others; don't (as you so often did and do) let every little feeling be read in your face and seen in your manner, pray don't give way to irritability before your ladies. All this I say with the love and affection I bear you—as I know what you have to contend with and struggle against.

> Letter to Princess Royal (September 27, 1858), *Dearest Child,* Roger Fulford, ed.
>
> *1964p*

* * *

8 He [Mr. Gladstone] speaks to Me as if I was a public meeting.

> Quoted in *Collections and Recollections* by G. W. E. Russell

68. Susan Warner
(1819–1885)

1 One chapter a day was all we took. We searched that carefully, and noted down with miser eagerness everything which seemed to us to have an important bearing upon any point in our scheme. . . . But by dint of this practice we ourselves grew daily in the power of judging; and not only that, but the skill and the power of seeing, too; till by the time we were half through the Bible, we were just fit to begin again at the beginning. And so we did. . . .

> *The Law and the Testimony,* Foreword   *1853*

2 Many a bit we passed in our ignorance, in the days when we could see no metal but what glittered on the surface; and many a good time we went back again, long afterward, and broke our rejected lump with great exultation to find it fat with the riches of the mind.

Ibid.

3 "There is a world there, Winthrop—another sort of world—where people know something; where other things are to be done than running plow furrows; where men may distinguish themselves!—where men may read and write; and do something great; and grow to be something besides what nature made them!—I want to be in that world."

The Hills of the Shatemuc, Ch. 1   *1856*

4   "Did it ever happen to you to want anything you could not have, Miss Elizabeth?"

"No—never," said Elizabeth slowly.

"You have a lesson to learn yet."

"I hope I sha'n't learn it," said Elizabeth.

"It must be learned," said Mrs. Landholm gently. "Life would not be life without it. It is not a bad lesson either."

Ibid., Ch. 10

5 "The back is fitted to the burden, they say; and I always *did* pray that if I had work to do, I might be able to do it; and I always was, somehow."

What She Could, Ch. 3   *1870*

6   "And I, Maria—am I not somebody?" her aunt asked.

"Well, we're all *somebody,* of course, in one sense. Of course we're not *nobody.*"

"I am not so sure what you think about it," said Mrs. Candy. "I think that in your language, who isn't somebody, is nobody."   *Ibid.,* Ch. 7

7 "He who serves God with what costs him nothing, will do very little service, you may depend on it."

Ibid., Ch. 11

8   "Why should not a woman be as brave as a man, and as strong—in one way?"

"I suppose, because she is not as strong in the other way."   *The House in Town,* Ch. 1   *1871*

94

69. Amelia C. Welby
(1819–1852)

* * *

1 As the dew to the blossom, the bud to the bee,
As the scent to the rose, are those memories to me.

"Pulpit Eloquence"

2 Ten thousand stars were in the sky,
Ten thousand on the sea.

"Twilight at Sea," St. 4

70. Susan B. Anthony
(1820–1906)

1 Men their rights and nothing more; women their rights
and nothing less.   Motto, *The Revolution*   *1868*

2 . . . gentlemen. . . . Do you not see that so long as
society says a woman is incompetent to be a lawyer,
minister or doctor, but has ample ability to be a
teacher, that every man of you who chooses this profession tacitly acknowledges that he has no more brains
than a woman?

Speech, State Convention of
Schoolteachers, *History of
Woman Suffrage*, Vol. I, with
Elizabeth Cady Stanton and
Mathilda Gage   *1881*

3 Of all the old prejudices that cling to the hem of the
woman's garments and persistently impede her progress, none holds faster than this. The idea that she owes
service to a man instead of to herself, and that it is her
highest duty to aid his development rather than her
own, will be the last to die.

"The Status of Women, Past, Present
and Future," *The Arena May, 1897*

4 While in most states the divorce laws are the same for
men and women, they never can bear equally upon
both while all the property earned during marriage belongs wholly to the husband.   Ibid.

5 Suffrage is the pivotal right. . . .

Ibid.

6 . . . there never will be complete equality until women themselves help to make laws and elect lawmakers.

Ibid.

7 . . . who can measure the advantages that would result if the magnificent abilities of [women] . . . could be devoted to the needs of government, society, home, instead of being consumed in the struggle to obtain their birthright of individual freedom?

Ibid.

8 . . . the day will come when men will recognize woman as his peer, not only at the fireside, but in the councils of the nation. Then, and not until then, will there be the perfect comradeship, the ideal union between the sexes that shall result in the highest development of the race.

Ibid.

9 As when the slaves who got their freedom had to take it over or under or through the unjust forms of the law, precisely so now must women take it to get their right to a voice in this government. . . .

Courtroom Speech (June 18, 1873),
Quoted in Jailed for Freedom
by Doris Stevens   1920p

10 . . . and I shall earnestly and persistently continue to urge all women to the practical recognition of the old Revolutionary maxim, "Resistance to tyranny is obedience to God."

Ibid.

11 Those of you who have the talent to do honor to poor womanhood, have all given yourself over to baby-making. . . .

Quoted in Elizabeth Cady Stanton, Vol. II, Theodore Stanton and Harriot Stanton Blatch, eds.
1922p

12 So, for the love of me and for the saving of the reputation of womanhood, I beg you, with one baby on your knee and another at your feet, and four boys whistling, buzzing, halooing "Ma, Ma," set yourself about the work.

Ibid.

13 And yet, in the schoolroom more than any other place, does the difference of sex, if there is any, need to be forgotten.

Ibid.

14 The rank and file are not philosophers, they are not educated to think for themselves, but simply to accept, unquestioned, whatever comes.

Speech, "Woman Wants Bread, Not the Ballot!," *The Life and Work of Susan B. Anthony,* Vol. II, Ida Husted, ed.   *1969p*

15 . . . just so long as there is a degraded class of labor in the market, it always will be used by the capitalists to checkmate and undermine the superior classes.

Ibid.

16 Failure is impossible.

Quoted by Carrie Chapman Catt in Her Speech "Is Woman Suffrage Progressing?" (1911), *Feminism,* Miriam Schneir, ed.   *1972p*

17 The fact is, women are in chains, and their servitude is all the more debasing because they do not realize it. O to compel them to see and feel and to give them the courage and the conscience to speak and act for their own freedom, though they face the scorn and contempt of all the world for doing it!

Quoted in *The Liberated Woman's Appointment Calendar,* Lynn Sherr and Jurate Kazickas, eds.   *1975p*

71. Urania Locke Bailey
(1820–1882)

* * *

1 I want to be an angel,
  And with the angels stand
A crown upon my forehead,
  A harp within my hand.

"I Want to Be an Angel," St. 1

72. Alice Cary
(1820–1871)

* * *

1 For the human heart is the mirror
    Of the things that are near and far;
Like the wave that reflects in its bosom
    The flower and the distant star.

"The Time to Be"

2 How many lives we live in one,
    And how much less than one, in all!

"Life's Mysteries"

3 Kiss me, though you make believe;
Kiss me, though I almost know
    You are kissing to deceive.

"Make Believe"

4 Three little bugs in a basket,
    And hardly room for two.

"Three Bugs"

5 True worth is in *being*, not *seeming*—
    In doing, each day that goes by,
Some little good—not in dreaming
    Of great things to do by and by.

"Nobility," St. 1

6 We cannot bake bargains for blisses,
    Nor catch them like fishes in nets;
And sometimes the thing our life misses
    Helps more than the thing which it gets.

Ibid., St. 4

7 Women and men in the crowd meet and mingle,
Yet with itself every soul standeth single. . . .

"Life," St. 2

8 Work, and your house shall be duly fed:
Work, and rest shall be won;
I hold that a man had better be dead
Than alive when his work is done.

"Work"

73. Lucretia Peabody Hale
(1820–1900)

1 It was one of the first of the spring days—one of the days that seemed to be promise and fulfillment in one. They are only of promise; for the east wind shuts them in, behind and before. But behind the east wind is hidden the summer, and in these early spring days we feel a little of its breath, its warmth, and its languor. The invitation it gives to come out from winter activities and winter confinements, into its soft lassitude, and all its offers of freedom.

The Struggle for Life, Ch. 4   *1867*

2 All the years before, she had lived in a roving, aimless way, and the old love of change came up often to assert its power. Often came back the old longing to live where she would not be bound to anybody—where she might be free, even if she were only free to starve.

Ibid., Ch. 18

3 It is so hard to melt away the influences of an early life, to counteract all the lessons of the first ten years, to tear up the weeds that are early planted. There are evil inheritances to be struggled with, childish prejudices and fancies banished.

Ibid., Ch. 33

4 They say that the lady from Philadelphia, who is staying in town, is very wise. Suppose I go and ask her what is best to be done?

The Peterkin Papers
(c.1870), Ch. 1   *1924p*

74. Jean Ingelow
((1820–1897)

* * *

1 A sweeter woman ne'er drew breath
Than my sonne's wife Elizabeth.
"The High Tide on the Coast of Lincolnshire"

2 O Land where all the men are stones,
Or all the stones are men.
"A Land That Living Warmth Disowns"

99

3 There's no dew left on the daisies and clover,
  There's no rain left in heaven:
I've said my "seven times" over and over,
  Seven times one are seven.
> "Seven Times One," St. 1, *Songs of Seven*

4 You Moon! Have you done something wrong in
  heaven,
  That God has hidden your face?
> Ibid., St. 4

75. Jenny Lind
(1820–1887)

1 The [unfortunate] experience has passed over my soul
like a beneficent storm which has broken through the
hard shell of my being and freed many little green
shoots to find their way to the sun. And I see quite
clearly how infinitely much there is for me to do with
my life. I have only one prayer, that I may be able to
show a pure soul to God. . . . I am glad and grateful
from morning to night! I do not feel lonely or bored,
and my only complaint is that the days fly by too
quickly. I have a brightness in my soul, which strains
toward Heaven. I am like a bird!
> Quoted in *Jenny Lind: The Swedish Nightingale*
> by Gladys Denny Shultz   *1962p*

2 I have appeared twice in *Norma*; and was called so
many times before the curtain that I was quite exhausted. Bah! I don't like it. Everything should be done
in moderation; otherwise it is not pleasing.
> Letter (April 27, 1846), *The Lost Letters of
> Jenny Lind,* W. Porter Ware and Thaddeus C.
> Lockard, Jr., eds.   *1966p*

3 I have often wished for the blessing of motherhood, for
it would have given me a much-needed focal point for
my affections. With it, and through the varied experiences that accompany it, I could perhaps have achieved
something better than that which I have attained up to
now.
> Ibid., Letter (July 11, 1849)

4 My voice is still the same, and this makes me beside myself with joy! Oh, *mon Dieu*, when I think what I might be able to do with it!

Ibid., Letter (January 10, 1855)

76. Mary Livermore
(1820?–1905)

1 For humanity has moved forward to an era when wrong and slavery are being displaced, and reason and justice are being recognized as the rule of life. . . . The age looks steadily to the redressing of wrong, to the righting of every form of error and injustice; and a tireless and prying philanthropy, which is almost omniscient, is one of the most hopeful characteristics of the time.

*What Shall We Do with
Our Daughters?*, Ch. 1   1883

2 Other books have been written by men physicians. . . . One would suppose in reading them that women possess but one class of physical organs, and that these are always diseased. Such teaching is pestiferous, and tends to cause and perpetuate the very evils it professes to remedy.

Ibid., Ch. 2

3 Almost every one of the great religions of the world has made special provision for them, and the woman who has preferred a celibate to a domestic life has been able to occupy a position of honor and usefulness.

Ibid., Ch. 7

4 Above the titles of wife and mother, which, although dear, are transitory and accidental, there is the title human being, which precedes and out-ranks every other.

Ibid.

77. Princess Mathilde
(1820–1904)

1 But I think him lost for ever for any kind of locomotion. Nowadays it is only his mind that travels; his body stays behind on the bank.

Quoted in *Revue Bleu*   *August 6, 1863*

2 He knew that his conversation had the power to fasci-
nate, and he used it like a prodigal man who knew he
had an everlasting fortune. . . .

Quoted in *Le Moniteur Universelle*
October 15, 1869

3 I was born in exile—civically dead. . . .

"Souvenirs des Années d'Exile,"
La Revue des Deux Mondes
December 15, 1927p

78. Florence Nightingale
(1820–1910)

1 But when you have done away with all that pain and
suffering, which in patients are the symptoms, not of
their disease, but of the absence of one or all of the
essentials to the success of Nature's reparative processes, we shall then know what the symptoms of, and
the sufferings inseparable from, the disease.

Notes on Nursing   1859

2 No *man*, not even a doctor, ever gives any other definition of what a nurse should be than this—"devoted and
obedient." This definition would do just as well for a
porter. It might even do for a horse. It would not do
for a policeman.

Ibid.

3 Merely looking at the sick is not observing.

Ibid.

4 It may seem a strange thing to begin a book with:—
This Book is not for any one who has time to read
it—but the meaning of it is: this reading is good only
as a preparation for work. If it is not to inspire life and
work, it is bad. Just as the end of food is to enable us
to live and work, and not to live and eat, so the end of
most reading perhaps, but certainly of mystical reading,
is not to read but to work.

Mysticism, Preface   1873

5 For what is Mysticism? Is it not the attempt to draw
near to God, not by rites or ceremonies, but by inward
disposition? It is not merely a hard word for "The
Kingdom of Heaven is within"? Heaven is neither a
place nor a time.

Ibid.

6 So I never lose an opportunity of urging a practical beginning, however small, for it is wonderful how often in such matters the mustard-seed germinates and roots itself.

"Health Missionaries for Rural India,"
India   December, 1896

7 Nothing ever laughs or plays [in Egypt]. Everything is grown up and grown old.

Quoted in *The Life of Florence Night-ingale* by Sir Edward Cook   *1913p*

8 I stand at the altar of the murdered men, and, while I live, I fight their cause.

Ibid., Private Note (1856)

9 Asceticism is the trifling of an enthusiast with his power, a puerile coquetting with his selfishness or his vanity, in the absence of any sufficiently great object to employ the first or overcome the last.

Ibid., Letter to Dr. Sutherland (1857)

10 I can stand out the war with any man.

Quoted in *The World Book Encyclopedia*   1972p

79. Margaret Preston
(1820–1897)

1 Pain is no longer pain when it is past.

"Nature's Lesson"   *c.1875*

2 'Tis the motive exalts the action;
'Tis the doing, and not the deed.

"The First Proclamation of Miles Standish"   *c.1875*

3 Whoso lives the holiest life
Is fittest far to die.

"Ready"   *c.1875*

80. Anna Sewell
(1820–1878)

1 "I never yet could make out why men are so fond of this sport; they often hurt themselves, often spoil good horses, and tear up the fields, and all for a hare, or a

fox, or a stag, that they could get more easily some other way; but we are only horses, and don't know."

Black Beauty, Pt. I, Ch. 2   *1877*

2 . . . he said that cruelty was the Devil's own trademark, and if we saw anyone who took pleasure in cruelty we might know whom he belonged to, for the Devil was a murderer from the beginning, and a tormentor to the end.

Ibid., Ch. 13

3 I am never afraid of what I know.

Ibid., Pt. II, Ch. 29

4   I said, "I have heard people talk about war as if it was a very fine thing."
"Ah!" said he, "I should think they never saw it. No doubt it is very fine when there is no enemy, when it is just exercise and parade, and sham fight. Yes, it is very fine then; but when thousands of good, brave men and horses are killed or crippled for life, if has a very different look."

Ibid., Pt. III, Ch. 34

5 "My doctrine is this, that *if we see cruelty or wrong that we have the power to stop, and do nothing, we make ourselves sharers in the guilt.*"

Ibid., Ch. 38

6 "Is it not better," she said, "to lead a good fashion than to follow a bad one?"

Ibid., Pt. IV, Ch. 46

81. Anna Bartlett Warner
(1820–1915)

* * *

1 Daffy-down-dilly came up in the cold. . . .

"Daffy-Down-Dilly"

2 Jesus loves me, this I know
For the Bible tells me so.

"Jesus Loves Me"

82. Clara Barton
(1821–1912)

1 It is wise statesmanship which suggests that in time of
peace we must prepare for war, and it is no less a wise
benevolence that makes preparation in the hour of
peace for assuaging the ills that are sure to accompany
war.

The Red Cross, Ch. 1   *1898*

2 An institution or reform movement that is not selfish,
must originate in the recognition of some evil that is
adding to the sum of human suffering, or diminishing
the sum of happiness. I suppose it is a philanthropic
movement to try to reverse the process.

Ibid.

83. Elizabeth Blackwell
(1821–1910)

1 Social intercourse—a very limited thing in a half civilized country, becomes in our centers of civilization a
great power. . . .

Medicine as a Profession for Women,
with Emily Blackwell   *1860*

2 . . . every advance in social progress removes us more
and more from the guidance of instinct, obliging us to
depend upon reason for the assurance that our habits
are really agreeable to the laws of health, and compel-
ling us to guard against the sacrifice of our physical or
moral nature while pursuing the ends of civilization.

Ibid.

3 Our school education ignores, in a thousand ways, the
rules of healthy development. . . .

Ibid.

4 . . . health has its science as well as disease. . . .

Ibid.

5 As teachers, then, to diffuse among women the physiological and sanitary knowledge which they need, we
found the first work for women physicians.

Ibid.

6 . . . the church, with its usual sagacity in availing itself of all talents, opens the attractive prospect of active occupation, personal standing and authority, social respect, and the companionship of intelligent co-workers, both men and women—the feeling of belonging to the world, in fact, instead of a crippled and isolated life. For though it is common to speak of the sisters as renouncing the world, the fact is that the members of these sisterhoods have a far more active participation in the interests of life than most of them had before.

Ibid.

7 Medicine is so broad a field, so closely interwoven with general interests, dealing as it does with all ages, sexes, and classes, and yet of so personal a character in its individual applications, that it must be regarded as one of those great departments of work in which the cooperation of men and women is needed to fulfill all its requirements.

Ibid.

8 How often homes, which should be the source of moral and physical health and truth, are centers of selfishness or frivolity!

Ibid.

9 For what is done or learned by one class of women becomes, by virtue of their common womanhood, the property of all women.

Ibid.

10 This failure to recognize the equivalent value of internal with external structure has led to such a crude fallacy as a comparison of the penis with such a vestige as the clitoris, whilst failing to recognize that vast amount of erectile tissue, mostly internal, in the female, which is the direct seat of sexual spasm.

The Human Element in Sex 1894

11 . . . the total deprivation of it [sex] produces irritability.

Ibid.

12 I must have something to engross my thoughts, some object in life which will fill this vacuum and prevent this sad wearing away of the heart.

Pioneer Work for Women 1914p

13 . . . I, who so love a hermit life for a good part of the day, find myself living in public, and almost losing my identity.

Ibid.

14 Do you think I care about medicine? Nay, verily, it's just to kill the devil, whom I hate so heartily—that's the fact, mother.

Letter to Mother, Quoted in
Those Extraordinary Blackwells
by Elinor R. Hays   *1967p*

84. Mary Baker Eddy
(1821–1910)

1 The prayer that reforms the sinner and heals the sick is an absolute faith that all things are possible to God—a spiritual understanding of Him, an unselfed love.

*Science and Health, with Key
to the Scriptures (1910 ed.)*   *1875*

2 The highest prayer is not one of faith merely; it is demonstration. Such prayer heals sickness, and must destroy sin and death.

Ibid.

3 Christian Science explains all cause and effect as mental, not physical.

Ibid.

4 Disease can carry its ill-effects no farther than mortal mind maps out the way.

Ibid.

5 If materialistic knowledge is power, it is not wisdom. It is but a blind force.

Ibid.

6 Sin makes its own hell, and goodness its own heaven.

Ibid.

7 We classify disease as error, which nothing but Truth or Mind can heal, and this Mind must be divine, not human.

Ibid.

107

8 Jesus of Nazareth was the most scientific man that ever trod the globe. He plunged beneath the material surface of things, and found the spiritual cause.

Ibid.

9 The basis of all health, sinlessness, and immortality is the great fact that God is the only Mind; and this Mind must be not merely believed, but it must be understood.

Ibid.

10 You conquer error by denying its verity.

Ibid.

11 Stand porter at the door of thought. Admitting only such conclusions as you wish realized in bodily results, you will control yourself harmoniously.

Ibid.

12 Disease is an image of thought externalized.

Ibid.

13 Sin brought death, and death will disappear with the disappearance of sin.

Ibid.

14 Health is not a condition of matter, but of Mind; nor can the maternal senses bear reliable testimony on the subject of health.

Ibid.

15 You command the situation if you understand that mortal existence is a state of self-deception and not the truth of being.

Ibid.

16 God is incorporeal, divine, supreme, infinite Mind, Spirit, Soul, Principle, Life, Truth, Love.

Ibid.

17 Spirit is the real and eternal; matter is the unreal and temporal.

Ibid.

18 Truth is immortal; error is mortal.

Ibid.

19 Sickness, sin and death, being inharmonious, do not originate in God, nor belong to his government.

Ibid.

20 Then comes the question, how do drugs, hygiene and animal magnetism heal? It may be affirmed that they do not heal, but only relieve suffering temporarily, exchanging one disease for another.

Ibid.

21 God is Mind, and God is infinite; hence all is Mind.

Ibid.

22 Disease is an experience of so-called mortal mind. It is fear made manifest on the body.

Ibid.

23 Divine Love always has met and always will meet every human need.

Ibid.

24 I would no more quarrel with a man because of his religion than I would because of his art.
Miscellaneous Writings (rev. as *The First Church of Christ, Scientist, and Miscellany, 1973*)   1883–1896

25 How would you define Christian Science? As the law of God, the law of good, interpreting and demonstrating the divine Principle and rule of universal harmony.
Rudimental Divine Science (*1908 ed.*)   1891

26 To live and let live, without clamor for distinction of recognition; to wait on Divine Love; to write truth first on the tablet of one's own heart—this is the sanity and perfection of living, and my human ideal.
Message to the Mother Church   1902

27 To live so as to keep human consciousness in constant relation with the divine, the spiritual and the eternal, is to individualize infinite power; and this is Christian Science.

The First Church of Christ, Scientist and Miscellany   1913

* * *

28 It matters not what be thy lot,
　　So Love doth guide;
For storm or shine, pure peace is thine
　　Whate'er betide.

"Satisfied," St. 1

29 My prayer, some daily good to do
    To Thine, for Thee;
  An offering pure of Love, whereto
    God leadeth me.

"Christ My Refuge," St. 7

85. Frances P. Cobbe
(1822–1904)

1 The time comes to every dog when it ceases to care for
people merely for biscuits or bones, or even for caresses, and walks out of doors. When a dog *really* loves,
it prefers the person who gives it nothing, and perhaps
is too ill to take it out for exercise, to all the liberal
cooks and active dog-boys in the world.

The Confessions of a Lost Dog   1867

2 I could discern clearly, even at that early age, the essential difference between people who are *kind* to dogs
and people who really *love* them.

Ibid.

3 Then the Sorcerer Science entered, and where e'er he
    waved his wand
  Fresh wonders and fresh mysteries rose on every hand.

"The Pageant of Time," St. 1 (December, 1859),
Rest in the Lord   1887

4 Is it to mock a world of woe
  The soft winds laugh, the clear streams flow?
  Is it a proof of wrath Divine
  That the earth is gilt by the bright sunshine?
  "A Vale of Tears"? Does not each sense
  Proclaim a good Omnipotence?

Ibid., "A Vale of Tears," Sts. 6–7

5 . . . I must avow that the halo which has gathered
round Jesus Christ obscures Him to my eyes.

Life of Frances Power Cobbe,
Vol. II, Ch. 15   1894

86. Caroline Dall
(1822–1912)

1 A solution of an old mystery must bring justification
and proof to every assertion.
The Romance of the Association, Preface   *1875*

2 I have seen no Hindu who seemed to me prepared intellectually and morally for the freedom he would find
in American society; nor are Americans prepared for
the air of innocence and exaltation worn by very un-
deserving Orientals.
The Life of Doctor Anandabai Joshee   1888

3 It is not learning intellect, subtlety, or imagination that
is wanting in the average Hindu; it is purity, faith, and
honesty.

Ibid.

4 Why is it that human hearts are so dead to the heroic?
Barbara Fritchie, Pt. I   *1892*

5 It was the glorious function of [John Greenleaf] Whittier to lift us nearer to the Infinite Spirit, to keep us
intent upon our immortal destiny, and to fill us with
that love of Beauty which is the love of God.

Ibid., "L'Envoi"

87. Julia Carney
(1823–1908)

1 Little drops of water, Little grains of sand,
Make the mighty ocean, And the pleasant land.
So the little minutes, Humble tho' they be,
Make the mighty ages Of Eternity!
"Little Things," St. 1   *1845*

2 Little deeds of kindness, little words of love,
Help to make earth happy, like the heaven above.

Ibid., St. 4

88. Mary Bokin Chesnut
(1823–1886)

1 "You know how women sell themselves and are sold in marriage, from queens downwards, eh? You know what the Bible says about slaves, and marriage. Poor women, poor slaves."
Diary from Dixie (March 4, 1861)   *1949p*

2 I think this journal will be disadvantageous for me, for I spend my time now like a spider spinning my own entrails, instead of reading as my habit was in all spare moments.
Ibid. (March 14, 1861)

3 Women—wives and mothers—are the same everywhere.
Ibid. (July 24, 1861)

4 You see, Mrs. Stowe did not hit the sorest spot. She makes Legree a bachelor.
Ibid. (August 27, 1861)

5 . . . those soul-stirring Negro camp-meeting hymns. To me this is the saddest of all earthly music, weird and depressing beyond my power to describe.
Ibid. (October 13, 1861)

6 They live in nice New England homes, clean, sweet-smelling, shut up in libraries, writing books which ease their hearts of their bitterness against us. What self-denial they do practice is to tell John Brown to come down here and cut our throats in Christ's name.
Ibid. (November 28, 1861)

7 I say we are no better than our judges in the North, and no worse. We are human beings of the nineteenth century and slavery has to go of course.
Ibid.

8 I hate slavery. I even hate the harsh authority I see parents think it is their duty to exercise toward their children.   Ibid.

9 Conscription has waked the Rip Van Winkles. To fight and to be made to fight are different things.
Ibid. (March 19, 1862)

10 Does anybody wonder so many women die. Grief and
   constant anxiety kill nearly as many women as men die
   on the battlefield.

   Ibid. (June 9, 1862)

11 "Hysterical grief never moves me. It annoys me. You
   think yourself a miracle of sensibility; but self-control is
   what you need. That is all that separates you from
   those you look down upon as unfeeling."

   Ibid. (December 7, 1863)

12 Is the sea drying up? It is going up into mist and coming down on us in this water spout, the rain. It raineth
   every day, and the weather represents our tearful despair on a large scale.

   Ibid. (March 5, 1865)

13 We are scattered, stunned, the remnant of heart left
   alive in us filled with brotherly hate. We sit and wait
   until the drunken tailor [President Andrew Johnson]
   who rules the United States issues a proclamation and
   defines our anomalous position.

   Ibid. (May 16, 1865)

89. Caroline Mason
(1823–1890)

1 Do they miss me at home—do they miss me?
  'Twould be an assurance most dear,
  To know that this moment some loved one
  Were saying, "I wish he were here."
          "Do They Miss Me at Home," St. 1   *1850*

* * *

2 . . . like a story well-nigh told,
  Will seem my life—when I am old.
                    "When I Am Old," St. 1

3 Ere I am old, O! Let me give
  My life to learning how to live.

                              Ibid., St. 8

4 His grave a nation's heart shall be,
  His monument a people free!
                         "President Lincoln's Grave"

90. Elizabeth Stoddard
(1823–1902)

1 A woman despises a man for loving her, unless she returns his love.

Two Men, Ch. 32   1888

91. Phoebe Cary
(1824–1871?)

* * *

1 And though hard be the task,
   "Keep a stiff upper lip."

"Keep a Stiff Upper Lip"

2 And wouldn't it be nicer
   For you to smile than pout,
And so make sunshine in the house
   When there is none without?

"Suppose," St. 2

3 And isn't it, my boy or girl,
   The wisest, bravest plan,
Whatever comes, or doesn't come,
   To do the best you can?

Ibid., St. 5

4   Charley Church, was a preacher who praught,
Though his enemies called him a screecher who
   scraught.

"The Lovers"

5 For of all the hard things to bear and grin,
   The hardest is being taken in.

"Kate Ketchem"

6 Give plenty of what is given to you,
   And listen to pity's call;
Don't think the little you give is great
   And the much you get is small.

"A Legend of the Northland," I, St. 8

7 I think true love is never blind
   But rather brings an added light,
An inner vision quick to find
   The beauties hid from common sight.

"True Love," St. 1

8 Sometimes, I think, the things we see
Are shadows of the things to be;
That what we plan we build. . . .
"Dreams and Realities," St. 7

9 There's many a battle fought daily
The world knows nothing about.
"Our Heroes," St. 2

10 Be steadfast, my boy, when you're tempted,
To do what you know to be right.
Stand firm by the colors of manhood,
And you will o'ercome in the fight.   Ibid., St. 3

11 Thou hast battled for the right
With many a brave and trenchant word
And shown us how the pen may fight
A mightier battle than the sword.
"John Greenleaf Whittier"

92. Julia Kavanagh
(1824–1877)

1 Most children are aristocratic. . . .
Daisy Burns, Vol. I   *1853*

2 Alas! why has the plain truth the power of offending so
many people. . . .   Ibid., Ch. 4

3 It is the culprit who must seek the glance of the judge,
and not the judge that must look at the culprit.
Natalie, Ch. 1   *1872*

4 A beauty must regret the past; a noble-born and impoverished lady cannot look with favour on a new order of things.   *Adele,* Ch. 2   *1872*

93. Adeline Dutton Whitney
(1824–1906)

* * *

1 I bow me to the thwarting gale:
I know when that is overpast,
Among the peaceful harvest days
An Indian Summer comes at last.
"Equinoctial," St. 6

94. Mrs. Alexander
(1825–1902)

1 ". . . it is impossible to rely on the prudence or common sense of any man. . . ."
Ralph Wilton's Weird, Ch. 1   1875

2 "There's nothing more mischievous than moping along and getting into the blue devils!—nothing more likely to drive a man to suicide or matrimony, or some infernal entanglement even worse!"
Ibid., Ch. 6

95. Antoinette Brown Blackwell
(1825–1921)

1 Mr. Darwin . . . has failed to hold definitely before his mind the principle that the difference of sex, whatever it may consist in, must itself be subject to natural selection and to evolution.
The Sexes Throughout Nature   1875

2 . . . the sexes in each species of beings . . . are always true equivalents—equals but not identicals. . . .
Ibid.

3 Any positive thinker is compelled to see everything in the light of his own convictions.
Ibid.

4 It is difficult to perceive what self-adjusting forces, in the organic world, have developed men everywhere the superiors of women, males characteristically the superiors of females.
Ibid.

5 I do not underrate the charge of presumption which must attach to any woman who will attempt to controvert the great masters of science and scientific inference. But there is no alternative!
Ibid.

6 All insect mothers act with the utmost wisdom and good faith, and with a beautiful instinctive love towards a posterity which they are directly never to caress or

116

nurture. . . . These tiny creatures work with the skill of carpenters and masons, and often with a prudence and forethought which is even more than human; for they never suffer personal ease or advantage to prevent their making proper provision for their young.

Ibid.

7 If woman's sole responsibility is of the domestic type, one class will be crushed by it, and the other throw it off as a badge of poverty. The poor man's motto, "Women's work is never done," leads inevitably to its antithesis—ladies' work is never begun.

Ibid.

8 Woman's share of duties must involve direct nutrition, man's indirect nutrition. She should be able to bear and nourish their young children, at a cost of energy equal to the amount expended by him as household provider. Beyond this, if human justice is to supplement Nature's provisions, all family duties must be shared equitably, in person or by proxy.

Ibid.

9 Work, alternated with needful rest, is the salvation of man or woman.

Ibid.

10 Nature is just enough; but men and women must comprehend and accept her suggestions.

Ibid.

11 Every nursing mother, in the midst of her little dependent brood, has far more right to whine, sulk, or scold, as temperament dictates, because beefsteak and coffee are not prepared for her and exactly to her taste, than any man ever had or ever can have during the present stage of human evolution.

Ibid.

12 The interests of their children *must not be sacrificed* by her over-exhaustion, even though she were willing and eager for the sacrifice of herself.

Ibid.

13 A woman finds the natural lay of the land almost unconsciously; and not feeling it incumbent on her to be guide and philosopher to any successor, she takes little pains to mark the route by which she is making her ascent.

Ibid.

14 The brain is not, and cannot be, the sole or complete organ of thought and feeling.

Ibid.

15 Conventionality has indeed curtailed feminine force by hindering healthful and varied activity. . . .

Ibid.

16 Women's thoughts are impelled by their feelings. Hence the sharp-sightedness, the direct instinct, the quick perceptions; hence also their warmer prejudices and more unbalanced judgments. . . . In this the child is like the woman.

Ibid.

17 The immediate sensation or perception seems also to be the impelling power of the savage and of all animal instincts. Call it automatic activity if you will; yet the incident force is real feeling, is perception, is intelligence. . . .

Ibid.

18 The law of grab is the primal law of infancy.

Ibid.

19 That she is not his peer in all intellectual and moral capabilities, cannot at least be very well provided until she is allowed an equally untrammelled opportunity to test her own strength.

Ibid.

20 There is a broader, not a higher, life outside, which she is impelled to enter, taking some share also in its responsibilities.

Ibid.

21 If Evolution, as applied to sex, teaches any one lesson plainer than another, it is the lesson that the monogamic marriage is the basis of all progress.

Ibid.

22 No theory of unfitness, no form of conventionality, can have the right to suppress any excellence which Nature has seen fit to evolve.

Ibid.

23 It had seemed to both Lucy Stone and myself in our student days that marriage would be a hindrance to our public work.

Quoted in *Antoinette Brown Blackwell: Biographical Sketch* by Sarah Gibson
1909

24 . . . you asked me one day if it seemed like giving up much for your sake. Only leave me free, as free as you are and everyone ought to be, and it is giving up nothing.   Ibid.

96. Julia Dorr
(1825–1913)

* * *

1 And the stately lilies stand
    Fair in the silvery light,
Like saintly vestals, pale in prayer.   "A Red Rose"

2 April's rare capricious loveliness.
                                                        "November"

3 Come, blessed Darkness, come and bring thy balm
    For eyes grown weary of the garish day!
    Come with thy soft, slow steps, thy garments grey,
Thy veiling shadows, bearing in thy palm
The poppy-seeds of slumber, deep and calm.
                                                        "Darkness"

4 Grass grows at last above all graves.
                                                "Grass-Grown"

5 O beautiful, royal Rose,
    O Rose, so fair and sweet!
Queen of the garden art thou,
    And I—the Clay at thy feet.
                                            "The Clay to the Rose"

6 O golden Silence, bid our souls be still,
And on the foolish fretting of our care
Lay thy soft touch of healing unaware!
                                                        "Silence"

7 Stars will blossom in the darkness,
    Violets bloom beneath the snow.
                                        "For a Silver Wedding"

8 What dost thou bring me, O fair To-day,
That comest o'er the mountains with swift feet?
                                                        "To-day"

9 Who soweth good seed shall surely reap;
The year grows rich as it groweth old,
And life's latest sands are its sands of gold!
                                            "To the 'Bouquet Club' "

97. Henrietta Heathorn
(1825–1915)

1 Be not afraid, ye waiting hearts that weep,
  For God still giveth His belovèd sleep,
  And if an endless sleep He wills—so best.*
                "Browning's Funeral"   *1889*

* * *

2 To all the gossip that I hear
  I'll give no faith; to what I see
  But only half, for it is clear
  All that led up is dark to me.
    Learn we the larger life to live,
    To comprehend is to forgive.
          "Tout Comprendre, C'est Tout Pardonner"

98. Adelaide Proctor
(1825–1864)

1 Dreams grow holy put in action.
        "Phillip and Mildred," *The Poems of*
                Adelaide Proctor   *1869p*

2 Half my life is full of sorrow,
  Half of joy, still fresh and new;
  One of these lives is a fancy,
  But the other one is true.
                Ibid., "Dream-Life"

3 Now Time has fled—the world is strange,
  Something there is of pain and change;
  My books lie closed upon the shelf;
  I miss the old heart in myself.
                Ibid., "A Student"

4 One by one the sands are flowing,
  One by one the moments fall;
  Some are coming, some are going;
  Do not strive to grasp them all.
           Ibid., "One by One," St. 1

* Epitaph on T. H. Huxley's tombstone.

5   Only heaven
    Means crowned, not conquered, when it says
    "Forgiven."

Ibid., "A Legend of Provence"

6 One dark cloud can hide the sunlight;
  Loose one string, the pearls are scattered;
  Think one thought, a soul may perish;
  Say one word, a heart may break.

Ibid., "Phillip and Mildred"

7 But I struck one chord of music,
  Like the sound of a great Amen.

Ibid., "A Lost Chord," St. 2

8 See how time makes all grief decay.

Ibid., "Life in Death"

9 O, there are Voices of the Past,
    Links of a broken chain,
  Wings that can bear me back to Times
  Which cannot come again. . . .

Ibid., "Voices of the Past"

10 Joy is like restless day; Peace divine
   Like quiet night. . . .

Ibid., "Per Pacem ad Lucem"

11 I know too well the poison and the sting
    Of things too sweet.   Ibid.

12 Tell her that the lesson taught her
   Far outweighs the pain.

Ibid., "Friend Sorrow"

13 Rise! for the day is passing
   And you lie dreaming on. . . .

Ibid., "Now," St. 1

14 The Past and the Future are nothing,
   In the face of the stern To-day.   Ibid.

99. Harriet Robinson
(1825–1911)

1 What if she did hunger and thirst after knowledge? She
could do nothing with it even if she could get it. So she
made a *fetish* of some male relative, and gave him the

mental food for which she herself was starving; and devoted all her energies towards helping him to become what she felt, under better conditions, she herself might have been. It was enough in those early days to be the *mother* or *sister* of somebody.

> "Early Factory Labor in New England,"
> *Massachusetts in the Woman Suffrage*
> *Movement   1883*

2 In those days there was no need of advocating the doctrine of the proper relation between employer and employed. *Help was too valuable to be ill-treated.* . . .

> Ibid.

3 Skilled labor teaches something not to be found in books or in colleges.

> Ibid.

100. Emily Blackwell
(1826–1911)

Co-author of *Medicine as a Profession for Women* with Elizabeth Blackwell. See 83:1–9.

101. Dinah Mulock Craik
(1826–1887)

1 . . . a Brownie is a curious creature. . . .
> *The Adventures of a Brownie   1872*

2 Altogether, his conscience pricked him a good deal; and when people's consciences prick them, sometimes they get angry with other people, which is very silly, and only makes matters worse.

> Ibid.

3 Now, I have nothing to say against uncles in general. They are usually very excellent people, and very convenient to little boys and girls.
> *The Little Lame Prince, Ch. 2   1875*

4 There is much that we do not know, and cannot understand—we big folks, no more than you little ones.

> Ibid., Ch. 6

5 It seemed as if she had given these treasures and left him alone—to use them, or lose them, apply them, or

misapply them, according to his own choice. That is all we can do with children, when they grow into big children, old enough to distinguish between right and wrong, and too old to be forced to do either.

Ibid., Ch. 7

6 "You are a child. Accept the fact. Be humble—be teachable. Lean upon the wisdom of others till you have gained your own."

Ibid., Ch. 10

7 "One cannot make oneself, but one can sometimes help a little in the making of somebody else. It is well."

Ibid.

8 Friend, what years could us divide?
"A Christmas Blessing," Thirty Years   1881

9 Those rooks, dear, from morning till night,
They seem to do nothing but quarrel and fight,
And wrangle and jangle, and plunder.
Ibid., "The Blackbird and the Rooks"

10 And when I lie in the green kirkyard,
　　With mould upon my breast,
Say not that she did well—or ill,
　　Only "she did her best."   "Obituary"   1887

* * *

11 Never was owl more blind than a lover.
Magnus and Morna

12 A secret at home is like rocks under tide.   Ibid., Sc. 2

13 Silence is sweeter than speech.

Ibid., Sc. 3

14 Wedlock's a lane where there is no turning.
Ibid.

15 Autumn to winter, winter into spring,
Spring into summer, summer into fall,—
So rolls the changing year, and so we change;
Motion so swift, we know not that we move.
"Immutable"

16 Duty's a slave that keeps the keys,
But Love the master goes in and out
Of his goodly chambers with song and shout,
Just as he pleases—just as he pleases.   "Plighted"

123

17 Faith needs her daily bread.

Fortune's Marriage, Ch. 10

18 Forgotten? No, we never do forget:
We let the years go by; wash them clean with tears,
Leave them to bleach out in the open day,
Or lock them careful by, like dead friends' clothes,
Till we shall dare unfold them without pain,—
But we forget not, never can forget.

"A Flower of a Day"

19 God rest ye, little children; let nothing you afright,
For Jesus Christ, your Saviour, was born this happy
night;
Along the hills of Galilee the white blocks sleeping lay,
When Christ, the child of Nazareth, was born on
Christmas day.

"Christmas Carol," St. 2

20 Hour after hour that passionless bright face
Climbs up the desolate blue.

"Moon-Struck"

21   Immortality
Alone could teach this mortal how to die.

"Looking Death in the Face"

22 Keep what is worth keeping—
And with the breath of kindness
Blow the rest away.

"Friendship"

23 Life bears love's cross, death brings love's crown.

"Lettice"

24 Lo! all life this truth declares,
Laborare est orare;
And the whole earth rings with prayers.

"Labour Is Prayer," St. 4

25 Love that asketh love again
Finds the barter nought but pain;
Love that giveth in full store
Aye receives as much, and more.

"Love That Asketh Love Again"

26 Oh my son's my son till he gets him a wife,
But my daughter's my daughter all her life.

"Young and Old"

27 O the green things growing, the green things growing,
   The faint sweet smell of the green things growing!
"Green Things Growing"

28 Pierce with thy trill the dark,
   Like a glittering music spark.
"A Rhyme About Birds"

29 Sing away, ay, sing away,
     Merry little bird
   Always gayest of the gay,
   Though a woodland roundelay
     You ne'er sung nor heard;
Though your life from youth to age
Passes in a narrow cage.
"The Canary in His Cage"

3 Sweet April-time—O cruel April-time!
"April"

31 There never was night that had no morn.
"The Golden Gate"

32 Tomorrow is, ah, whose?
"Between Two Worlds"

102. Mathilda Gage
(1826–1898)

Co-author of *History of Woman Suffrage*, Vols. I and
II, with Elizabeth Cady Stanton and Susan B. Anthony.
See 45:1–37.

103. Lucy Larcom
(1826–1893)

* * *

1 Breathe thy balm upon the lonely,
     Gentle Sleep!
"Sleep Song"

2 Each red stripe has blazoned forth
   Gospels writ in blood;
Every star has sung the birth
   Of some deathless good.
"The Flag"

3 He who plants a tree
   Plants a hope.

"Plant a Tree," St. 1

4 Canst thou prophesy, thou little tree,
   What the glory of thy boughs shall be?

Ibid.

5 I do not own an inch of land,
   But all I see is mine.

"A Strip of Blue"

6 If the world seems cold to you,
   Kindle fires to warm it!

"Three Old Saws"

7 If the world's a wilderness,
   Go, build houses in it!

Ibid.

8 June falls asleep upon her bier of flowers.

"Death of June"

9 Oh, her heart's adrift, with one
   On an endless voyage gone!
      Night and morning
   Hannah's at the window binding shoes.

"Hannah Binding Shoes," St. 2

10 The land is dearer for the sea,
   The ocean for the shore.

"On the Beach," St. 11

11 There is light in shadow and shadow in light,
   And black in the blue of the sky.

"Black in Blue Sky," St. 2

104. Dorothy Nevill
(1826–1913)

1 It seems to be that, had the educational authorities attempted to keep alive these local industries by encouraging the children under their charge not to abandon
them, they would have been doing much more good
than by teaching smatterings of many totally useless
subjects, which, imperfectly understood and soon forgotten, have but served to convert the English rustic
into a somewhat dissatisfied imitation of the Londoner,
whilst thoroughly stamping out that local character and

individuality which was such an admirable feature of old-time country life.

The Reminiscences of Lady Dorothy
Nevill, Ch. 3   1907

2 Society to-day and Society as I formerly knew it are two entirely different things; indeed, it may be questioned whether Society, as the word used to be understood, now exists at all. . . . Now all is changed, and wealth has usurped the place formerly held by wit and learning. The question is not now asked, "Is So-and-so clever?" but, instead, "Is So-and-so rich?"   Ibid., Ch. 8

3 It is, I think, a good deal owing to the preponderance of the commercial element in Society that conversation has sunk to its present dull level of conventional chatter. The commercial class has always mistrusted verbal brilliancy and wit, deeming such qualities, perhaps with some justice, frivolous and unprofitable.   Ibid.

4 The French I think are improved, not so childish—how refined their manners and talk and how dirty their habits—morality and decency they know nothing of, but yet with benefit we might exchange a little of our morality for some of their cooking virtues. . . .

Letter to a Friend (1871), *The Life and Letters*
of Lady Dorothy Nevill, Ralph Nevill, ed.

1919p

105. Jane Francesca Wilde
(1826–1896)

* * *

1 Weary men, what reap ye?—"Golden corn for the
   stranger."
What sow ye?—"Human corpses that await for the
   Avenger."
Fainting forms, all hunger-stricken, what see you in the
   offing?
"Stately ships to bear our food away amid the
   stranger's scoffing."
There's a proud array of soldiers—what do they round
   your door?
"They guard our master's granaries from the thin
   hands of the poor."

"Ballad on the Irish Famine"

106. Ethel Lynn Beers
(1827–1879)

1 All quiet along the Potomac to-night,
    No sound save the rush of the river,
While soft falls the dew on the face of the dead,
    The picket's off duty forever.

"The Picket Guard," St. 6 (1861),
*All Quiet Along the Potomac and
          Other Poems   1879*

* * *

2 Art thou a pen, whose task shall be
    To drown in ink
    What writers think?
    Oh, wisely write,
    That pages white
Be not the worse for ink and thee.

"The Gold Nugget"

3 Oh, Mother! Laugh your merry note,
    Be gay and glad, but don't forget
From baby's eyes look out a soul
    That claims a home in Eden yet.

"Weighing the Baby"

4 Only a mother's heart can be
Patient enough for such as he.

"Which Shall It Be"

107. Rose Terry Cooke
(1827–1892)

* * *

1 Darlings of the forest!
    Blossoming alone
When Earth's grief is sorest
    For her jewels gone. . . .

"Trailing Arbutus"

2 Yet courage, soul! nor hold thy strength in vain,
In hope o'er come the steeps God set for thee,
For past the Alpine summits of great pain
Lieth thine Italy.

"Beyond," St. 4

108. Ellen Howarth
(1827–1899)

* * *

1 Where is the heart that doth not keep,
   Within its inmost core,
Some fond remembrance hidden deep,
   Of days that are no more?
                    " 'Tis But a Little Faded Flower"

2 Who hath not saved some trifling thing
   More prized than jewels rare,
A faded flower, a broken ring,
   A tress of golden hair.

                                        Ibid.

3 I may not to the world impart
   The secret of its power,
But treasured in my inmost heart
   I keep my faded flower.

                                        Ibid.

109. Johanna Spyri
(1827–1901)

1   "You mischievous child!" she cried, in great excitement. "What are you thinking of? Why have you taken
everything off? What does it mean?"
     "I do not need them," replied the child, and did not
look sorry for what she had done.
                         Heidi, Ch. 1   —1885

2 "Oh, I wish that God had not given me what I prayed
for! It was not so good as I thought."

                                        Ibid., Ch. 11

3 "One must wait," she said after a while, "and must always think that soon the good God will bring something to make one happier; that something will come
out of the trouble, but I must keep perfectly quiet, and
not run away."

                                        Ibid., Ch. 17

4 "If your A B C is not learned to-day,
   Go to be punished to-morrow, I say."   Ibid., Ch. 19

129

5 "Anger has overpowered him, and driven him to a revenge which was rather a stupid one, I must acknowledge, but anger makes us all stupid."

Ibid., Ch. 23

110. Elizabeth Charles
(1828–1896)

1 To know how to say what others only know how to think is what makes men poets or sages; and to dare to say what others only dare to think makes men martyrs or reformers—or both.

Chronicle of the Schönberg-Cotta Family　　1863

111. Mary Jane Holmes
(1828–1907)

1 ". . . but needn't tell me that prayers made up is as good as them as isn't. . . ."

The Cameron Pride, Ch. 1　　1867

2 "Keep yourself unspotted from the world," Morris had said, and she repeated it to herself asking "how shall I do that? how can one be good and fashionable too?"

Ibid., Ch. 19

3 "If the body you bring back has my George's heart within it, I shall love you just the same as I do now. . . ."

Rose Mather, Ch. 3　　1868

112. Margaret Oliphant
(1828–1897)

1 The first thing which I can record concerning myself is, that I was born. . . . These are wonderful words. This life, to which neither time nor eternity can bring diminution—this everlasting living soul, *began.* My mind loses itself in these depths.

Memoirs and Resolutions of
Adam Graeme, of Mossgray
Vol. I, Bk. I, Ch. 1　　1852

2 "I am perfectly safe—nobody can possibly be safer than such a woman as I am, in poverty and middle age," said this strange acquaintance. "It is an immunity that women don't often prize, Mr. Vincent, but it is very valuable in its way."

Salem Chapel, Ch. 9   *1863*

3 ". . . the world does not care, though our hearts are breaking; it keeps its own time."

Ibid., Ch. 18

4 "There ain't a worm but will turn when he's trod upon. . . ."

The Perpetual Curate, Vol. II, Ch. 20   *1864*

5 It, the thirteenth century, possessed few of the virtues of civilization, had little time for thought and none for speculation, and was marked by all the rudeness of manners and morals, indifference to human life and callousness to suffering which are almost inseparable from continuous and oft-repeated wars.

Francis of Assisi, Introduction   *1871*

6 She was not clever; you might have said she had no mind at all; but so wise and right and tender a heart, that it was as good as genius.

A Little Pilgrim, Ch. 1   *1882*

7 "And we who were the workers began to contend one against another to satisfy the gnawings of the rage that was in our hearts. For we had deceived ourselves, thinking once more that all would be well; while all the time nothing was changed."

Ibid., Ch. 2

8 "One does not want to hear one's thoughts; most of them are not worth hearing."

Ibid., Ch. 3

9   "I am afraid; I am afraid!" I cried.
    "And I too am afraid; but it is better to suffer more and to escape than to suffer less and to remain."

Ibid.

10 It *was* a bore to go out into those aimless assemblies where not to go was a social mistake, yet to go was weariness of the flesh and spirit.

A Country Gentleman and His Family,
Vol. III, Ch. 5   *1866*

11 "A girl who has been talked about is always at a disadvantage. She had much better keep quite quiet until the story has all died away."

Ibid., Ch. 12

12 In the history of men and of commonwealth there is a slow progression, which, however faint, however deferred, yet gradually goes on, leaving one generation always a trifle better than that which preceded it, with some scrap of new possession, some right assured, some small inheritance gained.

The Literary History of England,
Introduction   *1889*

13 There are many variations in degree of the greatest human gifts, but they are few in kind.

Royal Edinburgh, Pt. IV, Ch. 3   *1890*

14 The highest ideal [in the fifteenth century] was that of war, war no doubt sometimes for good ends, to redress wrongs, to avenge injury, to make crooked things straight—but yet always war, implying a state of affairs in which the last thing that men thought of was the Golden Rule, and the highest attainment to be looked for was the position of a protector, doer of justice, deliverer of the oppressed.

Jeanne d'Arc, Ch. 1   *1896*

15 It is not necessary to be a good man in order to divine what in certain circumstances a good and pure spirit will do.

Ibid., Ch. 17

* * *

16 Imagination is the first faculty wanting in those that do harm to their kind.   "Innocent"

113. Elizabeth Doten
(1829–?)

1 God of the granite and the rose,
  Soul of the sparrow and the bee,
  The mighty tide of being flows
    Through countless channels, Lord, from
      Thee.

"Reconciliation"   *c.1870*

132

114. Edna Dean Proctor
(1829–1923)

* * *

1 Into Thy hands, O Lord,
Into Thy hands I give my soul.

"Columbus Dying"

2 Now God avenges the life he gladly gave,
Freedom reigns to-day!

"John Brown"

3   O there are tears for him,*
  O there are cheers for him—
Liberty's champion, Cid of the West.

"Cid of the West"

4 The fasts are done; the Aves said;
The moon has filled her horn,
And in the solemn night I watch
Before the Easter morn.

"Easter Morning"

115. Charlotte Barnard
(1830–1869)

1 I cannot sing the old songs,
Or dream those dreams again.
"I Cannot Sing the Old Songs"   *c.1860*

2 Take back the freedom thou cravest,
Leaving the fetters to me.
"Take Back the Heart"   *c.1860*

116. Helen Olcott Bell
(1830–1918)

1 To a woman, the consciousness of being well-dressed
gives a sense of tranquility which religion fails to be-
stow.
Letters and Social Aims: R. W. Emerson   1876

* Referring to Theodore Roosevelt.

133

117. Emily Dickinson
(1830–1886)

1 Angels—twice descending
  Reimbursed my store—
  Burglar! Banker!—Father!
  I am poor once more.

No. 49, St. 2   c.1858

2 I never lost as much but twice,
  And that was in the sod.
  Twice have I stood a beggar
  Before the door of God.

Ibid.

3 Surgeons must be very careful
  When they take the knife!
  Underneath their fine incisions
  Stirs the Culprit—Life!

No. 108   c.1859

4 Here a star, and there a star,
  Some lose their way!
  Here a mist, and there a mist,
  Afterwards—Day!

No. 113   c.1859

5 For each ecstatic instant
  We must an anguish pay
  In keen and quivering ratio
  To the ecstasy. . . .   No. 125, St. 1   c.1859

6 There are days when Birds come back—
  A very few—a Bird or two—
  To take a backward look.

  There are days when skies resume
  The old—old sophistries of June—
  A blue and gold mistake.

No. 130, Sts. 1–2   c.1859

7 Besides the Autumn poets sing
  A few prosaic days
  A little this side of the snow
  And that side of the Haze. . . .

No. 131, St. 1   1859

8 Just lost when I was saved!

No. 160, St. 1   *1860*

9 Inebriate of Air—am I—
And Debauchee of Dew—
Reeling through endless summer days—
From inns of Molten Blue.

No. 214, St. 2   *1860*

10 "Hope" is the thing with feathers
That perches in the soul
And sings the tune without the words
And never stops—at all. . . .

No. 254, St. 1   *1861*

11 There's a certain Slant of light,
Winter Afternoons—
That oppresses, like the Heft
Of Cathedral Tunes. . . .

No. 258, St. 1   *1861*

12 I'm nobody, Who are you?
Are you—Nobody,—too?

No. 288, St. 1   *1861*

13 How dreary—to be—Somebody!
How public—like a Frog—
To tell one's name—the livelong June—
To an admiring Bog!

Ibid., St. 2

14 I tasted—careless—then—
I did not know the Wine
Came once a World—Did you?

No. 296, St. 3   *1861*

15 The Soul selects its own Society—
Then—shuts the Door.

No. 303, St. 1   *1862*

16 I'll tell you how the Sun rose—
A ribbon at a time. . . .

No. 318   *1862*

17 Some keep the Sabbath going to Church—
I keep it, staying at Home—
With a bobolink for a Chorister—
And an Orchard, for a Dome. . . .

No. 324, St. 1   *1862*

18 After great pain, a formal feeling comes.

No. 341, St. 1   1862

19 Of Course—I prayed—
And did God Care?   No. 376   1862

20 Except Thyself may be
Thine Enemy—
Captivity is Consciousness—
So's Liberty.   No. 384, St. 4   1862

21 This is my letter to the World
That never wrote to Me. . . .

No. 441, St. 1   1862

22 I died for Beauty—but was scarce
Adjusted in the Tomb
When One who died for Truth, was lain
In an adjoining Room. . . .

No. 449, St. 1   1862

23 I reckon—when I count at all—
First—Poets—Then the Sun—
Then Summer—Then the Heaven of God—
And then—the List is done. . . .

No. 569, St. 1   1862

24 Afraid! Of whom am I afraid?
Not Death—for who is He?
The Porter of my Father's Lodge
As much abasheth me!

No. 608, St. 1   1862

25 The Brain—is wider than the Sky—
For—put them side by side—
The one the other will contain
With ease—and You—beside.

No. 632, St. 1   1862

26 I cannot live with You—
It would be Life—
And Life is over there—
Behind the Shelf.   No. 640, St. 1   1862

27 Pain—has an Element of Blank—
It cannot recollect
When it begun—or if there were
A time when it was not. . . .

No. 650, St. 1   1862

28 I dwell in Possibility—
A fairer House than Prose—
More numerous of Windows—
Superior—for Doors.

No. 657, St. 1   *1862*

29 The soul unto itself
Is an imperial friend—
Or the most agonizing Spy—
An Enemy—could send. . . .

No. 683, St. 1   *1862*

30 God gave a Loaf to every Bird—
But just a Crumb—to Me. . . .

No. 791, St. 1   *1863*

31 Truth—is as old as God—
His Twin identity
And will endure as long as He
A Co-Eternity. . . .

No. 836, St. 1   *1864*

32 Love—is anterior to Life—
Posterior—to Death—
Initial of Creation, and
The Exponent of Earth.

No. 917   *1864*

33 'Twas my one Glory—
Let it be
Remembered
I was owned of Thee. . . .

No. 1028   *1865*

34 Not to discover weakness is
The Artifice of strength. . . .

No. 1054, St. 1   *1865*

35 The Sweeping up the Heart,
And putting Love away. . . .

No. 1078, St. 2   *1866*

36 Truth is such a rare thing, it is delightful to tell it.

Letter to Thomas Wentworth
Higginson   *August, 1870*

37 A Word is dead
When it is said,
Some say.
I say it just
Begins to live
That day.

No. 1212   *1872*

38 Not with a Club, the Heart is broken
   Nor with a Stone—
   A Whip so small you could not see it
   I've known
   To lash the Magic Creature
   Till it fell.
                No. 1304, St. 1   *1874*

39 That short—potential stir
   That each can make but once.
                     No. 1307, St. 1   *1874*

40 A little Madness in the Spring
   Is wholesome even for the King.
                          No. 1333   *1875*

41 Bees are Black, with Gilt Surcingles—
   Buccaneers of Buzz.
                          No. 1405, St. 1   *1877*

42 Success is counted sweetest
      By those who ne'er succeed.
                  "Success," *Poems,* V   *1891p*

43 The distant strains of triumph
      Break agonized and clear.

                                              Ibid.

44 The pedigree of honey
      Does not concern the bee
   A clover, anytime, to him
      Is aristocracy.

                               Ibid., "The Bee"

45 His labor is a chant
      His idleness a tune;
   Oh, for a bee's experience
      Of clovers and of noon!

                                              Ibid.

46 So, instead of getting to Heaven at last—
   I'm going, all along.
              Ibid., VI, "A Service of Song," St. 3

47 Much madness is divinist sense
      To a discerning eye;
   Much sense the starkest madness.

                                       Ibid., XI

* * *

48 Because I could not stop for Death,
He kindly stopped for me.
"Because I Could Not Stop for Death"

49 Faith is a fine invention
For gentlemen who see;
But microscopes are prudent
In an emergency.

"Faith"

50 Great Spirit, give to me
A heaven not so large as yours
But large enough for me.

"A Prayer"

51 I believe the love of God may be taught not to seem
like bears.
"In Protest Over Severe Religious Ideas of Ancestors"

52 If I can stop one heart from breaking,
I shall not live in vain;
If I can ease one life the aching,
Or cool one pain,
Or help one fainting robin
Into his nest again,
I shall not live in vain.

"Life"

53 Parting is all we know of heaven,
And all we need of hell.

"Parting"

118. Marie Ebner von Eschenbach
(1830–1916)

1 "Good heavens!" said he, "if it be our clothes alone
which fit us for society, how highly we should esteem
those who make them."

The Two Countesses   1893

2 HE. You apparently occupy yourself but little with
reading?
I. Just enough to do penance for my sins, and to keep
up my English.

Ibid.

3 He says a learned woman is the greatest of all calami-
ties.   Ibid.

4 "Everyone plays at the game for a time, my dear Paula, because it is the correct thing to do. . . . But thinking persons cannot hide from themselves the consciousness of the hollowness of it all, and then they turn to the realities of life, often bitterly to repent of their wasted years."

Ibid.

5 "Nothing is too strong to express the humiliation of knowing the being one looks up to—or rather one should look up to—to be a non-entity, or the hypocrisy of seeming to defer to him one knows to be one's inferior."

Ibid.

6 Accident is veiled necessity.

Aphorism 1905

7 Fear not those who argue but those who dodge.

Ibid.

8 Conquer, but don't triumph.

Ibid.

9 To be content with little is hard, to be content with much, impossible.

Ibid.

10 No one is so eager to gain new experience as he who doesn't know how to make use of the old ones.

Ibid.

11 If there is a faith that can move mountains, it is faith in your own power.

Ibid.

12 He who believes in freedom of the will has never loved and never hated.

Ibid.

13 Whenever two good people argue over principles, they are both right.

Ibid.

14 Imaginary evils are incurable.

Ibid.

15 Many think they have a kind heart who only have weak nerves.

Ibid.

16 We don't believe in rheumatism and true love until after the first attack.

Ibid.

17 We are so vain that we even care for the opinion of those we don't care for.

Ibid.

18 Privilege is the greatest enemy of right.

Ibid.

19 As far as your self-control goes, as far goes your freedom.

Ibid.

20 Even a stopped clock is right twice a day.

Ibid.

21 Those whom we support hold us up in life.

Ibid.

22 Only the thinking man lives his life, the thoughtless man's life passes him by.

Ibid.

23 You can stay young as long as you can learn, acquire new habits and suffer contradiction.

Ibid.

24 In youth we learn; in age we understand.

Ibid.

25 Oh, say not foreign war! A war is never foreign.

Quoted in *War, Peace, and the Future* by Ellen Key   1916

119. Helen Fiske Hunt Jackson
(1830–1885)

1 There is nothing so skillful in its own defence as imperious pride.

Ramona, Ch. 13   1884

2 Wounded vanity knows when it is mortally hurt; and limps off the field, piteous, all disguises thrown away. But pride carries its banner to the last.

Ibid.

3 There cannot be found in the animal kingdom a bat, or any other creature, so blind in its own range of cir-

141

cumstance and connection, as the greater majority of human beings are in the bosoms of their families.

Ibid.

4 That indescribable expression peculiar to people who hope they have not been asleep, but know they have.

Ibid., Ch. 14

5 Words are less needful to sorrow than to joy.

Ibid., Ch. 17

6 My body, eh. Friend Death, how now?
   Why all this tedious pomp of writ?
Thou hast reclaimed it sure and slow
   For half a century, bit by bit.

"Habeas Corpus," St. 1   1885

* * *

7 And newest friend is oldest friend in this:
That, waiting him, we longest grieved to miss
One thing we sought.

"My New Friend"

8 Bee to the blossom, moth to the flame;
Each to his passion; what's in a name?

"Vanity of Vanities"

9 But all lost things are in the angels' keeping. . . .

"At Last," St. 6

10 Father, I scarcely dare to pray,
   So clear I see, now it is done,
How I have wasted half my day,
   And left my work but just begun.

"A Last Prayer"

11 Find me the men on earth who care
   Enough for faith or creed today
To seek a barren wilderness
   For simple liberty to pray.

"The Pilgrim Forefathers," St. 5

12 Great loves, to the last, have pulses red;
All great loves that have ever died dropped dead.

"Dropped Dead"

13 Love has a tide!   "Tides"

14 Oh, write of me, not "Died in bitter pains,"
But "Emigrated to another star!"

"Emigravit"

15 O suns and skies and clouds of June,
    And flowers of June together,
Ye cannot rival for one hour
    October's bright blue weather.
                    "October's Bright Blue Weather," St. 1

16 O Sweet delusive Noon,
    Which the morning climbs to find,
O moment sped too soon,
    And morning left behind.
                            "Noon," *Verses*

17 She said: "The daisy but deceives;
    'He loves me not,' 'He loves me well,'
    One story no two daisies tell."
Ah foolish heart, which waits and grieves
    Under the daisy's mocking spell.
                            "The Sign of the Daisy"

18 The mighty are brought low by many a thing
Too small to name. Beneath the daisy's disk
Lies hid the pebble for the fatal sling.
                            "Danger"

19 We sail, at sunrise, daily, "outward bound."
                            "Outward Bound"

20 When love is at its best, one loves
So much that he cannot forget.
                            "Two Truths"

21 Who longest waits of all most surely wins.
                    "The Victory of Patience"

120. Mother Jones
(1830–1930)

1 Sometimes I'm in Washington, then in Pennsylvania,
Arizona, Texas, Alabama, Colorado, Minnesota. My
address is like my shoes. It travels with me. I abide
where there is a fight against wrong.
                        Congressional Hearing,
                Quoted in *The Rebel Girl*, Pt. II, by
                Elizabeth Gurley Flynn   *1955p*

* * *

2 Pray for the dead and fight like hell for the living.
                            Motto

121. Belva Lockwood
(1830–1917)

1 I do not believe in sex distinction in literature, law, politics, or trade—or that modesty and virtue are more becoming to women than to men, but wish we had more of it everywhere.

> Quoted in *Lady for the Defense,* Pt. II,
> Ch. 8, by Mary Virginia Fox   *1975p*

2 I know we can't abolish prejudice through laws, but we can set up guidelines for our actions by legislation. If women are given equal pay for Civil Service jobs, maybe other employers will do the same.

> Ibid., Pt. III, Ch. 11

3 I have been told that there is no precedent for admitting a woman to practice in the Supreme Court of the United States. The glory of each generation is to make its own precedents. As there was none for Eve in the Garden of Eden, so there need be none for her daughters on entering the colleges, the church, or the courts.

> Ibid., Ch. 13

4 If nations could only depend upon fair and impartial judgments in a world court of law, they would abandon the senseless, savage practice of war.

> Ibid., Ch. 15

5 No one can claim to be called Christian who gives money for the building of warships and arsenals.

> Ibid., Address at Westminister Hall, London (c.1886)

122. Louise Michel
(1830–1905)

1 In rebellion alone, woman is at ease, stamping out both prejudices and sufferings; all intellectual women will sooner or later rise in rebellion.

> Attributed   *1890*

123. Christina Rossetti
(1830–1894)

1 Why strive for love when love is o'er. . . .
　　　　　　　　　"Hearts' Chill Between," St. 2
　　　　　　　　　　　September 22, 1847

2 When I am dead, my dearest,
　　Sing no sad songs for me;
Plant thou no roses at my head,
　　Nor shady cypress tree.
Be the green grass above me
　　With showers and dew drops wet:
And if thou wilt, remember,
　　And if thou wilt, forget.
　　　　　　　"Song," St. 1　　*December 12, 1848*

3 To-day is still the same as yesterday,
　　To-morrow also even as one of them;
　　　And there is nothing new under the sun. . . .
　　　　　　　　"One Certainty"　　*June 2, 1849*

4 O dream house sweet, too sweet, too bittersweet,
　　Whose wakening should have been in Paradise,
Where souls brimfull of love abide and meet;
　　Where thirsting longing eyes
　　　Watch the slow door
That opening, letting in, lets out no more.
　　　　　　　　"Echo," St. 2　　*December 18, 1854*

5 My friends had failed one by one,
　　Middle-aged, young, and old,
Till the ghosts were warmer to me
　　Then my friends that had grown cold.
　　　　　"A Chilly Night," St. 2　　*February 11, 1856*

6 We, one, must part in two:
　　Verily death is this:
　　　I must die.
　　　　　　　"Wife to Husband," St. 5　　*June 8, 1861*

7 Too late for love, too late for joy,
　　Too late, too late!
You loitered on the road too long,
　　You trifled at the gate. . . .
　　"The Prince's Progress," St. 1　　*November 11, 1861*

8 "Does the road wind up-hill all the way?"
  "Yes, to the very end."
"Will the day's journey take the whole long day?"
  "From morn to night, my friend."
"Up-Hill," St. 1   1861

9 "May not the darkness hide it from my face?"
  "You cannot miss that inn."
Ibid.

10 My heart is like a singing bird.
"A Birthday," St. 1   1861

11   Because the birth of my life
Is come, my love is come to me.
Ibid., St. 2

12 All earth's full rivers cannot fill
The sea, that drinking thirsteth still.
"By the Sea," Goblin Market   1862

13 Darkness more clear than noonday holdeth her,
Silence more musical than any song.
Ibid., "Rest"

14 For there is no friend like a sister
In calm or stormy weather;
To cheer one on the tedious way,
To fetch one if one goes astray,
To lift one if one totters down,
To strengthen whilst one stands.
Ibid., "Goblin Market"

15 One day in the country
Is worth a month in town.
Ibid., "Summer"

16 Remember me when I am gone away,
Gone far away into the silent land.
Ibid., "Remember"

17 Better by far that you should forget and smile
Than that you should remember and be sad.
Ibid. (July 25, 1849)

18 I might show facts as plain as day:
But, since your eyes are blind, you'd say,
"Where? What?" and turn away.
"A Sketch," St. 3   August 15, 1864

19 "I ate his life as a banquet,
    I drank his life as new wine,
    I've fattened upon his leanness,
Mine to flourish and his to pine."
                "Cannot Sweeten," St. 7   *March 8, 1866*

20 "For the nobility have blood, if you please, and the literary beggars are welcome to all the brains they've got" (the Doctor smiled, Allen winced visibly); "but you'll find it's us city men who've got backbone, and backbone's the best to wear. . . ."
        Commonplace, A Tale of Today, Ch. 6   *1870*

21 So gradually it came to pass that, from looking back together, they took also to looking forward together.
                              Ibid., Ch. 17

22 Glow-worms that gleam but yield no warmth in gleaming. . . .
                "Till To-morrow," St. 2   *c.1882*

23 If thou canst dive, bring up pearls. If thou canst not dive, collect amber.
                The Face of the Deep,
                Prefatory Note   *1892*

24 Multitude no less than Unity characterizes various types of God the Holy Spirit.
                            Ibid., Ch. 1

25 Rapture and rest, desire and satisfaction, perfection and progress, may seem to clash to-day: to-morrow the paradoxes of earth may reappear as the demonstrations of heaven.
                            Ibid., Ch. 4

26 Well spake that soldier who being asked what he would do if he became too weak to cling to Christ, answered, "Then I will pray Him to cling to me."
                          Ibid., Ch. 16

* * *

27 Hope is like a harebell trembling from its birth. . . .
                "Hope Is Like a Harebell"

28 No wonder that his soul was sad,
When not one penny piece he had.
                        "Johnny"

29 Snow had fallen, snow on snow,
   Snow on snow,
   In the bleak mid-winter,
   Long ago.

                                        "Mid-Winter"

30 Who has seen the wind?
      Neither you nor I:
   But when the trees bow down their heads,
      The wind is passing by.
                            "Who Has Seen the Wind?," St. 2

124. Amelia Barr
(1831–1919)

1 But what do we know of the heart nearest to our own?
What do we know of our own heart? Some ancestor
who sailed with Offa, or who fought with the Ironsides,
or protested with the Covenanters, or legislated with
the Puritans, may, at this very hour, be influencing us,
in a way of which we never speak, and in which no
other soul intermeddles.
              Jan Vedder's Wife, Ch. 1   *1885*

2 ". . . for still I see that forethought spares afterthought
and after-sorrow."

                                        Ibid., Ch. 5

3 "There is no corner too quiet, or too far away, for a
woman to make sorrow in it."

                                        Ibid., Ch. 9

4 " 'Is she not handsome, virtuous, rich, amiable?' they
asked. 'What hath she done to thee?' The Roman husband pointed to his sandal. 'Is it not new, is it not
handsome and well made? But none of you can tell
where it pinches me.' That old Roman and I are brothers. Everyone praises 'my good wife, my rich wife, my
handsome wife,' but for all that, the matrimonial shoe
pinches me."

                                        Ibid.

5 "Let me tell thee, time is a very precious gift of God;
so precious that He only gives it to us moment by moment. He would not have thee waste it."

                                        Ibid., Ch. 11

6 "It is a sin to be merciful to the wicked, it is that; and the kindness done to them is unblessed, and brings forth sin and trouble."

Ibid.

7 "It is little men know of women; their smiles and their tears alike are seldom what they seem."

Ibid.

8 That is the great mistake about the affections. It is not the rise and fall of empires, the birth and death of kings, or the marching of armies that move them most. When they answer from their depths, it is to the domestic joys and tragedies of life.

Ibid., Ch. 14

9 It is only in sorrow bad weather masters us; in joy we face the storm and defy it.

Ibid.

10 But the lover's power is the poet's power. He can make love from all the common strings with which this world is strung.

The Belle of Bolling Green, Ch. 3   *1904*

11 The fate of love is that it always seems too little or too much.

Ibid., Ch. 5

12 Now jealousy is only good when she torments herself. . . .   *Ibid.*

13 "When men make themselves into brutes it is just to treat them like brutes."   *Ibid.*, Ch. 8

14 I entered this incarnation on March-the-twenty-ninth, A.D. 1831, at the ancient town of Ulverston, Lancashire, England. My soul came with me. This is not always the case. Every observing mother of a large family knows that the period of spiritual possession varies. . . . I brought my soul with me—an eager soul, impatient for the loves and joys, the struggles and triumphs of the dear, unforgotten world.

All the Days of My Life, Ch. 1   *1913*

15 With renunciation life begins.   *Ibid.*, Ch. 9

16 The great difference between voyages rests not with the ships, but with the people you meet on them.

Ibid., Ch. 11

17 For moral and spiritual gifts are bought and not given. We pay for them in some manner, or we go empty away. It is *every day duty* that tells on life. Spiritual favors are not always to be looked for, and not always to be relied on.

Ibid., Ch. 19

18 What we call death was to him only emigration, and I care not where he now tarries. He is doing God's will, and more alive than ever he was on earth.

Ibid., Ch. 23

19 Old age is the verdict of life.

Ibid., Ch. 26

20 Whatever the scientists may say, if we take the supernatural out of life, we leave only the unnatural.

Ibid.

125. Elena Petrovna Blavatsky
(1831–1891)

1 We live in an age of prejudice, dissimulation and paradox, wherein, like dry leaves caught in a whirlpool, some of us are tossed helpless, hither and thither, ever struggling between our honest convictions and fear of that cruelest of tyrants—PUBLIC OPINION.
   "A Paradoxical World," *Lucifer*   February, *1889*

2 For fourteen years our Theosophical Society has been before the public. Born with the threefold object of infusing a little more mutual brotherly feeling in mankind; of investigating the mysteries of nature from the Spiritual and Psychic aspect. . . . If it did not do all the good that a richer Society might, it certainly did no harm.
   Ibid., "On Pseudo-Theosophy"   *March, 1889*

3 We must prepare and study truth under every aspect, endeavoring to ignore nothing, if we do not wish to fall into the abyss of the unknown when the hour shall strike.
Quoted in *La Revue Theosophique*   March *21, 1899*

4 Just back from under the far-reaching shadow of the Eighth Wonder of the World—the gigantic iron carrot that goes by the name of the Eiffel Tower. Child of its

country, wondrous in its size, useless in its object, as shaky and vacillating as the republican soil upon which it is built, it has not one single moral feature of its seven ancestors, not one trait of atavism to boast of.

"The Eighth Wonder," *Lucifer*   *October, 1891*

5 This idea of passing one's whole life in moral idleness, and having one's hardest work and duty done by another—whether God or man—is most revolting to us, as it is most degrading to human dignity.

The Keys to Theosophy, Sec. 5   *1893*

6 And so the only reality in our conception is the hour of man's *post mortem* life, when, disembodied—during the period of that pilgrimage which we call "the cycle of re-births"—he stands face to face with truth and not the mirages of his transitory earthly existences.

Ibid., Sec. 9

7 It is the worst of crimes and dire in its results. . . . Voluntary death would be an abandonment of our present post and of the duties incumbent on us, as well as an attempt to shirk karmic responsibilities, and thus involve the creation of new Karma.

Ibid., Sec. 12

8 For in this age of crass and illogical materialism, the Esoteric Philosophy [theosophy] alone is calculated to withstand the repeated attacks on all and everything man holds most dear and sacred in his inner spiritual life.

The Secret Doctrine, Introduction (1893)   *1918p*

9 If there were such a thing as a void, a vacuum in Nature, one ought to find it produced, according to a physical law, in the minds of helpless admirers of the "lights" of Science, who pass their time in mutually destroying their teachings.

Ibid., Sec. 17

126. Isabel Burton
(1831–1896)

1 Without any cant, does not Providence provide wonderfully for us?

Arabia Egypt India, Ch. 15   *1879*

2 Like most outsiders, I cannot see the difficulty of settling the Eastern Question (*malé pereat!*), but I thoroughly see the danger of leaving it, as at present, half
settled. Ibid., Ch. 20

3 I have no leisure to think of style or of polish, or to
select the best language, the best English—no time to
shine as an authoress. I must just think aloud, so as not
to keep the public waiting.

*The Life of Captain Sir Richard F.
Burton,* Foreword *1898p*

127. Rebecca Harding Davis
(1831–1910)

1 The idiosyncrasy of this town is smoke. It rolls solemnly in slow folds from the great chimneys of the
iron-foundries, and settles down in black, slimy pools
on the muddy streets. Smoke on the wharves, smoke on
the dingy boats, on the yellow river—clinging in a
coating of greasy soot to the house-front, the two faded
poplars, the faces of the passers-by.

"Life in the Iron Mills,"
Atlantic Monthly April, 1861

2 You, Egoist, or Pantheist, or Arminian, busy in making
straight paths for your feet on the hills, do not see it
clearly—this terrible question which men here have
gone mad and died trying to answer. I dare not put this
secret into words. I told you it was dumb. These men,
going by with drunken faces and brains full of unawak-
ened power, do not ask it of Society or of God. Their
lives ask it; their deaths ask it. Ibid.

3 There are moments when a passing cloud, the sun
glinting on the purple thistles, a kindly smile, a child's
face, will rouse him to a passion of pain—when his nature starts up with a mad cry of rage against God, man,
whoever it is that has forced this vile, slimy life upon
him. Ibid.

4 Be just—not like man's law, which seizes on one isolated fact, but like God's judging angel, whose clear,
sad eye saw all the countless cankering days of this
man's life. . . . Ibid.

152

5 He was . . . a man who sucked the essence out of a science or philosophy in an indifferent, gentlemanly way; who took Kant, Novalis, Humboldt, for what they were worth in his own scale; accepting all, despising nothing, in heaven, earth, or hell, but one-idea'd men; with a temper yielding and brilliant as summer water, until his Self was touched, when it was ice, though brilliant still. Such men are not rare in the States.

Ibid.

6 "I tell you, there's something wrong that no talk of *'Liberté'* or *'Egalité'* will do away. If I had the making of men, these men who do the lowest part of the world's work should be machines—nothing more— hands. It would be kindness. God help them! What are taste, reason, to creatures who must live such lives as that?"

Ibid.

7 "Reform is born of need, not pity. No vital movement of the people has worked down, for good or evil; fermented, instead, carried up the heaving, cloggy mass."

Ibid.

8 Something is lost in the passage of every soul from one eternity to the other—something pure and beautiful, which might have been and was not: a hope, a talent, a love, over which the soul mourns, like Esau deprived of his birthright.

Ibid.

9 Every child was taught from his cradle that money was Mammon, the chief agent of the flesh and the devil. As he grew up it was his duty as a Christian and a gentleman to appear to despise filthy lucre, whatever his secret opinion of it might be.

Bits of Gossip, Ch. 1   1904

10 Nowhere in this country, from sea to sea, does nature comfort us with such assurance of plenty, such rich and tranquil beauty as in those unsung, unpainted hills of Pennsylvania.

Ibid., Ch. 4

11 North and South were equally confident that God was on their side, and appealed incessantly to Him.

Ibid., Ch. 5

12 We don't look into these unpleasant details of our great
struggle [the Civil War]. We all prefer to think that
every man who wore the blue or gray was a Philip Sidney at heart. These are sordid facts that I have dragged
up. But—they are facts. And because we have hidden
them our young people have come to look upon war as
a kind of beneficent deity, which not only adds to the
national honor but uplifts a nation and develops patriotism and courage. That is all true. But it is only fair,
too, to let them know that the garments of the deity are
filthy and that some of her influences debase and befoul
a people.

Ibid.

13 But while the light burning within may have been divine, the outer case of the lamp was assuredly cheap
enough. [Walt] Whitman was, from first to last, a
boorish, awkward *poseur*.

Ibid., Ch. 8

128. Henrietta Dobree
(1831–1894)

* * *

1 Safely, safely, gather'd in,
Far from sorrow, far from sin.

"Child's Hymn Book"

129. Amelia Edwards
(1831–1892)

* * *

1 The Queen has lands and gold, Mother
The Queen has lands and gold,
While you are forced to your empty breast
A skeleton Babe to hold. . . .

"Give Me Three Grains of Corn, Mother," St. 4

2 What has poor Ireland done, Mother,
What has poor Ireland done,
That the world looks on, and sees us starve,
Perishing one by one?

Ibid., St. 5

154

3 There are rich and proud men there, Mother,
   With wondrous wealth to view
And the bread they fling to their dogs tonight
   Would give life to me and you.   Ibid., St. 6

130. Nora Perry
(1831–1896)

* * *

1 But not alone with the silken snare
Did she catch her lovely floating hair,
For, tying her bonnet under her chin,
She tied a young man's heart within.
                          "The Love-Knot," St. 1

2 Some day, some day of days, threading the street
   With idle, headless pace,
   Unlooking for such grace,
   I shall behold your face!
Some day, some day of days, thus may we meet.
                          "Some Day of Days"

3 What silences we keep, year after year,
With those who are most near to us,
   And dear!   "Too Late," St. 1

4 Who knows the thoughts of a child?
                          "Who Knows?," St. 1

131. Elizabeth Chase Akers
(1832–1911)

1 Backward, turn backward, O Time, in your flight,
Make me a child again, just for to-night!
          "Rock Me to Sleep, Mother"   *1860*

2 I have grown weary of dust and decay—
Weary of flinging my soul-wealth away;—
Weary of sowing for others to reap;
Rock me to sleep, Mother—rock me to sleep!
                          Ibid., St. 2

* * *

3 Blush, happy maiden, when you feel
The lips that press love's glowing seal.
But as the slow years darker roll,

Grown wiser, the experienced soul
Will own as dearer far than they
The lips which kiss the tears away.   "Kisses"

4 Carve not upon a stone when I am dead
The praises which remorseful mourners give
To women's graves—a tardy recompense—
    But speak them while I live.

"Till Death," St. 6

5 Though we be sick and tired and faint and worn,—
Lo, all things can be borne!   "Endurance," St. 5

6   Unremembered and afar
I watched you as I watched a star,
Through darkness struggling into view,
I loved you better than you knew.

"Left Behind," St. 5

132. Louisa May Alcott
(1832–1888)

1 A little kingdom I possess,
    Where thought and feelings dwell;
And very hard the task I find
    Of governing it well.
            "My Kingdom," St. 1   *c.1845*

2 I do not ask for any crown
    But that which all may win;
Nor try to conquer any world
    Except the one within.   Ibid., St. 4

3 Above man's aims his nature rose.
The wisdom of a just content
Made one small spot a continent,
And turned to poetry life's prose.

"Thoreau's Flute," St. 2, *Atlantic
Monthly*   September, *1863*

4 "Energy is more attractive than beauty in a man."
            Behind a Mask, Ch. 2   *1866*

5 "You *are* master here, but not of me, or my actions,
and you have no right to expect obedience or respect,
for you inspire neither."

Ibid., Ch. 4

6 ". . . rivalry adds so much to the charms of one's conquests."

Ibid., Ch. 7

7 "Christmas won't be Christmas without any presents."
Little Women, Pt. I   *1868*

8 "I shall have to toil and moil all my days, with only little bits of fun now and then, and get old and ugly and sour, because I'm poor, and can't enjoy my life as other girls do. It's a shame!"

Ibid.

9 "You have a good many little gifts and virtues, but there is no need of parading them, for conceit spoils the finest genius. There is not much danger that real talent or goodness will be overlooked long, and the great charm of all power is modesty."

Ibid.

10 ". . . It seems as if I could do anything when I'm in a passion. I get so savage I could hurt anyone and enjoy it. I'm afraid I *shall* do something dreadful some day, and spoil my life, and make everybody hate me. O Mother, help me. . . ."

Ibid.

11 "Housekeeping ain't no joke."

Ibid.

12 "November is the most disagreeable month in the whole year."

Ibid.

13 "People don't have fortunes left them . . . nowadays; men have to work, and women to marry for money. It's a dreadfully unjust world. . . ."

Ibid.

14 . . . love is a great beautifier.

Ibid.

15 It takes people a long time to learn the difference between talent and genius, especially ambitious young men and women.

Ibid., Pt. II

16 . . . she was one of those happily created beings who please without effort, make friends everywhere, and take life so gracefully and easily that less fortunate

157

souls are tempted to believe that such are born under a lucky star.

Ibid.

17 "My lady" . . . had yet to learn that money cannot buy refinement of nature, that rank does not always confer nobility, and that true breeding makes itself felt in spite of external drawbacks.

Ibid.

18 ". . . It's a great comfort to have an artistic sister."

Ibid.

19 ". . . elegance has a bad effect upon my constitution. . . ."

Ibid.

20 . . . she had a womanly instinct that clothes possess an influence more powerful over many than the worth of character or the magic of manners.

Ibid.

21 ". . . girls are so queer you never know what they mean. They say No when they mean Yes, and drive a man out of his wits for the fun of it. . . ."

Ibid.

22 . . . public opinion is a giant which has frightened stouter-hearted Jacks on bigger beanstalks than hers.

Ibid.

23 ". . . I don't believe I shall ever marry. I'm happy as I am, and love my liberty too well to be in any hurry to give it up for any mortal man."

Ibid.

24 ". . . Oh dear! How can girls like to have lovers and refuse them? I think it's dreadful."

Ibid.

25 "Rome took all the vanity out of me; for after seeing the wonders there, I felt too insignificant to live, and gave up all my foolish hopes in despair."

Ibid.

26 ". . . talent isn't genius, and no amount of energy can make it so. I want to be great, or nothing. I won't be a commonplace dauber, so I don't intend to try any more."

Ibid.

27 "It takes two flints to make a fire."

Ibid.

28 ". . . love is the only thing that we can carry with us when we go, and it makes the end so easy."

Ibid.

29 . . . when women are the advisers, the lords of creation don't take the advice till they have persuaded themselves that it is just what they intended to do; then they act upon it, and if it succeeds, they give the weaker vessel half the credit of it; if it fails, they generously give her the whole.

Ibid.

30 . . . when a man has a great sorrow, he should be indulged in all sorts of vagaries till he has lived it down.

Ibid.

31 ". . . I'm not afraid of storms, for I'm learning how to sail my ship."

Ibid.

32 ". . . What *do* girls do who haven't any mothers to help them through their troubles?"   Ibid.

33 "Help one another, is part of the religion of our sisterhood, Fan."

An Old-Fashioned Girl   1869

34 ". . . women have been called queens for a long time, but the kingdom given them isn't worth ruling."

Ibid.

35 I believe that it is as much a right and duty for women to do something with their lives as for men and we are not going to be satisfied with such frivolous parts as you give us.

Rose in Bloom   1876

36 "[Molly] remained a merry spinster all her days, one of the independent, brave and busy creatures of whom there is such need in the world to help take care of other people's wives and children, and to do the many useful jobs that married folk have no time for."

Jack and Jill   1880

37 "[I'm] very glad and grateful that my profession will make me a useful, happy and independent spinster."

Jo's Boys   1886

38 Now I am beginning to live a little, and feel less like a sick oyster at low tide.
Louisa May Alcott: Her Life, Letters, and Journals, Edna D. Cheney, ed.   *1889p*

39 My definition [of a philosopher] is of a man up in a balloon, with his family and friends holding the ropes which confine him to the earth and trying to haul him down.
Ibid.

40 Resolved to take Fate by the throat and shake a living out of her.
Ibid., Ch. 3

41 Father asked us what was God's noblest work. Anna said *men,* but I said *babies.* Men are often bad; babies never are.
Ibid., Early Diary Kept at Fruitlands (1843)

42 I had a pleasant time with my mind, for it was happy.
Ibid.

43 I have at last got the little room I have wanted so long, and am very happy about it. It does me good to be alone. . . .
Ibid. (1846)

44 Philosophers sit in their sylvan hall
And talk of the duties of man,
Of Chaos and Cosmos, Hegel and Kant,
With the Oversoul well in the van;
All on their hobbies they amble away
And a terrible dust they make;
Disciples devout both gaze and adore,
As daily they listen and bake.
"Philosophers" (1845), *Alcott and the Concord School of Philosophy,* Florence Whiting Brown, ed.   *1926p*

133. Mary Walker
(1832–1919)

1 If men were really what they profess to be they would not compel women to dress so that the facilities for vice would always be so easy.
Quoted in *Saturday Review*   *1935p*

134. Mary Woolsey
(1832–1864)

* * *

1 I lay me down to sleep with little thought or care
Whether my waking find me here, or there.

"Rest"

135. Gail Hamilton
(1833–1896)

1 Whatever an author puts between the two covers of his
book is public property; whatever of himself he does
not put there is his private property, as much as if he
had never written a word.

*Country Living and Country
Thinking*, Preface   *1862*

2 Every person is responsible for all the good within the
scope of his abilities, and for no more, and none can
tell whose sphere is the largest.

Ibid., "Men and Women"

* * *

3 What's virtue in man can't be virtue in a cat.

"Both Sides"

136. Julia Harris May
(1833–1912)

* * *

1   If we could know
Which of us, darling, would be the first to go,
Who would be first to breast the swelling tide
And step alone upon the other side—
     If we could know!

"If We Could Know"

137. Emily Miller
(1833-1913)

* * *

1 I love to hear the story
  Which angel voices tell.
> "I love to Hear," *The Little Corporal*

2 Then sing, young hearts that are full of cheer,
    With never a thought of sorrow;
  The old goes out, but the glad young year
    Comes merrily in tomorrow.
> "New Year Song"

138. Julia Woodruff
(1833-1909)

1 Out of the strain of the Doing,
  Into the race of the Done.
> "Harvest Home," *Sunday at Home*   *May, 1910p*

139. Annie Adams Fields
(1834-1915)

1 Woman of nerve and thought,
  Bring in the urn your power!
  By you is manhood taught
  To meet the supreme hour.
> "Give," St. 2, *The Singing Shepherd*   1895

2 Once men could walk these roads and hear no sound
  Save the sad ocean beating on the shore . . .
> Ibid., "Unchanged"

140. Katherine Hankey
(1834-1911)

* * *

1 Tell me the old, old story
  Of unseen things above,
  Of Jesus and His glory
  Of Jesus and His love.
> Hymn

141. Harriet Kimball
(1834–1917)

* * *

1 A very rapturing of white;
  A wedlock of silence and light:
  White, white as the wonder undefiled
  Of Eve just wakened in Paradise.   "White Azaleas"

142. Josephine Pollard
(1834–1892)

* * *

1 Though he had Eden to live in,
  Man cannot be happy alone.
                "We Cannot Be Happy Alone," St. 5

143. Ellen Palmer Allerton
(1835–1893)

* * *

1 Beautiful faces are those that wear
  Whole-souled honesty printed there.
                          "Beautiful Things"

144. Mary Bradley
(1835–1898)

* * *

1 Of all the flowers that come and go
    The whole twelve months together,
  This little purple pansy brings
  Thoughts of the sweetest, saddest things.   "Heartsease"

145. Augusta Evans
(1835–1909)

1 Money is everything in this world to some people and
  more than the next to other poor souls.
                          Beulah, Ch. 2   *1859*

2 Can the feeling that you are independent and doing
   your duty, satisfy the longing for other idyls? Oh! Duty
   is an icy shadow. It will freeze you. It cannot fill the
   heart's sanctuary.   Ibid., Ch. 13

3 Oh, has the foul atmosphere of foreign lands extin-
   guished *all* your self respect? Do you come back sordid
   and sycophantic, and the slave of opinions you would
   once have utterly detested?
                                                    Ibid., Ch. 18

4 Human genius has accomplished a vast deal for man's
   temporal existence. . . . But . . . what has it effected
   for philosophy, that great burden which constantly re-
   calls the fabled labors of Sisyphus and the Danaides?
   Since the rising of Bethlehem's star, in the cloudy sky
   of polytheism, what has human genius discovered of
   God, eternity, destiny?
                                                    Ibid., Ch. 41

5 Fortuitous circumstances constitute the moulds that
   shape the majority of human lives, and the hasty impress of an accident is too often regarded as the relentless decree of all ordaining fate. . . .
           Until Death Us Do Part, Ch. 1   *1869*

146. Ellen Gates
(1835–1920)

* * *

1 Sleep sweet within this quiet room,
     O thou! whoe'er thou art;
   And let no mournful yesterday,
     Disturb thy peaceful heart.

                                              "Sleep Sweet"

147. Louise Moulton
(1835–1908)

* * *

1 Bend low, O dusky night,
     And give my spirit rest,
     Hold me deep to your breast,
   And put old cares to flight.

                                                 "Tonight"

164

2 Give me back the lost delight
   That once my soul possessed,
   When love was loveliest.

Ibid.

3   The month it was the month of May,
   And all along the pleasant way,
  The morning birds were mad with glee,
  And all the flowers sprang up to see. . . .

"The Secret of Arcady"

4 This life is a fleeting breath. . . .

"When I Wander Away with Death"

148. Harriet Spofford
(1835–1921)

* * *

1 Beauty vanishes like a vapor,
  Preach the men of musty morals.

"Evanescence"

2 Something to live for came to the place,
   Something to die for maybe,
  Something to give even sorrow a grace,
   And yet it was only a baby!

"Only"

3 The awful phantom of the hungry poor.

"A Winter's Night"

149. Celia Thaxter
(1835–1894)

* * *

1 Across the narrow beach we flit,
  One little sandpiper and I.

"The Sandpiper," St. 1

2 Look to the East, where up the lucid sky
   The morning climbs! The day shall yet be fair.

"Faith"

3 Sad soul, take comfort, nor forget
  That sunrise never failed us yet.

"The Sunrise Never Failed Us Yet," St. 4

150. Mary Frances Butts
(1836–1902)

* * *

1 Build a little fence of trust
  Around today;
Fill the space with loving work,
  And therein stay.

"Trust"

151. Frances Ridley Havergal
(1836–1879)

* * *

1 Doubt indulged soon becomes doubt realized.
  "The Imagination of the Thoughts of
  the Heart," *Royal Bounty*

2 Love understands love; it needs no talk.
  "Loving Allegiance," *Royal Commandments*

3 Silence is no certain token
  That no secret grief is there;
Sorrow which is never spoken
  Is the heaviest load to bear.

"Misunderstood," St. 15

152. Marietta Holley
(1836?–1926)

1 Yes, this world is a curious place, very, and holler, holler as a drum. Lots of times the ground seems to lay
smooth and serene under your rockin' chair, when all
the time a earthquake may be on the very p'int of bust-
in' it open and swollerin' you up—chair and all.
  "Josiah Allen Gits a Stray," *My
  Wayward Pardner; or My Trials
  with Josiah, America, the Widow
  Bump, and Etcetery   1880*

2 We are blind creeters, the fur-seein'est of us; weak
creeters, when we think we are the strong-mindedest.
Now, when we hear of a crime, it is easy to say that the

one who committed that wrong stepped flat off from
goodness into sin, and should be hung. It is so awful
easy and sort of satisfactory to condemn other folks'es
faults that we don't stop to think that it may be that
evil was fell into through the weakness and blindness of
a mistake.

Ibid., "Kitty Smith and Caleb Cobb"

3 And then when we read of some noble, splendid act of
generosity, our souls burn within us, and it is easy to
say, the one who did that glorious deed should be
throned and crowned with honor—not thinkin' how,
mebby, unbeknown to us, that act was the costly and
glitterin' varnish coverin' up a whited sepulchre. That
deed was restin' on self-seekin', ambitious littleness.

Ibid.

4 But I am a-eppisodin', and a-eppisodin' to a length and
depth almost onprecedented and onheard on—and to
resoom and go on.
Samantha at the World's Fair, Ch. 4   1893

5 And I sez, "Children and trees have to be tackled
young, Josiah, to bend their wills the way you want 'em
to go."

*Around the World with Josiah Allen's
Wife,* Ch. 18   1899

153. Jane Ellice Hopkins
(1836–1904)

1 Gift, like genius, I often think only means an infinite
capacity for taking pains.
Work Amongst Working Men   1870

154. Mary Elizabeth Braddon
(1837–1915)

1 ". . . it is easy to starve, but it is difficult to stoop."
Lady Audley's Secret, Ch. 23   1862

2 "Let any man make a calculation of his existence, sub-
tracting the hours in which he has been *thoroughly*
happy—really and entirely at his ease, without one *ar-
rière pensée* to mar his enjoyment—without the most

167

infinitesimal cloud to overshadow the brightness of his horizon. Let him do this, and surely he will laugh in utter bitterness of soul when he sets down the sum of his felicity, and discovers the pitiful smallness of the amount." *Ibid., Ch. 25*

3 There can be no reconciliation where there is no open warfare. There must be a battle, a brave boisterous battle, with pennants waving and cannon roaring, before there can be peaceful treaties and enthusiastic shaking of hands. *Ibid., Ch. 32*

4 She was no longer innocent, and the pleasure we take in art and loveliness, being an innocent pleasure, had passed beyond her reach.

Ibid.

5 "Do you think that there will not come a day in which my meerschaums will be foul, and the French novels more than usually stupid, and life altogether such a dismal monotony that I shall want to get rid of it somehow or other?" *Ibid., Ch. 41*

6 "A priest can achieve great victories with an army of women at his command. How are our churches beautified, our sick tended, our poor fed, our children taught and cared for and civilised? Do you think the masculine element goes for much in these things? No, Westray; women are the Church's strong rock. As they were the last at the foot of the cross, so they have become the first at the altar."

Hostages to Fortune, Vol. I, Ch. 1   1875

7 "Progress is a grand word," he said at last, "but how few they are who have the elements of progress in their nature! To go up like a rocket and come down like a stick seems the natural tendency of human genius."

Ibid., Ch. 3

8 Life, which he had thought worn out and done with, save as a mere mechanical process, seems to have begun afresh for him—life and youth and happiness all renewed together like a second birth.

Ibid., Vol. II, Ch. 5

9 "After all, what the world says of a man never yet made his finger ache. But how many a heartache the slave of opinion gives himself!"

Ibid., Vol. III, Ch. 2

10 Paris is a mighty schoolmaster, a grand enlightener of the provincial intellect.

The Cloven Foot, Ch. 4   *1879*

11 He had lived for himself alone, and had sinned for his own pleasure; and if his life within the last decade had been comparatively pure and harmless, it was because the bitter apples of the Dead Sea could tempt him no longer by their outward beauty.

Dead-Sea Fruit, Vol. II, Ch. 1   *1868*

12 "I do not think the stage, as it is at present constituted, offers a brilliant prospect for any woman. Of course there are exceptional circumstances, and there is exceptional talent; but, unhappily, exceptional talent does not always win its reward unless favoured by exceptional circumstances."

Ibid., Ch. 4

13 "Are there not, indeed, brief pauses of mental intoxication, in which the spirit releases itself from its dull mortal bondage, and floats starward on the wings of inspiration?"

Ibid., Ch. 9

14 "I think that most wearisome institution, the honeymoon, must have been inaugurated by some sworn foe to matrimony, some vile misogynist, who took to himself a wife in order to discover, by experience, the best mode of rendering married life a martyrdom."

Ibid.

15 "My life was one long yawn—and if I still lived, it was only because I knew not what purgatory a perpetual *ennui* might await me on Acheron's further shore."

Ibid.

16 Flatterers fawned upon him, intimate acquaintances hung fondly upon him, reminding him pathetically that they knew him twenty years ago, when he hadn't a sixpence, as if that knowledge of bygone adversity were a merit and a claim.   Ibid., Ch. 14

17 The brother had strange views of life and duty, and a beautiful young woman, essentially worldly and modern, could hardly be expected to get on well with a young man whose master and guide was St. Francis of Assisi.

The White House, Ch. 1   *1906*

18 "A London house without visitors is so triste."

Ibid., Ch. 6

19 He had compelled her to think of the sons of toil as she had never thought before, this world outside the world of Skepton, the lower-grade labour, the unskilled, uncertain, casual work; a life in which thrift would seem impossible, since there was nothing to save, cleanliness and decency impracticable and drunken oblivion the only possible relief.

Ibid., Ch. 15

20 "I have heard that Africa is irresistible, that the man who has once been there, most of all who has lived there for years, must go back. The mountains and the lakes call him."

Ibid.

21 It may be that Miranda had enjoyed too much of the roses and the lilies of life, and that a girlhood of such absolute indulgence was hardly the best preparation for the battle which has to come in the lives of women—whatever their temporal advantages—the battle of the heart, or of the brain, the fight with fate, or the fight with man.

Miranda, Book I, Ch. 2   *1913*

22 "I hope they won't uglify the house," sighed Lady Laura. "People generally do when they try to improve a sweet, picturesque old place."

Ibid., Book II, Ch. 1

23 "Love is life, love is the lamp that lights the universe: without that light this goodly frame, the earth, is a barren promontory and man the quintessence of dust."

Ibid., Ch. 9

24 Be happy! What a cruel mockery that advice may sometimes sound in the patient's ear! How impossible to obey!

Ibid., Book III, Ch. 13

* * *

25 When once estrangement has arisen between those who truly love each other, everything seems to widen the breach.

Run to Earth, Ch. 8

26 "I'm an old stager, ma'am, and have seen a good deal of life, and I have generally found that people who are ready to promise so much before-hand, are apt not to give anything when their work has been done."

Ibid., Ch. 15

170

155. Jeanne Detourbey
(1837–1908)

1 Is it necessary to have read Spinoza in order to make out a laundry list?

> Quoted in *Forty Years of Parisian Society* by Arthur Meyer   *1912p*

2 Of course, fortune has its part in human affairs, but conduct is really much more important.

> Ibid.

3 So I cannot bear to be told that So-and-so is lucky. Too often the phrase is a covert attack upon the man; for what does it amount to in plain speech but that he is an idiot with nothing but his luck to recommend him?

> Ibid.

156. Mary Mapes Dodge
(1838?–1905)

1 Should this simple narrative . . . cause even one heart to feel a deeper trust in God's goodness and love, or aid any in weaving a life, wherein, through knots and entanglements, the golden thread shall never be tarnished or broken, the prayer with which it was begun and ended will have been answered.

Hans Brinker or The Silver Skates, Preface   *1865*

2 . . . in Holland ice is generally an all-winter affair.

> Ibid.

3 I'm as true a Protestant, in sooth, as any fine lady that walks into church, but it's not wrong to turn sometimes to the good St. Nicholas.

> Ibid.

4 To her mind, the poor peasant-girl Gretel was not a human being, a God-created creature like herself—she was only something that meant poverty, rags and dirt.

> Ibid.

5 This kind of work is apt to summon Vertigo, of whom good Hans Andersen writes—the same who hurls daring young hunters from the mountains, or spins them

from the sharpest heights of the glaciers, or catches them as they tread the stepping-stones of the mountain torrent.

Ibid., "Jacob Poot Changes the Plan"

6 What a dreadful thing it must be to have a dull father. . . .

Ibid., "Boys and Girls"

7 Ten years dropped from a man's life are no small loss; ten years of manhood, of household happiness and care; ten years of honest labor, of conscious enjoyment of sunshine and outdoor beauty; ten years of grateful life—one day looking forward to all this; the next, waking to find them passed, and a blank.

Ibid., "The Father's Return"

8 . . . the dame was filled with delightful anxieties caused by the unreasonable demands of ten thousand guilders' worth of new wants that had sprung up like mushrooms in a single night.

Ibid., "A Discovery"

9 "It is an ugly business, boy, this surgery," said the doctor, still frowning at Hans, "it requires great patience, self-denial and perseverance."

Ibid., "Broad Sunshine"

10 How faithfully those glancing eyes shall yet seek for the jewels that lie hidden in rocky schoolbooks!

Ibid.

11 "Modern ways are quite alarming,"
Grandma says, "but boys were charming"
(Girls and boys she means, of course) "long ago."

"The Minuet," St. 3   1879

* * *

12 All things ready with a will,
April's coming up the Hill.

"Now the Noisy Winds Are Still"

13 Life is a mystery as deep as ever death can be;
Yet oh, how dear it is to us, this life we live and see!

"The Two Mysteries," St. 3

14 But I believe that God is overhead;
And as life is to the living, so death is to the dead.

Ibid., St. 5

15 She wants from me, my lady Earth,
   Smiles and waits and sighs.

"How the Rain Comes"

157. Kate Field
(1838–1896)

* * *

1 They talk about a woman's sphere,
   As though it had a limit,
   There's not a place in earth or heaven,
   There's not a task to mankind given . . .
   Without a woman in it.

"Woman's Spirit"

158. Lydia Kamekeha Liliuokalani
(1838–1917)

1 The Hawaiian people have been from time immemorial
   lovers of poetry and music, and have been apt in im-
   provising historic poems, songs of love, and chants of
   worship, so that praises of the living or wails over the
   dead were with them but the natural expression of their
   feelings.

Hawaii's Story, Ch. 5   *1898*

2 Oh, honest Americans, as Christians hear me for my
   down-trodden people! Their form of government is as
   dear to them as yours is precious to you. Quite as
   warmly as you love your country, so they love theirs.
   With all your goodly possessions, covering a territory
   so immense that there yet remains parts unexplored,
   possessing islands that, although near at hand, had to
   be neutral ground in time of war, do not covet the little
   vineyard of Naboth's, so far from your shores, lest the
   punishment of Ahab fall upon you, if not in your day,
   in that of your children, for "be not deceived, God is
   not mocked."   Ibid., Ch. 57

* * *

3 Farewell to thee, farewell to thee,
   Thou charming one who dwells among the bowers,
   One fond embrace before I now depart
   Until we meet again.

"Aloha Oe"

159. Margaret Sangster
(1838–1912)

* * *

1 And hearts have broken from harsh words spoken
   That sorrow can ne'er set right.   "Our Own," St. 1

2 We have careful thought from the stranger,
   And smiles from the sometime guest;
   But oft from "our own" the bitter tone,
   Though we love our own the best.   Ibid., St. 3

3 And it isn't the thing you do, dear,
   It's the thing you leave undone
   Which gives you a bit of a heartache
   At the setting of the sun.   "The Sin of Omission"

4 Never yet was a springtime
   When the buds forgot to blow.

                                            "Awakening"

5 Not always the fanciest cake that's there
   Is the best to eat!

                                    "French Pastry," St. 3

6 Out of the chill and the shadow,
   Into the thrill and the shine;
   Out of the dearth and the famine,
   Into the fullness divine.

                                            "Going Home"

7 Prophet and priest he stood
   In the storm of embattled years;
   The broken chain was his heart's refrain,
   And the peace that is balm for tears.
                                "John Greenleaf Whittier"

160. Victoria Claflin Woodhull
(1838–1927)

1 I have an inalienable constitutional and natural right to
love whom I may, to love as long or as short a period
as I can, to change that love every day if I please!
                        Article in *Woodhull and Claflin's*
                        Weekly   November 20, 1871

2 A Vanderbilt may sit in his office and manipulate stocks or declare dividends by which in a few years he amasses fifty million dollars from the industries of the country, and he is one of the remarkable men of the age. But if a poor, half-starved child should take a loaf of bread from his cupboard to appease her hunger, she would be sent to the tombs.

Campaign Speech   1872

3 The wife who submits to sexual intercourse against her wishes or desires, virtually commits suicide; while the husband who compels it, commits murder. . . .

Speech, "The Elixir of Life,"
American Association of Spiritu-
alists (1873), Chicago, Feminism,
Miriam Schneir, ed.   1972p

4 It is a fact terrible to contemplate, yet it is nevertheless true, and ought to be pressed upon the world for its recognition: that fully one-half of all women seldom or never experience any pleasure whatever in the sexual act. Now this is an impeachment of nature, a disgrace to our civilization.

Ibid.

161. Mary Clemmer
(1839–1884)

* * *

1 A shining isle in a stormy sea,
   We seek it ever with smiles and sighs;
To-day is sad. In the bland To-be,
   Serene and lovely To-morrow lies.

"To-morrow"

2 I lie amid the Goldenrod,
I love to see it lean and nod.

"Goldenrod"

3 The Indian Summer, the dead Summer's soul.

"Presence"

4 To serve thy generation, this thy fate:
"Written in water," swiftly fades thy name;
But he who loves his kind does, first or late,
A work too great for fame.

"The Journalist"

5 Only a newspaper! Quick read, quick lost,
  Who sums the treasure that it carries hence?
  Torn, trampled under feet, who counts thy cost,
  Star-eyed intelligence?

Ibid.

162. Ouida
(1839–1908)

1 . . . with peaches and women, it's only the side next
  the sun that's tempting.

Strathmore   1865

2 What is it that love does to a woman? Without it she
  only sleeps; with it alone, she lives.

Wisdom, Wit and Pathos   1884

3 To vice, innocence must always seem only a superior
  kind of chicanery.

Ibid., "Two Little Wooden Shoes" (1874)

4 Fame has only the span of a day, they say. But to live
  in the hearts of the people—that is worth something.

Ibid., "Signa" (1875)

5 The song that we hear with our ears is only the song
  that is sung in our hearts.

Ibid., "Ariadne" (1877)

6 Petty laws breed great crimes.

Ibid., "Pipistrello" (1880)

7 Take hope from the heart of man, and you make him a
  beast of prey.

Ibid., "A Village Commune" (1881)

8 She knew how to be "so naughty and so nice" in the
  way that society in London likes and never punishes.

Ibid., "Moths"

9 A cruel story runs on wheels, and every hand oils the
  wheels as they run.

Ibid.

* * *

10 Christianity has ever been the enemy of human love.

"The Failure of Christianity"

11 Christianity has made of death a terror which was unknown to the gay calmness of the Pagan.

Ibid.

163. Frances Willard
(1839–1898)

1 Geology teaches that death was in the world before sin, which is contrary to the Bible. But it is nowhere stated in the Bible that sin was the cause of the death of any save man: he only has sinned. Any other idea is a superstition and without foundation.

Quoted in Frances Willard: Her Life
and Work, Ch. 2, by Ray Strachey   1912p

2 Here's a recipe for the abolishment of the Blues which
    is worth a dozen medical nostrums:
    Take one spoonful of Pleasant memories.
    Take two spoonfuls of Endeavours for the
      Happiness of others.
    Take two spoonfuls of Forgetfulness of
      Sorrow.
    Mix well with a half pint of Cheerfulness.
    Take a portion every hour of the day.

Ibid., Journal Entry (c.1860)

3 Germany is the purgatory of women and dogs.
Ibid., Journal Entry (November 30, 1868), Ch. 5

4 The world is wide, and I will not waste my life in friction when it could be turned into momentum.

Ibid., Ch. 6

5 Recognising that our cause is, and will be, combated by mighty, determined, and relentless forces, we will, trusting in Him who is the Prince of Peace, meet argument with argument, misjudgment with patience, denunciations with kindness, and all our difficulties and dangers with prayer.

Ibid., Ch. 7

6 Everything is not in the temperance movement, but the temperance movement should be in everything.

Ibid., Ch. 11

164. Mary Branch
(1840–1922)

* * *

1 So, I think, God hides some souls away,
Sweetly to surprise us, the last day.
"The Petrified Fern"

165. Elizabeth York Case
(1840?–1911)

* * *

1 There is no unbelief;
Whoever plants a seed beneath the sod
And waits to see it push away the clod,
He trusts in God.
"There Is No Unbelief"

166. Harriet King
(1840–1920)

* * *

1 Measure thy life by loss instead of gain,
Not by the wine drunk, but by the wine poured forth.
"The Disciples"

167. Helena Modjeska
(1840–1910)

1 Alas! it was not my destiny to die for my country, as
was my cherished dream, but instead of becoming the
heroine I had to be satisfied with acting heroines, exchanging the armor for tinsel, and the weapon for
words.
Memories and Impressions, Pt. I, Ch. 1   *1910*

2 It is never right to be more Catholic than the Pope.
Ibid., Ch. 25

3 . . . the word "great" is not sufficient anymore, if you
do not add to it, "Genius!" In Europe the word "gen-

178

ius" is only applied to the greatest of the world, but here [in America] it has become an everyday occurrence.

Ibid., Pt. III, Ch. 51

4 It seems to me that there are only two schools, one of good acting, the other of bad acting.

Ibid.

5 We foreigners, born outside of the magic pale of the Anglo-Saxon race, place Shakespeare upon a much higher pedestal. We claim that, before being English, he was human, and that his creations are not bound either by local or ethnological limits, but belong to humanity in general.

Ibid.

168. Marilla Ricker
(1840–1920)

1 The only thing that ever came back from the grave that we know of was a lie.
The Philistine, Vol. XXV   c.1901

2 He [Thomas Paine] was as democratic as nature, as impartial as sun and rain.

Ibid.

169. Katharine Walker
(1840–1916)

1 However divinity schools may refuse to "skip" in unison, and may butt and butter each other about the doctrine and origin of human depravity, all will join devoutly in the credo, I believe in the total depravity of inanimate things.
"The Total Depravity of Inanimate
Things," Atlantic Monthly   September, 1864

2 The elusiveness of soap, the knottiness of strings, the transitory nature of buttons, the inclination of suspenders to twist and of hooks to forsake their lawful eyes, and cleave only into the hairs of their hapless owner's head.

Ibid.

170. Elizabeth Wordsworth
(1840–1932)

1 If all the good people were clever,
   And all the clever people were good,
   The world would be nicer than ever
   We thought that it possibly could.

   But somehow, 'tis seldom or never
   The two hit if off as they should;
   The good are so harsh to the clever,
   The clever so rude to the good.

"The Good and the Clever,"
St. Christopher and Other Poems   *1890*

171. Mary Wood Allen
(1841–1908)

1 Woman embroiders man's life—Embroider is to beautify—The embroidery of cleanliness—Of a smile—Of
  gentle words.

What a Young Girl Ought to Know,
Summary   *1897*

172. Mathilde Blind
(1841–1896)

* * *

1 Children mothered by the saint . . .
  Blossoms of humanity!
  Poor soiled blossoms in the dust!

"The St.-Children's Dance"

2 The dead abide with us. Though stark and cold,
  Earth seems to grip them, they are with us still:
  They have forged our chains of being of good or ill,
  And their invisible hands these hands yet hold.

"The Dead"

3 The moon returns, and the spring; birds warble, trees
  burst into leaf,
  But love once gone, goes forever, and all that endures
  is the grief.   "Love Trilogy," No. 3

173. Sarah Knowles Bolton
(1841–1916)

* * *

1   He alone is great
Who by a life heroic conquers fate.

"The Inevitable"

174. Mary Lathbury
(1841–1913)

1 Day is dying in the west;
  Heaven is touching earth with rest.

"Day Is Dying in the West," St. 1   *1877*

* * *

2 Children of yesterday,
  Heirs of tomorrow,
What are you weaving?
  Labor and sorrow?

"Song of Hope," St. 1

175. Kate Brownlee Sherwood
(1841–1914)

1 One heart, one hope, one destiny, one flag from sea to
sea.

"Albert Sidney Johnstone,"
Dream of the Ages   *1893*

176. Sarah Sadie Williams
(1841–1868)

* * *

1 Is it so, O Christ in heaven, that the highest suffer
most,
That the strongest wander farthest, and more hope-
lessly are lost,
That the mark of rank in nature is capacity for pain,
That the anguish of the singer makes the sweetness of
the strain?

"Is It So, O Christ in Heaven?"

177. Mary Elizabeth Brown
(1842–1917)

* * *

1 I'll go where you want me to go, dear Lord,
   O'er mountain, or plain, or sea;
I'll say what you want me to say, dear Lord,
   I'll be what you want me to be.
          "I'll Go Where You Want Me to Go"

178. Ina Coolbrith
(1842–1928)

* * *

1 He walks with God upon the hills!
And sees, each morn, the world arise
New-bathed in light of paradise.

             "The Poet"

179. May Riley Smith
(1842–1927)

1 How these little hands remind us,
   As in snowy grace they lie,
Not to scatter thorns—but roses—
   For our reaping by and by.
       "If We Knew," St. 3   *1867*

2 Strange we never prize the music
Till the sweet-voiced bird has flown. . . .
            Ibid., St. 4

3 Let us gather up the sunbeams
   Lying all around our path;
Let us keep the wheat and roses,
   Casting out the thorns and chaff.
            Ibid., St. 6

4 God's plan, like lilies pure and white, unfold.
   We must not tear the close-shut leaves apart.
Time will reveal the calyxes of gold.
   "Sometime," *Sometime and Other Poems*   *1892*

* * *

5 My life's a pool which can only hold
   One star and a glimpse of blue.
                              "My Life Is a Bowl," St. 2

180. Sarah Doudney
(1843–1926)

1 Oh, the wasted hours of life
   That have drifted by!
 Oh, the good that might have been,
   Lost without a sigh.
              "The Lesson of the Water-Mill"   *1864*

2 "No," said Faith sternly, "we don't want this girl to be
 hanged; we wish her to spend a useful life, full of re-
 pentance and good deeds."
                    *Faith Harrowby; or, The Smuggler's
                         Cave*, Ch. 4   *1871*

3 "Ah, how good God is to me! He has not suffered me
 to be tried and tempted! Had I been in her place I
 might have done just the same."

                                              Ibid.

4 "There are no such things as mermaids," exclaimed
 Frank, her schoolboy brother; "and if there are, their
 company wouldn't suit you, Ada. How do you suppose
 you would get on under the sea, with no circulating
 library, no dressmakers and milliners, and knick
 knacks and fal-lals?"

                                      Ibid., Ch. 19

5 We love thee well, but Jesus loves thee best.
                    "The Christian's Good-Night"   *1892*

                    *   *   *

6 But the waiting time, my brothers,
 Is the hardest time of all.
              "The Hardest Time of All," *Psalms of Life*

7 Take the sweetness of a gift unsought,
 And for the pansies send me back a thought.
                                          "Pansies"

181. Violet Fane
(1843–1905)

* * *

1 Ah, "All things come to those who wait,"
  (I say these words to make me glad),
  But something answers soft and sad,
  "They come, but often come too late."

"Tout Vient à Qui Sait Attendre"

2 Let me arise and open the gate,
  To breathe the wild warm air of the heath,
  And to let in Love, and to let out Hate,
  And anger at living and scorn of Fate,
  To let in Life, and to let out Death.

"Reverie"

3 Nothing is right and nothing is just;
  We sow in ashes and reap in dust.

Ibid.

182. Anna Hamilton
(1843–1875)

* * *

1 This learned I from the shadow of a tree,
  That to and fro did sway against a wall,
  Our shadow selves, our influence, may fall
  Where we ourselves can never be.

"Influence"

183. Caroline Le Row
(1843–?)

* * *

1 But I will write of him who fights
    And vanquishes his sins,
  Who struggles on through weary years
    Against himself and wins.

"True Heroism"

184. Isabella Stephenson
(1843–1890)

* * *

1 Holy Father, in Thy mercy,
  Hear our anxious prayer,
Keep our loved ones, now far absent,
  'Neath thy care.

"Holy Father, in Thy Mercy"

185. Bertha von Suttner
(1843–1914)

1 After the verb "To Love," "To Help" is the most beautiful verb in the world!

"Epigram," *Ground Arms*   1892

186. Carmen Sylva
(1843–1916)

1 Life was a radiant maiden, the daughter of the Sun, endowed with all the charm and grace, all the power and happiness, which only such a mother could give to her child.

"The Child of the Sun," *Pilgrim Sorrow*   1884

2 But Truth was not in love, neither was it in renunciation, for I murmured and knew not why I should renounce.

Ibid., "A Life"

3 Surely he could never have borne such a life, and must have died of misery, save for one only consolation. Every man must have some such, be it only a dog, a flower, or a spider. Ovid had a snake, a tiny, bewitching snake. . . .

"The Serpent Isle," *Legends from River and Mountain*   1896

4 Complaints were heard no longer, for dull despair had reduced all men to silence; and when the starving people tore one another to pieces, no one even told it.

Ibid., "Rîul Doamnei"

5 " 'Tis the ignorant who boast. . . ."
Ibid., "The Nixies' Cleft"

6 . . . he hesitated to pluck the fruit, for fear it should leave a bitter taste behind.
Ibid., "A Doubting Lover"

7 "It seems to me," said a young man who, sitting by the fire in deep study over a roll of paper, had not yet spoken, "that in these tales of yours, only those came to harm who themselves sought after money, greedily, and merely for their own use. But methinks, after all, the best and safest way of getting wealth is to work for it. I, too, hope to find a pot of gold in the earth, but not by your manner of seeking it."
Ibid., "Seekers After Gold"

8 "Ill could I resign myself to dwell forever shut in between four walls. I must be free, free to roam where I please, like the birds in the woodlands."
"Carma, the Harp-Girl,"
Real Queen's Fairy Tales
1901

9 "One cannot help those who will not help themselves, so we felt it would be quite useless for us to come again."
Ibid., "The Little People"

10 There was another thing that did not exist in these islands; that was money. The swans would never have permitted anything so low and degrading to enter their domain. Gold they tolerated, but merely for ornamentation, where it could light up some dull surface. But to traffic with money, and to bargain, and barter—that was unheard of.
Ibid., "The Swan Lake"

11 "Our work was only play, we never knew what it was to feel fatigue; and as for loving others, since it has been granted to us to see how all things are, and have been, and must ever be, how should any feeling but love and infinite compassion fill our hearts for all who live?"
Ibid.

12   The pangs
Are hushed, for life is wild no more with strife,
Nor breathless uphill work, nor heavy with
The brewing tempests, which have torn away
So much, that nothing more remains to fear.
"A Friend," St. 3, *Sweet Hours*   *1904*

13   Our life is seldom open,
For love and fear have shut it.
Ibid., "Out of the Deep," St. 2

14   Great Solitude
Hath one thousand voices and a flood of light,
Be not afraid, enter the Sanctuary,
Thou wilt be taken by the hand and led
To Life's own fountain, never-ending Thought!
Ibid., "Solitude"

15   Ye not dare tell
Your heart what it has suffered, dare not look
Into the past again, for fear of turning
To stone, for white lipped fear of waking from
Its sleep that heart to make it throb again,
Like millstones.
Ibid., "Rest"

187. St. Bernadette
(1844–1879)

1 I fear only bad Catholics.
Quoted in Lourdes by Edith Sanders   1940p

188. Sarah Bernhardt
(1844–1923)

1 Cloister existence is one of unbroken sameness for all.
. . . The rumor of the outside world dies away at the
heavy cloister gate.
Memories of My Life, Ch. 3   1907

2 For the theatre one needs long arms; it is better to have
them too long than too short. An <i>artiste</i> with short
arms can never, never make a fine gesture.
Ibid., Ch. 6

3 Those who know the joys and miseries of celebrity . . .
know. . . . It is a sort of octopus with innumerable
tentacles. It throws out its clammy arms on the right
and on the left, in front and behind, and gathers into its
thousand little inhaling organs all the gossip and slan-
der and praise afloat to spit out again at the public
when it is vomiting its black gall.   Ibid., Ch. 22

189. Madeline Bridges
(1844–1920)

* * *

1 Then give to the world the best you have,
   And the best will come back to you.
                              "Life's Mirror," St. 1

2 And a smile that is sweet will surely find
   A smile that is just as sweet.

                                    Ibid., St. 3

3 When Psyche's friend becomes her lover,
   How sweetly these conditions blend!
   But, oh, what anguish to discover
   Her lover has become—her friend!
                              "Friend and Lover"

190. Bertha Buxton
(1844–1881)

1 After all, the eleventh commandment (thou shalt not
   be found out) is the only one that is virtually impossible to keep in these days.
          Jenny of the Princes, Ch. 3   *1879*

191. Mary Cassatt
(1844–1926)

1 I am independent! I can live alone and I love to work.
   Sometimes it made him [Degas] furious that he could
   not find a chink in my armor, and there would be
   months when we just could not see each other, and
   then something I painted would bring us together
   again. . . .
          Quoted in *Sixteen to Sixty, Memoirs
          of a Collector* by Louisine W.
          Havemeyer   *1930p*

2 A woman artist must be . . . capable of making the
   primary sacrifices.
          Quoted in "Mary Cassatt" by Forbes
          Watson, *Arts Weekly*   *1932p*

3 You know how hard it is to inaugurate anything like independent action among French artists, and we are carrying on a despairing fight and need all our forces, as every year there are new deserters. . . .

> Letter to J. Alden Weir, Paris
> (March 10, 1878), Quoted in
> *Mary Cassatt: A Biography
> of the Great American Painter*
> by Nancy Hale   *1975p*

4 The occasion [World's Colombian Exposition, Women's Building mural, 1893] is one of rejoicing, a great national fête. . . . I reserved all the seriousness for the execution, for the drawing and painting.

> Ibid., Letter to Mrs. Potter Palmer
> (October 11, 1892)

5 Yet in spite of the total disregard of the dictionary of manners, he [Cézanne] shows a politeness toward us which no other man here would have shown. . . . Cézanne is one of the most liberal artists I have ever seen. He prefaces every remark with *Pour moi* it is so and so, but he grants that everyone may be as honest and as true to nature from their convictions; he doesn't believe that everyone should see alike.

> Ibid., Letter to Mrs. Stillman (1894)

6 Why do people so love to wander? I think the civilized parts of the World will suffice for me in the future.

> Ibid., Letter to Louisine Havemeyer
> (February 11, 1911)

192. Elizabeth Stuart Phelps
(1844–1911)

1 Who originated that most exquisite of inquisitions, the condolence system?

> *The Gates Ajar*, Ch. 2   *1869*

2 That a girl could possibly be pretty with straight hair, had never once entered her mind. All the little girls in story-books had curls. Whoever heard of the straight-haired maiden that made wreaths of the rosebuds, or saw the fairies, or married the Prince?

> *Gypsy Breynton*, Ch. 1   *1876*

3 "There are several disadvantages in being a girl, my dear, as you will find out, occasionally," said Tom, with a lordly air.

Ibid., Ch. 4

4 I must say distinctly that, though after the act of dying I departed from the surface of the earth, and reached the confines of a different locality, I cannot yet instruct another *where* this place may be.

Beyond the Gates, Ch. 3   1883

5 The meaning of liberty broke upon me like a sunburst. Freedom was in and of itself the highest law. Had I thought that death was to mean release from personal obedience? Lo, death itself was but the elevation of moral claims, from lower to higher.

Ibid.

6 I mean that the *soul of a sense* is a more exquisite thing than what we may call the body of the sense, as developed to earthly consciousness.

Ibid., Ch. 11

7 The great law of denial belongs to the powerful forces of life, whether the case be one of coolish baked beans, or an unrequited affection.

A Singular Life, Ch. 1   1896

193. Margaret Sidney
(1844–1924)

1 The little old kitchen had quieted down from the bustle and confusion of mid-day; and now, with its afternoon manners on, presented a holiday aspect, that as the principal room in the brown house, it was eminently proper it should have.

"A Home View," *Five Little Peppers and How They Grew*   1881

2 "And you're very impertinent, too," said Miss Jerusha; "a good child *never* is impertinent."

Ibid., "New Friends"

3 . . . "we've got to do something 'cause we've begun. . . ."

Ibid., "Getting a Christmas for the Little Ones"

4 "It's better'n a Christmas," they told their mother, "to
get ready for it!"   Ibid.

5 . . . "it can't be Christmas all the time."
                                    Ibid., "Christmas Bells"

6 "Corners are for little folks; but when people who
know better, do wrong, there aren't any corners they
can creep into, or they'd get into them pretty quick!"
                  Ibid., "Which Treats of a Good Many Matters"

7 "You're just the splendidest, *goodest* mamsie in all the
world. And I'm a hateful cross old bear, so I am!"
                                    Ibid., "Polly's Dismal Morning"

194. Arabella Smith
(1844–1916)

* * *

1 Oh, friends! I pray to-night,
Keep not your roses for my dead, cold brow
The way is lonely, let me feel them now.
                                    "If I Should Die To-Night"

195. Sophie Tolstoy
(1844–1919)

1 One can't live on love alone; and I am so stupid that I
can do nothing but think of him.
                  A Diary of Tolstoy's Wife, 1860–1891
                  (November 13, 1862)   *1928p*

2 Of course I am idle, but I am not idle by nature; I
simply haven't yet discovered what I can do here. . . .
                                    Ibid. (November 23, 1862)

3 I am a source of satisfaction to him, a nurse, a piece of
furniture, a *woman*—nothing more.
                                    Ibid. (November 13, 1863)

4 As for me, I both *can* and *want* to do everything, but
after a while I begin to realize there is nothing to want,
and that I can't do anything beyond eating, drinking,
sleeping, nursing the children, and caring for them and
my husband. After all, this *is* happiness, yet why do I
grow sad and weep, as I did yesterday?
                                    Ibid. (February 25, 1865)

191

5 The thing to do is *not* to love, to be clever and sly, and to hide all one's bad points. . . .

Ibid. (September 12, 1865)

6 I want nothing but his love and sympathy, and he won't give it me; and all my pride is trampled in the mud; I am nothing but a miserable crushed worm, whom no one wants, whom no one loves, a useless creature with morning sickness, and a big belly, two rotten teeth, and a bad temper, a battered sense of dignity, and a love which nobody wants and which nearly drives me insane.

Ibid.

7 It makes me laugh to read over this diary. It's so full of contradictions, and one would think I was such an unhappy woman. Yet is there a happier woman than I?

Ibid. (July 31, 1868)

8 How deep is the unconscious hatred of even one's nearest people, and how great their selfishness.

Ibid. (October 25, 1886)

9 He would like to destroy his old diaries and to appear before his children and the public only in his patriarchal robes. His vanity is immense!

Ibid. (December 17, 1890)

10 It is sad that my emotional dependence on the man I love should have killed so much of my energy and ability; there was certainly once a great deal of energy in me.

Ibid. (December 31, 1890)

196. Tennessee Claflin
(1845–1923)

1 If the disenfranchised woman should still be compelled to remain the servile, docile, meekly-acquiescent, self-immolated and self-abnegative wife, there would be no difficulty about the voting. At the ballot-box is not where the shoe pinches. . . . It is at home where the husband . . . is the supreme ruler, that the little difficulty arises; he will not surrender this absolute power unless he is compelled.

"Constitutional Equality, a Right of Women" *1871*

2 A *free* man is a noble being; a *free* woman is a contemptible being. . . . In other terms, the use of this one word, in its two-fold application to men and to women, reveals the unconscious but ever present conviction in the public mind that men tend, of course, heavenward in their natures and development, and that women tend just as naturally hellward.

Article in *Woodhull and Claflin's Weekly*   1871

3 The revolt against any oppression usually goes to an opposite extreme for a time; and that is right and necessary.   Ibid.

4 The world enslaves our sex by the mere fear of an epithet; and as long as it can throw any vile term at us, before which we cower, it can maintain our enslavement.   Ibid.

5 He or she who would be free must defy the enemy, and must be *ultra* enough to exhaust the possibilities of the enemy's assault; and it will not be until women can contemplate and accept unconcernedly whatsoever imputation an ignorant, bitter, lying and persecuting world may heap on them that they will be really free.   Ibid.

6 When people had slaves, they expected that their pigs, chickens, corn and everything lying loose about the plantation would be stolen. But the planters began by stealing the liberty of their slaves, by stealing their labor, by stealing, in fact, all they had; and the natural result was that the slaves stole back all they could.

Ibid., "Which Is to Blame?"   1872

197. Susan Coolidge
(1845–1905)

* * *

1 "A commonplace life," we say and we sigh;
    But why would we sigh as we say?
The commonplace sun in the commonplace sky
    Makes up the commonplace day.

"Commonplace"

2 And God, who studies each commonplace soul,
    Out of commonplace things makes His beauty whole.
Ibid.

3 Men die, but sorrow never dies;
  The crowding years divide in vain,
And the wide world is knit with ties
  Of common brotherhood in pain.
                    "The Cradle Tomb in Westminster Abbey"

4 New morn has come
And with the morn the punctual tide again.
                                      "Floodtide"

5 Slow buds the pink dawn like a rose
  From out night's gray and cloudy sheath;
Softly and still it grows and grows,
  Petal by petal, leaf by leaf.
                  "The Morning Comes Before the Sun"

6 Yesterday's errors let yesterday cover.
                        "New Every Morning"

198. Emily Hickey
(1845–1924)

* * *

1 Beloved, it is morn!
  A redder berry on the thorn,
  A deeper yellow on the corn,
For this good day new-born!
  Pray, Sweet, for me
  That I may be
  Faithful to God and thee.   "Beloved, It Is Morn"

2 Strive we, and do, lest by-and-by we sit
  In that blind life to which all other fate
  Is cause for envy. . . .
                        "Michael Villiers, Idealist"

199. Margaret Janvier
(1845–1913)

* * *

1 You needn't try to comfort me—
  I tell you my dolly is dead!
There's no use in saying she isn't, with
  A crack like that in her head.
                          "The Dead Doll," St. 1

194

200. Katharine Bradley
(1846–1914)

* * *

1 Come, mete out my loneliness, O wind,
  For I would know
  How far the living who must stay behind
  Are from the dead who go.
          "Mete Out My Loneliness," with Edith Cooper

2 Sweet and of their nature vacant are the days I spend—
  Quiet as a plough laid by at the furrow's end.
                 "Old Age," with Edith Cooper

3 The enchanting miracles of change.
                 "Renewal," with Edith Cooper

201. Anna Dostoevsky
(1846–1918)

1 From a timid, shy girl I had become a woman of resolute character, who could not longer be frightened by
the struggle with troubles.
        Dostoevsky Portrayed by His Wife
            (c.1871)   *1926p*

2 It seems to me that he has never loved, that he has
only imagined that he has loved, that there has been no
real love on his part. I even think that he is incapable
of love; he is too much occupied with other thoughts
and ideas to become strongly attached to anyone
earthly.
                      Ibid. (1887)

202. Anna Green
(1846–1935)

* * *

1 Hath the spirit of all beauty
  Kissed you in the path of duty?

                  "On the Threshold"

203. Princess Kazu-no-miya
(1846–1877)

1 Please understand the heart of one who leaves as the water in the streams; never to return again.
Untitled Poem   *1861*

2 I wear the magnificent dress of brocade and damask in vain, now that you are not here to admire it.
Untitled Poem   *1866*

3 I would cross the river with you, if there were no barrier to stop me.
Untitled Poem   *1866*

204. Carry Nation
(1846–1911)

1 The women and children of Barber County are calling to you men for bread, for clothes, and education. . . . [Instead] men in Medicine Lodge and other towns of Barber County are selling whiskey. . . . No wonder the women want the ballot.
Quoted in *Cyclone Carry* by Carleton Beals   *1962p*

2 Who hath sorrow? Who hath woe?
They who do not answer no;
They whose feet to sin incline,
While they tarry at the wine.

Ibid., Ch. 12

3 A woman is stripped of everything by them [saloons]. Her husband is torn from her; she is robbed of her sons, her home, her food, and her virtue; and then they strip her clothes off and hang her up bare in these dens of robbery and murder. Truly does the saloon make a woman bare of all things!

Ibid. (c.1893), Ch. 14

4 You have put me in here [jail] a cub, but I will come out roaring like a lion, and I will make all hell howl!
Ibid. (c.1901)

205. Annie Wood Besant
(1847–1933)

1 There is no birthright in the white skin that it shall say that wherever it goes, to any nation, amongst any people, there the people of the country shall give way before it, and those to whom the land belongs shall bow down and become its servants. . . .
Wake Up, India: A Plea for Social Reform   1913

2 For I believe that the colour bar and all it implies are largely due to thoughtlessness, to silly pride, to the pride of race, which has grown mad in a country where there is no public opinion to check it.

Ibid.

3 . . . when there shall be no differences save by merit of character, by merit of ability, by merit of service to the country. Those are the true tests of the value of any man or woman, white or coloured; those who can serve best, those who help most, those who sacrifice most, those are the people who will be loved in life and honoured in death, when all questions of colour are swept away and when in a free country free citizens shall meet on equal grounds.

Ibid.

206. Mary Catherwood
(1847–1901)

1 They [the Chippewa] were a people ruled only by persuasive eloquence moving on the surface of their passion. . . .
The White Islander, Pt. I   1893

2 He reveled in this swimming of the wilderness. He had capacities for woodcraft. It gave freedom to a repressed and manly part of him, and in the darkness of the buried path he breathed largely.   Ibid., Pt. II

3 Two may talk together under the same roof for many years, yet never really meet; and two others at first speech are old friends.
"Marianson," *Mackinac and Lake Stories*   1899

4 Though in those days of the young century a man
   might become anything; for the West was before him,
   an empire, and woodcraft was better than learning.

                              Ibid., "The Black Feather"

5 She might struggle like a fly in a web. He wrapped her
   around and around with beautiful sentences.

                              Ibid., "The King of Beaver"

6 "O God, since Thou hast shut me up in this world, I
   will do the best I can, without fear or favor. When my
   task is done, let me out!"

                              Ibid.

7 The world of city-maddened people who swarmed to
   this lake for their annual immersion in nature. . . .

                              Ibid., "The Cursed Patois"

207. Alice Meynell
(1847–1922)

* * *

1   And when you go
There's loneliness in loneliness.

                              "Song"

2 A voice peals in this end of night
     A phrase of notes resembling stars,
Single and spiritual notes of light.
                              "A Thrush Before Dawn"

3 Dear Laws, be wings to me!
The feather merely floats, O be it heard
Through weight of life—the skylark's gravity—
That I am not a feather, but a bird!
                              "The Laws of Verse"

4 Flocks of the memories of the day draw near
The dovecote doors of sleep.

                              "At Night"

5 I come from nothing: but from where
come the undying thoughts I bear?
             "The Modern Poet, or a Song of Derivations"

6 I shall not hold my little peace; for me
There is no peace but one.

                              "The Poet to the Birds"

198

7 My heart shall be thy garden.

"The Garden"

8 New every year,
  New born and newly dear,
  He comes with tidings and a song,
  The ages long, the ages long.

"Unto Us a Son Is Given"

9 O Spring! I know thee.

"In Early Spring"

10 She walks—the lady of my delight—
   A shepherdess of sheep
   Her flocks are thoughts.

"The Shepherdess," St. 1

11 The sense of humour has other things to do than to
   make itself conspicuous in the act of laughter.

"Laughter"

12 With the first dream that comes with the first sleep
   I run, I run, I am gathered to thy heart.

"Renouncement"

208. Julia A. Moore
(1847–1920)

* * *

1 And now, kind friends, what I have wrote
  I hope you will pass over,
  And not criticize as some have done
  Hitherto herebefore.

"To My Friends and Critics"

2 Leave off the agony, leave off style,
  Unless you've got money by us all the while.

"Leave Off the Agony in Style"

209. Annie Rankin Annan
(1848–1925)

* * *

1 A dandelion in his verse,
  Like the first gold in childhood's purse.

"Dandelions"

199

210. Alice James
(1848–1892)

1 It is so comic to hear oneself called old, even at ninety I suppose!

> Letter to William James (June 14, 1889), *The Diary of Alice James,* Leon Edel, ed.   1964p

2 ... the immutable law that however great we may seem to our own consciousness no human being would exchange his for ours. ...   Ibid. (July 7, 1889)

3 Ah! Those strange people who have the courage to be unhappy! *Are* they unhappy, by-the-way?   Ibid.

4 How sick one gets of being "good," how much I should respect myself if I could burst out and make every one wretched for twenty-four hours; embody selfishness. ...   Ibid. (December 11, 1889)

5 It is an immense loss to have all robust and sustaining expletives refined away from one! At ... moments of trial refinement is a feeble reed to lean upon.

> Ibid. (December 12, 1889)

6 ... who would ever give up the reality of dreams for relative knowledge?

> Ibid.

7 Every hour I live I become an intenser devotee to common-sense!

> Ibid. (June 16, 1890)

8 I suppose one has a greater sense of intellectual degradation after an interview with a doctor than from any human experience.

> Ibid. (September 27, 1890)

9 Having it to look forward to for a while seems to double the value of the event. ...

> Ibid. (June 1, 1891)

10 The grief is all for K. and H.,* who will *see* it all [her death], whilst I shall only feel it. ...

> Ibid.

* K. is Katharine Loring Peabody, her companion and nurse; H. is Henry James, her brother.

11 The difficulty about all this dying is that you can't tell a fellow anything about it, so where does the fun come in?

Ibid. (December 11, 1891)

12 . . . I feel sure that it can't be possible but what the bewildered little hammer that keeps me going will very shortly see the decency of ending his distracted career; . . . physical pain however great ends in itself and falls away like dry husks from the mind, whilst moral discords and nervous horrors sear the soul.

Ibid. (March 4, 1892)

13 Notwithstanding the poverty of my outside experience, I have always had a significance for myself, and every chance to stumble along my straight and narrow little path, and to worship at the feet of my Deity, and what more can a human soul ask for?

Ibid. (1892)

211. Catherine Liddell
(1848–?)

* * *

1 "Isn't this Joseph's son?"—ah, it is He;
Joseph the carpenter—same trade as me.
"Jesus the Carpenter"

212. Ellen Terry
(1848–1928)

1 Imagination! imagination! I put it first years ago, when I was asked what qualities I thought necessary for success upon the stage. And I am still of the same opinion. Imagination, industry, and intelligence—"the three I's"—are all indispensable to the actress, but of these three the greatest is, without any doubt, imagination.
The Story of My Life, Ch. 2   1908

2 Some people are "tone-deaf," and they find it physically impossible to observe the law of contrasts. But even a physical deficiency can be overcome by that faculty for taking infinite pains which may not be genius but is certainly a good substitute for it.

Ibid., Ch. 4

3 What is a diary as a rule? A document useful to the person who keeps it, dull to the contemporary who reads it, invaluable to the student, centuries afterwards, who treasures it!

Ibid., Ch. 14

4 Wonderful women! Have you ever thought how much we all, and women especially, owe to Shakespeare for his vindication of women in these fearless, high-spirited, resolute and intelligent heroines?

"The Triumphant Women," Lecture
(1911), *Four Lectures on Shakespeare*
1932p

213. Frances Burnett
(1849–1924)

1 "Are you a 'publican, Mary?" "Sorra a bit," sez I; "I'm the bist o' dimmycrats!" An' he looks up at me wid a look that ud go to yer heart, an' sez he: "Mary," sez he, "the country will go to ruin." An' nivver a day since thin has he let go by widout argyin' wid me to change me polytics.

Little Lord Fauntleroy, Ch. 1   *1888*

2 It is astonishing how short a time it takes for very wonderful things to happen.

Ibid., Ch. 14

214. Sarah Orne Jewett
(1849–1909)

1 A harbor, even if it is a little harbor, is a good thing. . . . It takes something from the world and has something to give in return.

"River Driftwood," *Country By-Ways*   *1886*

2 This was one of those perfect New England days in late summer where the spirit of autumn takes a first stealthy flight, like a spy, through the ripening country-side, and, with feigned sympathy for those who droop with August heat, puts her cool cloak of bracing air about leaf and flower and human shoulders.

"The Courting of Sister Wisby,"
Atlantic Monthly   *1887*

3 "Now I'm a believer, and I try to live a Christian life, but I'd as soon hear a surveyor's book read out, figgers an' all, as try to get any simple truth out o' most sermons."

Ibid.

4 The thing that teases the mind over and over for years, and at last gets itself put down rightly on paper—whether little or great, it belongs to Literature.

Letter to Willa Cather in Preface,
*The Country of the Pointed Firs and
Other Stories*   1896

5 Wrecked on the lee shore of age.

Ibid., Ch. 7

6 Tact is after all a kind of mind reading.

Ibid., Ch. 10

7 "Yes'm, old friends is always best, 'less you can catch a new one that's fit to make an old one out of."

Ibid., Ch. 12

8 "T'ain't worthwhile to wear a day all out before it comes."

Ibid., Ch. 16

9 The road was new to me, as roads always are, going back.

Ibid., Ch. 19

10 So we die before our own eyes; so we see some chapters of our lives come to their natural end.   Ibid.

11 God bless them all who die at sea!
If they must sleep in restless waves,
God make them dream they are ashore,
With grass above their graves.

"The Gloucester Mother," St. 3   1908

* * *

12 A lean sorrow is hardest to bear.   *Life of Nancy*

215. Ellen Key
(1849–1926)

1 Poverty hinders suitable marriages.
The Century of the Child, Ch. 1   1909

2 . . . the emancipation of women is practically the greatest egoistic movement of the nineteenth century, and the most intense affirmation of the right of the self that history has yet seen. . . .

Ibid., Ch. 2

3 According to my method of thinking, and that of many others, not woman but the mother is the most precious possession of the nation, so precious that society advances its highest well-being when it protects the functions of the mother.

Ibid.

4 All philanthrophy—no age has seen more of it than our own—is only a savoury fumigation burning at the mouth of a sewer. This incense offering makes the air more endurable to passersby, but it does not hinder the infection in the sewer from spreading.

Ibid.

5 For success in training children the first condition is to become as a child oneself, but this means no assumed childishness, no condescending baby-talk that the child immediately sees through and deeply abhors. What it does mean is to be as entirely and simply taken up with the child as the child himself is absorbed by his life.

Ibid., Ch. 3

6 At every step the child should be allowed to meet the real experiences of life; the thorns should never be plucked from his roses.

Ibid.

7 Nothing would more effectively further the development of education than for all flogging pedagogues to learn to educate with the head instead of with the hand.

Ibid.

8 Anyone who would attempt the task of felling a virgin forest with a penknife would probably feel the same paralysis of despair that the reformer feels when confronted with existing school systems.   Ibid., Ch. 5

9 I wrote in the sand [at age ten], "God is dead." In doing so I thought, If there is a God, He will kill me now with a thunderbolt. But since the sun continued to shine, the question was answered for the time being; but it soon turned up again.   Ibid., Ch. 7

204

10 Corporal punishment is as humiliating for him who gives it as for him who receives it; it is ineffective besides. Neither shame nor physical pain have any other effect than a hardening one. . . .

Ibid., Ch. 8

11 A destroyed home life, an idiotic school system, premature work in the factory, stupefying life in the streets, these are what the great city gives to the children of the under classes. It is more astonishing that the better instincts of human nature generally are victorious in the lower class than the fact that this result is occasionally reversed.

Ibid.

12 Love is moral even without legal marriage, but marriage is immoral without love.

"The Morality of Woman," The
Morality of Woman and Other
Essays　1911

13 Purity is the new-fallen snow which can be melted or sullied; chastity is steel tempered in the fire by white heat.

Ibid.

14 . . . everything which is exchanged between husband and wife in their life together can only be the free gift of love, can never be demanded by one or the other as a right. Man will understand that when one can no longer continue the life of love then this life must cease; that all vows binding forever the life of feeling are a violence of one's personality, since one cannot be held accountable for the transformation of one's feeling.

Ibid.

15 After some generations . . . we shall see marriages such as even now not a few are seen, in which not observation of a duty but liberty itself is the pledge that assures fidelity.

Ibid.

16 My ideal picture of the woman of the future, and when one paints an ideal one does not need to limit one's imagination, is that she will be a being of profound contrasts which have attained harmony. She will appear as a great multiplicity and a complete unity; a rich plentitude and a perfect simplicity; a thoroughly educated creature of culture and an original spontaneous nature; a strongly marked human individuality and a complete manifestation of most profound womanliness.

Ibid., "The Woman of the Future"

17 Conventionality is the tacit agreement to set appearance before reality, form before content, subordination before principle.

Ibid., "The Conventional Woman"

18 The discovery that each personality is a new world—which in Shakespeare found its Columbus, a Columbus after whom new mariners immediately undertook new conquests—this discovery of literature has as yet only partially penetrated the universal consciousness, as a truth of experience.

Ibid.

19 For outside the field of immutable laws, children ought not to be constrained nor coerced against their nature and their disposition, against their healthy egoism and against their especial taste.

Ibid.

20 The educator must above all understand how to wait; to reckon all effects in the light of the future, not of the present.

Ibid.

21 The destruction of the personality is the great evil of the time.

Ibid.

22 Instead of defending "free love," which is a much-abused term capable of many interpretations, we ought to strive for the freedom of love; for while the former has come to imply freedom of any sort of love, the latter must only mean freedom for a feeling which is worthy the name of love. This feeling, it may be hoped, will gradually win for itself the same freedom in life as it already possesses in poetry.

Spreading Liberty and the Great
Libertarians   1913

23 Such conceptions as knightly honour or warrior pride, business integrity or artistic conscience, indicate a few of those unwritten laws [of convention] which proffer sufficient evidence that man in his sphere, to a greater extent perhaps than woman in hers, has been a maker of convention, objectionable and otherwise.

The Renaissance of Motherhood,
Pt. I, Ch. 1   *1914*

206

24 The home was a closed sphere touched only at its edge by the world's evolution.

Ibid.

25 Woman, however, as the bearer and guardian of the new lives, has everywhere greater respect for life than man, who for centuries, as hunter and warrior, learned that the taking of lives may be not only allowed, but honourable.

Ibid., Ch. 2

26 No emancipation must make women indifferent to sexual self-control and motherly devotion, from which some of the highest life values we possess on this earth have sprung.

Ibid., Ch. 4

27 . . . the child craves of the mother, the work craves of its creator; the vision, the waiting, the hope, the pure will, the faith, and the love; the power to suffer, the desire to sacrifice, the ecstasy of devotion. Thus, man also has his "motherliness," a compound of feelings corresponding to those with which the woman enriches the race, oftener than the work, but which in woman, as in man, constitutes the productive mental process without which neither new works nor new generations turn out well.

Ibid., Pt. II, Ch. 1

28 . . . art, that great undogmatized church. . . .

Ibid.

29 Motherhood has . . . for many women ceased to be the sweet secret dream of the maiden, the glad hope of the wife, the deep regret of the ageing woman who has not had this yearning satisfied.

Ibid., Ch. 3

30 The socially pernicious, racially wasteful, and soul-withering consequences of the working of mothers outside the home must cease. And this can only come to pass, either through the programme of institutional upbringing, *or* through the intimated renaissance of the home.

Ibid., Pt. III, Ch. 2

31 The belief that we some day shall be able to prevent war is to me one with the belief in the possibility of making humanity *really* human.

War, Peace, and the Future, Preface   *1916*

32 But the havoc wrought by war, which one compares with the havoc wrought by nature, is not an unavoidable fate before which man stands helpless. The natural forces which are the causes of war are human passions which it lies in our power to change.

Ibid., Ch. 1

33 Formerly, a nation that broke the peace did not trouble to try and prove to the world that it was done solely from higher motives. . . . *Now war has a bad conscience.* Now every nation assures us that it is bleeding for a human cause, the fate of which hangs in the balance of its victory. All now declare themselves to be fighting for right, against might, the very thing that the pacifists urged. No nation will admit that it was solely to insure its own safety and to increase its power that it declared war. No nation dares to admit the guilt of blood before the world.

Ibid.

34 Everything, everything in war is barbaric. . . . But the worst barbarity of war is that it forces men collectively to commit acts against which individually they would revolt with their whole being.

Ibid., Ch. 6

35 Every State that relies on its war-preparedness for its power, honour, and glory must look upon its mothers with the same eyes as the first Napoleon, of whom someone had said that "he looked as if he wished to rive new war material out of the wombs of the mothers."

Ibid., Ch. 9

36 Only calm thinking will lead one to the root of war. The peace movement that has only appealed to the emotions has never put the axe to the root of the problem. This movement, which was started in America and England, presupposed that Christianity is already realized.

Ibid., Ch. 10

37 . . . feelings of sympathy and admiration are the indispensable mortar that holds the stones of international justice together.

Ibid., Ch. 16

208

216. Marie La Coste
(1849–1936)

* * *

1 Into a ward of the whitewashed walls
   Where the dead and dying lay—
   Wounded by bayonets, shells, and balls—
   Somebody's darling was borne one day.
                                 "Somebody's Darling," St. 1

2 Tenderly bury the fair young dead,
   Pausing to drop on his grave a tear;
   Carve on the wooden slab at his head,
   "Somebody's darling lies buried here!"   Ibid., St. 5

217. Emma Lazarus
(1849–1887)

1 Give me your tired, your poor,
   Your huddled masses yearning to breathe free,
   The wretched refuse of your teeming shore,
   Send these, the homeless, tempest-tossed to me,
   I lift my lamp beside the golden door!
                           "The New Colossus"   *c.1886*

2 Here at our sea-washed, sunset gates shall stand
   A mighty woman with a torch, whose flame
   Is the imprisoned lightning, and her name
   Mother of exiles.   Ibid.

* * *

3 His cup is gall, his meat is tears,
   His passion lasts a million years.
                           "Crowing of the Red Cock"

4 Still on Israel's head forlorn,
   Every nation heaps its scorn.

                           "The World's Justice"

218. Pauline Roland
(fl. 1850s)

Co-author with Jeanne-Françoise Deroine. See 17:1–2.

219. Frances Xavier Cabrini
(1850–1917)

1 But don't think that my Institute can be confined to one city or to one diocese. The whole world is not wide enough for me.

> Quoted by Bishop Gelmini in
> *Too Small a World* by Theodore
> Maynard, Pt. I, Ch. 3   *1945p*

2 To become perfect, all you have to do is to obey perfectly. When you renounce your personal inclinations you accept a mortification counter-signed with the cross of Christ.

> Ibid., Ch. 3

3 God commands, the sea obeys. If also in religion every Sister would obey her superior—with perfect submission, that is, without relying on her own judgment—what peace, what paradisal sweetness would be hers.

> Ibid., Diary (1889), Pt. II, Ch. 7

4 I want all of you to take on wings and fly swiftly to repose in that blessed peace possessed by a soul that is all for God.

> Ibid.

5 Love is not loved, my daughters! Love is not loved! And how can we remain cold, indifferent and almost without heart at this thought? . . . If we do not burn with love, we do not deserve the title which ennobles us, elevates us, makes us great, and even a portent to the angels in heaven.

> Ibid., Diary (1891)

220. Emma Carleton
(1850–1925)

* * *

1 Reputation is a bubble which a man bursts when he tries to blow it for himself.

> *The Philistine,* Vol. XI, No. 82

221. Florence Earle Coates
(1850–1927)

* * *

1 Age, out of heart, impatient, sighed:—
  "I ask what will the *Future* be?"
  Youth laughed contentedly, and cried:—
  "The future leave to me!"
                                    "Youth and Age"

2 Ah me! the Prison House of Pain!—what lessons there
     are bought!—
  Lessons of a sublimer strain than any elsewhere taught.
                                    "The House of Pain"

3 Columbus! Other title needs he none.
                                    "Columbus"

4 Death—Life's servitor and friend—the guide
  That safely ferries us from shore to shore!
                                    "Sleep"

5 Fear is the fire that melts Icarian wings.
                                    "The Unconquered Air"

6 He turned with such a smile to face disaster
     That he sublimed defeat.   "The Hero"

7 I love, and the world is mine!   "The World Is Mine"

8 Though his beginnings be but poor and low,
  Thank God a man can grow!   "Per Aspera"

9 The soul hath need of prophet and redeemer:
     Her outstretched wings against her prisoning bars,
  She waits for truth; and truth is with the dreamer,—
     Persistent as the myriad light of stars!
                                    "Dream the Great Dream"

222. Geneviève
(1850–?)

1 The feminine chest was not made for hanging orders
  on.
                        Quoted in *Pomp and Circumstance*
                        — by E. de Gramont   *1929*

211

223. Margaret Collier Graham
(1850–1910)

1 . . . it's no more 'n fair to be civil to a man when you're gettin' the best of 'im; but I hain't.

"The Withrow Water Right,"
Stories of the Foot-hills   1875

2 "Harvest's a poor time fer wishin'; it's more prof'table 'long about seedin'-time. . . ."

Ibid., "Idy"

3 The mind of the most logical thinker goes so easily from one point to another that it is not hard to mistake motion for progress.

Gifts and Givers   1906

4 People need joy quite as much as clothing. Some of them need it far more.

Ibid.

5 We are all held in place by the pressure of the crowd around us. We must all lean upon others. Let us see that we lean gracefully and freely and acknowledge their support.

Ibid.

6 Conscience, as I understand it, is the impulse to do right because it is right, regardless of personal ends, and has nothing whatever to do with the ability to distinguish between right and wrong.

"A Matter of Conscience,"
Do They Really Respect Us?
and Other Essays   1911p

7 If any good results to a man from believing a lie, it certainly comes from the honesty of his belief.

Ibid., "Some Immortal Fallacy"

224. Jane Harrison
(1850–1928)

1 Youth and Crabbed Age stand broadly for the two opposite poles of human living, poles equally essential to any real vitality, but always contrasted. Youth stands

for rationalism, for the intellect and its concomitants, egotism and individualism. Crabbed Age stands for tradition, for the instincts and emotions, with their concomitant altruism. . . . The whole art of living is a delicate balance between the two tendencies. Virtues and vices are but convenient analytic labels attached to particular forms of the two tendencies.

"Crabbed Age and Youth,"
Alpha and Omega   1915

2 Any association of men begets a force, which is not the sum of the forces of its individual members; and this new force, this group-begotten potency, is more real, more living, than any orthodox divinity. Moreover, each group-god is necessarily a Unanimistic force. For better for worse it unites, not divides.

Ibid., "Unanimism and Conversion"

3 To be meek, patient, tactful, modest, honourable, brave, is not to be either manly or womanly; it is to be humane, to have social virtue. To be womanly is one thing, and one only; it is to be sensitive to man, to be highly endowed with the sex instinct; to be manly is to be sensitive to woman.

Ibid., "Homo Sum"

4 Your thoughts are—for what they are worth—self-begotten by some process of parthenogenesis. But there comes often to me, almost always, a moment when alone I cannot bring them to birth, when if companionship is denied, they die unborn.

Ibid., "Scientiae Sacra Fames"

5 A child's mind is, indeed, throughout the best clue to understanding of savage magic. A young and vital child knows no limit to his own will, and it is the only reality to him. It is not that he wants at the outset to fight other wills, but that they simply do not exist for him. Like the artist, he goes forth to the work of creation, gloriously alone.   Ibid., "Darwinism and Religion"

6 Whenever at an accusation blind rage burns up within us, the reason is that some arrow has pierced the joints of our harness. Behind our shining armour of righteous indignation lurks a convicted and only half-repentant sinner . . . [and] we may be almost sure some sharp and bitter grain of truth lurks within it, and the wound is best probed.   Ibid., "Epilogue on the War"

7 Here was a big constructive imagination; here was a mere doctor laying bare the origins of Greek drama as no classical scholar had ever done, teaching the anthropologist what was really meant by his *totem and taboo*, probing the mysteries of sin, of sanctity, of sacrament—a man who, because he understood, purged the human spirit from fear. I have no confidence in psycho-analysis as a method of therapeutics . . . but I am equally sure that for generations almost every branch of human knowledge will be enriched and illumined by the imagination of Freud.

*"Conclusion," Reminiscences of a
Student's Life   1925*

8 I have elsewhere tried to show that Art is not the handmaid of Religion, but that Art in some sense springs out of Religion, and that between them is a connecting link, a bridge, and that bridge is Ritual.   *Ibid.*

9 If I think of Death at all it is merely as a negation of life, a close, a last and necessary chord. What I dread is disease, that is, bad, disordered life, not Death, and disease, so far, I have escaped. I have no hope whatever of personal immortality, no desire even for a future life. My consciousness began in a very humble fashion with my body; with my body, very quietly, I hope it will end.   *Ibid.*

10 Marriage, for a woman at least, hampers the two things that made life to me glorious—friendship and learning.
Ibid.

11 Old age, believe me, is a good and pleasant thing. It is true you are gently shouldered off the stage, but then you are given such a comfortable front stall as spectator. . . .   *Ibid.*

225. Laura Howe Richards
(1850–1943)

1 "And the storm went on. It roared, it bellowed, and it screeched: it thumped and it kerwhalloped. The great seas would come bunt agin the rocks, as if they were bound to go right through to Jersey City, which they used to say was the end of the world."
Captain January, Ch. 2   1890

214

2 "A cap'n on a quarterdeck's a good thing; but a cap'n on a pint o' rock, out to sea in a northeast gale, might just as well be a fo'c'sle hand and done with it."

Ibid.

3 "There's times when a man has strength given to him, seemin'ly, over and above human strength. 'Twas like as if the Lord ketched holt and helped me: maybe he did, seein' what 'twas I was doing. Maybe he did!"

Ibid.

4 Be you clown or be you King,
  Still your singing is the thing.

"Dedication," Tirra Lirra   1890

5 Every little wave has its nightcap on.

Ibid., "Song for Hal," Refrain

6 Great is truth and shall prevail,
  Therefore must we weep and wail.

Ibid., "The Mameluke and the Hospodar," St. 4

7 Once there was an elephant
  Who tried to use the telephant—
  No! No! I mean an elephone
  Who tried to use the telephone.

Ibid., "Eletelephony," St. 1

8   Ponsonby Perks,
     He fought with Turks,
  Performing many wonderful works.

Ibid., "Nonsense Verses," St. 2

9 "Mighty poor country up that way. Some say the Rome folks don't see any garden-truck from year's end to year's end, and that if you ask a Rome girl to cook you up a mess of string beans, she takes the store beans and runs 'em on a string, and boils 'em that way. . . ."

Narcissa, Pt. II   1892

226. Rose Hartwick Thorpe
(1850–1939)

1 And her face so sweet and pleading, yet with sorrow
  pale and worn,
  Touched his heart with sudden pity—lit his eye with
  misty light;

215

"Go, your lover lives!" said Cromwell; "Curfew shall
not ring tonight!"
"Curfew Shall Not Ring Tonight" 1866

227. Nellie Cashman
(1851–1925)

1 When I saw something that needed doing, I did it.
Interview, *Daily British Colonist* 1898

228. Kate Chopin
(1851–1904)

1 In entering upon their new life they decided to be governed by no precedential methods. Marriage was to be
a form, that while fixing legally their relation to each
other, was in no wise to touch the individuality of either; that was to be preserved intact. Each was to remain a free integral of humanity, responsible to no
dominating exactness of so-called marriage laws. And
the element that was to make possible such a union was
trust in each other's love, honor, courtesy, tempered by
the reserving clause of readiness to meet the consequences of reciprocal liberty.
"A Point at Issue!" 1889

2 The mother-women seemed to prevail that summer at
Grand Isle. It was easy to know them, fluttering about
with extended, protecting wings when any harm, real
or imaginary, threatened their precious brood. They
were women who idolized their children, worshipped
their husbands, and esteemed it a holy privilege to ef-
face themselves as individuals and grow wings as minis-
tering angels.
The Awakening, Ch. 4 1889

3 A certain light was beginning to dawn dimly within
her—the light which, showing the way, forbids it. . . .
But the beginning of things, of a world especially, is
necessarily vague, tangled, chaotic, and exceedingly
disturbing. How few of us ever emerge from such beginning! How many souls perish in its tumult!
Ibid., Ch. 6

4 The voice of the sea speaks to the soul. The touch of the sea is sensuous, enfolding the body in its soft, close embrace.

Ibid.

5 "Pirate gold isn't a thing to be hoarded or utilized. It is something to squander and throw to the four winds, for the fun of seeing the golden specks fly."

Ibid., Ch. 12

6 The past was nothing to her; offered no lesson which she was willing to heed. The future was a mystery which she never attempted to penetrate. The present alone was significant. . . .

Ibid., Ch. 15

7 "The way to become rich is to make money, my dear Edna, not to save it. . . ."

Ibid., Ch. 18

8 It sometimes entered Mr. Pontellier's mind to wonder if his wife were not growing a little unbalanced mentally. He could see plainly that she was not herself. That is, he could not see that she was becoming herself and daily casting aside that fictitious self which we assume like a garment with which to appear before the world.

Ibid., Ch. 19

9 . . . "a wedding is one of the most lamentable spectacles on earth."

Ibid., Ch. 22

10 Alcée Arobin's manner was so genuine that it often deceived even himself.

Ibid., Ch. 25

11 ". . . when I left her today, she put her arms around me and felt my shoulder blades, to see if my wings were strong, she said. 'The bird that would soar above the level plain of tradition and prejudice must have strong wings. It is a sad spectacle to see the weaklings bruised, exhausted, fluttering back to earth.'"

Ibid., Ch. 27

12 "There are some people who leave impressions not so lasting as the imprint of an oar upon the water."

Ibid., Ch. 34

13 "The years that are gone seem like dreams—if one might go on sleeping and dreaming—but to wake up

and find—oh! well! perhaps it is better to wake up
after all, even to suffer, rather than to remain a dupe to
illusions all one's life."

Ibid., Ch. 38

14 The children appeared before her like antagonists who
had overcome her; who had overpowered and sought to
drag her into the soul's slavery for the rest of her days.

Ibid., Ch. 39

15 Only the birds had seen, and she could count on their
discretion.

"A Shameful Affair"   1891

16 There would be no one to live for her during these
coming years; she would live for herself. There would
be no powerful will bending hers in that blind persistence with which men and women believe they have a
right to impose a private will upon a fellow-creature.

"The Story of an Hour"   1894

17 What could love, the unsolved mystery, count for in
face of this possession of self-assertion which she suddenly recognized as the strongest impulse of her being!

Ibid.

18 "I don't hate him," Athenaise answered. . . . "It's jus'
being married that I detes' an' despise."

"Athenaise"   1895

229. Anna Garlin Spencer
(1851–1931)

1 The failure of woman to produce genius of the first
rank in most of the supreme forms of human effort has
been used to block the way of all women of talent and
ambition for intellectual achievement in a manner that
would be amusingly absurd were it not so monstrously
unjust and socially harmful.

Woman's Share in Social Culture   1912

2 The whole course of evolution in industry, and in the
achievements of higher education and exceptional talent, has shown man's invariable tendency to shut
women out when their activities have reached a highly
specialized period of growth.

Ibid.

3 And when her biographer says of an Italian woman poet, "during some years her Muse was intermitted," we do not wonder at the fact when he casually mentions her ten children.

Ibid.

4 It is not alone the fact that women have generally had to spend most of their strength in caring for others that has handicapped them in individual effort; but also that they have almost universally had to care wholly for themselves.

Ibid.

5 A successful woman preacher was once asked "what special obstacles have you met as a woman in the ministry?" "Not one," she answered, "except the lack of a minister's wife."

Ibid.

230. Mary Augusta Ward
(1851–1920)

1 "Propinquity does it"—as Mrs. Thornburgh is always reminding us.

Robert Elsmer, Bk. I, Ch. 2   *1888*

2 "Every man is bound to leave a story better than he found it."

Ibid., Ch. 3

3 One may as well preach a respectable mythology as anything else.

Ibid., Ch. 5

4 In my youth people talked about Ruskin; now they talk about drains.

Ibid., Bk. II, Ch. 12

5 This Laodicean* cant of tolerance.

Ibid.

6 "Put down enthusiasm." . . . The Church of England in a nutshell.

Ibid., Ch. 16

7 Conviction is the Conscience of the Mind.

Ibid., Bk., IV, Ch. 26

* Lukewarm.

8 All things change, creeds and philosophies and outward
 system—but God remains!

Ibid., Ch. 27

9 Truth has never been, can never be, contained in any
 one creed. Ibid., Bk. VI, Ch. 38

231. Mary A. Barr
(1852–?)

* * *

1 I sing the Poppy! The frail snowy weed!
  The flower of Mercy! That within its heart
 Doth keep "a drop serene" of human need,
  A drowsy balm of every bitter smart.
 For happy hours the rose will idly blow
 The Poppy hath a charm of pain and woe.

"White Poppies"

232. Martha Jane Burke
(1852–1903)

1 During the month of June I acted as a pony express
 rider carrying the U.S. mail between Deadwood and
 Custer, a distance of fifty miles. . . . It was considered
 the most dangerous route in the Hills, but as my reputation as a rider and quick shot was well known, I was
 molested very little, for the toll gatherers looked on me
 as being a good fellow, and they knew that I never
 missed my mark.
  Life and Adventures of Calamity Jane 1896

2 There are thousands of Sioux in this valley. I am not
 afraid of them. They think I am a crazy woman and
 never molest me. . . . I guess I am the only human
 being they are afraid of.

Letter to Daughter (September 28,
1877), Quoted in Calamity Was the
Name for Jane by Glenn Clairmonte
1959p

3 I Jane Hickok Burke better known as Calamity Jane of
 my own free will and being of sound mind do this day
 June 3, 1903 make this confession. I have lied about
 my past life. . . . People got snoopy so I told them

lies to hear their tongues wag. The women are all snakes and none of them I can call friends.

Ibid., Document to James O'Neill (June 3, 1903)

233. Vera Figner
(1852–1942)

1 Generally speaking, there was in her [Sofia Perovskaya] nature both feminine gentleness and masculine severity. Tender, tender as a mother with the working people, she was exacting and severe toward her comrades and fellow-workers, while towards her political enemies, the government, she could be merciless. . . .

Memoirs of a Revolutionist   *1927*

234. Mary Wilkins Freeman
(1852–1930)

1 . . . it took her a long time to prepare her tea; but when ready it was set forth with as much grace as if she had been a veritable guest to her own self.

A New England Nun   *1891*

2 Louisa's feet had turned into a path . . . so straight and unswerving that it could only meet a check at her grave, and so narrow that there was no room for anyone at her side.   Ibid.

3 She gazed ahead through a long reach of future days strung together like pearls in a rosary, every one like the others, and all smooth and flawless and innocent, and her heart went up in thankfulness.   Ibid.

235. Gertrude Kasebier
(1852–1934)

1 . . . from the first days of dawning individuality, I have longed unceasingly to make pictures of people . . . to make likenesses that are biographies, to bring out in each photograph the essential personality that is variously called temperament, soul, humanity.

Quoted in *The Woman's Eye*
by Anne Tucker   *1973p*

236. Lily Langtry
(1853–1929)

1 The sentimentalist ages far more quickly than the person who loves his work and enjoys new challenges.
Quoted in the *New York Sun*   *1906*

2 Anyone who limits his vision to his memories of yesterday is already dead.
Quoted in *Because I Loved Him*
by Noel B. Gerson   *1971p*

237. Mary Lease
(1853–1933)

1 What you Kansas farmers ought to do is to raise less corn and raise more hell.
Political Speech   *1890*

238. Sofia Perovskaya
(1853–1881)

1 . . . my lot is not at all such a dark one. I have lived as my convictions have prompted me; I could not do otherwise; therefore I await what is in store for me with a clear conscience.
Letter to Her Mother, *Woman as Revolutionary*,
Fred C. Giffin, ed.   *1973p*

239. Emilie Poulsson
(1853–1939)

* * *

1 Books are keys to wisdom's treasure;
Books are gates to lands of pleasure;
Books are paths that upward lead;
Books are friends. Come, let us read.
Inscription in Children's Reading
Room, Hopkington, Massachusetts

240. Jennie Jerome Churchill
(1854–1921)

1 The best society does not necessarily mean the "smart set."
Quoted in the *New York World*   *October 13, 1908*

2 Of all nationalities, Americans are the best in adapting themselves. With them, to see is to know—and to know is to conquer.
Ibid.

3 You may be a princess or the richest woman in the world, but you cannot be more than a lady. . . .
Ibid.

4 It is so tempting to try the most difficult thing possible.
Quoted in the *Daily Chronicle* (London)
July 8, 1909

5 BASIL. But remember, a man ends by hating the woman who he thinks has found him out.
His Borrowed Plumes   *1909*

6 ALMA. I rather suspect her of being in love with him.
MARTIN. Her own husband? Monstrous! What a selfish woman!   Ibid.

7 All natures are in nature.   Ibid.

8 What is love without passion?—A garden without flowers, a hat without feathers, tobogganing without snow.
Ibid.

9 Italians love—sun, sin and spaghetti.
Ibid.

10 We don't elope nowadays, and we don't divorce, except out of kindness.
The Bill   *1913*

11 Your castle in Spain has no foundations, that is why it is so easily built. . . .
"Mars and Cupid," *Pearson's*   *September, 1915*

12 . . . we owe something to extravagance, for thrift and adventure seldom go hand in hand. . . .
Ibid., "Extravagance"   *October, 1915*

13 Treat your friends as you do your pictures, and place them in their best light.

"Friendship," *Small Talk on Big Subjects*　1916

14 There is no such thing as a moral dress. . . . It's people who are moral or immoral. . . .

Quoted in the *Daily Chronicle*
(London)　*February 16, 1921*

15 It's a wise virgin who looks after her own lamp.

Quoted in *Bystander*　July 6, 1921

16 But I suppose experience of life will in time teach you that tact is a very essential ingredient in all things.

Letter to Winston Churchill (October 4, 1895),
Quoted in *Jennie*, Vol. II by Ralph G. Martin　*1971p*

17 Life is not always what one wants it to be, but to make the best of it as it is, is the only way of being happy. . . .

Ibid., Letter to Lord Kitchener
(November 27, 1896)

18 You seem to have no real purpose in life and won't realize at the age of twenty-two that for a man life means work, and hard work if you mean to succeed. . . .

Ibid., Letter to Winston Churchill
(February 26, 1897)

19 . . . be modest. . . . One must be tempted to talk of oneself . . . *but resist.* Let them *drag* things out.

Ibid. (November 4, 1897)

20 If we can alleviate sufferings and at the same time comfort the many aching and anxious hearts at home, shall we not be fulfilling our greatest mission in life? These are "Women's Rights" in the best sense of the word. We need no others.

Ibid., Speech, First Meeting of
General Committee for Hospital Ship
(November 18, 1899)

21 One is forever throwing away substance for shadows.

Ibid., Letter to her sister,
Leonie Leslie (July 24, 1914)

241. Eva March Tappan
(1854–1930)

* * *

1 We drove the Indians out of the land,
But a dire revenge those Redmen planned,
For they fastened a name to every nook,
And every boy with a spelling book
Will have to toil till his hair turns gray
Before he can spell them the proper way.

"On the Cape," St. 1

242. Edith Thomas
(1854–1925)

1 How on the moment all changes!
Quietude midmost the throng,
Peace amid tumult, and dissonance
Charmed into vespertine song!

Dew on the dust of the noontime,
Spring at the dead of the year,
Freedom discerned out of bondage,
Grace in condition austere!

"Optimi Consiliarii Mortui, XXXIV,"
Sts. 1–2, *The Inverted Torch*   *1890*

2 When the wind through the trees makes a path for the
moon!
Praise June!

"Praise June," *In Sunshine Land*   *1894*

3 Sweet, sweet, you've no reason
To hurry away;
Stay so, sweet Season,
Stay, oh stay!

Ibid., "Stay So, Sweet Season," St. 1

4 They troop to their work in the gray of the morning,
Each with a shovel swung over his shoulder . . .
You have cut down their wages without any warning—
Angry? Well, let their wrath smolder!

"Their Argument," St. 2,
The Guest at the Gate   *1909*

225

5 And Heaven gave me strivings blind
   By Justice to be schooled,
And purpose branded in the mind,
   To rule not, nor be ruled. . . .
                    Ibid., "Of the Middle World," St. 2

* * *

6 The God of Music dwelleth out of doors.
                         "The God of Music"

243. Mary Dow Brine
(1855?–1925?)

1 She's somebody's mother, boys, you know,
   For all she's aged, and poor, and slow.
                         "Somebody's Mother," St. 15,
                 Harper's Weekly   *March 2, 1878*

244. Margaret Wolfe Hungerford
(1855?–1897)

1 Beauty is in the eye of the beholder.
                    Molly Bawn   *1878*

245. Alice Freeman Palmer
(1855–1902)

* * *

1 Exquisite child of the air.

                         "The Butterfly"

246. Olive Schreiner
(1855–1920)

1 An ox at the roadside, when it is dying of hunger and
   thirst, does not lie down; it walks up and down—up
   and down, seeking it knows not what;—but it does not
   lie down.

              From Man to Man, Ch. 1   *1876*

2 "Nothing can ever alter, nothing can ever change, our
   happiness, that springs from such deep love. Death it-

self will be but going home to the Father's house to be made perfect there in that which made us loved and loving here." He looked up at her. "For those who love as we love, there is no parting, and no death, only eternal union."

Ibid., Ch. 4

3 "There are some men," said Lyndall, "whom you never can believe were babies at all; and others you never see without thinking how very nice they must have looked when they wore socks and pink sashes."

The Story of an African Farm, "Lyndall"   1883

4 They are called finishing-schools and the name tells accurately what they are. They finish everything. . . .

Ibid.

5 I have seen some souls so compressed that they would have fitted into a small thimble, and found room to move there—wide room.

Ibid.

6 . . . how hard it is to make your thoughts look anything but imbecile fools when you paint them with ink on paper.

Ibid.

7 "It is delightful to be a woman; but every man thanks the Lord devoutly that he isn't one."

Ibid.

8 "But this one thought stands, never goes—if I might but be one of those born in the future; then, perhaps, to be born a woman will not be to be born branded."

Ibid.

9 "Wisdom never kicks at the iron walls it can't bring down." Ibid.

10 "Everything has two sides—the outside that is ridiculous, and the inside that is solemn." Ibid.

11 "Look at this little chin of mine, Waldo, with the dimple in it. It is but a small part of my person; but though I had a knowledge of all things under the sun, and the wisdom to use it, and the deep loving heart of an angel, it would not stead me through life like this little chin. I can win money with it, I can win love; I can win power with it, I can win fame." Ibid.

12 "The less a woman has in her head the better she is for climbing."

Ibid.

13 "We fit our sphere as a Chinese woman's fits her shoe, exactly as though God had made both; and yet He knows nothing of either."

Ibid.

14 "We were equals once when we lay newborn babes on our nurse's knees. We shall be equals again when they tie up our jaws for the last sleep."

Ibid.

15 "If the bird *does* like its cage, and *does* like its sugar, and will not leave it, why keep the door so very carefully shut?"

Ibid.

16 "The surest sign of fitness is success."

Ibid.

17 "*We* bear the world, and we make it. . . . There was never a great man who had not a great mother—it is hardly an exaggeration."

Ibid.

18 "By every inch we grow in intellectual height our love strikes down its roots deeper, and spreads out its arms wider."

19 ". . . when love is no more bought or sold, when it is not a means of making bread, when each woman's life is filled with earnest, individual labor—then love will come to her. . . . Then, but not now. . . ."

Ibid.

20 ". . . till I have been delivered I can deliver no one."

Ibid.

21 "Men are like the earth and we are the moon; we turn always one side to them, and they think there is no other, because they don't see it—but there is."

Ibid.

22 All day, where the sunlight played on the seashore, Life sat.

"The Lost Joy," *Dreams* 1892

23 And he said, "I take it, ages ago the Aegis-of-Dominion-of-Muscular-Force found her, and when she

228

stooped low to give suck to her young, and her back was broad, he put his burden of subjection on to it, and tied it on with the broad band of Inevitable Necessity. Then she looked at the earth and the sky, and knew there was no hope for her; and she lay down on the sand with the burden she could not loosen. Ever since she has lain here, and the ages have come, and the ages have gone, but the band of Inevitable Necessity has not been cut."

Ibid., "Three Dreams in a Desert"

24 I said to God, "What are they doing?"
God said, "Making pitfalls into which their fellows may sink."
I said to God, "Why do they do it?"
God said, "Because each thinks that when his brother falls he will rise."

Ibid., "Across My Bed"

25 "There are only two things that are absolute realities, love and knowledge, and you can't escape them."

"The Buddhist Priest's Wife,"
Stories, Dreams, and Allegories 1892

26 "I suppose the most absolutely delicious thing in life is to feel a thing needs you, and to give at the moment it needs. Things that don't need you, you must love from a distance."

Ibid.

27 "No woman has the right to marry a man if she has to bend herself out of shape for him. She might wish to, but she could never be to him with all her passionate endeavor what the other woman could be to him without trying. Character will dominate over all and will come out at last."

Ibid.

28 "There is nothing ridiculous in love." *Ibid.*

29 There are artists who, loving their work, when they have finished it, put it aside for years, that, after the lapse of time, returning to it and reviewing it from the standpoint of distance, they may judge of it in a manner which was not possible while the passion of creation and the link of unbroken emotion bound them to it. What the artist does intentionally, life often does for us fortuitously in other relationships.

Thoughts on South Africa, Ch. 1 1892

30 If Nature here wishes to make a mountain, she runs a range for five hundred miles; if a plain, she levels eighty; if a rock, she tilts five thousand feet of strata on end; our skies are higher and more intensely blue; our waves larger than others; our rivers fiercer. There is nothing measured, small nor petty in South Africa.

Ibid.

31 Slavery may, perhaps, be best compared to the infantile disease of measles; a complaint which so commonly attacks the young of humanity in their infancy, and when gone through at that period leaves behind it so few fatal marks; but which when it normally attacks the full developed adult becomes one of the most virulent and toxic of diseases, often permanently poisoning the constitution where it does not end in death.

Ibid.

32 St. Francis of Assisi preached to the little fishes: we eat them. But the man who eats fish can hardly be blamed, seeing that the eating of fishes is all but universal among the human race!—if only he does not pretend that while he eats them he preaches to them!

Ibid., Ch. 4

33 The modern woman stands with the prospect of shrinking fields of labour on every hand. She is brought face-to-face with two possibilities. Either, on the one hand, she may remain quiescent and, as her old fields of labour fall from her, seek no new: in which case . . . she is bound to become more or less parasitic, as vast bodies of women in our wealthier and even our middle classes have already become. . . . On the other hand, woman may determine not to remain quiescent. As her old fields of labour slip from her under the inevitable changes of modern life, she may determine to find labour in the new and to obtain that training which, whether in the world of handicraft or the mental field of toil, increasingly all-important in our modern world, shall fit her to take as large a share in the labours of her race in the future as in the past.

Ibid.

34 "Yes, the life of the individual is short, but the life of the nation is long; and it is longer, and stronger, more vigorous and more knit, if it grows slowly and spontaneously than if formed by violence or fraud. The individual cannot afford to wait but the nation can and

must wait for true unity, which can only come as the result of internal growth and the union of its atoms, and in no other way whatsoever."

Ibid., Ch. 8

35 I know there will be spring; as surely as the birds know it when they see above the snow two tiny, quivering green leaves. Spring cannot fail us.

"The Woman's Rose" *1893*

36 The greatest nations, like the greatest individuals, have often been the poorest; and with wealth comes often what is more terrible than poverty—corruption.

An English South African's View of the Situation c.1899

37 I suppose there is no man who to-day loves his country who has not perceived that in the life of the nation, as in the life of the individual, the hour of external success may be the hour of irrevocable failure, and that the hour of death, whether to nations or individuals, is often the hour of immortality.

Ibid.

38 We have in us the blood of a womanhood that was never bought and never sold; that wore no veil and had no foot bound; whose realized ideal of marriage was sexual companionship and an equality in duty and labor.

Woman and Labor *1911*

39 We demand that . . . in this new world we also shall have our share of honored and socially useful human toil, our full half of the labor of the Children of Woman. We demand nothing more than this, and will take nothing less.

Ibid.

40 We have always borne part of the weight of war, and the major part. . . . Men have made boomerangs, bows, swords, or guns with which to destroy one another; we have made the men who destroyed and were destroyed! . . . *We pay the first cost on all human life.*
Ibid., Ch. 4

* * *

41 And it came to pass that after a time the artist was forgotten, but the work lived.

The Artist's Secret

231

247. Ella Wheeler Wilcox
(1855–1919)

1 Laugh and the world laughs with you;
   Weep, and you weep alone;
For the sad old earth must borrow its mirth,
   But has trouble enough of its own.
> "Solitude," St. 1, *New York Sun*
> *February 25, 1883*

*   *   *

2 And the life that is worth the honor of earth,
   Is the one that resists desire.
> "Worth While"

3 'Tis easy enough to be pleasant,
   When life flows along like a song;
But the man worth while is the one who will smile
   When everything goes dead wrong.
> Ibid.

4   Apart
Must dwell those angels known as Peace and Love,
For only death can reconcile the two.
> "Peace and Love"

5 A weed is but an unloved flower!
> "The Weed," St. 1

6 But with every deed you are sowing a seed,
   Though the harvest you may not see.
> "You Never Can Tell," St. 2

7 Distrust that man who tells you to distrust.
> "Distrust"

8 For why should I fan, or feed with fuel,
   A love that showed me but blank despair?
So my hold was firm, and my grasp was cruel—
   I meant to strangle it then and there!
> "Ad Finem," St. 2

9 Give us that grand word "woman" once again,
   And let's have done with "lady"; one's a term
Full of fine force, strong, beautiful, and firm,
   Fit for the noblest use of tongue or pen;
And one's a word for lackeys.   "Woman"

10 I love your lips when they're wet with wine
   And red with a wicked desire.
                                    "I Love You," St. 1

11 Not from me the cold calm kiss
   Of a virgin's bloodless love.
                                    Ibid., St. 2

12 I think of death as some delightful journey
   That I shall take when all my tasks are done.
                                    "The Journey"

13 It ever has been since time began,
     And ever will be, till time lose breath,
   That love is a mood—no more—to man,
     And love to a woman is life or death.
                                    "Blind," St. 1

14 Let there be many windows to your soul,
   That all the glory of the world
   May beautify it.
                                    "Progress," St. 1

15   Tear away
   The blinds of superstition; let the light
   Pour through fair windows broad as Truth itself
   And high as God.
                                    Ibid.

16 Sweep up the debris from decaying faiths;
   Sweep down the cobwebs of worn-out beliefs,
   And throw your soul open to the light
   Of Reason and Knowledge.
                                    Ibid., St. 2

17 Love lights more fires than hate extinguishes,
   And men grow better as the world grows old.
                                    "Optimism"

18 Talk happiness. The world is sad enough
   Without your woe. No path is wholly rough.
                                    Ibid., St. 1

19 No one will ever grieve because your lips are dumb.
                                    Ibid.

20 No! The two kinds of people on earth that I mean
   Are the people who lift and the people who lean.
                                    "To Lift or to Lean"

233

21 O man bowed down with labor,
       O woman young yet old,
   O heart oppressed in the toiler's breast
       And crushed by the power of gold—
   Keep on with your weary battle against triumphant
       might;
   No question is ever settled until it is settled right.
                                    "Settle the Question Right"

22 One ship drives east and another drives west
   With the selfsame winds that blow.
   'Tis the set of sails and not the gales
   Which tells us the way to go.
                                    "Winds of Fate," St. 1

23 The days grown shorter, the nights grow longer;
       The headstones thicken along the way;
   And life grows sadder, but love grows stronger
       For those who walk with us day by day.
                                    "Growing Old," St. 1

24 The splendid discontent of God
   With chaos, made the world.
   And from the discontent of man
       The world's best progress springs.   "Discontent"

25 We flatter those we scarcely know,
       We please the fleeting guest,
   And deal full many a thoughtless blow
       To those who love us best.   "Life's Scars," St. 3

26 Whatever is—is best.   "Whatever Is—Is Best"

27   Why, even death stands still,
   And waits an hour sometimes for such a will.
                                    "Will," St. 2

28 Why, half the gossip under the sun,
   If you trace it back, you will find begun
       In that wretched House of They.   "They Say"

248. Elisabeth Marbury
(1856–1933)

1 I began to realize that the world was divided into three
   groups: wasters, mollusks, and builders.
                              My Crystal Ball, Ch. 1   *1923*

2 "Ah, daughter," said Mother, "where there is room in
the heart, there is always room on the hearth."

Ibid.

3 I began to realize the woefulness of ignorance. Things
of unimportance fell into their proper places. I was in-
oculated with beauty and my feet became shod with a
sense of its value. . . .

Ibid., Ch. 3

4 Throughout my life, I have always found that events
which seemed at the time disastrous ultimately developed into positive blessings. In fact, I have never
known one instance when this has not proved to be the
case.

Ibid., Ch. 5

5 The praise of injudicious friends frequently fosters bad
mannerisms.

Ibid., Ch. 6

* * *

6 A caress is better than a career.

"Careers for Women"

7 No influence so quickly converts a radical into a reactionary as does his election to power.

Ibid.

8 The richer your friends, the more they will cost you.

Ibid.

249. Lizette Reese
(1856–1935)

* * *

1 A book may be a flower that blows;
A road to a far town;
A roof, a well, a tower;
A book
May be a staff, a crook.

"Books"

2 Creeds grow so thick along the way,
Their boughs hide God.

"Doubt"

3 Fame is a bugle call
Blown past a crumbling wall.

"Taps"

235

4 Glad that I live am I;
That the sky is blue;
Glad for the country lanes,
And the fall of dew.

"A Little Song of Life," St. 1

5 Oh, far, far, far,
As any spire or star,
Beyond the cloistered wall!
Oh, high, high, high,
A heart-throb in the sky—
Then not at all!

"The Lark"

6 The old faiths light their candles all about,
But burly Truth comes by and puts them out.

"Truth'

7 We that are twain by day, at night are one.
A dream can bring me to your arms once more.

"Compensation"

8 When I consider life and its few years—
A wisp of fog betwixt us and the sun;
A call to battle, and the battle done
Ere the last echo dies within our ears,
I wonder at the idleness of tears.

"Tears"

250. Kate Douglas Wiggin
(1856–1923)

1 Women never hit what they aim at: but if they just
shut their eyes and shoot in the air they generally find
themselves in the bull's eye.

New Chronicles of Rebecca   1907

* * *

2 My heart is open wide tonight
For stranger, kith or kin.
I would not bar a single door
Where love might enter in.

"The Romance of a Christmas Card"

251. Ada Alden
(1857–1936)

* * *

1 Can this by Italy, or but a dream
　　Emerging from the broken waves of sleep? . . .
This world of beauty, color, and perfume,
　　Hoary with age, yet of unaging bloom.
　　　　　　　　　　　　　　　　"Above Salerno"

2 The years shall right the balance tilted wrong,
The years shall set upon his* brows a star.　　"Ave"

252. Gertrude Atherton
(1857–1948)

1 We love the lie that saves their pride, but never an un-
flattering truth.
　　　　　　The Conqueror, Bk. III, Ch. 6　　*1902*

2 To put a tempting face aside when duty demands every
faculty . . . is a lesson which takes most men longest
to learn.　　　　　　　　　　　　　　　Ibid.

3 The perfect friendship of two men is the deepest and
highest sentiment of which the finite mind is capable;
women miss the best in life.

　　　　　　　　　　　　　　　　　　Ibid., Ch. 12

4 No matter how hard a man may labor, some woman is
always in the background of his mind. She is the one
reward of virtue.　　　　　　　Ibid., Bk. IV, Ch. 3

253. Alice Brown
(1857–1948)

* * *

1 And led by silence more majestical
Than clash of conquering arms, He comes! He comes!
And strikes out flame from the adoring hills.
　　　　　　　　　　"Sunrise on Mansfield Mountain"

* Referring to Woodrow Wilson.

2 Praise not the critic, lest he think
  You crave the shelter of his ink.   **"The Critic"**

3 Take with thee, too, our bond of gratitude
  That in a cynic and a tattle age
  Thou didst consent to write, in missal script,
  Thy name on the poor players' slandered page,
  And teach the lords of empty birth a king may walk
          the stage.   **"Edwin Booth"**

4 Yet thou, O banqueter on worms,
      Who wilt not let corruption pass!—
  Dost search out mildew, mould and stain,
      Beneath a magnifying-glass.   **"The Slanderer"**

254. Mary Lee Demarest
(1857–1888)

* * *

1 Like a bairn to his mither, a wee birdie to its nest,
  I wud fain be ganging nod unto my Saviour's breast;
  For he gathers in his bosom witless, worthless lambs
          like me,
  An' he carries them himsel' to his ain countree.
                          "My Ain Countree"

255. Fannie Farmer
(1857–1915)

1 Progress in civilization has been accompanied by progress in cookery.

                          The Boston Cooking-School
                          Cookbook, Ch. 2   *1896*

2 I certainly feel that the time is not far distant when a
  knowledge of the principles of diet will be an essential
  part of one's education. Then mankind will eat to live,
  be able to do better mental and physical work, and disease will be less frequent.

                  Ibid., Preface to the First Edition

3 . . . France, that land to which we ever look for gas-
  tronomic delights. . . .
          Chafing Dish Possibilities, Ch. 1   *1898*

256. Minna Irving
(1857–1940)

* * *

1 A nation thrills, a nation bleeds,
  A nation follows where it leads,
  And every man is proud to yield
  His life upon a crimson field
    For Betsy's battle flag.

"Betsy's Battle Flag"

2 He's cheerful in weather so bitterly cold
    It freezes your bones to the marrow;
  I'll admit he's a beggar, a gangster, a bum,
    But I take off my hat to the sparrow.

"The Sparrow"

3 I used to climb the garret stairs
    On a rainy day and lift the lid
  And loose the fragrance of olden times
    That under the faded finery hid.

"The Wedding Gift," St. 2

4 The flowery frocks and the ancient trunk,
    And Grandmother Granger, too, are dust,
  But something precious and sweet and rare
    Survives the havoc of moth and rust.

Ibid., St. 6

257. Edna Lyall
(1857–1903)

1 Two is company, three is trumpery, as the proverb
says.

Wayfaring Men, Ch. 24   *1897*

258. Agnes Mary Robinson
(1857–1944)

* * *

1 When I was young the twilight seemed too long.

"Twilight"

2 You hail from dream-land, Dragon fly?
A stranger hither? So am I.

"To a Dragonfly"

259. Ida Tarbell
(1857–1944)

1 The first and most imperative necessity in war is money, for money means everything else—men, guns, ammunition.

The Tariff in Our Times, Ch. 1   *1906*

2 There is no man more dangerous, in a position of power, than he who refuses to accept as a working truth the idea that all a man does should make for rightness and soundness, that even the fixing of a tariff rate must be moral.

Ibid., Ch. 12

3 Sacredness of human life! The world has never believed it! It has been with life that we settled our quarrels, won wives, gold and land, defended ideas, imposed religions. We have held that a death toll was a necessary part of every human achievement, whether sport, war, or industry. A moment's rage over the horror of it, and we have sunk into indifference.

New Ideals in Business, Ch. 3   *1914*

4 Those who talk of the mine, the mill, the factory as if they were inherently inhuman and horrible are those who never have known the miner, the weaver, or the steel or iron worker.

Ibid., Ch. 7

5 There is no more effective medicine to apply to feverish public sentiment than figures. To be sure, they must be properly prepared, must cover the case, not confine themselves to a quarter of it, and they must be gathered for their own sake, not for the sake of a theory. Such preparation we get in a national census.

The Ways of Woman, Ch. 1   *1914*

6 They did not understand it [culture] to be ripeness and sureness of mind, it was not taste, discrimination, judgment; it was an acquisition—something which came with diplomas and degrees and only with them.

Ibid., Ch. 5

7 A mind which really lays hold of a subject is not easily detached from it.

Ibid.

8 A mind truly cultivated never feels that the intellectual process is complete until it can reproduce in some media the thing which it has absorbed.

Ibid.

9 "Yes, sir; he was what I call a *godly* man. Fact is, I never knew anybody I felt so sure would walk straight into Heaven, everybody welcomin' him, nobody fussin' or fumin' about his bein' let in, as Abraham Lincoln."
In Lincoln's Chair   1920

10 "It takes God a long time to work out His will with men like us, Billy, bad men, stupid men, selfish men. But even if we're beat, there's a gain. There are more men who see clear now how hard it is for people to rule themselves, more people to determine government by the people shan't perish from the earth, more people willin' to admit that you can't have peace when you've got a thing like slavery goin' on. That something, that's goin' to help when the next struggle comes."   Ibid.

260. Martha Thomas
(1857–1935)

1 Women are one-half of the world but until a century ago . . . it was a man's world. The laws were man's laws, the government a man's government, the country a man's country. . . . The man's world must become a man's and a woman's world. Why are we afraid? It is the next step forward on the path to the sunrise, and the sun is rising over a new heaven and a new earth.
Address, North American
Woman Suffrage Association, Buffalo,
New York   *October, 1908*

261. Clara Zetkin
(1857–1933)

1 . . . women must remain in industry despite all narrow-minded caterwauling; in fact the circle of their

241

industrial activity must become broader and more secure daily. . . .

The Question of Women Workers and Women at the Present Time 1889

2 The organization and enlightenment of working women, the struggle to attain their economic and political equal rights is not only desirable for the socialist movement. It is and will become more and more a life-and-death question for it. . . .

Ibid.

3 The beginnings of the class-conscious organized proletarian woman's movement in Germany are indissolubly bound up with the coming into being and maturing of the socialist conception of society in the proletariat. . . .

Zur Geschichte der proletarischen Frauenbewegung Deutschlands 1928

4 The position of women could only be improved through the improvement of workers, that is, through abolition of the wage system.

Ibid.

5 . . . as the liberation of the proletariat is possible only through the abolition of the capitalist productive relation, so too the emancipation of woman is possible only through doing away with private property.　　Ibid.

6 All roads led to Rome. Every truly Marxist analysis of an important part of the ideological superstructure of society, of an outstanding social phenomenon, had to lead to an analysis of bourgeois society and its foundation, private property. It should lead to the conclusion that "Carthage must be destroyed."

"My Recollections of Lenin" (1925), Quoted in *The Emancipation of Women* 1966p

262. Dorothy Gurney
(1858–1932)

* * *

1 The kiss of sun for pardon,
　　The song of the birds for mirth—
One is nearer God's Heart in a garden
　　Than anywhere else on earth.

"The Lord God Planted a Garden," St. 3

263. Selma Lagerlöf
(1858–1940)

1 There were no accusers; there could be no judge.

The Story of Gösta Berling,
Introduction, Ch. 1   *1891*

2 Burdensome are the ways men have to follow here on
earth. They lead through deserts, and through marshes,
and over mountains. Why is so much sorrow allowed
to go on without interruption, until it loses itself in the
desert or sinks in the bog, or is killed in the mountains?
Where are the little flower-pickers, where are the little
princesses of the fairy tale about whose feet roses grow;
where are they who should strew flowers on the weary
path?

Ibid., Pt. II, Ch. 2

3 There was nothing to do but to rest after the endless
journey she had made. But that she could never do.
She began to weep because she would never reach her
journey's end. Her whole life long she would travel,
travel, travel, and never reach the end of her journey.

The Miracles of Anti-Christ,
Bk. I, Ch. 7   *1899*

4 Does it always end so with a woman? When they build
their palaces they are never finished. Women can do
nothing that has permanence.

Ibid., Bk. II, Ch. 2

5 It is a strange thing to come home. While yet on the
journey, you cannot at all realize how strange it will
be.

Ibid., Bk. III, Ch. 3

6 Just fancy what an effect his violin could have! It made
people quite forget themselves. It was a great power to
have at his disposal. Any moment he liked he could
take possession of his kingdom.

"The Story of a Country House,"
Ch. 1, *From a Swedish Homestead*   *1901*

7 In that region of terror, in that great desert, there had
at any rate grown one flower that had comforted him
with fragrance and beauty, and now he felt that love
would dwell with him forever. The wildflower of the

desert had been transplanted into the garden of life, and had taken root and grown and thriven, and when he felt this he knew he was saved; he knew that the darkness had found its master.

Ibid., Ch. 6

8 The fair sun is like a mother whose son is about to set out for a far-off land, and who, in the hour of the leave-taking, cannot take her eyes from the beloved.

Ibid., "Astrid," Ch. 3

9 There is nothing so terrible as perjury. There is something uncanny and awful about that sin. There is no mercy or condonation for it.

"The Girl from the Marsh Croft,"
The Girl from the Marsh Croft   1911

10 "When I see a stream like this in the wilderness," he thought, "I am reminded of my own life. As persistent as this stream have I been in forcing my way past all that has obstructed my path. Father has been my rock ahead, and Mother tried to hold me back and bury me between moss-tufts, but I stole past both of them and got out in the world. Hey-ho, hi, hi!"

Ibid., "The Musician"

11 Thinking is never so easy as when one follows a plow up a furrow and down a furrow.

Jerusalem, Bk. I, Ch. 1   1915

12 "The ways of Providence cannot be reasoned out by the finite mind," he mused. "I cannot fathom them, yet seeking to know them is the most satisfying thing in all the world."

Ibid., Bk. II

13 "It has been said, as you know," Hellgum went on, "that if somebody strikes us on one cheek we must turn the other cheek also, and that we should not resist evil, and other things of the same sort; all of which none of us can live up to. Why, people would rob you of your house and home, they'd steal your potatoes and carry off your grain, if you fail to protect what was yours."

Ibid.

14 Could I ever be happy again now that I knew there was so much evil in the world?

The Diary of Selma Lagerlöf
(March 24, 1872)   1936

15 To be sure, I believe in the power of the dead, but I
   also know that Selma Otillia Lovisa Lagerlöf is inclined
   to imagine things that are utterly impossible.

   Ibid. (March 26, 1872)

264. Edith Nesbit
(1858–1924)

* * *

1 Little brown brother, oh! little brown brother,
   Are you awake in the dark?

   "Baby Seed Song"

2 The chestnut's proud, and the lilac's pretty,
   The poplar's gentle and tall,
   But the plane tree's kind to the poor dull city—
   I love him best of all!

   "Child's Song in Spring"

265. Emmeline Pankhurst
(1858–1928)

1 It is time that the women took their place in Imperial
   politics.

   Quoted in *The Standard* (London) *October 5, 1911*

2 Those men and women are fortunate who are born at a
   time when a great struggle for human freedom is in
   progress.

   My Own Story   *1914*

3 I was transfixed with horror, and over me there swept
   the sudden conviction that hanging was a mistake—
   worse, a crime. It was my awakening to one of the
   most terrible facts of life—that justice and judgment lie
   often a world apart.   Ibid.

4 . . . if civilisation is to advance at all in the future, it
   must be through the help of women, women freed of
   their political shackles, women with full power to work
   their will in society. It was rapidly becoming clear to
   my mind that men regarded women as a servant class
   in the community, and that women were going to remain in the servant class until they lifted themselves
   out of it.   Ibid.

5 Women had always fought for men, and for their children. Now they were ready to fight for their own human rights. Our militant movement was established.

Ibid.

6 "I have never felt a prouder woman than I did one night when a police constable said to me, after one of these demonstrations, 'Had this been a man's demonstration, there would have been bloodshed long ago.' Well, my lord, there has not been any bloodshed except on the part of the women themselves—these so-called militant women. Violence has been done to us, and I who stand before you in this dock have lost a dear sister in the course of this agitation."

Ibid.

7 . . . I was sadly aware that we were but approaching a far goal. The end, though certain, was still distant. Patience and still more patience, faith and still more faith, well, we had called upon these souls' help before and it was certain that they would not fail us at this greatest crisis of all.

Ibid.

8 . . . I said [to the prison doctor]: "I will not be examined by you because your intention is not to help me as a patient, but merely to ascertain how much longer it will be possible to keep me alive in prison. I am not prepared to assist you or the government in any such way. I am not prepared to relieve you of any responsibility in this matter."

Ibid.

9 Why is it that men's blood-shedding militancy is applauded and women's symbolic militancy punished with a prison-cell and the forcible feeding horror? It means simply this, that men's double standard of sexual morals, whereby the victims of their lust are counted as outcasts while the men themselves escape all social censure, really applies to morals in all departments of life. Men make the moral code and they expect women to accept it.

Ibid.

10 It always seems to me when the anti-suffrage members of the Government criticize militancy in women that it is very like beasts of prey reproaching the gentler animals who turn in desperate resistance when at the point of death.

Ibid., Speech, "I Incite This Meeting
to Rebellion" (October 17, 1912)

11 There is something that governments care far more for than human life, and that is the security of property, and so it is through property that we shall strike the enemy. *Ibid.*

12 One thing is essential to an army, and that thing is made up of a two-fold requirement. In an army you need unity of purpose. In an army you also need unity of policy. *Ibid.*

13 How different the reasoning is that men adopt when they are discussing the cases of men and those of women.

Ibid., Speech, "When
Civil War Is Waged by Women"
(November 13, 1913)

14 You have to make more noise than anybody else, you have to make yourself more obtrusive than anybody else, you have to fill all the papers more than anybody else, in fact you have to be there all the time and see that they do not snow you under, if you are really going to get your reform realized. *Ibid.*

15 Some of the guards—I think men who had never known what it was to earn a living, who knew nothing of the difficulties of a man's life, let alone the difficulties of a woman's life—came out, and they said: "Why did you break our windows? We have done nothing." She said: "It is because you have done nothing I have broken your windows." *Ibid.*

16 We are driven to this. We are determined to go on with the agitation. We are in honour bound to do so until we win. Just as it was the duty of our forefathers to do it for you, it is our duty to make this world a better place for women.

Speech (1908), Quoted in
The Fighting Pankhursts
by David Mitchell   1967p

17 I am what you call a hooligan!

Ibid., Speech (1909)

18 I have no sense of guilt. I look upon myself as a prisoner of war. I am under no moral obligation to conform to, or in any way accept, the sentence imposed upon me.

Ibid., Speech to the Court (April, 1913)

19 Our sons and daughters must be trained in national service, taught to give as well as to receive.
> Ibid., Speech, British Columbia (May, 1920)

20 Help us to educate the people of the Dominion to the necessity of a single standard of morals—that of the highest. Teach your children reverence for the marriage vow of men and women. Instill into their minds the belief in purity of body, mind and soul.
> Ibid., Speech, Federated Women's
> Institutes, Ottawa (March, 1924)

21 I don't think they [women] have done badly, considering that it is so hard not to get wrapped up in the mere struggle for existence. Of course we expected a great deal from our enfranchisement. But so did men when they fought for theirs. It is the only way—to keep fighting, to believe that the miracle is going to happen.
> Ibid., Press Conference (1926)

22 We have taken this action, because as women . . . we realize that the condition of our sex is so deplorable that it is our duty even to break the law in order to call attention to the reasons why we do so.
> Speech to the Court (October 21,
> 1908), *Shoulder to Shoulder,*
> Midge Mackenzie, ed.   *1975p*

23 Over one thousand women have gone to prison in the course of this agitation, have suffered their imprisonment, have come out of prison injured in health, weakened in body, but not in spirit. . . . I ask you . . . if you are prepared to go on doing that kind of thing indefinitely, because that is what is going to happen. There is absolutely no doubt about it. . . . We are women, rightly or wrongly convinced that this is the only way in which we can win power to alter what for us are intolerable conditions, absolutely intolerable conditions. From the moment I leave this court I shall deliberately refuse to eat food—I shall join the women who are already in Holloway [Women's Prison] on the hunger strike. I shall come out of prison, dead or alive, at the earliest possible moment; and once again, as soon as I am physically fit I shall enter into this fight again. Life is very dear to all of us. I am not seeking, as was said by the Home Secretary, to commit suicide. I do not want to commit suicide. I want to see the

women of this country enfranchised, and I want to live until that is done.

Ibid., Speech to the Court (April 2, 1913)

24 In time of war the rules of peace must be set aside and we must put ourselves without delay upon a war basis, let the women stand shoulder to shoulder with the men to win the common victory which we all desire.

Ibid., Speech, London Pavilion (October 5, 1915)

25 Better that we should die fighting than be outraged and dishonoured. . . . Better to die than to live in slavery.

Ibid., Speech, Army and Navy Hall,
Petrograd (August, 1917)

26 What we want to proclaim to this meeting is that we want the bill, the whole bill, and nothing but the bill. . . . We want the vote so that we may serve our country better. We want the vote so that we shall be more faithful and more true to our allies. We want the vote so that we may help to maintain the cause of Christian civilisation for which we entered this war. We want the vote so that in future such wars if possible may be averted.

Ibid., Speech, Queen's Hall (April 23, 1917)

266. Agnes Repplier
(1858–1950)

1 . . . but the children of to-day are favored beyond their knowledge and certainly far beyond their deserts.

"Children, Past and Present,"
Books and Men   *1888*

2 And what universal politeness has been fostered by the terror that superstition breeds, what delicate euphemisms containing the very soul of courtesy!

Ibid., "On the Benefits of Superstition"

3 Again, in the stress of modern life, how little room is left for that most comfortable vanity which whispers in our ears that failures are not faults! Now we are taught from infancy that we must rise or fall upon our own merits; that vigilance wins success, and incapacity means ruin.

Ibid.

249

4 A happy commonplaceness is now acknowledged to be, next to brevity of life, man's best inheritance; but in the days when all the virtues and vices were flaunted in gala costume, people were hardly prepared for that fine simplicity which has grown to be the crucial test of art.

Ibid., "The Decay of Sentiment"

5 So if the masterpieces of the present, the triumphs of learned verbs and realistic prose, fail to lift their readers out of themselves, like the masterpieces of the past, the fault must be our own.

Ibid.

6 There is nothing in the world so enjoyable as a thorough-going monomania. . . .

Ibid.

7 We are tethered to our kind, and may as well join hands in the struggle.

Ibid.

8 But self-satisfaction, if as buoyant as gas, has an ugly trick of collapsing when full blown, and facts are stony things that refuse to melt away in the sunshine of a smile.

Ibid., "Some Aspects of Pessimism"

9 It is a humiliating fact that, notwithstanding our avaricious greed for novelties, we are forced, when sincere, to confess that *"les anciens ont tout dit,"* and that it is probable that contending schools of thought have always held the same relative positions they do now: Optimism glittering in the front ranks as a deservedly popular favorite; pessimism speaking with a still, persistent voice to those who, unluckily for themselves, have the leisure and the intelligence to attend.

Ibid.

10 The pessimist, however—be it recorded to his credit—is seldom an agitating individual. His creed breeds indifference to others, and he does not trouble himself to thrust his views upon the unconvinced.   Ibid.

11 Memory cheats us no less than hope by hazing over those things that we would fain forget; but who that has plodded on to middle age would take back upon his shoulders ten of the vanished years, with their mingled pleasures and pains? Who would return to the youth he is forever pretending to regret?   Ibid.

12 The great masterpieces of humor, which have kept men young by laughter, are being tried in the courts of an orthodox morality, and found lamentably wanting; or else, by way of giving them another chance, they are being subjected to the *peine forte et dure* of modern analysis, and are revealing hideous and melancholy meanings in the process.

"A Plea for Humor," *Points of View*   1891

13 Whatever has "wit enough to keep it sweet" defies corruption and outlasts all time; but the wit must be of that outward and visible order which needs no introduction or demonstration at our hands.

Ibid.

14 Sensuality, too, which used to show itself coarse, smiling, unmasked, and unmistakable, is now serious, analytic, and so burdened with a sense of its responsibility that it passes muster half the time as a new type of asceticism.

Ibid., "Fiction in the Pulpit"

15 Amusement is merely one side of pleasure, but a very excellent side, against which, in truth, I have no evil word to urge. The gods forbid such base and savorless ingratitude!

Ibid., "Pleasure: A Heresy"

16 A villain must be a thing of power, handled with delicacy and grace. He must be wicked enough to excite our aversion, strong enough to arouse our fear, human enough to awaken some transient gleam of sympathy. We must triumph in his downfall, yet not barbarously nor with contempt, and the close of his career must be in harmony with all its previous development.

"A Short Defence of Villains,"
Essays in Miniature   1892

17 We have but the memories of past good cheer, we have but the echoes of departed laughter. In vain we look and listen for the mirth that has died away. In vain we seek to question the gray ghosts of old-time revelers.

Ibid., "Humors of Gastronomy"

18 Philadelphians are every whit as mediocre as their neighbours, but they seldom encourage each other in mediocrity by giving it a more agreeable name.

Philadelphia: The Place and the People, Introduction   1898

19 It is hard for us who live in an age of careless and cheerful tolerance to understand the precise inconveniences attending religious persecution.

Ibid., Ch. 1

20 Necessity knows no Sunday. . . .

Ibid., Ch. 18

21 We have reached a point of idle curiosity which forces into print every pitiful scrap of correspondence which has lain sacred—or forgotten—in the bottoms of old desks, and every five minutes chat with people of distinction.

*"Memories and Biographies," Counsel
Upon the Reading of Books   1900*

22 Anyone, however, who has had dealings with dates knows that they are worse than elusive, they are perverse. Events do not happen at the right time, nor in their proper sequence. That sense of harmony with place and season which is so strong in the historian—if he be a readable historian—is lamentably lacking in history, which takes no pains to verify his most convincing statements.

To Think of Tea!, Ch. 1   1932

23 It has been well said that tea is suggestive of a thousand wants, from which spring the decencies and luxuries of civilization.

Ibid., Ch. 2

24 The English do not strain their tea in the fervid fashion we [Americans] do. They like to see a few leaves dawdling about the cup. They like to know what they are drinking.

Ibid., Ch. 13

25 No man pursues what he has at hand. No man recognizes the need of pursuit until that which he desires has escaped him.

In Pursuit of Laughter, Ch. 1   1936

26 People who cannot recognize a palpable absurdity are very much in the way of civilization.

Ibid., Ch. 9

27 It is not depravity that afflicts the human race so much as a general lack of intelligence.

Ibid.

28 The worst in life, we are told, is compatible with the best in art. So too the worst in life is compatible with the best in humour.

Ibid.

29 Wit is a pleasure-giving thing, largely because it eludes reason; but in the apprehension of an absurdity through the working of the comic spirit there is a foundation of reason, and an impetus to human companionship.

Ibid.

30 Humour brings insight and tolerance. Irony brings a deeper and less friendly understanding.

Ibid.

31 On the preservation of the Comic Spirit depends in some measure the ultimate triumph of civilization. Science may carry us to Mars, but it will leave the earth peopled as ever by the inept.   Ibid.

267. Beatrice Potter Webb
(1858–1943)

1 The underlying principle of the industrial revolution— the creed of universal competition—the firm faith that every man free to follow his own self-interest would contribute most effectually to the common weal, with the converse proposition that each man should suffer the full consequence of his own actions—this simple and powerful idea was enabling a rising middle class to break up and destroy those restraints on personal freedom, those monopolies for private gain, with which a Parliament of landowners had shackled the enterprise and weighted the energies of the nation.

*The Cooperative Movement in Great
Britain*, Ch. 1   *1891*

2 For the committee-man or officer who accepts a bribe or neglects his duty must be fully aware that he is not simply an indifferently honest man, like many of his fellows in private trade, but the deliberate betrayer of the means of salvation to thousands of his fellow-countrymen of this and all future generations.

Ibid., Ch. 7

3 The hand-to-mouth existence of the casual labourer . . . the restlessness or mortal weariness arising from lack of

nourishment, tempered by idleness, or intensified by physical exhaustion, do not permit the development, in the individual or the class, of the qualities of democratic association and democratic self-government.

Ibid., Ch. 8

4 The caprices of fashion, the vagaries of personal vanity and over-indulged appetites can find no satisfaction in an organization of industry based on the supply of rational and persistent wants.

Ibid.

5 But evidence drawn empirically from facts, though it may justify the action of the practical man, is not scientifically conclusive.

"The Economics of Factory Legislation," *Socialism and National Minimum*   1909

6 All along the line, physically, mentally, morally, alcohol is a weakening and deadening force, and it is worth a great deal to save women and girls from its influence.

Health of Working Girls, Ch. 10   1917

7 The inevitability of gradualness.

Presidential Address, British Labour Party Congress   1923

8 Beneath the surface of our daily life, in the personal history of many of us, there runs a continuous controversy between an Ego that affirms and an Ego that denies. On the course of this controversy depends the attainment of inner harmony and consistent conduct in private and public affairs.

My Apprenticeship, Introduction   1926

9 Religion is love; in no case is it logic.

Ibid., Ch. 2

10 For any detailed description of the complexity of human nature, of the variety and mixture in human motive, of the insurgence of instinct in the garb of reason, of the multifarious play of the social environment on the individual ego and of the individual ego on the social environment, I had to turn to novelists and poets. . . .

Ibid., Ch. 3

11 . . . if I had been a man, self-respect, family pressure and the public opinion of my class would have pushed

me into a money-making profession; as a mere woman
I could carve out a career of disinterested research.
Ibid., Ch. 8

12 . . . what we had to do was . . . to make medical
treatment not a favour granted to those in desperate
need but to compel all sick persons to submit to it . . .
to treat illness, in fact, as a public nuisance to be suppressed in the interests of the community.
Quoted by Anne Fremantle in
Woman as Revolutionary,
Fred C. Griffin, ed. 1973p

268. Eva Rose York
(1858–1925?)

* * *

1 I shall not pass this way again;
Then let me now relieve some pain,
Remove some barrier from the road,
Or brighten some one's heavy load.
"I Shall Not Pass This Way Again," St. 2

2 . . . I drunk the cup of bliss
Remembering not that those there be
Who drink the dregs of misery.
Ibid., St. 3

269. Katherine Lee Bates
(1859–1929)

1 O beautiful for spacious skies,
For amber waves of grain,
For purple mountain majesties
Above the fruited plain!
America! America!
God shed His grace on thee
And crown they good with brotherhood
From sea to shining sea!
"America the Beautiful," St. 1 1893

2 O beautiful for patriot dream
That sees beyond the years.
Thine alabaster cities gleam
Undimmed by human tears!
Ibid., St. 4

* * *

3 Dawn love is silver,
   Wait for the west:
Old love is gold love—
   Old love is best.

"For a Golden Wedding"

4 Nay, brother of the sod,
What part hast thou in God?
What spirit art thou of?
It answers, "Love."

"Laddie"

5 Spirit long shaping for sublime endeavor,
A sword of God, the gleaming metal came
From stern Scotch ancestry, where whatsoever
Was true, was pure, was noble, won acclaim.

"Woodrow Wilson"

270. Louise de Koven Bowen
(1859–1953)

1 I hated myself because I smelt of onions and meat, and
I seriously considered suicide in the cistern which supplied the house.

Growing Up with a City, Ch. 1   1926

2 By the time I made my entry into society I was ignorant in everything and accomplished in nothing.

Ibid.

3 It is always a real satisfaction to know that politics has
not yet dominated the Juvenile Court of Cook County;
that we still have these judges who are incorruptible
and devoted to their work.

Ibid., Ch. 4

271. Carrie Chapman Catt
(1859–1947)

1 The sacrifice of suffering, of doubt, of obloquy, which
has been endured by the pioneers in the woman movement will never be fully known or understood. . . .

Speech, "For the Sake of Liberty" (February
8–14, 1900), Quoted in History of Woman Suf-
frage, Vol. IV, by Susan B. Anthony and Ida
Husted   1902

2 There are two kinds of restrictions upon human liberty—the restraint of law and that of custom. No written law has ever been more binding than unwritten custom supported by popular opinion.

Ibid.

3 Once, this movement represented the scattered and disconnected protests of individual women. . . . Happily those days are past; and out of that incoherent and seemingly futile agitation, which extended over many centuries, there has emerged a present-day movement possessing a clear understanding and a definite, positive purpose.

Speech, "Is Woman Suffrage
Progressing?," Stockholm   *1911*

4 The Government evidently nurses a forlorn hope that by delay it may tire out the workers and destroy the force of the campaign.

Ibid.

5 When a just cause reaches its flood-tide, as ours has done in that country, whatever stands in the way must fall before its overwhelming power.

Ibid.

6 There they swell that horrid, unspeakably unclean peril of civilisation, prostitution—augmented by the White Slave Traffic and by the machinations of the male parasites who live upon the earnings of women of vice. . . . We must be merciful, for they are the natural and inevitable consequence of centuries of false reasoning concerning woman's place in the world. . . . Upon these women we have no right to turn our backs. Their wrongs are our wrongs. Their existence is part of our problem. They have been created by the very injustice against which we protest.

Ibid.

272. Helen Gray Cone
(1859–1934)

1 A song of hate is a song of Hell;
Some there be who sing it well.

"Chant of Love for England"   *1945p*

2 Bind higher, grind higher, burn higher with fire,
   Cast her ashes into the sea,—
She shall escape, she shall aspire,
   She shall arise to make men free.

Ibid.

* * *

3 Peerless, fearless, an army's flower!
Sterner soldiers the world never saw,
Marching lightly, that summer hour,
To death and failure and fame forever.

"Greencastle Jenny," St. 4

4 Upon a showery night and still,
   Without a second of warning,
A trooper band surprised the hill,
   And held it in the morning.
We were not waked by bugle notes,
   No cheer our dreams invaded,
And yet at dawn their yellow coats
   On the green slopes paraded.

"The Dandelions"

273. Eleanora Duse
(1859–1924)

1 Before passing my lips each word seemed to have
coursed through the ardor of my blood. There wasn't a
fiber in me that did not add its notes to the harmony.
Ah, grace—the state of grace!

Quoted in Il Fuoco by D'Annunzio   1900

2 I know nothing, nothing! I have everything to learn.
Twelve years ago, when I left the theatre, I did so with
no regrets. I was tired of living for others; I wanted to
live for myself and learn and learn!

Quoted in Errinerungen, Betrachtungen
und Brief by Edouard Schneider   1921

3 I did not use paint. I made myself up morally.

Quoted by Louis Schneider in
Le Gaulois   July 27, 1922

4 I'm only a little Italian actress. Nobody would understand me abroad. Let me first perfect myself in my art
which I dearly love, and don't try to lead me astray.

Quoted in Le Matin   April 12, 1924

5 Do you think one can speak about art? It would be like trying to explain love. There are many ways of loving and there are as many kinds of art. There is the love that elevates and leads to good—there is the love that absorbs all one's will, all one's strength and intelligence. In my opinion this is the truest love—but it is certainly fatal. . . . So is it with art. . . .

Quoted in *Eleanora Duse*
by C. Antonia-Traversi *1926p*

6 You never told me that life is vulgar, you—alone—sadly agreed with me that life is grievous.

Ibid.

7 Oh, art, that consumes my life! But what resource! I could not bear to live if I did not have it.

Quoted in *Signorelli* by
Olga Resnevic (1884) *1938p*

8 Work means so many things! So many! Among other things Work also means Freedom. . . . Without it even the miracle of love is only a cruel deception.

Quoted in *Vita de Arrigo Boito*
by Piero Nardi *1942p*

9 The strongest is the loneliest and the loneliest is the strongest. Ibid.

10 When moral sensibility alone is in question, I am won; but as soon as doctrinal intransigence and a purely ecclesiastical point of view enter in, I rebel.

Quoted in *The Mystic in the Theatre*
by Eva Le Gallienne *1965p*

274. Lady Gregory
(1859?–1932)

1 CHRISTIE. It's a grand thing to be able to take up your money in your hand and to think no more of it when it slips away from you than you would of a trout that would slip back into the stream.

Twenty Five 1903

2 MRS. TARPEY. Business, is it? What business would the people here have but to be minding one another's business?

Spreading the News 1905

3 MRS. DELANE. I'm not one that blames the police. Sure, they have their own bread to earn like every other one. And indeed it is often they will let a thing pass.
Hyacinth Halvey 1906

4 MRS. DONOHOE. There is many a thing in the sea is not decent, but cockles is fit to put before the Lord!
The Workhouse Ward 1908

5 HAZEL. To have no power of revenge after death! My strength to go nourish weeds and grass!
Coats 1910

6 MRS. BRODERICK. A splendid shot he was; the thing he did not see he'd hit it the same as the thing he'd see.
The Full Moon 1910

7 DARBY. I am maybe getting your meaning wrong, your tongue being a little hard and sharp because you are Englified, but I am without new learnments and so I speak flat.
The Bogiemen 1912

8 O'MALLEY. Well, there's no one at all, they do be saying, but is deserving of some punishment from the very minute of his birth. . . . Sure it is allotted to every Christian to meet with his share of trouble.
Shanwalla, Act II 1915

9 1ST POLICEMAN. There's nothing in the world more ignorant than to give any belief to ghosts. I am walking the world these twenty years, and never met anything worse than myself!
Ibid., Act III

10 GIANT. Fru, Fa, Fashog! I smell the smell of a melodious lying Irishman!
The Golden Apple, Act I, Sc. 4 1916

11 GIANT. One person to know it, and you to know him to know it, is the same as if it was known to all the world.
Ibid., Act II, Sc. 2

12 MOTHER. Them that have too much of it [learning] are seven times crosser than them that never saw a book.
Aristotle Bellows, Act I 1921

13 CELIA. It is better to be tied to any thorny bush than to be with a cross man.
Ibid.

14 JESTER. There's more learning than is taught in books.
The Jester, Act I   1923

15 OGRE. I'll take no charity! What I get I'll earn by taking it. I would feel no pleasure it being given to me, any more than a huntsman would take pleasure being made a present of a dead fox, in place of getting a run across country after it.

Ibid., Act II, Sc. 1

16 JOEL. That's the way of it! All the generations looking for him, and praying for him. We wanted him, and we got him, and what we did with him was to kill him. And that is the way it will be ever and always, so long as leaves grow upon the trees!

The Story Brought by Brigit,
Act III   1924

275. Florence Kelley
(1859–1932)

1 . . . the utter unimportance of children compared with products in the minds of the people. . . .
"My Philadelphia," *The Survey Graphic*
October 1, 1926

276. Nora Archibald Smith
(1859–1934)

* * *

1 They'd knock on a tree and would timidly say
To the spirit that might be within there that day:
"Fairy fair, Fairy fair, wish thou me well;
'Gainst evil witcheries weave me a spell!"
"Knocking on Wood," St. 3

277. Mary Gardiner Brainard
(fl. 1860s)

* * *

1 I would rather walk with God in the dark than go alone in the light.

"Not Knowing," St. 1

2 And what looks dark in the distance may brighten as I draw near.

Ibid., St. 2

278. Jane Addams
(1860–1935)

1 The new growth in the plant swelling against the sheath, which at the same time imprisons and protects it, must still be the truest type of progress.

"Filial Relations," Democracy and
Social Ethics   1907

2 The colleges have long been full of the best ethical teaching. . . . But while the teaching has included an ever-broadening range of obligation and has insisted upon the recognition of the claims of human brotherhood, the training has been singularly individualistic; it has fostered ambitions for personal distinction, and has trained the faculties almost exclusively in the direction of intellectual accumulation.

Ibid.

3 In our pity for Lear, we fail to analyze his character. . . . His paternal expression was one of domination and indulgence, without the perception of the needs of his children, without any anticipation of their entrance into a wider life, or any belief that they could have a worthy life apart from him.

Ibid.

4 Doubtless the clashes and jars which we feel most keenly are those which occur when two standards of morals, both honestly held and believed in, are brought sharply together.

Ibid.

5 A city is in many respects a great business corporation, but in other respects it is enlarged housekeeping. . . . May we not say that city housekeeping has failed partly because women, the traditional housekeepers, have not been consulted as to its multiform activities?

"Utilization of Women in City
Government," Newer Ideals of Peace   1907

6 Old-fashioned ways which no longer apply to changed conditions are a snare in which the feet of women have always become readily entangled.

Ibid.

7 . . . the administration of the household has suffered because it has become unnaturally isolated from the rest of the community.

Ibid.

8 Unless our conception of patriotism is progressive, it cannot hope to embody the real affection and the real interest of the nation.

Ibid.

9 Private beneficence is totally inadequate to deal with the vast numbers of the city's disinherited.

Twenty Years at Hull House   *1910*

10 Perhaps I may record here my protest against the efforts, so often made, to shield children and young people from all that has to do with death and sorrow, to give them a good time at all hazards on the assumption that the ills of life will come soon enough. Young people themselves often resent this attitude on the part of their elders; they feel set aside and belittled as if they were denied the common human experiences.

Ibid.

11 We were often distressed by the children of immigrant parents who were ashamed of the pit whence they were digged, who repudiated the language and customs of their elders, and counted themselves successful [when] they were able to ignore the past.

Ibid.

12 In his own way each man must struggle, lest the moral law become a far-off abstraction utterly separated from his active life.

Ibid.

13 You do not know what life means when all the difficulties are removed! I am simply smothered and sickened with advantages. It is like eating a sweet dessert the first thing in the morning.

Ibid.

14 Only in time of fear is government thrown back to its primitive and sole function of self-defense and the many interests of which it is the guardian become subordinated to that.

"Women, War and Suffrage," *Survey*
November 6, 1915

15 Each exponent in this long effort to place law above force was called a dreamer and a coward, but each did his utmost to express clearly the truth that was in him, and beyond that human effort cannot go.   Ibid.

16 . . . the fruitful processes of cooperation in the great experiment of living together in a world become conscious of itself.   Ibid.

17 Civilization is a method of living, an attitude of equal respect for all men.   Speech, Honolulu   *1933*

279. Marie Konstantinovna Bashkirtseff
(1860–1884)

1 Ah, when one thinks what a miserable creature man is! Every other animal can, at his will, wear on his face the expression he pleases. He is not obligated to smile if he has a mind to weep. When he does not wish to see his fellows he does not see them. While man is the slave of everything and everybody!
The Journal of a Young Artist
(May 6, 1873)   *1884*

2 To say that my grief will be eternal would be ridiculous—nothing is eternal.

Ibid. (October 17, 1873)

3 Let us love dogs; let us love only dogs! Men and cats are unworthy creatures. . . .

Ibid. (July 16, 1874)

4 In the studio all distinctions disappear. One has neither name nor family; one is no longer the daughter of one's mother, one is one's self—an individual—and one has before one art, and nothing else. One feels so happy, so free, so proud.

Ibid. (October 5, 1877)

5 . . . I write down everything, everything, everything. Otherwise why should I write?

Ibid. (May 1, 1884)

6 If I had been born a man, I would have conquered Europe. As I was born a woman, I exhausted my energy in tirades against fate, and in eccentricities.

Ibid. (June 25, 1884)

7 For my own part I think love—impossible—to one who looks at human nature through a microscope, as I do. They who see only what they wish to see in those around them are very fortunate.

Ibid. (August 1, 1884)

280. Ellen Thorneycroft Fowler
(1860–1929)

* * *

1 Though outwardly a gloomy shroud,
The inner half of every cloud
  Is bright and shining:
I therefore turn my clouds about
And always wear them inside out
  To show the lining.   "Wisdom of Folly"

281. Charlotte Perkins Gilman
(1860–1935)

1 "Your exercise depends on your strength, my dear," said he, "and your food somewhat on your appetite; but air you can absorb all the time."

"The Yellow Wall-Paper,"
New England Magazine   1891

2 I used to lie awake as a child and get more entertainment and terror out of blank walls and plain furniture than most children could find in a toy-store.   Ibid.

3 I do not want to be a fly,
I want to be a worm!

"A Conservative,"
In This Our World   1893

4 From the day laborer to the millionaire, the wife's worn dress or flashing jewels, her low roof or her lordly one, her weary feet or her rich equipage—these speak of the economic ability of the husband.

Women and Economics, Ch. 1   1898

5 Grateful return for happiness conferred is not the method of exchange in a partnership. The comfort a man takes with his wife is not in the nature of a business partnership, nor are her frugality and industry.

Ibid.

6 The labor of women in the house, certainly, enables men to produce more wealth than they otherwise could; and in this way women are economic factors in society. But so are horses.

Ibid.

7 The women who do the most work get the least money, and the women who have the most money do the least work.

Ibid.

8 It is not motherhood that keeps the housewife on her feet from dawn till dark; it is house service, not child service.

Ibid.

9 . . . with her overcharged sensibility, her prominent modesty, her "eternal feminity"—the female genus homo is undeniably over-sexed.

Ibid.

10 Boys and girls are expected, also, to behave differently to each other, and to people in general—a behavior to be briefly described in two words. To the boy we say, "Do"; to the girl, "Don't."

Ibid.

11 The transient trade we think evil. The bargain for life we think good.

Ibid., Ch. 4

12 To be surrounded by beautiful things has much influence upon the human creature: to make beautiful things has more.

Ibid.

13 Specialization and organization are the basis of human progress.   *Ibid.*

14 Where young boys plan for what they will achieve and attain, young girls plan for whom they will achieve and attain.   *Ibid., Ch. 5*

15 Marriage is the woman's proper sphere, her divinely ordered place, her natural end. It is what she is born for, what she is trained for, what she is exhibited for. It is, moreover, her means of honorable livelihood and advancement. *But*—she must not even look as if she wanted it!   *Ibid.*

16 Legitimate sex-competition brings out all that is best in man.

Ibid., Ch. 6

17 It is not for nothing that a man's best friends sigh when he marries, especially if he is a man of genius.

Ibid.

18 The world is quite right. It does not have to be consistent.

Ibid.

19 We have built into the constitution of the human race the habit and desire of taking, as divorced from its natural precursor and concomitant of making.

Ibid.

20 As the priestess of the temple of consumption, as the limitless demander of things to use up, her economic influence is reactionary and injurious.

Ibid.

21 The sexuo-economic relationship . . . sexualizes our industrial relationship and commericializes our sex-relation.

Ibid.

22 The female segregated to the uses of sex alone naturally deteriorates in racial development.

Ibid., Ch. 9

23 When we see great men and women, we give credit to their mothers. When we see inferior men and women— and that is a common circumstance—no one presumes to the question of the motherhood which has produced them.

Ibid.

24 The human mother does less for her young, both absently and proportionately, than any kind of mother on earth. . . . The necessary knowledge of the world, so indispensable to every human being, she cannot give, because she does not possess it.

Ibid.

25 "To bear and rear the majestic race to which they can never fully belong! To live vicariously forever, through their sons, the daughters being only another vicarious link! What a supreme and magnificent martyrdom!"

Ibid.

26 Maternal instinct, merely as an instinct, is unworthy of our superstitious reverence.

Ibid.

27 A family unity which is only bound together with a table-cloth is of questionable value.

Ibid., Ch. 11

28 The child learns more of the virtues needed in modern life—of fairness, of justice, of comradeship, of collective interest and action——in a common school than can be taught in the most perfect family circle.

Ibid., Ch. 13

29 Work the object of which is merely to serve one's self is the lowest. Work the object of which is merely to serve one's family is the next lowest. Work the object of which is to serve more and more people, in widening range . . . is social service in the fullest sense, and the highest form of service we can reach.

Ibid.

30 A baby who spent certain hours of every day among other babies, being cared for because he was a baby and not because he was "my baby," would grow to have a very different opinion of himself from that which is forced upon each new soul that comes among us by the ceaseless adoration of his own immediate family.

Ibid.

31 . . . while we flatter ourselves that things remain the same, they are changing under our very eyes from year to year, from day to day.

Ibid.

32 You cannot teach every mother to be a good school educator or a good college educator. Why should you expect every mother to be a good nursery educator?

Ibid.

33 The mother as a social servant instead of a home servant will not lack in true mother duty. . . . From her work, loved and honored though it is, she will return to the home life, the child life, with an eager, ceaseless pleasure, cleansed of all the fret and fraction and weariness that so mar it now.

Ibid.

34 Allegiance and long labor due my lord—
  Allegiance in an idleness abhorred—
I am the squaw—the slave—the harem beauty—
  I serve and serve, the handmaid of the world.
                    "Two Callings," *The Home*,
                    Introduction, Pt. I   *1910*

35 So when the great word "Mother!" rang once more,
    I saw at last its meaning and its place;
  Not the blind passion of the brooding past,
  But Mother—the World's Mother—come at last,
  To love as she had never loved before—
    To feed and guard and teach the human race.
                            Ibid., Pt. II

36 Habits of thought persist through the centuries; and
  while a healthy brain may reject the doctrine it no
  longer believes, it will continue to feel the same sentiments formerly associated with that doctrine.
                            Ibid., Ch. 3

37 The original necessity for the ceaseless presence of the
  woman to maintain that altar fire—and it was an altar
  fire in very truth at one period—has passed with the
  means of prompt ignition; the matchbox has freed the
  housewife from that incessant service, but the *feeling*
  that women should stay at home is with us yet.
                                        Ibid.

38 Noticed, studied, commented on, and incessantly inter-
  fered with; forced into miserable self-consciousness by
  this unremitting glare; our little ones grow up permanently injured in character by this lack of one of humanity's most precious rights—privacy.   Ibid.

39 Let us revere, let us worship, but erect and open-eyed,
  the highest, not the lowest; the future, not the past!
                                        Ibid.

40 It will be a great thing for the human soul when it
  finally stops worshiping backwards.
                                        Ibid.

41 You may observe mother instinct at its height in a fond
  hen sitting on china eggs—instinct, but no brains.
                                        Ibid.

42 Eternity is not something that begins after you are
  dead. It is going on all the time. We are in it now.
        Quoted in *The Forerunner Magazine*   *1909–1916*

43 How many a useless stone we find
   Swallowed in that capacious blind
   Faith-swollen gullet, our ancestral mind.

   Ibid.

44 There was a time when Patience ceased to be a virtue.
   It was long ago.

   Ibid.

45 Human life consists in mutual service. No grief, pain,
   misfortune, or "broken heart," is excuse for cutting off
   one's life while any power of service remains. But when
   all usefulness is over, when one is assured of an unavoidable and imminent death, it is the simplest of human rights to choose a quick and easy death in place of
   a slow and horrible one.

   Suicide Note   *August 17, 1935*

46 If love, devotion to duty, sublime self-sacrifice, were
   enough in child-culture, mothers would achieve better
   results; but there is another requisite too often lacking—knowledge.

   The Living of Charlotte Perkins Gilman   1935p

47 One may have a brain specialized in its grasp of ethics,
   as well as of mechanics, mathematics or music.

   Ibid.

48 It is told that Buddha, going out to look on life, was
   greatly daunted by death. "They all eat one another!"
   he cried, and called it evil. This process I examined,
   changed the verb, said, "They all feed one another,"
   and called it good.

   Ibid.

49 Death? Why this fuss about death. Use your imagination, try to visualize a world *without* death! . . .
   Death is the essential condition of life, not an evil.

   Ibid.

50 However, one cannot put a quart in a pint cup.

   Ibid.

51 The first duty of a human being is to assume the right
   functional relationship to society—more briefly, to find
   your real job, and do it.

   Ibid.

52 . . . love grows by service.

   Ibid.

53 We are told to hitch our wagons to a star, but why pick on Betelgeuse?*

Ibid.

54 . . . New York . . . that unnatural city where every one is an exile, none more so than the American.

Ibid.

55 Socialism, long misrepresented and misunderstood under the violent propaganda of Marxism, has been fairly obliterated in the public mind by the Jewish-Russian nightmare, Bolshevism.

Ibid.

56 But reason has no power against feeling, and feeling older than history is no light matter.

Ibid.

57 It is no wonder we behave badly, we are literally ignorant of the laws of ethics, which is the simplest of sciences, the most necessary, the most constantly needed.

Ibid.

58 There is no female mind. The brain is not an organ of sex. As well speak of a female liver.

Quoted in *The Liberated Woman's Appointment Calendar*, Lynn Sherr and Jurate Kazickas, eds.   *1975p*

* * *

59 A concept is stronger than a fact.

"Human Work"

60 To swallow and follow, whether old doctrine or new propaganda, is a weakness still dominating the human mind.

Ibid.

61 Cried this pretentious ape one day,
      "I'm going to be a Man!
And stand upright, and hunt, and fight,
      And conquer all I can."

"Similar Cases"

62 Cried all, "Before such things can come,
      You idiotic child,
You must alter Human Nature!"
And they all sat back and smiled.   *Ibid.*

* Largest star in the galaxy.

63 I ran against a Prejudice.
  That quite cut off the view.

"An Obstacle," St. 1

64 The people people have for friends
    Your common sense appall,
  But the people people marry
    Are the queerest folks of all.

"Queer People"

65 There's a whining at the threshold—
    There's a scratching at the floor—
  To work! To work! In heaven's name!
    The wolf is at the door!

"The Wolf at the Door," St. 6

66 We are the wisest, strongest race:
    Long may our praise be sung—
  The only animal alive
    That lives upon its young!

"Child Labor"

282. Amy Leslie
(1860–1939)

1 Those who make the most memorable racket are of
  two classes—wary diplomats looking for the best of a
  business proposition and irresponsible parrots who
  croak and yell and chatter simply because exclamation
  points and interrogatories swim through the misty Chicago air.

Amy Leslie at the Fair   1893

2 No animal is so inexhaustible as an excited infant.

Ibid.

3 When these marvels of art and architecture begin to
  crumble the hearts of nations will stand still. Now the
  city blooms apace like a great white rose perfuming the
  clouds and smiling out upon the waters, but it is to
  fade! It is to die and that is one of its most exquisite
  enchantments.

Ibid.

4 As a singer you're a great dancer.

Quoted by George Primrose in
They All Sang by E. W. Marks   1934

283. Juliette Low
(1860–1927)

1 To put yourself in another's place requires real imagination, but by so doing each Girl Scout will be able to
live among others happily.

> Letter to Girl Scouts of America
> (October 31, 1923),* *Juliette Low*
> *and the Girl Scouts,* Anne Hyde Choate
> and Helen Ferris, eds. *1928p*

2 I am like the old woman who lived in the shoe! And
now the shoe has become too small for the many children and we must have a building that will be large
enough for us all.

> Ibid. (October 31, 1924)*

3 I hope that during the coming year we shall all remember the rules of this Girl Scouting game of ours. They
are: To play fair. To play in your place. To play for
your side and not for yourself. And as for the score, the
best thing in a game is the fun and not the result. . . .

> Ibid.

284. Harriet Monroe
(1860–1936)

1 Great ages of art come only when a wide-spread creative impulse meets an equally wide-spread impulse of
sympathy. . . . The people must grant a hearing to
the best poets they have else they will never have better.

> Quoted in "Harriet Monroe," *Famous*
> *American Women* by Hope Stoddard
> *1970p*

2 . . . poetry, "The Cinderella of the Arts."

> Ibid.

3 Poetry has been left to herself and blamed for ineffi-
ciency, a process as unreasonable as blaming the desert
for barrenness.

> Ibid.

* Ms. Low's birthday.

4 . . . poetry might become the fashion—a real danger, because the poets need an audience not fitful and superficial, but loyal and sincere.

Ibid.

285. Grandma Moses
(1860–1961)

1 I don't advise any one to take it [painting] up as a business proposition, unless they really have talent, and are crippled so as to deprive them of physical labor, Then with help they might make a living, But with taxes and income tax there is little money in that kind of art for the ordinary artis [sic] But I will say that I have did remarkable for one of my years, and experience, As for publicity, that Im [sic] too old to care for now. . . .

"How Do I Paint?," *The New York Times*   *May 11, 1947*

2 What a strange thing is memory, and hope; one looks backward, the other forward. The one is of today, the other is the Tomorrow. Memory is history recorded in our brain, memory is a painter, it paints pictures of the past and of the day.

Grandma Moses, My Life's History, Ch. 1, Aotto Kallir, ed.   *1947*

3 If I didn't start painting, I would have raised chickens.
Ibid., Ch. 3

286. Annie Oakley
(1860–1926)

1 I can shoot as well as you [her husband]. I think I should be able to go on and trade shot for shot with you. You take one shot while I hold the object for you, and then I take the next one, you acting as object holder for me.

Quoted in *Annie Oakley: Woman at Arms*, Ch. 4, by Courtney Ryley Cooper   *1927p*

2 The contents of his [Sitting Bull's] pockets were often emptied into the hands of small, ragged little boys, nor

274

could he understand how so much wealth should go
brushing by, unmindful of the poor.

Ibid., Ch. 7

287. Minna Antrim
(1861–?)

1 Satan will be obliged to extend his courtyard, since
men insist upon furnishing him with such quantities of
paving material.
Naked Truth and Veiled Allusions 1902

2 Doing all we can to promote our friend's happiness is
better than to continually drink to his prosperity.

Ibid.

3 A homely face and no figure have aided many women
heavenward.

Ibid.

4 Smart society is a body of autocrats in deadly warfare
against plutocrats.

Ibid.

5 Gratitude is the rosemary of the heart.

Ibid.

6 Illusion is the dust the devil throws in the eyes of the
foolish.

Ibid.

7 Somnolence in society is a crime; better chatter like a
magpie than blink like an owl.

Ibid.

8 Being pertinently impertinent and properly improper
has often won an impecunious man social prestige.

Ibid.

9 A fool bolts pleasure, then complains of moral indiges-
tion.

Ibid.

10 Man forgives woman anything save the wit to outwit
him.

Ibid.

11 Experience has no text books nor proxies. She demands
that her pupils answer her roll-call personally. Ibid.

12 Satiety is a mongrel that barks at the heels of plenty.

Ibid.

13 Politeness is a guilt-edged investment that seldom misses a dividend.

Ibid.

14 To be loved is to be fortunate, but to be hated is to achieve distinction.

Ibid.

15 Sympatica is the touchstone that leads to talent's highest altitude.

Ibid.

16 To know one's self is wisdom, but to know one's neighbor is genius.

Ibid.

17 Between condolence and consolation there flows an ocean of tears.

Ibid.

18 Saying smart things achieves eclat, but doing them wins substance.

Ibid.

19 Man is kind only to be cruel; woman cruel only to be kind.

Ibid.

20 Smiles are the soul's kisses. . . .

Ibid.

21 The "Green-Eyed Monster" causes much woe, but the absence of this ugly serpent argues the presence of a corpse whose name is Eros.

Ibid.

22 To control a man a woman must first control herself.

Ibid.

23 Many women plume themselves upon their impregnable virtue, who have never met *the* man.

Ibid.

24 Experience is a good teacher, but she sends in terrific bills.

Ibid.

25 Golden fetters hurt as cruelly as iron ones.　　Ibid.

288. Mary Byron
(1861–?)

* * *

1 On gossamer nights when the moon is low,
　　And stars in the mist are hiding,
　Over the hill where the foxgloves grow
　　You may see the fairies riding.

"The Fairy Thrall"

289. Mary Coleridge
(1861–1907)

1 The fruits of the tree of knowledge are various; he must
be strong indeed who can digest all of them.

*Gathered Leaves from the Prose
of Mary E. Coleridge*　1910p

2 Solitude affects some people like wine; they must not
take too much of it, for it flies to the head.

Ibid.

* * *

3 Into the land of dreams I long to go.
　　Bid me forget!

"Mandragora"

4 Where is delight? and what are pleasures now?—
Moths that a garment fret.

Ibid.

5 Mother of God! No lady thou:
Common woman of common earth!

"Our Lady"

6 We were young, we were merry, we were very, very
　　wise,
　　And the door stood open at our feast,
When there passed us a woman with the West in her
　　eyes,
　　And a man with his back to the East.

"Unwelcome"

290. Clemence Dane
(1861–1965)

1 SYDNEY. It's extraordinary to me—whenever you middle-aged people want to excuse yourselves for anything you've done that you know you oughtn't have done, you say it was the war.
A Bill of Divorcement, Act I   1921

2 HILARY. I was a dead man. You know what the dead do in heaven? They sit on their golden chairs and sicken for home.
Ibid.

3 MARGARET. It's the things I might have said that fester.
Ibid., Act II

4 DR. ALLIOT. That young, young generation found out, out of their own unhappiness, the war taught them, what peace couldn't teach us—that when conditions are evil it is not your duty to submit—that when conditions are evil, your duty, in spite of protests, in spite of sentiment, your duty, though you trample on the bodies of your nearest and dearest to do it, though you bleed your own heart white, your duty is to see that those conditions are changed. If your laws forbid you, you must change your laws. If your church forbids you, you must change your church. And if your God forbids you, why then, you must change your God.
Ibid.

5 ZEDEKIAH. How else should I treat an idol but tread on it?
Naboth's Vineyard, Act I, Sc. 1   1925

6 JEZEBEL. How often must I stoop to hold you up?
Ibid., Sc. 2

7 JEZEBEL. Toss back the ball! Shall I flinch because a heavy hand flings it? At least it is a friend's hand.
Ibid.

8 JEZEBEL. What is it to sit on a throne? Weariness! But to shift the dolls that sit there, that's a game, Jehu, for a man or a woman! Let me teach you my game!
Ibid., Act II, Sc. 1

9 I think of our century as a sixty-year-old housewife in love with modern ideas.

> Speech, "Approach to Drama," London   *1961*

10 I suppose there is not one of us here who has not, at some time or other, evoked the good in which we believe to take our part, to speak for us, to put our case to the invisible evil (if it is evil) that thwarts and destroys our efforts toward happiness. . . .

> Ibid.

291. Dorothy Dix
(1861–1951)

1 It is only the women whose eyes have been washed clear with tears who get the broad vision that makes them little sisters to all the world.

> *Dorothy Dix, Her Book,* Introduction   *1926*

2 I have learned in the great University of Hard Knocks a philosophy that no woman who has had an easy life ever acquires. I have learned to live each day as it comes, and not to borrow trouble by dreading tomorrow. It is the dark menace of the future that makes cowards of us.

> Ibid.

3 Now one of the great reasons why so many husbands and wives make shipwreck of their lives together is because a man is always seeking for happiness, while a woman is on a perpetual still hunt for trouble.

> Ibid., Ch. 1

4 So many persons think divorce a panacea for every ill, who find out, when they try it, that the remedy is worse than the disease.

> Ibid., Ch. 13

5 Confession is always weakness. The grave soul keeps its own secrets, and takes its own punishment in silence.

> Ibid., Ch. 20

6 In reality, the mother who rears her children up to be monsters of selfishness has no right to expect appreciation and gratitude from them because she has done them as ill a turn as one human being can do another. She has warped their characters.   Ibid., Ch. 44

7 Extravagance. The price of indulging yourself in your youth in the things you cannot afford is poverty and dependence in your old age.

Ibid., Ch. 53

8 Women have changed in their relationship to men, but men stand pat just where Adam did when it comes to dealing with women.

Ibid., Ch. 59

9 For in all the world there are no people so piteous and forlorn as those who are forced to eat the bitter bread of dependency in their old age, and find how steep are the stairs of another man's house. Wherever they go they know themselves unwelcome. Wherever they are, they feel themselves a burden. There is no humiliation of the spirit they are not forced to endure. Their hearts are scarred all over with the stabs from cruel and callous speeches.

Ibid., Ch. 69

* * *

10 Nobody wants to kiss when they are hungry.

News Item

11 The reason that husbands and wives do not understand each other is because they belong to different sexes.

Ibid.

292. Frances Greville
(1861–1938)

1 Love and Misery proverbially go together. There is a popular notion . . . that a lover could not get along without a little misery. . . .

Quoted in the *Anglo-Saxon Review*   *June, 1900*

293. Louise Imogen Guiney
(1861–1920)

1 To be Anonymous is better than to be Alexander. Cowley said it engagingly, in his little essay on *Obscurity:* "*Bene qui latuit, bene vixit*; he lives well that has lain well hidden." The pleasantest condition of life is in incognito.

"On the Delights of an Incognito," *Patrins*   *1897*

2 A certain sesquipedalianism* is natural to Americans: witness our press editorials, our Fourth of July orations, and the public messages of all our Presidents since Lincoln.

Quoted in *Scribner's Magazine*   *January, 1911*

3 Quotations (such as have point and lack triteness) from the great old authors are an act of filial reverence on the part of the quoter, and a blessing to a public grown superficial and external.   Ibid.

* * *

4 A short life in the saddle, Lord!
Not long life by the fire.   "The Knight Errant," St. 2

5 He has done with roofs and men,
Open, Time, and let him pass.   "Ballad of Kenelm"

6 High above hate I dwell,
O storms! Farewell.

"The Sanctuary"

7 The fears of what may come to pass,
I cast them all away,
Among the clover scented grass,
Among the new-mown hay.

"A Song from Sylvan," St. 2

8 The fool who redeemed us once of our folly,
And the smiter that healed us, our right John Brown!
"John Brown: A Paradox"

9 To fear not sensible failure,
Nor covet the game at all,
But fighting, fighting, fighting,
Die, driven against the wall.

"The Kings"

294. Gracy Hebard
(1861–1936)

1 These indians [Shoshones] believe also that God pulled out the upper teeth of the elk because the elk were meant to be eaten by the indians, and not the indians by the elk.

Washakie   1930

* Use of long words.

2 The buffaloes were the original engineers, as they followed the lay of the land and the run of the water. These buffalo paths became indian trails, which always pointed out the easiest way across the mountain barriers. The white man followed in these footpaths. The iron trail finished the road.

The Pathbreakers from River to Ocean, Ch. 9   1932

3 While we are enjoying the luxuries of this new era of the great west let us not forget to honor those who endured hardships and privations, encountered dangers and peril; yes, even gave up their lives to make these things possible. . . . It is all a story that has never had its equal in the world's history. The great American desert is no more.

Ibid.

295. Katharine Tynan Hinkson
(1861–1931)

* * *

1 Good is an orchard. . . .

"Of an Orchard"

2 O you poor folk in cities,
A thousand, thousand pities!
Heaping the fairy gold that withers and dies;
One field in the June weather
Is worth all the gold ye gather,
One field in June weather—one Paradise.

"June Song"

3 The dear Lord God, of His glories weary—
    Christ our Lord had the heart of a boy—
Made Him birds in a moment merry,
    Bade them soar and sing for His joy.

"The Making of Birds"

4 To me the wonderful charge was given,
    I, even a little ass, did go
Bearing the very weight of heaven;
    So I crept cat-foot, sure and slow.

"The Ass Speaks"

296. Alice Hubbard
(1861–1915)

1 [Thomas] Paine was a Quaker by birth and a friend by
nature. The world was his home, mankind were his
friends, to do good was his religion.
An American Bible, Introduction   *1911*

297. Jessie Brown Pounds
(1861–?)

1 Somewhere, Somewhere, Beautiful Isle of
    Somewhere,
  Land of the true, where we live anew,
Beautiful Isle of Somewhere.
"Beautiful Isle of Somewhere"   *1901*

298. Corinne Roosevelt Robinson
(1861–1933)

1 Serene amid the clamor and the strife
  She bore the lily of a blameless life!
"To F.W.," *The Call of Brotherhood
and Other Poems*   *1912*

2 Stretch out your hand and take the world's wide gift
Of Joy and Beauty.
Ibid., "Stretch Out Your Hand"

3 Though Love be deeper, Friendship is more wide. . . .
Ibid., "Friendship"

4 Is life worth living?
  Aye, with the best of us,
  Heights of us, depths of us,—
Life is the test of us!
"Life, A Question," *One Woman to Another*   *1914*

5 Nothing is as difficult as to achieve results in this world
if one is filled full of great tolerance and the milk of
human kindness. The person who achieves must generally be a one-ideaed individual, concentrated entirely

on that one idea, and ruthless in his aspect toward other men and other ideas.

My Brother Theodore Roosevelt, Ch. 1   *1921*

6   Spirit of the air,
And of the seas, and of the fragrant earth,
I thank thee that thou didst attend my birth
To dower me with wonder. . . .

"The Gift of Wonder," *Out of Nymph*   *1930*

7 Thy love was like a royal accolade. . . .

Ibid., "Afterward"

299. Ernestine Schumann-Heink
(1861–1936)

1 One can never either hear or see himself, and there is a need—if one would make real progress in art—for constant criticism.

Quoted in *Schumann-Heink, the Last of the Titans* by Mary Lawton   *1935*

2 This shall be my parting word—know what you want to do—then do it. Make straight for your goal and go undefeated in spirit to the end.

Ibid.

300. Carrie Jacobs Bond
(1862–1946)

1 When God made up this world of ours,
    He made it long and wide,
And meant that it should shelter all,
    And none should be denied.

"Friends," St. 1, *Little Stories in Verse*   *1905*

2 Kind words smooth all the "Paths o' Life"
    And smiles make burdens light,
And uncomplainin' friends can make
    A daytime out o' night.

Ibid., "The Path o' Life," St. 11

3 And we find at the end of a perfect day,
The soul of a friend we've made.

"A Perfect Day," St. 2   *1926*

301. Edith Cooper
(1862–1913)

Co-author with Katharine Bradley. See 200:1–3.

302. Ella Higginson
(1862–1940)

* * *

1 Forgive you?—Oh, of course, dear,
    A dozen times a week!
We women were created
    Forgiveness but to speak.
                "Wearing Out Love," St. 1

2 One leaf is for hope, and one is for faith,
    And one is for love, you know,
And God put another in for luck.
                "Four-Leaf Clover," St. 2

303. Ada Leverson
(1862–1933)

1 Absurdly improbable things happen in real life as well
as in weak literature.
          The Twelfth Hour   1907

304. Ts'ai-t'ien Chang
(1862–1945)

1 ". . . I wanted to study and not to marry. My brother
and Mao Tse-tung also hated marriage and declared
they would never marry. . . ."
          Quoted in *Women in Modern China*
          by Helen Foster Snow   *1967p*

305. Ida B. Wells
(1862–1931)

1 Let the Afro-American depend on no party, but on
himself for his salvation. Let him continue to educa-

tion, character, and above all, put money in his purse. When he has a dollar in his pocket and many more in the bank, he can move from injustice and oppression and no one to say him nay. When he has money, and plenty of it, parties and races will become his servants.

"Iola's Southern Field," *The New York Age*   November *11, 1892*

2 The first excuse given to the civilized world for the murder of unoffending Negroes was the necessity of the white man to repress and stamp out "race riots." . . . It was always a remarkable feature in these insurrections and riots that only Negroes were killed during the rioting, and that all the white men escaped unharmed.

A Red Record   1895

3 True chivalry respects all womanhood, and no one who reads the record, as it is written in the faces of the million mulattoes in the South, will for a minute conceive that the southern white man had a very chivalrous regard for the honor due the women of his race or respect for the womanhood which circumstances placed in his power. . . . Virtue knows no color lines, and the chivalry which depends upon complexion of skin and texture of hair can command no honest respect.

Ibid.

4 I felt that one had better die fighting against injustice than to die like a dog or a rat in a trap. I had already determined to sell my life as dearly as possible if attacked. I felt if I could take one lyncher with me, this would even up the score a little bit.

The Autobiography of Ida B. Wells, Alfreda M. Duster, ed.   *1970p*

306. Edith Wharton
(1862–1937)

1 . . . he had been drawn to her by the unperturbed gaiety which kept her fresh and elastic at an age when most women's activities are growing either slack or febrile.

"The Other Two," Ch. 1, *The Descent of Man   1904*

2 A New York divorce is in itself a diploma of virtue. . . .

Ibid.

3 People shook their heads over him, however, and one grudging friend, to whom he affirmed that he took the step with his eyes open, replied oracularly: "Yes—and with your ears shut."

Ibid.

4 "It feels uncommonly queer to have enough cash to pay one's bills. I'd have sold my soul for it a few years ago!"

Ibid., Ch. 3

5 A man would rather think that his wife has been brutalized by her first husband than that the process has been reversed.

Ibid.

6 "I don't know as I think a man is entitled to rights he hasn't known how to hold on to. . . ."

Ibid., Ch. 4

7 Her pliancy was beginning to sicken him. Had she really no will of her own . . . ? She was "as easy as an old shoe"—a shoe that too many feet had worn.

Ibid.

8 He had fancied that a woman can shed her past like a man.

Ibid.

9 If he paid for each day's comfort with the small change of his illusions, he grew daily to value the comfort more and set less store upon the coin.   Ibid.

10 She keeps on being queenly in her own room with the door shut.   *The House of Mirth*   1905

11 When she spoke it was only to complain, and to complain of things not in his power to remedy; and to check a tendency to impatient retort he had first formed the habit of not answering her, and finally of thinking of other things while she talked.

Ethan Frome, Ch. 4   1911

12 Almost everybody in the neighborhood had "troubles," frankly localized and specified; but only the chosen had "complications." To have them was in itself a distinction, though it was also, in most cases, a death-warrant. People struggled on for years with "troubles," but they almost always succumbed to "complications."

Ibid., Ch. 7

13 . . . they seemed to come suddenly upon happiness as if they had surprised a butterfly in the winter woods. . . .
Ibid., Ch. 9

14 "Oh, what good'll writing do? I want to put my hand out and touch you. I want to do for you and care for you. I want to be there when you're sick and when you're lonesome."
Ibid.

15 Mrs. Ballinger is one of the ladies who pursue Culture in bands, as though it were dangerous to meet it alone.
"Xingu," *Xingu and Other Stories*   1916

16 To [Henry] James's intimates, however, these elaborate hesitancies, far from being an obstacle, were like a cobweb bridge flung from his mind to theirs, an invisible passage over which one knew that slur-footed ironies, veiled jokes, tiptoe malices, were stealing to explode a huge laugh at one's feet.
A Backward Glance, Ch. 8   1934

* * *

17 My little old dog:
A heart-beat at my feet.
"A Lyrical Epigram"

18 There are two ways of spreading light: to be
The candle or the mirror that receives it.
"Vesalius in Zante"

307. Annie Jump Cannon
(1863–1941)

1 . . . a life spent in the routine of science need not destroy the attractive human element of a woman's nature.
Quoted in *Science*   June 30, 1911

308. Elaine Goodale
(1863–1953)

1 We feel our savage kind,—
And thus alone with conscious meaning wear
The Indian's moccasin.
"Moccasin Flower," *In Berkshire with
the Wild Flowers*   1879

2 Bronzed and molded by wind and sun,
Maddening, gladdening everyone
With a gypsy beauty full and fine,—
A health to the crimson columbine!

"Columbine"

3 Nature lies disheveled, pale,
   With her feverish lips apart,—
Day by day the pulses fail,
   Nearer to her bounding heart.

"Goldenrod"

309. Mary Church Terrell
(1863–1954)

1 Lynching is the aftermath of slavery. The white men who shoot negroes to death and flay them alive, and the white women who apply flaming torches to their oil-soaked bodies today, are the sons and daughters of women who had but little, if any, compassion on the race when it was enslaved.

"Lynching from a Negro's Point of View," *North American Review*   *June, 1904*

2 The whole country seems tired of hearing about the black man's woes. The wrongs of the Irish, of the Armenians, of the Roumanian and Russian Jews, of the exiles of Russia and of every other oppressed people upon the face of the globe, can arouse sympathy and fire the indignation of the American public, while they seem to be all but indifferent to the murderous assaults upon the negroes in the South.

Ibid.

3 As a colored woman I might enter Washington any night, a stranger in a strange land, and walk miles without finding a place to lay my head. . . . The colored man alone is thrust out of the hotels of the national capital like a leper.

"What It Means to Be Colored in the Capital of the United States" (1907),
A Colored Woman in a White World   *1940*

4 It is impossible for any white person in the United States, no matter how sympathetic and broad, to realize what life would mean to him if his incentive to effort

were suddenly snatched away. To the lack of incentive to effort, which is the awful shadow under which we live, may be traced the wreck and ruin of scores of colored youth. And surely no where in the world do oppression and persecution based solely on the color of the skin appear more hateful and hideous than in the capital of the United States, because the chasm between the principles upon which this Government was founded, in which it still professes to believe, and those which are daily practiced under the protection of the flag, yawn so wide and deep.

Ibid.

5 Please stop using the word "Negro." . . . We are the only human beings in the world with fifty-seven variety of complexions who are classed together as a single racial unit. Therefore, we are really truly colored people, and that is the only name in the English language which accurately describes us.

Ibid., Letter to the Editor,
The Washington Post   *May 14, 1949*

6 Some of our group say they will continue to classify us as Negroes, until an individual referred to as such will be proud of that name. But that is a case of wishful thinking and nothing else.

Ibid.

310. Margot Asquith
(1864–1945)

1 Riches are overestimated in the Old Testament: the good and successful man received too many animals, wives, apes, she-goats and peacocks.

*The Autobiography of Margot
Asquith,* Vols. I and II   *1920–1922*

2 To marry a man out of pity is folly; and, if you think you are going to influence the kind of fellow who has "never had a chance, poor devil," you are profoundly mistaken. One can only influence the strong characters in life, not the weak; and it is the height of vanity to suppose that you can make an honest man of anyone.

Ibid., Ch. 6

3 There are big men, men of intellect, men of talent and men of action; but the great man is difficult to find, and it needs—apart from discernment—a certain graveness to find him. The Almighty is a wonderful handicapper: He will not give us everything.

Ibid., Ch. 7

4 The first element of greatness is fundamental humbleness (this should not be confused with servility); the second is freedom from self; the third is intrepid courage, which, taken in its widest interpretation, generally goes with truth; and the fourth—the power to love—although I have put it last, is the rarest.

Ibid.

5 Rich men's houses are seldom beautiful, rarely comfortable, and never original. It is a constant source of surprise to people of moderate means to observe how little a big fortune contributes to Beauty.

Ibid., Ch. 17

6 Haunted from my early youth by the transitoriness and pathos of life, I was aware that it was not enough to say, "I am doing no harm," I ought to be testing myself daily, and asking what I was really achieving.

My Impressions of America, Ch. 4   *1922*

7 Journalism over here [in America] is not only an obsession but a drawback that cannot be overrated. Politicians are frightened of the press, and in the same way as bull-fighting has a brutalising effect upon Spain (of which she is unconscious), headlines of murder, rape, and rubbish, excite and demoralise the American public.

Ibid., Ch. 10

8 It is always dangerous to generalise, but the American people, while infinitely generous, are a hard and strong race and, but for the few cemeteries I have seen, I am inclined to think they never die.

Ibid., Ch. 14

9 The ingrained idea that, because there is no king and they despise titles, the Americans are a free people is pathetically untrue. . . . There is a perpetual interference with personal liberty over there that would not be tolerated in England for a week.

Ibid., Ch. 17

10 . . . her one idea was to exercise a moderating influence; and without knowing it she would in a subtle and disparaging manner check the enthusiasm, dim the glow, and cramp the extravagance of everyone round her.

Octavia, Ch. 1   1928

11 "Women are like horses, and should never be ridden on the curb."

Ibid., Ch. 9

12 She wanted to *give* life; to warm the blood and kindle the hope of drab and cautious people. You could not make others live unless you had life yourself.

Ibid., Ch. 12

13 She was not an individual when she was with him, she was an audience—an audience that only came in at the end. When people clapped, was it the last sentence, or the whole speech they were applauding? Or was it merely relief that the speech was over?

Ibid.

14 Life was cruel, demanding wisdom from the young before they had the chance of acquiring it! Innocence was admired, ignorance despised: yet, in their effects, they had a dangerous resemblance.

Ibid., Ch. 22

311. Elinor Glyn
(1864–1943)

1 Marriage is the aim and end of all sensible girls, because it is the meaning of life.

"Letters to Caroline," *Harper's Bazaar*   September, 1913

312. Margaret P. Sherwood
(1864–1955)

* * *

1 Whisper some kindly word, to bless
A wistful soul who understands
That life is but one long caress
Of gentle words and gentle hands.

"In Memoriam—Leo: A Yellow Cat"

313. Wenonah Stevens Abbott
(1865–1950)

* * *

1 To-day the journey is ended,
   I have worked out the mandates of fate;
Naked, alone, undefended,
   I knock at the Uttermost Gate.

"A Soul's Soliloquy"

314. Evangeline Booth
(1865–1950)

* * *

1 Drink has drained more blood,
Hung more crepe,
Sold more houses,
Plunged more people into bankruptcy,
Armed more villains,
Slain more children,
Snapped more wedding rings,
Defiled more innocence,
Blinded more eyes,
Twisted more limbs,
Dethroned more reason,
Wrecked more manhood,
Dishonored more womanhood,
Broken more hearts,
Blasted more lives,
Driven more to suicide, and
Dug more graves than any other poisoned
Scourge that ever swept its death-
Dealing waves across the world.

"Good Housekeeping"

315. Mrs. Patrick Campbell
(1865–1940)

1 I believe I was impatient with unintelligent people from
the moment I was born: a tragedy—for I am myself
three-parts a fool.

My Life and Some Letters, Ch. 2   *1922*

2 I remember a certain dinner party given for me by a well-known Jewish financier, and being asked by him at table in an earnest, curious voice, what I kept in a small locket I wore on a chain round my neck. Everyone stopped talking and listened for my answer. I replied gravely, "One hair of a Jew's moustache."

Ibid., Ch. 6

3 To be made to hold his [George Bernard Shaw's] tongue is the greatest insult you can offer him—though he might be ready with a poker to make you hold yours.

Ibid., Ch. 16

4 . . . there can be a fundamental gulf of gracelessness in a human heart which neither our love nor our courage can bridge.

Ibid., Ch. 19

5 Wedlock—the deep, deep peace of the double bed after the hurly-burly of the chaise-longue.

Quoted in *Jennie* (1914), Vol. II,
by Ralph G. Martin   *1971p*

316. Edith Louisa Cavell
(1865–1915)

1 I realize that patriotism is not enough. I must have no hatred or bitterness towards anyone.

Last Words, Quoted in *The Times*
(London)   *October 23, 1915p*

317. Elsie De Wolfe
(1865–1950)

1 It is the personality of the mistress that the home expresses. Men are forever guests in our homes, no matter how much happiness they may find there.

The House in Good Taste, Ch. 1   *1920*

2 What a joyous thing is color! How influenced we all are by it, even if we are unconscious of how our sense of restfulness has been brought about.

Ibid., Ch. 6

3 It does not matter whether one paints a picture, writes a poem, or carves a statue, simplicity is the mark of a master-hand. Don't run away with the idea that it is easy to cook simply. It requires a long apprenticeship.

"Why I Wrote This Book," *Recipes for Successful Dining* 1934

318. Minnie Fiske
(1865–1932)

1 You must make your own blunders, must cheerfully accept your own mistakes as part of the scheme of things. You must not allow yourself to be advised, cautioned, influenced, persuaded this way and that.

Letter to Alexander Woollcott (1908), Quoted in *Mrs. Fiske* by Alexander Woollcott 1917

2 Among the most disheartening and dangerous of . . . advisors, you will often find those closest to you, your dearest friends, members of your own family, perhaps, loving, anxious, and knowing nothing whatever. . . .

Ibid.

3 "Bosh! do not talk to me about the repertory idea. It is an outworn, needless, impossible, *harmful* scheme. . . . This, my friend, is an age of specialization, and in such an age the repertory theatre is an anachronism, a ludicrous anachronism."

Ibid., Ch. 1

4 But there are times when the actor is an artist far greater and more creative than his material. . . .

Ibid., Ch. 5

5 The essence of acting is the conveyance of truth through the medium of the actor's mind and person. The science of acting deals with the perfecting of that medium. The great actors are the luminous ones. They are the great conductors of the stage.

Ibid.

319. Yvette Guilbert
(1865–1944)

1 Try to make a woman who does badly on the stage
understand that she might do better in trade, or in any
other occupation. She will never believe you. It seems
impossible to her to make linen garments or millinery,
but very simple to enact the dandy on the stage.
La Vedette 1902

2 Caper without cease, and caper again. . . . You are
gaiety, which passes away.

Ibid.

3 All women are alike. All demand stimulation for their
sense. . . . These ladies of society also feel the need
of language strong enough to stimulate them. . . .
Licentiousness takes them all in the same manner.

Ibid.

4 One cannot remain the same. Art is a mirror which
should show many reflections, and the artist should not
always show the same face, or the face becomes a
mask.

Ibid.

320. Laurence Hope
(1865–1904)

1 For this is wisdom: to love, to live,
To take what Fate, or the Gods, may give.
"The Teak Forest,"
India's Love Lyrics 1922

2 Speed passion's ebb as you greet its flow—
To have, to hold, and in time let go!

Ibid.

3 Less than the dust beneath thy chariot wheel,
Less than the weed that grows beside thy door,
Less than the rust that never stained thy sword,
Less than the need thou hast in life of me,
　　Even less am I.
Ibid., "Less Than the Dust," St. 1

4 Pale hands I loved beside the Shalimar,
  Where are you now? Who lies beneath your spell?

> Ibid., "Kashmiri Song," St. 1

* * *

5 Men should be judged, not by their tint of skin,
  The Gods they serve, the Vintage that they drink,
  Nor by the way they fight, or love, or sin,
  But by the quality of thought they think.

> "Men Should Be Judged"

6 Often devotion to virtue arises from sated desire.

> "I Arise and Go Down to the River," St. 6

7 Yet I, this little while ere I go hence,
  Love very lightly now, in self-defence.

> "Verse by Taj Mahomed"

8 Your work was waste? Maybe your share
  Lay in the hour you laughed and kissed;
  Who knows but that your son shall wear
  The laurels that his father missed?

> "The Masters"

321. Anandabai Joshee
(1865–1887)

1 Holes are bored through the lower part of the left nos-
  tril for the nose-ring, and all around the edge of the ear
  for jewels. This may appear barbarous to the foreign
  eye; to us it is a beauty! Everything changes with the
  clime.

> Letter to Mrs. Carpenter (1880), Quoted in *The
> Life of Anandabai Joshee* by Caroline H. Dall
> *1888p*

2 Your American widows may have difficulties and inconveniences to struggle with, but weighed in the scale
  against ours, all of them put together are but as a parti-
  cle against a mountain.

> Ibid.

3 When I think over the sufferings of women in India in
  all ages, I am impatient to see the Western light dawn
  as the harbinger of emancipation.

> Ibid.

4 Had there been no difficulties and no thorns in the way, then man would have been in his primitive state and no progress made in civilisation and mental culture.

> Ibid., Letter to Her Aunt (August 27, 1881)

5 . . . I regard irreligious people as pioneers. If there had been no priesthood the world would have advanced ten thousand times better than it has now.

> Ibid.

322. Nellie Melba
(1865?–1931)

1 The first rule in opera is the first rule in life: see to everything yourself.

> *Melodies and Memories* 1925

2 Music is not written in red, white and blue. It is written in the heart's blood of the composer.

> Ibid.

3 One of the drawbacks of Fame is that one can never escape from it. Ibid.

323. Baroness Orczy
(1865–1947)

1 A surging, seething, murmuring crowd of beings that are human only in name, for to the eye and ear they seem naught but savage creatures, animated by vile passions and by the lust of vengeance and of hate.

> *The Scarlet Pimpernel*, Ch. 1 1905

2 Marguerite St. Just was from principle and by conviction a republican—equality of birth was her motto—inequality of fortune was in her eyes a mere untoward accident, but the only inequality she admitted was that of talent. "Money and titles may be hereditary," she would say, "but brains are not. . . ." Ibid., Ch. 6

3 "I sometimes wish you had not so many lofty virtues. . . . I assure you little sins are far less dangerous and uncomfortable. But you *will* be prudent?" she added earnestly. Ibid., Ch. 7

4 "We seek him here, we see him there,
    Those Frenchies seek him everywhere.
    Is he in heaven?—Is he in hell?
    That damned elusive Pimpernel?"   Ibid., Ch. 12

5 It is only when we are very happy that we can bear to
    gaze merrily upon the vast and limitless expanse of wa-
    ter, rolling on and on with such persistent, irritating
    monotony, to the accompaniment of our thoughts,
    whether grave or gay. When they are gay, the waves
    echo their gaiety; but when they are sad, then every
    breaker, as it rolls, seems to bring additional sadness,
    and to speak to us of hopelessness and of the pettiness
    of all our joys.   Ibid., Ch. 21

6 The weariest nights, the longest days, sooner or later
    must perforce come to an end.   Ibid., Ch. 22

7 An apology? Bah! Disgusting! cowardly! beneath the
    dignity of any gentleman, however wrong he might be.
                        I Will Repay, Prologue   1906

8 "To love is to feel one being in the world at one with
    us, our equal in sin as well as in virtue. To love, for us
    men, is to clasp one woman with our arms, feeling that
    she lives and breathes just as we do, suffers as we do,
    thinks with us, loves with us, and, above all, sins with
    us. Your mock saint who stands in a niche is not a
    woman if she have not suffered, still less a woman if
    she have not sinned. Fall at the feet of your idol as you
    wish, but drag her down to your level after that—the
    only level she should ever reach, that of your heart."
                                            Ibid., Ch. 7

9 "We are not masters of our heart, Messire."
                        Leatherface, Bk. I, Ch. 3   1918

10 "But a wife! . . . What matters what she thinks and
    feels? if she be cold or loving, gentle or shrewish, sensi-
    tive to a kind word or callous to cruelty? A wife! . . .
    Well! so long as no other man hath ever kissed her lips—
    for that would hurt masculine vanity and wound the
    pride of possession!"
                                            Ibid.

11 This, mayhap, was not logic, but it was something
    more potent, more real than logic—the soft insinuating
    voice of Sentiment. . . .
                                    Ibid., Bk. II, Ch. 5

12 A blind, unreasoning rage, an irresistible thirst for revenge: a black hatred of all those placed in authority;
of all those who were rich, who were independent or
influential, filled André Vallon's young soul to the exclusion of every other thought and every other aspiration.

> *A Child of the Revolution,*
> Bk. II, Ch. 5 *1932*

13 "My dear, since the beginning of all times, men have
perpetrated horrors against one another. It is the devil
in them, but the devil would have no power over men
if God did not allow it. Could He not, if He so willed,
quell this revolution with His Word? Must we not
rather bow to His will and try to realize that something
great, something good, something, at any rate, that is in
accordance with the great scheme of the universe must
in the end come out of all this sorrow?"

> Ibid., Bk. III, Ch. 31

324. Emily James Putnam
(1865–1944)

1 But the typical lady everywhere tends to the feudal
habit of mind. In contemporary society she is an archa-
ism, and can hardly understand herself unless she
knows her own history.

> *The Lady,* Introduction *1910*

2 Sentimentally the lady has established herself as the criterion of a community's civilisation. . . . When it is
flatly put to her that she cannot become a human being
and yet retain her privileges as a non-combatant, she
often enough decides for etiquette.

> Ibid.

3 Maternity is on the face of it an unsocial experience.
The selfishness that a woman has learned to stifle or to
dissemble where she alone is concerned, blooms freely
and unashamed on behalf of her offspring.

> Ibid.

4 Until changing economic conditions made the thing actually happen, struggling early society would hardly
have guessed that woman's road to gentility would lie
through doing nothing at all.

> Ibid.

325. Louisa Thomas
(1865–?)

* * *

1 Charm is the measure of attraction's power
To chain the fleeting fancy of the hour.
"What Is Charm?," St. 1

326. Mary A. Arnim
(1866–?)

1 A marriage, she found, with someone of a different
breed is fruitful of small rubs. . . .
Mr. Skeffington, Ch. 1   *1940*

2 Life was certainly a queer business—so brief, yet such
a lot of it; so substantial, yet in a few years, which
behaved like minutes, all scattered and anyhow.
Ibid.

3 She had been dragged in the most humiliating of all
dusts, the dust reserved for older women who let themselves be approached, on amorous lines, by boys. . . .
It had all been pure vanity, all just a wish, in these wan-
ing days of hers, still to feel power, still to have the
assurance of her beauty and its effects.
Ibid., Ch. 3

4 . . . without it [love], without, anyhow, the capacity
for it, people didn't seem to be much good. Dry as
bones, cold as stones, they seemed to become, when
love was done; inhuman, indifferent, self-absorbed,
numb.   Ibid., Ch. 5

5 Strange that the vanity which accompanies beauty—
excusable, perhaps, when there is such great beauty, or
at any rate understandable—should persist after the
beauty was gone.   Ibid., Ch. 6

6 How could one live, while such things were going on?
How could one endure consciousness, except by giving
oneself up wholly and forever to helping, and comfort-
ing, and at last, at last, perhaps healing?
Ibid., Ch. 11

301

327. Martha Dickinson Bianchi
(1866–1943)

* * *

1 Deeper than chords that search the soul and die,
  Mocking to ashes color's hot array,—
  Closer than touch,—within our hearts they lie—
  The words we do not say.
                              "The Words We Do Not Say"

328. Voltairine de Cleyre
(1866–1912)

1 I had never seen a book or heard a word to help me in
  my loneliness.
                  "The Making of an Anarchist," *The
  Selected Works of Voltairine de Cleyre*   *1914p*

2 And Now, Humanity, I turn to you;
  I consecrate my service to the world!
                  Ibid., "The Burial of My Past Self" (1885)

3 [Anarchism] . . . not only the denial of authority,
  not only a new economy, but a revision of the principles of morality. It means . . . self-responsibility, not
  leader-worship.
                                      Ibid. (c. 1887)

4 Consider the soul reflected on the advertising page. . . .
  Commercial man has set his image therein; let him regard himself when he gets time.
                                                Ibid.

5 [Language] . . . this great instrument which men
  have jointly built . . . every word the mystic embodiment of a thousand years of vanished passion, hope,
  desire, thought.
                                                Ibid.

6 Do I repent? Yes, I do; but wait till I tell you of what I
  repent and why. I repent that I ever believed a man
  could be anything but a living lie!
                                      Ibid., "Betrayed"

7 I die, as I have lived, a free spirit, an Anarchist, owing
  no allegiance to rulers, heavenly or earthly. . . . If my

302

comrades wish to do aught for my memory, let them print my poems.

Ibid., Journal (1912)

329. Annie Johnson Flint
(1866–1932)

* * *

1 Have you come to the Red Sea place in your life
   Where, in spite of all you can do,
There is no way out, there is no way back,
   There is no other way but through?

"At the Place of the Sea," St. 1

2 The thrones are rocking to their fall—
It is the twilight of the Kings!

"The Twilight of the Kings"

330. Dora Read Goodale
(1866–1915)

* * *

1 The earth and sky, the day and night
Are melted in her depth of blue.

"Blue Violets"

2 The modest, lowly violet
In leaves of tender green inset,
So rich she cannot hide from view,
But covers all the bank with blue.

"Spring Scatters Far and Wide"

331. Eleanor Prescott Hammond
(1866–1933)

1 Prone on my back I greet arriving day,
   A day no different than the one just o'er;
When I will be, to practically say,
   Considerably like I have been before.
Why then get up? Why wash, why eat, why pray?
   —Oh, leave me lay!

"Oh, Leave Me Lay,"
Atlantic Monthly   August, 1922

332. Beatrix Potter
(1866–1943)

1 Once upon a time there were four little Rabbits, and their names were—Flopsy, Mopsy, Cottontail, and Peter.

The Tale of Peter Rabbit   1904

2 The water was all slippy-sloppy in the larder and the back passage. But Mr. Jeremy liked getting his feet wet; nobody ever scolded him, and he never caught a cold.

The Tale of Mr. Jeremy Fisher   1906

333. Annie Sullivan
(1866–1936)

1 I have thought about it a great deal, and the more I think the more certain I am that obedience is the gateway through which knowledge, yes, and love, too, enter the mind of the child.

Letter (March 11, 1887),
Quoted in *The Story of My Life*
by Helen Keller   1903

2 My heart is singing for joy this morning. A miracle has happened! The light of understanding has shone upon my little pupil's mind, and behold, all things are changed!

Ibid. (March 20, 1887)

3 I am beginning to suspect all elaborate and special systems of education. They seem to me to be built upon the supposition that every child is a kind of idiot who must be taught to think.

Ibid. (May 8, 1887)

4 It is a rare privilege to watch the birth, growth, and first feeble struggles of a living mind. . . .

Ibid. (May 22, 1887)

5 It's queer how ready people always are with advice in any real or imaginary emergency, and no matter how many times experience has shown them to be wrong,

they continue to set forth their opinions, as if they had received them from the Almighty!

Ibid. (June 12, 1887)

6 It's a great mistake, I think, to put children off with falsehoods and nonsense, when their growing powers of observation and discrimination excite in them a desire to know about things.

Ibid. (August 28, 1887)

7 . . . people seldom see the halting and painful steps by which the most insignificant success is achieved.

Ibid. (October 30, 1887)

8 She likes stories that make her cry—I think we all do, its so nice to feel sad when you've nothing particular to be sad about.

Ibid. (December 12, 1887)

9 I see no sense in "faking" conversation for the sake of teaching language. It's stupid and deadening to pupil and teacher. Talk should be natural and have for its object an exchange of ideas.

Ibid. (January 1, 1888)

10 The truth is not wonderful enough to suit the newspapers; so they enlarge upon it and invent ridiculous embellishments.

Ibid. (March 4, 1888)

11 Why, it is as easy to teach the name of an idea, if it is clearly formulated in the child's mind, as to teach the name of an object.

Ibid. (May 15, 1888)

12 Language grows out of life, out of its needs and experiences. . . . *Language* and *knowledge* are indissolubly connected; they are interdependent. Good work in language presupposes and depends on a real knowledge of things.

Ibid., Speech, American Association to Promote the Teaching of Speech to the Deaf (July, 1894)

13 I never taught language for the PURPOSE of teaching it; but invariably used language as a medium for the communication of *thought*; thus the learning of language was *coincident* with the acquisition of knowledge.

Ibid.

334. Pearl Craigie
(1867–1906)

1 To love is to know the sacrifices which eternity exacts
from life.

Schools of Saints, Ch. 25   1897

2 Women may be whole oceans deeper than we are, but
they are also a whole paradise better. She may have got
us out of Eden, but as a compensation she makes the
earth very pleasant.

The Ambassador, Act III   1898

3 A false success made by the good humor of outside
influences is always peaceful; a real success made by
the qualities of the thing itself is always a declaration of
war.

The Dream and the Business   1906

335. Marie Curie
(1867–1934)

1 Men of moral and intellectual distinction could scarcely
agree to teach in schools where an alien attitude was
forced upon them.

Pierre Curie   1923

2 All my life through, the new sights of Nature made me
rejoice like a child.

Ibid.

3 . . . I was taught that the way of progress is neither
swift nor easy. . . .

Ibid.

4 You cannot hope to build a better world without im-
proving the individuals. To that end each of us must
work for his own improvement, and at the same time
share a general responsibility for all humanity, our particular duty being to aid those to whom we think we
can be most useful.   Ibid.

5 One never notices what has been done; one can only
see what remains to be done. . . .

Ibid., Letter to Her Brother (March 18, 1894)

6 Indeed, if the mentality of the scholars of the various countries, as revealed by the recent war, often appears to be on a lower level than that of the less cultured masses, it is because there is a danger inherent in all power that is not disciplined and directed toward the higher aims which alone are worthy of it.

"Intellectual Co-operation,"
Memorandum (magazine)   *June 16, 1926*

7 After all, science is essentially international, and it is only through lack of the historical sense that national qualities have been attributed to it.

Ibid.

8 I have no dress except the one I wear every day. If you are going to be kind enough to give me one,* please let it be practical and dark so that I can put it on afterwards to go to the laboratory.

Letter to a Friend (1849), Quoted in
"She Did Not Know How to Be Famous,"
Party of One by Clifton Fadiman   *1955p*

336. Edith Hamilton
(1867–1963)

1 The fundamental fact about the Greek was that he had to use his mind. The ancient priests had said, "Thus far and no farther. We set the limits of thought." The Greeks said, "All things are to be examined and called into question. There are no limits set on thought."

The Greek Way   *1930*

2 The anthropologists are busy, indeed, and ready to transport us back into the savage forest where all human things, the Greek things, too, have their beginnings; but the seed never explains the flower.

Ibid., Ch. 1

3 The Greeks were the first intellectualists. In a world where the irrational had played the chief role, they came forward as the protagonists of the mind.

Ibid.

4 Mind and spirit together make up that which separates us from the rest of the animal world, that which en-

---

* A wedding gown.

ables a man to know the truth and that which enables him to die for the truth.

Ibid.

5 The spirit has not essentially anything to do with what is outside of itself. It is mind that keeps hold of reality.

Ibid., Ch. 3

6 The English method [of poetry] is to fill the mind with beauty; the Greek method was to set the mind to work.

Ibid., Ch. 4

7 None but a poet can write a tragedy. For tragedy is nothing less than pain transmuted into exaltation by the alchemy of poetry, and if poetry is true knowledge and the great poet's guides safe to follow, this transmutation has arresting implications.

Ibid., Ch. 11

8 A people's literature is the great textbook for real knowledge of them. The writings of the day show the quality of the people as no historical reconstruction can.

The Roman Way, Preface   1932

9 Theories that go counter to the facts of human nature are foredoomed.

Ibid., Ch. 1

10 A good-humored crowd, those people who filled the Roman theatre in its first days of popularity, easily appealed to by any sentimental interest, eager to have the wicked punished—but not too severely—and the good live happily after. No occasions wanted for intellectual exertion, no wit for deft malice; fun such as could be passably enjoyed, broad with a flavor of obscenity. Most marked characteristic of all, a love of mediocrity, a complete satisfaction with the average. The people who applauded these plays wanted nothing bigger than their own small selves. They were democratic.

Ibid., Ch. 2

11 There are few efforts more conducive to humility than that of the translator trying to communicate an incommunicable beauty. Yet, unless we do try, something unique and never surpassed will cease to exist except in the libraries of a few inquisitive book lovers.

Three Greek Plays, Introduction   1937

12 Christ must be rediscovered perpetually.
> *Witness to the Truth,* Ch. 1   *1948*

13 "Bless me," he [Socrates] said, looking around the
market where all an Athenian wanted lay piled in
glowing profusion, "what a lot of things there are a
man can do without."
> Ibid.

14 So Socrates loved the truth and so he made it live. He
brought it down into the homes and hearts of men because he showed it to them in himself, the spirit of
truth manifest in the only way that can be, in the flesh.
> Ibid.

15 A life can be more lasting than systems of thought.
> Ibid., Ch. 2

16 The power of Christianity, the power of all religion, is
sustained by that strange capacity we call faith, a word
very commonly used and very commonly misunderstood. Ages of faith and of unbelief are always said to
mark the course of history.
> Ibid., Ch. 9

17 But it is not hard work which is dreary; it is superficial
work. That is always boring in the long run, and it has
always seemed strange to me that in our endless discus-
sions about education so little stress is ever laid on the
pleasure of becoming an educated person, the enormous interest it adds to life. To be able to be caught up
into the world of thought—that is to be educated.
> Quoted in the *Bryn Mawr School Bulletin*   *1959*

337. Käthe Kollwitz
(1867–1945)

1 No longer diverted by other emotions, I work the way
a cow grazes.
> *Diaries and Letters* (April, 1910),
> Hans Kollwitz, ed.   *1955p*

2 Sensuality is burgeoning. . . . I feel at once grave, ill
at ease and happy as I watch our children—our *children*—growing to meet the greatest of instincts. May it
have mercy on them!
> Ibid. (May 5, 1910)

3 For the last third of life there remains only work. It alone is always stimulating, rejuvenating, exciting and satisfying.
Ibid. (January 1, 1912)

4 Where do all the women who have watched so carefully over the lives of their beloved ones get the heroism to send them to face the cannon?
Ibid. (August 27, 1914)

5 The grave mood that comes over one when one knows: there is war, and one cannot hold on to any illusions any more. Nothing is real but the fruitfulness of this state, which we almost grow used to.
Ibid. (September 30, 1914)

6 I do not want to die . . . until I have faithfully made the most of my talent and cultivated the seed that was placed in me until the last small twig has grown.
Ibid. (February 15, 1915)

7 Culture arises only when the individual fulfills his cycle of obligations.
Ibid.

8 When we married, we took a leap in the dark. . . . There were grave contradictions in my own feelings. In the end I acted on this impulse: jump in—you'll manage to swim.
Ibid. (1916)

9 Men without joy seem like corpses.
Ibid. (September 19, 1918)

10 Age remains age, that is, it pains, torments and subdues. When others see my scant achievements, they speak of a happy old age. I doubt that there is such a thing as a happy old age.
Ibid. (January 1, 1932)

11 I am afraid of dying—but being dead, oh yes, that to me is often an appealing prospect.
Ibid. (December, 1941)

12 Although my leaning toward the male sex was dominant, I also felt frequently drawn toward my own sex— an inclination which I could not correctly interpret until much later on. As a matter of fact I believe that bisexuality is almost a necessary factor in artistic production; at any rate, the tinge of masculinity within me helped me in my work.
Ibid. (1942)

338. Emmeline Pethick-Lawrence
(1867–?)

1 Under the flagstones of the pavements in London lie
the dormant seeds of life—ready to spring into blossom
if the opportunity should ever occur. And under our
cruel and repressive financial and economic system lie
dormant human energy and joy that are ready to burst
into flower. So far as a drop may be compared to the
ocean, we witnessed in many individual cases that re-
leasing of the spirit that is possible when the conditions
of life afford some modicum of dignity and of leisure.
My Part in a Changing World, Ch. 7   1938

2 I find in many writers of the present day a persistent
inclination to refer to the suffrage movement as inspired by enmity towards men. So far as my own experience goes, during the six years with which I was connected with the campaign no effort was spared to
instruct the public that we had no enemy except a Government that was false to its professions. We refused to
have any quarrel even with the police who, acting under their orders, did us violence, or the prison officials
and doctors who became the agents of torture in prison
because their livelihood depended upon their obedience.
Ibid., Ch. 19

3 A change of heart is the essence of all other change and
it is brought about by a re-education of the mind.
Ibid., Ch. 23

339. Laura Ingalls Wilder
(1867–1957)

1 But they didn't believe that Santa Claus could, really,
have given any of them nothing but a switch. That happened to some children, but it couldn't happen to them.
It was so hard to be good all the time, every day, for a
whole year.
Little House in the Big Woods, Ch. 4   1932

2 "Did little girls have to be as good as that?" Laura
asked, and Ma said: "It was harder for little girls. Be-

311

cause they had to behave like little ladies all the time, not only on Sundays. Little girls could never slide downhill, like boys. Little girls had to sit in the house and stitch on samplers." *Ibid.*, Ch. 5

3 "That machine's a great invention!" he said. "Other folks can stick to old-fashioned ways if they want to, but I'm all for progress. It's a great age we're living in." *Ibid.*, Ch. 12

340. Mary Hunter Austin
(1868–1934)

1 When a woman ceases to alter the fashion of her hair, you guess that she has passed the crisis of her experience.

The Land of Little Rain   1903

2 Life set itself to new processions of seed-time and harvest, the skin newly tuned to seasonal variations, the very blood humming to new altitudes. The rhythm of walking, always a recognizable background for our thoughts, altered from the militaristic stride to the job of the wide unrutted earth.

The American Rhythm   1923

* * *

3 Oh, the Shepards in Judea!
  Do you think the shepards know
    How the whole round world is brightened
    In the ruddy Christmas glow?
                    "The Shepards in Judea"

4 Never was it printed on a page,
Never was it spoken, never heard.
                    "Whisper of the Wind"

5 What need has he of clocks who knows
When highest peaks are gilt and rose
Day has begun?
                    "Clocks and Calendars," St. 1

341. Guida Diehl
(1868–?)

1 Never did Hitler promise to the masses in his rousing
speeches any material advantage whatever. On the contrary he pleaded with them to turn aside from every
form of advantage-seeking and serve the great thought:
Honor, Freedom, Fatherland!
  The German Woman and National Socialism   *1933*

2 We long to see Men and Heroes who scorn fate. . . .
Call us to every service, even to weapons!

Ibid.

342. Maude Glasgow
(1868–1955)

1 When new-born humanity was learning to stand upright, it depended much on its mother and stood close
to her protecting side. Then women were goddesses,
they conducted divine worship, woman's voice was
heard in council, she was loved and revered and
genealogies were reckoned through her.
  The Subjection of Women and the
  Traditions of Men   *1940*

2 As the race grew older, rationality flourished at the expense of moral sense.   Ibid.

343. Agnes Lee
(1868–1939)

* * *

1 Bed is the boon for me!
  It's well to bake and sweep,
But hear the word of old Lizette:
  It's better than all to sleep.
    "Old Lizette on Sleep," St. 1

2 But I'll not venture in the drift
Out of this bright security,
Till enough footsteps come and go
To make a path for me.   "Convention"

313

3 Oh, mine was rosy as a bough
Blooming with roses, sent, somehow,
To bloom for me!
His balmy fingers left a thrill
Deep in my breast that warms me still.

"Motherhood," St. 5

344. Caroline "La Belle" Otero
(1868–1965)

1 . . . Paco took care of me; protected me; taught me to
dance and sing, and was my lover. It was the first time
in over two years that I knew where I was going to
sleep every night, and the first time in my life that I
knew there would be something for me to eat when I
woke up. Then Paco fell in love with me; wanted me to
marry him, and spoiled everything.

Quoted in the Pittsburgh Leader   April 11, 1904

2 There are two things in Spain which are not found elsewhere—flowers, lovely flowers in such abundance, and
bull fights. I love both.

Quoted in the New York World   May 10, 1908

345. Eleanor H. Porter
(1868–1920)

1 "Oh, yes, the game was to just find something about
everything to be glad about—not matter what 'twas,"
rejoined Pollyanna earnestly. "And we began right
then—on the crutches."

"Well, goodness me! I can't see anythin' ter be glad
about—gettin' a pair of crutches when you wanted a
doll!" . . .

"Goosey! Why, just be glad because you *don't—
need—'em*! . . ."

Pollyanna, Ch. 5   1912

2 "Oh, but Aunt Polly, Aunt Polly, you haven't left me
any time at all just to—to live."

"To live, child! What do you mean? As if you weren't
living all the time!"

"Oh, of course I'd be *breathing* all the time I was
doing those things, Aunt Polly, but I wouldn't be liv-

314

ing. You breathe all the time you're sleep, but you aren't living. I mean *living*—doing the things you want to do. . . . That's what I call living, Aunt Polly. Just breathing isn't living!"

Ibid., Ch. 7

3 ". . . he said, too, that he wouldn't *stay* a minister a minute if 'twasn't for the rejoicing texts. . . . Of course the Bible didn't name 'em that. But it's all those that begin 'Be glad in the Lord,' or 'Rejoice greatly,' or 'Shout for joy,' and all that, you know—such a lot of 'em. Once, when father felt specially bad, he counted 'em. There were eight hundred of 'em."   Ibid., Ch. 22

4 "What men and women need is encouragement. Their natural resisting powers should be strengthened, not weakened. . . . Instead of always harping on a man's faults, tell him of his virtues. Try to pull him out of his rut of bad habits. Hold up to him his better self, his *real* self that can dare and do and win out! . . . The influence of a beautiful, helpful, hopeful character is contagious, and may revolutionize a whole town. . . . People radiate what is in their minds and in their hearts. If a man feels kindly and obliging, his neighbors will feel that way, too, before long. But if he scolds and scowls and criticizes—his neighbors will return scowl for scowl, and add interest!"   Ibid.

346. Margaret Fairless Barber
(1869–1901)

1 . . . Earth, my Mother, whom I love.
The Roadmender, Vol. I, Dedication   1900

2 The people who make no roads are ruled out from intellectual participation in the world's brotherhood.
Ibid., Ch. 5

3 Necessity can set me helpless on my back, but she cannot keep me there; nor can four walls limit my vision.
Ibid., Vol. II, Ch. 6

4 Revelation is always measured by capacity.
Ibid., Vol. III, Ch. 3

5 To look backward for a while is to refresh the eye, to restore it, and to render it the more fit for its prime function of looking forward.   Ibid.

315

6 This place is peace and would be silent peace were it not for an Eisteddfod of small birds outvying each other with an eagerness which cannot wait until the last candidate has finished.

> Letter (May 19, 1900), *The Complete Works of Michael Fairless*   *1932p*

7 "In my Father's house are many mansions," and I suppose we are stripped of something in each till at last we can do without the Tree of Life and the candle and the sun and the protecting gates, in the innermost mansion which is the Beatific Vision.

> Ibid.

8 Having first insulted you and then calmed you with poetry, I can sleep the sleep of drugs and justice.

> Ibid. (May 30, 1900)

347. Elsa Barker
(1869–1954)

1 They never fail who light
Their lamp of faith at the unwavering flame
Burnt for the altar service of the Race
Since the beginning.

> "The Frozen Grail"   *1910*

348. Olive Dargan
(1869–1968)

* * *

1 Be a God, your spirit cried;
Tread with feet that burn the dew;
Dress with clouds your locks of pride;
Be a child, God said to you.

> "To William Blake"

2 The mountains lie in curves so tender
I want to lay my arm about them
As God does.

> "Twilight"

349. Anna Bunston De Bary
(1869–?)

* * *

1 Close to the sod there can be seen
A thought of God in white and green.

"The Snowdrop"

350. Emma Goldman
(1869–1940)

1 The motto should not be: Forgive one another; rather,
Understand one another.

"The Tragedy of Women's Emancipation,"
Anarchism and Other Essays   1911

2 Merely external emancipation has made of the modern
woman an artificial being. . . . Now, woman is confronted with the necessity of emancipating herself from
emancipation, if she really desires to be free.

Ibid.

3 Corruption of politics has nothing to do with the morals, or the laxity of morals, of various political personalities. Its cause is altogether a material one.

Ibid.

4 Politics is the reflex of the business and industrial
world. . . .

Ibid.

5 There is no hope even that woman, with her right to
vote, will ever purify politics.

Ibid.

6 As to the great mass of working girls and women, how
much independence is gained if the narrowness and
lack of freedom of the home is exchanged for the narrowness and lack of freedom of the factory, sweatshop,
department store, or office?

Ibid.

7 Every movement that aims at the destruction of existing institutions and the replacement thereof with something more advanced, more perfect, has followers who

317

in theory stand for the most radical ideas, but who, nevertheless, in their every-day practice, are like the average Philistine, feigning respectability and clamoring for the good opinion of their opponents.

Ibid.

8 True, the movement for women's rights has broken many old fetters, but it has also forged new ones.

Ibid.

9 . . . the higher mental development of woman, the less possible it is for her to meet a congenial mate who will see in her, not only sex, but also the human being, the friend, the comrade and strong individuality, who cannot and ought not lose a single trait of her character.

Ibid.

10 And yet we find many emancipated women who prefer marriage, with all its deficiencies, to the narrowness of an unmarried life; narrow and unendurable because of the chains of moral and social prejudice that cramp and bind her nature.

Ibid.

11 These internal tyrants [conscience] . . . these busy-bodies, moral detectives, jailers of the human spirit, what will they say?

Ibid.

12 If love does not know how to give and take without restrictions, it is not love, but a transaction that never fails to lay stress on a plus and a minus.

Ibid.

13 Salvation lies in an energetic march onward towards a brighter and clearer future.

Ibid.

14 . . . true emancipation begins neither at the polls nor in courts. It begins in woman's soul.

Ibid.

15 . . . the most vital right is the right to love and be loved.
Ibid.

16 A true conception of the relationship of the sexes . . . knows of but one great thing: to give of one's self boundlessly, in order to find one's self richer, deeper, better.

Ibid.

17 It is significant that whenever the public mind is to be diverted from a great social wrong, a crusade is inaugurated against indecency, gambling, saloons, etc.

Ibid., "The Traffic in Women"

18 Whether our reformers admit it or not, the economic and social inferiority of women is responsible for prostitution.

Ibid.

19 As to a thorough eradication of prostitution, nothing can accomplish that save a complete transvaluation of all accepted values—especially the moral ones—coupled with the abolition of industrial slavery.

Ibid.

20 Those who sit in a glass house do wrong to throw stones about them; besides, the American glass house is rather thin, it will break easily, and the interior is anything but a gainly sight.

Ibid.

21 Marriage is primarily an economic arrangement, an insurance pact. . . . Its returns are insignificantly small compared with the investments. In taking out an insurance policy one pays for it in dollars and cents, always at liberty to discontinue payments. If, however, woman's premium is a husband, she pays for it with her name, her privacy, her self-respect, her very life, "until death doth part." . . . Man, too, pays his toll. . . .

Ibid., "Marriage and Love"

22 The important and only God of practical American life: Can the man make a living? Can he support a wife? That is the only thing that justifies marriage.

Ibid.

23 Yet, if motherhood be of free choice, of love, of ecstasy, of defiant passion, does it not place a crown of thorns upon an innocent head and carve in letters of blood the hideous epithet, Bastard?

Ibid.

24 Love, the strongest and deepest element in all life, the harbinger of hope, of joy, of ecstasy; love, the defier of all laws, of all conventions; love, the freest, the most powerful moulder of human destiny; how can such an all-compelling force be synonymous with that poor little State and Church-begotten weed, marriage?   Ibid.

25 Man has bought brains, but all the millions in the world have failed to buy love. Man has subdued bodies, but all the power on earth has been unable to subdue love. Man has conquered whole nations but all his armies could not conquer love. Man has chained and fettered the spirit, but he has been utterly helpless before love. High on a throne, with all the splendor and pomp his gold can command, man is yet poor and desolate, if love passes him by. And if it stays, the poorest hovel is radiant with warmth, with life and color. Thus love has the magic power to make of a beggar a king. Yes, love is free; it can dwell in no other atmosphere. In freedom it gives itself unreservedly, abundantly, completely.

Ibid.

26 Capitalism . . . has . . . grown into a huge insatiable monster.

"The Social Aspects of Birth Control,"
Mother Earth   *April, 1916*

27 And through its destructive machinery, militarism, capitalism proclaims, "Send your sons on to me, I will drill and discipline them until all humanity has been ground out of them; until they become automatons ready to shoot and kill at the behest of their masters." Capitalism cannot do without militarism and since the masses of people furnish the material to be destroyed in the trenches and on the battlefield, capitalism must have a large race.

Ibid.

28 . . . the soldier's business is to take life. For that he is paid by the State, eulogized by political charlatans and upheld by public hysteria. But woman's function is to give life, yet neither the State nor politicians nor public opinion have ever made the slightest provision in return for the life woman has given.

Ibid.

29 No, it is not because woman is lacking in responsibility, but because she has too much of the latter that she demands to know how to prevent conception.

Ibid.

30 After all, that is what laws are for, to be made and unmade.   *Ibid.*

31 But even judges sometimes progress.   *Ibid.*

32 I may be arrested, I may be tried and thrown into jail, but I never will be silent. . . .

> Ibid.

33 . . . the government will . . . go on in the highly democratic method of conscripting American manhood for European slaughter.

> "Address to the Jury,"
> *Mother Earth*   *July, 1917*

34 . . . all wars are wars among thieves who are too cowardly to fight and who therefore induce the young manhood of the whole world to do the fighting for them.

> Ibid.

35 . . . always and forever we have stood up against war, because we say that the war going on in the world is for the further enslavement of the people, for the further placing of them under the yoke of a military tyranny. . . .

> Ibid.

36 The conscientious objector, rightly or wrongly—that is a thing which you will have to argue with him—does not believe in war . . . because he insists that, belonging to the people whence he has come and to whom he owes his life, it is his place to stand on the side of the people, for the people and by the people and not on the side of the governing classes. . . .

> Ibid.

37 . . . the tree of Russian liberty is watered with the blood of Russian martyrs.

> Ibid.

38 . . . no great idea in its beginning can ever be within the law. How can it be within the law? The law is stationary. The law is fixed. The law is a chariot wheel which binds us all regardless of conditions or place or time.

> Ibid.

39 But progress is ever changing, progress is ever renewing, progress has nothing to do with fixity.

> Ibid.

40 . . . democracy must first be safe for America before it can be safe for the world.

> Ibid.

41 Anarchy stands for the liberation of the human mind from the dominion of religion; the liberation of the human body from the dominion of property; liberation from the shackles and restraints of government.

Anarchism   1917

42 . . . the experience of Russia, more than any theories, has demonstrated that *all* government, whatever its forms or pretenses, is a dead weight that paralyzes the free spirit and activities of the masses.

My Disillusionment in Russia   1923

43 The ultimate end of all revolutionary social change is to establish the sanctity of human life, the dignity of man, the right of every human being to liberty and well-being.

My Further Disillusionment in Russia   1924

44 No revolution ever succeeds as a factor of liberation unless the means used to further it be identified in spirit and tendency with the purpose to be achieved.

Ibid.

45 Anarchy asserts the possibility of organization without discipline, fear or punishment, and without the pressure of property.

Living My Life   1931

46 Revolution is but thought carried into action.

Quoted in *The Feminist Papers*,
Alice Rossi, ed.   1973p

47 There's never been a good government.

Quoted by Katherine Anne Porter in
the *Los Angeles Times*
July 7, 1974p

351. Corra May Harris
(1869–1935)

1 The deadly monotony of Christian country life where there are no beggars to feed, no drunkards to credit, which are among the moral duties of Christians in cities, leads as naturally to the outvent of what Methodists call "revivals" as did the backslidings of the people in those days.

A Circuit Rider's Wife, Ch. 3   1910

2 This is the wonderful thing about the pure in heart—
they do see God.

Ibid., Ch. 6

3 After you are dead it doesn't matter if you were not
successful in a business way. No one has yet had the
courage to memorialize his wealth on his tombstone. A
dollar mark would not look well there.

Ibid., Ch. 11

4 So long as a man attends to his business the public does
not count his drinks. When he fails they notice if he
takes even a glass of root beer.

Eve's Second Husband, Ch. 6   1910

5 Adam was a man who could believe any statement he
could evolve out of his ambitious imagination easier
than he could believe the literal facts of his life.

Ibid., Ch. 7

6 "The world smacks most of us out of shape so soon."
Ibid., Ch. 14

7 A woman would rather visit her own grave than the
place where she has been young and beautiful after she
is aged and ugly.

Ibid.

352. Else Lasker-Schuler
(1869–1945)

1 We shall rest from love like two rare beasts
In the high reeds behind this world.
"A Love Song" (c.1902), *The Other Voices,*
Carol Cosman, ed.   1975p

353. Charlotte Mew
(1869–1928)

1   . . . Oh! my God! the down,
The soft young down of her, the brown,
The brown of her. . . .
"The Farmer's Bride," *Collected Poems*   1916

2   When us was wed she turned afraid
Of love and me and all things human;
Like the shut of a winter's day.
Ibid.

354. Jessie Rittenhouse
(1869–1948)

* * *

1 I worked for a menial's hire,
  Only to learn, dismayed,
That any wage I had asked of life,
  Life would have paid.

"My Wage"

2 My debt to you, Beloved,
  Is one I cannot pay
In any coin of any realm
  On any reckoning day.

"Debt"

355. Carolyn Wells
(1869–1942)

1 Total is a book. We find it
  Just a little past its prime;
And departing leaves behind it
  Footprints on the sands of time.
    "Four," St. 3, *At the Sign of the Sphinx*   1896

2 There was a young man of St. Kitts
Who was very much troubled with fits;
  The eclipse of the moon
  Threw him into a swoon,
When he tumbled and broke into bits.
        "Limericks," No. 3, *The Book of
            Humorous Verse*   1920

3 A Tutor who tooted the flute
Tried to teach two young tutors to toot;
  Said the two to the Tutor,
  "Is it harder to toot, or
To tutor two tutors to toot?"   Ibid., No. 6

4 "Women are all right, in their place—which, by the
way, is not necessarily in the home—but a family feud,
of all things, calls for masculine management and
skill."

In the Onyx Lobby, Ch. 1   1920

5   "I'll bet Sherlock Holmes could find a lot of data just
by going over the floor with a lens."

"He could in a story book—and do you know why?
Because the clews and things, in a story, are all put
there for him by the property man. Like a salted mine.
But in real life, there's nothing doing of that sort."

Ibid., Ch. 5

6 The earth has rolled around again and harvest time is
   here,
The glory of the seasons and the crown of all the years.
     "The Meaning of Thanksgiving Day"   *1922*

* * *

6 A canner can can
     Anything that he can,
But a canner can't can a can, can he?

"The Canner"

8 But Woman is rare beyond compare,
     The poets tell us so;
How little they know of Woman
     Who only Women know!

"Woman"

9 I love the Christmas-tide, and yet;
     I notice this, each year I live;
I always like the gifts I get,
     But how I love the gifts I give!

"A Thought"

10 The books we think we ought to read are poky, dull,
     and dry;
The books that we would like to read we are ashamed
     to buy;
The books that people talk about we never can recall;
And the books that people give us, oh, they're the
     worst of all.

"On Books"

11 When Venus said "Spell no for me,"
     "N-O," Dan Cupid wrote with glee,
        And smiled at his success:
     "Ah, child," said Venus, laughing low,
     "We women do not spell it so,
        We spell it Y-E-S."

"The Spelling Lesson"

356. Elizabeth Botume
(fl. 1870s)

1 It was not an unusual thing to meet a woman coming
from the fields, where she had been hoeing cotton, with
a small bucket or cup on her head, and a hoe over her
shoulder, contentedly smoking a pipe and briskly knitting as she strode along. I have seen, added to all these,
a baby strapped to her back.
First Days Amongst the Contrabands   *1893*

357. Mrs. Edmund Craster
(fl. 1870s)

1 The Centipede was happy quite,
Until the Toad in fun
Said, "Pray which leg goes after which?"
And worked her mind to such a pitch,
She lay distracted in a ditch
Considering how to run.
"Pinafore Poems," *Cassell's Weekly*   *1871*

358. Clara Dolliver
(fl. 1870s)

1 No merry frolics after tea,
No baby in the house.

"No Baby in the House,"
No Baby in the House and Other
Stories for Children   *1868*

359. Mary Pyper
(fl. 1870s)

* * *

1 I sat me down; 'twas autumn eve,
And I with sadness wept;
I laid me down at night, and then
'Twas winter, and I slept.

"Epitaph: A Life"

360. Sarah Ann Sewell
(fl. 1870s)

1 It is a man's place to rule, and a woman's to yield. He
must be held up as the head of the house, and it is her
duty to bend so unmurmuringly to his wishes, that the
rest of the household will follow her example, and treat
him with the due respect his sex demands.
Woman and the Times We Live In   *1869*

361. Sharlot Mabridth Hall
(1870–1943)

1 I stayed not, I could not linger; patient, resistless,
    alone,
I hewed the trail of my destiny deep in the hindering
    stone.
"Song of the Colorado," *Cactus Pine*   *1910*

362. Florence Hurst Harriman
(1870–1967)

1 Next to entertaining or impressive talk, a thorough-
going silence manages to intrigue most people.
From Pinafores to Politics, Ch. 4   *1924*

363. Grace Hibbard
(1870?–1911)

* * *

1 "An Honest Lawyer"—book just out—
    What can the author have to say?
Reprint perhaps of ancient tome—
    A work of fiction anyway.   "Books Received"

364. Mary Johnston
(1870–1936)

1 "I am weary of swords and courts and kings. Let us go
into the garden and watch the minister's bees."
To Have and to Hold, Ch. 9   *1899*

365. Marie Lloyd
(1870–1922)

* * *

1 A little of what you fancy does you good.

Song

2 I'm one of the ruins that Cromwell knocked about a bit.

Ibid.

366. Rosa Luxemburg
(1870–1919)

1 . . . profits are springing, like weeds, from the fields of the dead.

*The Crisis in the German
Social Democracy* *1919*

2 Shamed, dishonored, wading in blood and dripping with filth, thus capitalist society stands.

Ibid.

3 Self-criticism, cruel, unsparing criticism that goes to the very root of the evil, is life and breath for the proletarian movement.

Ibid.

4 It is a foolish delusion to believe that we need only live through the war, as a rabbit hides under the bush to await the end of a thunderstorm, to trot merrily off in his old accustomed gait when all is over.

Ibid.

5 If the proletariat learns *from* this war and *in* this war to exert itself, to cast off its serfdom to the ruling classes, to become the lord of its own destiny, the shame and misery will not have been in vain.

Ibid.

6 . . . we will be victorious if we have not forgotten how to learn.

Ibid.

7 Passive fatalism can never be the role of a revolutionary party. . . .

Ibid.

328

8 Victory or defeat? It is the slogan of all-powerful militarism in every belligerent nation. . . . And yet, what can victory bring to the proletariat?

Ibid.

9 Reduced to its objective historic significance, the present world war as a whole is a competitive struggle of a fully developed capitalism for world supremacy, for the exploitation of the last remnant of noncapitalistic world zones.

Ibid.

10 The high stage of world-industrial development in capitalistic production finds expression in the extraordinary technical development and destructiveness of the instruments of war. . . .

Ibid.

11 This madness will not stop, and this bloody nightmare of hell will not cease until the workers . . . will drown the bestial chorus of war agitators and the hoarse cry of capitalist hyenas with the mighty cry of labor, "Proletarians of all countries, unite!"

Ibid.

12 Freedom for supporters of the government only, for the members of one party only—no matter how big its membership may be—is no freedom at all. Freedom is always freedom for the man who thinks differently.

Quoted in *Die Russische Revolution*
by Paul Froelich   *1940p*

13 Without general elections, without freedom of the press, freedom of speech, freedom of assembly, without the free battle of opinions, life in every public institution withers away, becomes a caricature of itself, and bureaucracy rises as the only deciding factor.

Ibid.

* * *

14 I hope to die at my post; on the street, or in prison.

Letter to Sonia Liebnecht

367. Lucia Clark Markham
(1870–?)

* * *

1 To-night from deeps of loneliness I wake in wistful wonder
To a sudden sense of brightness, an immanence of blue.

"Bluebells"

368. Maria Montessori
(1870–1952)

1 A single fact lies at the source of all deviations, viz., that the child has been prevented from fulfilling the original pattern of his development at the formative age. . . .

The Secret of Childhood   *1939*

2 . . . in nature nothing creates itself and nothing destroys itself.

Ibid.

3 The babies . . . sought to render themselves independent of adults in all the actions which they could manage on their own, manifesting clearly the desire not to be helped, except in cases of absolute necessity. And they were seen to be tranquil, absorbed and concentrating on their work, acquiring a surprising calm and serenity.

The Child in the Family   *1956p*

4 . . . humanity is still far from that stage of maturity needed for the realization of its aspirations, for the construction, that is, of a harmonious and peaceful society and the elimination of wars. Men are not yet ready to shape their own destinies, to control and direct world events, of which—instead—they become the victims.

The Absorbent Mind   *1967p*

5 And if education is always to be conceived along the same antiquated lines of a mere transmission of knowledge, there is little to be hoped from it in the bettering of man's future. For what is the use of transmitting knowledge if the individual's total development lags behind?

Ibid.

6 If help and salvation are to come, they can only come from the children, for the children are the makers of men.   *Ibid.*

7 The greatness of the human personality begins at the hour of birth. From this almost mystic affirmation there comes what may seem a strange conclusion: that education must start from birth.   *Ibid.*

8 The only language men ever speak perfectly is the one they learn in babyhood, when no one can teach them anything!

Ibid.

9 And so we discovered that education is not something which the teacher does, but that it is a natural process which develops spontaneously in the human being.

Ibid.

10 We teachers can only help the work going on, as servants wait upon a master.

Ibid.

11 How strange it is to observe that in times like ours, when war has achieved a destructiveness without parallel . . . future plans for unity are made, which means not only that love exists, but that its power is fundamental.

Ibid.

12 Love and the hope of it are not things one can learn; they are a part of life's heritage.

Ibid.

13 The child endures all things.

Ibid.

14 The Absorbent Mind welcomes everything, puts its hope in everything, accepts poverty equally with wealth, adopts any religion and the prejudices and habits of its countrymen, incarnating all in itself.

Ibid.

15 Strange, is it not, that among all the wonders man has worked, and the discoveries he has made, there is only one field to which he has paid no attention; it is that of the miracle that God has worked from the first: the miracle of children.

Ibid.

369. Alice Caldwell Rice
(1870–1942)

1 Life is made up of desires that seem big and vital one minute, and little and absurd the next. I guess we get what's best for us in the end.

A Romance of Billy-Goat Hill, Ch. 2   *1912*

2 To him work appeared a wholly artificial and abnormal action, self-imposed and unnecessary. The stage of life presented so many opportunities for him to exercise his histrionic ability, that the idea of settling down to a routine of labor seemed a waste of talent.

Ibid., Ch. 6

3 The arbitrary division of one's life into weeks and days and hours seemed, on the whole, useless. There was but one day for the men, and that was pay day, and one for the women, and that was rent day. As for the children, every day was theirs, just as it should be in every corner of the world.

Ibid., Ch. 15

4 "Fer my part I can't see it's to any woman's credit to look nice when she's got the right kind of a switch and a good set of false teeth. It's the woman that keeps her good looks without none of them luxuries that orter be praised."   *Calvary Alley*, Ch. 2   *1918*

5 When one has a famishing thirst for happiness, one is apt to gulp down diversions wherever they are offered. The necessity of draining the dregs of life before the wine is savored does not cultivate a discriminating taste.   *Ibid.*, Ch. 14

370. Helena Rubinstein
(1870–1965)

1 I have always felt that a woman has the right to treat the subject of her age with ambiguity until, perhaps, she passes into the realm of over ninety. Then it is better she be candid with herself and with the world.

My Life for Beauty, Pt. I, Ch. 1   *1966p*

2 There are no ugly women, only lazy ones.

Ibid., Pt. II, Ch. 1

3 But what parent can tell when some such fragmentary gift of knowledge or wisdom will enrich her children's lives? Or how a small seed of information passed from one generation to another may generate a new science, a new industry—a seed which neither the giver nor the receiver can truly evaluate at the time.

Ibid., Ch. 10

371. Maud Younger
(1870–1936)

1 We have so many ideas about things we have never tried.

"New York, May 6, 1907,"
McClure's Magazine   1907

2 It is not pleasant to have a stranger doubt your respectability.

Ibid.

3 "See here. How am I ever going to get experience if everyone tells me that I must have it before I begin?"

Ibid.

4 I did not know the working classes were so united. There is more affection and loyalty toward one another than among other people. Perhaps this is because the working people feel that there is a class struggle, and the leisure class does not know it yet.

Ibid., "New York, May 15"

5 "Then why don't all girls belong to unions?" I asked, feeling very much an outsider; but she of the gents' neckwear replied: "Well, there's some that thinks it ain't fashionable; there's some that thinks it ain't no use; and there's some that never thinks at all."

Ibid., "New York, June 8"

6 A trade unionist—of course I am. First, last, and all the time. How else to strike at the roots of the evils undermining the moral and physical health of women? How else grapple with the complex problems of employment, overemployment, and underemployment alike, resulting in discouraged, undernourished bodies, too tired to resist the onslaughts of disease and crime?

Speech, Quoted in *Ms.*   *January, 1973 p*

372. Emily Carr
(1871–1945)

1 I wonder why we are always sort of ashamed of our best parts and try to hide them. We don't mind ridicule

of our "sillinesses" but of our "sobers," oh! Indians are the same and even dogs.

Hundreds and Thousands
(November 23, 1930)   *1966p*

2 You come into the world alone and you go out of the world alone yet it seems to me you are more alone while living than even going and coming.

Ibid. (July 16, 1933)

3 Oh, the glory of growth, silent, mighty, persistent, inevitable! To awaken, to open up like a flower to the light of a fuller consciousness!

Ibid. (October 17, 1933)

4 It is not all bad, this getting old, ripening. After the fruit has got its growth it should juice up and mellow. God forbid I should live long enough to ferment and rot and fall to the ground in a squash.

Ibid. (December 12, 1933)

5 B-a-a-a-, old sheep, bleating for fellows. Don't you know better by now?

Ibid. (April 6, 1934)

6 Twenty can't be expected to tolerate sixty in all things, and sixty gets bored stiff with twenty's eternal love affairs.

Ibid. (August 12, 1934)

7 It is wonderful to feel the grandness of Canada in the raw, not because she is Canada but because she is something sublime that you were born into, some great rugged power that you are a part of.

Ibid. (April 16, 1937)

8 I am not half as patient with old women now that I am one. Ibid. (March 6, 1940)

9 Everything holds its breath except spring. She bursts through as strong as ever.   Ibid. (March 7, 1941)

373. Maxine Elliott
(1871–1940)

1 Beauty, what is that? There are phalanxes of beauty in every comic show. Beauty neither buys food nor keeps up a home.   News Item   *1908*

374. Margaret Witter Fuller
(1871–1954)

* * *

1 I am immortal! I know it! I feel it!
Hope floods my heart with delight!
Running on air, mad with life, dizzy, reeling,
Upward I mount—faith is sight, life is feeling,
Hope is the day-star of might!

"Dryad Song"

2 It was thy kiss, Love, that made me immortal.

Ibid.

375. Pamela Glenconner
(1871–1928)

1 Giving presents is a talent; to know what a person
wants, to know when and how to get it, to give it lov-
ingly and well. Unless a character possesses this talent
there is no moment more annihilating to ease than that
in which a present is received and given.

*Edward Wyndhan Tennant:
A Memoir,* Ch. 5　　1919

* * *

2 Bitter are the tears of a child:
　　Sweeten them.
Deep are the thoughts of a child:
　　Quiet them.
Sharp is the grief of a child:
　　Take it from him.
Soft is the heart of a child:
　　Do not harden it.　　　　　　　　"A Child"

376. Agnes C. Laut
(1871–1936)

1 They had reached the fine point where it is better for
the weak to die trying to overthrow strength, than to
live under the iron heel of brute oppression.

Vikings of the Pacific, Ch. 4　　1905

2 Countless hopes and fears must have animated at the breasts of the Frenchmen.* It is so with every venture that is based on the unknown. The very fact that possibilities *are* unknown gives scope to unbridled fancy and the wildest hopes; gives scope, too, when the pendulum swings the other way to deepest distrust.

The Conquest of the Great Northwest, Ch. 7   *1908*

3 The ultimate umpire of all things in life is—Fact.

Ibid., Ch. 20

4 Canada's prosperity is literally overflowing from a cornucopia of superabundant plenty. Will her Constitution, wrested from political and civil strife; will her moral stamina, bred from the heroism of an heroic past, stand the strain, the tremendous strain of the new conditions? . . . Above all, will she stand the strain, the tremendous strain, of prosperity, and the corruption that is attendant on prosperity? *Quien sabe?*

Canada, the Empire of the North, Ch. 16   *1909*

5 Yet when you come to trace when and where national consciousness awakened, it is like following a river back from the ocean to its mountain springs. . . . You can guess the eternal striving, the forward rush and the throwback that have carved a way through the solid rock; but until you have followed the river to its source and tried to stem its current you can not know.

The Canadian Commonwealth, Ch. 1   *1915*

377. Florence Sabin
(1871–1953)

1 The prohibition law, written for weaklings and derelicts, has divided the nation, like Gaul, into three parts—wets, drys and hypocrites.

Speech   *February 9, 1931*

---

* Radisson and Groseillers' voyage in 1668 to Hudson Bay.

378. Maude Adams
(1872–1953)

1 If I smashed the traditions it was because I knew no traditions.

> Quoted in *Maude Adams: A Biography*
> by Ada Patterson   *1907*

2 Genius is the talent for seeing things straight. It is seeing things in a straight line without any bend or break or aberration of sight, seeing them as they are, without any warping of vision. Flawless mental sight! That is genius.   Ibid.

379. Mary Reynolds Aldis
(1872–1949)

* * *

1 They flush joyously like a cheek under a lover's kiss;
They bleed cruelly like a dagger-wound in the breast;
They flame up madly of their little hour,
Knowing they must die.   "Barberries"

380. Eva Gore-Booth
(1872–1926)

* * *

1 The little waves of Breffney go stumbling through my soul.

> "The Little Waves of Breffney," *Poems*

381. Mildred Howells
(1872–1966)

* * *

1 And so it criticized each flower,
  This supercilious seed;
Until it woke one summer hour,
  And found itself a weed.

> "The Different Seed," St. 5

2 Oh, tell me how my garden grows,
   Where I no more may take delight,
And if some dream of me it knows,
   Who dream of it by day and night.
                "Oh, Tell Me How My Garden Grows," St. 5

382. Aleksandra Kollontai
(1872–1952)

1 In place of the indissoluble marriage based on the servitude of women, we shall see rise the free union, forti-
fied by the love and the mutual respect of the two
members of the workers' state, equal in their rights and
in their obligations. In place of the individual and ego-
tistic family, there will arise a great universal family of
workers, in which all the workers, men and women,
will be, above all, workers, comrades. . . .
                Communism and the Family   1918

2 The "upper" elements may divert the masses from the
straight road of history which leads toward communism only when the masses are mute, obedient, and
when they passively and credulously follow their leaders.
           The Workers' Opposition in Russia   c.1921

3 . . . beginning with the appointment of a sovereign for
the state and ending with a sovereign director for the
factory. This is the supreme wisdom of bourgeois
thought.
                                                    Ibid.

4 . . . the middle class with their hostility toward communism, and with their predilections toward the immutable customs of the past, with resentments and
fears toward revolutionary acts—these are the elements
that bring decay into our Soviet institutions, breeding
there an atmosphere altogether repugnant to the working class.   Ibid.

5 It is well known to every Marxian that reconstruction
of industry and development of creative forces of a
country depend on two factors: on the development of
technique, and the efficient organization of labor by
means of increasing productivity and finding new in-
centives to work.   Ibid.

6 Bureaucracy, as it is, is a direct negation of mass self-activity. . . .

Ibid.

7 Fear of criticism and freedom of thought by combining together with bureaucracy quite often produce ridiculous forms.

Ibid.

8 The practice of [political] appointments rejects completely the principle of collective work; it breeds irresponsibility.

Ibid.

383. Julia Morgan
(1872–1957)

1 I don't think you understand just what my work has been here. The decorative part was all done by a New York firm. My work was structural [on the rebuilding of the Fairmont Hotel following the 1906 earthquake].

Quoted in the San Francisco Call   1907

2 The building should speak for itself.

Quoted in "Some Examples of the
Work of Julia Morgan" by Walter T.
Steilberg, Architect and Engineer
November, 1918

3 Never turn down a job because you think it's too small, you don't know where it can lead.

Ibid.

384. Grace Seton-Thompson
(1872–1959)

1 . . . the outfit I got together for my first [hunting] trip appalled that good man, my husband, while the number of things I had to learn appalled me.

A Woman Tenderfoot, Ch. 1   1900

2 I know what it means to be a miner and a cowboy, and have risked my life when need be, *but,* best of all, I have felt the charm of the glorious freedom, the quick rushing blood, the bounding motion, of the wild life, the joy of the living and of the doing, of the mountain and the plain; I have learned to know and feel some, at least, of the secrets of the Wild Ones.

Ibid., Ch. 18

3 Courage! Speed the day of world perfection.
   Straining from the Wheel of Things,
   Let us break the bonds of lost direction!
   Godward! Borne on Freedom's Wings!

> "The Wheel of Life," St. 6,
> *The Singing Traveler*   1947

4 My Mother is everywhere . . .
   In the perfume of a rose,
   The eyes of a tiger,
   The pages of a book,
   The food that we partake,
   The whistling wind of the desert,
   The blazing gems of sunset,
   The crystal light of full moon,
   The opal veils of sunrise.

> Ibid., "Hindu Chant," St. 4

5 Beckon, dreams of passion, luring snare!
   Your guileful bed of satin-white
   Calls to lustful ease.

> Ibid., "Opium Poppy," St. 2

6 If I must suffer more re-birth
   Upon the weary plain of earth,
   Grant that my rest be deep,
   And happy be my sleep
   Until the turning Wheel of Life
   Wakes me to Illusion's strife.

> Ibid., "Goddess of Mercy," St. 1

7 Butterflies and birds fly over me unconcerned . . .
   The forest accepts me.

> Ibid., "Forest," St. 4

8 What is an eye?
   A strange device,
   A bit of film and nerve, the first camera obscura,
   A wonder steeped in mystery . . .
   Recording scenes and filing prints in cabinets of the
     brain?

> Ibid., "Windows of the Soul," St. 1

9 Many times I have looked into the eyes of wild animals
   And we have parted friends.
   What did they see, and recognize,
   Shining through the windows of a human soul?

> Ibid., St. 9

385. Leonora Speyer
(1872–1956)

1 I'll sing, "Here lies, here lies, here lies—"
  Ah, rust in peace below!
  Passers will wonder at my words,
  But your dark dust will know.

"I'll Be Your Epitaph,"
Fiddler's Farewell   1926

2 Poor patch-work of the heart,
  This healing love with love;
  Binding the wound to wound,
  The smart to smart!

Ibid., "Therapy," St. 3

3 Love has a hundred gentle ends.

Ibid., "Two Passionate Ones Part," St. 5

4 Houses are like the hearts of men,
  I think;
  They must have life within,
  (This is their meat and drink),
  They must have fires and friends and kin,
  Love for the day and night,
  Children in strong young laps:
  Then they live—then!

Ibid., "Abrigada," St. 10

5 You gave me wings to fly;
  Then took away the sky.   Ibid., Introduction, Pt. V

6 Let me declare
  That music never dies;
  That music never dies.

Ibid., "Fiddler's Farewell," St. 13

7 . . . no amount of study will contrive a talent, that
  being God's affair; but having the gift, "through
  Grace," as John Masefield says, it must be developed,
  the art must be learned.

"On the Teaching of Poetry,"
The Saturday Review of Literature   1946

8 There is not much stitching and unstitching in some of
  the hasty and cocksure writing of today.   Ibid.

341

9 . . . to be exact has naught to do with pedantry or
dogma. . . .

Ibid.

10 I believe in anthologies, although I know they offer
only a glimpse.

Ibid.

11 . . . I quote a good deal in my talks. . . . I do like to
call upon my radiant cloud of witnesses to back me up,
saying the thing I would say, and saying it so much
more eloquently.

Ibid.

12 I do not think that too severe comment is good teaching.

Ibid.

* * *

13 Sky, be my depth;
Wind, be my width and my height;
World, my heart's span:
Loneliness, wings for my flight!

"Measure Me, Sky"

14 Thunder crumples the sky,
Lightning tears at it.

"The Squall"

386. Willa Cather
(1873–1947)

1 No one can build his security upon the nobleness of
another person.

Alexander's Bridge, Ch. 8   *1912*

2 There are only two or three human stories, and they go
on repeating themselves as fiercely as if they had never
happened before.

O Pioneers!, Pt. II, Ch. 4   *1913*

3 The history of every country begins in the heart of a
man or woman.

Ibid.

4 I like trees because they seem more resigned to the way
they have to live than other things do.

Ibid., Ch. 8

5 "There was certainly no kindly Providence that directed one's life; and one's parents did not in the least care what became of one, so long as one did not misbehave and endanger their comfort. One's life was at the mercy of blind chance. She had better take it in her own hands and lose everything than meekly draw the plough under the rod of parental guidance. She had seen it when she was at home last summer—the hostility of comfortable, self-satisfied people towards serious effort." *The Song of the Lark* 1915

6 We all like people who do things, even if we only see their faces on a cigar-box lid. *Ibid.*

7 "I tell you there is such a thing as creative hate!"
Ibid., Pt. I

8 Artistic growth is, more than it is anything else, a refining of the sense of truthfulness. The stupid believe that to be truthful is easy; only the artist, the great artist, knows how difficult it is. *Ibid., Pt. VI, Ch. 11*

9 "Oh, better I like to work out of doors than in the house. . . . I not care that your grandmother says it makes me like a man. I like to be like a man."
My Antonia 1918

10 That is happiness; to be dissolved into something completely great.
Ibid., Bk. I, Ch. 2, Epitaph

11 Winter lies too long in country towns; hangs on until it is stale and shabby, old and sullen.
Ibid., Bk. II, Ch. 7

12 Old men are like that, you know. It makes them feel important to think they are in love with somebody.
Ibid., Bk. III, Ch. 4

13 This was a lie, but Paul was quite accustomed to lying; found it, indeed, indispensable for overcoming friction.
"Paul's Case," *Youth and the Bright Medusa* 1920

14 It was not that symphonies, as such, meant anything in particular to Paul, but the first sigh of the instruments seemed to free some hilarious spirit within him; something that struggled there like the Genius in the bottle found by the Arab fisherman.
Ibid.

15 It was a highly respectable street, where all the houses
were exactly alike, and where business men of moderate means begot and reared large families of children,
all of whom went to sabbath-school and learned the
shorter catechism, and were interested in arithmetic; all
of whom were as exactly alike as their homes, and of a
piece with the monotony in which they lived.

Ibid.

16 Perhaps it was because, in Paul's world, the natural
nearly always wore the guise of ugliness, that a certain
element of artificiality seemed to him necessary in
beauty.

Ibid.

17 He . . . knew now, more than ever, that money was
everything, the wall that stood between all he loathed
and all he wanted.

Ibid.

18 It was a losing game in the end, it seemed, this revolt
against the homilies by which the world is run.

Ibid.

19 Art, it seems to me, should simplify. That, indeed, is
very nearly the whole of the higher artistic process;
finding what conventions of form and what details one
can do without and yet preserve the spirit of the
whole. . . .

On the Art of Fiction   1920

20 There was this to be said for Nat Wheeler, that he liked
every sort of human creature; he liked good people and
honest people, and he liked rascals and hypocrites almost to the point of loving them.

One of Ours, Bk. I, Ch. 1   1922

21 The dead might as well try to speak to the living as the
old to the young.   Ibid., Bk. II, Ch. 6

22 The sun was like a great visiting presence that stimu-
lated and took its due from all animal energy. When it
flung wide its cloak and stepped down over the edge of
the fields at evening, it left behind it a spent and exhausted world.   Ibid.

23 Yes, inside of people who walked and worked in the
broad sun, there were captives dwelling in darkness,—
never seen from birth to death.   Ibid., Bk. III, Ch. 2

24 He was still burning with the first ardour of the enlisted man. He believed that he was going abroad with an expeditionary force that would make war without rage, with uncompromising generosity and chivalry.

Ibid., Ch. 10

25 "When I'm in normal health, I'm a Presbyterian, but just now I feel that even the wicked get worse than they deserve."

Ibid., Bk. IV, Ch. 9

26 They were mortal, but they were unconquerable.

Ibid., Bk. V, Ch. 18

27 Theoretically he knew that life is possible, maybe even pleasant, without joy, without passionate griefs. But it had never occurred to him that he might have to live like that.

The Professor's House 1925

28 That irregular and intimate quality of things made entirely by the human hand.

Death Comes for the Archbishop,
Bk. I, Ch. 3 1927

29 The miracles of the church seem to me to rest not so much upon faces or voices or healing power coming suddenly near to us from afar off, but upon our perceptions being made finer, so that for a moment our eyes can see and our ears can hear what is there about us always.

Ibid., Ch. 4

30 The universal human yearning for something permanent, enduring, without shadow of change.

Ibid., Bk. III, Ch. 3

31 CECILE. Do you think it wrong for a girl to know Latin?

PIERRE. Not if she can cook a hare or a partridge as well as Mademoiselle Auclaire! She may read all the Latin she pleases. *Shadows on the Rock* 1931

32 Only solitary men know the full joys of friendship. Others have their family; but to a solitary and an exile his friends are everything. *Ibid.*, Bk. III, Ch. 5

33 There are all those early memories; one cannot get another set; one has only those. *Ibid.*, Bk. IV, Ch. 2

345

34 One made a climate within a climate; one made the days—the complexion, the special flavor, the special happiness of each day as it passed; one made life.

Ibid., Ch. 3

35 Sometimes a neighbor whom we have disliked a lifetime for his arrogance and conceit lets fall a single commonplace remark that shows us another side, another man, really; a man uncertain, and puzzled, and in the dark like ourselves.

Ibid., Epilogue

36 "Nothing really matters but living—accomplishments are the ornaments of life, they come second."

Lucy Gayheart   1935

37 The revolt against individuals naturally calls artists severely to account, because the artist is of all men the most individual: those who were not have long been forgotten. The condition every art requires is, not so much freedom from restriction, as freedom from adulteration and from the intrusion of foreign matter, considerations and purposes which have nothing to do with spontaneous invention.

On Writing   1949p

38 Religion and art spring from the same root and are close kin. Economics and art are strangers.

Ibid.

* * *

39 Incapable of compromises,
     Unable to forgive or spare,
The strange awarding of the prizes
     He had no fortitude to bear.

"A Likeness"

40 So blind is life, so long at last is sleep,
And none but love to bid us laugh or weep.

"Evening Song"

41 Oh, this is the joy of the rose:
     That it blows,
     And goes.

"In Rose-Time"

42 Where are the loves that we have loved before
When once we are alone, and shut the door?

"L'Envoi"

387. Colette
(1873–1954)

1 All those beautiful sentiments I've uttered have made me feel genuinely upset.

> "The Journey"   1905

2 I look like a discouraged beetle battered by the rains of a spring night. I look like a molting bird. I look like a governess in distress. I look—Good Lord, I look like an actress on tour, and that speaks for itself.

> "On Tour," *Music Hall Sidelights*   1913

3 How can one help shivering with delight when one's hot fingers close around the stem of a live flower, cool from the shade and stiff with newborn vigor!

> Ibid.

4 Nothing ages a woman like living in the country.

> Ibid.

5 We don't feel at ease here: we are surrounded by too much beauty.

> Ibid.

6 A bed, a nice fresh bed, with smoothly drawn sheets and a hot-water bottle at the end of it, soft to the feet like a live animal's tummy.

> Ibid., "Arrival and Rehearsal"

7 Happy in our obtuse way, devoid of intuition or foresight, we give no thought to the future, to misfortune, to old age. . . .

> Ibid.

8 Privation prevents all thought, substitutes for any other mental image that of a hot, sweet-smelling dish, and reduces hope to the shape of a rounded loaf set in rays of glory.

> Ibid., "A Bad Morning"

9 Our goal, though difficult to attain, is not inaccessible. Words, as we cease to feel their urgency, become detached from us, like graceless chips from a precious gem. Invested with a subtler task than those who speak classical verse or exchange witticisms in lively prose, we are eager to banish from our mute dialogues the

347

earthbound word, the one obstacle between us and si- lence—perfect, limpid, rhythmic silence—proud to give expression to every emotion and every feeling, and ac- cepting no other support, no other restraint than that of music alone.

Ibid.

10 "My dear sir, *they* don't debate. Each of them merely issues an ultimatum, and in what a tone! It all goes to show what extraordinary people they are, each more unequivocal than the other."

"The Old Lady and the Bear" 1914

11 I hate guests who complain of the cooking and leave bits and pieces all over the place and cream-cheese sticking to the mirrors.

Cheri 1920

12 Years of close familiarity rendered silence congenial. . . .

Ibid.

13 Life is nothing but a series of crosses for us mothers.

Ibid.

14 . . . they had become mistrustful, self-indulgent, and cut off from the world, as women are who have lived only for love.

Ibid.

15 . . . her smile was like a rainbow after a sudden storm.

Ibid.

16 Give me a dozen such heart-breaks, if that would help me to lose a couple of pounds.

Ibid.

17 Life as a child and then as a girl had taught her pa- tience, hope, silence; and given her a prisoner's profi- ciency in handling these virtues as weapons.

Ibid.

18 You aren't frightened when a door slams, though it may make you jump. It's a snake creeping under it that's frightening.

Ibid.

19 . . . the sudden desire to look beautiful made her straighten her back. "Beautiful? For whom? Why, for myself, of course."

Ibid.

20 The divorce will be gayer than the wedding.

Ibid.

21 Let's go out and buy playing-cards, good wine, bridge-
scorers, knitting needles—all the paraphernalia to fill a
gaping void, all that's required to disguise that monster,
an old woman.

Ibid.

22 That lovely voice; how I should weep for joy if I could
hear it now!

"Where Are the Children,"
My Mother's House   1922

23 If there be a place of waiting after this life, then surely
she who so often waited for us has not ceased to tremble for those two who are yet alive.

Ibid.

24 "Where, oh where are the children . . . ?"

Ibid.

25 "What a nuisance! Why should one have to eat? And
what shall we eat this evening?"

Ibid., "Jealousy"

26 Blushing beneath the strands of her graying hair, her
chin trembling with resentment, this little elderly lady
is charming when she defends herself without so much
as a smile against the accusations of a jealous sexage-
narian. Nor does he smile either as he goes on to accuse
her now of "gallivanting." But I can still smile at their
quarrels because I am only fifteen and have not yet
divined the ferocity of love beneath his old man's eye-
brows, or the blushes of adolescence upon her fading
cheeks.

Ibid.

27   "What are you thinking about, Bel-Gazou?"
    "Nothing, Mother."
    An excellent answer. The same that I invariably gave
when I was her age.

Ibid., "The Priest on the Wall"

28 It is not a bad thing that children should occasionally,
and politely, put parents in their place.

Ibid.

29 I know that to her faithful nurse, my Bel-Gazou is alternately the center of the universe, a consummate

masterpiece, a possessed monster from whom the devil must hourly be exorcised, a champion runner, a dizzy abyss of perversity, a *dear little one*, and a baby rabbit. But who will tell me how my daughter appears to herself?

Ibid.

30 What's come over our daughters that they don't like essence of violet any more?

Ibid., "My Mother and Illness"

31 It's pretty hard to retain the characteristics of one's sex after a certain age.

Ibid.

32 You'll understand later that one keeps on forgetting old age up to the very brink of the grave.

Ibid.

33 Imagine killing all those young flowers for the sake of an old woman.

Ibid.

34 . . . she has lost her torturer, her tormentor, the daily poison, the lack of which may well kill her.

Ibid.

35 Those love children always suffer because their mothers have crushed them under their stays trying to hide them, more's the pity. Yet after all, a lovely unrepentant creature, big with child, is not such an outrageous sight.

Ibid.

36 But at my age there's only one virtue: not to make people unhappy.   Ibid.

37 . . . great joys must be controlled.

Ibid., "The Seamstress"

38 But it would seem that with this needleplay she has discovered the perfect means of adventuring, stitch by stitch, point by point, along a road of risks and temptations.   Ibid.

39 Oh, for those young embroiderers of bygone days, sitting on a hard little stool in the shelter of their mother's ample skirts! Maternal authority kept them there for years and years, never rising except to change the skein of silk or to elope with a stranger.   Ibid.

40 . . . the telephone shone as brightly as a weapon kept polished by daily use. . . .

The Last of Cheri   1926

41 I love my past. I love my present. I'm not ashamed of what I've had, and I'm not sad because I have it no longer.

Ibid.

42 If one wished to be perfectly sincere, one would have to admit there are two kinds of love—well-fed and ill-fed. The rest is pure fiction.

Ibid.

43 Whenever I feel myself inferior to everything about me, threatened by my own mediocrity, frightened by the discovery that a muscle is losing its strength, a desire its power, or a pain the keen edge of its bite, I can still hold up my head and say to myself: . . . "Let me not forget that I am the daughter of a woman who bent her head, trembling, between the blades of a cactus, her wrinkled face full of ecstasy over the promise of a flower, a woman who herself never ceased to flower, untiringly, during three quarters of a century."

Break of Day   1928

44 A second place [setting]. . . . If I say that it is to be taken away for good, no pernicious blast will blow suddenly from the horizon to make my hair stand on end and alter the direction of my life as once it did. If that plate is removed from my table, I shall still eat with appetite.

Ibid.

45 I instinctively like to acquire and store up what promises to outlast me.

Ibid.

46 My true friends have always given me that supreme proof of devotion, a spontaneous aversion for the man I loved.

Ibid.

47 For to dream and then to return to reality only means that our qualms suffer a change of place and significance.

Ibid.

48 I have suffered, oh yes, certainly I learned how to suffer. But is suffering so very serious? I have come to

doubt it. It may be quite childish, a sort of undignified pastime—I'm referring to the kind of suffering a man inflicts on a woman or a woman on a man. It's extremely painful. I agree that it's hardly bearable. But I very much fear that this sort of pain deserves no consideration at all.

Ibid.

49 "Love is not a sentiment worthy of respect."

Ibid.

50 O Man, my former loves, how one gains and learns in your company!

Ibid.

51 . . . that wild, unknown being, the child, who is both bottomless pit and impregnable fortress. . . .

"Look!" 1929

52 I have not forgotten how I used to take a child every year to the sea, as to a maternal element better fitted than I to teach, ripen, and perfect the mind and body that I had merely roughhewn.

Ibid.

53 I am seized with the itch to possess the secrets of a being who has vanished forever. . . .

"The Savages," Sido 1929

54 He was such an inoffensive little boy, she could find no fault with him, except his tendency to disappear.

Ibid.

55 "You don't like them? Then what was it you wanted?"
Rashly he confessed: "I wanted to ask for them."

Ibid.

56 When ordinary parents produce exceptional children they are often so dazzled by them that they push them into careers that they consider superior, even if it takes some lusty kicks on their behinds to achieve this result.

Ibid.

57 He finds him again without difficulty, slips into the light and nimble little body that he never leaves long, and roams through a century of the mind, where all is to the measure and liking of one who for sixty years has triumphantly remained a child.

Ibid.

58 The age we call awkward and the growing pains it inflicts on young bodies exact occasional sacrifices.

Ibid.

59 She [the cat] hasn't had her full ration of kisses-on-the-lips today. She had the quarter-to-twelve one in the Bois, she had the two o'clock one after coffee, she had the half-past-six one in the garden, but she's missed tonight's.

The Cat 1933

60 This life's idiotic: we're seeing far too much of each other and yet we never see each other properly.

Ibid.

61 He shut his eyes while Saha [the cat] kept vigil, watching all the invisible signs that hover over sleeping human beings when the light is put out.

Ibid.

62 He loved his dreams and cultivated them.

Ibid.

63 . . . that provisional tomb where the living exile sighs, weeps, fights, and succumbs, and from which he rises, remembering nothing, with the day.

Ibid.

64 "She never misses an opportunity to shrink away from anything that can be tasted or touched or smelled."

"Armande" 1944

65 "All women are monkeys. They're interested only in our absurdities and our love affairs and our illnesses."

Ibid.

66 He wondered why sexual shyness, which excites the desire of dissolute women, arouses the contempt of decent ones.

Ibid.

67 . . . love made him gloomy, jealous, self-conscious, unable to break down an obstacle between the two of them that perhaps did not exist.

Ibid.

68 "Drawers are one thing, decorum is another. . . ."

Gigi 1944

69 "If you didn't find *me* discouraging, then you'd find something else."

Ibid.

70 . . . she drew no advantage other than the close relationship of Gaston Lachaille and the pleasure to be derived from watching a rich man enjoying the comforts of the poor. . . .

Ibid.

71 "She's smart enough to keep herself to herself."

Ibid.

72 "If only her brain worked as well as her jaws!"

Ibid.

73 . . . pessimists have good appetites.

Ibid.

74   "Call your mother, Gigi! Liane d'Exelmans has committed suicide."
The child replied with a long drawn-out "Oooh!" and asked, "Is she dead?"
"Of course not. She knows how to do things."

Ibid.

75 "You must always start by refusing to give an interview to anybody. Then later you can fill the front page."

Ibid.

76 "The telephone is of real use only to important businessmen or to women who have something to hide."

Ibid.

77 "Instead of marrying 'at once,' it sometimes happens that we marry 'at last.' "

Ibid.

78 "Boredom helps one to make decisions."

Ibid.

79 "Explain yourself without gestures. The moment you gesticulate you look common."

Ibid.

80 "A pretty little collection of weaknesses and a terror of spiders are indispensable stock-in-trade with men."

Ibid.

81 "They forgive us—oh, for many things, but not for the absence in us of their own failings."   Ibid.

82   "All that's in the past. All that's over and done with."
"Of course, Tonton, until it begins again."   Ibid.

83 . . . he was always ready to part with twenty francs or
even a "banknote," so much so that he died poor, in
the arms of his unsuspected honesty.

"The Photographer's Missus"   *1944*

84 "Oh, you know, when it comes to pearls, it's very seldom there isn't some shady story behind them."

Ibid.

85 "In our part of the world, as you well know, they say
raw meat is for cats and the English."

Ibid.

86 "Don't be too nice to me. When anyone's too nice to
me, I don't know what I'm doing—I boil over like a
soup."

Ibid.

87 The unexpected sound of sobbing is demoralizing.

Ibid.

88 On this narrow planet, we have only the choice between two unknown worlds.

Ibid.

89 In the matter of furnishing, I find a certain absence of
ugliness far worse than ugliness.

Ibid.

90 Like so many saviors, heavenly or earthly, the angel
tended to overdo her part.

Ibid.

91 Sorrow, fear, physical pain, excessive heat and excessive cold, I can still guarantee to stand up to all these
with decent courage. But I abdicate in the face of boredom, which turns me into a wretched and, if necessary,
ferocious creature.

Ibid.

92 It is easy to relate what is of no importance.

Ibid.

93 "Such a happy woman, why exactly, that's what I
would have been if, here and there, in my trivial little
life, I'd had something great. What do I call great? I've
no idea, madame, because I've never had it!"

Ibid.

94 "But once I had set out, I was already far on my way."

Ibid.

95 "Madame, people very seldom die because they lost someone. I believe they die more often because they haven't had someone."

Ibid.

96 A mouth is not always a mouth, but a bit is always a bit, and it matters little what it bridles.

"The Sick Child"   *1944*

97 Exhausted under the burden of universal kindness, he shut his eyes. . . .

Ibid.

98 . . . the majesty that illness confers on children whom it strikes down. . . .

Ibid.

99 [There are] two forms of luxury: fastidiousness and pain.

Ibid.

100 . . . one word escaped, crisp and lively, and made a beeline for Jean, the word "crisis." Sometimes it entered ceremoniously, like a lady dressed up to give away prizes, with an *h* behind its ear and a *y* tucked into its bodice: Chrysis, Chrysis Salutari.

Ibid.

101 The confused murmur of his nights began to rise, expected but not familiar.

Ibid.

102 A boiled egg raised its little lid and revealed its buttercup yolk.   *Ibid.*

103 Slightly intoxicated with the power to work marvels, he called up his boon companions of the cruel but privileged hours: the visible sounds; the tangible images; the breathable seas; the nourishing, navigable air; the wings that mocked feet; the laughing suns.

Ibid.

104 A time comes when one is forced to concentrate on living. A time comes when one has to renounce dying in full flight.   *Ibid.*

105 My only remaining property is . . . a living beast, the fire . . . like all other beasts, it likes to have its belly scratched from underneath.

"The Blue Lantern"   *1949*

106 How pleasant a companion, the fire is
To the prisoner, during the long winter evenings!
Very near me a benevolent spirit warms itself
Who drinks or smokes or sings an old tune. . . .

Ibid.

107 A line of verse need not necessarily be beautiful for it
to remain in the depths of our memory and occupy
maliciously the place overrun by certain condemnable
but unerasable melodies.

Ibid.

108 . . . writing leads only to writing.   Ibid.

109 The more the wonders of the visible world become
inaccessible, the more intensely do its curiosities affect
us.

"Orchid," For a Flower   1949

388. Mary Elizabeth Crouse
(1873–?)

* * *

1 How often do the clinging hands, though weak,
Clasp round strong hearts that otherwise would break.

"Strength of Weakness"

389. Marie Dressler
(1873–1934)

1 Fate cast me to play the role of an ugly duckling with
no promise of swanning. Therefore, I sat down when a
mere child—fully realizing just how utterly "mere" I
was—and figured out my life early. Most people do it,
but they do it too late. At any rate, from the beginning
I have played my life as a comedy rather than the tragedy many would have made of it.

The Life Story of an Ugly Duckling,
Ch. 1   1924

2 . . . poor had no terror for me! It was pie for me! My
whole life had been a fight!   Ibid., Ch. 5

3 I was born serious and I have earned my bread making
other people laugh.

My Own Story, Ch. 1   1934p

4 It is well enough to be interested in one's profession, but to restrict one's leisure to association with the members of one's own guild, so to speak, is to be doomed to artificiality and eventually to sterility. In order to represent life on the stage, we must rub elbows with life, live ourselves.

Ibid., Ch. 3

5 Love is not getting, but giving. It is sacrifice. And sacrifice is glorious! I have no patience with women who measure and weigh their love like a country doctor dispensing capsules. If a man is worth loving at all, he is worth loving generously, even recklessly.

Ibid., Ch. 7

6 There is a vast difference between success at twenty-five and success at sixty. At sixty, nobody envies you. Instead, everybody rejoices generously, sincerely, in your good fortune.

Ibid., Ch. 17

7 By the time we hit fifty, we have learned our hardest lessons. We have found out that only a few things are really important. We have learned to take life seriously, but never ourselves.   Ibid.

390. Nellie McClung
(1873–1951)

1 When they felt tired, they called it laziness and felt disgraced, and thus they had spent their days, working, working from the grey dawn, until the darkness came again, and all for what? When in after years these girls, broken in health and in spirits, slipped away to premature graves, or, worse still, settled into chronic invalidism, of what avail was the memory of the cows they milked, the mats they hooked, the number of pounds of butter they made.

Sowing Seeds in Danny   1908

2 "While we are side by side" the violins sang, glad, triumphant, that old story that runs like a thread of gold through all life's patterns; that old song, old yet ever new, deathless, unchangeable, which maketh the poor man rich and without which the richest becomes poor!   Ibid.

391. Virginia Taylor McCormick
(1873–1957)

* * *

1 Not any leaf from any book
Can give what Pan, in going, took.

"Regret from Pan"

2 Now she is dead she greets Christ with a nod,—
(He was a carpenter)—*but she knows God.*

"The Snob"

392. Elizabeth Reeve Morrow
(1873–1955)

* * *

1 My friend and I have built a wall
Between us thick and wide:
The stones of it are laid in scorn
And plastered high with pride.

"Wall," St. 1

2 There is no lover like an island shore
For lingering embrace;
No tryst so faithful as the turning tide
At its accustomed place.

"Islands," St. 1

393. Daisy, Princess of Pless
(1873–?)

1 My parents, with hearts full of tender love, did nothing
whatever to prepare me for life and its ordeals. . . .
Without a rudder or chart, I was at the mercy of any
winds that blew close enough to reach me. Either of
my parents would have done anything in the world for
me—except tell me the truth.

Daisy, Princess of Pless, Ch. 1   1923

2 How seldom people find their happiness on a darkened
stage; they must turn up all the limelights to find it.

Entry (August 16, 1903),
From My Private Diary   1926

3 No theatre is prosperous, or a play complete, unless there is a bedroom scene in the second act. . . .

Ibid. (April 28, 1904)

4 It is no use having illusions about life. Life, as we live it, *is* commonplace unless one chooses to renounce the world, and live out of it, and therefore be different from others.

Ibid.

5 The souls we have loved here, we may love and meet again because we have once loved them; but our intercourse with them will not be tainted with the remembrance of this heartbreaking little world; we shall not recognize them in their personal limitations.

Ibid. (February 13, 1907)

6 I was always frank by nature and cannot understand the absurd reticences which many people seem to consider so necessary.

Better Left Unsaid, Ch. 1 *1931*

7 The Irish sit by a peat fire; the English by a coal one. That is the unbridgeable difference between the two peoples: We prefer the glamorous, the quick, the pungent; they the lasting and substantial.

What I Left Unsaid, Ch. 1 *1936*

8 For each of us, after middle-age, the world is always emptying.

Ibid., Ch. 3

394. Emily Post
(1873–1960)

1 Considering manners even in their superficial aspect, no one—unless he be a recluse who comes in contact with no other human being—can fail to reap the advantage of a proper, courteous and likeable approach, or fail to be handicapped by an improper, offensive and resented one.

Etiquette, Ch. 1 *1922*

2 Ideal conversation must be an exchange of thought, and not, as many of those who worry most about their shortcomings believe, an eloquent exhibition of wit or oratory.

Ibid., Ch. 6

3 . . . to do *exactly as your neighbors* do is the only sensible rule.

Ibid., Ch. 33

4 To the old saying that man built the house but woman made of it a "home" might be added the modern supplement that woman accepted cooking as a chore but man has made of it a recreation.

Ibid., Ch. 34

5 Far more important than any mere dictum of etiquette is the fundamental code of honor, without strict observance of which no man, no matter how "polished," can be considered a gentleman. The honor of a gentleman demands the inviolability of his word, and the incorruptibility of his principles. He is the descendant of the knight, the crusader; he is the defender of the defenseless and the champion of justice—or he is not a gentleman.

Ibid., Ch. 48

6 To tell a lie in cowardice, to tell a lie for gain, or to avoid deserved punishment—are all the blackest of black lies. On the other hand, to teach him to try his best to avoid the truth—even to press it when necessary toward the outer edge of the rainbow—for a reason of kindness, or of mercy, is far closer to the heart of truth than to repeat something accurately and mercilessly that will cruelly hurt the feelings of someone.

Children Are People, Ch. 11   1940

7 The natural impulses of every thoroughbred include his sense of honor; his love of fair play and courage; his dislike of pretense and of cheapness.

Ibid., Ch. 30

395. Dorothy Miller Richardson
(1873–1957)

1 "There; how d'ye like that, eh? A liberal education in twelve volumes, with an index."

Pilgrimage, Vol. II, Ch. 24   1938

2 . . . women stopped being people and went off into hideous processes.   Ibid.

3 If there was a trick, there must be a trickster.   Ibid.

4 It will all go on as long as women are stupid enough to go on bringing men into the world. . . .

Ibid.

5 They invent a legend to put the blame for the existence of humanity on women and, if she wants to stop it, they talk about the wonders of civilizations and the sacred responsibilities of motherhood. They can't have it both ways. Ibid.

6 No future life could heal the degradation of having been a woman. Religion in the world had nothing but insults for women.

Ibid.

7 *Coercion.* The unpardonable crime.
Ibid., Vol. IV, Ch. 9

8 In and out of every year of his ascent her life had been woven. She had been a witness, and was now a kind of compendium for him of it all, one of his supports, one of those who through having known the beginnings, through representing them every time she appeared, brought to him a realization of his achievements.

Ibid.

9 . . . she saw how very slight, how restricted and perpetually baffled must always be the communication between him and anything that bore the name of woman. Saw the price each one had paid with whom he had been intimate either in love or friendship, in being obliged to shut off . . . three-fourths of their being.

Ibid.

10 "Women carry all the domesticity they need about with them. That is why they can get along alone so much better than men."

Ibid.

11 "Religious people in general are in some way unsatisfactory. Not fully alive. Exclusive. Irreligious people are unsatisfactory in another way. Defiant."

Ibid.

12 . . . men want recognition of their work, to help them to believe in themselves.

Ibid.

13 With the familiar clothes, something of his essential self seemed to have departed. Ibid.

396. Margaret Baillie Saunders
(1873–1949?)

1 I've often known people more shocked because you are
not bankrupt than because you are.
A Shepherd of Kensington   1907

2 One's old acquaintances sometimes come upon one like
ghosts—and most people hate ghosts.

Ibid.

3 Very few men care to have the obvious pointed out to
them by a woman.

Ibid.

397. Janet Scudder
(1873–1940)

1 I don't believe artists should be subjected to experiences that harden the sensibilities; without sensibility
no fine work can ever be done.
Modeling My Life, Ch. 2   1925

2 Someone has said that even criticism is better than silence. I don't agree to this. Criticism can be very harmful unless it comes from a master; and in spite of the
fact that we have hundreds of critics these days, it is
one of the most difficult of professions.   Ibid.

398. Edith Franklin Wyatt
(1873–1958)

1 Every true poem is a lone fount, of whose refreshment
the traveler himself must drink, if he is to quench his
thirst for poetry.
"Modern Poetry," *Art and the
Worth-While,* Baker Brownell, ed.   1929

2 Our criticism is always devoting itself to . . .
watching the sticks and straws on the surface of the current, without interest, apparently, in the natural force
of the stream, the style and turn of the whole composi-
tion, its communicative social imagination.   Ibid.

399. Ch'iu Chin
(1874–1907)

1 We'll follow Joan of Arc—
With our own hands our land we shall regain!

> "Ch'iu Chin—A Woman Revolu-
> tionary," Quoted in *Women of
> China* by Fan Wen-Lan   *1956p*

2 "We want to unite our two hundred million sisters into
a solid whole, so that they can call to each other. Our
journal will act as the mouthpiece for our women. It is
meant to help our sisters by giving their life a deeper
meaning and hope and to advance rapidly towards a
bright, new society. We Chin women should become
the vanguard in rousing the people to welcome enlightenment."   Ibid. (1905)

400. Isabel La Howe Conant
(1874–?)

* * *

1 He who loves an old house
Never loves in vain.   "Old House," St. 1

401. Olive Custance
(1874–1944)

* * *

1 Spirit of Twilight, through your folded wings
I catch a glimpse of your averted face,
And rapturous on a sudden, my soul sings
"Is not this common earth a holy place?"

                                "Twilight"

402. Zona Gale
(1874–1938)

1 They were all dimly aware that something was escaping
them, some inheritance of joy which they had meant to
share. How was it they were not sharing it?

                        Birth, Ch. 1   *1918*

2 Loving, like prayer, is a power as well as a process. It's curative. It is creative.

Ibid., Ch. 3

3 DWIGHT. Energy—it's the driving power of the nation.
Miss Lulu Bett, Act I, Sc. 1   *1920*

4 NINIAN. Education: I ain't never had it and I ain't never missed it.

Ibid., Sc. 2

5 DWIGHT. I tell you of all history the most beautiful product is the family tie. Of it are born family consideration. . . .

Ibid., Act II, Sc. 2

6 He faced the blind wall of human loneliness. He was as one who, expecting to be born, is still-born, and becomes aware not of the cradle, but of eternity.

"The Biography of Blade,"
Century Magazine   *1924*

7 Always he had wanted to tell somebody about his life, but when he had tried, his confidante had looked at him.

"Evening," *The Book Man*   *1925*

8 But the romance, the true interpretation of any habit, of any convention, lies in this faint inner significance for which few have memory or attention.

"Modern Prose," *Art and the
Worth-While,* Baker Brownell, ed.   *1929*

9 The unexpressed, then, is always of greater value than the expressed.   *Ibid.*

* * *

10 He was integrated into life,
He was a member of life,
He was harmonized, orchestrated, identified with the
    program of being.   "Walt Whitman"

403. Theodosia Garrison
(1874–1944)

* * *

1 At first cock-crow the ghosts must go
Back to their quiet graves below.   "The Neighbors"

2 I have known laughter—therefore I
   May sorrow with you far more tenderly
   Than those who never guess how sad a thing
   Seems merriment to one heart's suffering.

                                    "Knowledge"

3 I never crossed your threshold with a grief
   But that I went without it.
                          "The Closed Door," St. 1

4 The hardest habit of all to break
   Is the terrible habit of happiness.

                                      "The Lake"

5 The kindliest thing God ever made,
   His hand of very healing laid
   Upon a fevered world, is shade.

                               "The Shade," St. 1

6 When the red wrath perisheth, when the dulled swords
      fail,
   These three who have walked with death—these shall
      prevail.
   Hell bade all its millions rise; Paradise sends three:
   Pity, and self-sacrifice, and charity.
                              "This Shall Prevail"

404. Ellen Glasgow
(1874–1945)

1 And the spring passed into Nicholas also. The wonderful renewal of surrounding life thrilled through the repression of his nature. With the flowing of the sap the
   blood flowed more freely in his veins. New possibilities
   were revealed to him; new emotions urged him into
   fresh endeavours. All his powerful, unspent youth
   spurred on to manhood.
        The Voice of the People, Bk. II, Ch. 3   *1900*

2 With a sudden shout Nicholas voiced the glorification
   of toil—of honest work well done. He felt with the
   force of a revelation that to throw up the clods of earth
   manfully is as beneficent as to revolutionise the world.
   It was not the matter of the work, but the mind that
   went into it, that counted—and the man who was not
   content to do small things well would leave great things
   undone.   Ibid., Ch. 4

3 "A farmer's got to be born, same as a fool. You can't make a corn pone out of flour dough by the twistin' of it."

Ibid.

4 "What a man marries for's hard to tell," she returned; "an' what a woman marries for's past findin' out."

Ibid., Bk. III, Ch. 1

5 "I ain't never seen no head so level that it could bear the lettin' in of politics. It makes a fool of a man and a worse fool of a fool. The government's like a mule, it's slow and it's sure; it's slow to turn, and it's sure to turn the way you don't want it."

Ibid., Ch. 2

6 "I d'clare if it don't beat all—one minute we're thar an' the next we're here. It's a movin' world we live in, ain't that so, Mum?"

The Deliverance, Bk. I, Ch. 1   *1904*

7 "Maria has been so long at her high-and-mighty boarding-school," he said, "that I reckon her head's as full of fancies as a cheese is of maggots."

Ibid., Ch. 3

8 "I haven't much opinion of words. . . . They're apt to set fire to a dry tongue, that's what I say."

Ibid., Bk. II, Ch. 4

9 "I hate lies, I have had so many of them, and I shall speak the truth hereafter, no matter what comes of it. Anything is better than a long, wearing falsehood, or than those hideous little shams that we were always afraid to touch for fear they would melt and show us our own nakedness."

Ibid., Bk. IV, Ch. 2

10 I wondered why anyone so rich and so beautiful should ever be unhappy—for I had been schooled by poverty to believe that money is the first essential of happiness—and yet her unhappiness was as evident as her beauty, or the luxury that enveloped her.

"The Past," *Good Housekeeping*   *1920*

11 "For once we were natural. . . . And it was a relief, even to the women, especially to the women, when the savage hunger broke through the thin crust we call civilization. It was a relief to us all, no doubt, to be able to

think murder and call it idealism. But the war wasn't the worst thing," he concluded grimly. "The worst thing is this sense of having lost our way in the universe. The worst thing is that the war has made peace seem so futile. It is just as if the bottom had dropped out of idealism. . . ."

They Stooped to Folly, Pt. I, Ch. 1 *1929*

12 "Oh, but it feels so nice to be hard! If I had known how nice it felt, I should have been hard all my life."

Ibid., Ch. 12

13 After all, you can't expect men not to judge by appearances.

The Sheltered Life *1932*

14 Shadows are not enough.

Ibid.

15 Women like to sit down with trouble as if it were knitting.

Ibid.

16 No idea is so antiquated that it was not once modern. No idea is so modern that it will not someday be antiquated.

Address, Modern Language Association *1936*

17 To seize the flying thought before it escapes us is our only touch with reality.

Ibid.

18 "Grandpa says we've got everything to make us happy but happiness."

In This Our Life, Pt. I, Ch. 1 *1941*

19 "Heaven knows, I'm not a snob, and I realize it's the fashion nowadays to climb down and not up; but all the radicals you see in the newspapers look so untidy, and I'm afraid when he gets middle-aged he will never want to brush his hair or wash his face."

Ibid., Ch. 9

20 "I don't like human nature, but I do like human beings."

Ibid., Pt. II, Ch. 1

21 "We didn't talk so much about happiness in my day. When it came, we were grateful for it, and, I suppose, a little went farther than it does nowadays. We may have

been all wrong in our ideas, but we were brought up to think other things more important than happiness."

Ibid., Ch. 10

22 No matter how vital experience might be while you lived it, no sooner was it ended and dead than it became as lifeless as the piles of dry dust in a school history book.

Ibid., Pt. II, Ch. 9

23 Tilling the fertile soil of man's vanity.
A Certain Measure 1943

405. Beatrice Hinkle
(1874–1953)

1 Fundamentally the male artist approximates more to the psychology of woman, who, biologically speaking, is a purely creative being and whose personality has been as mysterious and unfathomable to the man as the artist has been to the average person.
"The Psychology of the Artist,"
Recreating the Individual 1923

2 . . . woman is a being dominated by the creative urge and . . . no understanding of her as an individual can be gained unless the significance and effects of that great fact can be grasped.

Ibid.

3 . . . the artist has always been and still is a being somewhat apart from the rest of humanity.

Ibid.

4 When one looks back over human existence, however, it is very evident that all culture has developed through an *initial resistance against adaptation to the reality in which man finds himself.*

Ibid.

5 The mystics are the only ones who have gained a glimpse into what is possible. . . .   Ibid.

6 The amount which cannot be harnessed and domesticated, but insists on its own form of activity rather than one which is offered ready made, is the energy used for the creation of art.   Ibid.

7 The creator does not create only for the pleasure of creating but . . . he also desires to subdue other minds. Ibid.

8 The attitude and reactions of artists toward their art children reveal an attitude similar to that which mothers in general possess toward their children. There is the same sensitivity to any criticism, the same possessive pride, the same devotion and love, with the accompanying anxiety and distress concerning them. Ibid.

406. Bettina von Hutten
(1874–1957)

1 A good many women are good tempered simply because it saves the wrinkles coming too soon.
The Halo 1907

2 Everybody in the world ought to be sorry for everybody else. We all have our little private hell. Ibid.

407. Yamamuro Kieko
(1874–1915)

1 . . . I realize that were I a man, I would be at the battlefront fighting amidst bullets and explosives, instead of sitting serenely at my desk.
Untitled Essay 1895

408. Amy Lowell
(1874–1925)

1 Time! Joyless emblem of the greed
Of millions, robber of the best
Which earth can give. . . .
"New York at Night," *A Dome of Many*-Coloured *Glass* 1912

2 Brave idolatry
Which can conceive a hero! No deceit,
No knowledge taught by unrelenting years,
Can quench this fierce, untamable desire.
Ibid., "Hero-Worship"

3 Every castle of the air
 Sleeps in the fine black grains, and there
 Are seeds for every romance, or light
 Whiff of a dream for a summer night.
 "Sword Blades and Poppy Seeds,"
 Sword Blades and Poppy Seeds   *1914*

4 Visions for those too tired to sleep.
 These seeds cast a film over eyes which weep.
 Ibid., St. 3

5 All books are either dreams or swords,
 You can cut, or you can drug, with words.
 Ibid.

6 Happiness, to some, elation;
 Is, to others, mere stagnation.
 Ibid., "Happiness"

7 Marshalled like soldiers in gay company,
 The tulips stand arrayed. Here infantry
 Wheels out into the sunlight.
 Ibid., "A Tulip Garden"

8 My God, but you keep me starved! You write "No Entrance Here," over all the doors. . . . Hating bonds as
 you do, why should I be denied the rights of love if I
 leave you free?
 Ibid., "The Basket," III

9 My words are little jars
 For you to take and put upon a shelf.
 Ibid., "Gift"

10 Also the scent from them fills the room
 With sweetness of flowers and crushed grass.
 Ibid.

11 You are beautiful and faded,
 Like an old opera tune
 Played upon a harpsichord.
 Ibid., "A Lady," St. 1

12 I too am a rare
 Pattern. As I wander down
 The garden paths.
 "Patterns," *Men, Women, and Ghosts*   *1916*

13   A pattern called a war.
 Christ! What are patterns for?   Ibid., St. 7

14 The cost runs into millions, but a woman must have
   something to console herself for a broken heart.
   Ibid., "Malmaison," V

15 Art is the desire of a man to express himself, to record
   the reactions of his personality to the world he lives in.
   Tendencies in Modern American Poetry   1917

16 Youth condems; maturity condones.
   Ibid.

17 All Naples prates of this and that, and runs about its
   little business, shouting, bawling, incessantly calling
   its wares.
   "Sea-Blue and Blood-Red," II,
Can Grande's Castle   1918

18 Let the key-guns be mounted, make a brave show of
   waging war, and pry off the lid of Pandora's box
   once more.
   Ibid., "Guns as Keys: And the
Great Gate Swings," Pt. I

19 A wise man,
   Watching the stars pass across the sky,
   Remarked:
   In the upper air the fireflies move more slowly.
   "Meditation," *Picture of the
Floating World*   1919

20 Moon!
   Moon!
   I am prone before you.
   Pity me,
   And drench me in loneliness.
   Ibid., "On a Certain Critic"

21 If failure, then another long beginning.
   Why hope,
   Why think that Spring must bring relenting.
   "A Legend of Porcelain," St. 25, *Legends*   1921

22 "The sun weaves the seasons," thought Many Swans,
   "I have been under and over the warp of the
   world. . . ."
   Ibid., "Many Swans"

23 There are few things so futile, and few so amusing,
   As a peaceful and purposeless sort of perusing

Of old random jottings set down in a blank-book
You've unearthed from a drawer as you looked for
   your bank-book. . . .

"A Critical Fable," St. 1,
A Critical Fable   1922

24 A man must be sacrificed now and again
   To provide for the next generation of men.

Ibid., St. 2

25 I am sorry myself to be forced to distort a
   Fine line unduly, and if I or my thought err
   I am willing to own it without the least *hauteur.*

Ibid., St. 9

26 And the sight of a white church above thin trees in a
   city square
   Amazes my eyes as though it were the Parthenon.

"Meeting-House Hill,"
What's O'Clock   1925

27 And what are we?
   We, the people without a race,
   Without a language;
   Of all races, and of none;
   Of all tongues, and one imposed;
   Of all traditions and all pasts,
   With no tradition and no past.
   A patchwork and an altar-piece. . . .

Ibid., "The Congressional Liberty," St. 1

28 Heart-leaves of lilac all over New England,
   Roots of lilac under all the soil of New England,
   Lilac in me because I am New England.

Ibid., "Lilacs," St. 4

29 I went a-riding, a-riding,
   Over a great long plain.
   And the plain went a-sliding, a-sliding
   Away from my bridle-rein.

Ibid., "Texas," St. 1

30 Love is a game—yes?
   I think it is a drowning. . . .

Ibid., "Twenty-four Hokku on a
Modern Theme," XIX

31 Sappho would speak, I think, quite openly,
   And Mrs. Browning guard a careful silence,

373

But Emily would set doors ajar and slam them
And love you for your speed of observation.
Ibid., "The Sisters," St. 2

* * *

32 Finally, most of us [imagist poets] believe that concentration is the very essence of poetry.   "Imagist Poetry"

33 For books are more than books, they are the life
The very heart and core of ages past,
The reason why men lived and worked and died,
The essence and quintessence of their lives.
Untitled Poem, *The Boston Athenoeum*

409. Dorothy Reed Mendenhall
(1874–1964)

1 My early life had been fed with dreams and a deep feeling that if I waited, did my part and was patient, love would come to me and with it such a family life as fiction depicted and romance built up. It seems to me that I have always been waiting for something better—sometimes to see the best I had snatched from me.
Quoted in "Dorothy Mendenhall:
'Childbirth Is Not a Disease' "
by Gena Corea, *Ms.*   *April, 1974p*

2 When hurry in the attendant meets fear in the mother, the combination . . . militates against safe and sane obstetrics.   Ibid.

410. Alice Duer Miller
(1874–1942)

1 And now too late, we see these things are one:
That art is sacrifice and self-control,
And who loves beauty must be stern of soul.
"An American to France," *Welcome Home*   1928

2 When a woman like that whom I've seen so much
All of a sudden drops out of touch,
Is always busy and never can
Spare you a moment, it means a Man.
"Forsaking All Others,"
Forsaking All Others   1931

3   Frenchmen, when
The ultimate menace comes, will die for France
Logically as they lived.

Ibid., XXI

4 Good manners are the technique of expressing consideration for the feelings of others.

"I Like American Manners,"
Saturday Evening Post   *August 13, 1932*

5 The white cliffs of Dover, I saw rising steeply
Out of the sea that once made her [England] secure.

"The White Cliffs," St. 1,
The White Cliffs   1940

6   I am American bred,
I have seen much to hate here—much to forgive,
    But in a world where England is finished and dead,
I do not wish to live.

Ibid., St. 52

411. Lucy Montgomery
(1874–1942)

1 "Isn't it splendid to think of all the things there are to find out about? It just makes me feel glad to be alive—it's such an interesting world. It wouldn't be half so interesting if we knew all about everything, would it? There'd be no scope for imagination then, would there?"

Anne of Green Gables, Ch. 2   1908

2 "There's such a lot of different Annes in me. I sometimes think that is why I'm such a troublesome person. If I was just one Anne it would be ever so much more comfortable, but then it wouldn't be half so interesting."

Ibid., Ch. 20

3 "As for Horace Baxter, he was in financial difficulties a year ago last summer, and he prayed to the Lord for help; and when his wife died and he got her life insurance he said he believed it was the answer to his prayer. Wasn't that like a man?"

Anne's House of Dreams, Ch. 15   1917

4 "When a man is alone he's mighty apt to be with the
  devil—if he ain't with God. He has to choose which
  company he'll keep, I reckon."

Ibid.

5 The point of good writing is knowing when to stop.

Ibid., Ch. 24

412. Roselle Mercier Montgomery
(1874–1933)

1 I would always be with the thick of life,
  Threading its mazes, sharing its strife;
      Yet—somehow, singing!
          "Somehow, Singing," *Ulysses Returns*   1925

2 Never a ship sails out of the bay
  But carries my heart as a stowaway.

Ibid., "The Stowaway"

3 Put by, O waiting ones, put by your weaving,
  Unlike Ulysses, love is unreturning.

Ibid., "Counsel"

4 . . . to that they know, their dearest never guess!

Ibid., "Penelope Speaks"

5 The fates are not quite obdurate.
      They have a grim, sardonic way
  Of granting men who supplicate
      The things they wanted—yesterday!
          "The Fates," *Many Devices*   1929

* * *

6 Companioned years have made them comprehend
  The comradeship that lies beyond a kiss.

"For a Wedding Anniversary"

413. Angela Morgan
(1874?–1957)

* * *

1 A courage mightier than the sun—
  You rose and fought and, fighting, won!

"Know Thyself"

2 God, when you thought of a pine tree,
  How did you think of a star?

> "God, the Artist," St. 1

3 I will hew great windows for my soul.

> "Room"

4 Lad, you took the world's soul,
  Thrilled it by your daring,
  Lifted the uncaring
  And made them joyous men.

> "Lindbergh"

5 O thrilling age,
  O willing age!

> "Today," St. 1

6 The signals of the century
  Proclaims the things that are to be—
  The rise of woman to her place,
  The coming of a nobler race.

> Ibid., St. 3

7 To be alive in such an age—
    To live in it,
    To give to it!

> Ibid., St. 4

8 Praised be the gods that made my spirit mad;
  Kept me aflame and raw to beauty's touch.

> "June Rapture"

9 Work!
  Thank God for the swing of it,
  For the clamoring, hammering ring of it,
  Passion of labor daily hurled
  On the mighty anvils of the world.

> "Work: A Song of Triumph"

414. Rose O'Neill
(1874–1944)

1 Remember, men of guns and rhymes,
    And kings who kill so fast,
  That men you kill too many times
    May be too dead at last.

> "When the Dead Men Die,"
> *The Master's Mistress*   1922

2 "My face is a caricature of her, and her soul is a caricature of mine. In fact, she has no soul. She is my substance. She robbed me of substance in the womb. That's why I named her Narcissa. . . . She grew her beauty on me like a flower on a dunghill. She is my material. I am her soul. We are that perilous pair."

Garda, Ch. 1   1929

3 "When we are in bed, or floating in water, is the only time when we are really out of pain. In every other situation there is always some stress."

Ibid., Ch. 5

4 Her mind was as spry as a humming bird, but its beak was not so long for the inward flower of things. Still, she had always been looked upon as a wit; and when a creature is witty enough, he will occasionally say something that smacks of the profound.

Ibid., Ch. 11

5 They lose least who have least to lose.

Ibid.

6 It was not her way to invent obstacles, that blood-thinning process of the sickly imaginative.

Ibid., Ch. 15

415. Josephine Preston Peabody
(1874–1922)

* * *

1 That you should follow our poor humanhood,
Only because you would!

"To a Dog"

2   . . . The elements rehearse
Man's urgent utterance, and his words traverse
The spacious heav'ns like homing birds.

"Wireless"

3 The little Road says, Go;
The little House says, Stay;
And oh, it's bonny here at home,
But I must go away.

"The House and the Road"

416. Gertrude Stein
(1874–1946)

1 Honesty is a selfish virtue. Yes, I am honest enough.
"Adele," *Q.E.D.*, Bk. I   *1903*

2 I simply contend that the middle-class ideal which demands that people be affectionate, respectable, honest and content, that they avoid excitements and cultivate serenity is the ideal that appeals to me, it is in short the ideal of affectionate family life, of honorable business methods.

Ibid.

3 "You are so afraid of losing your moral sense that you are not willing to take it through anything more dangerous than a mud-puddle."

Ibid.

4 "I never wanted to be a hero, but on the other hand I am not anxious to cultivate cowardice."

Ibid.

5 "I could undertake to be an efficient pupil if it were possible to find an efficient teacher."

Ibid.

6 One must either accept some theory or else believe one's instinct or follow the world's opinion.
Ibid., "Helen," Bk. III

7 I am writing for myself and strangers. This is the only way that I can do it.
The Making of Americans   *1906–1908*

8 "Rose is a rose is a rose is a rose."
"Sacred Emily"   *1913*

9 I suppose I pose I expose, I repose, I close the door when the sun shines so, I close the door when the wind is so strong and the dust is not there. . . .
"Mildred's Thoughts"   *1922*

10 You are all a lost generation.
Letter to Ernest Hemingway   *1926*

11 Pigeons on the grass alas.
Four Saints in Three Acts   *1927*

379

12 Before the flowers of friendship faded friendship faded.
*Before the Flowers of Friendship
Faded Friendship Faded* 1931

13 Remarks are not literature.
*The Autobiography of
Alice B. Toklas* 1933

14 She always says she dislikes the abnormal, it is so obvious. She says the normal is so much more simply complicated and interesting.
Ibid.

15 America is my country and Paris is my hometown. And it is as it has come to be. After all anybody is as their air and land is. Anybody is as the sky is low or high, the air heavy or clear and anybody is as there is wind or no wind there. It is that which makes them and the arts they make and the work they do and the way they eat and the way they drink and the way they learn and everything. And so I am an American and I have lived half my life in Paris, not the half that made me but the half in which I made what I made.
"An American and France" 1936

16 In the United States there is more space where nobody is than where anybody is. That is what makes America what it is.
The Geographical History of America 1936

17 Everybody knows if you are too careful you are so occupied in being careful that you are sure to stumble over something.
Everybody's Autobiography, Ch. 1 1937

18 . . . native always means people who belong somewhere else, because they had once belonged somewhere. That shows that the white race does not really think they belong anywhere because they think of everybody else as native.
Ibid.

19 . . . one never discusses anything with anybody who can understand one discusses things with people who cannot understand. . . .
Ibid.

20 . . . if anything is a surprise then there is not much difference between older or younger because the only thing that does make anybody older is that they cannot be surprised.
Ibid., Ch. 2

21 . . . money . . . is really the difference between men and animals, most of the things men feel animals feel and vice versa, but animals do not know about money, money is purely a human conception and that is very important to know very very important.

Ibid.

22 A distraction is to avoid the consciousness of the passage of time.

Ibid.

23 . . . considering how dangerous everything is nothing is really very frightening.

Ibid.

24 . . . what is the use of thinking if after all there is to be organization.

Ibid.

25 More great Americans were failures than they were successes. They mostly spent their lives in not having a buyer for what they had for sale.

Ibid.

26 It is funny the two things most men are proudest of is the thing that any man can do and doing does in the same way, that is being drunk and being the father of their son.

Ibid.

27 It takes a lot of time to be a genius, you have to sit around so much doing nothing, really doing nothing.

Ibid.

28 . . . understanding is a very dull occupation.

Ibid.

29 I am also fond of saying that a war of fighting is like a dance because it is all going forward and back, and that is what everybody likes they like that forward and back movement, that is the reason that revolutions and Utopias are discouraging they are up and down and not forward and back.

Ibid., Ch. 3

30 The minute you or anybody else knows what you are you are not it, you are what you or anybody else knows you are and as everything in living is made up of finding out what you are it is extraordinarily difficult really not to know what you are and yet to be that thing.

Ibid.

31 Too few is as many as too many.

Ibid.

32 America is not old enough yet to get young again.

Ibid.

33 I am always ready to sign anything a bank tells me to sign but anything else fills me with suspicion.

Ibid.

34 Counting is the religion of this generation it is its hope and its salvation.

Ibid.

35 I understand you undertake to overthrow my undertaking.

Ibid.

36 . . . I do want to get rich but I never want to do what there is to do to get rich.

Ibid.

37 That is natural enough when nobody has had fathers they begin to long for them and then when everybody has had fathers they begin to long to do without them.

Ibid.

38 If things happen all the time you are never nervous it is when they are not happening that you are nervous.

Ibid., Ch. 4

39 In America if they do not do it right away they do not do it at all in France they very often seem not to be going to do it at all but if it has ever really been proposed at all sometimes it really is done.

Ibid.

40 The only thing that anybody can understand is mechanics and that is what makes everybody feel that they are something when they talk about it. About every other thing nobody is of the same opinion nobody means the same thing by what they say as the other one means and only the one who is talking thinks he means what he is saying even though he knows very well that that is not what he is saying.

Ibid.

41 . . . what is the use of being a little boy if you are going to grow up to be a man.

Ibid.

42 . . . it is a peaceful thing to be one succeeding.

Ibid.

43 She was thinking about it she was thinking about life.
She knew it was just like that through and through.
She never did not want to leave it.
She did not want to stop thinking about it thinking
about life, so that is what she was thinking about.

"Ida"   1941

44 Nothing has happened today except kindness. . . .

"A Diary," *Alphabets and Birthdays*   1957p

45 A diary means yes indeed. . . .

Ibid.

46 What is the answer? (I was silent.) In that case, what
is the question?

Quoted in *What Is Remembered*
by Alice B. Toklas   1963p

47 You know very well that it is not necessary to explain
to an intelligent person—one only explains to a stupid
one.

Quoted in *Playing on Alone: Letters*
of Alice B. Toklas, Ed Burns, ed.   1973p

48 And how do you look backward. By looking forward.
And what do they see. As they look forward. They see
what they had to do before they could look backward.
And there we have it all.

"Thoughts on an American
Contemporary Feeling" (1932),
Reflection on the Atomic Bomb, Vol. I   1973p

49 Everybody gets so much information all day long that
they lose their common sense.

Ibid., Untitled Essay (1946)

417. Etsu Inagaki Sugimoto
(1874?–1950)

1 A careless or perturbed state of mind always betrays
itself in the intricate shadings of ideographs, for each
one requires absolute steadiness and accuracy of touch.
Thus, in careful guidance of the hand were we children
taught to hold the mind in leash.

A Daughter of the Samurai, Ch. 2   1925

2 "Look in the mirror every day," she said, "for if scars of selfishness or pride are in the heart, they will grow into the lines of the face. Watch closely. Be strong like the pine, yield in gentle obedience like the swaying bamboo, and yet, like the fragrant plum blossoming beneath the snow, never lose the gentle perseverance of loyal womanhood."

Ibid., Ch. 6

418. Mary McLeod Bethune
(1875–1955)

1 If our people are to fight their way up out of bondage we must arm them with the sword and the shield and the buckler of pride. . . .

"Clarifying Our Vision with the Facts,"
Journal of Negro History   *January, 1938*

2 Mr. Lincoln had told our race we were free, but mentally we were still enslaved.

"Faith That Moved a Dump Heap,"
Who, The Magazine About People   *June, 1941*

3 "For God so loved the world, that He gave His only begotten Son, that whosoever believeth in Him should not perish, but have everlasting life." With these words the scales fell from my eyes and the light came flooding in. My sense of inferiority, my fear of handicaps, dropped away. "Whosoever," it said. No Jew nor Gentile, no Catholic nor Protestant, no black nor white; just "whosoever." It meant that I, a humble Negro girl, had just as much chance as anybody in the sight and love of God. These words stored up a battery of faith and confidence and determination in my heart, which has not failed me to this day. . . .

Ibid.

4 I never stop to plan. I take things step by step. For thirty-five years we [Bethune-Cookman College] have never had to close our doors for lack of food or fuel, although often we had to live from day to day. . . .   Ibid.

5 For I am my mother's daughter, and the drums of Africa still beat in my heart. They will not let me rest while there is a single Negro boy or girl without a chance to prove his worth.   Ibid.

6 I do feel, in my dreamings and yearnings, so undiscovered by those who are able to help me. . . . The burden is so heavy just now, the task is so great, that
speedy reinforcement is needed. My mind is over-
taxed. Brave and courageous as I am I feel that creeping on of that inevitable thing, a breakdown, if I cannot
get some immediate relief. I need somebody to come
and get me.

> Letter to George R. Arthur
> (November 1, 1930), *Black Women
> in White America,* Gerda Lerner, ed.   *1972p*

7 The true worth of a race must be measured by the
character of its womanhood. . . .

> Ibid., Address, "A Century of
> Progress of Negro Women,"
> Chicago Women's Federation (June 3, 1933)

419. Anna Hempstead Branch
(1875–1937)

1 His screaming stallions maned with whistling wind.

> "Nimrod Wars with the Angels"   *1910*

* * *

2 God wove a web of loveliness,
  Of clouds and stars and birds,
But made not anything at all
  So beautiful as words.

> "Songs for My Mother: Her Words," St. 5

3 If there is no God for thee
Then there is no God for me.

> "To a Dog"

4 Oh, grieve not, ladies, if at night
  Ye wake to feel your beauty going.
It was a web of frail delight,
  Inconstant as an April snowing.

> "Grieve Not, Ladies," St. 1

5   Order is a lovely thing;
  On disarray it lays its wing,
  Teaching simplicity to sing.

> "The Monk in the Kitchen"

420. Abbie Farwell Brown
(1875–1927)

* * *

1 No matter what my birth may be,
   No matter where my lot is cast,
I am the heir in equity
   Of all the precious past.

"The Heritage," St. 1

2 They named their rocky farmlands,
   Their hamlets by the sea,
For the mother-towns that bred them
   In racial loyalty.

"Names," St. 7

421. Louise Driscoll
(1875–1957)

* * *

1 Power and gold and fame denied,
Love laughs glad in the paths aside.

"The Highway"

2 Some men die early and are spared much care,
   Some suddenly, escaping worse than death;
But he is fortunate who happens where
   He can exult and die in the same breath.

"The Good Hour"

3 There you will find what
   Every man needs,
Wild religion
   Without any creeds.

"Spring Market," St. 5

4 When youth is spent, a penny at a fair,
The old men tell of the bargains there.
There was this and that for a price and a wage,
But when they came away they had all bought age.

"Bargain"

422. Anne Crawford Flexner
(1875?–1955)

1 MRS. FROST: If there were no women in the world, what would become of you men?
FROST: We would be scarce, Emily, but we might be happier.

The Marriage Game, Act I   *1913*

2 FROST: Every man can get on with the woman he hasn't married.

Ibid.

3 KEATS: One must have health! You may banish money—banish sofas—banish wine! but right Jack Health, true Jack Health, honest Jack Health—banish health, and you banish all the world!

Aged Twenty-six, Act II, Sc. 3   *1937*

423. Minnie Haskins
(1875–1957)

1 And I said to the man who stood at the gate of the year:
"Give me a light that I may tread safely into the Unknown."
And he replied: "Go out into the darkness and put your hand
Into the hand of God. That shall be to you better than light
And safer than a known way."

"The Desert"   *1908*

424. Helen Huntington
(1875?–1950)

* * *

1 With the bitter past I will deck to-morrow.

"The Wayfarer"

425. Marie Lenéru
(1875–1940)

1 To be deaf is perhaps not to hear, but certainly it is
this: to hold your tongue. Whatever spontaneous feelings may move you, to resist the impulse to communicate them, to remember that *your* world, your moment,
are not other people's: to hold your tongue . . . a
haute école of self-control, of nonspontaneousness, of
solitude and indifference.

Journal   1945p

2 Books, books, these are the only things that have come
to my aid! In the end, it makes one terribly arrogant,
always to do without one's equals!

Ibid.

3 One *sees* intelligence far more than one hears it. People
do not always say transcendental things, but if they are
capable of saying them, it is always visible.

Ibid.

4 Isolation has led me to reflection, reflection to doubt,
doubt to a more sincere and intelligent love of God.

Ibid. (1896)

5 I will never abdicate. I shall always want everything.
To accept my life I must prefer it.

Ibid. (1898)

6 I have discovered that in an intellectual society individual intelligence is no more frequent than anywhere else,
and its absence is more tedious, for not to speak in a
superior manner of superior subjects is both boring and
ridiculous.

Ibid.

7 If I were honest, I would admit that money is one half
of happiness; it makes it so much more attractive!

Ibid.

8 To succeed in nothing, it's an accident. But to feel no
doubts about oneself is something very different: it is
character.

Ibid.

426. Belle Livingstone
(1875–1957)

1 That winter two things happened which made me see that the world, the flesh, and the devil were going to be more powerful influences in my life after all than the chapel bell. First, I tasted champagne; second, the theatre.

Belle Out of Order   1959p

2 Like Moses, I wasn't born. I was found.

Ibid., Pt. I, Ch. 1

3 Odd how the erotic appeal has swung away from legs; today a smart girl takes her legs for granted and gets herself a good sweater.

Ibid., Ch. 2

4 The courtesan, alas, is gone, extinct as the American buffalo. . . . Anyone can become a mistress; one has to be born a courtesan.

Ibid.

5 Much has been written about the beauty, the stillness, the terror of the desert but little about its flies.

Ibid., Ch. 5

6 Oddly enough, a gambler never entertains the thought of loss. He can't afford to. No one who has never gambled can possibly understand the projects, plans, dreams a gambler can create on the turn of a card or the chance of a horse going to the post.

Ibid., Ch. 9

7 . . . I had swallowed the sugar-coated pill of Rabelaisian philosophy—that life is its own justification and we need not live depriving ourselves of anything.

Ibid., Pt. II, Ch. 1

8 It is a truism that most people take their adventures vicariously.

Ibid., Epilogue

427. Vilda Sauvage Owens
(1875–1950)

* * *

1 If ever I have time for things that matter,
  If ever I have the smallest chance,
  I'm going to live in
  Little Broom Gardens,
  Moat-by-the-Castle,
  Nettlecombe, Hants.
       "If Ever I Have Time for Things That Matter," St. 1

428. Anne Goodwin Winslow
(1875–?)

* * *

1 And how can curses make him yours
  When kisses could not make him so?
                                    "The Beaten Path"

429. Josephine Dodge Bacon
(1876–1961)

1 "Girls, it isn't likely that we'll win, *but we can give 'em
  something to beat*!"
                         "The Emotions of a Sub-Guard,"
                         Smith College Stories   1900

2 Life in all its phases possessed for him unsounded
  depths of entertainment, and in the intervals of uncon-
  trolled laughter at the acts and words of his astonished
  elders he gave way to frequent subtle smiles resulting
  from subjectively humorous experiences unguessed by
  the world at large.
           The Memoirs of a Baby, Ch. 2   1904

3 You mustn't say anything that won't be perfectly true
  when he's grown up, you see. It's learning two sets of
  things that makes a child distrust you.

                                    Ibid., Ch. 6

4 You mark my words, Toots, if you ever hear a darn-
  fool thing to-day, you can make up your mind some

woman said it that writes books. . . . It ought to be a crime for any woman to have children that writes books.

The Biography of a Boy, Ch. 2   *1910*

5 Starved once and forever,
  By a cruel love.
  I lost my life—
  The public gained it.

Truth o' Women, Ch. 15   *1923*

6 I do not see how there can be any real respect,
  Or any real privacy such as women love,
  When you marry a man.
    A man makes trouble.   Ibid., Ch. 20

7 To you in reality dead,
  Dragging your bodies after you,
  Persistently vital,
  I say this:
  Death will come. Be patient.   Ibid., Ch. 42

430. Mary Ritter Beard
(1876–1958)

1 The prosecution of modern wars rests completely upon the operation of labor in mines, mills and factories, so that labor fights there just as truly as the soldiers do in the trenches.

A Short History of the American Labor Movement, Ch. 1   *1920*

2 The trade agreement has become a rather distinct feature of the American labor movement. It does not represent any revolutionary tendency in industry. It is based on the idea that labor shall accept the capitalist system of production and makes terms of peace with it.

Ibid., Ch. 9

3 Viewed narrowly, all life is universal hunger and an expression of energy associated with it.

Understanding Women, Ch. 1   *1931*

4 In their quest for rights they [women] have naturally placed emphasis on their wrongs, rather than their achievements and possessions, and have retold history as a story of their long Martyrdom.   Ibid.

5 Unless one's philosophy is all-inclusive, nothing can be understood.

Ibid., Ch. 4

6 In matters pertaining to the care of life there has been no marked gain over Greek and Roman antiquity.

Ibid., Ch. 5

7 In other words, those who sit at the feast will continue to enjoy themselves even though the veil that separates them from the world of toiling reality below has been lifted by mass revolts and critics.

Ibid., Ch. 6

8 The emphasis in Communism, if its ideal is realized, will be on woman as a worker, and the opportunities for a life of leisure, patronage, noblesse oblige, religious service and idle curiosity will vanish.

Ibid.

9 If this analysis of history is approximately sound and if the future like the past is to be crowded with changes and exigencies, then it is difficult to believe that the feminism of the passing generation, already hardened into dogma and tradition, represents the completed form of woman's relations to work, interests and society.

Ibid.

10 The dogma of woman's complete historical subjection to men must be rated as one of the most fantastic myths ever created by the human mind.

Woman as a Force in History   1946

11 . . . history has been conceived—and with high justification in the records—as the human struggle for civilization against barbarism in different ages and places, from the beginning of human societies.

Ibid., Ch. 12

12 Beneath the surface of civilian interests and capitalistic enterprises smoldered embers of the world's war spirit—humanity's traditional flare—now to be enflamed by new instruments for fighting and the associated aspiration for world trade and world power.

*The Force of Women in Japanese
History*, Ch. 9   1963p

431. Anne Bronaugh
(1876–1961)

* * *

1 Life is patchwork—here and there,
Scraps of pleasure and despair
Join together, hit or miss.

"Patchwork"

432. Sarah Norcliffe Cleghorn
(1876–1959)

1 The golf links lie so near the mill
That almost every day
The laboring children can look out
And watch the men at play.
"The Conning Tower," *New York Tribune*
January 1, 1915

2 Since more than half my hopes came true
And more than half my fears
Are but the pleasant laughing-stock
Of these my middle years . . .
Shall I not bless the middle years?
Not I for youth repine
While warmly round me cluster lives
More dear to me than mine.
"Contented at Forty"   *1916*

3 Come, Captain Age,
With your great sea-chest full of treasure!
Under the yellow and wrinkled tarpaulin
Disclose the carved ivory
And the sandalwood inlaid with pearl:
Riches of wisdom and years.
"Come, Captain Age," *Three Score*   *1936*

* * *

4 "The unfit die—the fit both live and thrive."
Alas, who say so? They who do survive.
"The Survival of the Fittest"

433. Mata Hari
(1876–1917)

1 The dance is a poem of which each movement is a
word.

Scrapbook   *1905*

2 The [military] officer is a being apart, a kind of artist
breathing the grand air in the brilliant profession of
arms, in a uniform that is always seductive. . . . To
me the officer is a separate race.

Life   *1906*

3 I firmly believe that the only means of living in beauty
consists in avoiding the thousand and one daily annoy-
ances which interfere with an existence in the full ideal.
That is why I cannot tolerate European things, not
even the religion.

Quoted in *Mata Hari* (1917),
by Major Thomas Coulson, O.B.E.
1930p

434. Norah M. Holland
(1876–1925)

* * *

1 Life has given me of its best—
Laughter and weeping, labour and rest,
Little of gold, but lots of fun;
Shall I then sigh that all is done?

"Life"

435. Sally Kinsolving
(1876–?)

1 Ships, young ships,
I do not wonder men see you as women—
You in the white length of your loveliness
Reclining on the sea!

"Ships," *Many Waters*   *1942*

436. Mary Sinton Leitch
(1876–1954)

* * *

1 And deaf, he sings of nightingales
   Or, blind, he sings of stars.

"The Poet"

2 He who loves the ocean
   And the ways of ships
   May taste beside a mountain pool
   Brine on his lips.

"He Who Loves the Ocean"

3 They would not be the great, were not the cause
   They love so great that it must needs be lost.

"Pity the Great"

4 While far below men crawl in clay and cold,
   Sublimely I shall stand alone with God.

"The Summit, Mt. Everest"

437. Grace Fallow Norton
(1876–1926)

* * *

1 I have loved many, the more and the few—
   I have loved many that I might love you.

"Song of the Sum of All"

2 Take me upon thy breast,
   O River of Rest.
   Draw me down to thy side,
   Slow-moving tide.

"O Sleep"

438. Mary Roberts Rinehart
(1876–1958)

1 There is something magnificent, a contagion of enthusiasm, in the sight of a great volunteer army. The North and the South knew the thrill during our own great war. Conscription may form a great and admirable ma-

chine, but it differs from the trained army of volunteers as a body differs from a soul. But it costs a country heavy in griefs, does a volunteer army; for the flower of the country goes.

Kings, Queens, and Pawns, Introduction   1915

2 War is a thing of fearful and curious anomalies. . . .
It has shown that government by men only is not an appeal to reason, but an appeal to arms; that on women, without a voice to protest, must fall the burden. It is easier to die than to send a son to death. It has shown that a single hatred may infect a world, but it has shown that mercy too may spread among nations. That love is greater than cannon, greater than hate, greater than vengeance; that it triumphs over wrath, as good triumphs over evil.   Ibid., Ch. 37

3 What was I to do? You may say what you like—a lot of married women get into things they never meant to simply because they are kind-hearted and hate to be called quitters.
"Affinities," *Affinities and Other Stories*   1920

4 "You're a perfect child, a stubborn child! Your mind's in pigtails, like your hair."
Ibid., "The Family Friend"

5 "Nurses in hospitals are there to carry out the doctor's orders. Not to think or to say what they think unless they are asked."
"Twenty-Two," *Love Stories*   1920

6 The great God endows His children variously. To some He gives intellect—and they move the earth. To some He allots heart—and the beating pulse of humanity is theirs. But to some He gives only a soul, without intelligence—and these, who never grow up, but remain always His children, are God's fools, kindly, elemental, simple, as if from His palette the Artist of all had taken one colour instead of many.
Ibid., "God's Fool"

7 Men deceive themselves; they look back on the children who were once themselves, and attempt to reconstruct them. But they can no longer think like the child, and against the unpleasant and the horrid the mind has set up the defensive machinery of forgetfulness.   *My Story,* Ch. 1   1931

8 But it is interesting to see how the Socialist becomes the conservative when given power; Mussolini, Briand, Masaryk, all considered radicals at one time. Or is it that our own ideas change, and that we are after all moving slowly toward greater justice?

Ibid., Ch. 40

9 Will we never learn? Is our cupidity greater than our patriotism? And is our generosity greater than our common sense?

My Story, Ch. 19, Rev. Ed.   *1948*

439. Helen Rowland
(1876–1950)

1 Woman: the peg on which the wit hangs his jest, the preacher his text, the cynic his grouch, and the sinner his justification.

Reflections of a Bachelor Girl   *1903*

2 When you see what some girls marry, you realize how they must hate to work for a living.

Ibid.

3 Love, the quest; marriage, the conquest; divorce, the inquest.

Ibid.

4 Marriage: a souvenir of love.

Ibid.

5 The follies which a man regrets most in his life are those which he didn't commit when he had the opportunity.

Ibid.

6 It takes a woman twenty years to make a man of her son, and another woman twenty minutes to make a fool of him.

Ibid.

7 To a woman the first kiss is the end of the beginning; to a man it is the beginning of the end.   Ibid.

8 One man's folly is another man's wife.   Ibid.

9 Never trust a husband too far, nor a bachelor too near.
The Rubaiyat of a Bachelor   *1915*

10 A husband is what is left of the lover after the nerve has been extracted.

Ibid.

11 Better a lively old epigram than a deadly new one.
"The World in Epigram," *The Book of Diversion*,
F. P. Adams, D. Taylor, J. Bechdolt, eds.   *1925*

12 The woman who appeals to a man's vanity may stimulate him; the woman who appeals to his heart may attract him; but it's the woman who appeals to his imagination who *gets* him.

Ibid., "Personally Speaking"

13 A man may talk inspiringly to a woman about love in the abstract—but the look in his eyes is always perfectly concrete.

Ibid.

14 Nothing annoys a man as to hear a woman promising to love him "forever" when he merely wanted her to love him for a few weeks.

Ibid.

15 A bachelor has to have an inspiration for making love to a woman—a married man needs only an excuse.

Ibid.

16 At twenty, a man feels awfully aged and blasé; at thirty, almost senile; at forty, "not so old"; and at fifty, positively skittish.

Ibid.

17 Courtship is a republic; marriage, a monarchy; divorce, a soviet.

Ibid.

18 Alas, why will a man spend months trying to hand over his liberty to a woman—and the rest of his life trying to get it back again?   *Ibid.*

19 Honeymoons are the beginning of wisdom—but the beginning of wisdom is the end of romance.   *Ibid.*

20 The same woman may be a goddess to a boy, a temptation to a married man, and a "menace" to a bachelor.

Ibid.

21 The honeymoon is not actually over until we cease to stifle our sighs and begin to stifle our yawns.   *Ibid.*

22 True love says, "Love me—or I suffer!" Infatuation says, "Love me—or I'll make *you* suffer!"

Ibid.

23 The feminine vanity-case is the grave of masculine illusions.

Ibid.

24 Marriage is the only thing that affords a woman the pleasure of company and the perfect sensation of solitude at the same time.

Ibid.

25 A man always mistakes a woman's clinging devotion for weakness, until he discovers that it requires the strength of Samson, the patience of Job, and the finesse of Solomon to untwine it.

Ibid.

440. Helen L. Sumner
(1876–1933)

1 The story of women's work in gainful employments is a story of constant changes or shiftings of work and workshop, accompanied by long hours, low wages, insanitary conditions, overwork, and the want on the part of the woman of training, skill, and vital interest in her work.

Senate Report, History of Women in
Industry in the United States, Vol IX
1911

2 . . . the history of women's work in this country shows that legislation has been the only force which has improved the working conditions of any large number of women wage-earners.

Ibid.

441. Katharine Anthony
(1877–1965)

1 For mothers who must earn, there is indeed no leisure time problem. The long hours of earning are increased by the hours of domestic labor, until no slightest margin for relaxation or change of thought remains.

Mothers Who Must Earn, Ch. 6   1914

2 Personal ambitions and disappointments, personal desire and weaknesses, personal shrewdness or slackness play their part in these narrow homes as they do in more spacious ones.

Ibid., Ch. 8

3 Beyond all superficial differences and incidental forms, the vision of the emancipated woman wears the same features, whether she be hailed as *frau, fru,* or *woman.* The disfranchisement of a whole sex, a condition which has existed throughout the civilized world until a comparatively recent date, has bred in half the population an unconscious internationalism. The man without a country was a tragic exception; the woman without a country was the accepted rule.

Feminism in Germany and
Scandinavia, Ch. 1   *1915*

4 The cult of "arms and the man" must reckon with a newer cult, that of "schools and the woman." Schools, which exalt brains above brawn, and women, who exalt life-giving above life-taking, are the natural allies of the present era.

Ibid., Ch. 2

5 The struggle for self-consciousness is the essence of the feminist movement. Slowly but inevitably, the soul of a sex is emerging from the dim chamber of instinct and feeling into the strong sunshine of reason and will.

Ibid., Ch. 9

6 There can be no doubt as to who began the literary war between the sexes. Also there is no comparison between the severity and harshness of the tone of criticism in the opposing camps. If we search the polemic writings of the most militant feminists, we can nowhere find expressions which compare in venom and ruthlessness with the woman-eating sentiments of certain medieval "saints" and modern "philosophers."

Ibid.

7 The generosity of childless people toward the children of near relatives and favorite friends strikes one as mere justice and propriety, after all, and such voluntary acts of evening-up between one generation and the next are not at all uncommon among the families and classes who can afford to be kind.

The Endowment of Motherhood, Preface   *1920*

8 Principles are a dangerous form of social dynamite. . . .

> Ibid., Introduction

9 Foremost among the barriers to equality is the system which ignores the mother's service to Society in making a home and rearing children. The mother is still the unchartered servant of the future, who receives from her husband, at *his* discretion, a share of *his* wages.

> Ibid.

10 To the biographer all lives bar none are dramatic constructions.

> "Writing Biography," *The Writer's
> Book,* Helen Hull, ed.   *1950*

11 . . . people . . . seem to think that life began with the achievement of personal independence.

> Ibid.

12 The lovers of romance can go elsewhere for satisfaction but where can the lovers of truth turn if not to history?

> Ibid.

13 Persons who are born too soon or born too late seldom achieve the eminence of those who are born at the right time.

> Ibid.

442. Grace Noll Crowell
(1877–1965?)

1 I am one ever journeying toward the "light that never was on land or sea," and yet ever beckons one onward and upward to the glory ahead.

> Quoted in *Grace Noll Crowell,*
> Foreword, by Beatrice Plumb
> *1938*

* * *

2 God wrote His loveliest poem on the day
He made the first tall silver poplar tree.

> "Silver Poplars," St. 1

3 The woman who can move about a house,
Whether it be a mansion or a camp,
And deftly lay a fire, and spread a cloth,
And light a lamp,
And by the magic of a quick touch give

The look of home wherever she may be—
Such a woman always will seem great
And beautiful to me.

"The Home Makers," St. 1

4 Home may be near,
Home may be far—
But it is anywhere love
And a few plain household treasures are.

Ibid.

443. Isabelle Eberhardt
(1877–1904)

1 For those who know the value and the exquisite taste
of solitary freedom (for one is only free when alone),
the act of leaving is the bravest and most beautiful of
all.

Journal Entry, Quoted in The Destiny
of Isabelle Eberhardt by Cecily
Mackworth   1975p

2 In the staid costume of a European girl I would never
have seen anything. The world would have been closed
to me, for . . . external life seems to have been made
for man, not for woman.

Ibid.

3 I love to dive into the bath of street life, the waves of
the crowd flowing over me, to impregnate myself with
the fluids of the people.

Ibid.

4 Death does not frighten me, but dying obscurely and
above all uselessly does.   Ibid.

444. Rose Fyleman
(1877–1957)

* * *

1 The Fairies have never a penny to spend,
They haven't a thing put by,
But theirs is the dower of bird and of flower,
And theirs are the earth and the sky.

"The Fairies Have Never a Penny to Spend," St. 1

2 There are fairies at the bottom of our garden.
"The Fairies," St. 1

3 The queen—now can you guess who that could be
(She's a little girl by day, but at night she steals
away)?
Well—it's me!

Ibid., St. 3

445. Mary Garden
(1877?–1967)

1 That was my first real flutter. I am sure Mr. Smith
never knew, for he never paid the slightest attention to
me except as a pupil. But *I* knew—I was in such a state
of excitement every time I came back for a lesson; but
my Mr. Smith never noticed it and to the end was as
correct as a metronome, and as cold.

Mary Garden's Story, Ch. 1,
with Louis Biancolli   *1951*

2 I have never been nervous in all my life and I have no
patience with people who are. If you know what you're
going to do, you have no reason to be nervous. And I
knew what I was going to do.   Ibid., Ch. 3

3 If I ever had complete charge of an opera house, the
chances are I wouldn't get anybody to sing for me. I
would be very emphatic about some things. I would
never have a curtain call. I would never allow an en-
core. I would never permit a claque. There would be
only art in my theatre.   Ibid., Ch. 11

4 I used my voice to color my roles. Salomé was blood
red. Melissande was ice, melting ice. . . .

Ibid., Ch. 21

446. Virginia Gildersleeve
(1877–1965)

1 Medicine is a profession which naturally appeals deeply
to women, as they are instinctively concerned with conserving life.

"The Advancement of Women,"
Many a Good Crusade   *1954*

2 The delicate first moment of dawn, before its mystery is invaded by the clatter of daily living, the bright hour of sunset before it is quenched in darkness, the last days of health unbroken, the last year of man's assurance that his civilization moves "ever upward and onward"—these are the moments, hours, days, years that have for us a poignant significance.

Ibid., "The Turning of the Tide"

3 I well know from my own experience how essential it is for the survival of our democracy that scholars and teachers should have freedom of the mind to pursue truth "with clear eyes unafraid." Now our witchhunters are trying to drive students and teachers into conformity with a rigid concept of Americanism defined by ignorant and irresponsible politicians. If we do not check this movement, we shall become a totalitarian state like the Fascist and Communist models and our colleges and universities will produce frightened rabbits instead of scholars with free minds.

Ibid., "The Inescapable Desert"

447. Mathilda von Kemnitz
(1877–?)

1 Since the fundamental principle of eroticism imperiously governs every human life, since the manner of the first erotic happiness determines in a far-reaching manner the laws of the individual's eroticism throughout his entire life, the majority of men have become entirely incapable of concentrating their erotic will consistently on one human being; therefore, they have become incapable of monogamy.

The Triumph of the Immortal Will   1932

2 The man experiences the highest unfolding of his creative powers not through asceticism but through sexual happiness.   Ibid.

448. Marian Le Sueur
(1877–1954)

1 The American destiny is what our fathers dreamed, a land of the free, and the home of the brave; but only

the brave can be free. Science has made the dream of today's reality for all the earth if we have the courage and vision to build it. American Democracy must furnish the engineers of world plenty—the builders of world peace and freedom.

Quoted in *Crusaders* by Meridel Le Sueur   *1955p*

449. Anne Shannon Monroe
(1877–1942)

1 I have never been much cheered by the "stenciled smile," the false front, the pretending that there was no trouble when trouble stalked, that there was no death when Death laid his cold hand upon one dearer to us than life: but I have been tremendously cheered by the *brave* front; the imagination that could travel past the trouble and see that there were still joys in the world. . . .

Singing in the Rain, Ch. 1   *1926*

2 For loneliness is but cutting adrift from our moorings and floating out to the open sea; an opportunity for finding ourselves, our *real* selves, what we are about, where we are heading during our little time on this beautiful earth.

Ibid., Ch. 6

3 "Don't get hung up on a snag in the stream, my dear. Snags alone are not so dangerous—it's the debris that clings to them that makes the trouble. Pull yourself loose and go on."

Ibid., Ch. 13

450. Maude Royden
(1877–1956)

1 The belief that the personality of men and women are of equal dignity in the sight of God is necessary to a right moral standard.

The Church and Woman   *c.1920*

451. Rosika Schwimmer
(1877–1948)

1 I am no uncompromising pacifist. . . . I have no sense of nationalism, only a cosmic consciousness of belonging to the human family.
>Court Testimony, Citizenship Hearings   *1928*

2 Women's rights, men's rights—human rights—all are threatened by the ever-present spectre of war so destructive now of human material and moral values as to render victory indistinguishable from defeat.
>Speech, Centennial Celebration of
>Seneca Falls Convention of
>Women's Rights   *July, 1948*

3 We who successfully freed half of the human race without violence must now undertake with equal devotion, perseverance and intelligence the supreme act of human statesmanship involved in the creation of institutions of government on a world scale.
>Ibid.

4 Women's function of homemaker, we once dreamed, would extend into politics and economics our highest creative and conserving instincts. Let us go back to the task of building that safe, decent and wholesome home for the entire human family to which we once pledged ourselves.
>Ibid.

452. Laura Simmons
(1877–1949)

* * *

1 The face within that passport book
Will rise to haunt you yet.
>"Your Passport Picture"

453. Alice B. Toklas
(1877–1967)

1 What is sauce for the goose may be sauce for the gander, but is not necessarily sauce for the chicken, the duck, the turkey or the guinea hen.
> *The Alice B. Toklas Cook Book*   1954

2 She quoted a friend who used to say any advice is good as long as it is strong enough.
> Letter to Carl Van Vechten (September 3, 1946), *Staying On Alone*, Ed Burns, ed.   *1973p*

3 I am staying on here alone now.
> Ibid., Letter to Julian Beck (September 8, 1946)

4 Now I ask you what is the impulse that comes from the possession of even the kindest heart compared to real faith in God and a hereafter. Without it one just plods on. . . .
> Ibid., Letter to Fania Marinoff Van Vechten (February 21, 1948)

5 Austerity has gone so far that the population has become submissive through lack of physical resistance.
> Ibid., Letter to Donald Gallup (October 12, 1948)

6 . . . he [Basket, a dog] has filled the corners of the room and the minutes and me so sweetly these last years.
> Ibid., Letter to Thornton Wilder (April 5, 1949)

7 Well, I've gotten to the end of the subject—of the page—of your patience and my time.
> Ibid., Letter to Elizabeth Hansen (July 19, 1949)

8 The young men of today seem mostly to be interested in the manner rather than the matter.
> Ibid., Letter to Mark Lutz (August 16, 1951)

9 I love Spain and things Spanish and Picasso!
> Ibid., Letter to Louise Taylor (August 16, 1951)

10 Haven't you learned yet that it isn't age but lack of experience that makes us fall off ladders or have radiators fall on us.
> Ibid., Letter to Princess Dilkusha de Rohan (March 5, 1955)

11 . . . the past is not gone—nor is Gertrude.
     Ibid., Letter to Samuel Steward (August 7, 1958)

12 Dawn comes slowly but dusk is rapid.
     Ibid., Letter to Virginia Knapik (August 9, 1960)

454. Elizabeth Arden
(1878–1966)

1 Nothing that costs only a dollar is worth having.
     Quoted in "In Cosmetics the Old
     Mystique Is No Longer Enough"
     by Eleanore Carruth, *Fortune*
     October, 1973p

455. Florence Ayscough
(1878–1942)

1 Ideals determine government, and government determines social life, and social life, with all that the term connotes, is the essence of every literature.
     Fir-Flower Tablets, Introduction   *1921*

456. Amelia Burr
(1878–1940?)

1 Because I have loved life, I shall have no sorrow to die.
     "A Song of Living," St. 3
     Life and Living   *1916*

2 Spring comes laughing down the valley
  All in white, from the snow
Where the winter's armies rally
  Loth to go.   *Ibid.,* "New Life"

* * *

3 But I have certainty enough,
  For I am sure of you.   "Certainty Enough"

4 Swift and sure go the lonely feet,
    And the single eye sees cold and true,
And the road that has room and to spare for one
    May be sorely narrow for two.   "To Lovers"

457. Grace H. Conkling
(1878–1958)

* * *

1 I have an understanding with the hills.

"After Sunset"

2 Invisible beauty has a world so brief
A flower can say it or a shaken leaf,
But few may ever snare it in a song.

Ibid.

3 I wonder if it *is* a bird
That sings within the hidden tree,
Or some shy angel calling me
To follow far away?

"Nightingale"

4 Mountains are good to look upon
But do not look too long.
They are made of granite. They will break your heart.

"Mountains"

5 Over the stones to lull and leap
Herding the bubbles like white sheep;
The claims of worry to deny,
And whisper sorrow into sleep.

"The Whole Duty of Berkshire Brooks"

6 To build the trout a crystal stair.

Ibid.

7 The forest looks the way
Nightingales sound.

"Frost on a Window"

458. Adelaide Crapsey
(1878–1914)

* * *

1 If I'd as much money as I could tell,
I never would cry my songs to sell.

"Vendor's Song"

2 Is it as plainly in our living shown,
By slant and twist, which way the wind hath blown?

"On Seeing Weather-Beaten Trees"

409

3 These be
Three silent things:
The falling snow . . . the hour
Before the dawn . . . the mouth of one
Just dead.

"Cinquain: Triad"

4 Wouldst thou find my ashes? Look
In the pages of my book;
And, as this thy hands doth turn,
Know here is my funeral urn.

"The Immortal Residue"

459. Isadora Duncan
(1878–1927)

1 America has all that Russia has not. Russia has things
America has not. Why will America not reach out a
hand to Russia, as I have given my hand?

Curtain Speech, Symphony Hall, Boston   1922

2 You were once wild here. Don't let them tame you!

Ibid.

3 All Puritan vulgarity centers in Boston. The Back Bay
conservatives are impoverished by custom and taboo.
They are the lifeless and sterile of this country.

Interview, Boston   1922

4 . . . [I] would rather live in Russia on black bread
and vodka than in the United States at the best hotels.
America knows nothing of food, love or art.

Interview Aboard Ship   1922

5 So that ends my first experience with matrimony,
which I always thought a highly overrated performance.

Interview, The New York Times   1923

6 . . . the artist is the only lover, he alone has the pure
vision of beauty, and love is the vision of the soul when
it is permitted to gaze upon immortal beauty. . . .

My Life   1927

7 I have discovered the dance. I have discovered the art
which has been lost for two thousand years.

Ibid.

8 . . . when I listened to music the rays and vibrations of the music streamed to this one fount of light within me—there they reflected themselves in Spiritual Vision, not the brain's mirror, but the soul's, and from the vision I could express them in Dance. . . .

Ibid.

9 . . . I believe, as a wage-earning woman, that if I make the great sacrifice of strength and health and even risk my life, to have a child, I should certainly not do so if, on some future occasion, the man can say that the child belongs to him by law and he will take it from me and I shall see it only three times a year!

Ibid.

10 Any intelligent woman who reads the marriage contract, and then goes into it, deserves all the consequences.

Ibid.

11 With what a price we pay for the glory of motherhood. . . .

Ibid.

12 It is unheard of, uncivilized barbarism that any woman should still be forced to bear such monstrous torture. It should be remedied. It should be stopped. It is simply absurd that with our modern science painless childbirth does not exist as a matter of course. . . . I tremble with indignation when I think of . . . the unspeakable egotism and blindness of men of science who permit such atrocities when they can be remedied. . . .

Ibid.

13 . . . now that I had discovered that Love might be a pastime as well as a tragedy, I gave myself to it with pagan innocence. Men seemed so hungry for Beauty, hungry for that love which refreshes and inspires without fear or responsibility.

Ibid.

14 . . . if you have a body in which you are born to a certain amount of pain . . . why should you not, when the occasion presents, draw from this same body the maximum of pleasure?

Ibid.

15 No composer has yet caught this rhythm of America—it is too mighty for the ears of most. Ibid.

16 And this dance will have nothing in it of the inane co-
quetry of the ballet, or the sensual convulsion of the
Negro. It will be clean.

Ibid.

17 The real American type can never be a ballet dancer.
The legs are too long, the body too supple and the
spirit too free for this school of affected grace and toe
walking. *Ibid.*

18 . . . let [them] come forth with great strides, leaps
and bounds, with lifted forehead and farspread arms, to
dance the language of our Pioneers, the Fortitude of
our heroes, the Justice, Kindness, Purity of our statesmen, and all the inspired love and tenderness of our
Mothers. *Ibid.*

19 She [Eleanora Duse] never said, "Cease to grieve" but
she grieved with me. *Ibid.*

20 The whole world is absolutely brought up on lies. We
are fed nothing but lies. It begins with lies and half our
lives we live with lies.
"Memoirs" (1924), *This Quarter   Autumn, 1929p*

21 Art is not necessary at all. All that is necessary to make
this world a better place to live in is to love—to love as
Christ loved, as Buddha loved. *Ibid.*

22 Lenin was God, as Christ was God, because God is
love and Christ and Lenin were all love.

Ibid.

23 So long as little children are allowed to suffer, there is
no true love in this world. *Ibid.*

24 People do not live nowadays—they get about ten percent out of life. *Ibid.*

460. Edith Ronald Mirrielees
(1878–1962)

1 In the thinking out of most stories, the thing the story
is about, as apart from merely what happens in it, is of
the utmost importance. For a story is not the sum of its
happenings.

"The Substance of the Story,"
Story Writing   1947

2 Incident piled on incident no more makes life than brick piled on brick makes a house.

Ibid.

3 . . . belief that persistence is all and is bound to be rewarded has no . . . foundation. . . .

Ibid.

4 Experience shows that exceptions are as true as rules.
Ibid.

461. Ethel Watts Mumford
(1878–1940)

1 There was a young lady named Julie,
Who was terribly fond of patchouli;
   She used bottles seven,
   'Til smelt up to heaven,
Which made all the angels unruly.

"Lavishness," The Limerick
Up to Date Book   1903

2 There was a young person of Tottenhem,
Whose manners, good Lord! she'd forgotten 'em.

Ibid., "Good Manners"

3 There was a young lady from Skye,
With a shape like a capital I;
   She said, "It's too bad!
   But then I can pad,"
Which shows you that figures can lie.

Ibid., "Appearances Deceitful"

4 There was a young damsel named Nell,
Who considered herself quite a belle.
   She sat on the sand,
   And held her own hand,
And never got on to the swell.

Ibid., "Self-Sufficiency"

5 Said a Rooster, "I'd have you all know
I am nearly the whole of the show;
   Why, the Sun every morn
   Gets up with the dawn
For the purpose of hearing me crow!"

Ibid., "Know Your Own Worth"

462. Bertha Runkle
(1878–1958)

* * *

1 We own the right of roaming, and the world is wide.
"Songs of the Sons of Esau"

463. Nancy Astor
(1879–1964)

1 I can conceive of nothing worse than a man-governed
world—except a woman-governed world.
"America," *My Two Countries*, Ch. 1   *1923*

2 Mercifully, we have no political past; we have all the
mistakes of one-sex legislation, with its appalling failures, to guide us. We should know what to avoid. It is
no use blaming the men—we made them what they
are—and now it is up to us to try and make ourselves—the makers of men—a little more responsible.
Ibid.

3 In passing, also, I would like to say that the first time
Adam had a chance he laid the blame on woman. . . .
Ibid.

4 I believe that the safest and surest way to get out of
war is to join some sort of league of nations. That misrepresented and much despised League has already
prevented three small wars, it has registered over one
hundred treaties, has repatriated nearly four hundred
thousand prisoners—not a bad record for only a half a
league.
Ibid., Ch. 2

5 The most practical thing in the world is common sense
and common humanity.
Ibid., Ch. 7

6 Real education should educate us out of self into something far finer—into a selflessness which links us with
all humanity. Political education should do the same.
Ibid.

7 A fool without fear is sometimes wiser than an angel with fear.

Ibid., Ch. 8

8 My vigor, vitality and cheek repel me. I am the kind of woman I would run from.

News Item   1955

464. Ethel Barrymore
(1879–1959)

1 That's all there is, there isn't any more.

Curtain Speech After Performance of
Sunday   1904

2 For an actress to be a success she must have the face of Venus, the brains of Minerva, the grace of Terpsichore, the memory of Macaulay, the figure of Juno, and the hide of a rhinoceros.

Quoted in *The Theatre in the Fifties*
by George Jean Nathan   1953

465. Catherine Carswell
(1879–1946)

1 . . . it wasn't a woman who betrayed Jesus with a kiss.

The Savage Pilgrimage   1932

466. Mabel Dodge
(1879–1962)

1 . . . she [Frieda Lawrence] had to see life from the sex center, she endorsed or repudiated experience from that angle. She was the mother of orgasm and of the vast, lively mystery of the flesh. But no more.

Lorenzo in Taos   1932

2 The womb behind the womb—the significant, extended and transformed power that succeeds primary sex, that he [D. H. Lawrence] was ready, long since, to receive from woman.

Ibid.

3 The groping, suffering, tragic soul of man was so much filthiness to that healthy creature.

Ibid.

4 . . . I knew instinctively that the strongest, surest way to the soul is through the flesh.

Ibid.

467. Dorothy Canfield Fisher
(1879–1958)

1 "He divides us all into two kinds: the ones that get what they want by taking it away from other people— those are the dolichocophalic blonds—though I believe it doesn't refer to the color of their hair. The other kind are the white folks, the unpredatory ones who have scruples, and get pushed to the wall for their pains."
The Bent Twig, Bk. I, Ch. 5   *1915*

2 No European could have conceived how literally it was true that the birth or wealth or social position of a child made no difference in the estimation of his mates. There were no exceptions to the custom of considering the individual on his own merits.

Ibid., Ch. 7

3 "I am thinking that I am being present at a spectacle which cynics say is impossible, the spectacle of a woman delighting—and with most obvious sincerity— in the beauty of another."

Ibid., Bk. III, Ch. 23

4 A mother is not a person to lean on but a person to making leaning unnecessary.
Her Son's Wife   *1926*

5 This was a nighttime memory, one of those that never come to you at all in daylight, but when you get about so far asleep, start to unroll themselves in the dark.
The Deepening Stream, Pt. I, Ch. 2   *1930*

6 "Father sticks to it that anything that promises to pay too much can't help being risky. He always says he doesn't adivse people against taking risks. . . . 'What is life but one long risk?' . . . You know how father talks."

Ibid., Pt. II, Ch. 1

7 "I've seen children before who'd had too great a fright. They are always imbeciles. . . ." There had been long periods in her youth when she too had crept into a corner and turned her face away from what life seemed to be.

Ibid., Pt. III, Ch. 11

8 The skull of life suddenly showed through its smile.
Bonfire   1933

9 Freedom is not worth fighting for if it means no more than license for everyone to get as much as he can for himself. And freedom *is* worth fighting for. Because it does mean more than unrestricted grabbing. He saw in imagination those young faces looking up at him attentively, and told them, "Laugh in the faces of the Fascist priests who chant the new Black Mass, when they tell you boys and girls that democratic government means nothing but license for the money-getters."
Seasoned Timber   1939

468. Katherine Gerould
(1879–1944)

1 There are only three things worth while—fighting, drinking, and making love.
"The Tortoise," *Vain Oblations*   1914

2 The commonest field may be chosen by opposing generals to be decisive; and in a day history is born where before only the quiet wheat has sprung.
Ibid., "The Case of Paramore"

3 You don't care about this State: you want to put it into white petticoats and see it across a muddy street.
"The Knights' Move," *Atlantic Monthly*   1917

4 . . . I have always, privately and humbly, thought it a pity that so good a word [as culture] should go out of the best vocabularies; for when you lose an abstract term, you are very apt to lose the thing it stands for.
"The Extirpation of Culture,"
Modes and Morals   1920

5 . . . it is one thing to sow your wild oats in talk, and quite another to live by your own kaleidescopic paradoxes. The people who frowned on the manifestations

of "temperament" were merely those logical creatures who believed that if you expressed your opinions regardless of other people's feelings, you probably meant what you said. They did not know the pathology of epigram, the basic truth of which is that word-intoxicated people express an opinion long before they dream of holding it.

> Ibid., "Tabu and Temperament"

6 We were a plutocracy; which means that so long as a man had the house and the drinks, you asked no questions. The same rule holds—allowing for their dizzier sense of figures—in New York and Chicago.

> "French Eva," *Scribner's Magazine*   1920

7 Politics, which, the planet over, are the fly in the amber, the worm in the bud, the rift in the loot, had, with great suddenness, deprived Wharton Cameron of a job.

> *Conquistador,* Ch. 1   1923

8 Codes cohabit easily until it comes to women. Then jungle and steppe, delta and forest, proceed to argue their differences.

> Ibid., Ch. 5

469. Wanda Landowska
(1879–1959)

1 Music of the past has become a distant and vague country where everything is totally different from our surroundings, our life, our art, our impressions, and our concepts.

> "Music of the Past" (1905),
> *Landowska on Music,*
> Denise Resout, ed.   *1964p*

2 Obviously the good lady [melody] has a tough constitution. The more attempts made against her, the more she blooms with health and rotundity. It is interesting to note that all those accused of being her murderers are becoming, in turn, her benefactors and her saviors.

> Ibid., "Why Does Modern Music Lack
> Melody?" (February 9, 1913)

3 In this obstinate race after the original—while avoiding thoroughly that which has already been said and taking refuge on an island that we thought was uninhabited—

do we not risk running into a good old acquaintance who has just been dropped? . . . Is is really indispensable to believe with such seriousness that every little change will, at last, bring the definitive salvation? If it gives us a thrill, it is already delightful enough; and if this thrill reminds us of the dear caresses of old, it is all for the best!

Ibid., Book Review (1923)

4 To embrace an epoch in all its splendor and truth, to understand the fluctuations of taste, one needs perspective.

Ibid., Letter (September 8, 1948)

5 But I cannot help it if, having never stopped working, I have learned a great deal, especially about this divine freedom that is to music the air without which it would die. What would you say of a scientist or of a painter who, like stagnant water, would stop his experimentation and remain still?

Ibid., Letter to a Former Pupil (1950)

6 The most beautiful thing in the world is, precisely, the conjuction of learning and inspiration. Oh, the passion for research and the joy of discovery!

Ibid.

470. Frieda Lawrence
(1879–1956)

1 Everything he met had the newness of a creation, just that moment come into being.

Not I, But the Wind . . . 1934

2 In spite of his age and strong passions he [D. H. Lawrence] had never let himself go. Sex was suppressed in him with ferocity. He had suppressed it so much, put it away so entirely, that now, married, it overwhelmed him.

Frieda Lawrence: The Memoirs and Correspondence, E. W. Tedlock, ed. 1961p

3 He loved me absolutely, that's why he hates me absolutely. . . .

Ibid., Letter to Edward Garnett (c.1914)

4 . . . he hated me for being miserable, not a moment of misery did he put up with; he denied all the suffering and suffered all the more. . . .

Ibid.

5 But it was nice to feel him at the back of her days, solid and firm her rock of ages. He bored her a bit occasionally.

Ibid., Letter (1938 or 1939)

471. Lilian Leveridge
(1879–1953)

1 Brother, little brother, your childhood is passing by,
And the dawn of a noble purpose I see in your thoughtful eye.

"A Cry from the Canadian Hills,"
St. 6, Over the Hills of Home   1918

2 Laddie! Laddie! Laddie! "Somewhere in France" you sleep,
Somewhere 'neath alien flowers and alien winds that weep,
Bravely you marched to battle, nobly your life laid down,
You unto death were faithful, laddie; yours is the victor's crown.

Ibid., St. 9

3 Over the hills of home, laddie, over the hills of home.

Ibid.

472. Sarojini Naidu
(1879–1949)

1 *To-day* it is spring!

"Ecstasy," The Golden Threshold   1890

2 What hope shall we gather, what dreams shall we sow?
Where the wind calls our wandering footsteps we go.
No love bids us tarry, no joy bids us wait;
The voice of the wind is the voice of our fate.

Ibid., "Wandering Singers," St. 3

3 And spirits of Truth were the birds that sang,
  And spirits of Love were the stars that glowed,
  And spirits of Peace were the streams that flowed
  In that magical wood in the land of sleep.

> Ibid., "Song of a Dream," St. 1

4 O Bird of Time on your fruitful bough
  What are the songs you sing?

> "The Bird of Time," St. 1
> *The Bird of Time*   1912

5 Shall hope prevail where clamorous hate is rife,
  Shall sweet love prosper or high dreams find place
  Amid the tumult of reverberant strife.

> Ibid., "At Twilight," St. 2

6 What do you know in your blithe, brief season
  Of dreams deferred and a heart grown old?

> Ibid., "A Song in Spring," St. 2

7 The Indian woman of to-day is once more awake and
  profoundly alive to her splendid destiny as the guardian
  and interpreter of the Triune Vision of national life—
  the Vision of Love, the Vision of Faith, the Vision of
  Patriotism.

> *The Broken Wing*, Foreword   1916

8 Can ye measure the grief of the tears I weep
  Or compass the woe of the watch I keep?

> Ibid., "The Gift of India," St. 3

9 Thy changing kings and kingdoms pass away
  The gorgeous legends of a bygone day,
  But thou dost still immutably remain
  Unbroken symbol of proud history, unageing priestess
    of old mysteries
  Before whose shrine the spells of Death are vain.

> Ibid., "Imperial Delhi," St. 2

10 Two gifts for our portion
   We ask thee, O Fate,
   A maiden to cherish,
   A kinsman to hate.

> "A Song of the Khyber Pass," St. 2,
> *The Feather of the Dawn*   1927

11 What, O my heart, though tomorrow be tragic,
   Today is inwoven of rapture and magic.

> Ibid.,, "Spring in Kashmir," St. 9

473. Alma Mahler Werfel
(1879–1964)

1 Mahler, ascetic though he was, had a lurid reputation. In fact, he was a child and women were his dread. It was only because I was a stupid, inexperienced girl that I took him off his guard.

"First Meeting," *Gustav Mahler*   *1946*

2 From the moment of his spiritual triumph, too, he looked down on me and did not recover his love for me until I had broken his tyranny. Sometimes he played the part of a school-master, relentlessly strict and unjust. He soured my enjoyment of life and made it an abomination. That is, he tried to. Money—rubbish! Clothes—rubbish! Beauty—rubbish! Traveling—rubbish! Only the spirit was to count. I know today that he was afraid of my youth and beauty. He wanted to make them safe for himself by simply taking from me any atom of life in which he himself played no part. I was a young thing he had desired and whose education he now took in hand.

Ibid., "Marriage and Life Together"

3 I can never forget his dying hours and the greatness of his face as death drew nearer. His battle for the eternal values, his elevation above trivial things and his unflinching devotion to truth are an example of the saintly life.   Ibid., "The End"

474. Beth Slater Whitson
(1879–1930)

1 Meet me in Dreamland, sweet dreamy Dreamland,
There let my dreams come true.

"Meet Me To-Night in Dreamland"   *1909*

475. Alice Williams Brotherton
(fl. 1880s–1930)

* * *

1 Books we must have though we lack bread.

"Ballade of Poor Bookworms"

2 Heap high the board with plenteous cheer, and gather
    to the feast,
  And toast the sturdy Pilgrim band whose courage never
    ceased.
                          "The First Thanksgiving Day"

476. Ophelia Guyon Browning
(fl. 1880s)

1 She knows Omnipotence has heard her prayer
  And cries, "It shall be done—sometime, somewhere."
                          "Pray Without Ceasing,"
                    Singing with Grace   1882

477. Mrs. E. T. Corbett
(fl. 1880s)

1 Ef you want to be sick of your life,
  Jest come and change places with me a spell—for I'm
  an inventor's wife.
                    The Inventor's Wife   1883

478. Ellen M. Hutchinson
(fl. 1880s—1933)

* * *

1 They are all in the lily-bed, cuddled close together—
  Purple, yellow-cap, and baby-blue;
  How they ever got there you must ask the April
    weather,
    The morning and the evening winds, the sunshine
    and the dew.   "Vagrant Pansies"

479. Meta Orred
(fl. 1880s)

1 In the gloaming, O, my darling!
  When the lights are dim and low,
  And the quiet shadows falling
  Softly come and softly go.
                          "In the Gloaming"   1890

480. Helen Keller
(1880–1968)

1 . . . we could never learn to be brave and patient, if there were only joy in the world.
Quoted in the *Atlantic Monthly*   May, 1890

2 Literature is my Utopia. Here I am not disenfranchised. No barrier of the senses shuts me out from the sweet, gracious discourse of my book friends. They talk to me without embarrassment or awkwardness.
The Story of My Life   1903

3 There is no king who has not had a slave among his ancestors, and no slave who has not had a king among his.
Ibid., Ch. 1

4 . . . I find that fact and fancy look alike across the years that link the past with the present.
Ibid.

5 There is nothing more beautiful, I think, than the evanescent fleeting images and sentiments presented by a language one is just becoming familiar with—ideas that flit across the mental sky, shaped and tinted by capricious fancy.
Ibid., Ch. 16

6 I hung about the dangerous frontier of "guess," avoiding with infinite trouble to myself and others the broad valley of reason.
Ibid., Ch. 17

7 Everything had its wonders, even darkness and silence, and I learn, whatever state I may be in, therein to be content.
Ibid., Ch. 22

8 . . . a people's peace—a peace without victory, a peace without conquests or indemnities.
Ibid.

9 . . . militarism . . . is one of the chief bulwarks of capitalism, and the day that militarism is undermined, capitalism will fail.
Ibid.

10 Now I feel as if I should succeed in doing something in mathematics, although I cannot see why it is so very important. . . . The knowledge doesn't make life any sweeter or happier, does it?

Ibid., Pt. II, Letter to Laurence Hutton

11 Now, however, I see the folly of attempting to hitch one's wagon to a star with a harness that does not belong to it.

Ibid., Letter to Charles T. Copeland

12 "I never fight," she replied, "except against difficulties."

Ibid., Pt. III

13 Toleration . . . is the greatest gift of the mind; it requires the same effort of the brain that it takes to balance oneself on a bicycle.

Ibid.

14 I know that daisies and pansies come from seeds which have been put in the ground; but children do not grow out of the ground. I am sure. I have never seen a plant child. . . .

Ibid., Quoted in Annie Sullivan's Report of 1891

15 One can never consent to creep when one feels an impulse to soar.

Ibid., Speech, Mt. Airy

16 Every industry, every process, is wrought by a hand, or by a superhand—a machine whose mighty arm and cunning fingers the human hand invents and wields.

"The Hand of the World,"
American Magazine
December, 1912

17 Study the hand, and you shall find in it the true picture of man, the story of human growth, the measure of the world's greatness and weakness.

Ibid.

18 . . . as the eagle was killed by the arrow winged with his own feather, so the hand of the world is wounded by its own skill.

Ibid.

19 Rebuffed, but always persevering; self-reproached, but ever regaining faith; undaunted, tenacious, the heart of man labors toward immeasurably distant goals.

Ibid.

20 How reconcile this world of fact with the bright world of my imagining? My darkness has been filled with the light of intelligence, and behold, the outer day-light world was stumbling and groping in social blindness.

Quoted in The Cry for Justice,
Upton Sinclair, ed.   1915

21 Let us start a world-encircling revolt, a revolt which shall make a junk heap out of the civilization of Kaisers and Kings and all the things that make of a man a brute and of God a monster.

Speech, New York City
December 19, 1915

22 The burden of war always falls heaviest on the toilers.

"Menace of the Militarist Program,"
New York Call   December 20, 1915

23 The only moral virtue of war is that it compels the capitalist system to look itself in the face and admit it is a fraud. It compels the present society to admit that it has no morals it will not sacrifice for gain.   Ibid.

24 I look upon the whole world as my fatherland, and every war has to me a horror of a family-feud. I look upon true patriotism as the brotherhood of man and the service of all to all.   Ibid.

25 The few who profit by the labor of the masses want to organize the workers into an army which will protect the interests of the capitalists.

Speech, New York City   December, 1916

26 Security is mostly a superstition. It does not exist in nature, nor do the children of men as a whole experience it. Avoiding danger is no safer in the long run than outright exposure. Life is either a daring adventure, or nothing.

The Open Door   1957

481. Sophie Kerr
(1880–1965)

1 Freud and his three slaves, Inhibition, Complex and Libido.

"The Age of Innocence," Saturday Evening Post   April 9, 1932

2 The longing to produce great inspirations didn't produce anything but more longing.
The Man Who Knew the Date, Ch. 1   *1951*

3 If peace, he thought (as he had often thought before), only had the music and pageantry of war, there'd be no more wars.

Ibid., Ch. 8

482. Edith Lewis
(1880?–1955?)

1 . . . it is not in any form of biographical writing, but in art alone, that the deepest truth about human beings is to be found.
Willa Cather Living   *1953*

483. Kathleen Norris
(1880–1966)

1 "If you have children, you never have anything else!"
Mother, Ch. 2   *1911*

2 We cooked, cleaned, laboured, worried, planned, we wept and laughed, we groaned and we sang—but we never despaired. All this was but a passing phase; "we will certainly laugh at this someday," we all said buoyantly, laughing even then.
Noon, Ch. 1   *1924*

3 And so came middle-age, for I have discovered that middle-age is not a question of years. It is that moment in life when one realizes that one has exchanged, by a series of subtle shifts and substitutes, the vague and vaporous dreams of youth for the definite and tangible realization.
Ibid., Ch. 3

4 Never in the history of the big round world has anything like us occurred. A country without caste, without serfs, peons or slaves, without banishment or exile or whipping post, without starvation and oppression!
Home   *1928*

5 Home ought to be our clearinghouse, the place from which we go forth lessoned and disciplined, and ready for life.
Ibid.

6 When they were going to be flagrantly, brutally selfish, how men did love to talk of being fair!
Bread into Roses, Ch. 2   1936

7 The bright panorama was only a panorama, that was the trouble. Under its undeniable joy and excitements . . . there was a strange emptiness, a feeling that somehow reality was escaping her, that the business of being amused was altogether too successful. Life wasn't, after all, only amusement—or was it?
Ibid., Ch. 11

8 But somehow one never had time to stop and savor the taste of life as the stream of it flowed by. It would be good to find some quiet inlet where the waters were still enough for reflection, where one might sense the joy of the moment, rather than plan breathlessly for a dozen mingled treats in the future.   Ibid.

9 "There seems to be so much more winter than we need this year."   Ibid., Ch. 14

484. Christabel Pankhurst
(1880–1958)

1 We are not ashamed of what we have done, because, when you have a great cause to fight for, the moment of greatest humiliation is the moment when the spirit is proudest. The women we do pity, the women we think unwomanly, the women for whom we have almost contempt, if our hearts could let us have that feeling, are the women who can stand aside, who take no part in this battle—and perhaps even more, the women who know what the right path is and will not tread it, who are selling the liberty of other women in order to win the smiles and favour of the dominant sex.
Speech, Albert Hall, London   *March 19, 1908*

2 We are here to claim our rights as women, not only to be free, but to fight for freedom. It is our privilege, as well as our pride and our joy, to take some part in this militant movement, which, as we believe, means the regeneration of all humanity. Nothing but contempt is due to those people who ask us to submit to unmerited oppression. We shall not do it.
Speech   *March 23, 1911*

3 What we suffragettes aspire to be when we are enfranchised is ambassadors of freedom to women in other parts of the world, who are not so free as we are.

Speech, "America and the War,"
Carnegie Hall, New York
October 25, 1915

4 Some people are tempted to say that all war is wrong, and that both sides to every war must be in the wrong. I challenge that statement and deny it utterly, absolutely, and with all the power I have at my disposal. All wars are not wrong. Was your war against a British Government wrong? As an Englishwoman, I say that when you fought us for the principle of freedom, for the right of self-government, you did right. I am glad you fought us and I am glad you beat us.

Ibid.

5 I have known passion that strengthens one for endurance, shakes one with its mighty force, makes humans god-like, fills them with creative force. The passion of my life has been for the freeing of women, not only for reasons political and economic.

"Confessions of Christabel: Why I
Never Married," *Weekly Dispatch*
(London)　　*April, 1921*

6 Never lose your temper with the Press or the public is a major rule of political life.

Unshackled　　1959p

7 The spirit of the movement was wonderful. It was joyous and grave at the same time. Self seemed to be laid down as the women joined us. Loyalty, the greatest of the virtues, was the keynote of the movement—first to the cause, then to those who were leading, and member to member. Courage came next, not simply physical courage, though so much of that was present, but still more the moral courage to endure ridicule and misunderstandings and harsh criticism and ostracism. There was a touch of the "impersonal" in the movement that made for its strength and dignity. Humour characterized it, too, in that our militant women were like the British soldier who knows how to joke and smile amid his fighting and trials.

Ibid.

8 I go about with the Bible in one hand and a newspaper in the other. The two go well together, for the concen-

429

trated study of the newspapers is a Christian's duty as this Age draws to its close.

> Speech, Albert Hall, London
> (September, 1926), Quoted in
> *The Fighting Pankhursts*
> by David Mitchell   *1967p*

9 We are suffering today from a greed for knowledge of evil. Moral disease and sin is rampant. Groups here and there are striving to keep us from slipping back into barbarism. But nothing can save us but divine intervention. . . .

> Ibid., Speech, California (1930)

485. Jeannette Rankin
(1880–   )

1 As a woman I can't go to war, and I refuse to send anyone else.

> Quoted in *Jeannette Rankin: First
> Lady in Congress,* Prologue
> (c.1941), by Hannah Josephson
> *1974*

2 You take people as far as they will go, not as far as you would like them to go.

> Ibid.

3 The individual woman is required . . . a thousand times a day to choose either to accept her appointed role and thereby rescue her good disposition out of the wreckage of her self-respect, or else follow an independent line of behavior and rescue her self-respect out of the wreckage of her good disposition.

> Ibid., Ch. 3

4 Establish democracy at home, based on human rights as superior to property rights. . . .

> Ibid., Ch. 6

5 You can no more win a war than you can win an earthquake.

> Ibid., Ch. 8

486. Ruth St. Denis
(1880–1968)

1 I used to say that if a person wanted to keep alive, in distinction to merely existing, he should change his occupation every ten years. . . . Our individuality is based upon something much vaster than a circumscribed profession. We should be in a position to bring our intelligence to any challenging objective and be at no disadvantage.

Ruth St. Denis: An Unfinished Life, Ch. 3   *1939*

2 I am a child of nature. Too much civilization and a touch of luxury have only depressed me. I must find a way to live more simply.   Ibid., Ch. 6

3 I want to dance always, to be good and not evil, and when it is all over not to have the feeling that I might have done better.   Ibid.

4 The human tragedy of artists must, at some time, bring itself to the attention of all earnest thinkers and seekers after truth. That something is terribly wrong with the whole round of artists' lives must be apparent to anyone who takes the trouble to observe it.

Ibid., Ch. 15

5 We were a Poet* and a Dancer; and we became lovers. And let it be said of us that Beauty was our god whom we worshipped in rites of such pure loveliness that he became my Emperor and I became Moon to his Imperial Sun. Poems, like shy white birds, rose from our union: records of the strange drama of our love.

Ibid.

487. Marie Carmichael Stopes
(1880–1958)

1 The surface freedom of our women has not materially altered the pristine purity of a girl of our northern race.
Married Love   *1918*

---

* Referring to her husband, Ted Shawn.

2 Each heart knows instinctively that it is only a mate who can give full comprehension of all the potential greatness in the soul, and have tender laughter for all the childlike wonder that lingers so enchantingly even in the white-haired.

Ibid., Ch. 1

3 An impersonal and scientific knowledge of the structure of our bodies is the surest safeguard against prurient curiosity and lascivious gloating.

Ibid., Ch. 5

4 . . . each coming together of man and wife, even if they have been mated for many years, should be a fresh adventure; each winning should necessitate a fresh wooing.

Ibid., Ch. 10

5 So deeply are we woven I can lend
You outwardly to other hands who clutch
Small corners of your heart, greedy that such
Resplendence should its rays to darkness send.

"You," St. 2, *Joy and Verity*   *1952*

6 London, scarred mistress of proud Freedom's heart,
The love we bear you has no counterpart.

Ibid., "London"

7 We are not much in sympathy with the typical hustling American business man, but we have often felt compunction for him, seeing him nervous and harassed, sleeplessly, anxiously hunting dollars and all but overshadowed by his over-dressed, extravagant and idle wife, who sometimes insists that her spiritual development necessitates that she shall have no children. Such husbands and wives are also found in this country; they are a growing produce of the upper reaches of the capitalist system. Yet such wives imagine that they are upholding women's emancipation.

Article in *Dreadnought* (c.1919),
Quoted in *The Fighting Pankhursts*
by David Mitchell   *1967p*

488. Nancy Byrd Turner
(1880–1954?)

* .* *

1 Burn, wood, burn—
    Wood that once was a tree, and knew
Blossom and sheaf, and the Spring's return,
    Nest, and singing, and rain, and dew—
Burn, wood, burn!   "Flame Song"

2 Death is only an old door
Set in a garden wall.

                        "Death Is a Door"

3 Men climb tall hills to suffer and die.

                               "Hills"

489. Margaret Widdemer
(1880–   )

1 I have shut my little sister in from light and life
    (For a rose, for a ribbon, for a wreath across my hair),
I have made her restless feet still until the night,
Locked from sweets of summer and from wild spring
    air.
             "The Factories," St. 1   *c.1916*

2 The old road to Paradise
Easy it is missed!
      "The Old Road to Paradise," St. 2   *1919*

3 To grown people a girl of fifteen and a half is a child
still; to herself she is very old and very real; more real,
perhaps, than ever before or after. . . .
                      "The Changeling,"
                  The Boardwalk   *1920*

4 She was poor, and she was broken. But the young are
improvident—not having yet learned how hard to come
by money is and of how little account are other things.
                  Ibid., "The Congregation"

5 No one had told them that Age was a place
Where you sat with a curious mask on your face.
        "Old Ladies," St. 6, *Hill Garden*   *1936*

6 "It only was gifts that I let them take.
  I never gave dreams away."

  Ibid., "Spendthrift Nancy," St. 3

* * *

7 And all that you are sorry for is what you haven't
  done.

  "De Senectute"

8 I am the Dark Cavalier; I am the Last Lover:
  My arms shall welcome you when other arms are tired.
  "The Dark Cavalier"

9 Love and grief and motherhood,
    Fame and mirth and scorn—
  These are all shall befall
    Any woman born.

  "A Cyprian Woman"

490. Mary Antin
(1881–1949)

1 "So at last I was going to America! Really, really
  going, at last! The boundaries burst. The arch of
  heaven soared. A million suns shone out of every star.
  The winds rushed into outer space, roaring in my ears,
  'America! America!' "

  The Promised Land   *1912*

491. Mary Breckinridge
(1881–1965)

1 To meet the needs of the frontierman's child, you must
  begin before he is born and carry him through the hazards of childbirth. This means that the nurses who
  serve him must be midwives. . . . Even after his birth,
  the young child is not an isolated individual. His care
  not only means the care of the mother before, during
  and after his birth, but the care of his whole family as
  well. . . . Health teaching must also be on a family
  basis—in the homes.

  Quoted in "Birth Control Gains in the
  Mountains of Kentucky" by Kenneth
  Reich, *Los Angeles Times*
  May 9, 1975p

492. Grace Stone Coates
(1881–?)

* * *

1 Now, no doubt, my friend and I
  Will proceed to lie and lie
  To ourselves, till we begin
  To act the truth and call it sin.   "As It Is"

493. Alice Corbin
(1881–1949)

* * *

1 Then welcome Age and fear not sorrow;
  Today's no better than tomorrow.   "Two Voices"

2 I know we grow more lovely
  Growing wise.   Ibid.

494. Rose Macaulay
(1881–1958)

1 "You, you see, have seemed equally happy for a time,
  equally unhappy after a time, in all the creeds or no-
  creeds. And equally good, my dear. I suppose I may
  say that I believe in none of them, or believe in all. In
  any case, it matters very little."
                    Told by an Idiot, Pt. I, Ch. 14   *1923*

2 Decades have a delusive edge to them. They are not, of
  course, really periods at all, except as any other ten
  years would be. But we, looking at them, are caught by
  the different name each bears, and give them different
  attributes, and tie labels on them, as if they were flowers in a border.   Ibid., Pt. II, Ch. 1

3 Sleeping in a bed—it is, apparently, of immense importance. Against those who sleep, from choice or necessity, elsewhere society feels righteously hostile. It is
  not done. It is disorderly, anarchical.
                    "Beds and 'Omes," *A Casual*
                    Commentary   *1925*

435

4 Does conduct rank with food, wine, and weather as a department of life in which goodness is almost universally admired?

> Ibid., "A Platonic Affection"

5 Cranks live by theory, not by pure desire. They want votes, peace, nuts, liberty, and spinning-looms not because they love these things, as a child loves jam, but because they think they ought to have them. That is one element which makes the crank.

> Ibid., "Cranks"

6 Yet, because prolonged anarchy is impossible to man's law-bound nature, as to that of the universe which bore him, each attempt at it defeats itself. . . .

> Catchwords and Claptrap   1926

7 . . . he desired to exaggerate. And here we have what may be called a primary human need, which should be placed by psychologists with the desire for nourishment, for safety, for sense-gratifications, and for appreciation, as one of the elemental lusts of man.

> Ibid.

8 In our attacks on conduct we mislike, we wave the corpses of women and children about us like banners as we charge.

> Ibid.

9. "The century of the common man": ominous phrase, that he and his friends like to turn on their tongues with relishing distaste; lacking this bogy, this sense of there being massed against them a Philistine, vocal army terrible with slogans, illiterate cries, and destructive leveling aims, the young gentlemen would have been less happy, less themselves.

> The World My Wilderness, Ch. 2   1950

10 . . . the desire not to work; indeed, I share it to the full. As to one's country, why should one feel any more interest in its welfare than in that of any other countries? And as to the family, I have never understood how that fits in with the other ideals—or, indeed, why it should be an ideal at all. A group of closely related persons living under one roof; it is a convenience, often a necessity, sometimes a pleasure, sometimes the reverse; but who first exalted it as admirable, an almost religious ideal?

> Ibid., Ch. 20

11 "Take my camel, dear," said my aunt Dot, as she climbed down from this animal on her return from High Mass.

The Towers of Trebizond, Ch. 1   *1956*

495. Anna Pavlova
(1881–1931)

1 . . . although one may fail to find happiness in theatrical life, one never wishes to give it up after having once tasted its fruits. To enter the School of the Imperial Ballet is to enter a convent whence frivolity is banned, and where merciless discipline reigns.

"Pages of My Life," *Pavlova:*
A Biography, A. H. Franks, ed.
1956p

2 As is the case in all branches of art, success depends in a very large measure upon individual initiative and exertion, and cannot be achieved except by dint of hard work. Even after having reached perfection, a ballerina may never indulge in idleness.

Ibid.

3 To tend, unfailingly, unflinchingly, towards a goal, is the secret of success. But success? What exactly is success? For me it is to be found not in applause, but in the satisfaction of feeling that one is realising one's ideal. When a small child . . . I thought that success spelled happiness. I was wrong. Happiness is like a butterfly which appears and delights us for one brief moment, but soon flits away.

Ibid.

496. Mary Heaton Vorse
(1881–1966)

1 "Some folks is born in the world feeling it and knowing it in their hearts that creation don't stop where the sight of the eyes stop, and the thinner the veil is the better, and something in them sickens when the veil gets too thick."

"The Other Room," *McCall's*   *1919*

2 He had seized the one loophole that life had given her and had infused her relentless courage into another's veins.

"The Wallow of the Sea," Harper's   1921

497. Mary Webb
(1881–1927)

1 The past is only the present become invisible and mute; and because it is invisible and mute, its memoried glances and its murmurs are infinitely precious. We are tomorrow's past.

Precious Bane, Foreword   1924

2 It made me gladsome to be getting some education, it being like a big window opening.

Ibid., Bk. I, Ch. 5

3 Saddle your dreams afore you ride 'em.

Ibid., Ch. 6

4 If you stop to be kind, you must swerve often from your path.   Ibid., Bk. II, Ch. 3

5 It's the folks that depend on us for this and for the other that we most do miss.   Ibid., Bk. IV, Ch. 4

498. Marie Bonaparte
(1882–1962)

1 The residue of virility in the woman's [sexual] organism is utilized by nature in order to eroticize her: otherwise the functioning of the maternal apparatus would wholly submerge her in the painful tasks of reproduction and motherhood.

"Passivity, Masochism, and
Femininity" (1934), International
Journal of Psycho-Analysis,
Vol. 16   1935

2 On the one hand, then, in the reproduction functions proper—menstruation, defloration, pregnancy and parturition—woman is biologically doomed to suffer. Nature seems to have no hesitation in administering to her strong doses of pain, and she can do nothing but submit passively to the regimen prescribed. On the other

hand, as regards sexual attraction, which is necessary for the act of impregnation, and as regards the erotic pleasure experienced during the act itself, the woman may be on equal footing with the man.

Ibid.

3 Now every living organism dreads invasion from without, and this is a dread bound up with life itself and governed by the biological law of self-preservation. Moreover . . . little girls . . . bear imprinted on their minds from earliest childhood the terrifying vision of a sexual attack by a man upon a woman, which they believe to be the cause of the [menstrual] bleeding. It follows therefore that, in spite of the instinct, which urges them forward, they draw back from the feminine erotic function itself, although of all the reproductive functions of woman this is the only one which should really be free from suffering and purely pleasurable.

Ibid.

499. Charlotte Brown
(1882–1961)

1 . . . I propose the raising of dollars to $500,000 as an endowment. . . . This seems tremendous, I know, for me to undertake but folks don't seem to pay much attention nowadays to anything that's small and a fund like this places a sort of permanence to the thing.

Letter to Mr. and Mrs. Galen Stone
(June 19, 1920), *Black Women in White
America,* Gerda Lerner, ed.   *1972p*

2 A few of us must be sacrificed perhaps in order to get a step further.

Ibid., Letter to F. P. Hobgood, Jr. (October 19, 1921)

3 Now that things are turning and many are opening their eyes to what I've tried to do and desiring to have a share in the same, the question in my heart and mind, and God only knows how it hurts, is just what are they going to ask me to submit to as a negro woman to get their interest for there are some men who occupy high places who feel that no negro woman whether she be cook, criminal or principal of a school should ever be addressed as *Mrs.*

Ibid., Letter Fragment

4 As a part of my argument for education for Negroes I used the incident as illustration that most white people looked upon every Negro, regardless of his appearance, modulated tones that reflected some culture and training, as a servant. . . .

Ibid., Autobiographical Sketch

500. Susan Glaspell
(1882–1948)

1 HENRIETTA. It is through suppression that hells are formed in us.

Suppressed Desires, Sc. 1   *1914*

2 MABEL. I think it's perfectly wonderful! Why, if it wasn't for psychoanalysis you'd never find out how wonderful your own mind is!

Ibid., Sc. 2

3 "We live close together and we live far apart. We all go through the same things—it's all just a different kind of the same thing!"

"A Jury of Her Peers," *Every Week*   *1917*

4 FATHER. But in a world that won't have visions—why not study Sanscrit while such a world is being made over—into another such world.

Bernice, Act I   *1919*

5 Those who were neither mourning nor rejoicing were being kept awake by mourners or rejoicers. All the while, diluted whiskey that could be bought on the quiet was in use for the deadening or the heightening of emotion.

"Government Goat," *The Pictorial Review*   *1919*

6 GRANDMOTHER. That's the worst of a war—you have to go on hearing about it so long.

Inheritors, Act I   *1921*

7 GRANDMOTHER. Seems nothing draws men together like killing other men.

Ibid.

8 HOLDEN. And I think a society which permits things to go on which I can prove go on in our federal prisons had better stop and take a fresh look at itself. To stand

for that and then talk of democracy and idealism—oh, it shows no mentality, for one thing.

Ibid., Act. II, Sc. 2

9 A new town was only the same town in a different place. . . .

"His Smile," The Pictorial Review   1921

501. Emma Jung
(1882–1955)

1 Neither arrogance nor presumption drives us to the audacity of wanting to be like God—that is, like man; we are not like Eve of old, lured by the beauty of the fruit of the tree of knowledge, nor does the snake encourage us to enjoy it. No, there has come to us something like a command; we are confronted with the necessity of biting into this apple, whether we think it good to eat or not, confronted with the fact that the paradise of naturalness and unconsciousness, in which many of us would only too gladly tarry, is gone forever.

"On the Nature of Animus" (1931),
Animus and Anima   1957p

2 The real thinking of woman . . . is preeminently practical and applied. It is something we describe as sound common sense, and is usually directed to what is close at hand and personal. . . . In general, it can be said that feminine mentality manifests an undeveloped, childlike, or primitive character; instead of the thirst for knowledge, curiosity; instead of judgment, prejudice; instead of thinking, imagination or dreaming; instead of will, wishing. Where a man takes up objective problems, a woman contents herself with solving riddles; where he battles for knowledge and understanding, she contents herself with faith or superstition, or else she makes assumptions.

Ibid.

3 Very frequently, feminine activity also expresses itself in what is largely a retrospectively oriented pondering over what we ought to have done differently in life, and how we ought to have done it; or, as if under compulsion, we make up strings of causal connections. We like to call this thinking; though, on the contrary, it is a form of mental activity that is strangely pointless and

441

unproductive, a form that really leads only to self-torture.

Ibid.

4 And now we come to the magic of words. A word, also, just like an idea, a thought, has the effect of reality upon undifferentiated minds. Our Biblical myth of creation, for instance, where the world grows out of the spoken word of the Creator, is an expression of this.

Ibid.

5 For by her unconsciousness, woman exerts a magical influence on man, a charm that lends her power over him. Because she feels this power instinctively and does not wish to lose it, she often resists to the utmost the process of becoming conscious. . . . Many men take pleasure in woman's unconsciousness. They are bent on opposing her development of greater consciousness in every possible way, because it seems to them uncomfortable and unnecessary.

Ibid.

6 Learning to cherish and emphaisze feminine values is the primary condition of our holding our own against the masculine principle. . . .

Ibid.

502. Winifred Letts
(1882–?)

1 Age after age the children give
Their lives that Herod still may live.

"The Children's Ghosts,"
Hallow-e'en, and Poems of War   1916

2 God rest you, happy gentlemen,
  Who laid your good lives down,
Who took the khaki and the gun
  Instead of cap and gown.

"The Spires of Oxford," St. 4,
The Spires of Oxford and
Other Poems</i>   1917</div>

* * *

3 I do be thinking God must laugh
The time he makes a boy,

442

All element the creatures are,
And divilment and joy.

"Boys"

4 That God once loved a garden
We learn in Holy writ.
And seeing gardens in the spring
I well can credit it.

"Stephen's Green," St. 1

503. Anne O'Hare McCormick
(1882?–1954)

1 Whoever goes to Russia discovers Russia.
The Hammer and the Scythe, Ch. 1   1927

2 The peasant wanders; he is still a nomad, a creature of pilgrimages and excursions, harnessed to rather than rooted in the soil.

Ibid., Ch. 6

3 There is no place where you can see more human nature in a few hours than in a session of the Parliament of Italy, and no place where you are more impressed by the unchanging tradition of the Catholic Church than at a consistory at the Vatican.

"A Papal Consistory and a Political
Debut" (July 24, 1921), *Vatican
Journal, 1921–1954*, Marion
Turner Sheehan, ed.   1957p

4 A new Italy demands a new Rome.
Ibid., "A New Rome Arises to Rival
the Old" (January 16, 1927)

5 One little angry, brooding man [Hitler] has put the whole world on wartime. A man who could never keep step with anybody has forced millions of free and intelligent human beings to keep the time he sets.
Ibid., "Reflections in Time of War" (April 4, 1942)

6 For what is the naked issue of the most universal war in history but the right of man to be himself?
Ibid., "Where the Christmas Lights
Are Out" (December 25, 1943)

504. Sylvia Pankhurst
(1882–1960)

1 English is the most modern of the great languages, the most widely spoken, and the most international. . . . Its swiftness and transparent accuracy of expression, and especially the fact that it has shed most of the old grammatical forms which time has rendered useless and scarcely intelligible, have made English a model, pointing the way which must be followed in building the Interlanguage. . . .

Delphos, Ch. 5   1926

2 The Interlanguage will provide a means by which the thoughts and emotions of mankind, as expressed in language, may achieve a world-comprehension, which is to-day possible only in music. There is work here for our teachers and students, our pacifists, and our sociologists. Let them rally to the standard of Interlanguage—to perfect it, and to advance it.

Ibid., Ch. 7

3 We do not make beams from the hollow, decaying trunk of the fallen oak. We use the upsoaring tree in the full vigour of its sap.

Quoted in the *Evening Standard*
(London)   *March 5, 1930*

4 Hourly the War drew nearer; threat followed threat; ultimatum, ultimatum. My mind shrank from the menace sweeping down on us, as children's do from belief in death and misfortune, vainly clinging to the fancy that great disasters only happen to other people.

The Home Front, Ch. 1   1932

5 The machinery of succour might be preparing; but the people were hungry.

Ibid., Ch. 2

6 I could not give my name to aid the slaughter in this war, fought on both sides for grossly material ends, which did not justify the sacrifice of a single mother's son. Clearly I must continue to oppose it, and expose it, to all whom I could reach with voice or pen.

Ibid., Ch. 25

7 Racked with pain, prostrate with headache, at times I might be, yet within me was a rage at this merciless War, this squalor of poverty! Oh! that all the wealth and effort the nation was squandering might be to re-build these slums, to restore these faded women, these starved and stunted children.

Ibid., Ch. 58

8 The cause of Ethiopia cannot be divorced from the cause of international justice, which is permanent and is not to be determined by ephemeral military victories. . . . *New Times* is opposed to the conception of dictatorship. It understands that Fascism destroys all personal liberty and is in fundamental opposition to all forms of intellectual and moral progress.

Quoted in the *New Times &*
Ethiopia News   May 5, 1936

9 My belief in the growth and permanence of democracy is undimmed. I know that the people will cast off the new dictatorships as they did the old. I believe as firmly as in my youth that humanity will surmount the era of poverty and war. Life will be happier and more beautiful for all. I believe in the GOLDEN AGE.

Essay in *Myself When Young,*
Margot Asquith, ed.   *1938*

10 The discerning traveler who records what appears to the citizens of a country [to be] commonplace performs a service to posterity.

Ethiopia, Preface   *1955*

11 I am proud to call myself a Bolshevist.

Article in *Dreadnought* (1918),
Quoted in *The Fighting Pankhursts*
by David Mitchell   *1967p*

12 We have only one life in this world. Can't we see the revolution in our time? Can't we live in it and enjoy it? I want to see the beginning. I want to see something done. When are you going to begin? If the police came here tonight and killed some of us, I think it would do a great deal of good!

Ibid., Speech, "Hands Off Russia"
Rally, London (January, 1919)

13 . . . but all my experience showed that it was useless trying to palliate an impossible system. It is a *wrong*

system and has got to be smashed. I would give my life to smash it. You cannot frighten me with any sentence you may impose. . . . You will not stop this agitation. The words that are being written in my paper [*Dreadnought*] will be as common as daily bread.

Ibid., Courtroom Speech (October 28, 1919)

14 I have gone to war too. . . . I am going to fight capitalism even if it kills me. It is wrong that people like you should be comfortable and well fed while all around you people are starving.

Ibid., (January, 1921)

15 Love and freedom are vital to the creation and upbringing of a child. I do not advise anyone to rush into either legal or free marriage without love, sympathy, understanding, friendship and frankness. These are essentials, and having these, no legal forms are necessary. Indifference, hostility and compulsion are the factors to be feared, and the influences that lead to sorrow for the individual and danger to the progress of the race.

Ibid., Article in *News of the World* (April, 1928)

16 Socialism is the greatest thing in life for me. You will never crush it out of me or kill it. I am only one of thousands or millions. Socialists make it possible to practise what you say in church, that we should love our neighbours as ourselves. If you work against socialism, you are standing with reaction against life, standing with the dead past against the coming civilization.

Ibid., Pt. II, Ch. 4

17 The emancipation of today displays itself mainly in cigarettes and shorts. There is even a reaction from the ideal of an intellectual and emancipated womanhood, for which the pioneers toiled and suffered, to be seen in painted lips and nails, and the return of trailing skirts and other absurdities of dress which betoken the slave-woman's intelligent companionship.

Ibid., Pt. V, Ch. 3

505. Frances Perkins
(1882–1965)

1 In America, public opinion is the leader.

People at Work, Sec. I   1934

2 But with the slow menace of a glacier, depression came on. No one had any measure of its progress; no one had any plan for stopping it. Everyone tried to get out of its way.

Ibid., Sec. IV

3 To one who believes that really good industrial conditions are the hope for a machine civilization, nothing is more heartening than to watch conference methods and education replacing police methods.

Ibid., Sec. VIII

4 The quality of his [F. D. Roosevelt] being one with the people, of having no artificial or natural barriers between him and them, made it possible for him to be a leader without ever being or thinking of being a dictator.

The Roosevelt I Knew, Ch. 7   1946

5 He [F. D. Roosevelt] didn't like concentrated responsibility. Agreement with other people who he thought were good, right-minded, and trying to do the right thing by the world was almost as necessary to him as air to breathe.

Ibid., Ch. 12

506. Mabel Ulrich
(1882?–?)

1 A man, it seems, may be intellectually in complete sympathy with a woman's aims. But only about ten percent of him is his intellect—the other ninety his emotions.

"A Doctor's Diary, 1904–1932,"
Scribner's Magazine   June, 1933

2 It can't be so easy being the husband of a "modern" woman. She is everything his mother wasn't—and nothing she was.

Ibid.

3 But, oh, what a woman I should be if an able young man would consecrate his life to me as secretaries and technicians do to their men employers.   Ibid.

4 Verily what bishops are to the English, bankers are to Americans.   Ibid.

507. Virginia Verona
(1882–)

1 I blame the unions, first, last and all the time. The nation has gotten to the place where unskilled labor is getting paid more than skilled. The unions have gone too far. They rule this country, and they have no compassion, no mercy for people, not even other union members.

> Quoted in "Fighting for Her—and
> Our—Rights" by Ursula Vils,
> *Los Angeles Times*   January 5, 1975

2 People are too easygoing. The American people will not stand up for their rights. They'll be violent, of course, but they will not stand up for their rights.

> Ibid.

508. Virginia Woolf
(1882–1941)

1 "Doesn't one always think of the past, in a garden with men and women lying under the trees? Aren't they one's past, all that remains of it, those men and women, those ghosts lying under the trees . . . one's happiness, one's reality?"

> *Kew Gardens*   1919

2 Desiring truth, awaiting it, laboriously distilling a few words, for ever desiring . . . truth.
> "Monday or Tuesday," *Monday or Tuesday*   1921

3 Life's what you see in people's eyes; life's what they learn, and having learnt it, never, though they seek to hide it, cease to be aware of what? That life's like that, it seems.

> Ibid., "An Unwritten Novel"

4 We all know—the *Times* knows—but we pretend we don't.

> Ibid.

5 The eyes of others our prisons; their thoughts our cages.   Ibid.

6 But when the self speaks to the self, who is speaking?—
the entombed soul, the spirit driven in, in, in to the
central catacomb; the self that took the veil and left the
world—a coward perhaps, yet somehow beautiful, as it
flits with its lantern restlessly up and down the dark
corridors.

Ibid.

7 Life's bare as a bone.

Ibid.

8 I too sit passive on a gilt chair, only turning the earth
above a buried memory, as we all do, for there are
signs, if I'm not mistaken, that we're all recalling something, furtively seeking something.

Ibid., "The String Quartet"

9 How lovely goodness is in those who, stepping lightly,
go smiling through the world!

Ibid.

10 The older one grows the more one likes indecency.

Ibid.

11 In people's eyes, in the swing, tramp, and trudge; in the
bellow and uproar; the carriages, motor cars, omni-
buses, vans, sandwich men shuffling and swinging;
brass bands; barrel organs; in the triumph and the jin-
gle and the strange high singing of some aeroplane
overhead was what she loved; life; London; this moment in June.

Mrs. Dalloway   1925

12 The word-coining genius, as if thought plunged into a
sea of words and came up dripping.

"An Elizabethan Play,"
The Common Reader   1925

13 Those comfortably padded lunatic asylums which are
known, euphemistically, as the stately homes of England.

Ibid., "Lady Dorothy Nevill"

14 Trivial personalities decomposing in the eternity of
print.

Ibid., "The Modern Essay"

15 The beauty of the world has two edges, one of laughter,
one of anguish, cutting the heart asunder.

A Room of One's Own   1929

16 If truth is not to be found on the shelves of the British Museum, where, I asked myself, picking up a notebook and a pencil, is truth?

Ibid., Ch. 2

17 How shall I ever find the grains of truth embedded in all this mass of paper?

Ibid.

18 Why are women . . . so much more interesting to men than men are to women?

Ibid.

19 Yet it is in our idleness, in our dreams, that the submerged truth sometimes comes to the top.

Ibid.

20 When an arguer argues dispassionately he thinks only of the argument.

Ibid.

21 Without self-confidence we are as babes in the cradle. And how can we generate this imponderable quality, which is yet so invaluable, most quickly? By thinking that other people are inferior to oneself.

Ibid.

22 Women have served all these centuries as looking-glasses possessing the magic and delicious power of reflecting the figure of man at twice its natural size.

Ibid.

23 Indeed, I thought, slipping the silver into my purse, it is remarkable, remembering the bitterness of those days, what a change of temper a fixed income will bring about.

Ibid.

24 Great bodies of people are never responsible for what they do.

Ibid.

25 . . . for fiction, imaginative work that is, is not dropped like a pebble upon the ground, as science may be; fiction is like a spider's web, attached ever so lightly perhaps, but still attached to life at all four corners.

Ibid., Ch. 3

26 . . . women have burnt like beacons in all the works of all the poets from the beginning of time.　　Ibid.

27 When, however, one reads of a witch being ducked, of a woman possessed by devils, of a wise woman selling herbs, or even a very remarkable man who had a mother, then I think we are on the track of a lost novelist, a suppressed poet . . . indeed, I would venture to guess that Anon, who wrote so many poems without signing them, was often a woman.

Ibid.

28 Chastity . . . has, even now, a relative importance in a woman's life, and has so wrapped itself round with nerves and instincts that to cut it free and bring it to the light of day demands courage of the rarest.

Ibid.

29 For surely it is time that the effect of discouragement upon the mind of the artist should be measured, as I have seen a dairy company measure the effect of ordinary milk and Grade A milk upon the body of the rat.

Ibid.

30 The history of men's opposition to women's emancipation is more interesting perhaps than the story of that emancipation itself.

Ibid.

31 Literature is strewn with the wreckage of men who have minded beyond reason the opinions of others.

Ibid.

32 . . . the mind of an artist, in order to achieve the prodigious effort of freeing whole and entire the work that is in him, must be incandescent. . . . There must be no obstacle in it, no foreign matter unconsumed.

Ibid.

33. . . virility has now become self-conscious.

Ibid., Ch. 6

34 . . . it is fatal for anyone who writes to think of their sex. It is fatal to be a man or woman pure and simple; one must be woman-manly or man-womanly.

Ibid.

35 . . . anything written with . . . conscious bias is doomed to death.

Ibid.

36 Everybody looked overdressed or badly dressed—some, indeed, looked positively dirty beside him. His clothes

451

seemed to melt into each other with the perfection of their cut and the quiet harmony of their color. Without a single point of emphasis everything was distinguished. . . . He was the personification of freshness and cleanliness and order.

"Beau Brummell," *The Second Common Reader*   1932

37 And then he said very cutting things about other people. They were not exactly witty; they were certainly not profound; but they were so skillful, so adroit—they had a twist in them which made them slip into the mind and stay there when more important phrases were forgotten.

Ibid.

38 To enjoy freedom, if the platitude is pardonable, we have of course to control ourselves. We must not squander our powers, helplessly and ignorantly, squirting half the house in order to water a single rose-bush; we must train them, exactly and powerfully, here on the very spot.

Ibid., "How Should One Read a Book?"

39 I have sometimes dreamt, at least, that when the Day of Judgment dawns and the great conquerors and lawyers and statesmen come to receive their rewards— their crowns, their laurels, their names carved indelibly upon imperishable marble—the Almighty will turn to Peter and will say, not without a certain envy when he sees us coming with our books under our arms, "Look, these need no reward. We have nothing to give them here. They have loved reading."

Ibid.

40 But what have I done with my life? thought Mrs. Ramsay, taking her place at the head of the table, and looking at all the plates making white circles on it.

To the Lighthouse   1937

41 She took up once more her old painting position with the dim eyes and the absent-minded manner, subduing all her impressions as a woman, to something more general; becoming once more under the power of that vision which she had been clearly once and must now grope for among hedges and houses and children—her picture.

Ibid.

42 If people are highly successful in their professions they lose their senses. Sight goes. They have no time to look at pictures. Sound goes. They have no time to listen to music. Speech goes. They have no time for conversation. They lose their sense of proportion—the relations between one thing and another. Humanity goes. . . .

Three Guineas   *1938*

43 How can we enter the professions and yet remain civilized human beings?

Ibid.

44 To make ideas effective, we must be able to fire them off. We must put them into action. . . . "I will not cease from mental fight," Blake wrote. Mental fight means thinking against the current, not with it. The current flows fast and furious. It issues a spate of words from the loudspeakers and the politicians. Every day they tell us that we are a free people fighting to defend freedom. That is the current that has whirled the young airman up into the sky and keeps him circulating there among the clouds. Down here, with a roof to cover us and a gas mask handy, it is our business to puncture gas bags and discover the seeds of truth.

Article in the *New Republic*   *October 21, 1940*

45 Surely it was time someone invented a new plot, or that the author came out from the bushes.

Between the Acts   *1941*

46 If you do not tell the truth about yourself you cannot tell it about other people.

The Moment and Other Essays   *1952p*

47 It is worth mentioning, for future reference, that the creative power which bubbles so pleasantly in beginning a new book quiets down after a time, and one goes on more steadily. Doubts creep in. Then one becomes resigned. Determination not to give in, and the sense of an impending shape keep one at it more than anything.

A Writer's Diary (May 11, 1919),
Leonard Woolf, ed.   *1954p*

48 Why is life so tragic; so like a little strip of pavement over an abyss. I look down; I feel giddy; I wonder how I am ever to walk to the end.

Ibid. (October 25, 1920)

453

49 But as I said, I must face the despicable vanity which is at the root of all this niggling and haggling.

Ibid. (April 8, 1921)

50 I get such a sense of tingling and vitality from an evening's talk like that; one's angularities and obscurities are smoothed and lit.

Ibid. (October 27, 1928)

51 How physical the sense of triumph and relief is!

Ibid. (February 7, 1931)

52 Odd how the creative power at once brings the whole universe to order.

Ibid. (July 27, 1934)

53 I mark Henry James' sentence: observe perpetually. Observe the oncome of age. Observe greed. Observe my own despondency. By that means it becomes serviceable.

Ibid. (March 8, 1941)

54 Occupation is essential.   *Ibid.*

509. Dorothy Brett
(1883–?)

1 She [Mabel Dodge] had an insatiable appetite for tasting life in all its aspects. She tasted and spat it out.

"My Long and Beautiful Journey,"
South Dakota Review
Summer, 1967

510. Nannie Helen Burroughs
(1883–1961)

1 In fact, America will destroy herself and revert to barbarism if she continues to cultivate the things of the flesh and neglect the higher virtues. The Negro must not, therefore, contribute to her doom, but must ransom her. Furthermore it will profit the Negro nothing to enter into ungodly competition for material possessions when he has gifts of greater value.

"With All They Getting,"
The Southern Workman
July, 1927

454

2 When the Negro learns what manner of man he is spiritually, he will wake up all over. He will stop playing white even on the stage. He will rise in the majesty of his own soul. He will glorify the beauty of his own brown skin. He will stop thinking white and go to thinking straight and living right. He will realize that wrong-reaching, wrong-bleaching and wrong-mixing have "most nigh ruin't him" and he will redeem his body and rescue his soul from the bondage of that death. . . .

Ibid.

3 The aim of the National Training School is to give a training of head, hand and heart and develop a definite and active social interest in the spiritual and moral forces that make the human welfare. . . .

Quoted in "That's
Nannie Burroughs' Job, And She Does
It" by Floyd Calvin, *Pittsburgh Courier*
June 8, 1929

4 Chloroform your "Uncle Toms." The Negro must unload the leeches and parasitic leaders who are absolutely eating the life out of the struggling, desiring mass of people. Negroes like that went out of style seventy years ago. They are relics and good for museums.

Article in *The Louisiana Weekly*
December 23, 1933

5 Don't wait for deliverers. . . . I like that quotation, "Moses, my servant, is dead. Therefore, arise and go over Jordan." There are no deliverers. They're all dead. We must arise and go over Jordan. We can take the promised land.   *Ibid.*

6 This nation openly endorses, tolerates and legalizes the very abuses against which she originally waged a bloody revolution. A colored boy, a nickel penknife and a screaming woman were no more the cause of the Harlem uprising in 1935 than was a shipload of tea in the Boston harbor, in 1773, the cause of the Revolutionary War.

"Declaration of 1776 Is Cause of
Harlem Riot," *The Afro-American*
April 13, 1935

7 The framers of the Declaration of Independence prophesied that uprisings would occur "in the course of

human events," if people are denied those inalienable rights to which the "laws of nature and of nature's God entitle them." Reread their prophecy. . . . If that's Red, then the writers of the Declaration of Independence were very Red. They told Americans not to stand injustice after "patient sufferance."

Ibid.

8 We specialize in the wholly impossible.
Motto, National Training School for
Girls, Washington, D.C. (c.1909),
Black Women in White America,
Gerda Lerner, ed.   *1972p*

511. Coco Chanel
(1883–1971)

1 There goes a woman who knows all the things that can be taught and none of the things that cannot be taught.
Quoted in *Coco Chanel, Her Life, Her
Secrets* by Marcel Haedrich   *1971*

2 Youth is something very new: twenty years ago no one mentioned it.

Ibid.

3 A fashion for the young? That is a pleonasm: there is no fashion for the old.

Ibid.

4 Great loves too must be endured.

Ibid.

5 You see, that's what fame is: solitude.

Ibid.

6 My friends, there are no friends.

Ibid.

7 Since everything is in our heads, we had better not lose them.

Ibid.

8 Legend is the consecration of fame.

Ibid.

9 I am no longer what I was. I will remain what I have become.

Ibid.

10 Silence is the cruelty of the provincial.

Ibid.

11 "Where should one use perfume?" a young woman
asked. "Wherever one wants to be kissed," I said.

Ibid.

12 Love? For whom? An old man? How horrible. A
young man? How shameful.

Ibid.

13 Elegance does not consist in putting on a new dress.

Ibid.

14 I am doing an optimistic collection because things are
going badly.

Ibid.

15 Fashion is architecture: it is a matter of proportions.

Ibid.

16 Nothing is ugly as long as it is alive.

Ibid.

17 In order to be irreplaceable one must always be different.   Ibid.

512. Imogen Cunningham
(1883–1976)

1 People who are living aren't famous—they're just infamous.

Quoted in Never Give Up,
a Film by Ann Hershey   1975

2 One thing about being born without beauty—you don't
look for it.   Ibid.

513. Elsa Maxwell
(1883–1963)

1 Fade little searchlight, fade forever.
Please go without a fuss,
For you don't interfere
With the Zeppelins, dear,
But you do interfere with us.

"Shine Little Searchlight"   1912

2 I married the world—the world is my husband. That is why I'm so young. No sex. Sex is the most tiring thing in the world.

"I Married the World," *This Fabulous Century: 1930–1940*   1940

3 First I want a woman guest to be beautiful. Second, I want her to be beautifully dressed. Third, I demand animation and vivacity. Fourth, not too many brains. Brains are always awkward at a gay and festive party.

Interview, *New York Mirror*   1938

4 Most rich people are the poorest people I know.

R.S.V.P., Ch. 1   1954

5 Giving parties is a trivial avocation, but it pays the dues for my union card in humanity.

Ibid., Ch. 16

6 Intolerance of mediocrity has been the main prop of my independence. . . .

Ibid.

7 Yet "old friends" always seemed a contradiction to me. Age cannot wither nor custom stale the infinite variety of friends who, as long as you know them, remain as vibrant and stimulating as the day you first met them.

Ibid.

8 I have lived by my wits all my life and I thank the Lord they are still in one, whole piece. I don't need glasses, Benzedrine or a psychiatrist.

Ibid.

9 Anatomize the character of a successful hostess and the knife will lay bare the fact that she owes her position to one of three things: either she is liked, or she is feared, or she is important.

How to Do It, Ch. 3   1957

514. Frances Newman
(1883?–1928)

1 . . . she did not understand how her father could have reached such age and such eminence without learning that all mothers are as infallible as any pope and more righteous than any saint.

The Hard-Boiled Virgin   1926

2 Katherine Faraday's mother had heard in her cradle that a nation which could prefer a Lincoln to a Breckenridge was unlikely to return to the conviction that elegance is the greatest of human virtues, and she had even heard delicate suggestions that a god who could look down unmoved on the triumph of a Grant over a Lee could hardly expect to be acquitted of increasingly Democratic sympathies.

Ibid.

3 For the first time, she realised that conversation might have been entirely satisfactory if women had been allowed to admit they understood the limited number of subjects men were interested in, and she was so excited by her idea that she almost committed the social crime of allowing a conversation to pause.

Ibid.

4 And while she wondered at all the things civilization can teach a woman to endure, she was able to take Mrs. Abbott's departing hand, and to watch Mrs. Abbott walk out of a door into the temporary silence civilization would require of her until she found another acquaintance on whom her conversation could pour as if she were emerging from a year and a day of solitary confinement.

Dead Lovers Are Faithful Lovers   1928

5 But she was disturbed when her mind astonished something which she did not think was her mind, and which she called herself.

Ibid.

515. Mabel Louise Robinson
(1883?–1962)

1   "Can't you have sense?"
Thankful, [the girl] hurried him on. "Not if I can have anything else."

Bright Island, Pt. I   1937

2 We have thought that because children are young they are silly. We have forgotten the blind stirrings, the reaching outward of our own youth.

"Writing for the Younger Generation,"
The Writer's Book, Helen Hull, ed.   1950

459

3 What if the truth does make them sad, what if it haunts them? Better be saddened than dead.

Ibid.

4 If this generation, like those before it, repeats the blunders of the past, we might possibly be to some degree at fault.

Ibid.

5 From the dog's point of view his master is an elongated and abnormally cunning dog.

Quoted in *The New York Times*
Magazine   *May 14, 1967p*

516. Margaret Sanger
(1883–1966)

1 Women of the working class, especially wage workers, should not have more than two children at most. The average working man can support no more and the average working woman can take care of no more in decent fashion.

Family Limitations   *1917*

2 A mutual and satisfied sexual act is of great benefit to the average woman, the magnetism of it is health giving. When it is not desired on the part of the woman and she has no response, *it should not take place*. This is an act of prostitution and is degrading to the woman's finer sensibility, all the marriage certificates on earth to the contrary notwithstanding.

Ibid.

3 The problem of birth control has arisen directly from the effort of the feminine spirit to free itself from bondage.

Women and the New Race   *1920*

4 A free race cannot be born of slave mothers.

Ibid.

5 Women are too much inclined to follow in the footsteps of men, to try to think as men think, to try to solve the general problems of life as men solve them. . . . The woman is not needed to do man's work. She is not needed to think man's thoughts. . . . Her mission is not to enhance the masculine spirit, but to express the

feminine; hers is not to preserve a man-made world, but to create a human world by the infusion of the feminine element into all of its activities.

Ibid.

6 Woman must not accept; she must challenge. She must not be awed by that which has been built up around her; she must reverence that woman in her which struggles for expression.

Ibid.

7 She goes through the vale of death alone, each time a babe is born.

Ibid.

8 Diplomats make it their business to conceal the facts. . . .

Ibid.

9 Behind all war has been the pressure of population . . . let countries become overpopulated and war is inevitable. It follows as daylight follows the sunrise. . . .

Ibid.

10 . . . behind all the slogans and shibboleths coined out of the ideals of the peoples for the uses of imperialism, women must and will see the iron hand of that same imperialism, condemning women to breed and men to die for the will of the rulers.

Ibid.

11 Upon women the burden and the horrors of war are heaviest. . . . When she sees what lies behind the glory and the horror, the boasting and the burden, and gets the vision, the human perspective, she will end war. She will kill war by the simple process of starving it to death. For she will refuse longer to produce the human food upon which the monster feeds.

Ibid.

12 When we voice, then, the necessity of setting the feminine spirit utterly and absolutely free, thought turns naturally not to rights of the woman, nor indeed of the mother, but to the rights of the child—of all children in the world.

Ibid.

13 When motherhood becomes the fruit of a deep yearning, not the result of ignorance or accident, its children will become the foundation of a new race.

Ibid.

461

14 Like begets like. We gather perfect fruit from perfect trees. . . . Abused soil brings forth stunted growths.

Ibid.

15 Custom controls the sexual impulse as it controls no other.

Interview, *American Mercury* 1924

16 The menace of another pregnancy hung like a sword over the head of every poor woman. . . .

"Awakening and Revolt,"
My Fight for Birth Control 1931

17 "Yes, yes—I know, Doctor," said the patient with trembling voice, "but," and she hesitated as if it took all of her courage to say it, "*what* can I do to prevent getting that way again?"

"Oh ho!" laughed the doctor good naturedly. "You want your cake while you eat it too, do you? Well, it can't be done. . . . I'll tell you the only sure thing to do. Tell Jake to sleep on the roof!"

Ibid.

18 I seemed chained hand and foot, and longed for an earthquake or a volcano to shake the world out of its lethargy into facing these monstrous atrocities.

Ibid.

19 Awaken the womanhood of America to free the motherhood of the world!

Ibid.

20 . . . there was not a darkened tenement, hovel, or flat but was brightened by the knowledge that motherhood could be voluntary; that children need not be born into the world unless they are wanted and have a place provided for them.

Ibid., "A Public Nuisance"

21 . . . we were dispossessed by the law as a "public nuisance." In Holland the clinics were called "public utilities."

Ibid.

22 . . . I wondered, and asked myself *what* had gone out of the race. Something had gone from them which silenced them, made them impotent to defend their rights.

Ibid.

23 I was resolved to seek out the root of the evil, to do something to change the destiny of mothers whose miseries were as vast as the sky.

An Autobiography   1938

517. Florida Scott-Maxwell
(1883–   )

1 Age puzzles me. I thought it was a quite time. My seventies were interesting and fairly serene, but my eighties are passionate. I grow more intense as I age.

The Measure of My Days   1972

2 No matter how old a mother is she watches her middle-aged children for signs of improvement.

Ibid.

3 If a grandmother wants to put her foot down, the only safe place to do it these days is in a note book.

Ibid.

4 Age is a desert of time—hours, days, weeks, years perhaps—with little to do. So one has ample time to face everything one has had, been, done; gather them all in: the things that came from outside, and those from inside. We have time at last to make them truly ours.

Ibid.

5 You need only claim the events of your life to make yourself yours.

Ibid.

6 Is there any stab as deep as wondering where and how much you failed those you loved?

Ibid.

7 I wonder why love is so often equated with joy when it is everything else as well. Devastation, balm, obsession, granting and receiving excessive value, and losing it again. It is recognition, often of what you are not but might be. It sears and it heals. It is beyond pity and above law. It can seem like truth.

Ibid.

8 I have made others suffer, and if there are more lives to be lived, I believe I ought to do penance for the suffering I have caused. I should experience what I have

made others experience. It belongs to me, and I should
learn it.   Ibid.

9 Is life a pregnancy? That would make death a birth.
                                                             Ibid.

10 Order, cleanliness, seemliness make a structure that is
half support, half ritual, and—if it does not create it—
maintains decency.   Ibid.

518. Marguerite Wilkinson
(1883–1928)

* * *

1 God bless pawnbrokers!
They are quiet men.   "Pawnbrokers"

2 My father got me strong and straight and slim
    And I give thanks to him.
My mother bore me glad and sound and sweet,
    I kiss her feet!   "The End"

519. Laura Benét
(1884–   )

* * *

1 Lost in the spiral of his conscience, he
Detachedly takes rest.   "The Snail"

2 No voice awoke. Dwelling sedate, apart
Only the thrush, the thrush that never spoke,
Sang from her bursting heart.   "The Thrush"

520. Helene Deutsch
(1884–   )

1 They have an extraordinary need of support when engaged in any *activity directed outward*, but are absolutely independent in such feeling and thinking as related to their inner life, that is to say, in their *activity
directed inward*. Their capacity for identification is not
an expression of inner poverty but of inner wealth.
    The Psychology of Women, Vol. I   1944–1945

2 All observations point to the fact that the intellectual woman is masculinized; in her, warm, intuitive knowledge has yielded to cold unproductive thinking.

Ibid.

3 After all, the ultimate goal of all research is not objectivity, but truth.

Ibid.

4 It is interesting to note that in every phase of life feminine masochism finds some form of expression.

Ibid., Ch. 1

5 The very fact that the youthful soul feels insecure strengthens its active aspiration to master its insecurity.

Ibid., Ch. 2

6 . . . adolescence is the period of the decisive last battle fought before maturity. The ego must achieve independence, the old emotional ties must be cast off, and new ones created.

Ibid.

7 It is no exaggeration to say that among all living creatures, only man, because of his prehensile appendages, is capable of rape in the full meaning of this term—that is, sexual possession of the female against her will.

Ibid., Ch. 6

8 The vagina—a completely passive, receptive organ—awaits an active agent to become a functioning excitable organ.

Ibid.

9 The embattled gates to equal rights indeed opened up for modern women, but I sometimes think to myself: "That is not what I meant by freedom—it is only 'social progress.'"

Confrontations with Myself, Ch. 1   1973

10 She [Rosa Luxemburg] was too great to be considered "only a woman," even by her enemies.

Ibid., Ch. 7

11 Psychoanalysis was my last and most deeply experienced revolution; and Freud, who was rightly considered a conservative on social and political issues, became for me the greatest revolutionary of the century.

Ibid., Ch. 10

521. Caroline Giltinan
(1884–   )

* * *

1 Betrayer of the Master,
  He sways against the sky,
  A black and broken body,
  Iscariot—or I?

"Identity"

2 Let me keep my eyes on yours;
  I dare not look away
  Fearing again to see your feet
  Cloven and of clay.

"Disillusioned"

522. Texas Guinan
(1884–1933)

1 Fifty million Frenchmen can be wrong.

Quoted in the
New York World-Telegram
March 21, 1931

* * *

2 I've been married once on the level, and twice in
  America.

Nightclub Act

3 Success has killed more men than bullets.

Ibid.

523. Rose Henniker Heaton
(1884–?)

* * *

1 She left no little things behind
  Excepting loving thoughts and kind.

"The Perfect Guest"

524. Fanny Heaslip Lea
(1884–1955)

* * *

1 It's odd to think we might have been
  Sun, moon and stars unto each other—
  Only, I turned down one little street
  As you went up another.

"Fate," St. 5

525. Alice Roosevelt Longworth
(1884–   )

1 He [Coolidge] looks as if he had been weaned on a
  pickle.

Crowded Hours   1934

2 Were it not for Czolgosz [the assassin of President
  McKinley], we'd all be back in our brownstone-front
  houses. That's where we'd be. And I would have married for money and been divorced for good cause.

Quoted by Jean Vanden Heuvel in the
Saturday Evening Post
December 4, 1965

3 I have a simple philosophy. Fill what's empty. Empty
  what's full. And scratch where it itches.

Quoted in *The Best* by Peter Russell
and Leonard Ross   1974

526. Adela Pankhurst
(1884?–?)

1 We have no religious doctrine to preach, only a morality that is big enough to include all religions and that
  should give offence to none.

Quoted in *The Fighting Pankhursts*
by David Mitchell   1967

2 We do not want strong leaders in Parliament, but servants who will carry out the dictates of the industrial
  bodies.

Ibid., Article in *The Socialist*

3 Profits and prostitution—upon these empires are built
and kingdoms stand. . . .

Ibid., "Communism and Social
Purity," *Dreadnought*, London
(February, 1921)

4 Their [politicians'] most outstanding characteristic, I
should say, would be their inability to manage anything
properly. What industry have they ever promoted but
the gambling industry? What have they ever produced
but strife and deficits? What resolve have they shown
but a determination to grab for themselves, their
friends and supporters whatever is available to grab?

Ibid., Speech (c.1929)

5 Capital and labour in alliance will require neither government control nor political interference, and the vast
network of government which is impoverishing us to-
day will become useless and will shrivel up and die
away.

Ibid.

527. Ruth Mason Rice
(1884–1927)

1 An oval, placid woman who assuaged men's lives;
Her comely hands wrought forth a century
Of oval, placid women who engaged, as wives,
In broideries and tea.

"Queen Victoria," *Afterward*   1927

2 But now—a loaf's an easy thing;
Made quickly by a blind machine;
And still—I find me hungering
For fare—unseen.

Ibid., "Daily Bread"

3 Your people build—to gain the firmaments;
They dig—to reach the sunken heart of hell;
They question every answer Life presents;
For they are sons of Lucifer—who fell.
Where are you going, multitude of feet?

Ibid., "New York"

528. Eleanor Roosevelt
(1884–1962)

1 No one can make you feel inferior without your consent.

This Is My Story   1937

2 A democratic form of government, a democratic way of life, presupposes free public education over a long period; it presupposes also an education for personal responsibility that too often is neglected.

"Let Us Have Faith in Democracy,"
Land Policy Review, Department of
Agriculture   *January, 1942*

3 I think if the people of this country can be reached with the truth, their judgment will be in favor of the many, as against the privileged few.

Quoted in the *Ladies' Home Journal*
May, 1942

4 Perhaps in His wisdom the Almighty is trying to show us that a leader may chart the way, may point out the road to lasting peace, but that many leaders and many peoples must do the building.

"My Day" Newspaper Column   *April 16, 1945*

5 Perhaps nature is our best assurance of immortality.

Ibid.   *April 24, 1945*

6 We must be willing to learn the lesson that cooperation may imply compromise, but if it brings a world advance it is a gain for each individual nation.

Ibid.   *January 21, 1946*

7 I am sorry that Governments in all parts of the world have not seen fit to send more women as delegates, alternates or advisors to the Assembly [U.N.]. I think it is in these positions that the women of every nation should work to see that equality exists.

Ibid.   *January 28, 1946*

8 None of us has lived up to the teachings of Christ.

Ibid.   *February 14, 1946*

9 It is not fair to ask of others what you are not willing to do yourself.   Ibid.   *June 15, 1946*

10 If I do not run for office, I am not beholden to my Party. What I give, I give freely and I am too old to want to be curtailed in any way in the expression of my own thinking.

"Why I Do Not Choose to Run,"
Look   *July 9, 1946*

11 . . . a trait no other nation seems to possess in quite the same degree that we do—namely, a feeling of almost childish injury and resentment unless the world as a whole recognizes how innocent we are of anything but the most generous and harmless intentions.

"My Day" Newspaper Column   *November 11, 1946*

12 It is very difficult to have a free, fair and honest press anywhere in the world. In the first place, as a rule, papers are largely supported by advertising, and that immediately gives the advertisers a certain hold over the medium which they use.

If You Ask Me   *1946*

13 It is not that you set the individual apart from society but that you recognize in any society that the individual must have rights that are guarded.

Quoted in *The New York Times*
February 4, 1947

14 I used to tell my husband that, if he could make *me* understand something, it would be clear to all the other people in the country.

"My Day" Newspaper Column   *February 12, 1947*

15 The economy of Communism is an economy which grows in an atmosphere of misery and want.

Ibid.   *March 15, 1947*

16 Franklin had a good way of simplifying things. He made people feel that he had a real understanding of things and they felt they had about the same understanding.

Interview in *PM*   *April 6, 1947*

17 . . . I deplore . . . the attitude of self-righteous governments. . . . Our own Government's position has never gone beyond pious hopes and unctuous words.

"My Day" Newspaper Column   *April 26, 1947*

18 Justice cannot be for one side alone, but must be for both. . . .

Ibid.   *October 15, 1947*

19 . . . certain rights can never be granted to the government, but must be kept in the hands of the people.

Quoted in *The New York Times*   *May 3, 1948*

20 A society in which everyone works is not necessarily a free society and may indeed be a slave society; on the other hand, a society in which there is widespread economic insecurity can turn freedom into a barren and vapid right for millions of people.

Speech, "The Struggle
for Human Rights," Paris
September 27, 1948

21 We must preserve our right to think and differ. . . . The day I'm afraid to sit down with people I do not know because five years from now someone will say five of those people were Communists and therefore you are a Communist—that will be a bad day.

Speech, Americans for Democratic
Action   *April 2, 1950*

22 My own feeling is that the Near East, India and many of the Asiatic people have a profound distrust of white people. This is understandable since the white people they have known intimately in the past have been the colonial nations and in the case of the United States, our businessmen. . . .

Report to President Truman   *1950*

23 For it isn't enough to talk about peace. One must believe in it. And it isn't enough to believe in it. One must work at it.

Broadcast, Voice of America
November 11, 1951

24 I believe that it is a great mistake not to stand up for people, even when you differ with them, if you feel that they are trying to do things that will help our country.

Quoted in *The Nation*   *June 7, 1952*

25 There is a small articulate minority in this country which advocates changing our national symbol which is the eagle to that of the ostrich and withdrawing from the United Nations.

Speech, Democratic National Convention
July 23, 1952

26 Too often the great decisions are originated and given form in bodies made up wholly of men, or so com-

471

pletely dominated by them that whatever of special value women have to offer is shunted aside without expression.

Speech, United Nations   *December, 1952*

27 Go down and answer up if you can. . . . It's not easy.
Quoted in the *New York Post*
May 13, 1953

28 You have to accept whatever comes and the only important thing is that you meet it with courage and with the best that you have to give.

Essay in *This I Believe,*
Edward P. Morgan, ed.   *1953*

29 Life has got to be lived—that's all there is to it. At 70, I would say the advantage is that you take life more calmly. You know that "this, too, shall pass!"
Quoted in *The New York Times*   *October 8, 1954*

30 As for accomplishments, I just did what I had to do as things came along.

Ibid.

31 I would like . . . to see us take hold of ourselves, look at ourselves and cease being afraid.

Ibid.   *October 12, 1954*

32 A mature person is one who does not think only in absolutes, who is able to be objective even when deeply stirred emotionally, who has learned that there is both good and bad in all people and in all things, and who walks humbly and deals charitably with the circumstances of life, knowing that in this world no one is all-knowing and therefore all of us need both love and charity.

It Seems to Me   *1954*

33 The only hope for a really free press is for the public to recognize that the press *should* not express the point of view of the owners and the writers but be factual; whereas the editorials *must* express the opinions of owners and writers.

Ibid.

34 Our party may be the oldest democratic party, but our party must live as a young party, and it must have a young leadership.

Speech, Democratic National
Convention   *August 13, 1956*

35 Could we have the vision of doing away in this great country with poverty? . . . what can make us not only the nation that has some of the richest people in the world, but the nation where there are no people that have to live at a substandard level. That would be one of the very best arguments against Communism that we could possibly have.

Ibid.

36 I have always felt that anyone who wanted an election so much that they would use those* methods did not have the character that I really admired in public life.
"Meet the Press," NBC-TV   *September 16, 1956*

37 . . . you always admire what you really don't understand.

Ibid.

38 I have a great objection to seeing anyone, particularly anyone whom I care about, lose his self-control.
"My Day" Newspaper Column   *February 3, 1958*

39 When the Tammany Hall boss bossed the convention it meant the defeat of the democratic process.
Quoted in the *New York Post*   *November 5, 1958*

40 Where, after all, do universal human rights begin? In small places, close to home—so close and so small that they cannot be seen on any maps of the world. Yet they *are* the world of the individual persons; the neighborhood he lives in; the school or college he attends; the factory, farm or office where he works. Such are the places where every man, woman and child seeks equal justice, equal opportunity, equal dignity without discrimination. Unless these rights have meaning there, they have little meaning anywhere. Without concerned citizen action to uphold them close to home, we shall look in vain for progress in the larger world.
Speech, "The Great Question,"
United Nations   *1958*

41 You can't move so fast that you try to change the mores faster than people can accept it. That doesn't mean you do nothing, but it means that you do the things that need to be done according to priority.
On My Own   *1958*

* Referring to Richard Nixon's smear campaign against Helen Gahagan Douglas.

473

42 We cannot exist as a little island of well-being in a world where two-thirds of the people go to bed hungry every night. I want unity but above everything else, I want a party that will fight for the things that we know to be right at home and abroad.

Speech, Democratic Fund-Raising
Dinner   December 8, 1959

43 We have to face the fact that either all of us are going to die together or we are going to learn to live together and if we are to live together we have to talk.

Quoted by A. David Gurewitsch in
The New York Times   October 15, 1960

44 Everybody wants something.

Interview with Maureen Corr   1960

45 You gain strength, courage, and confidence by every experience in which you really stop to look fear in the face.

"You Learn by Living"   1960

46 You must do the thing you think you cannot do.

Ibid.

47 . . . I could not, at any age, be content to take my place in a corner by the fireside and simply look on. Life was meant to be lived. Curiosity must be kept alive. The fatal thing is the rejection. One must never, for whatever reason, turn his back on life.

Quoted by Emma Bugbee in the
New York Herald Tribune
October 11, 1961

48 Both the President and his wife can never give way to apprehension even though they are probably more aware than most citizens of the dangers which may surround us. If the country is to be confident, they must be confident.

"My Day" Newspaper Column   May 29, 1962

49 You get well but is it really worth it?

Ibid.   August 14, 1962

50 They [Israelis] are still dreamers, but they make their dreams come true. . . .

Quoted by Ruth G. Michaels in
Hadassah   December, 1962

51 This I know. This I believe with all my heart. If we want a free and peaceful world, if we want to make the deserts bloom and man grow to greater dignity as a human being—*we can do it!*
Tomorrow Is Now   1963

52 . . . when you know to laugh and when to look upon things as too absurd to take seriously, the other person is ashamed to carry through even if he was serious about it.
Letter to Harry S. Truman
(May 14, 1945), Quóted in
Eleanor: The Years Alone
by Joseph P. Lash   *1972p*

53 So—against odds, the women inch forward, but I'm rather old to be carrying on this fight!
Ibid., Letter to Joesph P. Lash (February 13, 1946)

54 Not all Jewish people want a nation and a national home. . . .
Ibid., Letter to Miss Siegel (September 5, 1946)

55 . . . we do not always like what is good for us in this world.
Ibid., Letter to Miss Binn (October 24, 1947)

56 . . . perhaps man's spirit, his striving, is indestructible. It is set back but it does not die and so there is a reason why each one of us should do our best in our own small corner. Do you think I'm too optimistic?
Ibid., Letter to A. David Gurewitsch
(December 18, 1947)

57 I cannot believe that war is the best solution. No one won the last war, and no one will win the next war.
Ibid., Letter to Harry S. Truman
(March 22, 1948)

58 The President [Harry S. Truman] is so easily fooled in spite of his good intentions.
Ibid., Letter to Joseph P. Lash
(November 5, 1948)

59 Our real battlefield today is Asia and our real battle is the one between democracy and communism. . . . We have to prove to the world and particularly to downtrodden areas of the world which are the natural prey

to the principles of communist economics that democracy really brings about happier and better conditions for the people as a whole.

Ibid., Memo to Harry S. Truman
(December 28, 1948)

60 Spiritual leadership should remain spiritual leadership and the temporal power should not become too important in any Church.

Ibid., Letter to Cardinal Francis
Spellman (July 23, 1949)

61 . . . there is no complete unanimity here on what course should be followed any more than at home but fear is unanimous!

Ibid., Letter to Trude Lash (June 18, 1950)

62 We need our heroes*. . . .

Ibid., Letter to Joseph Lash (January 21, 1952)

63 The Jews in their own country are doing marvels and should, once the refugee problem is settled, help all the Arab countries.

Ibid., Letter to Maude Gray (March 5, 1952)

64 Television has completely revolutionized what should go on at a convention.

Ibid., Letter to Frank E. McKinney
(July 13, 1952)

65 It isn't within my hands to resign or not to resign. Each of us does that automatically. . . .

Ibid., Letter to Bernard Baruch (November 18, 1952)

66 . . . I have spent many years of my life in opposition and I rather like the role.

Ibid.

67 It is always hard to tell people that it is the causes of war which bring about such things as Hiroshima, and that we must try to eliminate these causes because if there is another Pearl Harbor there will be undoubtedly another Hiroshima.

Ibid., Letter to John Golden (June 12, 1953)

68 I believe that it is essential to our leadership in the world and to the development of true democracy in our country to have no discrimination in our country what-

* Referring to General Dwight D. Eisenhower.

soever. This is most important in the schools of our country.

Ibid., Letter to Richard Bolling (January 20, 1956)

69 I doubt if Eisenhower can stand a second term and I doubt if the country can stand Nixon as President.

Ibid., Letter to Lord Elibank (January 20, 1956)

70 Mr. Dulles has just frightened most of our allies to death with a statement that there is an art in actually threatening war and coming to the brink but retreating from the brink.

Ibid., Letter to Gus Ranis (January 23, 1956)

71 They [Russians] love to keep you waiting . . . but they hate you to deviate from a plan you once make!

Ibid., Letter to Joseph and Trude Lash (September 20, 1957)

72 It seems to me . . . we have reached a place where it is not a question of "can we live in the same world and cooperate" but "we must live in the same world and learn to cooperate."

Ibid., Letter to Queen Juliana of the Netherlands (February 14, 1958)

73 When you cease to make a contribution you begin to die.

Ibid., Letter to Mr. Horne (February 19, 1960)

74 I cannot, of course, ever feel safe . . . because with Mr. Nixon I always have the feeling that he will pull some trick at the last minute.

Ibid., Letter to John F. Kennedy (August 27, 1960)

75 To say he [John F. Kennedy] would not make mistakes would be silly. Anyone would make mistakes with the problems that lie ahead of us.

Ibid., Letter to Peter Kamitchis (October 21, 1960)

76 . . . on the whole, life is rather difficult for both the children and their parents in the "fish bowl" that lies before you.

Ibid., Letter to Jacqueline Kennedy (December 1, 1960)

77 You seem to think that everyone can save money if they have the character to do it. As a matter of fact, there are innumerable people who have a wide choice between saving and giving their children the best possi-

ble opportunities. The decision is usually in favor of the children.

> Ibid., Letter to Franklin Roosevelt III
> (January 15, 1962)

78 . . . I must reluctantly admit that I am not quite as I was. . . .

> Ibid., Letter to Tom Stix (May 10, 1962)

79 I'm so glad I never *feel* important, it does complicate life.

> Ibid., Ch. 2

529. Sara Teasdale
(1884–1933)

1 Let it be forgotten for ever and ever,
Time is a kind friend, he will make us old.
> "Let It Be Forgotten," St. 1   *1921*

* * *

2 I shall not let a sorrow die
    Until I find the heart of it,
Nor let a wordless joy go by
    Until it talks to me a bit.

> "Servitors"

3 Joy was a flame in me
    Too steady to destroy.

> "The Answer"

4 I found more joy in sorrow
Than you could find in joy.
> Ibid.

5 My soul is a broken field
    Ploughed by pain.

> "The Broken Field"

6 No one worth possessing
Can be quite possessed.

> "Advice to a Girl"

7 O beauty, are you not enough?
Why am I crying after love?

> "Spring Night"

8 Of my own spirit let me be
In sole though feeble mastery.   "Mastery"

9 One by one, like leaves from a tree,
All my faiths have forsaken me.

"Leaves"

10 Spend all you have for loveliness.

"Barter"

11 Strephon's kiss was lost in jest,
    Robin's lost in play,
But the kiss in Colin's eyes
    Haunts me night and day.

"The Look," St. 2

12 Then, like an old-time orator
    Impressively he rose;
"I make the most of all that comes
    And the least of all that goes."

"The Philosopher," St. 4

13 When I am dead and over me bright April
Shakes out her rain-drenched hair,
Though you should lean above me broken-hearted,
I shall not care.

"I Shall Not Care," St. 1

14 When I can look Life in the eyes,
Grown calm and very coldly wise,
Life will have given me the Truth,
And taken in exchange—my youth.

"Wisdom"

530. Sophie Tucker
(1884–1966)

1 Success in show business depends on your ability to
make and keep friends.

Some of These Days, with
Dorothy Giles, Ch. 4   *1945*

2 From birth to age eighteen, a girl needs good parents.
From eighteen to thirty-five, she needs good looks.
From thirty-five to fifty-five, she needs a good person-
ality. From fifty-five on, she needs good cash.

Attributed   *1953*

3 Keep breathing.

Anniversary Speech   *January 13, 1964*

531. Sophie Tunnell
(1884–?)

* * *

1 Fear is a slinking cat I find
  Beneath the lilacs of my mind.

"Fear"

532. Anna Wickham
(1884–1947)

1 I desire Virtue, though I love her not—
  I have no faith in her when she is got:
  I fear that she will bind and make me slave
  And send me songless to the sullen grave.

"Self-Analysis," St. 3,
The Contemplative Quarry   1915

2 When I am sick, then I believe in law.   Ibid., St. 4

3 'Tis folly to my dawning, thrifty thought
  That I must run, who in the end am caught.

Ibid., "The Contemplative Quarry"

4 I smother in the house in the valley below,
  Let me out to the night, let me go, let me go!

"Divorce," The World Split Open,
Louise Bernikow, ed.   1974p

* * *

5 Alas! For all the pretty women who marry dull men,
  Go into the suburbs and never come out again.

"Meditation at Kew"

6 Because of the body's hunger we are born,
  And by contriving hunger are we fed;
  Because of hunger is our work well done,
  And so our songs well sung, and things well said.

"Sehnsucht"

7 Desire and longing are the whips of God.   Ibid.

8 But the true male never yet walked
  Who liked to listen when his mate talked.

"The Affinity"

9 I have to thank God I'm a woman,
   For in these ordered days a woman only
   Is free to be very hungry, very lonely.

                                        Ibid.

10 If I had peace to sit and sing,
   Then I could make a lovely thing. . . .

                                   "The Singer"

11 I have been so misued by chaste men with one wife
   That I would live with satyrs all my life.
                                "Ship Near Shoals"

12 Oh, give me a woman of my race
   As well controlled as I,
   And let us sit by the fire,
   Patient till we die!

                                 "The Tired Man"

13 Think how poor Mother Eve was brought
   To being as God's afterthought.

                                     "To Men"

533. Helen M. Cam
(1885–1968)

1 We must not read either law or history backwards.
                    Introduction to *Selected Essays of
                    F. W. Maitland*, H. D. Hazeltine,
         G. Gapsley, P. H. Winfield, eds.   *1936*

2 The authority of a statute made in Parliament is universally recognized as superior to that of any other leg-
   islative act.
          England Before Elizabeth, Ch. 12   *1950*

3 Feudalism, for all its insistence on priority and place,
   had proved inadequate for the needs of government,
   however much its traditions of deference and responsibility might linger in the English social system.

                                        Ibid.

4 If civilisation is the art of living together with people
   not entirely like oneself, the first step in civilisation is
   not so much the invention of material tools as the regu-
   larisation of social habits. As soon as you begin to say
   "We always do things this way" the foundations are
   laid. "Custom is before all law." As soon as you begin

                        481

to say "We have always done things this way—perhaps *that* might be a better way," conscious law-making is beginning. As soon as you begin to say "*We* do things this way—*they* do things that way—what is to be done about it?" men are beginning to feel towards justice, that resides between the endless jar of right and wrong.

Lecture, "Law as It Looks to a
Historian," Girton College
February 18, 1956

5 Law offers a guiding thread to us . . . one of purpose—and a purpose infinitely worthwhile, for in the long view it is more important that human beings should learn to get on with each other than that they should be more comfortable materially and safer physically.

Ibid.

6 Historical fiction is not only a respectable literary form: it is a standing reminder of the fact that history is about human beings.

Historical Novel   1961

7 What the rule of law means for Englishmen, what due process of law means to Americans, is inseparably bound up with our traditional notions of Magna Carta. Whether all that has been read into the document is historically or legally sound, is not of the first importance; every historian knows that belief itself is a historical fact, and that legend and myth cannot be left out of account in tracing the sequence of cause and effect.

Lecture, "Magna Carta—Event
or Document?," Old Hall of
Lincoln's Inn   *July 7, 1967*

534. Gladys Cromwell
(1885–1919)

* * *

1 Sorrow can wait,
  For there is magic in the calm estate
  Of grief; low, where the dust complies
  Wisdom lies.

"Folded Power"

535. Isak Dinesen
(1885–1962)

1 "What is man, when you come to think upon him, but a minutely set, ingenious machine for turning, with infinite artfulness, the red wine of Shiraz into urine?"
Seven Gothic Tales   1934

2 Woman. I understand the word itself, in that sense, has gone out of the language. Where we talk of woman . . . you talk of women, and all the difference lies therein. . . .
Ibid., "The Old Chevalier"

3 I do not know if you remember the tale of the girl who saves the ship under mutiny by sitting on the powder barrel with her lighted torch . . . and all the time knowing that it is empty? This has seemed to me a charming image of the women of my time. There they were, keeping the world in order . . . by sitting on the mystery of life, and knowing themselves that there was no mystery.
Ibid.

4 "If only I could so live and so serve the world that after me there should never again be birds in cages. . . ."
Ibid., "The Deluge at Norderney"

5 I have seen a herd of elephants traveling through dense native forest . . . pacing along as if they had an appointment at the end of the world.
Out of Africa, Pt. I, Ch. 1   1938

6 The giraffe, in their queer, inimitable, vegetating gracefulness, as if it were not a herd of animals but a family of rare, long-stemmed, speckled gigantic flowers slowly advancing.
Ibid.

7 If I knew a song of Africa—I thought of the giraffe, and the African new moon lying on her back, of the plows in the fields, and the sweaty faces of the coffee-pickers—does Africa know a song for me?
Ibid., Ch. 4

8 I have before seen other countries, in the same manner, give themselves to you when you are about to leave them.

Ibid., Pt. V, Ch. 1

9 "But the trouble is not as you think now, that we have put up obstacles too high for you to jump, and how could we possibly do that, you great leaper? It is that we have put up no obstacles at all. The great strength is in you, Lulu, and the obstacles are within you as well, and the thing is, that the fullness of time has not yet come."

Ibid.

10 The true aristocracy and the true proletariat of the world are both in understanding with tragedy. To them it is the fundamental principle of God, and the key, the minor key, to existence. They differ in this way from the bourgeoisie of all classes, who deny tragedy, who will not tolerate it, and to whom the word tragedy means in itself unpleasantness."

Ibid.

11 "All Natives are masters in the art of the pause, and thereby give perspective to a discussion."

Ibid.

12 When Africans speak of the personality of God, they speak like the Arabian Nights or the last chapters of the Book of Job; it is . . . the infinite power of imagination with which they are impressed.

Ibid.

13 She was like a man who has been given an elephant gun and asked to shoot little birds.

Winter's Tales 1942

14 But she was badly hurt and disappointed because the world was not a much greater place . . . and because nothing more colossal, more like the dramas of the stage, took place in it.

Ibid.

536. Malvina Hoffman
(1885–1966)

1 My true center of work was not commissions. It was an enormous capacity for falling in love with everything around me. . . .

> Quoted in "Malvina Hoffman,"
> *Famous American Women*
> by Hope Stoddard   *1970p*

2 . . . at heart we are really working for the angels. . . . What counts is the lasting integrity of the artist and the enduring quality of his work.

> Ibid.

537. Karen Horney
(1885–1952)

1 Psychoanalysis is the creation of a male genius, and almost all those who have developed his ideas have been men. It is only right and reasonable that they should evolve more easily a masculine psychology and understand more of the development of men than of women.

> "The Flight from Womanhood,"
> *Feminine Psychology*   *1926*

2 Like all sciences and all valuations, the psychology of women has hitherto/ been considered only from the point of view of men.

> Ibid.

3 Is not the tremendous strength in men of the impulse to creative work in every field precisely due to their feeling of playing a relatively small part in the creation of living beings, which constantly impels them to an overcompensation in achievement?

> Ibid.

4 It seems to me impossible to judge to how great a degree the unconscious motives for the flight from womanhood are reinforced by the actual social subordination of women.

> Ibid.

5 . . . it is necessary not to be too easily satisfied with
ready-at-hand explanations for a disturbance.

Self-Analysis   1942

6 . . . concern should drive us into action and not into a
depression.

Ibid.

7 But miracles occur in psychoanalysis as seldom as anywhere else.

Ibid.

8 . . . a person who feels helplessly caught in his neurotic entanglements tends to hope against hope for a
miracle.

Ibid.

9 Fortunately [psycho]analysis is not the only way to resolve inner conflicts. Life itself still remains a very effective therapist.

Our Inner Conflicts   1945

538. Frances Parkinson Keyes
(1885–1970)

1 Women were cats, all of them, unless they were fools,
and there was no way of getting even with them, ever,
except by walking off with the men they wanted. . . .
The Great Tradition, Pt. I, Ch. 3   1939

2 "I can't see that the Nazis are any different from the
Communists, except that they're cleaner and better
looking and better drilled. They're both stirring up
trouble, they're both bent on destruction and despotism, they're both ready to go to any lengths to gain
their ends!"

Ibid., Pt. V, Ch. 15

3 Folks with their wits about them knew that advertise-
ments were just a pack of lies—you had only to look at
the claims of patent medicines!
Blue Camellia, Pt. I, Ch. 3   1957

4 "Well, it's a good thing to trust in Providence. But I
believe the Almighty likes a little cooperation now and
again."

Ibid., Pt. III, Ch. 10

5 ". . . young folks, them, don' never think 'bout nothin'
only spend, spend, spend money, instead of save, save,
save money, like us used to do, us. It's education, or
either it's clothes, or either it's something else, as long
as somebody got to spend, spend, spend. Boys is plenny
bad, I got to admit, yes, but girls is even worser."
Ibid., Pt. V, Ch. 22

539. Marie Laurencin
(1885–1956)

1 Why should I paint dead fish, onions and beer glasses?
Girls are so much prettier.
Quoted in *Time*   *June 18, 1956p*

540. Ettie Lee
(1885–1974)

1 Every child has a right to a good home.
Quoted in the *Los Angeles Times*   *April 27, 1974p*

541. Aline Triplett Michaelis
(1885–?)

* * *

1 Alone, yet never lonely,
  Serene, beyond mischance,
The world was his, his only,
  When Lindbergh flew to France.   "Lindbergh"

542. Constance Rourke
(1885–1941)

1 Ardent and tired and overwrought, in that sensitive
state where the imagination grows fluid, where inner
and outer motives coalesce. . . .
The Trumpets of Jubilee   *1927*

2 An emotional man may possess no humor, but a humorous man usually has deep pockets of emotion,
sometimes tucked away or forgotten.
American Humor, Ch. 1   *1931*

3 Comic resilience swept through them in waves, transcending the past, transcending terror, with a sense of comedy, itself a wild emotion.

Ibid., Ch. 2

4 It is a mistake to look for the social critic—even Manqué—in Mark Twain. In a sense the whole American comic tradition had been that of social criticism: but this had been instinctive and incomplete, and so it proved to be in Mark Twain. . . . He was primarily a *raconteur*. . . . He was never the conscious artist, always the improvisor.

Ibid., Ch. 7

5 In comedy, reconcilement with life comes at the point when to the tragic sense only an inalienable difference or dissension with life appears.

Ibid., Ch. 8

6 Humor has been a fashioning instrument in America, cleaving its way through the national life, holding tenaciously to the spread elements of that life. Its mode has often been swift and coarse and ruthless, beyond art and beyond established civilization. It has engaged in warfare against the established heritage, against the bonds of pioneer existence. Its objective—the unconscious objective of a disunited people—has seemed to be that of creating fresh bonds, a new unity, the semblance of a society and the rounded completion of an American type.

Ibid., Ch. 9

543. Marjorie Allen Seiffert
(1885–1968)

1 For to your heart
Beauty is a burned-out torch,
And Faith, a blind pigeon,
Friendship, a curious Persian myth,
And love, blank emptiness,
Bearing no significance
Nor any reality.

Only Weariness is yours. . . .

"Singalese Love Song, II," Sts. 2–3,
A Woman of Thirty   1919

2 And when I search your soul until
  I see too deeply and divine
  That you can never love me—Still
  I hold you fast for you are mine!

  Ibid., "Possession," St. 3

3 Sorrow stands in a wide place,
  Blind—blind—
  Beauty and joy are petals blown
  Across her granite face,
  They cannot find sight or sentience in stone.

  Yesterday's beauty and joy lie deep
  In sorrow's heart, asleep.   Ibid., "Sorrow"

4 Spring raged outside, but ghostly in my bed
  A dead self lay and knew itself for dead.
              "A Full Storm," *The King with Three
              Faces and Other Poems*   1929

5 "Pay as you enter!" is written on heaven's door.
  The beggar may go in velvet or in tatters,
  Hell's rubbish heap is the unpaid bills he scatters,
  And love is worth what it cost you, nothing more.

  Ibid., "The Horse-Leech's Daughter"

6 We are damned with the knowledge of good and evil:
      they,
  Whose new estate is freedom, suffer worse
  And find life empty, trivial and boring,
  A sort of game that every one must play,
  And no one knows the rules, and no one's scoring,
  And nothing's at stake, for youth has lost its purse.

  Ibid., "Youth Visits Our Inferno"

* * *

7 Lust is the oldest lion of them all.

  "An Italian Chest"

544. Clare Sheridan
(1885–?)

1 At the end of her days, she became superbly squaw-
  like, and would sit impassively for hours, staring into
  the fire, her head shrouded in a shawl. A figure of
  great moral fortitude and self-oblation was gradually
  fading out.   *To the Four Winds*   1955

545. Bess Truman
(1885–   )

1 I deplore any action which denies artistic talent an opportunity to express itself because of prejudice against race origin.

Quoted by Helen Weigel Brown in
Liberty   June 9, 1945

546. Elinor Wylie
(1885–1928)

1 Avoid the reeking herd,
    Shun the polluted flock,
Live like that stoic bird
    The eagle of the rock.

"The Eagle and the Mole," St. 1
(1921), Collected Poems   1932p

2 If you would keep your soul
    From spotted sight and sound,
Live like the velvet mole,
    Go burrow underground.   Ibid., St. 5

3 I was, being human, born alone;
I am, being woman, hard beset;
I live by squeezing from a stone
The little nourishment I get.

In masks outrageous and austere
The years go by in single file;
But none has merited my fear,
And none has quite escaped my smile.

Ibid., "Let No Charitable Hope," Sts. 2–3 (1923)

4   Honeyed words like bees,
Gilded and sticky, with a little sting.

Ibid., "Pretty Words"

5 I love smooth words, like gold-enameled fish
Which circle slowly with a silken swish. . . .   Ibid.

6 If any has a stone to throw
It is not I, ever or now.   Ibid., "The Pebble"

7 I've played the traitor over and over;
I'm a good hater but a bad lover.

Ibid., "Peregrine"

8 The worst and best are both inclined
To snap like vixens at the truth;
But, O, beware the middle mind
That purrs and never shows a tooth!

Ibid., "Nonsense Rhyme," St. 2

547. Zoë Akins
(1886–1958)

1 LADY HELEN. To accuse is so easy that it is infamous to do so where proof is impossible!

Déclassé, Act I   *1919*

2 LADY HELEN. My life is like water that has gone over the dam and turned no mill wheels. Here I am, not happy, but not unhappy, as my days run on to the sea, idly—but not too swiftly—for I love living.

Ibid.

3 LADY HELEN. Englishmen are like that. They love life more and value it less than any other people in the world.

Ibid., Act II

4 SOLOMON. Like a fool I thought I was the arbiter of her destiny; and all the time Fate had happier plans for her.

Ibid., Act III

5 EDITH. . . . there's a great strangeness about love. . . . Yes, I'm very sure that love is the strangest thing in the world—much stranger than death—or—or just life.

Daddy's Gone A-Hunting, Act I   *1921*

6 OSCAR. But you've got a wife. It's all right to tell a wife the brutal truth, but you've got to go sort of easy with your lady-love.

Ibid., Act II

7 MRS. DAHLGREN. Shutting one's eyes is an art, my dear. I suppose there's no use trying to make you see that—but that's the only way one *can* stay married.

Ibid.

8 EDITH. This world is a very unsafe place. It's all shifting sands, Ned. Shifting sands and changing winds.

Ibid., Act III

9 TILLERTON. "To him that hath it shall be given—" She hath . . . that's all. That's greatness.

PRESCOTT. One sort of greatness, maybe.

TILLERTON. Even the great can have only their own sort of greatness.

PRESCOTT. And it's often only that they're great sponges. . . .

TILLERTON. Often, yes, or great roses for whose blooming the trees have been pruned and stripped. But they make the beauty of the world and that's enough.

Greatness, Act I   1922

10 CANAVA. The success-haters. . . . That's what I call them—the people who have never got what they want and turned sour on everybody who has. The world's full of them. . . . As soon as you've made good they begin to watch for you to fail. . . .

Ibid.

11 TILLERTON. And I wonder if peace is enough for any man. . . .

Ibid., Act II

12 RAYMOND. No one can ever help loving anyone.

Ibid., Act III

13 SENTONI. My cousin Cleofante does not believe in inspiration. She shuns the false energy of all stimulants, even those of criticism and sympathy, when she sets herself to a task. What she does, she does alone—unencouraged, unadvised, unmoved. She has a man's broad and vital technique, and a man's ability for thinking straight and far. For years I have watched her work—coldly, intelligently, solely with the power of her brain—achieving effects that are in no way miracles, but are matters of technique and deliberation.

The Portrait of Tiero   1924

14 CLEOFANTE. Work alone qualifies us for life, Sentoni. It is much more exquisite to be blown from the tree as a flower than to be shaken down as a shriveled and bitter fruit.

Ibid.

492

15 And they shall know that in the ordering
  Of every world to come the law shall read
  That he who dares be lawless wears the wing

  Of bird and prophet and his light shall lead
  On through the darkness to eventual light,
  To undiscovered wealth, to newer need. . . .
                    "The Anarchist, III," *The Hills Grow
                        Smaller*, Sts. 15–16   *1937*

16 Mine was a love so exquisite that I
  Rather than watch it wither chose to die:
  So dress my grave, O friend, with no poor flower
  Which in your quiet garden blooms an hour!
                              Ibid., "Epitaph"

17 And have we lost the right
  To look on a blooming bough
  Without remembering how
  Once with high promising
  We were a part of spring—
  We who are now the dead
  Leaves of other years strewn where flowers spread?
                        Ibid., "Jazz Nocturne," St. 3

18 I know not where I go; I scarcely feel
  The menacing fatigue about my feet,
  The skies that scourge, the distances that cheat, the
      constant wounds that neither hurt nor heal.
                          Ibid., "Lethargy," St. 2

19 Indifferent to all the fun of chance
  I watched black spiders of inertia spin
  The far-flung web which I was strangling in.
                          Ibid., "Indifference," St. 1

20 In all my locked-up songs
  No one but you belongs.
                          Ibid., "To H.R.," St. 1

548. Margaret Ayer Barnes
(1886–1967)

1 There they were. Opinions. Jane bumped into them,
  tangible obstacles in her path, things to be recognized,
  and accepted or evaded, as the exigencies of the situation demanded.
                Years of Grace, Pt. I, Ch. 1   *1930*

2 "Curious, isn't it," he went on airily, "that 'talking with the right people' means something so very different from 'talking with the right person'?"

Ibid., Pt. III, Ch. 1

3 Childless women, Olivia reflected, slipped gracefully into middle age. There was no one particular awkward moment when they climbed up on the shelf.

Westward Passage, Ch. 1   *1931*

4 "There's nothing half so real in life as the things you've done," she whispered. "Inexorably, unalterably *done.*"

Ibid., Ch. 4

5 Sentiment, crystallized, grows into sentimentality. It lost all spontaneity, which was the essence of feeling. It was dated—old-fashioned.

"Prelude," *Within This Present*   *1933*

6 "Character comes before scholarship. . . ."

Ibid., Pt. I, Ch. 1

549. Frances Darwin Cornford
(1886–?)

* * *

1 O fat white woman whom nobody loves,
Why do you walk through the fields in gloves?

"To a Fat Lady Seen from the Train"

2 Magnificently unprepared
For the long littleness of life.

"Rupert Brooke"

550. Hilda Doolittle
(1886–1961)

* * *

1 Egypt had maimed us,
offered dream for life,
an opiate for a kiss,
and death for both.

"Egypt"

551. Florence Kiper Frank
(1886?–?)

1 The canny among the publishers know that an enormous popular appetite for the insulting of the famous must be gratified, and the modern biographer emerges from the editorial conference a sadist and a wiser man.
Morrow's Almanac   *1929*

* * *

2 Pooh-Men!
We are done with them now,
Who had need of them then,—
I and you!

"Baby"

552. Hazel Hall
(1886–1924)

* * *

1 *I am the dance of youth, and life is fair!*
Footfall, footfall;
I am a dream, divinely unaware!
Footfall, footfall;
I am the burden of an old despair!
Footfall.

"Footsteps"

553. Radclyffe Hall
(1886–1943)

1 Acknowledge us, o God, before the whole world. Give us also the right to our existence.
The Well of Loneliness   *1928*

2 "You're neither unnatural, nor abominable, nor mad; you're as much a part of what people call nature as anyone else; only you're unexplained as yet—you've not got your niche in creation."

Ibid.

3 But the intuition of those who stand midway between the two sexes is so ruthless, so poignant, so accurate, so deadly as to be in the nature of an added scourge.

Ibid.

4 They had sought among the ruins of a dead civilization for the beauty they missed subconsciously in their own.
A Saturday Life, Ch. 1   1930

5 But when told that to appear naked in a drawing-room might be considered somewhat odd, since it was no longer the custom, she had argued that our bodies were very unimportant, only there so that people might perceive us. "We couldn't see each other without them, you know," she had said, smiling up at her mother.

Ibid.

6 At a time of great strain and unhappiness a comparatively insignificant event may discover the chink in our armour; an event connected, as likely as not, with an equally insignificant person. . . .
The Master of the House, Ch. 25   1932

7 Cry out until the world shook with her cries: "You shall not take him, I care nothing for honour. I care only for the child that my womb has held, that my pain has brought forth, that my breasts have nourished. I care nothing for your wars. He was born of love; shall the blossom of love be destroyed by your hatreds? I care nothing. . . ."

Ibid., Ch. 41

554. Elizabeth Kenny
(1886–1952)

1 . . . panic plays no part in the training of a nurse.
And They Shall Walk, with
Martha Ostenso   1943

2 . . . it is easier to recount grievances and slights than it is to set down a broad redress of such grievances and slights. The reason is that one fears to be thought of as an arrant braggart.

Ibid.

3 The record of one's life must needs prove more interesting to him who writes it than to him who reads what has been written.   Ibid., Foreword

4 O sleep, O gentle sleep, I thought gratefully, Nature's gentle nurse!

Ibid., Ch. 2

5 Fortunately, perhaps, I was completely ignorant of the orthodox theory of the disease [poliomyelitis].

Ibid.

3 He looked at the book, took my name, and consulted his records. Then he informed me that I had been lost at sea and was dead. Under the circumstances, he could not possibly give me any money. . . . Even the fact that he was dealing with someone who had been dead for several days failed to awaken the slightest interest in his official heart.

Ibid., Ch. 3

7 I was wholly unprepared for the extraordinary attitude of the medical world in its readiness to condemn anything that smacked of reform or that ran contrary to approved methods of practice.

Ibid., Ch. 6

8 Some minds remain open long enough for the truth not only to enter but to pass on through by way of a ready exit without pausing anywhere along the route.

Ibid.

9 My mother used to say, "He who angers you, conquers you!" But my mother was a saint.

Ibid., Ch. 7

10 His response was remarkable for its irrelevance, if for nothing else.   *Ibid.*

11 A measure of victory has been won, and honors have been bestowed in token thereof. But honors fade or are forgotten, and monuments crumble into dust. It is the battle itself that matters—and the battle must go on.

Ibid., Ch. 14

555. Frances Marion
(1886–1973)

1 The thought had taken root in his imagination and grown as a tree grows from a tiny seed until it crowded out all other thoughts in his mind.

Westward the Dream, Pt. I, Ch. 1   *1948*

2 The land around San Juan Capistrano is the pocket where the Creator keeps all his treasures. Anything will grow there, from wheat and beans to citrus fruit.

Ibid., Ch. 3

3 "Do we really know anybody? Who does not wear one face to hide another?"

Ibid., Ch. 10

4 What a strange pattern the shuttle of life can weave. . . .
Ibid., Pt. II, Ch. 14

5 This is not dead land, it is only thirsty land.

Ibid., Ch. 22

6 "A coin, Mr. Fox, can only fall heads or tails, and I'll gamble on heads, they last longer."
Off with Their Heads   1972

7 I shall refrain from mentioning to our southern neighbors that San Franciscans look upon the City of the Queen of the Angels as California's floating kidney transplanted from the Middle West.
Ibid., "1914 Through 1924"

8 Promises that you make to yourself are often like the Japanese plum tree—they bear no fruit.

Ibid.

9 We have a little catch phrase in our family which somehow fits almost everyone in the movie colony: "Spare no expense to make everything as economical as possible."

Ibid.

10 One thing you learned when you wrote for the movies: all nationalities were sensitive except Americans. The Arabs were always to be pictured as a sweet, friendly people. So were the Greeks, the Dutch, Turks, Laps, Eskimoes, and so on down the line. Everyone was honest and virtuous, except Americans. You could make them the most sinister villains and never hear a word of protest from Washington, Chicago, Kalamazoo, or all points south. But should you describe a villain belonging to any country but America, you found yourself spread-eagled between the Board of Censors and the diplomatic service of some foreign power.
Ibid., "1925 Through 1928"

556. Mary Wigman
(1886–1973)

1 Strong and convincing art has never arisen from theories.

"The New German Dance,"
Modern Dance, Virginia
Stewart, ed.   *1935*

2 Art is communication spoken by man for humanity in a language raised above the everyday happening.

Ibid.

3 During the process of artistic creation, man descends into the primordial elements of life. He reverts to himself to become lost in something greater than himself, in the immediate, indivisible essence of life.

Ibid.

557. Anzia Yezierska
(1886–1970)

1 "If you have no luck in this world, then it's better not to live."

"The Fat of the Land," *The Century*   *1919*

2 "The world is a wheel always turning," philosophized Mrs. Pelz. "Those who were high go down low, and those who've been low go up higher."

Ibid.

558. Ruth Benedict
(1887–1948)

1 No man ever looks at the world with pristine eyes. He sees it edited by a definite set of customs and institutions and ways of thinking.

Patterns of Culture, Ch. 1   *1934*

2 War is, we have been forced to admit, even in the face of its huge place in our own civilization, an asocial trait.

Ibid.

3 If we justify war, it is because all peoples always justify the traits of which they find themselves possessed, not because war will bear an objective examination of its merits.

Ibid.

4 Racism is the new Calvinism which asserts that one group has the stigmata of superiority and the other has those of inferiority. . . . For racism is an *ism* to which everyone in the world today is exposed; for or against, we must take sides. And the history of the future will differ according to the decision which we make.

Race: Science and Politics, Ch. 1   1940

5 "Hybrid vigor" has been shown in studies of American Indian-White mixture, stature in the half-breeds being greater than that of either race contributing to the cross. Mixed bloods also show over and over again evidence of increased fertility. . . . Nature apparently does not condemn the half-caste to physiological inferiority. The rule for the breeding of good human stock is that both parents be of good physique and good mental ability.

Ibid., Ch. 4

6 Racism in its nationalistic phase, therefore, has been a politician's plaything. . . . It is a dangerous plaything, a sword which can be turned in any direction to condemn the enemy of the moment.

Ibid., Ch. 7

7 But the Thai have an indestructible conviction that existence is good, and they have characteristically placed the promised rewards of Buddhism in this life rather [than] in the life to come.

Thai Culture and Behavior,
Pt. II, Ch. 5   1943

8 Everybody repeats the proverbial maxim: "In this world everything changes except good deeds and bad deeds; these follow you as the shadow follows the body."

Ibid.

9 The Japanese are, to the highest degree, both aggressive and unaggressive, both militaristic and aesthetic, both insolent and polite, rigid and adaptable, submissive and resentful of being pushed around, loyal and

500

treacherous, brave and timid, conservative and hospitable to new ways.

The Chrysanthemum and the Sword, Ch. 1   *1946*

10 Love, kindness, generosity, which we value just in proportion as they are given without strings attached, necessarily must have their strings in Japan. And every such act received makes one a debtor.

Ibid., Ch. 5

11 A man's indebtedness . . . is not virtue; his repayment is. Virtue begins when he dedicates himself actively to the job of gratitude.

Ibid., Ch. 6

12 I have always used the world of make-believe with a certain desperation.

Quoted in *An Anthropologist at Work*
by Margaret Mead   *1951p*

13 . . . the passionate belief in the superior worthwhileness of our children. It is stored up in us as a great battery charged by the accumulated instincts of uncounted generations.

Ibid.

14 Life was a labyrinth of petty turns and there was no Ariadne who held the clue.

Ibid. (October, 1912)

15 So much of the trouble is because I am a woman.

Ibid.

16 If we are not to have the chance to fulfill our one potentiality—the power of loving—why were we not born men? At least we could have had an occupation then.

Ibid.

17 The trouble is not that we are never happy—it is that happiness is so episodical.

Ibid.

18 We turn in our sleep and groan because we are parasites—we women—because we produce nothing, say nothing, find our whole world in the love of a man.—For shame! We are become the veriest Philistines—in this matter of woman's sphere. I suppose it is too soon to expect us to achieve perspective on the problem of women's rights. . . .

Ibid.

19 We hurt each other badly, for words are clumsy things, and he is inexorable. But, at any rate, he does not baby me, and honesty helps even when it is cruel.

Ibid. (Christmas, 1916)

20 I long to speak out the intense inspiration that comes to me from the lives of strong women.

Ibid. (January, 1917)

21 . . . it is my necessary breath of life to understand and expression is the only justification of life that I can feel without prodding.

Ibid. (October, 1920)

22 . . . work even when I'm satisfied with it is never my child I love nor my servant I've brought to heel. It's always busy work I do with my left hand, and part of me watches grudging the wastes of a lifetime.

Ibid. (June 9, 1934)

559. Jessie Chambers
(1887–1944)

1 So instead of a release and deliverance from bondage, the bondage was glorified and made absolute. His [D. H. Lawrence's] mother conquered indeed, but the vanquished one was her son.

D. H. Lawrence: A Personal Record   1935

560. Elizabeth Drew
(1887–1965)

1 But though personality is a skin that no writer can slip, whatever he may write about: though it is a shadow which walks inexorably by his side, so also is the age he lives in.

"The Novel and the Age,"
The Modern Novel   1926

2 The world is not run by thought, nor by imagination, but by opinion. . . .

Ibid., "Sex Simplexes and Complexes"

3 Sown in space like one among a handful of seeds in a suburban garden, the earth exists; a revolving, tepid sphere, whose every rotation brings it relentlessly

nearer to the moon's dim, white, rotten desolation. Dwelling in this spinning island of terror, under immutable sentence of death, is Man, who, whether we regard him with the Psalmist as a little lower than the angels, or as "an ape, reft of his tail and grown rusty at climbing"; whether we see him shouting exultantly that he is the captain of his soul, or meeting his fate with all the lumbering discomfort of a cow being hustled into a railway truck, remains yet the ultimate mystery.

> Ibid., "The New Psychology"

4 The test of literature is, I suppose, whether we ourselves live more intensely for the reading of it. . . .

> Ibid., "Is There a 'Feminine' Fiction?"

5 In spite of equal education and equal opportunity, the *scope* of woman remains still smaller than the scope of man. . . . Just as it is still in her close personal relationships that woman most naturally uses her human genius and her artistry in life, so it is still in the portrayal of those relationships that she perfects her most characteristic genius in writing.   Ibid.

6 How poetry comes to the poet is a mystery.

> Quoted in "On the Teaching of Poetry" by Leonora Speyer, *The Saturday Review of Literature*   1946

7 We read poetry because the poets, like ourselves, have been haunted by the inescapable tyranny of time and death; have suffered the pain of loss, and the more wearing, continuous pain of frustration and failure; and have had moods of unlooked-for release and peace. They have known and watched in themselves and others. . . . Sympathy and empathy, feeling with and feeling into, are the bases for his search for the true embodiment in words of his perception, great or small.

> *Poetry: A Modern Guide to Its Understanding and Enjoyment,*   Pt. II, Ch. 7   *1959*

8 The pain of loss, moreover, however agonizing, however haunting in memory, quiets imperceptibly into acceptance as the currents of active living and of fresh emotions flow over it. Worse, perhaps, than the sufferings of grief are the torments that man endures from the conflicts within his own being.

> Ibid., Ch. 9

9 Propaganda has a bad name, but its root meaning is simply to disseminate through a medium, and all writing therefore is propaganda for *something*. It's a seeding of the self in the consciousness of others.

Ibid., Ch. 10

10 The torment of human frustration, whatever its immediate cause, is the knowledge that the self is in prison, its vital force and "mangled mind" leaking away in lonely, wasteful self-conflict.

Ibid., Ch. 13

11 But it is true that the inspired scribbler always has the gift for gossip in our common usage too; he or she can always inspire the commonplace with an uncommon flavor, and transform trivialities by some original grace or sympathy or humor or affection.

"The Literature of Gossip,"
The Literature of Gossip 1964

12 How frail and ephemeral too is the material substance of letters, which makes their very survival so hazardous. Print has a permanence of its own, though it may not be much worth preserving, but a letter! Conveyed by uncertain transportation, over which the sender has no control; committed to a single individual who may be careless or inappreciative; left to the mercy of future generations, of families maybe anxious to suppress the past, of the accidents of removals and house-cleanings, or of mere ignorance. How often it has been by the veriest chance that they survived at all.

Ibid.

561. Edna Ferber
(1887–1968)

1 Roast Beef, Medium, is not only a food. It is a philosophy. Seated at Life's Dining Table, with the menu of Morals before you, your eye wanders a bit over the entrées, the hors d'oeuvres, and the things *à la* though you know that Roast Beef, Medium, is safe and sane, and sure.

Roast Beef, Medium, Foreword 1911

2 From supper to bedtime is twice as long as from breakfast to supper.
Ibid., Ch. 1

3 "Music! That's my gift. And I varied it. Why? Because
the public won't take a fat man seriously. When he sits
down at the piano they begin to howl for Italian rag."
Ibid., Ch. 2

4 "There's certain things always go hand-in-hand in your
mind. You can't think of one without the other. Now,
Lillian Russell and cold cream is one; and new potatoes
and brown crocks is another."
Ibid., Ch. 5

5 Even in her childhood she extracted from life double
enjoyment that comes usually only to the creative
mind. "Now I am doing this. Now I am doing that,"
she told herself while she was doing it. Looking on
while she participated.
So Big, Ch. 1   *1924*

6 "There are only two kinds of people in the world that
really count. One kind's wheat and the other kind's em-
eralds."
Ibid.

7 But young love thrives on colour, warmth, beauty. It
becomes prosaic and inarticulate when forced to begin
its day at four in the morning . . . and to end that
day at nine, numb and sodden with weariness, after
seventeen hours of physical labour.
Ibid., Ch. 8

8 "Woman's work! Housework's the hardest work in the
world. That's why men won't do it."
Ibid.

9 "But 'most any place is Bagdad if you don't know what
will happen in it."
Ibid., Ch. 10

10 "Any piece of furniture, I don't care how beautiful it is,
has got to be lived with, kicked about, and rubbed
down, and mistreated by servants, and repolished, and
knocked around and dusted and sat on or slept in or
eaten off of before it develops its real character," Salina
said. "A good deal like human beings."   Ibid., Ch. 15

11 But his gifts were many, and not the least of them was
the trick of appearing sartorially and tonsorially flawless when dishevelment and a stubble were inevitable in
any other male.   *Show Boat*, Ch. 1   *1926*

12 . . . the Negroes whose black faces dotted the boards of the Southern wharves as thickly as grace notes sprinkle a bar of lively music.

Ibid., Ch. 2

13 They . . . never exchanged civilities. This state of affairs lent spice to an existence that might otherwise have proved too placid for comfort. The bickering acted as a safety valve.

Ibid., Ch. 5

14 "Don't you believe 'em when they say that what you don't know won't hurt you. Biggest lie ever was. See it all and go your own way and nothing'll hurt you. If what you see ain't pretty, what's the odds! See it anyway. Then next time you don't have to look."

Ibid., Ch. 13

15 Faro was not a game with Ravenal—it was for him at once his profession, his science, his drug, his drink, his mistress. He had, unhappily, as was so often the case with your confirmed gambler, no other vice.

Ibid.

16 There was about her—or them—nothing of genius, of greatness, of the divine fire. But the dramatic critics of the younger school who were too late to have seen past genius in its hey-day and for whom the theatrical genius of their day was yet to come, viewed her performance and waxed hysterical, mistaking talent and intelligence and hard work and ambition for something more rare.

Ibid., Ch. 19

17 Wasn't marriage, like life, unstimulating and unprofitable and somewhat empty when too well ordered and protected and guarded. Wasn't it finer, more splendid, more nourishing, when it was, like life itself, a mixture of the sordid and the magnificent; of mud and stars; of earth and flowers; of love and hate and laughter and tears and ugliness and beauty and hurt? Ibid.

18 It had no definite expression. It was not in their bearing; it could not be said to look out from the dead, black, Indian eye, nor was it anywhere about the immobile, parchment face. Yet somewhere black implacable resentment smoldered in the heart of this dying race. *Cimarron,* Ch. 3   *1929*

19 "The difference in America is that the women have always gone along. When you read the history of France you're peeking through a bedroom keyhole. The history of England is a joust. The womenfolks were always Elaineish and anemic, it seems. . . . But here in this land, Sabra, my girl, the women, they've been the real hewers of wood and drawers of water. You'll want to remember that."

Ibid.

20 "The gaudiest star-spangled cosmic joke that ever was played on a double-dealing government burst into fireworks today when, with a roar that could be heard for miles around, thousands of barrels of oil shot into the air on the miserable desert land known as the Osage Indian reservation and occupied by those duped and wretched—!"

Ibid., Ch. 20

21 "If American politics are too dirty for women to take part in, there's something wrong with American politics."

Ibid., Ch. 23

22 "I am not belittling the brave pioneer men, but the sunbonnet as well as the sombrero has helped to settle this glorious land of ours."

Ibid.

23 The goat's business is none of the sheep's concern.
Saratoga Trunk, Ch. 2   1941

24 Adventurers, both. . . . They were like two people who, searching for buried treasure, are caught in a quicksand. Every struggle to extricate themselves only made them sink deeper.

Ibid., Ch. 6

25 "Men often marry their mothers. . . ."

Ibid.

26 "You lose in the end unless you know how the wheel is fixed or can fix it yourself."   Ibid., Ch. 14

27 "Most people don't know how to have a good time, any more than spoiled children. I show them. I spend their money for them, and they're grateful for it. I've got nothing to lose, because I live by my wits. They can't take that away from me."   Ibid.

28 It was part of the Texas ritual. We're rich as son-of-a-
bitch stew but look how homely we are, just as plain-
folksy as Grandpappy back in 1836. We know about
champagne and caviar but we talk hog and hominy.

Giant, Ch. 2   *1952*

29 But undeniably there was about these three young
women an aura, a glow, a dash of what used to be
called diablerie that served as handily as beauty and
sometimes handier. These exhilarating qualities wore
well, too, for they lasted the girls their lifetime, which
beauty frequently fails to do.   *Ibid.*, Ch. 5

30 "Texas air is so rich you can nourish off it like it was
food."   *Ibid.*, Ch. 9

31 A woman can look both moral and exciting—if she
also looks as if it was quite a struggle.

Quoted in *Reader's Digest*   December, *1954*

562. Helen Hoyt
(1887–?)

* * *

1 My heart led me past and took me away;
And yet it was my heart that wanted to stay.

"In the Park"

563. Agnes Meyer
(1887–1970?)

1 When you travel through the wheat fields of Kansas for
a day and a night and see endless herds grazing on the
pastureland, when you have spent weeks visiting factory after factory in city after city producing at top
speed, when you have seen the tireless effort, the intelligent application of management and labor and their
ever-increasing co-operation, you realize that there are
enough resources, actual and potential, enough brains
and good will in this country to turn the whole world
into a paradise.

"Juvenile Delinquency and Child
Labor," *Washington Post*
March 14, 1943

2 What the Nation must realize is that the home, when both parents work, is non-existent. Once we have honestly faced that fact, we must act accordingly.

> Ibid., "Living Conditions of the Woolworker"   *April 10, 1943*

3 We have forgotten that democracy must live as it thinks and think as it lives.

> *Journey Through Chaos,* Introduction   *1943*

4 An orderly existence creates primarily an unconscious relation to the silent progression of the days, seasons, and the music of the spheres.

> *Out of These Roots*   *1953*

5 Fortunate are the people whose roots are deep.

> Ibid., Ch. 1

6 In pursuit of an educational program to suit the bright and the not-so-bright we have watered down a rigid training for the elite until we now have an educational diet in many of our public high schools that nourishes neither the classes nor the masses.

> Ibid., Ch. 2

7 Let us hope that in the process of integration in our society, which fortunately is now well underway, the Negro will not allow the American steam roller of conformity to destroy his creative gifts.

> Ibid., Ch. 8

8 The children are always the chief victims of social chaos.

> Ibid., Ch. 13

9 Science was the method used in the struggle by which mankind has passed from habit, routine, and caprice, from efforts to use nature magically, to intellectual self-control.

> Lecture, "Democracy and Clericalism"
> *May 21, 1954*

10 Christianity must now rise above the limitations of orthodoxy just as the free world must rise above the limitations of nationalism if we are not to pull the civilized world down around our ears.

> Ibid.

11 There is a need for heroism in American life today.

> *Education for a New Morality,* Ch. 1   *1957*

12 We Americans must now throw off our childishness and parochialism and create a new idea of man acceptable to thinking people the world over.

Ibid.

13 From the nineteenth-century view of science as a god, the twentieth century has begun to see it as a devil. It behooves us now to understand that science is neither one nor the other.

Ibid., Ch. 3

14 We can never achieve absolute truth but we can live hopefully by a system of calculated probabilities. The law of probability gives to natural and human sciences—to human experience as a whole—the unity of life we seek.

Ibid., Ch. 3

15 We are immoral in America today precisely because our existing institutions do not perform their function of abolishing our inherited dualism between thought and action, between our American ideals and what we do about them. Let us bear in mind that idealism when separated from empirical methods and experimental utilization in concrete social situations is vague, semantic mouthing. . . .

Ibid., Ch. 16

16 It certainly must have been a relief for the women of the country to realize that one could be a woman and a lady and yet be thoroughly political.

Letter to Eleanor Roosevelt
(July 25, 1952), Quoted in
Eleanor: The Years Alone
by Joseph P. Lash   *1972p*

564. Marianne Moore
(1887–1972)

1   The monkeys
winked too much and were afraid of
        snakes. The zebras, supreme in
their abnormality; the elephants, with
        their fog-colored skin
and strictly practical appendages
        were there.   "The Monkeys"   *1921*

510

2 I, too, dislike it: there are things that are important
   beyond all this fiddle.
                    "Poetry," *Collected Poems*   1935

3 There is a great amount of poetry in unconscious fastidiousness.
                    Ibid., "Critics and Connoisseurs"

4 I wonder what Adam and Eve
   think of it by this time.
                                    Ibid., "Marriage"

5 My father used to say,
   "Superior people never make long visits,"
   Have to be shown Longfellow's grave
   or the glass flowers at Harvard.
                                    Ibid., "Silence"

6 The deepest feeling always shows itself in silence;
   not in silence, but restraint. . . .
                                                Ibid.

7   What is our innocence,
   what is our guilt? All are
      naked, none is safe.
                        "What Are Years?," St. 1,
                        Collected Poems   1941

8 . . . satisfaction is a lowly
   thing, how pure a thing is joy.
                                          Ibid., St. 3

9 Denunciations do not affect
   the culprit; nor blows, but it
   is torture to him not to be spoken to.
                    Ibid., "Spenser's Ireland," St. 1

10 I am troubled, I'm dissatisfied, I'm Irish.
                                                Ibid.

11   Among animals, one has a sense of humor.
    Humor saves a few steps, it saves years.
                        Ibid., "The Pangolin," St. 1

12   As contagion
    of sickness makes sickness,
   contagion of trust can make trust.
                        "In Distrust of Merits," St. 2,
                        Collected Poems   1944

13 . . . "When a man is prey to anger,
he is moved by outside things; when he holds
 his ground in patience patience
  patience, that is action or
 beauty."

Ibid., St. 6

14 . . . The world's an orphan's home. . . .

Ibid., St. 7

15 Beauty is everlasting
 And dust is for a time.

Ibid.

16 Three foremost aids to persuasion which occur to me
are humility, concentration, and gusto.

Speech, "Humility, Concentration,
and Gusto," Grolier Club December 21, 1948

17 [The] whirlwind fife-and-drum of the storm bends the
 salt
 marsh grass, disturbs stars in the sky and the
star on the steeple; it is a privilege to see so
much confusion.

"The Steeple-Jack," Collected Poems 1951

18 One must be as clear as one's natural reticence allows
one to be.

Quoted in "Reading Contemporary
Poetry" by Louise Bogan,
College English February, 1953

19 Verbal felicity is the fruit of art and diligence and refusing to be false.

Ibid.

20 Since writing is not only an art but a trade embodying
principles attested by experience, we wou'd do well not
to forget that it is an expedient for making oneself understood and that what is said should at least have the
air of having meant something to the person who wrote
it—as is the case with Gertrude Stein and James Joyce.

Lecture, "Idiosyncrasy and Technique,"
Oxford University June, 1956

21   O to be a dragon
a symbol of the power of Heaven—of silkworm
size or immense; at times invisible.
 Felicitous phenomenon!

"O to Be a Dragon" 1959

22 To wear the arctic fox
  you have to kill it.
                "The Arctic Fox (Or Goat)"   *1959*

23 Camels are snobbish
  and sheep, unintelligent;
      water buffaloes, neurasthenic—
  even murderous.
  Reindeer seem over-serious.   Ibid.

565. Georgia O'Keeffe
(1887–   )

1 Those hills! They go on and on—it was like looking at
  two miles of gray elephants.
                Quoted in *Time*   *October 12, 1970*

2 I grew up pretty much as everybody else grows up, and
  one day . . . [in 1916] found myself saying to myself—I can't live where I want to—I can't go where I
  want to—I can't do what I want to—I can't even say
  what I want to—School and things that painters have
  taught me even keep me from painting as I want to. I
  decided I was a very stupid fool not to at least paint as
  I wanted to and say what I wanted to when I painted as
  that seemed to be the only thing I could do that didn't
  concern anybody but myself—that was nobody's business but my own. . . .
                Quoted in *Georgia O'Keeffe* by Lloyd
                Goodrich and Doris Bry   *1970*

3 . . . nobody sees a flower—really—it is so small—we
  haven't time—and to see takes time like to have a
  friend takes time. If I could paint the flower exactly as
  I see it no one would see what I see because I would
  paint it small like the flower is small. So I said to myself—I'll paint what I see—what the flower is to me
  but I'll paint it big and they will be surprised into
  taking time to look at it—I will make even busy New
  Yorkers take time to see what I see of flowers. . . .
  Well, I made you take time to look at what I saw and
  when you took time to really notice my flower you
  hung all your own associations with flowers on my
  flower and you write about my flower as if I think and
  see what you think and see of the flower—and I don't.
                Ibid. (c.1939)

4 This is the only place that I really belonged [the Texas panhandle], that I really felt at home. This is my country—terrible winds and wonderful emptiness.

> Quoted in "Flowers, Bones, and the Blue" by Alfred Frankenstein (c. 1919), *San Francisco Examiner & Chronicle*　　　*March 14, 1971*

5 . . . that Blue [of the sky] . . . will always be there as it is now after all man's destruction is finished.

> *Ibid.*

6 I don't very much enjoy looking at paintings in general. I know too much about them. I take them apart.

> Quoted in "An Artist of Her Own School" by Alexander Fried, *San Francisco Examiner & Chronicle*　　　*March 16, 1971*

7 The desert is the last place you can see all around you. The light out here makes everything close, and it is never, never the same. Sometimes the light hits the mountains from behind and front at the same time, and it gives them the look of Japanese prints, you know, distances in layers.

> Quoted in "A Visit with Georgia O'Keeffe" by Beth Coffelt, *San Francisco Examiner & Chronicle*　　　*April 11, 1971*

566. Edith Sitwell
(1887–1964)

1 Every one hundred years or so it becomes necessary for a change to take place in the body of poetry. . . . A fresh movement appears and produces a few great men, and once more the force and vigour die from the results of age; the movement is carried on by weak and worthless imitators, and a change becomes necessary again.

> *Poetry and Criticism*　　　*1926*

2 Still falls the Rain—
Dark as the world of man, black as our loss—
Blind as the nineteen hundred and forty nails
Upon the Cross.

> "Still Falls the Rain"　　　*1940*

3 Daisy and Lily
  Lazy and silly. . . . .
  "Facade" (1922), *Facade and Other Poems 1902–1935*   1950

4 But a word stung him like a mosquito. . . .
  Ibid., "I do like to be beside the Seaside" (1922)

5 The air still seems to reverberate with the wooden sound of numskulls being soundly hit.
  "Dylan Thomas," *Atlantic Monthly February, 1954*

6 He had full eyes . . . giving at first the impression of being unseeing, but seeing all, looking over immeasurable distances.   Ibid.

7 Alas, that he who caught and sang the sun in flight, yet was the sun's brother, and never grieved it on its way, should have left us with no good-by, good night.
  Ibid.

8 After the first death, there is no other. . . .   Ibid.

9 I'm not the man to baulk at a low smell,
  I'm not the man to insist on asphodel.
  This sounds like a He-fellow, don't you think?
  It sounds like that. I belch, I bawl, I drink.
  "One-Way Song," *Collected Poems*   1954

10 Jane, Jane
   Tall as a crane,
   The morning light creaks down again.
   Ibid., "Aubade"

11 My poems are hymns of praise to the glory of life.
   Ibid., "Some Notes on My Poetry"

12   A lady asked me why, on most occasions,
   I wore black. "Are you in mourning?"
      "Yes."
      "For whom are you in mourning?"
      "For the world."
   Taken Care Of, Ch. 1   1965p

13 . . . I have never, in all my life, been so odious as to regard myself as "superior" to any living being, human or animal. I just walked alone—as I have always walked alone.   Ibid., Ch. 2

14 By the time I was eleven years old, I had been taught that nature, far from abhorring a Vacuum, positively adores it.

Ibid., Ch. 3

15 I have lived through the shattering of two civilizations, have seen two Pandora's boxes opened. One contained horror, the other emptiness. . . . In both the new worlds hatched in those Pandora's boxes, mud and flies had taken over the spirit.

Ibid., Ch. 7

16 At last the day drifted into a long lacquered afternoon.

Ibid., Ch. 13

17 We stand on one leg and put our heads under our arms, and when the blood rushes into our heads we are in the full state of Awareness and the Cosmos is just round the corner, and we rush to it and rebound right into the Fourth Dimension. . . .

Ibid.

18 MR. MUGGLEBY LION. I hate to disturb you, but I have just finished a *Little Sonnet*, that I *must* read to you.

HIERATIC WOMAN (coldly). It can't be a *Little* Sonnet, Mr. Muggleby Lion. Sonnets are all of the same size.

Ibid.

19 Rhythm is one of the principal translators between dream and reality. Rhythm might be described, as to the world of sound, what light is to the world of sight. It shares and gives new meaning. Rhythm was described by Schopenhauer as melody deprived of its pitch.

Ibid., Ch. 14

20 Eccentricity is *not,* as dull people would have us believe, a form of madness. It is often a kind of innocent pride, and the man of genius and the aristocrat are frequently regarded as eccentrics because genius and aristocrat are entirely unafraid of and uninfluenced by the opinions and vagaries of the crowd.   Ibid., Ch. 15

21 A pompous woman of his acquaintance, complaining that the head-waiter of a restaurant had not shown her and her husband immediately to a table, said, "We had to tell him who we were." Gerald [Lord Berners], interested, enquired, "And who were you?"   Ibid.

22 Vulgarity is, in reality, nothing but a modern, chic, pert descendant of the goddess Dullness.

Ibid., Ch. 19

23 I do not know how to address you. I cannot call you a goose, as geese saved the capitol of Rome, and no amount of cackling on your part would awaken anybody! Nor can I call you an ass, since Balaam's constant companion saw an angel, and recognised it.

Ibid., Ch. 22

24 . . . the heartless stupidity of those who have never known a great and terrifying poverty.

Ibid.

25 When we think of cruelty, we must try to remember the stupidity, the envy, the frustration from which it has arisen.

Ibid.

26 Winter is the time for comfort, for good food and warmth, for the touch of a friendly hand and for a talk beside the fire: it is the time for home.

Ibid., Ch. 22

27 Then all will be over, bar the shouting and the worms.

Ibid.

* * *

28 Remember only this of our hopeless love
That never till time is done
Will the fire of the heart and the fire of the mind be
one.

"Heart and Mind"

29 Under great yellow flags and banners of the ancient
Cold
Began the huge migrations
From some primeval disaster in the heart of Man.

"The Shadow of Cain"

567. Anna Akhmatova
(1888?–1966)

1 What hangs in the balance is nowise in doubt;
We know the event and we brave what we know;
Our clocks are all striking the hour of courage.

"Courage"   1942

2   O great language we love:
It is you, Russian tongue, we must save, and we swear
We will give you unstained to the sons of our sons;
You shall live on our lips, and we promise you—never
A prison shall know you, but you shall be free
Forever.

Ibid.

568. Vicki Baum
(1888–1960)

1 Fame always brings loneliness. Success is as ice cold
and lonely as the north pole.

Grand Hotel   1931

2 A woman who is loved always has success.

Ibid.

3 Marriage always demands the greatest understanding of
the art of insincerity possible between two human
beings.

And Life Goes On   1932

4 Pity is the deadliest feeling that can be offered to a
woman.

Ibid.

5 To be a Jew is a destiny.

Ibid.

569. Marjorie Bowen
(1888–1952)

1   "But will it last?"
"What a ridiculous question," returned the colonel
blandly. "Will you, or I, or anything last? Flesh is
grass, my dear Count."

General Crack, Ch. 1   1928

2 Useless for one who did not believe in Heaven to renounce the World: that would be to fall into a void.

Ibid., Ch. 10

3 "If you live in the world you must live on the world's
terms."   *Ibid.*

4 "I thought," sighed the young man, "that you might
tell me the secret of peace."

"How can I tell you that? It's like talking to a general who wants to know how to set various troops in
order. If you have not the power of authority, no one
can give it to you. If you can't command your own
soul, how can I give you enlightenment how to do so?"

Ibid.

5 "Why do I concern myself with all these passions, that
to me are withered as the last leaf on a dead tree?"

Ibid., Ch. 35

6 "What is the most dangerous possession in the world,
Mr. Falkland?"

"No use at riddles," replied the young man cau-
tiously.

Dobree picked up the speaking-tube.

"Someone else's secret," he remarked. . . .

The Shadow on Mockways, Ch. 2   1932

7 "If I continue to drink I shall soon be like these—how
long would it take? It has not really got hold of me yet.
I could stop it if I wanted. Sometimes I take nothing
for days together—yes, if it were worth while and
something else offered, I could stop. But it is not worth
while and nothing else offers."

Moss Rose   1935

8 . . . she was cured of love as she was cured of drunk-
enness. Indulgence had soon brought her to a point of
nausea; she had never given anyone tenderness or affection, and the recollection of dead passions that had
ended in disgust or rage was like the recollection of the
stench of decay.   *Ibid.*

9 "It is more difficult, my lord, to rule the King's favourites than for the favourites to rule the King."

My Tattered Loving, Ch. 1   1937

10 Meanwhile, he continued to search for a brisk and subtle poison, for it seemed to him that one who could
make the discovery of such a weapon as this would be
more powerful than the greatest of kings.

Ibid., Ch. 2

11 But it had not needed much of a turn of fortune's wheel
for the Frenchman to have been the quack counting up

his illicit gains and the Englishman to have been the courtly physician to whom all the great ones ran for help in their distresses.

Ibid.

12 As civilisation advanced, people began to discover that more was to be gained by flattery than by force—and that flattery had a larger purchasing power than coin of the realm.

"The Art of Flattery,"
World's Wonder   1937

13 Flattery is so necessary to all of us that we flatter one another just to be flattered in return. . . .

Ibid.

14   "Leave well alone, my dear Miss Lawne."
    "But perhaps we are leaving evil alone," replied the lady, smiling.
    "In that case, also, have nothing to do with it."

Mignonette, Ch. 1   1948

15 "Rich and free," Barbara repeated to herself. It was hard to accept the meaning of the words. There was no one to thwart her, to scold her, to warn her, to advise her; there was only Mr. Bompast who had no authority over her and whose dry prudence would be ignored. She could not even be checked if she did anything eccentric.

Ibid.

16 Custom   reclaimed   her. . . . So,   insidiously,   her middle-class respectability hemmed in Barbara Lawne. . . . Only in her dreams did she explore wild and darkling landscapes. . . .

Ibid., Ch. 2

* * *

17 Even a fool can deceive a man—if he be a bigger fool than himself.

"The Glen o' Weeping"

570. Aline Murray Kilmer
(1888–1941)

* * *

1 For there is only sorrow in my heart;
    There is no room for fear.
But how I wish I were afraid again,
    My dear, my dear.

"I Shall Not Be Afraid"

2 I'm sorry you are wiser,
   I'm sorry you are taller;
I liked you better foolish,
   And I liked you better smaller.
        "For the Birth of a Middle-Aged Child," St. 1

3 I cannot see myself as I once was;
   I would not see myself as I am now.
             "To Aphrodite: With a Mirror"

4 I sing of little loves that glow
   Like tapers shining in the rain,
Of little loves that break themselves
   Like moths against the window-pane.

                  "Prelude"

5 Things have a terrible permanence
When people die.
              "Things," St. 6

6 When people inquire I always just state,
"I have four nice children, and hope to have eight."
             "Ambition"

571. Olga Knopf
(1888–   )

1 . . . the sexes are living, we might say, in a vast communal neurosis; a highly contagious neurosis which parents pass on to their children and men and women pass on to each other.
    The Art of Being a Woman   1932

2 The art of being a woman can never consist of being a bad imitation of a man.

                  Ibid.

3 The outer limitations to woman's progress are caused by the fact we are living in a man's culture.
    Women on Their Own   1935

572. Clare Kummer
(1888–1948)

1 ETHEL. Did you sell your verses to Binder?

JENNINGS. No—he seemed to think they were indecent

and when I explained to him that they weren't he lost
interest in them—so that's all.

Good Gracious, Annabelle, Act I   *1916*

2 STEIN. It's the public. You can't count on it. Give 'em
something good and they'll go to see something bad.
Give 'em something bad and they don't like that either.

Rollo's Wild Oat, Act I, Sc. 1   *1922*

3 STEIN. Pictures are a great business. You take a picture
and you got something.

MRS. PARK-GALES. Yes, but what?

STEIN. You get all through with the actors and there
they are playing for you every night. If they are sick or
dead, it don't make any difference. They are working
just the same.

LUCAS. Anything to make us work for nothing!

Ibid., Sc. 2

4 AUNT MIN. He should have started worrying before he
had things to worry about.

Her Master's Voice, Act I   *1933*

5 QUEENA. Don't you know when people are in love they
don't think? Merciful heavens!

AUNT MIN. Well, they ought to. I don't know of any
time when it's more important for them to think. In
love! In foolishness!

Ibid., Act II

* * *

6 Oh, there was a woman-hater hated women all he
  could,
And he built himself a bungle in a dingle in the wood;
Here he lived and said of ladies things I do not think
  he should,
"If they're good they're not good-looking; if good-
  looking, they're not good."

"In the Dingle-Dongle Bell"

573. Lotte Lehmann
(1888–1976)

1 But to me the actual sound of the words is all-important; I feel always that the words complete the music and must never be swallowed up in it. The music is the shining path over which the poet travels to bring his song to the world.

"The Singing Actor," *Players at Work*, Morton Eustis, ed.   *1937*

2 I have never understood the star who enjoys playing with a mediocre cast in order to shine out the more brilliantly himself, for the essence of any fine dramatic or operatic production is harmonious integration of all performances.

Ibid.

3 Imitation is, and can only be, the enemy of artistry. Everything which breathes the breath of life is changeable. . . . Only from life itself may life be born.

More Than Singing, Introduction   *1945*

4 That fine God-given instrument—the voice—must be capable of responding with the greatest subtlety to every shade of each emotion. But it must be subordinate, it must only be the foundation, the soil from which flowers true art.

Ibid.

5 Do not become paralyzed and enchained by the set patterns which have been woven of old. No, build from your own youthful feeling, your own groping thought and your own flowering perception—and help to further that beauty which has grown from the roots of tradition. . . .

Ibid.

6 . . . if your soul can soar above technique and float in the lofty regions of creative art, you have fulfilled your mission as a singer. For what mission can be greater than that of giving to the world hours of exaltation in which it may forget the misery of the present, the cares of everyday life and lose itself in the eternally pure world of harmony. . . .   Ibid.

574. Katherine Mansfield
(1888–1923)

1 How idiotic civilization is! Why be given a body if you
have to keep it shut up in a case like a rare, rare fiddle?
"Bliss," *Bliss and Other Stories*   1920

2 ". . . Why! Why! Why is the middle-class so stodgy—
so utterly without a sense of humour!"
Ibid.

3 . . . roses are the only flowers that impress people at
garden-parties; the only flowers that everybody is certain of knowing.
"The Garden Party"   1922

4 Hundreds, yes, literally hundreds, had come out in a
single night; the green bushes bowed down as though
they had been visited by archangels.
Ibid.

5 Fancy cream puffs so soon after breakfast. The very
idea made one shudder. All the same, two minutes later
Jose and Laura were licking their fingers with that absorbed inward look that only comes from whipped
cream.
Ibid.

6 "If you're going to stop a band playing every time
someone has an accident, you'll lead a very strenuous
life."
Ibid.

7 There lay a young man, fast asleep—sleeping so
soundly, so deeply, that he was far, far away from them
both. Oh, so remote, so peaceful. He was dreaming.
Never wake him up again.
Ibid.

8 Although over six years had passed away, the boss
never thought of the boy except as lying unchanged,
unblemished in his uniform, asleep for ever.
"The Fly," *The Dove's Nest*   1923

9 How on earth could he have slaved, denied himself,
kept going all those years without the promise for ever

before him of the boy's stepping into his shoes carrying on where he left off?

Ibid.

10 It is as though God opened his hand and let you dance on it a little, and then shut it . . . so tight that you could not even cry.

The Journal of Katherine Mansfield
(February, 1914)   1927p

11 Oh, the times when she had walked upside down on the ceiling . . . floated on a lake of light . . . !

Ibid. (December 31, 1918)

12 There is no limit to human suffering. When one thinks "Now I have touched the bottom of the sea—now I can go no deeper," one goes deeper. . . . Suffering is boundless, is eternity. One pang is eternal torment. Physical suffering is—child's play.

Ibid. (December 19, 1920)

13 Everything in life that we really accept undergoes a change. So suffering must become Love. That is the mystery.

Ibid.

14 As in the physical world, so in the spiritual world, pain does not last forever.

Ibid.

15   "Do you know what individuality is?"
     "No."
     "Consciousness of will. To be conscious that you have a will and can act."
     Yes, it is. It's a glorious saying.

Ibid. (September 30, 1922)

16 Nearly all my improved health is pretence—acting. What does it amount to? . . . I am an absolutely helpless invalid. What is my life? It is the existence of a parasite.

Ibid. (October 14, 1922)

17 Risk! Risk anything! Care no more for the opinions of others, for those voices. Do the hardest thing on earth for you. Act for yourself. Face the truth.   Ibid.

18 By health I mean the power to live a full, adult, living, breathing life in close contact with . . . the earth and the wonders thereof—the sea—the sun.   Ibid.

19 To be wildly enthusiastic, or deadly serious—both are
wrong. Both pass. One must keep ever present a sense
of humor.

Ibid. (October 17, 1922)

20 Now perhaps you understand what "indifference"
means. It is to learn not to mind, and not to show your
mind.

Ibid.

20 *Important.* When we can begin to take our failures
nonseriously, it means we are ceasing to be afraid of
them. It is of immense importance to learn to laugh at
ourselves.

Ibid. (October, 1922)

22 Whenever I prepare for a journey I prepare as though
for death. Should I never return, all is in order. This is
what life has taught me.

Ibid. (1922)

23 I want, by understanding myself, to understand others.
I want to be all that I am capable of becoming. . . .
This all sounds very strenuous and serious. But now that
I have wrestled with it, it's no longer so. I feel happy—
deep down. *All is well.*

Ibid.

24 I feel like a fly who has been dropped into the milk-jug
and fished out again, but is still too milky and drowned
to start cleaning up yet.

*Katherine Mansfield's Letters to John
Middleton Murry, 1913–1922*   *1951p*

575. Carlotta Monterey O'Neill
(1888–1970)

1 To understand his [Eugene O'Neill's] work you must
understand the man, for the work and the man are one.

Quoted in *O'Neill* by Arthur
and Barbara Gelb   *1960*

2 He got a racing car, a Bugatti, and when he was very
nervous and tired he would go out in it and drive
ninety-five miles an hour and come back looking nineteen years old and perfectly relaxed.

Ibid., Ch. 4

3 O'Neill was a tough mick, and never loved a woman who walked. He loved only his work. But he had respect for me. I had an independent income, and I told him I'd marry him if he would let me pay half of all the household expenses. . . . He said he needed a home. "I want a home properly run," he told me. And that is what I did for him, I saw to it that he was able to work.

Ibid.

4 I had to work like a dog. I was Gene's secretary, I was his nurse. His health was always bad. I did everything. He wrote the plays, but I did everything else. I loved it. It was a privilege to live with him, because he was mentally stimulating. My God, how many women have husbands who are very stimulating?

Ibid.

576. Agnes Sligh Turnbull
(1888–   )

1 "Now ain't that funny! I thought it was you, an' you thought it was me; an' begob, it's *nayther* of us!"

The Rolling Years, Bk. I, Ch. 6   1936

2 "The older I get, Jeannie, the more I wonder whether a life shouldn't perhaps be like a river—flowing along in the channel God gave it. Not too many radical deflections."

Ibid., Bk. II, Ch. 1

3 "That's it! The long look ahead. Doesn't it change things, though? Staking neck or nothing on a life to come! Keeps us from being too fussy over affairs here, I guess."

Ibid., Ch. 4

4 "There is still vitality under the winter snow, even though to the casual eye it seems to be dead."

Ibid.

5 "It's the trail of the old Puritan over us. We assume that the only natural course of events is the wrath of God and the miseries of this life. We're afraid to believe that the Creator might sometimes actually wish us well!"

Ibid.

6 "The trouble with the average human being is that he never goes on mountain journeys. He stops at the first way station and refuses to believe there is country beyond."

Ibid., Ch. 5

7 "You must learn to drink the cup of life as it comes, Connie, without stirring it up from the bottom. That's where the bitter dregs are!"

Ibid.

8 "Wasn't it [religion] invented by man for a kind of solace? It's as though he said, 'I'll make me a nice comfortable garment to shut out the heat and the cold'; and then it ends by becoming a straitjacket."

Ibid., Ch. 6

9 "I don't know that I care so much about going far," he said at last; "but I should like to go *deep* where I go."

Ibid., Epilogue

10 "You can put city polish *on* a man, but by golly, it seems you can't ever rub it off him."

The Golden Journey, Ch. 2   1955

11 "The idea of perfection always gives one a chance to talk without knowing facts."

Ibid., Ch. 4

12 "The older you get the more you realize that gray isn't such a bad color. And in politics you work with it or you don't work at all."

Ibid., Ch. 7

13 There would seem to be a law operating in human experience by which the mind once suddenly aware of a verity for the first time immediately invents it again.

Ibid., Ch. 10

14 Oh, the utter unpredictability of a quarrel! How inflammable words were to ignite each other until the blaze of them scorched and seared.

Ibid.

15 "Do you know that the tendrils of graft and corruption have become mighty interlacing roots so that even men who would like to be honest are tripped and trapped by them?"

Ibid., Ch. 11

16 Defeat in itself was part and parcel of the great gambling game of politics. A man who could not accept it and try again was not of the stuff of which leaders are made.

> Ibid., Ch. 12

17 . . . she *was* a widow, that strange feminine entity who had once been endowed with a dual personality and was now only half of what she had been.

> *The Flowering*, Ch. 1   1972

18 "Dogs' lives are too short. Their only fault, really."

> Ibid., Ch. 2

19 "If you keep things long enough, some fool or other will come along an' buy 'em."

> Ibid., Ch. 3

20 Girls! Girls! Girls!
With platted hair an' mebbe curls
Singin' in a *chorus!*
Lord have mercy o'er us.

> Ibid., Ch. 4

577. Mary Day Winn
(1888–1965)

1 Sex is the tabasco sauce which an adolescent national palate sprinkles on every course in the menu.

> *Adam's Rib*   1931

2 In the argot of the sub-deb, "U.S.A." has long ago lost its patriotic meaning. It now stands for "Universal Sex Appeal."

> Ibid.

578. Enid Bagnold
(1889–   )

1 "She keeps 'er brains in 'er 'eart. An' that's where they ought ter be. An' a man or woman who does that's one in a million an' 'as got my backing."

> *National Velvet*   1935

2 "Things come suitable to the time. Childbirth. An' bein' in love. An' death. You can't know 'em till you come to them. No use guessing an' dreading."   Ibid.

3 "There's men . . . as can see things in people. There's men . . . as can choose a horse, an' that horse'll win. It's not the look of the horse, no, nor of the child, nor of the woman. It's the thing *we* can see. . . .

Ibid.

4 "*You're all faith*. An' that's the kind of power that dumb animal can understand."

Ibid.

5 "What's the use of £7000 to me? . . . I shouldn't know what to do with it. What'd I do? It would give me the itch."

Ibid.

6 "This living in the middle of fame's upsetting. It's been like them sweepstakes you read of break up the home."

Ibid.

7 "Love don't seem dainty on a fat woman."

Ibid.

8 LAUREL. She says true devotion is only to be got when a man is worked to death and has no rival.

The Chalk Garden, Act I   1953

9 MAITLAND. Madame loves the unusual! It's a middle-class failing—she says—to run away from the unusual.

Ibid.

10 MRS. ST. MAUGHAM. You can't fit false teeth to a woman of character. As one gets older and older, the appearance becomes such a bore.

Ibid.

11 MRS. ST. MAUGHAM. Life without a room to oneself is a barbarity.

Ibid.

12 MRS. ST. MAUGHAM. Privilege and power make selfish people—but gay ones.

Ibid.

13 MAITLAND. Praise is the only thing that brings to life again a man that's been destroyed.

Ibid.

14 MRS. ST. MAUGHAM. Love can be had any day! Success is far harder.

Ibid.

15 MADRIGAL. Truth doesn't ring true in a court of law.
>Ibid., Act II

16 JUDGE. Judges don't age. Time decorates them.
>Ibid.

17 OLIVIA. The thoughts of a *daughter* are a kind of memorial.
>Ibid., Act III

18 SHE. But it's dishonest to make friends with the next generation.
>*The Chinese Prime Minister*, Act I, Sc. 1   *1964*

19 SHE. And that's the real truth about people! They are not types. They aren't mothers-in-law and daughters-in-law! They are creatures ardently engaged on themselves!
>Ibid.

20 ALICE. Oh—a girl's looks are *agony*!
>Ibid.

21 SHE. Yes, I was kind. But kindness is so fugitive. It comes like a gust into the heart. And blows out again.
>Ibid.

22 SHE. I want to get *out*! (*Picking up and shaking the engagement book.*) *Out* of this book—with its procession—moving me on!
>Ibid.

23 SHE. It was charming of God! I never expected it! . . . That as beauty vanishes the eyes grow dimmer.
>Ibid., Act II

24 SHE. If you fight an old battle—where are the witnesses! And the evidence—obliterated!
>Ibid.

25 SIR GREGORY. Marriage. The beginning and the end are wonderful. But the middle part is hell.
>Ibid.

26 ALICE. It must be pleasant to reach that age when one can go to the lavatory without explanation.
>Ibid.

27 BENT. So few people achieve the final end. *Most* are caught napping.
>Ibid., Act III

28 SHE. We were so different that when two rooms separated us for half an hour—we met again as strangers.

Ibid.

29 SHE. The using-up of grandmothers is not for me. It was pre-Christian! Now only the Latins and the natives do it! . . . I *had* my babies—it was like love! But I won't do things twice!

Ibid.

30 SHE. And if I die in ten years—or ten minutes—you can't measure Time! In ten minutes everything can be felt! In four minutes you can be born! Or live. In two minutes God may be understood! And what one woman grasps—all men may get nearer to.

Ibid.

31 SHE. I have always been a punctual woman. I have never glanced at the sea as I drove to the station. If God had been stoking the engine I wouldn't have seen Him!

Ibid.

579. Mildred Cram
(1889–?)

1 Publicity tripped upon the heels of publicity.
"Billy," *Harper's Bazaar*   1924

2 He was capitalized, consolidated, incorporated, copyrighted, limited, protected, insured, and all rights reserved, including the Scandinavian.

Ibid.

3 "I am vulgar, my friend! I mix tears with idiocy. I put the grotesque into love. I tickle sluggish minds. My recipe is a mixture of legend and pep, pantomime and beauty, artifice and art."   Ibid.

580. Fannie Hurst
(1889–1968)

1 It's hard for a young girl to have patience for old age sitting and chewing all day over the past.
"Get Ready the Wreaths," *Cosmopolitan*   1917

2 It is doubtful if in all its hothouse garden of women the Hotel Bon Ton boasted a broken finger-nail or that little brash place along the forefinger that tattles so of potato peeling or asparagus scraping.

"She Walks in Beauty," *Cosmopolitan* 1921

3 "I always say he wore himself out with conscientiousness."

Ibid.

4 To housekeep, one had to plan ahead and carry items of motley nature around in the mind and at the same time preside, as mother had, at table, just as if everything, from the liver and bacon, to the succotash, to the French toast and strawberry jam, had not been matters of forethought and speculation.

Imitation of Life, Ch. 2 1932

5 He had always said of himself that people first tasted the command in his voice and then came nibbling at his products.

Ibid., Ch. 14

6 "I know, it, and when I knows a thing wid my knowin', I knows it."

Ibid., Ch. 33

7 "Honey-chile, it will shore seem a funny world up dar widout washin'. If de Lawd's robes only needed launderin', I'd do his tucks de way He's never seen 'em done."

Ibid., Ch. 36

8 Papa lived so separately within himself that I retreated to Mama, who wore herself on the outside. Everything about her hung in view like peasant adobe houses with green peppers and little shrines, drying diapers and cooking utensils on the facade.

Anatomy of Me, Bk. I 1958

9 This anatomy of me is serving the double purpose of revealing me to myself.

Ibid., Bk. III

581. Elsie Janis
(1889–1956)

1 When I think of the hundreds of things I might be,
  I get down on my knees and thank God that I'm me.

"Compensation," *Poems Now and Then* c.1927

2 Why do we do it?
  Oh, Hell! What's the use?
  Why battle with the universe?
  Why not declare a truce?

Ibid., "Why?"

3 Up and down the burning sidewalks
  Praying ever for a job,
  In my heart a curse for mankind,
  In my pocket not a bob.

Ibid., "The Actor's Lament"

4 It was Mother who fought. Fought! To keep me up to
  par! To make me study and improve. Fought! To keep
  my name in the large type she believed I merited.
  Fought for heat in trains to protect my health. Fought
  to make ends meet, when each week she had finished
  sending money to the many dependents that automatically arrived on the high heels of success. Invincible!
  best describes her.

So Far, So Good!, Pt. I   *1931*

5 I realize, at least, that I have never been really virtuous, I have only been egotistical.

Ibid., Pt. VI

6 Life is marvelous! There is no death! It's a pity, everything that goes up must come down.

Ibid.

582. Dorothy McCall
(1889–   )

1 One cannot have wisdom without living life.
  Quoted in the *Los Angeles Times*   *March 14, 1974*

2 Lawmakers and employers should not be allowed to
  continue their shameful practice of punishing still-
  producing and competent people merely because of
  age.

Ibid.

3 Technology dominates us all, diminishing our freedom.
Ibid.

583. Gabriela Mistral
(1889–1957)

1 A son, a son, a son! I wanted a son of yours and mine,
in those distant days of burning bliss when my bones
would tremble at your least murmur
and my brow would glow with a radiant mist.
"Poem of the Son," St. 1, *Desolacion*   1922

2 he kissed me and now I am someone else; someone
else in the pulse that repeats the pulse of my
own veins and in the breath that mingles with my
breath. Now my belly is as noble as my heart.
Ibid., "He Kissed Me," St. 1

3   When he shall roam free on the
highways, even though he is far away from me, the
   wind that
lashes him will tear at my flesh, and his cry will be in
   my
throat, too. My grief and my smile begin in your face,
   my
son.   Ibid., "Eternal Grief," St. 2

4 Blushing, full of confusion, I talked with her about my
worries and the fear in my body. I fell on her breast,
and all over again I became a little girl sobbing in her
arms at the terror of life.   Ibid., "Mother," St. 2

5 I have a true happiness
and a happiness betrayed,
the one like a rose,
the other like a thorn.   "Richness," *Tala*   1938

6 I love the things I never had
along with those I have no more.
Ibid., "Things," St. 1

584. Julia Seton
(1889–?)

1 Dancing is a universal instinct—zoölogic, a biologic
impulse, found in animals as well as in man.
"Why Dance?," *The Rhythm of the Redman*   1930

2 In its natural, primitive form, dancing is vigorous muscular action to vent emotion. Originally, it was the natural expression of the basic impulses of a simple form of life. Triumph, defeat, war, love, hate, desire, propitiation of the gods—all were danced by the hero or the tribe to the rhythm of beaten drums.

> Ibid., "Dance in the Animal World"

3 I have listened by a thousand fires as the Buffalo Wind blew through our lives. . . . And so would come a flood of revelation, an unceasing flow of inspiration such as could not be courted. Many a time have I sat by the embers, in motionless silence for hours, while the words came in unhesitating rhythm of passionate life—for we did not measure our life together with a shallow cup. Each time we dipped, we brought up the chalice brimming full and running over.

> *By a Thousand Fires*, Prologue   *1967*

4 But life has taught me that it knows better plans than we can imagine, so that I try to submerge my own desires, apt to be too insistent, into a calm willingness to accept what comes, and to make the most of it, then wait again. I have discovered that there is a Pattern, larger and more beautiful than our short vision can weave. . . .

> Ibid., Epilogue

585. Mary E. Buell
(fl. 1890s)

* * *

1 Something made of nothing, tasting very sweet,
A most delicious compound, with ingredients complete;
But if, as on occasion, the heart and mind are sour,
It has no great significance, and loses half its power.

> "The Kiss"

586. Harriet L. Childe-Pemberton
(fl. 1890s)

1 As I allays say to my brother,
If it isn't one thing it's the tother.

> "Geese: A Dialogue," *Dead Letters and Other Narrative and Dramatic Pieces*   *1896*

2 MURIEL. In fact you expect me to submit to your un-
reasonableness because you haven't the courage to be
honest. How like a man!   Ibid., "The Deuce of Clubs"

3 MRS. CATERMOLE MACFADIE. No one will deny that
things that are wrong frequently have their roots in
things that are right; therefore, things that are right are
things that are wrong. We are nothing if not logical;
and when you have once become a member of the Sour
Grape Club, of the Ishamelites Club, and of the Clean-
Sweepers League, you will understand these matters
with a more enlightened apprehension.   Ibid.

4 Whenever any one tells me that he or she has a headache, has business letters to write,—doesn't want to be
disturbed,—I take it for granted that he or she is engaged in something nothing less than wicked—and naturally I don't want to know anything about it!
                      Ibid., "Smoke: A Monologue"

5 O beautiful Earth! alive, aglow,
    With your million things that grow,
  I would lay my head on your ample knee. . . .
        "Songs of Earth," I, St. 1, *Nenuphar*   *1911*

6 Earth rules all her children by the solar clock;—
    Should they dare to mock,
  Running loose before she gives them leave,
  They assuredly will grieve.   Ibid., II, St. 2

7 For Passion has come to the verge and leaps
    Headlong to the blind abyss,
  Yet gathers thereby the strength of deeps,
  And eddies a moment and swirls and sweeps
    Till peril is one with bliss!
                      Ibid., "Songs of Water," IV, St. 4

8 O sensitive Air who are one with Thought,
    To my seeking soul you have brought
  (On wings of silence or breeze or gale,)
    Your manifold messages. . . .
                      Ibid., "Songs of Air," X, St. 1

9 "There is no fear for those who truly see
    What is, or will be, springs from all that was,—
  How all that happens fitly has to be,
    And what ye name 'effect' and 'cause'
      Make up but one decree."
                      Ibid., "Songs of Fire," IX, St. 7

587. Lina Eckenstein
(fl. 1890s–1931)

1 The contributions of nuns to literature, as well as incidental remarks, show that the curriculum of study in the nunnery was as liberal as that accepted by the monks, and embraced all available writing whether by Christian or profane authors.

Women Under Monasticism   1896

588. Anita Owen
(fl. 1890s)

1 And in these eyes the love-light lies
And lies—and lies and lies!

"Dreamy Eyes"   *c.1894*

2 . . . Daisies won't tell.

"Sweet Bunch of Daisies"   *1894*

589. Hattie Starr
(fl. 1890s)

1 Nobody loves me, well do I know,
Don't all the cold world tell me so?

"Nobody Loves Me"   *1893*

2 Somebody loves me; How do I know?
Somebody's eyes have told me so!

"Somebody Loves Me"   *1893*

590. Daisy Ashford
(1890?–1972)

1 I am parshial [sic] to ladies if they are nice. I suppose it is my nature. I am not quite a gentleman but you would hardly notice it.

*The Young Visitors,** Ch. 1   *1919*

2 You look rather rash my dear your colours don't quite match your face.   Ibid., Ch. 2

* Written when the author was nine years old.

3 Here I am tied down to this life he said. . . . Being
royal has many painful drawbacks.

Ibid., Ch. 6

4 My life will be sour grapes and ashes without you.

Ibid., Ch. 8

591. Elizabeth Gurley Flynn
(1890–1964)

1 He was *an agitator*, born of the first national awakening of American labor. The shame of servitude and the
glory of struggle were emblazoned in the mind of every
worker who heard [Eugene V.] Debs.

"Eugene V. Debs," *Debs, Haywood,*
Ruthenberg   1939

2 We study their lives to understand better the past, as
lessons for the present and inspiration for the future.
The past is the background, the struggle part. . . .

Ibid., Conclusion

3 Time was, when the ACLU was young, they were An-
archists, Socialists, Christian pacifists, trade unionists,
I.W.W., Quaker, Irish Republican and Communist! To-
day, they are no longer heretics, non-conformists, radicals—they are respectable.

"I Am Expelled from Civil Liberties!,"
Sunday Worker   March 17, 1940

4 History has a long-range perspective. It ultimately passes stern judgment on tyrants and vindicates those who
fought, suffered, were imprisoned, and died for human
freedom, against political oppression and economic
slavery. Pioneers who were reviled, persecuted, ridi-
culed, and abused when they fought for free public
schools, woman's suffrage against chattel slavery, for
labor unions, are honored and revered today.

Labor's Own: William Z. Foster   1949

5 We know that the solid foundation of a Communist
Party are the workers and that our Party must be
rooted in their struggle. . . . A study of the inner
workings of capitalism with all its failures and contradictions, its excesses and abuses, will convince them
that capitalism's days are numbered; it has been tried
and found wanting; it hampers progress. . . . Negro

and white workers, young workers, women workers—
will come to understand the need of being a member of
the Communist Party. . . .

Ibid.

6 We hated the rich, the trusts they owned, the violence
they caused, the oppression they represented.
The Rebel Girl, Pt. I   1955

7 I said then and am still convinced that the full opportunity for women to become free and equal citizens with
access to all spheres of human endeavor cannot come
under capitalism, although many demands have been
won by organized struggle.

Ibid.

8 "What freedom?" we asked again. To be wage-slaves,
hired and fired at the will of a soulless corporation,
paid low wages for long hours, driven by the speed of a
machine? What freedom? To be clubbed, jailed, shot
down—and while we spoke, the hoofs of the troopers'
horses clattered by on the street.

Ibid., Pt. III

9 So confident was he [Nicola Sacco] of his innocence
that sunny afternoon that he had no fear. He was sure
when he told his story in court he would go free. He
did not know that he was approaching the valley of the
shadow of death. He feared no evil because the truth
was with him. But greed, corruption, prejudice, fear
and hatred of radical foreign-born workingmen were
weaving a net around him.

Ibid., Pt. VII

10 I was a convict, a prisoner without rights, writing a
censored letter. But my head was unbowed. Come what
may, *I was a political prisoner* and proud of it, at one
with some of the noblest of humanity who had suffered
for conscience's sake. I felt no shame, no humiliation,
no consciousness of guilt. To me my number 11710 was
a badge of honor.

The Alderson Story,* Ch. 3   1963

11 One of my correspondents asked me: "What do you
think are the main differences between a women's
prison and a men's prison?" I replied: "You would

* The Federal Reformatory for Women at Alderson, West Virginia.

never see diapers hung on a line at a men's prison or hear babies crying in the hospital on a quiet Sunday afternoon." The physiological differences—menstruation, menopause, and pregnancy—create intense emotional problems among many women in prison.

Ibid., Ch. 13

12 A popular saying in Alderson went as follows: "They work us like a horse, feed us like a bird, treat us like a child, dress us like a man—and then expect us to act like a lady."

Ibid., Ch. 25

13 We who are members of the Communist Party repudiate the exclusive identification of democracy with capitalism. We declare that democracy can be widened, take on new aspects, become truly a rule of the people, only when it is extended to the economic life of the people, as in the Soviet Union. As far as women are concerned, the U.S.S.R. is a trailblazer for equal rights and equal opportunities.

Defense Speech (May 7, 1940), The
Trial of Elizabeth Gurley Flynn by
the American Civil Liberties Union,
Corliss Lamont, ed.   1968

592. Frances Noyes Hart
(1890–1943)

1 "I cried at first . . . and then, it was such a beautiful day, that I forgot to be unhappy."

"Green Garden," Scribner's Magazine   1921

593. Hedda Hopper
(1890–1966)

1 At one time I thought he wanted to be an actor. He had certain qualifications, including no money and a total lack of responsibility.

From Under My Hat   1952

2 I decided that [Arthur] Brisbane was a member of the 7-H club—Holy howling hell, how he hates himself.

Ibid.

3 His footprints* were never asked for, yet no one has ever filled his shoes.

Ibid.

4 In Hollywood gratitude is Public Enemy Number One.

Ibid.

594. Rose Fitzgerald Kennedy
(1890–   )

1 The secret of the Kennedy successes in politics was not money but meticulous planning and organization, tremendous effort and the enthusiasm and devotion of family and friends.

Times to Remember   1974

2 Sedentary people are apt to have sluggish minds. A sluggish mind is apt to be reflected in flabbiness of body and in a dullness of expression that invites no interest and gets none.

Ibid.

3 Birds sing after a storm; why shouldn't people feel as free to delight in whatever remains to them?

Ibid.

4 We cannot always understand the ways of Almighty God—the crosses which He sends us, the sacrifices which He demands of us. . . . But we accept with faith and resignation His holy will with no looking back to what might have been, and we are at peace.

Ibid., Television Broadcast After
Robert Kennedy's Death (1968)

595. Beatrice Llewellyn-Thomas
(1890–?)

* * *

1 O We have a desperate need of laughter!
Give us laughter, Puck!

"To Puck"

* Referring to D.W. Griffith and Grauman's Theatre in Hollywood.

596. Mariia, Grand Duchess of Russia
(1890–1958)

1 . . . death, the mysterious disillusion and disappearance, of a human being.
Education of a Princess, Ch. 1   *1930*

2 Girls' games never have any interest for me; I hated dolls; the congealed expression on their porcelain faces provoked me. It was with lead soldiers that we played, without ever growing tired.

Ibid., Ch. 3

3 Russia still writhed and stumbled. The wave of revolts and uprisings, the constant agitations, the incessant inflammatory orations of men possessed of little political competence, had by this time cowed the emperor and the ruling class into bewildered and sullen inertia.

Ibid., Ch. 8

4 The mouthpiece of the so-called public opinion; those men, who by high-sounding formulas had so impressed the densely ignorant masses. . . . They had neither sufficient moral force nor experience necessary to build up a new system. Their mental store was limited to theories, often excellent but inapplicable to reality.

Ibid.

597. Aimee Semple McPherson
(1890–1944)

1 O Hope! dazzling, radiant Hope!—What a change thou bringest to the hopeless; brightening the darkened paths, and cheering the lonely way.
This Is That, Pt. I, Ch. 1   *1923*

2 We are all making a crown for Jesus out of these daily lives of ours, either a crown of golden, divine love, studded with gems of sacrifice and adoration, or a thorny crown, filled with the cruel briars of unbelief, or selfishness, and sin, and placing it upon His brow.

Ibid., Pt. II, "What Shall I Do with Jesus"

3 Right here let us make it plain, that each individual is either a sinner or a saint. It is impossible to be both; it

is impossible to be neutral; there is no half-way business in God. Either you are the child of the Lord or you are serving the devil—there is no middle territory.

Ibid., "The Two Houses"

4 "Pit-a-pat! Pit-a-pat!"—say the hundreds and thousands of feet, surging by the church doors of our land. "Pat! Pat! Pit-a-pat!"—hurrying multitudes, on business and pleasure bent.

Ibid., "Is Jesus Christ the Great 'I Am' or Is He the Great 'I Was'?"

598. Katherine Anne Porter
(1890–   )

1 She had sat down and read the letter over again; but there were phrases that insisted on being read many times, they had a life of their own separate from the others. . . .

"Theft," *Flowering Judas and Other Stories*   1930

2 In this moment she felt that she had been robbed of an enormous number of valuable things, whether material or intangible: things lost or broken by her own fault, things she had forgotten and left in houses when she moved: books borrowed from her and not returned, journeys she had planned and had not made, words she had waited to hear spoken to her and had not heard, and the words she meant to answer with. . . .

Ibid.

3 . . . all that she had had, and all that she had missed, were lost together, and were twice lost in this landslide of remembered losses.

Ibid.

4 She laid the purse on the table and sat down with the cup of chilled coffee, and thought: I was right not to be afraid of any thief but myself, who will end by leaving me nothing.   Ibid.

5   "*What* could you buy with a hundred dollars?" she asked fretfully.

"Nothing, nothing at all," said their father, "a hundred dollars is just something you put in the bank."

Old Mortality, Pt. II   1936

6 "It don't *look* right," was his final reason for not doing anything he did not wish to do.

Noon Wine 1937

7 "I don't see no reason to hold it against a man because he went loony once or twice in his lifetime and so I don't expect to take no steps about it. Not a step. I've got nothin' against the man, he's always treated me fair. They's things and people," he went on, "'nough to drive any man loony. The wonder to me is, more men don't wind up in straitjackets, the way things are going these days and times."

Ibid.

8 Nothing is mine, I have only nothing but it is enough, it is beautiful and it is all mine. Do I even walk about in my own skin or is it something I have borrowed to spare my modesty?

Pale Horse, Pale Rider 1939

9 After working for three years on a morning newspaper she had an illusion of maturity and experience; but it was fatigue merely. . . .

Ibid.

10 "Adam," she said, "the worst of war is the fear and suspicion and the awful expression in all the eyes you meet . . . as if they had pulled down the shutters over their minds and their hearts and were peering out at you, ready to leap if you make one gesture or say one word they do not understand instantly."

Ibid.

11 "The mind and the heart sometimes get another chance, but if anything happens to the poor old human frame, why, it's just out of luck, that's all."

Ibid.

12 No more war, no more plague, only the dazed silence that follows the ceasing of the heavy guns; noiseless houses with the shades drawn, empty streets, the dead cold light of tomorrow. Now there would be time for everything.

Ibid.

13 All believed they were bound for a place for some reason more desirable than the place they were leaving, but it was necessary to make the change with the least possible delay and expense. Delay and expense had

been their common portion at the hands of an army of professional tip-seekers, fee-collectors, half-asleep consular clerks and bored migration officials who were not in the least concerned whether the travelers gained their ship or dropped dead in their tracks.

Ship of Fools, Pt. I   1962

14 "People on a boat, Mary, can't seem to find any middle ground between stiffness, distrust, total rejection, or a kind of evasive, gnawing curiosity. Sometimes it's a friendly enough curiosity, sometimes sly and malicious, but you feel as if you were being eaten alive by fishes."

Ibid., Pt. II

15 Miracles are instantaneous, they cannot be summoned, but come of themselves, usually at unlikely moments and to those who least expect them.

Ibid., Pt. III

16 They exchanged one or two universal if minor truths— pleasure was so often more exhausting then the hardest work; they had both noticed that a life of dissipation sometimes gave to a face the look of gaunt suffering spirituality that a life of asceticism was supposed to give and quite often did not.

Ibid.

17 "The real sin against life is to abuse and destroy beauty, even one's own—even more, one's own, for that had been put in our care and we are responsible for its well-being. . . ."

Ibid.

18 Such ignorance. All the boys were in military schools and all the girls were in the convent, and that's all you need to say about it.

Quoted in "Lioness of Literature
Looks Back" by Henry Allen,
Los Angeles Times   July 7, 1974

19 It is disaster to have a man fall in love with me. They aren't content to take what I can give; they want everything from me.

Ibid.

20 Evil puts up a terrible fight. And it always wins in the end. I do not understand the world, but I watch its progress. I am not reconciled. I will not forgive it.

Ibid.

21 No man can be explained by his personal history, least of all a poet. *Ibid.*

22 My grandmother, when she heard that Mr. Lincoln had abolished slavery and the Negroes were free, was heard to say "I hope it works both ways," and lived to realize that it did not.
"Notes on the Texas I Remember,"
The Atlantic   *March, 1975*

599. Rachel
(1890–1931)

1 Like a bird in the butcher's palm you flutter in my hand, insolent pride.
"Revolt," *Poems from the Hebrew*,
Robert Mezey, ed.   *1973p*

2 This is a bond nothing can ever loosen.
What I have lost: what I possess forever.
Ibid., "My Dead"

600. Ellen West
(1890?–1923?)

1 I am twenty-one years old and am supposed to be silent and grin like a puppet.
Diary Entry (c.1911), Quoted in
Women and Madness by
Phyllis Chesler   *1972p*

601. Margaret Culkin Banning
(1891–   )

1 I get a little angry about this highhanded scrapping of the looks of things. What else have we to go by? How else can the average person form an opinion of a girl's sense of values or even of her chastity except by the looks of her conduct?   *Letters to Susan*   1936

2 You wouldn't be caught wearing cheap perfume, would you? Then why do you want to wear cheap perfume on your conduct?   *Ibid.*

3 Did it ever occur to you that there's something almost crooked in the way decent girls nowadays use the shelter of their established respectability to make things awkward for men?

Ibid.

4 It isn't easy to be the person who sometimes has to try to preserve your happiness at the expense of your fun.

Ibid.

5 The women's magazines are advertising mediums as well as publishers of fiction and articles on current subjects. They are fashion and marketing experts, instructors in home economics.

Ibid.

602. Fanny Brice
(1891–1951)

1 Your audience gives you everything you need. They tell you. There is no director who can direct you like an audience.

Quoted in The Fabulous Fanny, Ch. 6
by Norman Katkov   1952p

2 Being a funny person does an awful lot of things to you. You feel that you mustn't get serious with people. They don't expect it from you, and they don't want to see it. You're not entitled to be serious, you're a clown, and they only want you to make them laugh.

Ibid., Ch. 9

3 After the emotion is ended in your life, I found I got great joy from just being myself and relaxing. When love is out of your life, you're through in a way. Because while it is there it's like a motor that's going, you have such vitality to do things, big things, because love is goosing you all the time. I found, after the love, that I needed help to keep going.

Ibid., Ch. 19

4 Let the world know you as you are, not as you think you should be, because sooner or later, if you are posing, you will forget the pose, and then where are you?

Ibid., Ch. 24

603. Agatha Christie
(1891–1975)

1 Curious things, habits. People themselves never knew they had them.
Witness for the Prosecution 1924

2 "My friend—I had to save him. The evidence of a woman devoted to him would not have been enough— you hinted as much yourself. But I know something of the psychology of crowds. Let my evidence be wrung from me, as an admission, damning me in the eyes of the law, and a reaction in favor of the prisoner would immediately set in."
Ibid.

3 It is completely unimportant. That is why it is so interesting.
The Murder of Roger Ackroyd 1926

4 LADY ANGKATELL. People are quite right when they say nature in the mild is seldom raw.
The Hollow, Act I 1952

5 LADY ANGKATELL. Tradespeople are just like gardeners. They take advantage of your not knowing.
Ibid.

6 GUDGEON. The trouble is there are no proper *employers* nowadays.
Ibid.

7 HENRIETTA. I say the word, you know, over and over again to myself. Dead-dead-dead-dead—and soon it hasn't any meaning, it hasn't any meaning at all. Just a funny little word like the breaking of a rotten branch. Dead-dead-dead-dead-dead.
Ibid., Act II, Sc. 2

8 CLARISSA. Oh dear, I never realized what a terrible lot of explaining one has to do in a murder!
Spider's Web, Act II, Sc. 1 1956

9 SIR ROWLAND. You must know better than I do, Inspector, how very rarely two people's account of the same thing agrees. In fact, if three people were to agree ex-

actly, I should regard it as suspicious. Very suspicious, indeed.

Ibid., Sc. 2

10 TREVES. If one sticks too rigidly to one's principles one would hardly see anybody.

Toward's Zero, Act I   1957

11 TREVES. In my experience, pride is a word often on women's lips—but they display little sign of it where love affairs are concerned.

Ibid.

12 Is there ever any particular spot where one can put one's finger and say, "It all began that day, at such a time and such a place, with such an incident?"

Endless Night, Bk. I, Ch. 1   1967

13 . . . money isn't so hot, after all. What with incipient heart attacks, lots of bottles of little pills you have to take all the time, and losing your temper over the food or the service in hotels. Most of the rich people I've known have been fairly miserable.

Ibid., Ch. 3

14 I didn't want to work. It was as simple as that. I distrusted work, disliked it. I thought it was a very bad thing that the human race had unfortunately invented for itself.

Ibid.

15 One of the oddest things in life, I think, is the things one remembers.

Ibid.

16 "Look here," I said, "people like to collect disasters."

Ibid., Ch. 5

17 To put it quite crudely . . . the poor don't really know how the rich live, and the rich don't know how the poor live, and to find out is really enchanting to both of them.

Ibid., Bk. II, Ch. 9

18 "Doctors can do almost anything nowadays, can't they, unless they kill you first while they're trying to cure you."

Ibid., Ch. 11

19 Every Night and every Morn
 Some to Misery are born.
 Every Morn and every Night
 Some are born to Sweet Delight,
 Some are born to Endless Night.

Ibid., Ch. 14

20 One doesn't recognize in one's life the really important
 moments—not until it's too late.

Ibid.

21 It's astonishing in this world how things don't turn out
 at all the way you expect them to!

Ibid., Ch. 15

22 Where large sums of money are concerned, it is advis-
 able to trust nobody.

Ibid.

604. Laura Gilpin
(1891–   )

1 A river seems a magic thing. A magic, moving, living
 part of the very earth itself—for it is from the soil, both
 from its depth and from its surface, that a river has its
 beginning.

The Rio Grande, Introduction   *1949*

2 . . . much earnest philosophical thought is born of the
 life which springs from close association with nature.

Ibid., "The Source"

3 Since the earliest-known existence of human life in the
 Western World, all manner of men have trod the river's
 banks. With his progressing knowledge and experience,
 man has turned these life-giving waters upon the soil,
 magically evoking an increasing bounty from the arid
 land. But through misuse of its vast drainage areas—
 the denuding of forest lands and the destruction of soil-
 binding grasses—the volume of the river has been dim-
 inished, as once generous tributaries have become
 parched *arroyos*. Will present and future generations
 have the vision and wisdom to correct these abuses,
 protect this heritage, and permit a mighty river to fulfill its highest destiny?

Ibid., "The Delta"

605. Vivian Yeiser Laramore
(1891–?)

* * *

1 I've shut the door on yesterday
   And thrown the key away—
To-morrow holds no fears for me,
   Since I have found to-day.   "To-day"

2 Talk to me tenderly, tell me lies;
  I am a woman and time flies.

                 "Talk to Me Tenderly"

606. Irene Rutherford McLeod
(1891–1964?)

1 I'm a lean dog, a keen dog, a wild dog, and alone.
     "Lone Dog," *Songs to Save a Soul*   1919

607. Anne Nichols
(1891–1966)

1 MRS. COHEN. How early it iss of late!
           Abie's Irish Rose, Act I   1922

2 FATHER WHALEN. Shure, we're all trying to get to the
same place when we pass on. We're just going by different routes. We can't all go on the same train.

   RABBI. And just because you are not riding on my
train, why should I say your train won't get there?
                 Ibid., Act II

608. Victoria Ocampo
(1891–   )

1 Some regions of the earth, which are not rich or picturesque, attract us because of a mysterious relationship
we have with them.
        "A Man of the Desert," *338171TE*
        (Lawrence of Arabia)   1947

2 He [T. E. Lawrence] was of the same stuff as the saints, and like them he had to find perfection in himself, and not like a great artist in the work he had conceived and executed.

Ibid., "Childhood"

3 In literature homosexuality is always the occasion for detailed grandiloquent justifications and scientific reflections, or of obscure unclean explanation mixed up with a sense of guilt, or a weakness which turns out to be bragging. You apologize and then preen yourself upon it.

Ibid., "Homosexuality"

4 Sadism, masochism, neuroses, suppressed desires, complexes, all those things which psychoanalysis invents in order to debunk the scruples and ardent aspirations of mankind and their rebirth in secular disguises, are not sufficient to explain them.

Ibid., "The Flesh"

5 . . . there is a touch of optimism in every worry about one's own moral cleanliness.

Ibid., "Scruples and Ambitions"

6 Moral, like physical, cleanliness is not acquired once and for all: it can only be kept and renewed by a habit of constant watchfulness and discipline.

Ibid.

7 This eagerness to seek hidden but necessary connections, connections that revealed a close relationship between the world where I was born in the flesh and the other worlds where I was reborn, has been the enterprise of my whole life.

Speech, American Academy of Arts
and Letters, New York   1973

609. Ruth Law Oliver
(1891?–1970)

1 I had a great desire to take off and go somewhere in flight, never having done it.

Quoted in *The American Heritage*
History of Flight, Ch. 4   1962

610. Marie Rambert
(1891–   )

1 We want to create an atmosphere in which creation is possible.

Quoted in "Ballet Rambert: The
Company That Changed Its Mind"
by John Percival, *Dancemagazine*
February, 1973

2 I don't do cartwheels any more, but I still do a *barre* to keep supple.

Ibid., "Old School Tights"
by Beryl Hilary Ostlere

611. Nelly Sachs
(1891–1970)

1 O you chimneys,
O you fingers
And Israel's body as smoke through the air!

"O the Chimneys," St. 4,
O the Chimneys   1967

2 When sleep leaves the body like smoke
and man, sated with secrets,
drives the overworked nag of quarrel
out of its stall,
then the fire-breathing union begins anew. . . .

Ibid., "When Sleep Enters the Body
Like Smoke," St. 3

3 Peoples of the earth,
leave the words at their source,
for it is they that can nudge
the horizons into the true heaven. . . .

Ibid., "People of the Earth," St. 4

4 You, the inexperienced, who learn nothing in the nights.
Many angels are given you
But you do not see them.

"Chorus of Clouds," *The Seeker
and Other Poems*   1970

5 Are graves breath-space for longing?
>   *Ibid.*, "Are Graves Breath-Space for Longing?"

6 But how shall time be drawn
> from the golden threads of the sun?
> Wound
> for the cocoon of the silken butterfly
> night?

>   *Ibid.*, "Hunter"

612. Mary Ambrose
(1892–)

1 The true vocation [of a nun is] settled on the day the girl looks around her and sees a young woman her own age in pretty clothes wheeling a baby carriage by the convent. Then her heart takes an awful flop and she knows what it is God really is asking of her.

>   Quoted in *Life*   *March 15, 1963*

613. Djuna Barnes
(1892–)

1 She knew what was troubling him, thwarted instincts, common beautiful instincts that he was being robbed of.

>   "A Night Among the Horses,"
>   *The Little Review*   *1918*

2 No man needs curing of his individual sickness; his universal malady is what he should look to.

>   *Nightwood*   *1937*

3 No, I am not a neurasthenic; I haven't that much respect for people—the basis, by the way, of all neurasthenia.

>   *Ibid.*

614. Stella Benson
(1892–1933)

1 Call no man foe, but never love a stranger.
Build up no plan, nor any star pursue.
Go forth in crowds, in loneliness is danger.

Thus nothing fate can send,
And nothing fate can do
Shall pierce your peace, my friend.

"To the Unborn," St. 3,
This Is the End   1917

2 Family jokes, though rightly cursed by strangers, are the bond that keeps most families alive.

Pipers and a Dancer, Ch. 9   1924

615. Pearl S. Buck
(1892–1973)

1 It is better to be first with an ugly woman than the hundreth with a beauty.

The Good Earth, Ch. 1   1931

2 "We will eat meat that we can buy or beg, but not that which we steal. Beggars we may be but thieves we are not."

Ibid., Ch. 12

3 "Hunger makes a thief of any man."

Ibid., Ch. 15

4 "I do not need to tell you that there are no honorable rulers, and the people cry out under the cruelties and oppression of those who ought to treat them as fathers treat their sons."

Sons   1932

5 "Now we revolutionists are against every sort of god; our own or foreign, we are against them all and someday we will tear down temples, we will tear down gods. But if men in their ignorance must believe for a while in some god, let it be their own and not a foreign superstition such as these preach."

The Young Revolutionist, Ch. 6   1932

6 "Men do not take good iron to make nails nor good men to make soldiers."

Ibid., Ch. 8

7 "There was an old abbot in one temple and he said something of which I think often and it was this, that when men destroy their old gods they will find new ones to take their place."   Ibid., Ch. 15

8 "A woman must learn to obey. We must not ask why. We cannot help our birth. We must accept it and do the duty that is ours in this lifetime."

"The First Wife," *First Wife and Other Stories* 1933

9 Man was lost if he went to a usurer, for the interest ran faster than a tiger upon him. . . .

Ibid., "The Frill"

10 "But that land—it is one thing that will still be there when I come back—land is always there. . . ."

A House Divided, Ch. 1 1935

11 They were all trying so hard to live as they felt it beautiful to live, and their houses were so small—too small and too close, so that they had constantly to hush the crying of their children and their own laughter or anger or weeping as well. They had only silence to keep them private from each other. And they needed privacy, since they were not ignorant people and since decency was a necessity to them. They could make a joke of poverty and did.

This Proud Heart, Ch. 1 1938

12 Travel, the casual come and go of strange faces, people for whom she cared nothing and who did not care for her, these were not her life. She had to live not in that passing world but in her own deeps.

Ibid., Ch. 2

13 I feel no need for any other faith than my faith in human beings.

I Believe 1939

14 There were many ways of breaking a heart. Stories were full of hearts broken by love, but what really broke a heart was taking away its dream—whatever that dream might be.

The Patriot, Pt. II 1939

15 "We shall fight until all anti-Japanese feeling is stamped out and the Chinese are ready to co-operate with us."

I-wan stared at him, not believing what he heard.

"You mean," he repeated, "you will kill us and bomb our cities—and—and—rape our women—until we learn to love you?"

Ibid.

16 When hope is taken away from the people moral degeneration follows swiftly after.

Letter to the Editor,
The New York Times
November 14, 1941

17 . . . the basic discovery about any people is the discovery of the relationship between its men and women.

Of Men and Women, Ch. 1   *1941*

18 It is worse than folly . : . not to recognize the truth, for in it lies the tinder for tomorrow.

"Tinder for Tomorrow," *Asia*   *March, 1942*

19 For our democracy has been marred by imperialism, and it has been enlightened only by individual and sporadic efforts at freedom.

Speech, "Freedom for All," New York
March 14, 1942

20   I remember as a child hearing my impatient missionary father . . . [as] he explained to an elderly Chinese gentleman, "Does it mean nothing to you that if you reject Christ you will burn in hell?"
   The Chinese gentleman smiled as he replied, "If, as you say, my ancestors are all in hell at this moment, it would be unfilial of me not to be willing to suffer with them."

Speech, "The Chinese Mind and
India," Boston   *April 28, 1942*

21 One faces the future with one's past. . . .

Lecture, "China Faces the Future,"
New York   *October 13, 1942*

22 There is no way of dividing us. We are different races, and that is a division. We are of different nations, and that is a division. Religion is a division, and wealth is a division, and education is a division. Climate and geography and food have their dividing effects, and so has history. But war is the great simplifier.

"The Spirit Behind the Weapon,"
Survey Graphics   *November, 1942*

23 Fate proceeds inexorably . . . only upon the passive individual, the passive people. . . . Fate may be foreseen unacknowledged.

Address to Nobel Prize Winners,
New York   *December 10, 1942*

24 Every era of renaissance has come out of new freedoms for peoples. The coming renaissance will be greater than any in human history, for this time all the peoples of the earth will share in it.

What America Means to Me,
Introduction   1942

25 Every great mistake has a halfway moment, a split second when it can be recalled and perhaps remedied.

Ibid., Ch. 10

26 But when you remember the suffering, which you have not deserved, do not think of vengeance, as the small man does. Remember, rather, as the great remember, that which they have unjustly suffered, and determine only that such suffering shall not be possible again for any human being anywhere.

"A Letter to Colored Americans,"
American Unity and Asia   1942

27   "Who knows what you'll tell?" Wang Ma said severely.
    "I never tell anything I know," Peony said demurely.
    Wang Ma put down the bowl. "What do you know?" she inquired.
    "Now you want me to tell," Peony said, smiling.

The Bondsmaid, Ch. 1   1949

28 "Believing in gods always causes confusion."

Ibid.

29 She had always been too wise to tell him all she thought and felt, knowing by some intuition of her own womanhood that no man wants to know everything of any woman.

— Ibid., Ch. 4

30 Self-expression must pass into communication for its fulfillment. . . .

"In Search of Readers," *The Writer's Book,* Helen Hull, ed.   1950

31 The average person, fool that he often is, interests and amuses me more than the rare and extraordinary individual. The ways of common people are enchanting and funny and profound.   Ibid.

32 There are persons who honestly do not see the use of books in the home, either for information—have they

not radio and even television?—or for decoration—is there not the wallpaper?

Ibid.

33 Introversion, at least if extreme, is a sign of mental and spiritual immaturity.

Ibid.

34 Endurance can be a harsh and bitter root in one's life, bearing poisonous and gloomy fruit, destroying other lives. Endurance is only the beginning. There must be acceptance and the knowledge that sorrow fully accepted brings its own gifts. For there is an alchemy in sorrow. It can be transmuted into wisdom. . . .

The Child Who Never Grew, Ch. 1   1950

35 Americans are all too soft. I am not soft. It is better to be hard, so that you can know what to do.

Ibid.

36 Euthanasia is a long, smooth-sounding word, and it conceals its danger as long, smooth words do, but the danger is there, nevertheless.

Ibid., Ch. 2

37 Ours is an individualistic society, indeed, and the state must do for the individual what the family does for the older civilizations.

Ibid.

38 Children who never grow are human beings, and suffer as human beings, inarticulately but deeply nevertheless. The human creature is always more than an animal.

Ibid., Ch. 3

39 We had no police and needed none, because the family was responsible for all its members. . . . The child in Asia is loved not only for its own sake but as a symbol of hope for the future of both family and nation.

Children for Adoption, Ch. 1   1964

40 The American woman, when she is an unmarried mother, simply disappears for a while from her community and then comes back, childless, her secret hidden for life.

Ibid.

41 What is a neglected child? He is a child not planned for, not wanted. Neglect begins, therefore, before he is born.

Ibid., Ch. 3

42 The community must assume responsibility for each child within its confines. Not one must be neglected whatever his condition. The community must see that every child gets the advantages and opportunities which are due him as a citizen and as a human being.
Ibid., Ch. 4

43 The problem of the mixed-race child, born displaced in the world community, must be faced in its entirety. It can be no credit to the United States to have half-American children running about as beggars and potential criminals in the streets of Asian cities and on the islands of the Pacific.
Ibid., Ch. 7

44 If our American way of life fails the child, it fails us all.
Ibid., Ch. 9

45 It is indeed exasperating to have a memory that begins too young and continues too long. I know, because this is my memory. It goes back too far, it holds everything too fast, it does not forget anything—a relentless, merciless, disobedient memory, for there are some things I would like to forget. But I never forget.
China, Past and Present, Ch. 1 *1972*

46 Nothing and no one can destroy the Chinese people. They are relentless survivors. They are the oldest civilized people on earth. Their civilization passes through phases but its basic characteristics remain the same. They yield, they bend to the wind, but they never break.
Ibid.

47 Ah well, perhaps one has to be very old before one learns how to be amused rather than shocked.
Ibid., Ch. 6

48 No one really understood music unless he was a scientist, her father had declared, and not just a scientist, either, oh, no, only the real ones, the theoreticians, whose language was mathematics. She had not understood mathematics until he had explained to her that it was the symbolic language of relationships. "And relationships," he had told her, "contained the essential meaning of life."
The Goddess Abides, Pt. I *1972*

49 I contemplate death as though I were continuing after its arrival. I, therefore, survive since I can contemplate myself afterward as well as before.

Ibid.

50 "A hand is not only an implement, it's a sense organ. It's the eye of a blind man, it's the tone of those who cannot speak."

Ibid., Pt. II

* * *

51 Be born anywhere, little embryo novelist, but do not be born under the shadow of a great creed, not under the burden of original sin, not under the doom of salvation.   "Advice to Unborn Novelists"

52 Go out and be born among gypsies or thieves or among happy workaday people who live with the sun and do not think about their souls.

Ibid.

616. Ivy Compton-Burnett
(1892–1969)

1 "But a gentlewoman is not able to spin gold out of straw; it required a full princess to do that."
A House and Its Head, Ch. 1   1935

2 "We do not discuss the members of our family to their faces. . . ."

Ibid., Ch. 11

3 "It is no good to think that other people are out to serve our interests."
Elders and Betters, Ch. 1   1944

4 "It is a lonely business, waiting to be translated to another sphere."   Ibid., Ch. 7

5 "The relationship is only a shadow, but a shadow is not always easy to elude."
Two Worls and Their Ways, Ch. 3   1949

6 "I do like approving of things. It is disapproving of them that is disturbing."   Ibid., Ch. 4

7 "Parents have too little respect for their children, just as the children have too much for the parents. . . ."
Ibid., Ch. 5

8 "We will let the dead past bury its dead, and go back to the old days and the old ways and the old happiness."

Ibid.

9 "We can build upon foundations anywhere, if they are well and truly laid."

Ibid., Ch. 7

10 "We are all children up to a point in our own homes. I expect it is the same with all of you. And we shall have plenty of time to be grown-up."

"If I were not a child with my parents, they would be more unloving towards me," said Gwendolen.

Ibid.

11 "My youth is escaping without giving me anything it owes me."

A Heritage and Its History,
Ch. 1   1959

12 "There is no change. That is your trouble. You want me to be altered by my father's death. And I have not been, and shall not be. I am what I am."

Ibid., Ch. 3

13 "Civilised life exacts its toll."

Ibid., Ch. 9

14 "There is no need to act on a truth that might never have emerged. It would not have in most cases, should not have, to my mind. Many must lie unsaid. We can put it from us and go forward."

Ibid., Ch. 10

15 "A thing is not nothing, when it is all there is."

Ibid.

16 "She should be thinking of higher things."

"Nothing could be higher than food," said Leah.

The Mighty and Their Fall, Ch. 1   1961

17 "Destiny is over all of us, high or low."

Ibid., Ch. 2

18 "They must release each other in time for their lives to grow."

Ibid., Ch. 3

19 "Fancy daring to ask so much for yourself!" said Hugo.

"The more we ask, the more we have. And it is fair enough: asking is not always easy."

"And it is said to be hard to accept," said Lavinia. "So no wonder we have so little."

" 'Nothing venture, nothing have' is a heartless saying," said Egbert. "Fancy recognising that we may have nothing!"

"And we are to value things more when they don't come easily. There is no limit to the heartlessness."

Ibid., Ch. 7

20 "You and Ninian will have each other," said Hugo. "That foolish thing that is said, when that is all people have. As if they did not know it! It is the whole trouble."

"It is not only trouble," said Ninian, smiling at Teresa. "Or it is trouble shared and therefore less."

Ibid., Ch. 13

21 I have had such an uneventful life that there is little to say.

A Family and a Fortune   1962

22 When an age is ended you see it as it is.
Quoted in *The Life of Ivy Compton-Burnett* by Elizabeth Sprigge   1973p

23 Life makes great demands on people's characters, and gives them great opportunities to serve their own ends by the sacrifice of other people. Such ill doing may meet with little retribution, may indeed be hardly recognized, and I cannot feel so surprised if people yield to it.

Ibid.

617. Diana Cooper
(1892–   )

1 Naturally good until now, I had never lied, for nothing tempted me to lie except fear of wounding and I had nothing to fear. But now with the advent of the young men—benign serpents—came the apple . . . and many little lies to save her [mother's] disappointment in me. I felt that it was for happiness, and the only difficulties of the untruths were the crimson blushes and fears of detection. Childhood was over.

The Rainbow Comes and Goes, Ch. 5   1958

2 In astrology there is room for precaution and obstruction; the disaster is not inevitable. One can dodge the stars in their courses.

Trumpets from the Steep   1960

3 Childhood is stamped on the fair face of one's uncluttered memory as clearly as morning, and a heart beating with love, enterprise and procreancy seemed recordable, but when I come to armies clashing in the dark, to destruction, to the rulers and their strength, shortcomings or ambivalence . . . I am lost in a rabble of stampeding thoughts that can never be rounded up.

Ibid., Ch. 2

4 It helped me in the air to keep my small mind contained in earthly human limits, not lost in vertiginous space and elements unknown.

Ibid., Ch. 5

5 I'll write no more memories. They would get too sad, tender as they are. Age wins and one must learn to grow old. As I learnt with the loss of a nurse to put childish things behind me, as I learnt when the joys of dependence were over to embrace with fear the isolation of independence, so now I must learn to walk this long unlovely wintry way, looking for spectacles, shunning the cruel-looking glass, laughing at my clumsiness before others mistakenly condole, not expecting gallantry yet disappointed to receive none, apprehending every ache of shaft of pain, alive to blinding flashes of mortality, unarmed, totally vulnerable.

Ibid., Ch. 8

618. Janet Flanner
(1892–1978)

1 Never have nights been more beautiful than these nights of anxiety. In the sky have been shining in trinity the moon, Venus and Mars. Nature has been more splendid than man.

"Letter from Paris," *The New Yorker*
September 10, 1939

2 Paris is now the capital of limbo.

"Paris Germany," *The New Yorker*
December 7, 1940

3 The German passion for bureaucracy—for written and
signed forms, for files, statistics, and lists, and for
printed permissions to do this or that, to go here or
there, to move about, to work, to exist—is like a steel
pin pinning each French individual to a sheet of paper,
the way an entymologist pins each specimen insect past
struggling to his laboratory board.

Ibid.

4 In place of certainty there is only a vast, tangled ball of
rumor. In place of sensible, humane procedure, now
destroyed by wars, revenge, suspicion and power politics, petty official strictures have been built up against
which the individual is as helpless as a caged animal.

"The Escape of Mrs. Jeffries,"
The New Yorker
May 22, May 29, and June 5, 1943

619. Edna St. Vincent Millay
(1892–1950)

1 For my omniscience paid I toll
In infinite remorse of soul.

"Renascence," St. 2, *Renascence*
and Other Poems   1917

2 A grave is such a quiet place.

Ibid., St. 4

3 God, I can push the grass apart
And lay my finger on Thy heart.

Ibid., St. 7

4 The soul can split the sky in two,
And let the face of God shine through.

Ibid., St. 8

5 The room is full of you!

Ibid., "Interim," St. 1

6   What is the need of Heaven
When earth can be so sweet?

Ibid., St. 7

7   Strange how few,
After all's said and done, the things that are
Of moment.

Ibid., St. 8

8 I think our heart-strings were, like warp and woof
In some firm fabric, woven in and out. . . .

> *Ibid.*, St. 12

9   Not Truth, but Faith, it is
That keeps the world alive.

> *Ibid.*, St. 15

10 "Lonely I came, and I depart alone. . . ."

> *Ibid.*, "The Suicide," St. 1

11   "Father, I beg of Thee a little task
To dignify my days,—'tis all I ask. . . ."

> *Ibid.*, St. 12

12 Who told me time would ease me of my pain!

> *Ibid.*, "Time does not bring relief"

13 Life goes on forever like the gnawing of a mouse.

> *Ibid.*, "Ashes of Life," St. 3

14 O world, I cannot hold thee close enough!

> *Ibid.*, "God's World," St. 1

15 COLUMBINE. I cannot *live*
Without a macaroon!

> *Aria Da Capo*   1920

16 PIERROT. You see, I am always wanting
A little more than what I have,—or else
A little less.

> *Ibid.*

17 PIERROT. I am become a socialist. I love
Humanity; but I hate people.

> *Ibid.*

18 CORYDON. "Here is an hour,—in which to think
A mighty thought, and sing a trifling song,
And look at nothing."

> *Ibid.*

19 CORYDON. *Your* sheep! You are mad, to call them
Yours—mine—they are all one flock!

> *Ibid.*

20 CORYDON. We seem to be forgetting
It's only a game. . . .
But one of us has to take a risk, or else,
Why, don't you see?—the game goes on forever!

> *Ibid.*

21 PIERROT. Your mind is made of crumbs. . . .

Ibid.

22 COLUMBINE. If there's one thing I hate
Above everything else,—even more than getting my
feet wet—
It's clutter!

Ibid.

23 I had a little Sorrow,
Born of a little Sin.

"The Penitent," St. 1, *A Few
Figs from Thistles* 1920

24 My candle burns at both its ends;
    It will not last the night;
But oh, my foes, and oh, my friends—
    It gives a lovely light.

Ibid., "First Fig"

25 Whether or not we find what we are seeking
Is idle, biologically speaking.

Ibid., "I shall forget you presently"

26 We talk of taxes, and I call you friend.   Ibid.

27 After the feet of beauty fly my own.

Ibid., "Oh, think not I am faithful"

28 The fabric of my faithful love
    No power shall dim or ravel
Whilst I stay here,—but oh, my dear,
    If I should ever travel!

Ibid., "To the Not Impossible Him," St. 3

29 With him for a sire and her for a dam,
What should I be but just what I am?

Ibid., "The Singing-Woman
from the Wood's Edge," St. 9

30 Was it for this I uttered prayers,
And sobbed and cursed and kicked the stairs,
That now, domestic as a plate,
I should retire at half-past eight?   Ibid., "Grown-Up"

31 Cut if you will, with Sleep's dull knife,
    Each day to half its length, my friend,—
The years that time takes off my life,
    He'll take from off the other end!

Ibid., "Midnight Oil"

32 You leave me much against my will.
> Ibid., "To S.M. (If He Should Lie A-dying)"

33 Yet woman's ways are witless ways,
> As any sage will tell,—
And what am I, that I should love
> So wisely and so well?
>> Ibid., "The Philosopher," St. 4

34 Life in itself
Is nothing,
An empty cup, a flight of uncarpeted stairs.
> "Spring," *Second April*   1921

35   All my life,
Following Care along the dusty road,
Have I looked back at loveliness and sighed. . . .
> Ibid., "Journey," St. 1

36 Spring will not ail nor autumn falter;
> Nothing will know that you are gone. . . .
>> Ibid., "Elegy Before Death," St. 3

37 I make bean-stalks, I'm
> A builder, like yourself.
>> Ibid., "The Bean-Stalk," St. 4

38 Life is a quest and love a quarrel. . . .
> Ibid., "Weeds," St. 1

39 I am waylaid by Beauty.
> Ibid., "Assault," St. 2

40 *Down you mongrel, Death!*
> *Back into your kennel!*
>> Ibid., "The Poet and His Book," St. 1

41 Read me, do not let me die!
> Search the fading letters, finding
> Steadfast in the broken binding
All that once was I!
>> Ibid., St. 6

42 My heart is what it was before,
> A house where people come and go. . . .
>> Ibid., "Alms," St. 1

43 Many a bard's untimely death
Lends unto his verses breath. . . .
> Ibid., "To a Poet That Died Young," St. 3

44 Life must go on;
   I forget just why.

Ibid., "Lament"

45 Always I climbed the wave at morning,
   Shook the sand from my shoes at night,
That now am caught beneath great buildings,
   Stricken with noise, confused with light.

Ibid., "Exiled," St. 4

46 And what did I see I had not seen before?
   Only a question less or a question more. . . .

Ibid., "Wild Swans"

47 Longing alone is singer to the lute. . . .

Ibid., "Into the golden vessel of great song"

48 I turn away reluctant from your light,
   And stand irresolute, a mind undone,
A silly, dazzled thing deprived of sight
   From having looked too long upon the sun.

Ibid., "When I too long have looked
upon your face"

49 Your body was a temple to Delight. . . .

Ibid., "As to some lovely temple, tenantless"

50 I drank at every vine.
   The last was like the first.
I came upon no wine
   So wonderful as thirst.

"Feast," St. 1, The Harp-Weaver
and Other Poems   1923

51 I only know that summer sang in me
   A little while, that in me sings no more.

Ibid., "What lips my lips have
kissed, and where, and why"

52 Pity me that the heart is slow to learn
   What the swift mind beholds at every turn.

Ibid., "Pity me not because the light of day"

53 I would blossom if I were a rose.

Ibid., "Three Songs from the
Lamp and the Bell," I, St. 1

54 The heart grows weary after a little
   Of what it loved for a little while.

Ibid., II, St. 1

55 If ever I said, in grief or pride,
   I tired of honest things, I lied. . . .
                        Ibid., "The Goose-Girl"

56 He laughed at all I dared to praise,
   And broke my heart, in little ways.
                        Ibid., "The Spring and the Fall," St. 2

57 (Love, by whom I was beguiled,
   Grant I may not bear a child.)
                        Ibid., "Humoresque," St. 1

58 He that would eat of love must eat it where it hangs.
                        Ibid., "Never May the Fruit Be Plucked"

59 That Love at length should find me out. . . .
                        Ibid., "That love at length
                           should find me out and bring"

60   Well I know
   What is this beauty men are babbling of;
   I wonder only why they prize it so.
                        Ibid., "Love is not blind. I see with single eye"

61 I know I am but summer to your heart,
   And not the full four seasons of the year. . . .
                        Ibid., "I know I am but summer to your heart"

62 Oh, oh, you will be sorry for that word!
   Give back my book and take my kiss instead.
   Was it my enemy or my friend I heard,
   "What a big book for such a little head!"
                        Ibid., "Oh, oh, you will be sorry for that word!"

63 She said at length, feeling the doctor's eyes,
   "I don't know what you do exactly when a person
      dies."
                        Ibid., "Sonnets from an Ungrafted Tree," XVI

64 Sweet sounds, oh, beautiful music, do not cease!
   Reject me not into the world again.
                        "On Hearing a Symphony of
                        Beethoven," St. 1, *The Buck
                        in the Snow*   1928

65 Music my rampart, and my only one.
                        Ibid.

66 I am not resigned to the shutting away of loving hearts
      in the hard ground

                        571

So it is, and so it will be, for so it has been, time out of
   mind:
Into the darkness they go, the wise and the lovely.
   Crowned
With lilies and with laurel they go; but I am not re-
   signed.
Ibid., "Dirge Without Music," St. 1

67 April is upon us, pitiless and young and harsh.
Ibid., "Northern April," St. 2

68 The anguish of the world is on my tongue.
My bowl is filled to the brim with it; there is more than
   I can eat.
Happy are the toothless old and the toothless young,
That cannot rend this meat.
Ibid., "The Anguish," St. 2

69 Not for you was the pen bitten,
And the mind wrung, and the song written.
Ibid., "To Those Without Pity"

70 Night is my sister. . . .
"Fatal Interview," VII
Fatal Interview   *1931*

71 Life has no friend. . . .
Ibid., VIII

72 Unnatural night, the shortest of the year,
Farewell! 'Tis dawn. The longest day is here.
Ibid., XIII

73 Time, and to spare, for patience by and by,
Time to be cold and time to sleep alone. . . .
Ibid., XXII

74 I know the face of Falsehood and her tongue
Honeyed with unction, plausible with guile. . . .
Ibid., XXIII

75 Youth, have no pity; leave no farthing here
For age to invest in compromise and fear.
Ibid., XXIX

76 Desolate dreams pursue me out of sleep;
Weeping I wake; waking, I weep, I weep.
Ibid., XXXIII

77 My kisses now are sand against your mouth,
Teeth in your palm and pennies on your eyes.

Ibid., XXXIX

78 The heart once broken is a heart no more,
And is absolved from all a heart must be;
All that it signed or chartered heretofore
Is cancelled now, the bankrupt heart is free. . . .

Ibid., L

79 All skins are shed at length, remorse, even shame.

Wine from These Grapes, "Time, that
renews the tissues of this frame"   *1934*

80 I dread no more the first white in my hair,
Or even age itself, the easy shoe,
The cane, the wrinkled hands, the special chair:
Time, doing this to me, may alter too
My anguish, into something I can bear.

Ibid.

81 There it was I saw what I shall never forget
And never retrieve.

Ibid., "The Fawn," St. 1

82 Childhood is the Kingdom Where Nobody Dies.

Ibid., "Childhood Is the Kingdom
Where Nobody Dies," III

83 To be grown up is to sit at the table with people who
have died, who neither listen nor speak. . . .

Ibid., St. 6

84 Soar, eat ether, see what has never been seen; depart,
be lost,
But climb.

Ibid., "On Thought in Harness," St. 3

85 Breed, crowd, encroach, expand, expunge yourself, die
out,
Homo called *sapiens*.

Ibid., "Apostrophe to Man"

86 I shall die, but that is all that I shall do for Death; I am
not on his pay-roll.

Ibid., "Conscientious Objector," St. 3

87 Am I a spy in the land of the living, that I should deliver men to Death?

Ibid., St. 4

88   . . . what frosty fate's in store
     For the warm blood of man,—man, out of ooze
     But lately crawled, and climbing up the shore?
>> Ibid., "Epitaph for the
>> Race of Man," III

89 Man, with his singular laughter, his droll tears,
     His engines and his conscience and his art,
     Made but a simple sound upon your ears. . . .
>> Ibid., "O Earth, unhappy
>> planet born to die," IV

90 Ease has demoralized us, nearly so; we know
     Nothing of the rigours of winter. . . .
>> "Underground System," St. 2,
>> *Huntsman, What Quarry?*   1939

91 Heart, do not stain my skin
     With bruises; go about
     Your simple function. Mind,
     Sleep now; do not intrude;
     And do not spy; be kind.

     Sweet blindness, now begin.
>> Ibid., "Theme and Variations," II, Sts. 5–6

92 Even the bored, insulated heart,
     That signed so long and tight a lease,
     Can break its contract, slump in peace.
>> Ibid., IV, St. 6

93 Infinite Space lies curved within the scope
     Of the hand's cradle.
>> Ibid., "Truce for a Moment," St. 2

94   . . . I shall love you always.
     No matter what party is in power;
     No matter what temporarily expedient combination of
        allied interests wins the war;
     Shall love you always.
>> Ibid., "Modern Declaration," St. 2

95   . . . my heart is set
     On living—I have heroes to beget
     Before I die. . . .
>> Ibid., "Thou famished grave,
>> I will not fill thee yet"

96 No, no, not love, not love. Call it by name,
　　Now that it's over, now that it is gone and cannot hear
　　　　us.
　　It was an honest thing. Not noble. Yet no shame.
　　　　　　　　　　　Ibid., "What Savage Blossom," Sts. 3–4

97 Night falls fast.
　　Today is in the past.
　　　　　　　　　　　　　Ibid., "Not So Far as
　　　　　　　　　　　　　　the Forest," I, St. 3

98 O Life, my little day, at what cost
　　Have you been purchased!
　　　　　　　Ibid., "Be sure my coming was a sharp offense".

99 Parrots, tortoises and redwoods
　　Live a longer life than men do,
　　Men a longer life than dogs do,
　　Dogs a longer life than love does.
　　　　　　　　　　Ibid., "Pretty Love I Must Outlive You"

100 See how these masses mill and swarm
　　And troop and muster and assail:
　　God! we could keep this planet warm
　　By friction, if the sun should fail.
　　　　　　　　　　Ibid., "Three Sonnets in Tetrameter," I

101 Love does not help to understand
　　The logic of the bursting shell.
　　　　　　　　　　　　　　　　　Ibid., III

102 The oils and herbs of mercy are so few;
　　Honour's for sale; allegiance has its price;
　　The barking of a fox has bought us all;
　　We save our skins a craven hour or two. . . .
　　　　　　　　　　　　Ibid., "Czecho-Slovakia"

103 You think we build a world; I think we leave
　　Only these tools, wherewith to strain and grieve.
　　　　　　　　　　　　Ibid., "Count them unclean,
　　　　　　　　　　　　these tears that turn no mill"

104 Wisdom enough to leech us of our ill
　　Is daily spun; but there exists no loom
　　To weave it into fabric. . . .
　　　　　　　　　　　　Ibid., "Upon this age, that
　　　　　　　　　　　　never speaks its mind"

105 It's not true that life is one damn thing after an-
other—it's one damn thing over and over.
Letters of Edna St. Vincent Millay,
Allen R. Macdougall, ed.   *1952p*

106 A person who publishes a book willfully appears before the populace with his pants down. . . .
Ibid.

620. Vita Sackville-West
(1892–1962)

1 So prodigal was I of youth,
Forgetting I was young;
I worshipped dead men for their strength,
Forgetting I was strong.
"MCMXIII," St. 1, *Poems of
West and East   1917*

2 We have tasted space and freedom, frontiers falling as
we went,
Now with narrow bonds and limits, never could we be
content,
For we have abolished boundaries, straitened borders
had we rent,
And a house no more confines us than the roving nomads' tent.
Ibid., "Nomads," St. 6

3 Travel is the most private of pleasures. There is no
greater bore than the travel bore. We do not in the
least want to hear what he has seen in Hong-Kong.
Passenger to Teheran, Ch. 1   *1926*

4 For observe, that to hope for Paradise is to live in Paradise, a very different thing from actually getting there.
Ibid.

5 This question of horizon, however; how important it is;
how it alters the shape of the mind; how it expresses,
essentially, one's ultimate sense of country! That is
what can never be told in words: the exact size, proportion, contour; the new standard to which the mind
must adjust itself.   Ibid., Ch. 4

6 If you are wise you will not look upon the long period
of time thus occupied in actual movement as the mere

gulf dividing you from the end of your journey, but rather as one of those rare and plastic seasons of your life from which, perhaps, in after times, you may love to date the moulding of your character—that is, your very identity. Once feel this, and you will soon grow happy and contented in your saddle home.

Ibid., Ch. 6

7 . . . besides, the fingers which had once grown accustomed to a pen soon itch to hold one again: it is necessary to write, if the days are not to slip emptily by. How else, indeed, to clap the net over the butterfly of the moment? for the moment passes, it is forgotten; the mood is gone; life itself is gone. That is where the writer scores over his fellows: he catches the changes of his mind on the hop. Growth is exciting; growth is dynamic and alarming. Growth of the soul, growth of the mind. . . .

Twelve Days, Ch. 1   1928

8 Those who have never dwelt in tents have no idea either of the charm or of the discomfort of a nomadic existence. The charm is purely romantic, and consequently very soon proves to be fallacious.

Ibid., Ch. 6

9 Perhaps it would be better to go the whole hog and cut oneself off entirely from the outside world. A merely negative form of protest, I fear, against conditions one does not like; for resentment is vain unless one has an alternative to offer. Flight is no alternative; it is only a personal solution. But as a personal experiment it certainly offers material for reflection to the curious.

Ibid., Ch. 15

10 Among the many problems which beset the novelist, not the least weighty is the choice of the moment at which to begin his novel.

The Edwardians, Ch. 1   1930

11 If this is Society, thought Anguetil, God help us, for surely no fraud has ever equalled it.

Ibid.

12 For a young man to start his career with a love affair with an older woman was quite de rigueur. . . . Of course, it must not go on too long.

Ibid., Ch. 3

13 All the world of feminine voluptuousness seemed to be gathered up and released in that one divine curving of the loosened lips. There was no humour in it, but there was an indescribable caress.

Ibid.

14 The inner knowledge that he was behaving not only badly but histrionically increased his obstinacy. He was acutely ashamed of himself, since, for the first time in his life, he saw himself through other eyes; and saw his selfishness, his self-indulgence, his arrogance, his futile philandering, for what they were worth. Still he would not give way.

Ibid., Ch. 4

15 Click, clack, click, clack, went their conversation, like so many knitting-needles, purl, plain, purl plain, achieving a complex pattern of references, cross-references, Christian names, nicknames, and fleeting allusions. . . .

Ibid., Ch. 6

16 And as her legal authority shrivelled, so did her personal authority turn suddenly into a thing which had never enjoyed any real existence.

Ibid., Ch. 7

17 Men do kill women. Most women enjoy being killed; so I'm told.

All Passion Spent 1931

18 Now to my little death the pestering clock
Beckons,—but who would sleep when he might wake?
"Solitude" 1938

19 I suppose the pleasure of country life lies really in the eternally renewed evidences of the determination to live. That is a truism when said, but anything but a truism when daily observed. Nothing shows up the difference between the thing said or read, so much as the daily experience of it.

Country Notes 1940

20 It is very necessary to have makers of beauty left in a world seemingly bent on making the most evil ugliness.

Ibid.

21 I have grown wise, after many years of gardening, and no longer order recklessly from wildly alluring descrip-

tions which make every annual sound easy to grow and as brilliant as a film star. I now know that gardening is not like that.

"January," *In Your Garden Again*   1953

22 I have come to the conclusion, after many years of sometimes sad experience, that you cannot come to any conclusion at all.

Ibid., "May"

23 "It is lucky for some people," I say to Laura, "that they can live behind their own faces."

No Signposts in the Sea   1961

24 Ambition, old as mankind, the immemorial weakness of the strong.

Ibid.

25 When, and how, and at what stage of our development did spirituality and our strange notions of religion arise? the need for worship which is nothing more than our frightened refuge into propitiation of a Creator we do not understand? A detective story, the supreme Who-done-it, written in undecipherable hieroglyphics, no Rosetta stone supplied, by the consummate mystifier to tease us poor fumbling unravellers of his plot.

Ibid.

26 My whole curse has been a duality with which I was too weak and too self-indulgent to struggle.

Quoted in *Portrait of a Marriage*
by Nigel Nicolson   1973p

27 Women, like men, ought to have their youth so glutted with freedom they hate the very idea of freedom.

Ibid., Letter to Harold
Nicolson (June 1, 1919)

28 You have met and understood me on every point. It is this which binds me to you through every storm, and makes you so unalterably the one person whom I trust and love.

Ibid. (November 1, 1919)

29 I advance, therefore, the perfectly accepted theory that cases of dual personality do exist, in which the feminine and masculine elements alternately preponderate. I advance this in an impersonal and scientific spirit, and claim that I am qualified to speak with the intimacy a

professional scientist could acquire only after years of
study and indirect information, because I have the object of study always at hand, in my own heart.

Ibid., "Autobiography"
(September 27, 1920)

30 . . . I hold the conviction that as centuries go on, and
the sexes become more nearly merged on account of
their increasing resemblances, I hold the conviction
that such connections will to a very large extent cease
to be regarded as merely unnatural, and will be understood far better, at least in their *intellectual* if not in
their physical aspect.

Ibid.

31 Since "unnatural" means "removed from nature," only
the most civilized, because the least natural, class of
society can be expected to tolerate such a product of
civilization.

Ibid.

32 Things were not tragic for us then, because although
we cared passionately we didn't care deeply.

Ibid., (September 29, 1920)

33 Of course I wish now that I had never made these discoveries. One doesn't miss what one doesn't know, and
now life is made wretched by privations. I often long
for ignorance and innocence.   Ibid.

621. Alfonsina Storni
(1892–1938)

1 I gutted your belly as I would a doll's
Examining its artifice of cogs
And buried deep within its golden pulleys
I found a trap bearing this label: sex.

"To Eros," *Mask and Trefoil*   c.1930

2 . . . Ah, one favor:
If he telephones again,
Tell him it's no use, that I've gone out. . . .

"I Shall Sleep,"* *La Nacion*
(Buenos Aires newspaper)   1938p

* * *

* Sent to *La Nacion* the day before she drowned herself.

3 I was in your cage, little man
   Little man, what a cage you have given me,
   I say little because you do not understand me;
   You will never understand me.
                                   "Dear Little Man"

4 To tell you, my love, that I desired you
   With no instinctive hypocritic blush,
   I was incapable, as tightly bound as Prometheus,
   Until one day I burst my bonds.
                                   "Twenty Centuries"

5 You want me to be white
   (God forgive you)
   You want me to be chaste
   (God forgive you)
   You want me to be immaculate!
                               "You Want Me White"

622. Ruth Suckow
(1892–1960)

1 To have someone tell his boys to do this and that! To
   take away his help on the farm just when he needed it
   most! To have somebody just step in and tell him
   where they had to go! Was that what happened in this
   country? Why had his people left the old country, then,
   if things were going to be just the same?
            Country People, Pt. II, Ch. 4   *1924*

2 All women were that way—except his mother and sister and aunt, whom he unconsciously excluded (since
   they need not count in the way of desire) and did not
   place under the head of "Woman." He scorned, so he
   thought, all that had to do with them, and declared
   only "men's books" worth reading—adventure, travel;
   scorned "Woman" for not having brains, and despised
   the ones who had.
                       The Odyssey of a Nice Girl,
                       Pt. IV, Ch. 2   *1925*

3 To most of the people it [World War I] had seemed
   far away, something that could never come close. Some
   resented it, others seized upon it now to help break up
   the long monotony of everyday living—more terribly
   thrilling than a fire in the business district, a drowning
   in the river, or the discovery that the cashier of the

Farmers' Bank had been embezzling. Something had come, it seemed, to shake up that placid, solid, comfortable life of home, changing things around, shifting values that had seemed to be fixed.

Ibid., Ch. 3

4 Exercises, songs and recitations—pieces by children whose mothers would be offended if they were left off the program: good or bad, the audience clapped.

"Eminence," Children and
Other People　1931

5 That would be the most terrible thing of all, if she began to forget. Then her heart would have to close. Yes, but if she kept it open, to feel the happiness, then she would have to feel the rest, too. . . . She would have to feel again, like blows on her open heart, every cruel detail of Harold's suffering, and the awful blank fact of his death.

Ibid., "Experience"

623. Mae West
(1892–　)

1 "You're a fine woman, Lou. One of the finest women that ever walked the streets."

She Done Him Wrong　1932

2 TIRA. She's the kind of girl who climbed the ladder of success, wrong by wrong.

I'm No Angel　1933

3 FRISCO DOLL. Between two evils, I always pick the one I never tried before.

Klondike Annie　1936

4 FLOWER BELLE LEE. I generally avoid temptation unless I can't resist it.

My Little Chickadee　1940

I believe in the single standard for men and women.

The Wit and Wisdom of Mae West,
Joseph Weintraub, ed.　1967

6 It's hard to be funny when you have to be clean.

Ibid.

7 It is better to be looked over than overlooked.　Ibid.

8 It's not the men in my life that counts—it's the life in my men.

Ibid.

9 Too much of a good thing can be wonderful.

Ibid.

10 I used to be Snow White . . . but I drifted.

Ibid.

11 The best way to hold a man is in your arms.

Ibid.

12 He who hesitates is last.   Ibid.

13 When women go wrong, men go right after them.

Ibid.

624. Rebecca West
(1892–   )

1 Literature must be an analysis of experience and a synthesis of the findings into a unity.
Ending in Earnest   1931

2 When a book of great literary merit is denounced the first line of defence always is to point out that that kind of book, which conscientiously analyzes a human experience and gives its findings honestly, cannot do those who read it any harm, since it adds to the knowledge of reality by which man lives.
Ibid., "Concerning the Censorship"

3 Yes, if an age would deal fairly well with its children and let them do what they can!
Ibid., *"Manibus Date Lilia Plenis"*

4 It is not that they have any faith in Marxian or any other kind of Socialism, so much as that they believe a Labour government would scrap tradition and make a fresh start.
Ibid., "Feminist Revolt, Old and New"

5 Infantilism is not a happy state. The childhood of the individual and the race is full of fears, and panic-stricken attempts to avert what is feared by placating the gods with painful sacrifices.
Ibid., "Journey's End"

6 Most works of art, like most wines, ought to be consumed in the district of their fabrication.

Ibid., " 'Journey's End' Again"

7 It was true that her avarice operated continuously, collecting from him jewels and furs over and above her regular allowance at regular periods, but as at the beginning it was always as nicely calculated in relation to his means as if she had a highly-paid statistician working for her.

The Abiding Vision   1935

8 "We're on a permanent plateau of prosperity. There's never been anything like it before. It's America."

Ibid.

9 "That's what's wrong with us!" he exclaimed, getting up and walking about the room. "We can't talk. Nobody but writers know how to put things into words, and everybody goes around stuffed up with things they want to say and can't." It seemed to him that he had put his finger on the secret of all human sorrow.

Life Sentence   1935

10 There is no such thing as conversation. It is an illusion. There are intersecting monologues, that is all.

There Is No Conversation, Ch. 1   1935

11 It is queer how it is always one's virtues and not one's vices that precipitate one into disaster.

Ibid.

12 It appears that even the different parts of the same person do not converse among themselves, do not succeed in learning from each other what are their desires and their intentions.

Ibid., Ch. 2

13   "But then what did you want me to forgive you for?"
"I wanted you to forgive me for being mean," he said, "and having to be what I am, and do what I have done." A smile passed over his lips. "Just as you might ask me to forgive you for being you."

The Salt of the Earth, Ch. 2   1935

14 "Why must you always try to be omnipotent, and shove things about? Tragic things happen sometimes that we just have to submit to."

Ibid.

15 "The point is that nobody likes having salt rubbed into their wounds, even if it is the salt of the earth."

Ibid.

16 All the world over, the most good-natured find enjoyment in those who miss trains or sit down on frozen pavements.

"A Day in the Town," *The New Yorker*   *January 25, 1941*

17 For power claims to know what life is going to be about and what prescription to offer, and authority claims to be able to enforce that prescription. But the Slav knows . . . that life . . . is in essence unpredictable, that she often produces events for which there is no apt prescription, and that she can be as slippery as an eel when wise men attempt to control her; and they know that it is life, not power or authority, that gives us joy, and this often when she is least predictable.

"Dalmatia," *Black Lamb and Grey Falcon*   *1941*

18 But there are other things than dissipation that thicken the features. Tears, for example.

Ibid., "Serbia"

19 There is . . . the mystic who went into the desert because his head was so full of ideas about the spiritual world that everyday talk was in his ears as a barrel-organ playing outside a concert-hall is to a musician, the mystic who does not want to eat or drink or sleep with women because that is to take time off from the ecstatic pleasure of pursuing the ramifications of good and evil through his bosom and through the universe. . . . If a naked woman appeared before him she would not be a temptation but an offence, offending as a person in a library who begins chatting to a student who has found a long-sought reference a few minutes before closing time. Life is not long enough for these men to enjoy the richness of their own perceptions, to transmute them into wisdom.

Ibid., "Old Serbia"

20 Now different races and nationalities cherish different ideals of society that stink in each other's nostrils with an offensiveness beyond the power of any but the most monstrous private deed.   *Ibid.*, Epilogue

21 The intellectual world is largely of English creation, yet our authors write of ideas as if they were things to pick and choose, even though the choice might be pushed to the extremity of martyrdom, as if they could be left alone, as if they came into play only as they were picked and chosen. But that ideas are the symbols of relationships among real forces that make people late for breakfast, that take away their breakfast, that makes them beat each other across the breakfast-table, is something which the English do not like to realize. Lazy, bone-lazy, they wish to believe that life is lived simply by living.

Ibid.

22 . . . any authentic work of art must start an argument between the artist and his audience.

The Court and the Castle,
Pt. I, Ch. 1   *1957*

23 But humanity is never more sphinxlike than when it is expressing itself.

Ibid., Pt. II, Ch. 1

24 It is so difficult to become a specialist that the mediocre man has been very eager to cry wolf to the specialist, often before it was actually necessary.

Speech, "McLuhan and the
Future of Literature"   *1969*

625. Margaret Anderson
(1893–1973)

1 I have never been able to accept the two great laws of humanity—that you're always being suppressed if you're inspired and always being pushed into a corner if you're exceptional. I won't be cornered and I won't stay suppressed.

My Thirty Years' War   *1930*

2 My unreality is chiefly this: I have never felt much like a human being. It's a splendid feeling.

Ibid.

3 I didn't know what to do about life—so I did a nervous breakdown that lasted many months.

Ibid.

4 I have always had something to live besides a private life.

Ibid.

5 In real love you want the other person's good. In romantic love you want the other person.

The Fiery Fountains   1969

626. Faith Baldwin
(1893–   )

1 The kiss was so much a part of the routine that it embarrassed him to withhold it.

Alimony, Ch. 2   1928

2   "Compromises aren't enough."
   "But," he protested, stupidly, "they're life, aren't they?"
   "If they are, then life isn't enough either!"

Ibid., Ch. 8

3 He made more money than he could spend. His tastes were sound, not extravagant. There was no one dependent on him. He had a few close friends among his colleagues and a thousand pleasant acquaintances. Women had been kind to him and he had so arranged his life that he had been able to enjoy their generosity with discretion. He had recreations. . . . He liked to travel. . . . He liked his work. In short, the world with a fence around it was his.

Medical Center, Pt. I, Ch. 3   1938

4 Sometimes entering the ward he felt himself a god, with the gifts of life, of hope, of alleviation, of promise in his hands.

Ibid., Pt. V, Ch. 28

5 . . . it is hard to convince editors . . . that people of—or past—forty are not senile, and might even have problems, emotions and—*mirabile dictu*—romances, licit and illicit.

"Writing for the Women's Magazines,"
The Writer's Book, Helen Hull, ed.   1950

6 Oh well, one must adopt a New England attitude, saying not yea, nor nay, but perhaps, maybe, and sometimes.

Ibid.

7 The shadow of fear and uncertainty lies over most of us; for us the future seems far from being as clear and open as we believed it would be.

Ibid.

8 Gratitude is a humble emotion. It expresses itself in a thousand ways, from a sincere thank you to friend or stranger, to the mute, upreaching acknowledgement to God—not for the gifts of this day only, but for the day itself; not for what we believe will be ours in the future, but for the bounty of the past.

"December," *Harvest of Hope*   1962

3 One thing I know about March—whether it storms or shines, it is the key to spring. It can be a sun-warmed key, or a wet one, or a cold; but a key just the same.

Ibid., "March"

10 Men's private self-worlds are rather like our geographical world's seasons, storm, and sun, deserts, oases, mountains and abysses, the endless-seeming plateaus, darkness and light, and always the sowing and the reaping.

Ibid., "April"

11 Character builds slowly, but it can be torn down with incredible swiftness.

Ibid., "July"

12 . . . my temperament's temperature does not rise and fall with thermometers or barometers.

Ibid., "September"

* * *

13 I think that life has spared these mortals much—
And cheated them of more—who have not kept
A breathless vigil by the little bed
Of some beloved child.

"Vigil"

627. Bessie Breuer
(1893–   )

1 The habit of worry had settled so firmly into her mother's being that her worries were her aspects of love. . . .

The Actress, Ch. 1   1955

2 Hollywood . . . scripts . . . a medium where both
syntax and the language itself were subjected to horrid
mutilation by young men who thought of themselves as
writers and who proved it by the enormous salaries
they received from those higher up who were even less
knowledgeable of the mother tongue.

Ibid., Ch. 15

3 When they first brought the baby in to her . . . she
stared, inert, and thought, This is the author of my
pain.

Ibid., Ch. 21

4 But why, she begged the doctor. "We must stimulate
those secretions . . . or else . . ." and he walked
away. Why did he always walk away with these half-
explanations floating after him? Ibid.

5 Did I stay with him the very next night because I, way
deep down, thought I would learn the secret of acting
by sleeping with him; was that it—the way women are
always snatching at poets and composers and writers to
bedizen themselves with a rag, a knuckle, a toe, the
sacred toe of art? Ibid., Ch. 32

6 Lust, this muscular dilation and contraction, this in itself, was that it—the ding an sich, memory of a college
course? Ibid., Ch. 36

628. Vera Brittain
(1893–1970)

1 I thought that spring must last forevermore,
  For I was young and loved, and it was May.

"May Morning," St. 4 (May, 1916),
Poems of the War and After 1934

2 Hope has forsaken me, by death removed,
  And love that seemed so strong and gay has proved
  A poor crushed thing, the toy of cruel chance.

Ibid., St. 7

3 Have I so changed, since sorrow set her seal
  On my lost youth, and left me solitary. . . .

Ibid., "After Three Years," St. 2
(December, 1918)

4 I found in you a holy place apart,
   Sublime endurance, God in man revealed,
   Where mending broken bodies slowly healed
   My broken heart.
              Ibid., "Epitaph on My Days in Hospital" (1919)

5 He was of those whose vanity untold
   Builds up complacency to shut out loss,
   Who, snatching after dross, believe it gold,
   And throw away unvalued gold as dross.
                        Ibid., "The Fool," St. 1 (1920)

6 Meek wifehood is no part of my profession;
   I am your friend, but never your possession.
                        Ibid., "Married Love" (1926)

7 For the courage of greatness is adventurous and knows
      not withdrawing,
   But grasps the nettle, danger, with resolute hands,
   And ever again
   Gathers security from the sting of pain.
                 Ibid., "Evening in Yorkshire," St. 4
                                      (December, 1932)

8 For though I must die, youth itself is immortal; its star
   begins to ascend the heaven of the future as mine sinks
   below the brief zenith of my generation.
                   England's Hour, Ch. 24   1941

9 The idea that it is necessary to go to a university in
   order to become a successful writer, or even a man or
   woman of letters (which is by no means the same
   thing), is one of those phantasies that surround authorship.
                   On Being an Author, Ch. 2   1948

10 His secret realisation of his physical cowardice led him
   to underrate his exceptional moral courage. . . .
                        Born, Pt. I, Ch. 1   1949

11 He had never been afraid of death, which was still unreal to him, but he dreaded the end of the world.
                                      Ibid., Ch. 6

12 "There is a spiritual fellowship in suffering which
   unites men and women as nothing else can. Perhaps it
   will be by the world-wide members of this fellowship,
   in which those whom we call our enemies share, that

the temple of civilisation will be rebuilt when peace returns."

Ibid., Pt. II, Ch. 8

13 The history of men and women in the past fifty years suggests that the old conflict between male and female will ultimately reach reconciliation in a new synthesis which is already in sight. The organic type of human being which will emerge from that synthesis may well be the constructive achievement of the next half-century.

Lady into Woman, Ch. 1   1953

14 It is probably true to say that the largest scope for change still lies in men's attitude to women, and in women's attitude to themselves.

Ibid., Ch. 15

15 Politics are usually the executive expression of human immaturity.

The Rebel Passion, Ch. 1   1964

16 At no previous period has mankind been faced by a half-century which so paradoxically united violence and progress. Its greater and lesser wars and long series of major assassinations have been strangely combined with the liberation of more societies and individuals than ever before in history, and by the transformation of millions of second-class citizens—women, workers, and the members of subject races—to a stage at which first-rate achievement is no longer inhibited even if opportunities are not yet complete.

Ibid., Ch. 12

17 Nuclear weapons immediately vitiated campaigning methods of the secular pacifist society, since the individual renunciation of war, while retaining its moral authority, had lost its political validity. Wars would not now cease if the common man refused to fight when governments possessed weapons which were capable of annihilating both the enemy and his opponent.

Ibid.

18 The pacifists' task today is to find a method of helping and healing which provides a revolutionary constructive substitute for war.

Ibid.

629. Elizabeth Coatsworth
(1893–   )

* * *

1 To a life that seizes
  Upon content,
  Locality seems
  But accident.

"To Daughters, Growing Up," St. 1

630. Elizabeth Cotten
(1893–   )

1 But I didn't know people could takes songs from you.

Quoted by Stephen March
in Southern Voices
August/September, 1974

* * *

2 Freight train, freight train, goin' so fast. . . .

"Freight Train"

3 This life I been livin' is very hard.
  Work all the week, honey
  and I give it all to you.
  Honey, baby, what more can I do?

"Babe, It Ain't No Lie"

631. Lillian Day
(1893–?)

1 A lady is one who never shows her underwear unintentionally.

Kiss and Tell   1931

632. Marie Gilchrist
(1893–   )

1 But the life of poetry lies in fresh relationships between words, in the spontaneous fusion of hitherto unrelated words.

Writing Poetry, Ch. 1   1932

2 All American Indian poems are songs, and an Indian was once asked which came first, the words or the music. "They come together," he replied.

Ibid., Ch. 3

3 Nouns and verbs are almost pure metal; adjectives are cheaper ore.

Quoted in "On the Teaching of
Poetry" by Leonora Speyer, *The*
Saturday Review of Literature   *1946*

633. Helen Hathaway
(1893–1932)

* * *

1 More tears have been shed over men's lack of manners than their lack of morals.

Manners for Men

634. Margery Eldredge Howell
(1893–?)

* * *

1 There's dignity in suffering—
Nobility in pain—
But failure is a salted wound
That burns and burns again.

"Wormwood"

635. Emily Beatrix Jones
(1893–?)

* * *

1 The pools of art and memory keep
Reflections of our fallen towers,
And every princess there asleep,
Whom once we kissed, is always ours.

"Middle-Age"

636. Suzanne LaFollette
(1893–   )

1 There is nothing more innately human than the tendency to transmute what has become customary into what has been divinely ordained.

"The Beginnings of Emancipation,"
Concerning Women   *1926*

2 The revolutionists did not succeed in establishing human freedom; they poured the new wine of belief in equal rights for all men into the old bottle of privilege for some; and it soured.

Ibid.

3 . . . most people, no doubt, when they espouse human rights, make their own mental reservations about the proper application of the word "human."

Ibid.

4 . . . where divorce is allowed at all . . . society demands a specific grievance of one party against the other. . . . The fact that marriage may be a failure spiritually is seldom taken into account.

Ibid.

5 . . . laws are felt only when the individual comes into conflict with them.

Ibid.

6 For the wage-earner gets his living on sufferance: while he continues to please his employer he may earn a living. . . .

Ibid.

7 . . . the economic conditions brought about by the State operate to make marriage the State's strongest bulwark. . . .

Ibid.

8 It is a commonplace in this century that women form the leisure class; and this leisure class of women, like leisured classes everywhere, has its leisure at the expense of other people, who in this case are the husbands.

Ibid.

9 If responsibility for the upbringing of children is to continue to be vested in the family, then the rights of children will be secured only when parents are able to make a living for their families with so little difficulty that they may give their best thought and energy to the child's development. . . .

Ibid.

10 . . . where is the society which does not struggle along under a dead-weight of tradition and law inherited from its grandfathers?

Ibid.

11 All political and religious systems have their root and their strength in the innate conservatism of the human mind, and its intense fear of autonomy.

Ibid.

12 . . . people never move towards revolution; they are pushed towards it by intolerable injustices in the economic and social order under which they live.

Ibid.

13 For man, marriage is regarded as a station; for women, as a vocation.

Ibid., "Women and Marriage"

14 . . . nothing could be more grotesquely unjust than a code of morals, reinforced by laws, which relieves men from responsibility for irregular sexual acts, and for the same acts drives women to abortion, infanticide, prostitution and self-destruction.

Ibid.

15 The claim for alimony . . . implies the assumption that a woman is economically helpless. . . .

Ibid.

16 . . . when one hears the argument that marriage should be indissoluble for the sake of children, one cannot help wondering whether the protagonist is really such a firm friend of childhood. . . .

Ibid.

17 . . . to institutionalize means in great degree to mechanize.

Ibid.

18 It is necessary to grow accustomed to freedom before one may walk in it sure-footedly. *Ibid.*

19 It is impossible for a sex or a class to have economic freedom until everybody has it, and until economic freedom is attained for everybody, there can be no real freedom for anybody.

Ibid., "What Is to Be Done"

20 Rights that depend on the sufferance of the State are of uncertain tenure. . . .

Ibid.

21 No system of government can hope long to survive the cynical disregard of both law and principle which government in America regularly exhibits.

Ibid.

22 . . . the automobile had not yet come in and the family had not yet gone out.

Letter to Alice Rossi (July, 1971),
The Feminist Papers, Alice Rossi, ed.
1973

23 No one . . . who has not known that inestimable privilege can possibly realize what good fortune it is to grow up in a home where there are grandparents.

Ibid.

24 I . . . watch with growing concern the disintegration of the Western World—above all our own country—and the steady growth of totalitarian influence and power. . . .

Ibid.

637. Margaret Leech
(1893–   )

1 England was the friend whose policy stood like a bulwark against Continental animosity to the ambitions of the American republic.

In the Days of McKinley, Ch. 11   *1959*

2 Charity stood ready to atone for the heartlessness of the War Department.

Ibid., Ch. 13

3 The colonial fever was mildly infectious in Washington. Some of the President's closest friends and counselors came down with it.

Ibid., Ch. 17

4 Never in history had the Union of the States been joined in such universal sorrow. North and South, East and West, the people mourned [William McKinley] a father and a friend, and the fervent strains of "Nearer, My God, to Thee"* floated, like a prayer and a leave-taking, above the half-masted flags in every city and town.

Ibid., Ch. 26

5 Yet, for a space, Americans turned from the challenge and the strangeness of the future. Entranced and regretful, they remembered McKinley's firm, unquestioning faith; his kindly, frock-coated dignity; his accessibility and dedication to the people: the federal simplicity that would not be seen again in Washington.

Ibid.

6 The nation felt another leadership, nervous, aggressive, and strong. Under command of a bold young captain [Theodore Roosevelt], America set sail on the stormy voyage of the twentieth centry.

Ibid., Epilogue

638. Hesper Le Gallienne
(1893–?)

* * *

1 The loose foot of the wanderer
  Is curst as well as blest!
It urges ever, ever on
  And never gives him rest.   "The Wanderer"

639. Anita Loos
(1893–   )

1 "She always believed in the old adage: 'Leave them while you're looking good.' "
          Gentlemen Prefer Blondes, Ch. 1   1925

2 "I really think that American gentlemen are the best after all, because . . . kissing your hand may make you feel very, very good, but a diamond and sapphire bracelet lasts forever."   *Ibid.*, Ch. 4

* McKinley's favorite hymn and last words.

3 So this gentleman said, "A girl with brains ought to do something else with them besides think."

Ibid.

4 . . . I always say that a girl never really looks as well as she does on board a steamship, or even a yacht.

Ibid.

5 JUDGE. Always go to a solitary drinker for the truth!
Happy Birthday, Act I   1947

6 ADDIE. I've always been my own best company, Mr. Bishop.

Ibid.

7 ADDIE. Why, Benjamin Franklin says a man without a woman is like a half a pair of scissors.

Ibid., Act II

8 ADDIE. I was making love to a man, a man I hardly even know. He was kissing the face off me and I was kissing the face off him. And I found it highly satisfactory.

Ibid.

9 Of course, everybody knows that the greatest thing about Motherhood is the "Sacrifices," but it is quite a shock to find out that they begin so far ahead of time.
A Mouse Is Born, Ch. 1   1951

10 So after a Star has received five or six million of those Fan letters, you begin to realize you must be wonderful without having to read all those monitinous [sic] letters.

Ibid.

11 For the most outstanding shock that Tourists ever get is to find out that "Hollywood" is meerly [sic] one of unnumerable other spots, which we Citizens term "Hollywood" as a "cover-up" for the whole accumilation [sic].

Ibid., Ch. 6

12 So I am beginning to wonder if maybe girls wouldn't be happier if we stopped demanding so much respeckt for ourselves and developped [sic] a little more respeckt for husbands.

Ibid., Ch. 19

13 "Why, with a mental equipment which allows me to tell the difference between hot and cold, I stand out in this community like a modern-day Cicero. Dropped into any other city of the world, I'd rate as a possibly adequate night watchman. And let's be fair, old pal, you yourself, a leader of public thought in Hollywood, wouldn't have sufficient mental acumen anywhere else to hold down a place in a bread line!"

No Mother to Guide Her, Ch. 3   1961

14 "Childish" is the word with which the intelligentsia once branded Hollywood. And yet, those movies, which depicted Life as life can never be, were fairy tales for the adult. Today there are no fairy tales for us to believe in, and this is possibly a reason for the universal prevalence of mental crack-up. Yes, if we were childish in the past, I wish we could be children once again.

Ibid., Ch. 10

15 . . . the Welsh are a very peculiar breed, poetic, unpredictable, remote, and fiercely independent. For such a man [D. W. Griffith] to be in love must be terribly frustrating, because his deepest instinct is to be a loner.

A Girl Like I   1966

16 . . . memory is more indelible than ink.

Kiss Hollywood Goodby, Ch. 1   1974

17 That our popular art forms become so obsessed with sex has turned the U.S.A. into a nation of hobbledehoys; as if grown people don't have more vital concerns, such as taxes, inflation, dirty politics, earning a living, getting an education, or keeping out of jail. It's true that the French have a certain obsession with sex, but it's a particularly adult obsession. France is the thriftiest of all nations; to a Frenchman sex provides the most economical way to have fun. The French are a logical race.

Ibid., Ch. 21

18 There's nothing colder than chemistry.

Ibid.

640. Dorothy Parker
(1893–1967)

1 The affair between Margot Asquith and Margot Asquith will live as one of the prettiest love stories in all literature.

Book Review, The New Yorker   1922

2 (All your life you wait around for some damn man!)

"Chant for Dark Hours," Enough Rope   1927

3 By the time you swear you're his,
   Shivering and sighing,
And he vows his passion is
   Infinite, undying—
Lady, make a note of this:
   One of you is lying.

Ibid., "Unfortunate Coincidence"

4 Four be the things I am wiser to know:
Idleness, sorrow, a friend, and a foe.

Four be the things I'd be better without:
Love, curiosity, freckles, and doubt.

Ibid., "Inventory," Sts. 1–2

5 . . . the heart is bold
That pain has made incapable of pain.

Ibid.

6 Inertia rides and riddles me;
The which is called Philosophy.

Ibid., "The Veteran"

7 Lilacs blossom just as sweet
Now my heart is shattered.
If I bowled it down the street,
Who's to say it mattered?

Ibid., "Threnody," St. 1

8 Men seldom make passes
At girls who wear glasses.

Ibid., "News Item"

9 My soul is crushed, my spirit sore;
I do not like me any more.
I cavil, quarrel, grumble, grouse.

600

I ponder on the narrow house.
I shudder at the thought of men . . .
I'm due to fall in love again.

Ibid., "Symptom-Recital"

10 Oh, life is a glorious cycle of song,
   A medley of extemporanea;
   And love is a thing that can never go wrong;
   And I am Marie of Roumania.

Ibid., "Comment"

11 Razors pain you
   Rivers are damp;
   Acids stain you;
   And drugs cause cramp.
   Guns aren't lawful;
   Nooses give;
   Gas smells awful;
   You might as well live.   *Ibid.,* "Resumé"

12 Scratch a lover, and find a foe.
          Ibid., "Ballade of a Great Weariness," St. 1

13   This is what I know:
   Lover's oaths are thin as rain;
   Love's a harbinger of pain—
        Would it were not so!

Ibid., "Somebody's Song," St. 3

14 Travel, trouble, music, art,
     A kiss, a frock, a rhyme—
   I never said they feed my heart,
     But still they pass my time.

Ibid., "Faute de Mieux"

15 Where's the man could ease a heart
   Like a satin gown?

Ibid., "The Satin Dress," St. 1

16 Authors and actors and artists and such
   Never know nothing, and never know much.
          "Bohemia," *Sunset Gun*   1928

17 But ever does experience
   Deny me wisdom, calm, and sense!

Ibid., "A Fairly Sad Tale"

18 Byron and Shelley and Keats
   Were a trio of lyrical treats.

Ibid., "A Pig's-Eye View of Literature"

601

19 What time the gifted lady took
   Away from paper, pen, and book,
   She spent in amorous dalliance
   (They do those things so well in France).
                    Ibid., "George Sand"

20 Her mind lives tidily, apart
       From cold and noise and pain,
   And bolts the door against her heart,
       Out wailing in the rain.
                    Ibid., "Interior," St. 3

21 It costs me never a stab nor squirm
   To tread by chance upon a worm.
   "Aha, my little dear," I say,
   "Your clan will pay me back one day."
                    Ibid., "Thought for a Sunshiny Morning"

22 The love that sets you daft and dazed
   Is every love that ever blazed;
   The happier, I, to fathom this:
   A kiss is every other kiss.
                    Ibid., "Incurable"

23 They sicken of the calm, who knew the storm.
                    Ibid., "Fair Weather," St. 1

24 They that have roses
       Never need bread.
                    Ibid., "There Was One," St. 4

25 This living, this living, this living
       Was never a project of mine.
                    Ibid., "Coda"

26 Popularity seemed to her to be worth all the work that
   had to be put into its achievement.
                    "Big Blonde," Pt. I, *Laments*
                    for the Living   1929

27 She could not laugh at his whimsicalities, she was so
   tensely counting his indulgences. And she was unable
   to keep back her remonstrances. . . .
                    Ibid.

28 There was nothing separate about her days. Like drops
   upon a window-pane, they ran together and trickled
   away.
                    Ibid.

29 They resumed friendly relations only in the brief magnanimity caused by liquor, before more liquor drew
them into new battles.

Ibid.

30 She commenced drinking alone, short drinks all
through the day. . . . It blurred sharp things for her.
She lived in a haze of it. Her life took on a dream-like
quality. Nothing was astonishing.

Ibid.

31 She was always pleased to have him come and never
sorry to see him go.

Ibid., Pt. II

32 The thought of death came and stayed with her and
lent her a sort of drowsy cheer. It would be nice, nice
and restful, to be dead.

Ibid.

33 She had spent the golden time in grudging its going.

Ibid., "The Lovely Leave"   1929

34 Drink and dance and laugh and lie,
   Love, the reeling midnight through,
For tomorrow we shall die!
   (But, alas, we never do.)

"The Flaw in Paganism,"
Death and Taxes   1931

35   Here's my bitterness:
Would I knew a little more,
   Or very much less!

Ibid., "Summary"

36 Kings are shaped as other men.

Ibid., "Salome's Dancing-Lesson," St. 2

37 Death's the rarest prize of all!

Ibid.

38 Scratch a king and find a fool!

Ibid., St. 3

39 He lies below, correct in cypress wood,
   And entertains the most exclusive worms.

Ibid., "III. The Very Rich Man"

40 Poets alone should kiss and tell.

Ibid., "Ballade of a Talked-Off Ear," St. 3

41 The bird that feeds from off my palm
Is sleek, affectionate, and calm,
But double, to me, is worth the thrush
A-flickering in the elder-bush.
Ibid., "Ornithology for Beginners"

42 There was nothing more fun than a man!
Ibid., "The Little Old Lady in Lavendar Silk," St. 3

43 Women and elephants never forget.
Ibid., "Ballade of Unfortunate Mammals," St. 1

44 Brevity is the soul of lingerie.
Quoted in *While Rome Burns*
by Alexander Woollcott   *1934*

45 Constant use had not worn ragged the fabric of their
friendship.
The Standard of Living   *1944*

46 Wit has truth in it; wisecracking is simply calisthenics
with words.
Quoted in *Paris Review*   *Summer, 1956*

47 As artists [lady novelists] they're rot, but as providers
they're oil wells—they gush.
Quoted in *The Years with Ross*
by James Thurber   *1959*

48 She [Katharine Hepburn] runs the gamut of emotions
from A to B.
Quoted in *Publisher's Weekly*   *June 19, 1967p*

49 The only "ism" she believes in is plagiarism.
Ibid.

50 I was following in the exquisite footsteps of Miss Edna
St. Vincent Millay, unhappily in my own horrible
sneakers.
Ibid.

51 I heard someone say, and so I said it too, that ridicule
is the most effective weapon. Well, now I know. I know
that there are things that never have been funny, and
never will be. And I know that ridicule may be a
shield, but it is not a weapon.
Quoted in *You Might as Well Live*
by John Keats   *1970p*

* * *

604

52 Excuse my dust.

"Epitaph"

53 Accursed from their birth they be
   Who seek to find monogamy,
   Pursuing it from bed to bed—
   I think they would be better dead.

"Reuben's Children"

54 . . . art is a form of catharsis. . . .

"Art"

641. Mary Pickford
(1893–   )

1 I was forced to live far beyond my years when just a child, now I have reversed the order and I intend to remain young indefinitely.

Quoted in "How Mary Pickford Stays
Young" by Athene Farnsworth,
Everybody's Magazine   May, 1926

2 I left the screen because I didn't want what happened to Chaplin to happen to me. When he discarded the little tramp, the little tramp turned around and killed him.

Quoted in "America's Sweetheart
Lives" by Aljean Harmetz,
The New York Times   March 28, 1971

642. Dorothy L. Sayers
(1893–1957)

1 "A man goes and fights for his country, gets his inside gassed out, and loses his job, and all they give him is the privilege of marching past the Cenotaph once a year and paying four shillings in the pound income-tax."

The Unpleasantness at the
Bellona Club, Ch. 1   1928

2 The planet's tyrant, dotard Death, had held his gray mirror before them for a moment and shown them the image of things to come.

Ibid., Ch. 2

3 "I'm determined never to be a parent. Modern manners and the break-up of the fine old traditions have simply ruined the business. I shall devote my life and fortune to the endowment of research on the best method of producing human beings decorously and unobtrusively from eggs. All parental responsibility to devolve upon the incubator."

Ibid., Ch. 3

4 "Very dangerous things, theories."

Ibid., Ch. 4

5 "But I don't believe women ever get sensible, not even through prolonged association with their husbands."

Ibid., Ch. 8

6 "And a continued atmosphere of hectic passion is very trying if you haven't got any of your own."

Ibid., Ch. 10

7 Death seems to provide the minds of the Anglo-Saxon race with a greater fund of amusement than any other single subject. . . .

The Third Omnibus of Crime,
Introduction   *1935*

8 "If you want to set up your everlasting rest, you are far more likely to find it in the life of the mind than the life of the heart."

Gaudy Night   *1936*

9 "A desire to have all the fun," he says, "is nine-tenths of the law of chivalry."

Ibid.

10 "People who make some other person their job are dangerous."

Ibid.

11 "Once lay down the rule that the job comes first, and you throw that job open to every individual . . . who is able to do that job better than the rest of the world."

Ibid.

12 "There is perhaps one human being in a thousand who is passionately interested in his job for the job's sake. The difference is that if that one person in a thousand is a man, we say, simply, that he is passionately keen on his job; if she is a woman, we say she is a freak."

Ibid.

13 ". . . of all devils let loose in the world there [is] no devil like devoted love. . . ."

Ibid.

14 ". . . love's a nervous, awkward, overmastering brute; if you can't rein him, it's best to have no truck with him."

Ibid.

15 "The only sin passion can commit is to be joyless."

Busman's Honeymoon   1947

16 ". . . a human being must have occupation if he or she is not to become a nuisance to the world."

Ibid.

17 "Many words have no legal meaning. Others have a legal meaning very unlike their ordinary meaning. For example, the word 'daffy-down-dilly.' It is a criminal libel to call a lawyer a 'daffy-down-dilly.' Ha! Yes, I advise you never to do such a thing. No, I certainly advise you *never* to do it."

Unnatural Death, Ch. 14   1955

18 "Contrast," philosophized Lord Peter sleepily, "is life. . . ."

Clouds of Witness, Ch. 1   1956

19 ". . . What? Sunday morning in an English family and no sausages? God bless my soul, what's the world coming to, eh . . . ?"

Ibid., Ch. 2

20 "Lawyers enjoy a little mystery, you know. Why, if everybody came forward and told the truth, the whole truth, and nothing but the truth straight out, we should all retire to the workhouse."

Ibid., Ch. 3

21 "She always says, my lord, that facts are like cows. If you look them in the face hard enough they generally run away."

Ibid., Ch. 4

22   "But after all, what's money?"
    "Nothing, of course," said Peter. "But if you've been brought up to havin' it, it's a bit awkward to drop it suddenly. Like baths, you know."

Ibid., Ch. 7

23 "Well-bred English people never have imagination. . . ."
Ibid., Ch. 11

24 ". . . And the w'y they speak—that took some gettin'
used to. Call that English, I useter say, give me the
Frenchies in the Chantycleer Restaurong, I ses."
Ibid.

25 "Time and trouble will tame an advanced young
woman, but an advanced old woman is uncontrollable
by any earthly force."
Ibid., Ch. 16

* * *

26 The keeping of an idle woman is a badge of superior
social status.
Essay

643. Evelyn Scott
(1893–1963)

1 If I could only *feel* the child! I imagine the moment of
its quickening as a sudden awakening of my own being
which has never before had life. I want to *live* with the
child, and I am as heavy as a stone.
Escapade   1913

2 Inwardly shrinking and cold with an obscure fear, I
make it a point to look very directly at all the men who
speak to me. I want to shame them by the straightfor-
wardness of my gaze.
Ibid.

3 I realized a long time ago that a belief which does not
spring from a conviction in the emotions is no belief at
all.
Ibid.

4 Yes, I want to be an outcast in order to realize fully
what human beings are capable of. Now I know that
fear and cruelty underlie all of society's protestations in
favor of honesty and moral worth.
Ibid.

5 To have one's individuality completely ignored is like
being pushed quite out of life. Like being blown out as
one blows out a light.
Ibid.

608

6 Anything which is entirely beyond my control fascinates me and seems to me to have some awful and particular significance. . . . It is impossible to control creation.

Ibid.

7 If nobody recognizes me, then it is a sign that I have ceased to exist.

Ibid.

8 People think that in order to give up financial security one must be intoxicated.

Ibid.

9 . . . pain is timeless, absolute. It has removed itself from space. It always has been and always will be for it exists independent of relations.

Ibid.

10 He was too young to want milk but I held his face against my breast. In all my desire for him I was conscious of a heavy sensuality, a massiveness of appreciation.

Ibid.

644. Madame Sun Yat-sen
(1893–   )

1 Liberty and equality, those two inalienable rights of the individual . . . but there is still Fraternity to be acquired. . . . And it may be for China, the oldest of nations, to point the way to this Fraternity.

Quoted in *The Wesleyan*   *April, 1912*

2 In the last analysis, all revolutions must be social revolutions, based upon fundamental changes in society; otherwise it is not revolution, but merely a change of government. . . .

Article in the *People's Tribune*   *July 14, 1927*

3 . . . I want especially to say to our young people . . . learn from Sun Yat-sen! Imbibe his continuous zeal, study his demand for constant progress, emulate his lack of subjectiveness, his humbleness and his closeness to the people. Make these characteristics part of your own makeup. With these you can surely go forward to build a great socialist China.

"The Chinese Women's
Fight for Freedom," *Asia*
July-August, 1956

4 Let us exert every ounce of man's energy and everything produced by him to ensure that everywhere the
common people of the world get their due from life.
This is to say that our task does not end until every
hovel has been rebuilt into a decent house, until the
products of the earth are within easy reach of all, until
the profits from the factories are returned in equal
amount to the effort exerted, until the family can have
complete medical care from the cradle to the grave.

Ibid., Address (September 21, 1949)

5 Civil war cannot bring unity, liberation or livelihood.
. . . The peasants will support the Communists, who
give them land and lower taxes. . . . Why then do the
reactionaries inflame a war which *they cannot win?*

Public Statement (1947), Quoted in
Women in Modern China
by Helen Foster Snow   *1967*

645. Clara Thompson
(1893–1958)

1 Although this is a special group within the culture [the
upper classes], it is an important group because, on the
whole, it is a thinking group, nonconformist, and seeking to bring about changes in the cultural situation.

"The Role of Women in This Culture,"
Psychiatry, Vol. IV   *1941*

2 The question of her inferiority scarcely troubles her
when her life is happily fulfilled, even though she lives
in relative slavery.

Ibid.

3 Industry has been taken out of the home.

Ibid.

4 The women of past generations had no choice but to
bear children. Since their lives were organized around
this concept of duty, they seldom became aware of dislike of the situation, but there must have been many
unwanted children then. Nowadays, when women have
a choice, the illusion is to the effect that unwanted children are less common, but women still from neurotic
compulsion bear children they cannot love.

Ibid.

5 Sexual freedom [for women] can be an excellent instrument for the expression of neurotic drives arising
outside the strictly sexual sphere, especially drives ex-
pressive of hostility to men, or of the desire to be a
man. Thus promiscuity may mean the collecting of
scalps with the hope of hurting men, frustrating them,
or taking away their importance, or in another case it
may mean to the woman that she is herself a man.
Ibid.

6 The question that is raised in any study of change,
whether by evolution or revolution, takes the form:
Can one say that people are more benefited or harmed?
Ibid.

7 People who have a low self-esteem . . . have a ten-
dency to cling to their own sex because it is less frighten-
ing.
"Changing Concepts of Homosexuality
in Psychoanalysis," *A Study of*
Interpersonal Relations, New
Contributions to Psychiatry,
Patrick Mullahy, ed.   *1949*

8 The fact that one is married by no means proves that
one is a mature person.   *Ibid.*

646. Sylvia Townsend Warner
(1893–   )

1 Blest fertile Dullness! mothering surmise, rumor, report, as stagnant water, flies, whose happy votaries,
stung by every hatch, divinely itch, and more divinely
scratch!   *Opus Seven*   *1931*

2 "PANSY. *Pheonix phoenixissima formosissima arabiana.*
This rare and fabulous bird is UNIQUE. The World's Old
Bachelor. Has no mate and doesn't want one. When
old, sets fire to itself and emerges miraculously reborn.
Specially imported from the East."
"The Phoenix," *The Cat's Cradle-Book*   *1940*

3 It was the ambiguous interval of winter nightfall when
one seems to be wading through darkness as through
knee-high water while there is still light overhead.
"A Stranger with a Bag," *Swans*
on an Autumn River   *1966*

4 But no one would possibly listen to her. No one ever listened to one unless one said the wrong thing.

> Ibid., "Fenella"

5 . . . somewhere out to sea . . . was a bell buoy, rocking and ringing. It seemed as though a heart were beating—a serene, impersonal heart that rocked on a tide of salt water.

> Ibid., "Heathy Landscape with Dormouse"

6 You are only young once. At the time it seems endless, and is gone in a flash; and then for a very long time you are old.

> Ibid., "Swans on an Autumn River"

7 . . . Audrey carried in *The Daily Telegraph*. Mother turned with avidity to the Deaths. When other helpers fail and comforts flee, when the senses decay and the mind moves in a narrower and narrower circle, when the grasshopper is a burden and the postman brings no letters, and even the Royal Family is no longer quite what it was, an obituary column stands fast.

> Ibid., "Their Quiet Lives"

8 There are some women, Meg was one of them, in whom conscience is so strongly developed that it leaves little room for anything else. Love is scarcely felt before duty rushes to encase it, anger impossible because one must always be calm and see both sides, pity evaporates in expedients, even grief is felt as a sort of bruised sense of injury, a resentment that one should have grief forced upon one when one has always acted for the best.

> Ibid., "Total Loss"

9 Efficient people are always sending needless telegrams.

> Ibid., "The View of Rome"

647. Katherine Bowditch
(1894–1933)

* * *

1 And what am I but love of you made flesh,
Quickened by every longing love may bring,
A pilgrim fire, homeless and wandering.

> "Reincarnation"

648. Rachel Lyman Field
(1894–1942)

1 You won't know why, and you can't say now
  Such a change upon you came,
  But—once you have slept on an island
  You'll never be quite the same!
                    "If Once You Have Slept on an
        Island," *Taxis and Toadstools*   1926

* * *

2 Doorbells are like a magic game,
    Or the grab-bag at a fair—
  You never know when you hear one ring
    Who may be waiting there.

                              "Doorbells"

649. Esther Forbes
(1894–1967)

1 Women have almost a genius for anti-climaxes.
                  O Genteel Lady!   1926

2 Most American heroes of the Revolutionary period are
  by now two men, the actual man and the romantic image. Some are even three men—the actual man, the
  image, and the debunked remains.
                  Paul Revere   1942

650. Martha Graham
(1894–   )

1 Nothing is more revealing than movement.
                  "The American Dance," *Modern
        Dance*, Virginia Stewart, ed.   1935

2 America does not concern itself now with Impression-
  ism. We own no involved philosophy. The psyche of
  the land is to be found in its movement. It is to be felt
  as a dramatic force of energy and vitality. We move;
  we do not stand still. We have not yet arrived at the
  stock-taking stage.
                              Ibid.

3 We look at the dance to impart the sensation of living
in an affirmation of life, to energize the spectator into
keener awareness of the vigor, the mystery, the humor,
the variety, and the wonder of life. This is the function
of the American dance.

Ibid.

651. Agnes Kendrick Gray
(1894–?)

* * *

1 Sure, 'tis God's ways is very quare,
    An' far beyont my ken,
How o' the selfsame clay he makes
    Poets an' useful men.

"The Shepherd to the Poet," St. 4

652. Osa Johnson
(1894–1953)

1 "A woman that's too soft and sweet is like tapioca pud-
ding—fine for them as likes it."

I Married Adventure, Ch. 10   1940

2 Theirs, it might be said, was a Utopian existence, for
they [pygmies] showed neither hate, greed, vanity, nor
any other of the dominatingly unpleasant emotions of
our so-called civilized world. Each dusky hop-o'-my-
thumb plays his pleasant game of life with no desire to
interfere with, and caring little about, the conduct of
his fellows.

Ibid., Ch. 27

3 When I was most tired, particularly after a hot safari in
the dry, dusty plains, I always found relaxation and refreshment in my garden. It was my shop window of
loveliness, and Nature changed it regularly that I might
feast my hungry eyes upon it. Lone female that I was,
this was my special world of beauty: these were my
changing styles and my fashion parade.

Ibid., Ch. 9

4 "We must string him up in the presence of the chief
and the villagers. . . . We have to break this murder
madness on the island; we must make a show of force

that they will remember every time they want to go on a
rampage and give them a picture of retribution they
can't doubt and will not forget."

Bride in the Solomons, Ch. 1   1944

5 "Animals and primitive people are alike in one thing,"
he said. "They know when you are friendly, they can
sense it. . . . They can even smell fear."

Ibid., Ch. 18

653. Jean Rhys
(1894–   )

1 . . . Miss Bruce, passing by a shop, with the perpetual
hunger to be beautiful and that thirst to be loved which
is the real curse of Eve. . . . Then must have begun
the search for *the* dress, the perfect Dress, beautiful,
beautifying, possible to be worn. And lastly, the search
for illusion—a craving, almost a vice, the stolen waters
and the bread eaten in secret of Miss Bruce's life.

"Illusion," *The Left Bank*   1927

2 "I don't get any *kick* out of Anglo-Saxons," she said
out loud. "They don't . . . they *don't* stimulate my
imagination!"

Ibid., "Tout Montparnasse and Lady"

3 She respected Americans: they were not like the English, who, under a surface of annoying moroseness of
manner, were notoriously timid and easy to turn round
your finger.

Ibid., "Mannequin"

4 "But I do not wish to sell my pictures. And, as I do not
wish to sell them, exhibiting is useless. My pictures are
precious to me. They are precious, most probably, to
no one else."

Ibid., "Tea with an Artist"

5 For the first time she had dimly realized that only the
hopeless are starkly sincere and that only the unhappy
can either give or take sympathy—even some of the
bitter and dangerous voluptuousness of misery.

Ibid., "In the Rue de l'Arrivée"

6 Saved, rescued, fished-up, half-drowned, out of the
deep, dark river, dry clothes, hair shampooed and

set. Nobody would know I had ever been in it. Except,
of course, that there always remains something. Yes,
there always remains something. . . . Never mind,
here I am, sane and dry, with my place to hide in.
What more do I want?

Good Morning, Midnight, Pt. I   1939

7 We can't all be happy, we can't all be rich, we can't all
be lucky—and it would be so much less fun if we were.
Isn't it so, Mr. Blank? There must be the dark background to show off the bright colours. Some must cry
so that others may be able to laugh the more heartily.
Sacrifices are necessary. . . . Let's say you have this
mystical right to cut my legs off. But the right to ridicule me afterwards because I am a cripple—no, that I
think you haven't got.

Ibid.

8 Next week, or next month, or next year I'll kill myself.
But I might as well last out my month's rent, which has
been paid up, and my credit for breakfast in the morning.

Ibid., Pt. II

9 "I often want to cry. That is the only advantage women
have over men—at least they can cry."   Ibid.

654. Dora Russell
(1894–?)

1 Marriage, laws, the police, armies and navies are the
mark of human incompetence.

The Right to Be Happy   1927

655. Adela Rogers St. Johns
(1894–   )

1 The modern woman is the curse of the universe. A disaster, that's what. She thinks that before her arrival on
the scene no woman ever did anything worthwhile before, no woman was ever liberated until her time, no
woman really ever amounted to anything. . . .

Quoted in "Some Are Born Great"
by Mert Guswiler, *Los Angeles
Herald-Examiner*   October 13, 1974

2 About twenty-five years ago . . . I made three resolutions of what I would never do again. They were: to put on a girdle, to wear high heels, and to go out to dinner. *Ibid.*

3 I think every woman's entitled to a middle husband she can forget.

Quoted in "She's Had the Last Word
for Sixty Years" by Joyce Haber,
Los Angeles Times   *October 13, 1974*

4 Roosevelt had great class. He not only handled them [the press], he used them. F.D.R. would send for reporters and pick their brains. . . . He adored Eleanor. He had mistresses, but let's face facts. If more people would face facts, there'd be fewer broken marriages. *Ibid.*

5 I've often thought with Nixon that if he'd made the football team, his life would have been different. *Ibid.*

6 Why keep the [Watergate] tapes around? It's like you left the corpse in the bullring. *Ibid.*

7 Mrs. [Margaret] Sanger said the best birth control is to make your husband sleep on the roof.

Some Are Born Great   1974

8 People don't think the only American saint is a woman [Mother Cabrini]. I knew her and didn't know she was a saint. She didn't know, either. She built the first school and first hospital in every town. *Ibid.*

656. Genevieve Taggard
(1894–1948)

* * *

1 Try tropic for your balm,
Try storm,
And after storm, calm.
Try snow of heaven, heavy, soft and slow,
Brilliant and warm.
Nothing will help, and nothing do much harm.

"Of the Properties of Nature for
Healing an Illness," St. 1

657. Dorothy Thompson
(1894–1961)

1 But I do not think that Communism as a belief, apart
from overt and illegal actions, can be successfully com-
batted by police methods, persecution, war or a mere
anti spirit. The only force that can overcome an idea
and a faith is another and better idea and faith, positively and fearlessly upheld.

Quoted in the *Ladies' Home Journal*   *October, 1954*

2 The United States is the only great and populous
nation-state and world power whose people are not ce-
mented by ties of blood, race or original language. It is
the only world power which recognizes but one nationality of its citizens—American. . . . How can such a
union be maintained except through some idea which
involves loyalty?

Ibid.

3 Of all forms of government and society, those of free
men and women are in many respects the most brittle.
They give the fullest freedom for activities of private
persons and groups who often identify their own interests, essentially selfish, with the general welfare.

On the Record   *May, 1958*

4 It is not the fact of liberty but the way in which liberty
is exercised that ultimately determines whether liberty
itself survives.

Ibid.

5 They have not wanted *Peace* at all; they have wanted
to be spared war—as though the absence of war was
the same as peace.   Ibid.

658. Babette Deutsch
(1895–   )

1 But the poet's job is, after all, to translate God's poem
(or is it the Fiend's?) into words.

"Poetry at the Mid-Century,"
The Writer's Book,
Helen Hull, ed.   *1950*

2 The poets were among the first to realize the hollowness of a world in which love is made to seem as stan-
dardized as plumbing, and death is actually a mecha-
nized industry. . . .

> Ibid.

3 . . . the poet . . . like the lover . . . is a person unable to reconcile what he knows with what he feels. His
peculiarity is that he is under a certain compulsion to
do so.

> Ibid.

* * *

4 Their memories: a heap of tumbling stones,
Once builded stronger than a city wall.

> "Old Women"

5 You, also, laughing one,
Tosser of balls in the sun,
Will pillow your bright head
By the incurious dead.

> "A Girl"

659. Juana de Ibarbourou
(1895–   )

1 I give you my naked soul
Like a statue unveiled.

> "The Hour," *Diamond Tongues*   1919

2 For if I am so rich, if I have so much,
If they see me surrounded by every luxury,
It is because of my noble lineage
That builds castles on my pillow.

> Ibid., "Small Woman"

660. Dolores Ibarruri
(1895–   )

1 It is better to die on your feet than to live on your
knees!

> Radio Speech   *July 18, 1936*

2 It is better to be the widow of a hero than the wife of a
coward.

> Speech, Valencia   *1936*

3 . . . the working people of the whole world know that if fascism were to triumph in Spain, every democratic country in the world would be confronted with the fascist danger.

Speeches and Articles, 1936–1938   1938

4 Wherever they pass they [the fascists] sow death and desolation.

Ibid.

5 We shall very soon achieve victory and return to our children. . . .

Ibid.

6 Women have always played a prominent part, supporting the men in the struggle for liberty and showing them by their example that it is better to die than to bow to the butchers and oppressors of the people.

Ibid.

7 We dip our colours in honour of you, dear women comrades, who march into battle together with the men.

Ibid.

8 Never shall we see you again, yet we feel your closeness.

Ibid.

9 The lost their way and found themselves in the enemy's lines. They were surrounded and defended themselves until the bullets in their revolvers were exhausted. Lena kept the last bullet for herself. She committed suicide so as not to fall into the hands of the enemy.

Ibid.

661. Bessie Rowland James
(1895–?)

* * *

1 No matter how lofty you are in your department, the responsibility for what your lowliest assistant is doing is yours.

Adlai's Almanac

662. Dorothea Lange
(1895–1965)

1 These [country women] are women of the American
soil. They are a hardy stock. They are the roots of our
country. . . . They are not our well-advertised women
of beauty and fashion. . . . These women represent a
different mode of life. They are of *themselves* a very
great American style. They live with courage and purpose, a part of our tradition.

> Quoted in *The Woman's Eye*
> by Anne Tucker   *1973p*

663. Susanne K. Langer
(1895–   )

1 Feeling, in the broad sense of whatever is felt in any
way, as sensory stimulus or inward tension, pain, emotion or intent, is the mark of mentality.

> *Mind, An Essay on Human*
> *Feeling,* Vol. I, Pt. I, Ch. 1   *1967*

2 The secret of the "fusion" is the fact that the artists's
eye sees in nature . . . an inexhaustible wealth of tension, rhythms, continuities and contrasts which can be
rendered in line and color; and those are the "internal
forms" which the "external forms"—paintings, musical
or poetic compositions or any other works of art—
express for us.

> Ibid., Pt. II, Ch. 4

3 Art is the objectification of feeling. . . .   Ibid.

4 Every artistic form reflects the dynamism that is constantly building up the life of feeling. It is this same
dynamism that records itself in organic forms; growth
is its most characteristic process, and is the source of
almost all familiar living shape. Hence the kinship between organic and artistic forms, though the latter need
not be modeled on any natural object at all. If a work
of art is a projection of feeling, that kinship with organic nature will emerge, no matter through how many
transformations, logically and inevitably.

> Ibid., Ch. 7

5 "Consciousness" is not an entity at all, let alone a special cybernetic mechanism. It is a condition built up out of mental acts of a particular life episode. . . .

Ibid., Ch. 11

664. Monica Baldwin
(1896–?)

1 . . . all the magic of the countryside which is ordained from the healing of the soul.

I Leap Over the Wall   1950

2 You might have been standing in the heart of an iceberg, so strange it was, so silent, so austere.

Ibid.

665. Ruth Gordon
(1896–   )

1 MAX. I *always* get seventy-eight. No more, no less. It's nerve-wracking. I'd almost rather flunk once in a while.

Over Twenty-One, Act I   1943

2 POLLY. People like us and people born to be soldiers are kind of getting to be one and the same.

GOW. They are not—they're just all dressing alike. A uniform doesn't make a soldier. It takes aptitude, just like anything else.

Ibid., Act II

3 MAX. Say, is it too early for a drink?

POLLY. What's early about it? It's tomorrow in Europe and yesterday in China.

Ibid., Act III

4 POLLY. Do you realize you've come damn close to breaking a man's spirit?

GOW. Well, it was his spirit or my bank account.

Ibid.

5 JOE. You hit it! The truth's no good to me, Polly! History just isn't practical. . . . We can't stick to history. History's unbelievable! And it's up to us to make it seem real.

622

POLLY. Honest to God, Joe, you must have a brain of solid popcorn. *Ibid.*

6 CLYDE. Nothing dates one so dreadfully as to think someplace is uptown. . . . At our age one must be watchful of these conversational gray hairs.
The Leading Lady, Act I 1948

7 CLYDE. I'm sure the way to be happy is to live well beyond your means! *Ibid.*

8 CLYDE. The best impromptu speeches are the ones written well in advance.
Ibid.

9 GAY. So easy to fall into a rut, isn't it? Why should ruts be so comfortable and so unpopular?
Ibid., Act II

10 BENJY. The kiss. There are all sorts of kisses, lad, from the sticky confection to the kiss of death. Of them all, the kiss of an actress is the most unnerving. How can we tell if she means it or if she's just practicing?
Ibid.

11 MRS. GILSON. The circle comes around for everyone. It dips, but it comes round. Seven lean years and seven fat ones. And seven lean and seven fat. It doesn't always have to be seven, but some number! Never knew anyone didn't have the balloon go up and down.
Ibid., Act III

12 MRS. GILSON. Up and the world is your oyster! This time you can't miss! Whack comes down the old shillaly and you're down again bitin' the dust! Can't face it! Screeching into your pillow nights! Put back your smile in the morning, trampin' to managers' offices! Home again in the evenin' ready to give up the ghost. Somebody comes by, to tell you: "Go see Frohman nine-thirty sharp!" Luck's turned, you're on the trolley again! Curl up your ostrich feathers! Sponge off the train of your skirt! Because it's all aboard tomorrow. . . .
Ibid.

13 At seventy-four I look better than seventy-three. If you make it through seventy-four years, can it be that things shape up?
"Myself Among Others,"
Myself Among Others 1948

14 To get it right, be born with luck or else make it. *Never* give up. Get the knack of getting people to help you and also pitch in yourself. A little money helps, but what *really* gets it right is to *never*—I repeat—*never* under any condition face the facts.

Ibid.

15 "The good that men do lives after them." That's a quote from myself. I know the correct one, but I don't think so. I think the *good* lives after. The evil gets accepted or forgotten. Or becomes hearsay. The *good* lives on and does us all some good.

Ibid., "The Good That Men Do"

666. Vivien Kellems
(1896–1975)

1 Our tax law is a 1,598-page hydra-headed monster and I'm going to attack and attack and attack until I have ironed out every fault in it.

Quoted in "Vivien Kellems, Crusader
Against IRS" by Narda Z. Trout,
Los Angeles Times   January 26, 1975

2 Of course I'm a publicity hound. Aren't all crusaders? How can you accomplish anything unless people know what you're trying to do?

Quoted in "Unforgettable Vivien
Kellems" by Gloria Swanson,
Reader's Digest   October, 1975p

3 Men always try to keep women out of business so they won't find out how much fun it really is.

Ibid.

4 . . . the IRS has stolen from me over the past 20 years because I am single. It is unconstitutional to impose a penalty tax of 40 percent on me because I have no husband.

Ibid., (c.1969)

667. Martha Martin
(1896–1959)

1 I killed a sea otter today. I actually did kill a sea otter. I killed him with the ax, dragged him home, and skinned him.

O Rugged Land of Gold   1952

2 This awful deep snow and hard cold is going to kill off much of our wild life. Poor creatures, what a pity they can't all be like bears and sleep the winter through.

Ibid.

3 I have never seen a child born. I always felt inadequate to help and was too modest to want to be a spectator. I have never seen anything born—not even a cat. . . . I am no longer afraid, yet I do wish someone were with me to help me take care of the child. . . .

Ibid.

4 My darling little girl-child, after such a long and troublesome waiting I now have you in my arms. I am alone no more. I have my baby.

Ibid.

5 I told her the deer are our helpers and our friends, our subjects and our comfort, and they will give us food and clothing according to our needs. I told her of the birds. . . . Told her of the fishes. . . . Told her of the mink and the otter, and the great brown bear with his funny, furry cub. Told her of the forest and of the things it will give us . . . of the majestic mountain uprising behind us with a vein of gold-bearing ore coming straight from its heart. Told her that all these things were ours to have and to rule over and care for.

Ibid.

6 The Indians have come, good, good Indians. Shy, fat, smelly, friendly, kindhearted Indians.

Ibid.

668. Beata Rank
(1896–1967)

1 . . . examine the personality of the mother, who is the medium through which the primitive infant transforms himself into a socialized human being.

> "Adaptation of the Psychoanalytical
> Technique . . . ," *American Journal
> of Orthopsychiatry*   *January, 1949*

2 Because she is so barren of spontaneous manifestations of maternal feelings, she studies vigilantly all the new methods of upbringing and reads treatises about physical and mental hygiene.

> Ibid.

669. Marjorie Kinnan Rawlings
(1896–1953)

1 There was something about the most fertile field that was beyond control. A man could work himself to skin and bones, so that there was no flesh left on him to make sweat in the sun, and a crop would get away from him. There was something about all living that was uncertain.

> *South Moon Under*, Ch. 3   *1933*

2 Sorrow was like the wind. It came in gusts, shaking the woman. She braced herself.

> Ibid., Ch. 9

3 You can't change a man, no-ways. By the time his mummy turns him loose and he takes up with some innocent woman and marries her, he's what he is.

> "Benny and the Bird Dogs"   *1938*

4 It seemed a strange thing to him, when earth was earth and rain was rain, that scrawny pines should grow in the scrub, while by every branch and lake and river there grew magnolias. Dogs were the same everywhere, and oxen and mules and horses. But trees were different in different places.

> *The Yearling*, Ch. 1   *1938*

5 The game seemed for him to be two different animals. On the chase, it was the quarry. He wanted only to see it fall. . . . When it lay dead and bleeding, he was sickened and sorry. . . . Then when it was cut into portions . . . his mouth watered at its goodness. He wondered by what alchemy it was changed, so that what sickened him one hour, maddened him with hunger the next. It seemed as though there were either two different animals or two different boys.

Ibid., Ch. 8

6 "A woman has got to love a bad man once or twice in her life, to be thankful for a good one."

Ibid., Ch. 12

7 Living was no longer the grief behind him, but the anxiety ahead.

Ibid., Ch. 33

8 "You figgered I went back on you. Now there's a thing ever' man has got to know. Mebbe you know it a'ready. 'Twa'n't only me. 'Twa'n't only your yearlin' deer havin' to be destroyed. Boy, life goes back on you."

Ibid.

9 "Ever' man wants life to be a fine thing, and a easy. 'Tis fine, boy, powerful fine, but 'tain't easy. Life knocks a man down and he gits up and it knocks him down agin. I've been uneasy all my life."

Ibid.

10 He was the delight of fine cooks, who took his absent-minded capacity for appreciation.

The Sojourner, Ch. 1   *1953*

11 He found himself denying this so-called force of gravity. It could not be what tied men to earth. It was a heavy weight, an unendurable pressure from the outerland, and if a man could once break through it, soar high like a bird, he would be free, would meet, would join, something greater than he, and be complete at last.

Ibid., Ch. 15

12 They were all too tightly bound together, men and women, creatures wild and tame, flowers, fruits and leaves, to ask that any one be spared. As long as the whole continued, the earth could go about its business.

Ibid., Ch. 20

670. Betty Smith
(1896–1972)

1 There's a tree that grows in Brooklyn. Some people call
it the Tree of Heaven. No matter where its seed falls, it
makes a tree which struggles to reach the sky. It grows
in boarded-up plots and out of neglected rubbish heaps.
It grows up out of cellar gratings. It is the only tree
that grows out of cement. It grows lushly . . . survives
without sun, water, and seemingly without earth. It
would be considered beautiful except that there are too
many of it.

> *A Tree Grows in Brooklyn*   1958

2 "If it makes her feel better to throw it away rather than
to drink it, all right. *I* think it's good that people like us
can waste something once in a while and get the feeling
of how it would be to have lots of money and not have
to worry about scrounging."

> Ibid., Ch. 1

3 "My Francie wears no hair bow but her hair is long
and shiny. Can money buy things like that? That
means there must be something bigger than money."

> Ibid., Ch. 27

4 Miss Gardner had nothing in all the world excepting a
sureness about how right she was.

> Ibid., Ch. 42

5 "The difference between rich and poor," said Francie,
"is that the poor do everything with their own hands
and the rich hire hands to do things."

> Ibid., Ch. 45

6 "Is it not so that a son what is bad to his mother," he
said, "is bad to his wife?"

> *Maggie—Now*, Ch. 1   1958

7 She felt, vaguely, that she had given away her childhood that night. She had given it to him or he had
taken it from her, and made it into something wonderful. In a way, her life was his now.   Ibid., Ch. 23

8 ". . . I can never give a 'yes' or a 'no.' I don't believe
everything in life can be settled by a monosyllable."

> Ibid., Ch. 39

671. Dodie Smith
(1896–   )

1 I have found that sitting in a place where you have
never sat before can be inspiring.
I Capture the Castle   1948

2 Noble deeds and hot baths are the best cures for depression.
Ibid., Ch. 3

3 . . . miserable people cannot afford to dislike each
other. Cruel blows of fate call for extreme kindness in
the family circle.
Ibid., Ch. 6

4 Oh, it was the most glorious morning! I suppose the
best kind of spring morning is the best weather God
has to offer. It certainly helps one to believe in Him.
Ibid.

5 ". . . she happens to belong to a type [of American
woman] I frequently met—it goes to lectures. And entertains afterwards. . . . Amazing, their energy," he
went on. "They're perfectly capable of having three or
four children, running a house, keeping abreast of art,
literature and music—superficially of course, but good
lord, that's something—and holding down a job into
the bargain. Some of them get through two or three
husbands as well, just to avoid stagnation."
Ibid., Ch. 7

6 What a difference there is between wearing even the
skimpiest bathing-suit and wearing nothing! After a few
minutes I seemed to live in every inch of my body as
fully as I usually do in my head and my hands and my
heart. I had the fascinating feeling that I could think as
easily with my limbs as with my brain. . . .
Ibid., Ch. 12

7 Perhaps the effect wears off in time, or perhaps you
don't notice it if you are born to it, but it does seem to
me that the climate of richness must always be a little
dulling to the senses. Perhaps it takes the edge off joy
as well as off sorrow.
Ibid., Ch. 14

8 ". . . I don't like the sound of all those lists he's making—it's like taking too many notes at school; you feel
you've achieved something when you haven't."

Ibid., Ch. 15

672. Charlotte Whitton
(1896–1975?)

1 Whatever women do they must do twice as well as men
to be thought half as good. Luckily, this is not difficult.

Quoted in Canada Month June, 1963

673. Dixie Wilson
(1896–?)

* * *

1 He may look just the same to you,
 And he may be just as fine,
But the next-door dog is the next-door dog,
 And mine—is—mine!

"Next-Door Dog"

674. Wallis Simpson Windsor
(1896–)

1 I don't remember any love affairs. One must keep love
affairs quiet.

Quoted in the Los Angeles Times April 11, 1974

675. Elizabeth Asquith Bibesco
(1897–1945)

1 I have made a great discovery.
What I love belongs to me. Not the chairs and
tables in my house, but the masterpieces of the world.
It is only a question of loving them enough.

"Balloons" 1922

2 Being in a hurry is one of the tributes he pays to life.

Ibid.

630

3 It is sometimes the man who opens the door who is the last to enter the room.

The Fir and the Palm, Ch. 13 *1924*

4 You are such a wonderful Baedeker to life. All the stars are in the right places.

Ibid.

5 It is never any good dwelling on good-byes. It is not the being together that it prolongs, it is the parting.

Ibid., Ch. 15

676. Catherine Drinker Bowen
(1897–)

1 I know what these people want; I have seen them pick up my violin and turn it over in their hands. They may not know it themselves, but they want music, not by the ticketful, the purseful, but music as it should be had, music at home, a part of daily life, a thing as necessary, as satisfying, as the midday meal. They want to *play.* And they are kept back by the absurd, the mistaken, the wicked notion that in order to play an instrument one must be possessed by that bogey called Talent. . . .

Friends and Fiddlers, Ch. 2 *1934*

2 "We don't want her to take music too seriously." Real concern came into her voice. "We don't want her to become intense over something, and warped and queer. Such women are unhappy in later life. They don't," she rang the bell for more tea, "they don't make good wives."

Ibid., Ch. 4

3 Many a man who has known himself at ten forgets himself utterly between ten and thirty. . . .

Ibid., Ch. 9

4 The professors laugh at themselves, they laugh at life; they long ago abjured the bitch-goddess Success, and the best of them will fight for his scholastic ideals with a courage and persistence that would shame a soldier. The professor is not afraid of words like *truth*; in fact he is not afraid of words at all.

Adventures of a Biographer, Ch. 5 *1946*

5 For your born writer, nothing is so healing as the realization that he has come upon the right word.

Ibid., Ch. 11

6 There is a marvelous turn and trick to British arrogance; its apparent unconsciousness makes it twice as effectual.

Ibid., Ch. 14

7 In writing biography, fact and fiction shouldn't be mixed. And if they are, the fictional points should be printed in red ink, the facts printed in black ink.

Quoted in *Publisher's Weekly*   *March 24, 1958*

8 People who carry a musical soul about them are, I think, more receptive than others. They smile more readily. One feels in them a pleasing propensity toward the lesser sins, a pleasing readiness also to admit the possibility that on occasion they may be in the wrong—they may be mistaken.

Speech, "The Nature of the Artist,"
Scripps College   *April 27, 1961*

9 I have noted that, barring accidents, artists whose powers wear best and last longest are those who have trained themselves to work under adversity. . . . Great artists treasure their time with a bitter and snarling miserliness.

Ibid.

10 Your great artist looks on his talent as a responsibility laid on him by God, or perhaps a curse set on him by the devil. Whichever way he looks at it, while he is writing that book or composing that symphony, DOOM hangs over him. He is afraid something will interfere to stop him. . . . Artists often think they are going to die before their time. They seem to possess a heightened sense of the passing of the hours. . . . I think . . . artists dread death because they love life. Artists, even at their gloomiest, seem to maintain a constant love affair with life, marked by all the ups and downs, the depressions and ecstasies of infatuation. Artists have so much to do, and so little time to do it! Ibid.

11 The things we believe in and want done will not be done until women are in elective office.

Quoted in *National Business Week*
September, 1974

677. Catherine Cate Coblentz
(1897–   )

* * *

1 Life is an archer, fashioning an arrow
With anxious care, for in it life must trust;
A single flash across the earthly spaces
Straight to the throat of death—one conquering thrust!
"Life"

678. Dorothy Day
(1897–   )

1 Tradition! We scarcely know the word any more. We
are afraid to be either proud of our ancestors or
ashamed of them. We scorn nobility in name and in
fact. We cling to a bourgeois mediocrity which would
make it appear we are all Americans, made in the image and likeness of George Washington, all of a pattern, all prospering if we are good, and going down in
the world if we are bad.
The Long Loneliness, Pt. I   *1952*

2 . . . who were the mad and who the sane? . . .
People sold themselves for jobs, for the pay check, and if
they only received a high enough price, they were honored. If their cheating, their theft, their lies, were of
colossal proportions, if it were successful, they met with
praise, not blame.

Ibid.

3 In our disobedience we were trying to obey God rather
than men, trying to follow a higher obedience. We did
not wish to act in a spirit of defiance and rebellion.
Loaves and Fishes, Ch. 16   *1963*

4 One of the greatest evils of the day among those outside
of prison is their sense of futility. Young people say,
What is the sense of our small effort? They cannot see
that we must lay one brick at a time, take one step at a
time; we can be responsible only for the one action of
the present moment. But we can beg for an increase of
love in our hearts that will vitalize and transform all
our individual actions, and know that God will take

633

them and multiply them, as Jesus multiplied the loaves and fishes.

Ibid.

5 Much of the world has changed to a new society where collective and communal ownership is being emphasized to handle the matter of man and his work. But these changes have been brought about by violence and coercion, at the expense of man's freedom. The greatest challenge of the day is: how to bring about a revolution of the heart, a revolution which has to start with each one of us? When we begin to take the lowest place, to wash the feet of others, to love our brothers with that burning love, that passion, which led to the Cross, then we can truly say, "Now I have begun."

Ibid., Ch. 19

679. Hermione Gingold
(1897–   )

1 My father dealt in stocks and shares and my mother also had a lot of time on her hands.

The World Is Square, Pt. I   1945

2 To call him a dog hardly seems to do him justice, though inasmuch as he had four legs, a tail, and barked, I admit he was, to all outward appearances. But to those of us who knew him well, he was a perfect gentleman.

Ibid., Pt. II

3 This isn't a recipe for soup, although it can land you right in the *potage* if you aren't careful.

"I Make Summer Stock,"
*Sirens Should Be Seen and
Not Heard*   1963

4   "Have you anything to back up your theory?"
"I cannot truthfully say I have," Mr. Smith replied. "I just believe implicitly."
"Well," I said, "I suppose it's like believing in the creation. There is much less to back up that theory these scientific days, and yet in spite of everything people still believe."

Ibid., "The Bomb That Had
Mr. Smith's Name on It"

680. Iréne Joliot-Curie
(1897–1956)

1 That one must do some work seriously and must be independent and not merely amuse oneself in life—this our mother [Marie Curie] has told us always, but never that science was the only career worth following.

> Quoted in *A Long Way from Missouri,*
> Ch. 10, by Mary Margaret McBride
> *1959p*

681. Caroline Lejeune
(1897–1973)

1 Nothing is said that can be regretted. Nothing is said that can even be remembered.

> "Dietrich as an Angel,"
> *The Observer* (London) *1936*

2 Not the least remarkable thing about this remarkable picture is its apparent power of dormant development.

> Ibid., "The Truth About Balaklava," *1937*

3 In a world as ravaged as ours there is still room for joy over the maturing of a great talent.

> Ibid., "The Little Man Grows Up," *1940*

4 . . . for a good book has this quality, that it is not merely a petrifaction of its author, but that once it has been tossed behind, like Deucalion's little stone, it acquires a separate and vivid life of its own.

> *Chestnuts in Her Lap, 1936–1946*
> Introduction *1947*

5 It's odd how large a part food plays in memories of childhood. There are grown men and women who still shudder at the sight of spinach, or turn away with loathing from stewed prunes and tapioca. . . . Luckily, however, it's the good tastes one remembers best.

> *Thank You for Having Me*, Ch. 1 *1964*

6 Sometimes it seems to me as if the only quality admired in modern writing, or play-making, or film-making, is truth-and-ugliness. This, for some reason, is

described as realism; as if nothing could be real that is not sordid, disagreeable or violent.

Ibid., Ch. 21

7 I learned a lesson about retirement that was certainly true for me, and might be a help to many other people. When you finish with a job it is wiser to make the break completely. Cut off the old life, clean and sharp. If your mind is tired, that is the only way. If your mind is lively you will soon find other interests.

Ibid., Ch. 22

682. Ruth Pitter
(1897–   )

* * *

1 I go about, but cannot find
The blood-relations of the mind.

"The Lost Tribe," St. 1

2 Though our world burn, the small dim words
Stand here in steadfast grace,
And sing, like the indifferent birds
About a ruined place.   "On an Old Poem," St. 2

683. Lillian Smith
(1897–1966)

1 Faith and doubt both are needed—not as antagonists but working side by side—to take us around the unknown curve.

The Journey   1954

2 To believe in something not yet proved and to underwrite it with our lives: it is the only way we can leave the future open. Man, surrounded by facts, permitting himself no surprise, no intuitive flash, no great hypothesis, no risk, is in a locked cell. Ignorance cannot seal the mind and imagination more securely.   *Ibid.*

3 . . . I am caught again in those revolving doors of childhood.

Killers of the Dream
(Rev. Ed.), Foreword   *1961*

4 *Segregation* . . . a word full of meaning for every person on earth. A word that is both symbol and symptom of our modern, fragmented world. We, the earth people, have shattered our dreams, yes; we have shattered our own lives, too, and our world.

Ibid.

5 Man is a broken creature, yes; it is his nature as a human being to be so; but it is also his nature to create relationships that can span the brokenness. This is his first responsibility; when he fails, he is inevitably destroyed.

Ibid.

6 The human heart dares not stay away too long from that which hurt it most. There is a return journey to anguish that few of us are released from making.

Ibid., Pt. I, Ch. 1

7 I knew, though I would not for years confess it aloud, that in trying to shut the Negro race away from us, we have shut ourselves away from so many good, creative, honest, deeply human things in life. I began to understand slowly at first but more clearly as the years passed, that the warped, distorted frame we have put around every Negro child from birth is around every white child also. Each is on a different side of the frame but each is pinioned there. And I knew that what cruelly shapes and cripples the personality of one is as cruelly shaping and crippling the personality of the other.

Ibid.

8 When . . . [people] unite in common worship and common fear of one idea we know it has come to hold deep and secret meanings for each of them, as different as are the people themselves. We know it has woven itself around fantasies at levels difficult for the mind to touch, until it is a part of each man's internal defense system, embedded like steel in his psychic fortifications. And, like the little dirty rag or doll that an unhappy child sleeps with, it has acquired inflated values. . . .

Ibid., Ch. 4

9 Sometimes we blame Mom too much for all that is wrong with her sons and daughters. After all, we might well ask, who started the grim mess? Who long ago made Mom and her sex "inferior" and stripped her of

her economic and political and sexual rights? . . .
Man, born of woman, has found it a hard thing to forgive
her for giving him birth. The patriarchal protest against
the ancient matriarch has borne strange fruit through
the years. . . .

Ibid., Pt. II, Ch. 4

10 It is a man's dreams that make him human or inhuman
and a man who knows few words to dream with, who
has never heard, in words said aloud, other men's
dreams of human dignity and freedom and tender love,
and brotherhood, who has never heard of man the creator of truth and beauty, who has never even seen
man-made beauty, but has heard only of man the
killer, and words about sex and "race" which fill him
with anger and fear and lust, and words about himself
that make him feel degraded, or blow him up crazily
into paranoid "superiority"—how can he know the
meaning of *human*! How can he know that?

Ibid., Pt. III, Ch. 1

11 Education is a private matter between the person and
the world of knowledge and experience, and has little
to do with school or college. . . .

"Bridges to Other People," Redbook
September, 1969p

12 When you stop learning, stop listening, stop looking
and asking questions, always new questions, then it is
time to die. . . .   Ibid.

684. Margaret Chase Smith
(1897–   )

1 I believe that in our constant search for security we can
never gain any peace of mind until we secure our own
soul. And this I do believe above all, especially in my
times of greater discouragement, *that I must believe*—
that I must believe in my fellow men—that I must believe in myself—that I must believe in God—if life is to
have any meaning.

Essay in This I Believe,
Raymond Swing, ed.   1952

2 My creed is that public service must be more than
doing a job efficiently and honestly. It must be a com-

plete dedication to the people and to the nation with full recognition that every human being is entitled to courtesy and consideration, that constructive criticism is not only to be expected but sought, that smears are not only to be expected but fought, that honor is to be earned but not bought.

"My Creed," *Quick*   *November 11, 1953*

3 In these perilous hours, I fear that the American people are ahead of their leaders in realism and courage—but behind them in knowledge of the facts because the facts have not been given to them.

Address, U.S. Senate   *September 21, 1961*

4 Strength, the American way, is not manifested by threats of criminal prosecution or police state methods. Leadership is not manifested by coercion, even against the resented. Greatness is not manifested by unlimited pragmatism, which places such a high premium on the end justifying *any* means and *any* methods.

Address, National Republican
Women's Conference Banquet
April 16, 1962

5 In today's growing, but tragic, emphasis on materialism, we find a perversion of the values of things in life as we once knew them. For example, the creed once taught children as they grew up was that the most important thing was not in whether you won or lost the game but rather in "how you played the game." That high level attitude that stresses the moral side no longer predominates in this age of pragmatic materialism that increasingly worships the opposite creed that "the end justifies the means" or the attitude of get what you can in any way, manner, or means that you can.

RCA Victor Recording   *1964*

6 We are rapidly approaching a day when the United States will be subject to all sorts of diplomatic blackmail and a strategy of terror waged by the Soviet Union.

"It's Time to Speak Up for National
Defense," *Reader's Digest*
March, 1972

7 We are sick to death of war, defense spending and all things military. We are disgusted with and weary of the vilification that has been heaped upon us, at home as

well as abroad, for our attempts to block communist enslavement in Southeast Asia. We yearn to turn away from foreign entanglements and to begin making our own house a better place to live in.   Ibid.

8 The key to security is public information.

Ibid.

9 There are enough mistakes of the Democrats for the Republicans to criticize constructively without resorting to political smears. . . . Freedom of speech is not what it used to be in America.
Declaration of Conscience   *1972*

10 Before you can become a statesman you first have to get elected, and to get elected you have to be a politician pledging support for what the voters want.
Ibid., "Nuclear Test Ban Treaty"

685. Berenice Abbott
(1898–   )

1 Photography can never grow up if it imitates some other medium. It has to walk alone; it has to be itself.
"It Has to Walk Alone,"
Infinity (magazine)   *1951*

2 If a medium is represented by nature of the realistic image formed by a lens, I see no reason why we should stand on our heads to distort that function. On the contrary, we should take hold of that very quality, make use of it, and explore it to the fullest.

Ibid.

686. Judith Anderson
(1898–   )

1 There is nothing enduring in the life of a woman except what she builds in a man's heart.
News Item   *March 8, 1931*

687. Louise Bogan
(1898–1970)

1 The art of one period cannot be approached through the attitudes (emotional or intellectual) of another.
> "Reading Contemporary Poetry,"
> *College English*   February, 1953

2 The simile has been superseded by the metaphor and the metaphor is often reduced to the image or the symbol.   Ibid.

3 There is no way of reading as one runs, or looking as one runs, when we come to the examination of any highly developed art.
> Ibid.

4 True revolutions in art restore more than they destroy.
> Ibid.

5 Fear kept for thirty-five years poured through his mane,
and retribution equally old, or nearly, breathed through his nose.
> "The Dream," *Collected Poems*
> *(1923–1953)*   1954

6 The terrible beast, that no one may understand,
Came to my side, and put down his head in love.
> Ibid.

7 Now, innocent, within the deep
Night of all things you turn the key,
Unloosing what we know in sleep.
> Ibid., "M., Singing"

8 The good novelist is distinguished from the bad one chiefly by a gift of choice. Choice, itself a talent, as taste is a talent, is not, however, enough. Only extreme sanity and balance of selection can give to prose fiction the dignity and excitement inherent in more rigid forms of writing: drama, poetry, and the expositions of ideas.
> "Colette," *Selected Criticism*
> *(1930)*   1955

9 It is a dangerous lot, that of the charming, romantic public poet, especially if it falls to a woman. . . . it is

almost impossible for the poetess, once laurelled, to take off the crown for good or to reject values and taste of those who tender it.*

Ibid., "Unofficial Feminine Laureate" (1939)

10 But is there any reason to believe that a woman's spiritual fibre is less sturdy than a man's? Is it not possible for a woman to come to terms with herself if not with the world; to withdraw more and more, as time goes on, her own personality from her productions; to stop childish fears of death and eschew charming rebellions against facts?

Ibid.

11 But childhood prolonged, cannot remain a fairyland. It becomes a hell.†

Ibid., "Childhood's False Eden" (1940)

12 The reiterated insinuation that formal art is fraudulent because it is difficult to understand and makes no effort to appeal to the majority—that it is, in fact, somehow treasonable to mankind's higher purposes and aims—is a typical bourgeois notion that has been around for a long time.

Ibid., "Some Notes on Popular and Unpopular Art" (1943)

13 The intellectual is a middle-class product; if he is not born into the class he must soon insert himself into it, in order to exist. He is the fine nervous flower of the bourgeoisie.

Ibid.

14 Because language is the carrier of ideas, it is easy to believe that it should be very little else than such a carrier.

"A Revolution in European Poetry" (1941), A Poet's Alphabet   1970

15 Once form has been smashed, it has been smashed for good, and once a forbidden subject has been released it has been released for good.

Ibid., "Experimentalists of A New Generation" (1957)

---

* Referring to Edna St. Vincent Millay.
† Referring to Katherine Mansfield.

16 The verbal arts, which forty years or so ago were supposed to be spiralling upward toward an ultimately ex-
pressive richness and freedom, at present, according
to one gloomy set of prophets, are gyrating downward
toward silence. It must be remarked, however, that
they are being excessively noisy on their downward
way.   Ibid., "Pro-Tem" (1967)

17 How fortunate the rich and/or married, who have servants and *wives* to expedite matters.
                            *What the Woman Lived: Selected
                            Letters 1920–1970,* Ruth Limmer, ed.
                                                    1974p

18 I don't like quintessential certitude.
                            Ibid., Letter to Rolfe Humphries

19 . . . I wish there was something between love and
friendship that I could tender him [William Maxwell];
and some gesture, not quite a caress, I could give him.
A sort of smoothing. . . . I simply love him like a
brother.
                                                    Ibid.

20 The reason I get so mad at the comrades is that they
always sound as though they had discovered everything
yesterday. . . .
                                                    Ibid.

21 What we suffer, what we endure, what we muff, what
we kill, what we miss, what we are guilty of, is done by
us, as individuals, in private.
                                                    Ibid.

22 A second blooming and the bough can scarcely bear it.
                                                    Ibid.

23 Wifehood is too damned full of hero-husband-worship
for one of my age and disabusedness.
                                                    Ibid.

24 I cannot believe that the inscrutable universe turns on
an axis of suffering; surely the strange beauty of the
world must somewhere rest on pure joy!
                            Ibid., Letter to John Hall Wheelock

25 How good life is! How complicated! . . . I love and
revere life; and intend to keep on being vulgarly alive
just as long as possible.   Ibid.

* * *

26 I'll lie here and learn How, over their ground,
Trees make a long shadow And a light sound.

"Knowledge"

27 Men loved wholly beyond wisdom
Have the staff without the banner.

"Men Loved Wholly"

28 Women have no wilderness in them,
They are provident instead,
Content in the tight hot cell of their hearts
To eat dusty bread.

"Women"

688. Madame Chiang Kai-shek
(1898–   )

1 Of all the inventions that have helped to unify China
perhaps the airplane is the most outstanding. Its ability
to annihilate distance has been in direct proportion to
its achievements in assisting to annihilate suspicion and
misunderstanding among provincial officials far removed from one another or from the officials at the
seat of government.

"Wings Over China," *Shanghai
Evening Post*   *March 12, 1937*

2 There is no shadow of protection to be had by shelter-
ing behind the slender stockades of visionary speculation, or by hiding behind the wagon-wheels of pacific
theories.

Quoted in the *New York Herald
Tribune*   *March 21, 1938*

3 This changing world is rolling towards the abyss of self-
destruction with a breath-taking rapidity.

Speech, International Women's
Conference, Sydney, Australia
(February, 1938), *War Messages
and Other Selections*   *1938*

4 My friends, the world situation is so grave that we can
no longer afford to congratulate each other upon the
splendid success that we have achieved internationally.
It is imperative that we be frank, honest, and effective.
As a first step, I propose that we recognize our failure
mercilessly, even at the expense of our personal pride.

We are guilty, every one of us. Let us say *"mea culpa"* and not blame the rest of the world for what is happening around us.

Ibid.

5 Machinery should be used to make necessities which hands cannot make, but there it should stop.

Ibid., Letter to a Friend (May 14, 1938)

6 No nation that descends to murder, rape and rapine can expect to prosper or be respected.

Ibid., Article in the *Birmingham Post,*
England (May, 1938)

7 The faults of a government can be removed by the citizens, but the citizens must first remove their own faults, and learn in full what self-sacrifice really means. They must be self-reliant, and have self-respect.

Ibid. (1938)

8 Out of the ashes which the Japanese are spreading over our country will arise a phoenix of great national worth.

Ibid., "People's Spiritual Mobilization"
(March 18, 1939)

9 Hammered out on the anvil of experience are four cardinal principles of life, as we Chinese understand life: 1. The way in which human beings behave one toward another. 2. Justice for all classes within our social framework. 3. Honesty in public administration and in business. 4. Self-respect, and a profound sense of the value of personality.

This Is Our China, Sec. I, Ch. 1   1940

10 I am convinced that we must train not only the head, but the heart and hand as well.

Ibid., Sec. II

11 If one task is more outstandingly important than any other in connection with the reform and rehabilitation of our country it must be the eradication of the criminal stagnation that has for so many generations stifled the natural development of our economic life and stood upon our horizon like a grim spectre of predestined rule.

China Shall Rise Again
Pt. I, Ch. 6   1941

12 Cliques seem to hold sway in many places. They are like dry rot in the administration. They stifle enterprise and initiative. They operate to oust honesty and efficiency by preventing a patriotic "outsider," or a stranger to the clique, from gaining a position, no matter how capable he may be. And they eject, or try to, any one of any independence of character or mind who may happen to be near them but not of them. Every clique is a refuge for incompetence. It fosters corruption and disloyalty, it begets cowardice, and consequently is a burden upon and a drawback to the progress of the country. Its instincts and actions are those of the pack.   *Ibid.*, Ch. 8

13 They [the Chinese people] will remember never to believe in international promises or professions—no matter how well-intentioned they may appear to be; no matter how many imposing-looking seals may adorn the documents. To be sure this new wisdom of theirs has been dearly paid for; it will have to be paid for over and over again in more loss of blood and life. But, then I suppose they will have to learn the lesson of life that where there are no pains, there can be no real gains.   *Ibid.*, Pt. III, Ch. 23

14 America is not only the cauldron of democracy, but the incubator of democratic principles.
                    Speech, U.S. House of Representatives
                                    February 18, 1943

15 The universal tendency of the world as represented by the United Nations is as patent and inexorable as the enormous sheets of ice which float down the Hudson in winter. The swift and mighty tide is universal justice and freedom.
                        Speech, Madison Square Garden
                                    March 3, 1943

16 For is it not true that human progress is but a mighty growing pattern woven together by the tenuous single threads united in a common effort?
                            Speech, Wellesley College
                                    March 7, 1943

17 . . . is it not true that faith is the substance of things hoped for, the evidence of things not seen?
                                    Speech, Chicago
                                    March 22, 1943

18 China's struggle now is the initial phase of a gigantic conflict between good and evil, between liberty and communism.

Radio Address, New York
January 9, 1950

19 Truth requires that each people live according to its own traditions in a climate of human liberty and dignity. That has been the soul of Chinese civilization.

Ibid.

689. Amelia Earhart
(1898–1937)

1 Courage is the price that Life exacts for granting peace.
Courage 1927

2 There are two kinds of stones, as everyone knows, one of which rolls.

20 Hours: 40 Minutes—Our Flight in the Friendship, Ch. 1 1928

3 There is so much that must be done in a civilized barbarism like war.
Ibid.

4 In soloing—as in other activities—it is far easier to start something than it is to finish it. Ibid., Ch. 2

5 Of course I realized there was a measure of danger. Obviously I faced the possibility of not returning when first I considered going. Once faced and settled there really wasn't any good reason to refer to it [the "Friendship" flight] again. Ibid., Ch. 5

690. Gracie Fields
(1898–)

1 You can get good fish and chips at the Savoy; and you can put up with fancy people once you understand that you don't have to be like them.

Sing as We Go, Ch. 4 1960

2 Now sometimes it can be a very dangerous thing to go in search of a dream for the reality does not always match it. . . .

Ibid.

691. Cecily R. Hallack
(1898–1938)

1 Make me a saint by getting meals, and washing up the plates!

"The Divine Office of the Kitchen,"
St. 1   *c.1928*

692. Beatrice Lillie
(1898–   )

1 I'll simply say here that I was born Beatrice Gladys Lillie at an extremely tender age because my mother needed a fourth at meals.

Every Other Inch a Lady, Ch. 1   *1927*

2 In my experience, anyone can paint if he doesn't have to. . . . During my apprentice days I felt encouraged by the advice of Winston Churchill, who used to say, "Don't be afraid of the canvas." I have now reached the point where the canvas is afraid of me.

Ibid., Ch. 15

3 I took up knitting from time to time as a relaxation, but I always put it down again before going out to buy a rocking chair.   Ibid.

4 The vows one makes privately are more binding than any ceremony or even a Shubert contract.   Ibid.

693. Golda Meir
(1898–1978)

1 Can we today measure devotion to husband and children by our indifference to everything else? Is it not often true that the woman who has given up all the external world for her husband and her children has done it not out of a sense of duty, out of devotion and love, but out of incapacity, because the soul is not able to take into itself the many-sidedness of life, with its sufferings but also with its joys?

The Plough Woman   *c.1930*

2 I can honestly say that I was never affected by the question of the success of an undertaking. If I felt it was the right thing to do, I was for it regardless of the possible outcome.

Quoted in Golda Meir: Woman with a Cause by Marie Syrkin   1964

3 . . . sitting in America and talking about hard work is easier than doing the work. To deny oneself various comforts is also easier in talk than in deed.

Ibid., Letter to her Brother-in-law (August 24, 1921)

4 There is only one way: he who is a Zionist, he who cannot rest in the *Galuth** must come here, but he must be ready for anything.   *Ibid.*

5 I ask only one thing, that I be understood and believed. My social activities are not an accidental thing; they are an absolute necessity for me.

Ibid., Letter to Her Sister Shana (1929)

6 There are not enough prisons and concentration camps in Palestine to hold all the Jews who are ready to defend their lives and property.

Ibid., Speech (May 2, 1940)

7 If a Jew or Jewess who uses firearms to defend himself against firearms is a criminal, then many new prisons will be needed.

Ibid., Sirkin-Richlin Arms Trials (September, 1943)

8 We only want that which is given naturally to all peoples of the world, to be masters of our own fate, only of *our* fate, not of others, and in cooperation and friendship with others.

Ibid., Address, Anglo-American Committee of Inquiry (March 25, 1946)

9 Hebrew is our language, just as English is your language, just as French is the language of the French and Chinese the language of China. None of these probably would be questioned as to why they spoke their language.   *Ibid.*

10 The spirit is there. This spirit alone cannot face rifles and machine guns. Rifles and machine guns without

* Forced exile.

spirit are not worth very much. But spirit without these in time can be broken with the body.

Ibid., Address, Council of Jewish
Federation (January 21, 1949)

11 We are not a better breed; we are not the best Jews of the Jewish people. It so happened that we are there and you are here. I am certain that if you were there and we were here, you would be doing what we are doing there, and you would ask us who are here to do what you will have to do.

Ibid.

12 Religious families have sons as well as daughters. If army life is degrading why are they not concerned for the morals of their sons?

Ibid., Address (1953)

13 There is no Zionism except the rescue of Jews.

Quoted in *As Good as Golda* (1943),
Israel and Mary Shenker, eds.   *1970*

14 A leader who doesn't hesitate before he sends his nation into battle is not fit to be a leader.

Ibid. (1967)

15 I want to be able to live without a crowded calendar. I want to be able to read a book without feeling guilty, or go to a concert when I like. . . . But I do not intend to retire to a political nunnery.

Ibid., Comment on Resignation (1968)

16 We intend to remain alive. Our neighbors want to see us dead. This is not a question that leaves much room for compromise.

Quoted in "The Indestructible
Golda Meir" by David Reed,
Reader's Digest   *July, 1971*

17 Being seventy is not a sin.

Ibid.

18 Women's Liberation is just a lot of foolishness. It's the men who are discriminated against. They can't bear children. And no one's likely to do anything about that.

Quoted in *Newsweek*   *October 23, 1972*

19 I believe there are a couple of gross injustices in the world: against African blacks and against Jews. More-

650

over, I think these two instances of injustice can only be remedied by Socialist principles.

Quoted by Oriana Fallaci in *L'Europeo*   1973

20 How can one accept crazy creatures who deem it a misfortune to get pregnant and a disaster to give birth to children? When it's the greatest privilege we women have compared with men!

Ibid.

21 At work, you think of the children you've left at home. At home, you think of the work you've left unfinished. Such a struggle is unleashed within yourself: your heart is rent.

Ibid.

22 Those who do not know how to weep with their whole heart don't know how to laugh either.

Ibid.

23 Show me the sensible person who likes himself or herself! I know myself too well to like what I see. I know but too well that I'm not what I'd like to be.

Ibid.

24 If you knew how often I say to myself: to hell with everything, to hell with everybody, I've done my share, let the others do theirs now, enough, enough, enough!

Ibid.

25 I must govern the clock, not be governed by it.

Ibid.

26 . . . old age is like a plane flying through a storm. Once you're aboard, there's nothing you can do. You can't stop the plane, you can't stop the storm, you can't stop time. So one might as well accept it calmly, wisely.

Ibid.

27 I hate fashion, I've always hated it. Fashion is an imposition, a rein on freedom.

Ibid.

28 . . . there's no difference between one's killing and making decisions that will send others to kill. It's exactly the same thing, or even worse.   Ibid.

29 I have had enough.

Statement upon Resignation as Prime Minister of Israel   *April 11, 1974*

30 For me party discipline is a sacred matter, not just lust
   for power as some people claim: I was brought up that
   way all my life.

                                                      Ibid.

31 Once in a Cabinet we had to deal with the fact that
   there had been an outbreak of assaults on women at
   night. One minister suggested a curfew: women should
   stay home after dark. I said, "But it's the men who are
   attacking the women. If there's to be a curfew, let the
   men stay home, not the women."

               Quoted in *Against Rape*, Andra Medea
               and Kathleen Thompson, eds.   *1974*

694. Bessie Smith
(1898–1937)

1 I woke up this mornin', can't even get out of my do',
  There's enough trouble to make a poor girl wonder
      where she wanna go.
                           "Back Water Blues"   *1927*

2 No time to marry, no time to settle down;
  I'm a young woman, and I ain't done runnin' aroun'.
                     "Young Woman's Blues"   *1927*

3 While you're living in your mansion, you don't know
      what hard times mean.
  Poor working man's wife is starving; your wife is living
      like a queen.
                           "Poor Man's Blues"   *1930*

4 It's a long old road, but I know I'm gonna find the end.
                           "Long Old Road"   *1931*

695. Dorothy Speare
(1898–1951)

1 The intoxication of rouge is an insidious vintage known
  to more girls than mere man can ever believe.
                     Dancers in the Dark   *1922*

696. Elizabeth Bowen
(1898–1973)

1 "The best type of man is no companion."

The Hotel 1928

2 "I have a horror, I think, of not being, and of my friends not being, quite perfectly balanced."

Ibid.

3 "There being nothing was what you were frightened of all the time, eh? Yes."

The Little Girls 1963

4 "Did you exchange embraces of any kind?"
"No. She was always in a hurry."

Eva Trout 1968

697. Indra Devi
(1899–)

1 Like an ugly bird of prey, tension hovers over the heads of millions of people, ready to swoop down on its victims at any time and in any place. More and more men, women, and even children are caught up in its cold grip and held for years, sometimes for the whole of their lives. Tension, in fact, is probably one of the greatest menaces the civilized world must face these days.

Renewing Your Life Through Yoga, Ch. 1 1963

2 Tranquilizers do not change our environment, nor do they change our personalities. They merely reduce our responsiveness to stimuli. They dull the keen edge of the angers, fears, or anxiety with which we might otherwise react to the problems of living. Once the response has been dulled, the irritating surface noise of living muted or eliminated, the spark and brilliance are also gone.

Ibid.

3 Like water which can clearly mirror the sky and the trees only so long as its surface is undisturbed, the mind can only reflect the true image of the Self when it

653

is tranquil and wholly relaxed. A ghost of wind—and the rippling waters will distort the reflection; a storm—and the reflection disappears altogether. . . . It therefore becomes necessary to learn how to clear the mind of all clouds, to free it of all useless ballast and debris by dismissing the burden of too much concern with material things.

Ibid.

4 Our body is a magnificently devised, living, breathing mechanism, yet we do almost nothing to insure its optimal development and use. . . . We must begin at the beginning, just as the gardener who wants beautiful flowers in summer must start by cultivating the soil and properly nourishing the seedlings that come up in the early spring. The human organism needs an ample supply of good building material to repair the effects of daily wear and tear.

Ibid., Ch. 2

5 Yoga is not a religion, nor is it a magic formula or some form of calisthenics. In the country of its origin it is called a science—the science of living a healthy, meaningful, and purposeful life—a method of realizing the true self when the body, mind, and spirit blend into one harmonious whole. The system of Yoga, as developed by the ancient Indian philosophers and sages, has no temples, religious creed, or rites. . . . Yoga is a philosophy, a way of life, and organized religion forms no part of it. . . . The word Yoga symbolizes the unity of body, mind and spirit. It is derived from the Sanskrit word *yuj* which means a joining, a union, a reintegration. This actually is the aim of Yoga—to achieve union between man who is finite and the Spirit which is infinite.

Ibid., Ch. 10

698. Marguerite Harris
(1899–   )

1 In tidy terminal homes,
  agape at the stalking Rorschach
  shapes that menace our cosmos,
  pawns now, we itch and surmise.
"The Chosen," St. 1, The East Side
Scene, Allen de Loach, ed.   1968

699. Emily Kimbrough

(1899–   )

Co-author of *Our Hearts Were Young and Gay* with Cornelia Otis Skinner. See 744:4.

700. Eva Le Gallienne

(1899–   )

1 . . . no mechanical device can ever, it seems to me, quite take the place of that mysterious communication between players and public, that sense of an experience directly shared, which gives to the living theatre its unique appeal.

> *The Mystic in the Theatre:*
> *Eleanora Duse,* Ch. 1   *1965*

2 Innovators are inevitably controversial.

> Ibid.

3 People who are born even-tempered, placid and untroubled—secure from violent passions or temptations to evil—those who have never needed to struggle all night with the Angel to emerge lame but victorious at dawn, never become great saints.

> Ibid., Ch. 2

4 But the breathtaking part of it all was not so much the planning as the fantastic skill with which the planning was concealed.   Ibid., Ch. 5

5 There can be no generalizations as far as the art of acting is concerned. There can be no over-all "method"—above all no short cuts. Each actor must find his own way for himself.   Ibid., Ch. 6

701. Mary Margaret McBride

(1899–   )

1 Yes, we have a good many poor tired people here already, but we have plenty of mountains, rivers, woods, lots of sunshine and air, for tired people to rest in. We have Kansas wheat and Iowa corn and Wisconsin

cheese for them to eat, Texas cotton for them to wear. So give us as many as come—we can take it, and take care of them.

America for Me, Ch. 1   1941

2 It takes time to straighten these things out, but the big item is that we're still moving. This country began with people moving, and we've been moving ever since. . . . As long as we keep at that I guess we'll be all right.

Ibid., Ch. 2

3 "Terrible things happen to young girls in New York City. . . ."

A Long Way from Missouri, Ch. 1   1959

702. Helen Hill Miller
(1899–   )

1 France prides itself on being very old, on being not only the first-born among modern nations but the heir of the ancient world, the transmitter to the West of Mediterranean civilization.

Pamphlet, "The Spirit of Modern France"   1934

2 Logical clarity is the genius of the French language.

Ibid.

3 Then, the word tyrant did not carry the pejorative meaning it conveys today. Tyrants seized and held their power by force, exercised it subject to no restraint, and perpetrated notorious cruelties. But many of them were great generals who fought wide-sweeping wars, lavish patrons of the arts, public figures who brought their cities riches and renown. The times combined civilization and savagery.

Sicily and the Western Colonies of Greece   1965

4 "It isn't very often that a person who has been at the very center of one period in the life of a political party has the forward-lookingness and the resilience to note the transition to a new time, much less to bring it forcefully to the attention to the current members of the party."

Letter to Eleanor Roosevelt (1956),
Quoted in *Eleanor: The Years Alone*
by Joseph P. Lash   1972

703. Gloria Swanson
(1899–   )

1 When I die, my epitaph should read: *She Paid the Bills*. That's the story of my private life.

Quoted in "Gloria Swanson Comes Back" by S. Frank, *Saturday Evening Post*   *July 22, 1950*

Biographical Index

Biographical Index

NOTES TO BIOGRAPHICAL INDEX

Every contributor is listed alphabetically and her contributor number given (these numbers will be found in page headings throughout the Quotations section). If a woman is well known by a name other than the one used at the heading of her entry in the Quotations section, that name is cross-indexed here. All co-authors are listed here except "as told to" authors.

Brief biographical information is given for each woman: her full name (those parts of her name not used at the heading of her quotations are in brackets), and any hereditary or honorary title she is known to hold; her nationality, and—if different—her country of residence (i.e., Am./It. indicates a woman was born in the United States but has lived most of her life in Italy); her profession; her family relationship to other well-known persons; any major awards or honors she is known to have received; any "firsts" or outstanding achievements for which she is responsible; any other names by which she is known.

Abbreviations (other than nationality) are: m.–married name; w.–wife of; d.–daughter of; s.–sister of; pseud.–fictitious name used specifically in her work; aka (also known as)–nicknames, aliases, and any other names by which she was known.

The term educator encompasses teachers, professors—whether full, associate or assistant—and other instructors; college administrators are specifically designated. The term composer is used in reference to classical music; composers of popular music are designated as songwriters.

The term (cont./no date) denotes contemporary/no date. This was utilized in the case of women who are alive but for whom no birth date could be found.

Biographical Index

B

670

G

Glaspell, Susan (1882–1948) 500
Am. writer, playwright, actress; widow of George
Cram Cook; w. Norman H. Matson; co-founder of
Provincetown Players; Pulitzer Prize, 1931

Glenconner, Lady Pamela [Wyndham] (1871–1928) 375
Eng. writer; née Gray

Glyn, Elinor (1864–1943) 311
Eng. writer; née Sutherland

Goldman, Emma (1869–1940) 350
Russ./Am. anarchist, political agitator and organ-
izer, lecturer, editor; founder of *Mother Earth,* 1906

Goodale, Dora Read (1866–1915) 330
Am. poet; s. Elaine Goodale

Goodale, Elaine (1863–1953) 308
Am. poet; m. Eastman; s. Dora Read Goodale

Gordon, Ruth (1896–) 665
Am. actress, playwright, scenarist; née Jones; w.
Garson Kanin

Gore-Booth, Eva (1872–1926) 380
Ir. poet

Gorenko, Anna Andreevna (*see* Akhmatova, Anna)

Graham, Margaret Collier (1850–1910) 223
Am. writer

Graham, Martha (1894–) 650
Am. dancer, choreographer, educator; direct descendant of Miles Standish; founder of Martha Graham Dance Company

Gray, Agnes Kendrick (1894–) 651
Ir. poet

Green, Anna [Katharine] (1846–1935) 202
Am. writer

Green, Mary A. E. (1818?–1895) 58
Eng. writer, historian, editor; née Everett

Gregory, Lady [Augusta] (1859?–1932) 274
Ir. writer, playwright, director; née Persse; one of
the founders of Irish National Theatre Society,
1902; director of Abbey Theatre

Greville, Frances [Evelyn Maynard] (1861–1938) 292
Eng. writer; aka Countess of Warwick

Guilbert, Yvette (1865–1944) 319
Fr. actress, entertainer; née Emma Laure Esther
Guilbert

Guinan, [Mary Louise Cecilia] Texas (1884–1933) 522
Am. entertainer, actress, circus performer

Subject Index

Subject Index

NOTES TO SUBJECT INDEX

The numbers preceding the colons are contributor numbers; guides to these numbers are found at the top of each page in the Quotations section. The numbers following the colons refer to the specific quotations.

Entries are in the form of nouns, present participles, or proper names. Because of the amorphous nature of the English language, however, where the use of a noun might be confusing, "the" has been added for clarification (e.g., the obvious), or a noun is given in its plural form to clarify the author's use of the word (e.g., appearance has a different connotation than appearances, speech than speeches).

In subentries the symbol ~ is used to replace the main word; it is placed either before or after the subentry, whichever makes a whole phrase. For example, overpopulation is listed under population as over~, while marriage laws are listed under marriage as ~ laws.

Where there are two words in a main entry with a slash between them, the broader term appears first (e.g., barbarism/barbarian; nursing/nurse). This has been done when there were too few quotations under one or the other of such related subjects to warrant a separate listing.

For a statement on the purpose and style of the Subject Index, please see the Author's Preface.

Subject Index

291:9; 337:3; 359:1; 387:32, 36; 408:11; 416:20; 489:5; 582:2; 617:5; 646:6; 658:4; 693:26

agelessness, 306:1

agitation/agitator, 120:1; 237:1; 265:16, 17, 23; 504:13; 591:1

agreement, 505:5; 603:9

agriculture (*also see* farming), 565:2; 604:3

airplane, 688:1

alcoholism (*also see* liquor), 569:7; 640:30

alienation, 127:5

alimony, 636:15

aloneness (*also see* solitude), 387:44; 453:3

alphabet, 109:4

alter ego, 687:6

altruism, 19:51; 29:3; 45:39; 63:6; 78:8; 84:26; 132:36; 161:4; 268:1; 326:6; 328:2; 350:16; 387:36; 615:26

ambition (*also see* aspiration), 15:29, 36; 19:2; 31:29; 36:29; 57:8; 132:26; 246:24; 416:36; 480:11; 620:24

America (*see* United States)

American Civil Liberties Union, 591:3

Americans (*also see* United States), 240:2; 310:8; 408:27; 416:25; 459:2; 487:7; 528:3, 11; 563:12; 615:35, 40; 662:1; 678:1; 684:3

amnesia, 156:7

amusements (*also see* pleasure), 67:3; 266:15; 483:7; 640:14

anachronism, 278:6; 665:6

analysis, 64:59

anarchy/anarchist, 328:3, 7; 350:41, 42, 45; 494:6

ancestor, 124:1; 480:3

androgyny, 19:19; 31:11, 15; 233:1; 337:12; 508:34; 620:29

angel, 71:1; 137:1

anger, 64:15; 109:5; 564:13; 590:2

Anglo-Saxon, 642:7; 653:2

anguish, 19:8; 210:12; 619:68; 683:6

animal (*also see* individual species; wildlife), 29:9; 10; 64:4; 294:2; 295:4; 332:1; 416:21; 419:1; 453:6; 564:1,

11, 23; 578:4; 652:5

anonymity, 293:1; 508:27

answer (*also see* solution), 528:27; 670:8

anthology, 385:10

anthropology/anthropologist, 336:2

anticipation (*also see* expectation), 64:23; 193:4; 210:19

antiquity (*also see* history), 5:1; 48:1; 430:6

anxiety (*see* stress; worry)

apathy (*also see* passivity), 45:15; 516:22

apology, 323:7

appearance, physical, 192:2; 369:4; 387:19; 426:3; 578:20

appearances, 45:28; 118:1; 159:5; 404:13; 461:3; 576:4; 639:1, 4

applause, 75:2

appreciation (*also see* gratitude; respect), 31:31; 179:2; 619:69

apprehension (*see* dread; fear)

apprentice, 104:1

approval, 418:16; 508:5; 616:6

April, 96:2; 101:30; 156:12; 619:67

architecture, 383:1, 2

argument (*also see* bickering; quarrel), 56:6; 387:19; 508:20

aristocracy/aristocrat, 535:10; 566:20

armed forces, 24:1; 265:12; 619:100; 637:2; officer in ~, 433:2; sexism in ~, 693:12; volunteer ~, 438:1

army (*see* armed forces)

arrogance, 425:2; 676:6; 687:20

art (*also see specific arts*), 15:13, 14; 31:30; 43:4; 49:1, 2; 191:4; 215:28; 224:8; 246:41; 266:4, 28; 273:5, 7; 279:4; 284:1; 319:4; 386:19, 38; 405:6, 8; 408:15; 410:1; 459:21; 539:1; 556:1, 2; 565:3, 6; 573:3, 4, 6; 624:6, 22; 639:17; 640:54; 663:2, 3, 4; 687:1, 3, 4, 12

artist, 45:26; 191:3; 246:29, 41; 285:1; 319:4; 386:8, 37; 397:1; 405:3, 7, 8; 459:6; 508:32; 536:2; 640:16; 663:2; 676:9, 10; French ~, 191:3; man ~, 405:1; struggle of ~, 486:4; 495:2; 508:29; woman ~, 191:2; 229:3

asceticism, 78:9; 646:8

Asia (*also see* the East), 528:59; children in ∼, 615:39, 43

aspiration (*also see* ambition), 45:43; 207:3; 281:53; 480:15; 608:4; 611:3; 619:84

assertiveness, 228:17

assessment, 101:22

assistance (*see* help)

assurance, 154:26; 692:4

astrology, 617:2

atheism, 36:12; 615:5

athletics (*see* sports)

attention, need for, 623:**7**

audience, 310:13; 602:**1**

austerity, 453:5

author (*see* writer)

authority (*also see* power), 132:5; 569:4; 580:5; 620:16; 624:17

autobiography, 554:**3**

autocracy, 287:4

automobile, 575:**2**

autonomy, 529:8

autumn, 117:7; 214:2

avarice (*see* greed)

award, 554:11; scholarship ∼, 61:**6**

awareness, 64:41; 566:17; 603:20; 619:68

B

baby (*also see* children), 45:59; 62:1; 95:18; 106:3; 132:41; 148:2; 281:30; 282:2; 358:1; 368:3; 429:2; 627:3; 643:10

bachelor (*also see* singleness), 439:9, **15**

backlash, 36:**27**

banality, 681:1

banker, 506:4

bankruptcy, 396:1

barbarism/barbarian, 12:**1**; 45:20; 124:13; 484:9; 516:18; 702:3

barroom/bartender, 204:**3**

bathroom, 578:**26**

beauty, 15:30; 19:33; 42:**1**; 55:14; 92:4; 117:22; 143:1; 148:1; 244:1; 246:11; 248:3; 281:12; 298:2; 321:1; 326:5; 353:1; 373:1; 387:5; 408:11; 410:1; 413:8; 419:4; 433:3; 457:2; 512:2; 529:7, 10; 543:3;

553:4; 561:29; 564:15; 578:23; 598:17; 619:27, 39, 60; 620:20; 640:24

bed, 387:6; 494:3

bee, 41:1; 117:41, 44, 45

begging/beggar, 117:2; 615:**2**

beginning, 78:6; 112:1; 193:3; 228:3; 336:2; 368:7; 387:94; 603:12; 620:10; 624:4

behavior (*see* human nature)

belief (*also see* faith), 223:7; 494:1; 643:3; 683:2; 684:1

betrayal, 465:1; 583:6

bewilderment (*also see* confusion), 508:40; 547:18; 574:24

Bible, 18:3; 45:46, 47, 52, 53, 54; 68:1; 81:2; 88:1; 163:1; 310:1; 345:3

bickering (*also see* argument; quarrel), 508:49; 561:13

biography/biographer, 387:53; 441:10; 482:1; 561:1; 558:20; 591:2; 676:7

bird (*also see individual species*), 13:2; 101:9, 29; 149:1; 249:5; 256:2; 295:3; 346:6; 416:11; 457:3; 519:2; 535:4; 640:41; 646:2; caged ∼, 101:29; 246:15; 535:4; ∼ song, 101:28; 207:2

birth (*also see* childbirth), 480:14

birth control, 350:29; 516:3, 11, 17, 20, 21; 615:41; 655:7

birthday, 123:11

bisexuality (*also see* homosexuality; sex), 337:12; 553:3

bitterness, 36:38; 547:10; 640:33

blacks, 36:17; 309:5; 510:1; 561:12; 563:7; autonomy of ∼, 305:1; 510:4; heritage of ∼, 418:5; music of ∼, 88:5; oppression of ∼, 305:2; 309:1, 2, 4; 683:7, 10; ∼ pride, 309:6; 418:1; 510:2; religion and ∼, 418:3; ∼ women, 499:3

Blake, William, 348:1

blindness, 480:20

bliss, 55:10; 72:6; 117:5; 268:**2**

blue, 330:1

bluebell, 367:1

blush, 7:1

body, human, 43:2; 61:7; 553:5; 574:1; 598:11; 619:49; awareness of ∼, 15:6; care of ∼, 594:2; 697:4

705

209:1; 272:4; 308:2; 330:1, 2;
349:1; 367:1; 379:1; 386:41;
387:3; 408:7, 28; 416:8; 478:1;
565:3; 574:4, 17; 588:2; 640:4

flying, 609:1; 617:4; 689:4, 5

follower, 247:20; 350:7

food, 34:1; 387:25; 616:16;
669:5; 681:5

fool, 64:26; 287:9; 438:6; 566:23;
569:17

foolishness, 64:13; 439:5, 8;
532:3; 566:3

foresight, 123:21; 124:2; 346:4;
416:48; 572:4; 702:4

forest, 457:7

forgetfulness, 15:45; 101:18;
438:7

forgetting, 123:2, 17; 622:5

forgiveness, 98:5; 263:13; 302:1;
615:8; 624:13

foundation, strong, 616:9

foundling, 426:2

France (also see the French),
125:4; 255:3; 416:39; 618:3;
702:1

free enterprise (see capitalism)

freedom (also see liberation;
liberty), 5:5; 10:2; 24:4; 36:10,
11; 46:1, 2, 5; 65:1, 2; 70:17;
95:24; 115:2; 186:8; 196:5;
265:2, 25; 366:12, 13; 384:3;
467:9; 484:2; 508:38; 516:4;
543:6; 620:2, 27; 636:18;
640:41; 669:11; 688:15; economic ~, 636:19; limitations
of ~, 657:3; ~ of press,
528:12, 33; ~ of speech,
528:24; ~ of thought, 382:7

free will, 15:2; 118:12

French, the (also see France),
104:4; 410:3; 522:1; 639:17

Freud, Sigmund, 224:7; 481:1;
520:11; 537:1

friction, 132:27; 619:100

friend, 38:1; 64:4, 35; 101:8;
119:7; 123:5; 206:3; 240:13;
248:8; 281:64; 287:2; 300:3;
387:46; 511:6; 513:7; 578:18;
619:26; obligation to ~,
36:37; old ~, 214:7; 396:2

friendship (also see companionship), 31:37; 45:63; 55:4;
64:50; 101:22; 189:3; 252:3;
298:3; 386:32; 416:12; 548:2;
640:45; ~ between women

(see women, in relation to
women); breach in ~, 392:1;
lasting ~, 395:8

frigidity, 15:4, 8; 353:2; 387:64

fulfillment, 15:50; 68:4; 159:6;
337:6; 486:3; 574:23

fund-raising, 499:1

funeral, 387:33

furniture, 561:10

furs, 564:22

futility, 331:1

future, the (also see tomorrow),
15:44, 58; 19:48; 31:25; 45:84;
101:32; 174:2; 228:6; 246:8;
277:2; 281:39; 291:2; 346:5;
350:13; 413:6; 430:9; 493:1;
504:9; 615:21; 626:7

G

gambling/gambler, 426:6; 561:15

games (see playing)

garden/gardening, 31:25; 101:27;
262:1; 381:2; 502:4; 619:37;
620:21; 652:3

gay liberation movement (see
homosexuality)

generation gap, 224:1; 372:6;
386:21; 387:30; 578:18; 580:1

generosity, 91:6; 250:2; 286:2;
387:83

Genesis, 263:7

genitals, 83:10

genius (also see greatness), 5:21;
19:43; 31:24, 36; 132:15, 26;
145:4; 153:1; 167:3; 378:2;
416:27; 561:16; 566:20

gentility, 132:17; 210:5; 324:4;
580:2

gentleman, 12:8; 47:11; 57:11;
394:5, 7; 590:1

gentleness, 312:1

Germany, 163:3; 618:3; women
in ~, 261:3

ghost, 13:2; 123:5; 274:9; 403:1

gift (see presents; talent)

giraffe, 535:6

girl (also see children), 132:21;
192:3; 489:3; 576:20; conditioning of ~ (also see women,
conditioning of), 56:7; 339:2;
387:17; 409:1; 676:2

Girl Scouts, 283:1, 3

goal (also see purpose), 30:5;
234:2; 265:7; 299:2; 354:1;
480:19; 497:4; 619:25

713

God, 8:20; 11:5; 16:1, 3; 18:6, 18; 19:6, 27, 28, 37, 44; 29:1; 43:4; 49:1, 3; 52:1, 2; 53:2, 3; 55:7; 63:1; 64:12, 14, 62; 68:7; 84:7, 9, 16, 19, 21; 109:3; 113:1; 117:19, 31; 123:24; 126:1; 156:14; 164:1; 179:4; 184:1; 197:2; 215:9; 219:3; 230:8; 246:13; 263:12; 277:1; 300:1; 310:3; 323:13; 413:2; 419:3; 425:4; 438:6; 459:22; 484:9; 502:4; 528:4; 535:12; 538:4; 574:10; 576:5; 594:4; 597:3; 619:3, 4; 651:1; faith in ~, 163:5; 165:1; 418:3; 423:1; laws of ~, 5:18; love of ~, 15:41; 84:23, 28; 117:51; will of ~, 5:17; 177:1; 259:10

gods, the, 19:50; 615:5, 28

good and evil, 15:12; 19:50; 20:8; 290:10; 543:6; 597:3

goodness, 19:56; 55:14; 79:3; 84:6; 111:2; 112:15; 163:5; 170:1; 179:1, 3; 210:4; 247:17; 339:1; 387:90; 508:9; 665:15

goodwill, lack of, 315:4

gossip, 64:46; 97:2; 112:11; 162:9; 188:2; 247:28; 306:4; 387:72, 92; 560:11; 646:1

government (also see nation), 19:46; 45:18; 265:11; 271:4; 278:14; 350:42, 47; 404:5; 455:1; 463:1; 526:5; 528:19; 622:1; democratic ~, 467:9; 657:3; duplicity of ~, 350:17; faults of ~, 636:21; 684:3; 688:12; responsibility of ~, 20:7; 684:8; self-determination of ~, 259:10; women in ~, 278:5; 528:7, 26; world ~, 451:3

grammar, 632:3

grandparents, 5:22; 517:3; 578:29; 636:23

grass, 37:1

gratitude (also see appreciation), 75:1; 249:4; 287:5; 518:2; 558:11; 593:4; 626:8

graves (also see cemetery), 96:4; 619:2

gravity, 669:11

Great Britain (see England)

greatness (also see genius), 15:40;

19:19; 64:60; 173:1; 251:2; 310:3, 4; 387:93; 436:3; 520:10; 547:9; 628:7

greed, 186:7; 438:9; 624:7; 665:4; 684:5

Greeks, ancient, 336:1, 3

grief (also see mourning; sorrow), 19:10, 56; 32:5; 88:10; 98:8; 279:2; 403:4; 459:19; 472:8; 534:1; 560:8

Griffith, D. W., 593:3; 639:15

grooming, 508:36

growing up, 19:7; 36:6; 471:1; 570:2

growth, 15:46; 31:15; 45:77; 64:30; 78:6; 246:18; 278:1; 283:2; 372:3; 511:9; 573:5; 620:7; 683:12

guest (also see visit), 387:11; 513:3; 523:1; 564:5

guilt, 54:4; 80:5; 92:3; 101:2; 193:6; 224:6; 521:1; 564:7

gullibility, 281:60; 528:58

gun, 274:6; 408:18

gynecology (see medical profession)

Gypsy, 67:4

H

habit (also see custom), 402:8; 603:1

hair, 192:2; 353:1

hand, 480:16, 17; 615:50; 619:93

handicap, 212:2; physical ~, 111:3

happiness (also see joy), 15:33, 37; 123:10; 154:2, 24; 195:4; 247:18; 306:13; 345:1; 369:5; 386:10; 387:7, 93; 393:2; 403:3, 5; 404:18, 21; 408:6; 425:7; 495:3; 558:17; 576:7; 583:5; 619:53

harbor, 214:1

hardship (see life, struggle of)

harmony (also see cooperation), 31:12; 36:21; 402:10

harvest, 223:1; 355:6

hatred, 64:27; 195:8; 272:1; 287:14; 316:1; 386:7; 470:3

Hawaii/Hawaiians, 158:1, 2

healing, 84:7; 619:79; 656:1

health, 45:76; 61:7; 76:2; 83:4; 84:14; 246:16; 281:1; 422:3; 574:18; 610:2

insight (*also see* perceptiveness), 578:3

insignificance, 112:3; 553:6

inspiration, 31:19; 154:13; 310:12; 348:1; 469:6; 481:2; 547:13; 584:3

instinct, 31:19; 83:2; 95:16, 17; 580:6; 613:1; maternal ~, 45:62; 281:26, 41

integration, racial, 563:7

integrity (*also see* principle), 19:57; 270:3; 386:39; 684:5

intellectualism/intellectual, 336:3; 687:13; anti-~, 615:52

intelligence (*also see* the mind), 15:31; 18:5; 425:3, 6; 438:6; 555:6; 578:1; 619:21; 639:13

intensity, 36:45

interdependence, 223:5; 266:7; 486:5; 669:12

interior decorating, 387:89

introspection, 88:2

invention/inventor, 477:1; 480:16

invincibility, 386:26

Ireland, 27:2; 129:2; 380:1

Irish, the, 5:11; 31:42; 274:11; 393:7; 564:10

irony, 266:30

irrelevance, 554:10; 561:23

irritability, 36:36; 274:13; 624:15

island, 392:2; 648:1

isolation, 31:22; 425:4; 619:10

isolationism, 528:42

Israel/Israelis, 217:4; 528:50, 54, 63; 693:8

Italy/Italians, 19:47; 107:2; 240:9; 251:1; 503:3, 4

J

James, Henry, 306:16

Janus, 22:1

Japan/Japanese, 24:1; 558:9, 10

jealousy (*also see* envy), 21:2; 64:15, 21; 124:12; 287:21; 387:26

Jesus (*see* Christ, Jesus)

Jew (*see* Judaism)

jewelry, 387:84; 639:2

Johnson, Andrew, 88:13

Johnson, Lyndon B., 871:1

journalist (*also see* writer), 161:4

journey (*see* travel)

joy (*also see* happiness), 98:2, 10; 124:9; 223:4; 298:2; 319:2;
337:9; 386:27; 387:37; 529:2, 3; 543:3; 564:8; 594:3; 687:24

Joyce, James, 564:20

Judaism/Jew, 45:74; 64:47; 217:3; 528:54, 63; 568:5; 693:6, 7, 11, 13, 19; persecution of ~, 611:1

judge (*also see* the judiciary), 270:3; 350:31; 578:16

judgment (*also see* opinion), 47:12, 15; 263:1; 320:5; 601:1; 620:22

Judgment Day, 164:1

judiciary, the (*also see* judge; jury), 578:15

June, 103:8; 242:2; 295:2

jury (*see* the judiciary)

justice, 5:18; 60:2, 6; 127:4; 181:3; 265:3; 271:5; 386:25; 528:18; 533:4; international ~, 215:37; 504:8; 688:15

K

Kansas, 45:41

karma, 125:7; 517:8

Keats, John, 640:18

Kennedy, John F., 528:75

Kennedy family, the, 594:1

killing (*also see* murder), 414:1; 500:7; 619:86, 87; 693:28

kindness, 19:5; 47:4; 87:2; 300:2; 345:4; 387:86, 97; 416:44; 497:4; 578:21

King Lear, 278:3

kiss, 64:36; 72:3; 131:3; 291:10; 374:2; 387:59; 439:7; 529:11; 583:2; 585:1; 626:1; 639:8; 640:22; 665:10

knitting, 692:3

kitchen, 193:1

knowledge (*also see* wisdom), 19:18; 80:3; 84:5; 98:12; 156:10; 240:2; 246:25; 247:16; 289:1; 333:12; 370:3; 487:3; 501:1; 508:4; 561:14; 619:1; 620:33; 640:35; lack of ~, 101:4

L

labor (*see* work)

labor movement (*also see* union, labor), 430:2

717

lady, 240:3; 247:9; 324:1, 2; 580:2; 590:1; 631:1

land, 103:10; 615:10; 620:5; un-cultivated ~, 555:5

language, 57:12; 328:5; 333:12; 480:5; 564:19; 687:2, 14; English ~, 504:1; French ~, 702:2; Hebrew ~, 693:9; international ~, 504:1, 2; learning of ~, 368:8; Russian ~, 567:2

lasciviousness (also see lust), 319:3; 487:3; 572:1

laughter, 207:11; 247:1; 595:1; 693:22

law, 8:17; 47:16; 64:16; 121:2; 162:6; 271:2; 350:30, 38; 532:2; 533:1, 5; 636:5, 10; international ~, 121:4; origins of ~, 533:4; sexism in ~, 45:33, 34; 636:14; unjust ~, 70:9; women and ~, 440:2

lawlessness, 278:15; 547:15

Lawrence, D. H., 470:2; 559:1

Lawrence, Frieda, 466:1

Lawrence, T. E., 608:2

lawyer, 363:1; 642:17, 20

laziness, 331:1; 566:3, 16; 598:6

leader, 114:3; 247:20; 259:2; 528:4; 576:16; 693:14; oppres-sive ~, 615:4

leadership, 485:2; 505:4; 596:4; 637:6; 684:4; difficulties of ~, 569:9; spiritual ~, 528:60

League of Nations, 463:4

learning, 31:39; 61:5, 6; 109:4; 273:2; 274:12, 14; 366:6; 469:6; 480:5; 548:6; 683:12

legacy (also see inheritance), 45:83; 64:60; 256:4; 458:4; 558:13

legend, 511:8

Legree, Simon, 88:4

leisure, 532:10

Lenin, Vladimir Ilyich, 459:22

lesbianism/lesbian (see homo-sexuality)

letters, 32:4; 306:14; 560:12; 598:1; writing of ~, 64:54

liberation (also see freedom; rights; specific movements), 8:25; 246:20; 350:44; women's ~ (also see feminism), 45:29, 54; 63:3; 215:2, 26; 261:5; 265:4; 350:2, 9, 14; 441:3;

484:5; 487:1; 504:17; 508:30; 516:3, 12; 693:18

liberty (also see freedom), 10:3; 19:50; 46:5; 59:3; 132:23; 192:5; 310:9; 535:4; 657:4; 693:15

lie/lying, 168:1; 223:7; 232:3; 252:1; 328:6; 386:13; 394:6; 404:9; 429:3; 459:20; 492:1; 588:1; 617:1; 619:74; 640:3

life (also see existence), 19:17, 18, 34, 40, 55; 26:3; 30:5; 45:44; 47:1; 50:1; 63:5; 72:2; 89:2, 3; 99:1; 117:26; 118:22; 123:8; 132:38; 147:4; 152:1; 166:1; 179:5; 181:2; 186:1, 13; 189:1; 206:6; 240:17; 246:22, 37; 249:8; 259:3; 263:3, 10; 266:28; 273:6; 281:48; 298:4; 312:1; 329:1; 340:2; 345:2; 355:5; 369:2; 372:2; 386:27, 33, 34, 36; 387:13, 88, 93, 104; 393:4; 402:10; 416:43; 426:7; 429:2; 430:3, 6; 431:1; 434:1; 441:11; 456:1; 459:24; 460:2; 480:26; 508:3, 7, 40; 509:1; 517:9; 528:29, 47; 529:14; 549:2; 555:4; 569:3; 573:3; 576:7; 581:6; 586:1, 9; 619:6, 13, 20, 24, 34, 38, 44, 71, 95, 98, 105; 624:21; 625:3, 4; 626:2; 640:25; 642:18; 675:2; 677:1; 687:25; 694:4; civilized ~, 616:13; cycles of ~, 557:2; 665:11; daily ~, 36:9; 597:2; difficulties of ~, 68:4; 132:13; 192:7; 558:14; 574:6; fear of ~, 186:6; injustice of ~, 669:8; inner ~, 615:12; lessons of ~, 584:4; 688:13; mystery of ~, 156:13; 535:3; priorities in ~, 120:2; 468:1; 472:10; 508:42; public ~, 83:13; 429:5; purpose of ~, 127:2; 508:8; respect for ~, 215:25; sacrifice of ~, 259:3; simple ~, 486:2; spiritual ~, 442:1; struggle of ~, 5:9; 40:11; 91:9; 163:4; 247:21; 291:2; 508:48; 546:3; 554:11; 619:90; 630:3; 669:7, 9; transience of ~, 98:4; 326:2; unpredictability of ~, 624:17

lifelessness, 543:4

light, 103:11

615:29; 620:17; 623:13; role of ~, 360:1

mental health, 513:8

mental illness (*also see* madness), 6:1, 4; 598:7

mental retardedness, 615:38

merchandising (*see* advertising; publicity)

mercy, 19:5; 64:12, 24; 124:6; 619:102

mermaid, 180:4

metaphor, 687:2

Mexican-Americans, 561:22

middle age (*see* age, middle)

middle class (*see* bourgeoisie; classes, middle)

middle of the road, 546:8; 626:6

militancy, 265:9; 484:2

militarism, 121:5; 215:35; 350:27; 366:8; 480:9; 516:10; 684:7; opposition to ~, 441:4

military, the (*see* armed forces)

Millay, Edna St. Vincent, 687:9

mime, 387:9

mind, the (*also see* intelligence; reason), 61:7; 117:25; 336:4, 5; 500:2; 642:8; 682:1; 697:3; cultivated ~, 259:7, 8; flexibility of ~, 368:14; state of ~, 417:1

miracle, 386:29; 537:7; 598:15

mischief, 9:6; 395:3

misery, 64:31; 292:1; 470:4; 603:19; 671:3

mishap, 624:16

misogyny, 154:14; 572:6; 622:2

missionary, 615:20

mistake, 84:10, 18; 98:6; 152:2; 318:1; 408:25; 528:75; 615:25

mistress, 426:4; 624:7; 642:26

moderation, 75:2; 576:12; 603:4

modernity, 156:11

modesty, 8:6; 132:9; 240:19; 273:4

monarchy, 25:1

money, 14:1; 57:11; 127:9; 132:13, 17; 145:1; 186:10; 208:2; 228:5; 274:1; 305:1; 306:4; 386:17; 404:10; 416:21; 425:7; 454:1; 489:4; 578:5; 598:5; 603:13, 22; 642:22; 670:3; acquisition of ~, 228:7; saving ~, 528:77

monogamy, 95:21; 447:1; 532:11; 640:53

moon, 74:4; 101:20; 408:20

morale, 693:10

morality, 12:10; 18:11, 15; 20:2; 125:5; 148:1; 240:14; 265:9, 20; 278:4, 12; 350:3; 416:3; 450:1; 453:1; 468:8; 526:1; 563:15; 586:3, 5; 608:6; 633:1; 684:5

morning, 198:1

mortality, 91:10

motherhood/mother (*also see* parents), 19:31; 36:25; 45:42, 46, 58, 73; 75:3; 88:3; 95:6, 11, 12; 132:32; 193:7; 215:3, 27, 29; 243:1; 246:17; 281:23, 25, 32, 35; 291:6; 324:3; 343:3; 384:4; 387:13, 22, 23, 34, 43; 441:9; 459:11; 467:4; 514:1; 516:13, 19, 23; 517:2; 518:2; 551:2; 570:6; 581:4; 583:4; 639:9; 667:4; 668:1, 2; 683:9; glorification of ~, 281:26; inadequacies of ~, 281:24, 46; ~ in relation to children, 228:14; 439:6; 553:7; overbearing ~, 559:1; overprotective ~, 228:2; rights of ~, 459:9; unwed ~, 387:35; 615:40; working ~, 215:30; 281:33; 441:1

mountain (*also see* hill), 348:2; 436:4; 457:4

mourning (*also see* grief), 12:7; 29:5; 36:39; 55:2; 500:5; 566:12; 637:4

movement, physical, 650:1, 2

movement, social (*see specific movements*)

movie (*see* film)

murder (*also see* killing), 309:1; 603:8; 652:4

music (*also see* opera; singing; song; symphony), 15:22; 31:32; 98:7; 242:6; 263:6; 322:2; 385:6; 386:14; 459:8; 469:1, 2, 5; 481:3; 615:48; 619:64, 65; 676:1; American ~, 459:15; ~ lover, 676:8; ~ lyrics, 573:1

musical instruments, 355:3

musician, 31:32; 263:6

muteness, 425:1

mysticism, 78:5

mythology, 22:1; 230:3

N

nagging, 306:11
naiveté, 32:6; 270:2; 386:24; 472:7; 687:20
name, 45:78
Naples, Italy, 408:17
Napoleon, 19:4
narcissism, 31:38; 640:1
narrow-mindedness, 246:5; 459:3; 554:8; 683:2
nation, 19:53; 246:36, 37; 688:6; confidence in ~, 528:48; differences between ~, 624:20; hypocrisy of ~, 215:33
national defense, 688:2
nationalism (*also see* patriotism), 376:1; 451:1; 563:10
national security, 684:8
natives, 416:18; 535:11
naturalness, 5:15; 61:1
nature (*see* human nature)
Nature, 11:1; 12:6; 15:11, 27, 28; 31:16; 36:50; 45:16; 61:9; 85:4; 95:10, 22; 103:5; 117:9; 127:10; 156:15; 246:30; 269:1; 294:1; 308:3; 335:2; 349:1; 368:2; 384:4, 7; 385:13; 387:109; 413:2; 528:5; 566:14; 574:18; 586:5; 603:4; 604:2; 618:1; 619:3; 643:6; 667:5; 669:12
Nazi, 538:2
nearness, 230:1; 306:14
neatness (*see* orderliness)
necessity, 15:1; 44:1; 246:23; 266:20; 346:3; 619:15
needs, 388:1
negligence, 55:21; 615:41
Negro (*see* blacks)
nervousness, 416:38; 445:2
Netherlands, the (*see* Holland)
neurosis, 537:8; 571:1; 613:3
New England (*also see* United States), 214:2; 408:28; 626:6; slavery in ~, 36:23
news, unexpected, 36:19
newspaper, 161:5; 484:8; exaggeration in ~, 333:10; sensationalism in ~, 310:7
newspapermen (*see* journalist)
New Year, 137:2
New York City, 281:54; 468:6; 527:3; 701:3

night, 13:1; 147:1; 618:1; 619:70, 72
Nixon, Richard M., 528:36, 69, 74; 655:5
nonconformity, 228:11; 453:1; 494:3
normalcy, 416:14
North, the/Northerners, U.S. (*also see* United States), 11:4; 88:7
nose, 12:2
nosiness, 232:3; 274:2; 315:2; 561:23
nostalgia, 256:3
nothing, 616:15; 696:3
novel (*also see* fiction; writing), 620:10
novelist (*see* writer)
November, 132:12
nudity, 109:1; 553:5; 671:6
nun, 83:6; 219:3, 5; 612:1; education of ~, 587:1
nursing/nurse, 45:61; 78:2; 438:5; 491:1; 554:1; 628:4
nutrition, 255:2

O

obedience, 219:2, 3; 333:1
obesity, 549:1; 561:3
objectification (*see* dehumanization)
objectivity (*also see* detachment), 246:29; 299:1; 528:32
obligation (*also see* duty; responsibility), 45:69; 50:2; 112:10; 337:7; 528:10; 558:10; 578:22; 619:35
observation, 15:27; 78:3; 508:53; 565:3; 578:3
obsession (*also see* compulsion), 555:1; 563:1
obstacle (*also see* adversity), 203:3; 392:1; 414:6; 449:3; 535:9
obstetrics (*also see* medical profession), 409:2
obstinance, 36:40, 41; 123:18; 281:62; 438:4; 576:6; 620:14
ocean (*see* sea)
October, 119:15
odds and ends, 169:2; 576:19
odor, 15:22
Oedipus complex, 561:25

repetition, 387:82; 619:105

repression (*also see* suppression), 36:48; 386:23; 624:9; 687:5

reprieve, 226:1

reputation, 112:11; 220:1

rescue, 117:8; 653:6

research, 508:17; 520:3

resentment, 620:9

resigning, 528:65; 693:24, 29

resilience, 480:19; 615:46; 702:4

resistance, 15:3; 528:66; passive ~, 263:13

resolution, 555:8; 655:2

resourcefulness, 41:1; 513:8; 561:27

respect (*also see* appreciation), 36:4; 132:5; 639:12

respectability, 371:2; 601:3; middle-class ~, 569:16

responsibility (*also see* duty; obligation), 54:3; 80:5; 135:2; 508:24; 528:9; 642:10; 661:1; 687:21; family ~, 615:39; social ~, 63:6; 615:42

rest (*also see* relaxation), 95:9; 123:13; 437:2

restlessness, 619:24; 640:23

restraint (*also see* limitations), 64:52; 115:2; 186:8; 246:15; 287:25; 387:37; 564:6

results, 36:4, 30; 247:6; 248:4

reticence, 564:18

retirement, 582:2; 681:7

retribution (*also see* vengeance), 381:1; 529:13; 687:5

returning, 214:9

revolt (*also see* riot), 47:6; 196:3

revolution, 15:13; 17:1; 18:12; 26:2; 45:50; 246:34; 350:7, 43, 44, 46; 366:7; 399:1; 416:29; 480:21; 504:12; 636:12; 644:2; 678:5

revolutionary, 615:5; 636:2

reward, 33:1; 61:5

rhythm, 566:19

rich, the (*also see* classes, upper; wealth), 468:6; 591:6; 603:13; 670:5; 687:17; 694:3

ridicule, 640:51

righteousness, 127:11; 670:4

rights (*also see* liberation), 18:14, 17; 306:6; 350:15; 451:2; 528:2; 528:13, 19, 40; 636:20; children's ~, 516:12; 540:1; 636:9; civil ~, 70:1; individual

~, 46:5; 503:6; women's ~, 45:6, 32, 64, 82; 56:3; 63:4, 7; 121:2; 215:2; 240:20; 246:39; 265:5; 350:8; 430:4; workers' ~, 242:4; 505:3; 642:11

riot (*also see* revolt), race, 305:2; 510:6

risk (*also see* danger), 386:5; 467:6; 543:6; 619:20; 693:2

ritual, 224:8

river, 604:1

role playing, 600:1; 602:4

Roman Catholic Church, 45:40; 83:6; 167:1, 2; 187:1; 386:29; 503:3

romance, 439:19

Romans, ancient, 336:10

Rome, Italy, 132:25

Roosevelt, Eleanor, 563:16

Roosevelt, Franklin Delano, 505:4, 5; 528:16; 655:4

Roosevelt, Theodore, 114:3; 637:6

rose, 96:5; 416:8; 574:17; 640:24

route, 294:2

royalty, 25:1; 58:1; 290:8; 329:2; 590:3; 616:1; 640:36, 38

rules, 31:16; 460:4

Russia (*see* USSR)

Russian Revolution, 596:3

Russians (*also see* USSR), 503:2; 528:71

S

Sacco and Vanzetti, 591:9

sacrifice, 15:19; 19:3; 36:47; 334:1; 389:5; 408:24; 499:2; 639:9

safety (*also see* security), 45:14; 112:2; 128:1

sages, 624:19

sailor, 225:2

saint, 655:8; 700:3

saintliness, 36:31; 473:3

St. Nicholas, 156:3

salvation, 263:7; 350:13; 368:6

Sand, George, 19:19; 31:11; 640:19

sandpiper, 149:1

Sanger, Margaret, 655:7

sanity, 117:47

Santa Claus, 339:1

Sappho, 408:31

728

733

The DECLINE and FALL of the LOVE GODDESSES

Patrick Agan

☐ **40-623-1   304 pages   illustrated   8½″ x 11″ $7.95**

Between the covers of this book are the dazzling, behind-the-klieg lights stories of ten internationally famous film stars who made it to the top, held the world in the palm of their hands, then let it all slip through their fingers…victims of their own weaknesses, of changing times, of men who used them. With photographs as poignant as his words, Patrick Agan delves behind the headlines to present the *real* story—what made them tick, and what made the ticking stop.

The Love Goddesses: Rita Hayworth, Jayne Mansfield, Betty Hutton, Linda Darnell, Veronica Lake, Betty Grable, Susan Hayward, Dorothy Dandridge, Frances Farmer, and of course, Marilyn Monroe.